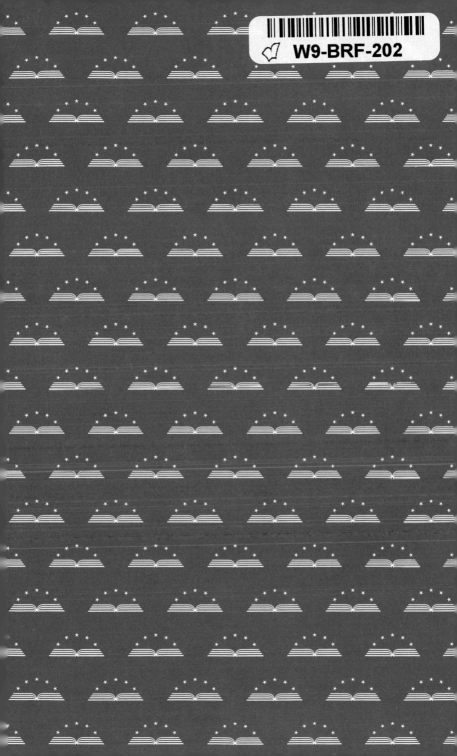

AMERICAN SPEECHES:

ABRAHAM LINCOLN TO BILL CLINTON

AMERICAN SPEECHES

POLITICAL ORATORY FROM
ABRAHAM LINCOLN TO BILL CLINTON

THE LIBRARY OF AMERICA

Some of the material in this volume is reprinted by
permission of the holders of copyright and publication rights
Acknowledgments will be found on pages 802–9.

The paper used in this publication meets the
minimum requirements of the American National Standard for
Information Sciences—Permanence of Paper for Printed
Library Materials, ANSI z39.48—1984.

Distributed to the trade in the United States
by Penguin Putnam Inc.
and in Canada by Penguin Books Canada Ltd.

Library of Congress Catalog Number: 2006040928
For cataloging information, see end of Index.
ISBN 978–1–931082–98–3
ISBN 1–931082–98–7

———

First Printing
The Library of America—167

Manufactured in the United States of America

TED WIDMER
IS THE EDITOR OF THIS VOLUME

American Speeches
is published with support from

THE ACHELIS FOUNDATION
and
THE BODMAN FOUNDATION

Contents

Abraham Lincoln: *Speech on Reconstruction*
Washington, D.C., April 11, 1865   1

Thaddeus Stevens: *Speech in Congress on Reconstruction*
Washington, D.C., December 18, 1865   6

Sojourner Truth: *Speech at Meeting Commemorating
      Emancipation*
Boston, January 1, 1871   19

Susan B. Anthony: *Is It a Crime for a Citizen of the
      United States to Vote?*
Monroe County, N.Y., March–April 1873;
      Ontario County, N.Y., May–June 1873   22

Robert Brown Elliott: *Speech in Congress on the Civil
      Rights Bill*
Washington, D.C., January 6, 1874   48

Benjamin F. Butler: *Speech in Congress on the Civil
      Rights Bill*
Washington, D.C., January 7, 1874   67

Frederick Douglass: *Oration in Memory of Abraham Lincoln*
Washington, D.C., April 14, 1876   74

Robert G. Ingersoll: *Speech Nominating James G. Blaine*
Cincinnati, June 15, 1876   85

Chief Joseph: *Reply to General Howard*
Bear Paw Mountains, Montana Territory, October 5, 1877 . .   88

Oliver Wendell Holmes, Jr.: *Memorial Day Address*
Keene, N.H., May 30, 1884   89

Grover Cleveland: *Address at the Dedication of the
      Statue of Liberty*
New York City, October 28, 1886   98

Elizabeth Cady Stanton: *The Solitude of Self*
Washington, D.C., January 18, 1892   99

Ida B. Wells: *Lynch Law in All Its Phases*
Boston, February 13, 1893   110

xi

John Peter Altgeld: *Labor Day Address*
Chicago, September 8, 1893   129

Booker T. Washington: *Address at the Atlanta Exposition*
September 18, 1895   137

William Jennings Bryan: *Speech to the Democratic
National Convention*
Chicago, July 9, 1896   142

Theodore Roosevelt: *The Strenuous Life*
Chicago, April 10, 1899   150

Carl Schurz: *The Policy of Imperialism*
Chicago, October 17, 1899   161

Theodore Roosevelt: *The Man with the Muck-Rake*
Washington, D.C., April 14, 1906   195

Mary Church Terrell: *What It Means to be Colored in the
Capital of the United States*
Washington, D.C., October 10, 1906   204

Theodore Roosevelt: *The New Nationalism*
Osawatomie, Kansas, August 31, 1910   213

John Jay Chapman: *Speech at Prayer Meeting*
Coatesville, Pennsylvania, August 18, 1912   229

Woodrow Wilson: *First Inaugural Address*
Washington, D.C., March 4, 1913   233

Woodrow Wilson: *Address to Congress on War
with Germany*
Washington, D.C., April 2, 1917   238

Robert M. La Follette, Sr.: *Speech in the Senate on
Free Speech in Wartime*
Washington, D.C., October 6, 1917   247

Carrie Chapman Catt: *Address to Woman Suffrage
Convention*
Washington, D.C., December 1917   286

Eugene V. Debs: *Speech to the Court*
Cleveland, September 14, 1918   308

Woodrow Wilson: *Address to the Senate on
the League of Nations*
Washington, D.C., July 10, 1919   314

Henry Cabot Lodge: *Speech in the Senate on
the League of Nations*
Washington, D.C., August 12, 1919   327

Herbert Hoover: *"Rugged Individualism" Speech*
New York City, October 22, 1928   356

Franklin D. Roosevelt: *Speech to the Democratic
National Convention*
Chicago, July 2, 1932   373

Franklin D. Roosevelt: *Speech to the Commonwealth Club*
San Francisco, September 23, 1932   384

Franklin D. Roosevelt: *First Inaugural Address*
Washington, D.C., March 4, 1933   398

Huey Long: *Every Man a King*
Washington, D.C., February 23, 1934   403

Franklin D. Roosevelt: *Speech to the Democratic
National Convention*
Philadelphia, June 27, 1936   415

Franklin D. Roosevelt: *Second Inaugural Address*
Washington, D.C., January 20, 1937   421

Franklin D. Roosevelt: *"Arsenal of Democracy"
Fireside Chat*
Washington, D.C., December 29, 1940   426

Franklin D. Roosevelt: *Eighth Annual Address to Congress*
Washington, D.C., January 6, 1941   437

Franklin D. Roosevelt: *Address to Congress on
War with Japan*
Washington, D.C., December 8, 1941   447

George S. Patton: *Speech to Third Army Troops*
England, Spring 1944   449

Dwight D. Eisenhower: *Address to the Allied
Expeditionary Forces*
England, June 6, 1944   453

Harry S. Truman: *Statement on the Atomic Bomb*
Washington, D.C., August 6, 1945   454

J. Robert Oppenheimer: *Speech to Los Alamos Scientists*
Los Alamos, N.M., November 2, 1945   458

George C. Marshall: *Speech at Harvard University*
Cambridge, Massachusetts, June 5, 1947   472

Hubert H. Humphrey: *Speech to the Democratic
National Convention,*
Philadelphia, July 14, 1948   476

Harry S. Truman: *Speech to the Democratic National
Convention*
Philadelphia, July 15, 1948   480

Margaret Chase Smith: *Declaration of Conscience*
Washington, D.C., June 1, 1950   487

William Faulkner: *Nobel Prize Address*
Stockholm, December 10, 1950   493

Douglas MacArthur: *Address to Congress*
Washington, D.C., April 19, 1951   495

Richard M. Nixon: *"Checkers" Speech*
Hollywood, California, September 23, 1952   504

Martin Luther King, Jr.: *Speech to the Montgomery
Improvement Association*
Montgomery, Alabama, December 5, 1955   516

Dwight D. Eisenhower: *Second Inaugural Address*
Washington, D.C., January 21, 1957   520

John F. Kennedy: *Speech to the Greater Houston
Ministerial Association*
Houston, September 12, 1960   525

Dwight D. Eisenhower: *Farewell Address*
Washington, D.C., January 17, 1961   529

John F. Kennedy: *Inaugural Address*
Washington, D.C., January 20, 1961   535

John F. Kennedy: *Address at American University*
Washington, D.C., June 10, 1963   539

John F. Kennedy: *Address to the Nation on Civil Rights*
Washington, D.C., June 11, 1963   548

John F. Kennedy: *Speech in the Rudolph Wilde Platz*
Berlin, June 26, 1963   554

Martin Luther King, Jr.: *Address at the March
on Washington*
August 28, 1963   556

Betty Friedan: *The Crisis in Women's Identity*
San Francisco, 1964   561

Malcolm X: *The Ballot or the Bullet*
Cleveland, April 3, 1964   574

Barry Goldwater: *Speech to the Republican National
   Convention*
San Francisco, July 16, 1964   595

Ronald Reagan: *Speech on Behalf of Barry Goldwater*
Los Angeles, October 27, 1964   604

Mario Savio: *Speech in Sproul Plaza*
Berkeley, California, December 2, 1964   616

Martin Luther King, Jr.: *Nobel Prize Address*
Oslo, December 10, 1964   619

Lyndon B. Johnson: *Address to Congress on Voting Rights*
Washington, D.C., March 15, 1965   623

Lyndon B. Johnson: *Address at Howard University*
Washington, D.C., June 4, 1965   633

Robert F. Kennedy: *Address at the University of
   Cape Town*
South Africa, June 6, 1966   641

Martin Luther King, Jr.: *Speech on the Vietnam War*
New York City, April 4, 1967   651

Martin Luther King, Jr.: *Sermon at National Cathedral*
Washington, D.C., March 31, 1968   668

Martin Luther King, Jr.: *Speech at Mason Temple*
Memphis, April 3, 1968   681

Robert F. Kennedy: *Remarks on the Assassination of
   Martin Luther King*
Indianapolis, April 4, 1968   693

Barbara Jordan: *Statement to the House Judiciary
   Committee*
Washington, D.C., July 25, 1974   695

Richard M. Nixon: *Remarks on Leaving the White House*
Washington, D.C., August 9, 1974   700

Jimmy Carter: *Address to the Nation on Energy Policy*
Washington, D.C., July 15, 1979   705

Edward M. Kennedy: *Speech to the Democratic National Convention*
New York City, August 12, 1980   715

Ronald Reagan: *Address to Members of Parliament*
London, June 8, 1982   724

Ronald Reagan: *Address at Pointe-du-Hoc*
Normandy, June 6, 1984   736

Jesse Jackson: *Speech to the Democratic National Convention*
San Francisco, July 17, 1984   741

Ronald Reagan: *Address to the Nation on the* Challenger *Disaster*
Washington, D.C., January 28, 1986   754

Ronald Reagan: *Speech at the Brandenburg Gate*
Berlin, June 12, 1987   756

William J. Clinton: *Speech at Mason Temple*
Memphis, November 13, 1993   763

William J. Clinton: *Speech at Central High School*
Little Rock, Arkansas, September 25, 1997   773

Biographical Notes   783
Note on the Texts   801
Notes   810
Index   859

ABRAHAM LINCOLN

Speech on Reconstruction

Washington, D.C., April 11, 1865

W E MEET this evening, not in sorrow, but in gladness of heart. The evacuation of Petersburg and Richmond, and the surrender of the principal insurgent army, give hope of a righteous and speedy peace whose joyous expression can not be restrained. In the midst of this, however, He, from Whom all blessings flow, must not be forgotten. A call for a national thanksgiving is being prepared, and will be duly promulgated. Nor must those whose harder part gives us the cause of rejoicing, be overlooked. Their honors must not be parcelled out with others. I myself, was near the front, and had the high pleasure of transmitting much of the good news to you; but no part of the honor, for plan or execution, is mine. To Gen. Grant, his skilful officers, and brave men, all belongs. The gallant Navy stood ready, but was not in reach to take active part.

By these recent successes the re-inauguration of the national authority—reconstruction—which has had a large share of thought from the first, is pressed much more closely upon our attention. It is fraught with great difficulty. Unlike the case of a war between independent nations, there is no authorized organ for us to treat with. No one man has authority to give up the rebellion for any other man. We simply must begin with, and mould from, disorganized and discordant elements. Nor is it a small additional embarrassment that we, the loyal people, differ among ourselves as to the mode, manner, and means of reconstruction.

As a general rule, I abstain from reading the reports of attacks upon myself, wishing not to be provoked by that to which I can not properly offer an answer. In spite of this precaution, however, it comes to my knowledge that I am much censured for some supposed agency in setting up, and seeking to sustain, the new State Government of Louisiana. In this I have done

just so much as, and no more than, the public knows. In the
Annual Message of Dec. 1863 and accompanying Proclamation,
I presented *a* plan of reconstruction (as the phrase goes) which,
I promised, if adopted by any State, should be acceptable to,
and sustained by, the Executive government of the nation. I
distinctly stated that this was not the only plan which might
possibly be acceptable; and I also distinctly protested that the
Executive claimed no right to say when, or whether members
should be admitted to seats in Congress from such States. This
plan was, in advance, submitted to the then Cabinet, and distinctly approved by every member of it. One of them suggested that I should then, and in that connection, apply the
Emancipation Proclamation to the theretofore excepted parts
of Virginia and Louisiana; that I should drop the suggestion
about apprenticeship for freed-people, and that I should omit
the protest against my own power, in regard to the admission
of members to Congress; but even he approved every part and
parcel of the plan which has since been employed or touched
by the action of Louisiana. The new constitution of Louisiana,
declaring emancipation for the whole State, practically applies
the Proclamation to the part previously excepted. It does not
adopt apprenticeship for freed-people; and it is silent, as it
could not well be otherwise, about the admission of members
to Congress. So that, as it applies to Louisiana, every member
of the Cabinet fully approved the plan. The Message went to
Congress, and I received many commendations of the plan,
written and verbal; and not a single objection to it, from any
professed emancipationist, came to my knowledge, until after
the news reached Washington that the people of Louisiana had
begun to move in accordance with it. From about July 1862, I
had corresponded with different persons, supposed to be interested, seeking a reconstruction of a State government for
Louisiana. When the Message of 1863, with the plan before
mentioned, reached New-Orleans, Gen. Banks wrote me that
he was confident the people, with his military co-operation,
would reconstruct, substantially on that plan. I wrote him, and
some of them to try it; they tried it, and the result is known.
Such only has been my agency in getting up the Louisiana government. As to sustaining it, my promise is out, as before stated.
But, as bad promises are better broken than kept, I shall treat

this as a bad promise, and break it, whenever I shall be convinced that keeping it is adverse to the public interest. But I
have not yet been so convinced.

I have been shown a letter on this subject, supposed to be an
able one, in which the writer expresses regret that my mind has
not seemed to be definitely fixed on the question whether the
seceded States, so called, are in the Union or out of it. It would
perhaps, add astonishment to his regret, were he to learn that
since I have found professed Union men endeavoring to make
that question, I have *purposely* forborne any public expression
upon it. As appears to me that question has not been, nor yet
is, a practically material one, and that any discussion of it,
while it thus remains practically immaterial, could have no effect other than the mischievous one of dividing our friends. As
yet, whatever it may hereafter become, that question is bad, as
the basis of a controversy, and good for nothing at all—a
merely pernicious abstraction.

We all agree that the seceded States, so called, are out of
their proper practical relation with the Union; and that the sole
object of the government, civil and military, in regard to those
States is to again get them into that proper practical relation. I
believe it is not only possible, but in fact, easier, to do this,
without deciding, or even considering, whether these states
have even been out of the Union, than with it. Finding themselves safely at home, it would be utterly immaterial whether
they had ever been abroad. Let us all join in doing the acts
necessary to restoring the proper practical relations between
these states and the Union; and each forever after, innocently
indulge his own opinion whether, in doing the acts, he brought
the States from without, into the Union, or only gave them
proper assistance, they never having been out of it.

The amount of constituency, so to speak, on which the new
Louisiana government rests, would be more satisfactory to all,
if it contained fifty, thirty, or even twenty thousand, instead of
only about twelve thousand, as it does. It is also unsatisfactory
to some that the elective franchise is not given to the colored
man. I would myself prefer that it were now conferred on the
very intelligent, and on those who serve our cause as soldiers.
Still the question is not whether the Louisiana government, as
it stands, is quite all that is desirable. The question is "Will it

be wiser to take it as it is, and help to improve it; or to reject, and disperse it?" "Can Louisiana be brought into proper practical relation with the Union *sooner* by *sustaining*, or by *discarding* her new State Government?"

Some twelve thousand voters in the heretofore slave-state of Louisiana have sworn allegiance to the Union, assumed to be the rightful political power of the State, held elections, organized a State government, adopted a free-state constitution, giving the benefit of public schools equally to black and white, and empowering the Legislature to confer the elective franchise upon the colored man. Their Legislature has already voted to ratify the constitutional amendment recently passed by Congress, abolishing slavery throughout the nation. These twelve thousand persons are thus fully committed to the Union, and to perpetual freedom in the state—committed to the very things, and nearly all the things the nation wants—and they ask the nations recognition, and it's assistance to make good their committal. Now, if we reject, and spurn them, we do our utmost to disorganize and disperse them. We in effect say to the white men "You are worthless, or worse—we will neither help you, nor be helped by you." To the blacks we say "This cup of liberty which these, your old masters, hold to your lips, we will dash from you, and leave you to the chances of gathering the spilled and scattered contents in some vague and undefined when, where, and how." If this course, discouraging and paralyzing both white and black, has any tendency to bring Louisiana into proper practical relations with the Union, I have, so far, been unable to perceive it. If, on the contrary, we recognize, and sustain the new government of Louisiana the converse of all this is made true. We encourage the hearts, and nerve the arms of the twelve thousand to adhere to their work, and argue for it, and proselyte for it, and fight for it, and feed it, and grow it, and ripen it to a complete success. The colored man too, in seeing all united for him, is inspired with vigilance, and energy, and daring, to the same end. Grant that he desires the elective franchise, will he not attain it sooner by saving the already advanced steps toward it, than by running backward over them? Concede that the new government of Louisiana is only to what it should be as the egg is to the fowl, we shall sooner have the fowl by hatching the egg than by smashing it?

Again, if we reject Louisiana, we also reject one vote in favor of the proposed amendment to the national constitution. To meet this proposition, it has been argued that no more than three fourths of those States which have not attempted secession are necessary to validly ratify the amendment. I do not commit myself against this, further than to say that such a ratification would be questionable, and sure to be persistently questioned; while a ratification by three fourths of all the States would be unquestioned and unquestionable.

I repeat the question. "Can Louisiana be brought into proper practical relation with the Union *sooner* by *sustaining* or by *discarding* her new State Government?"

What has been said of Louisiana will apply generally to other States. And yet so great peculiarities pertain to each state; and such important and sudden changes occur in the same state; and, withal, so new and unprecedented is the whole case, that no exclusive, and inflexible plan can safely be prescribed as to details and colatterals. Such exclusive, and inflexible plan, would surely become a new entanglement. Important principles may, and must, be inflexible.

In the present "*situation*" as the phrase goes, it may be my duty to make some new announcement to the people of the South. I am considering, and shall not fail to act, when satisfied that action will be proper

THADDEUS STEVENS

Speech in Congress on Reconstruction

Washington, D.C., December 18, 1865

A CANDID examination of the power and proper principles of reconstruction can be offensive to no one, and may possibly be profitable by exciting inquiry. One of the suggestions of the message which we are now considering has special reference to this. Perhaps it is the principle most interesting to the people at this time. The President assumes, what no one doubts, that the late rebel States have lost their constitutional relations to the Union, and are incapable of representation in Congress, except by permission of the Government. It matters but little, with this admission, whether you call them States out of the Union, and now conquered territories, or assert that because the Constitution forbids them to do what they did do, that they are therefore only dead as to all national and political action, and will remain so until the Government shall breathe into them the breath of life anew and permit them to occupy their former position. In other words, that they are not out of the Union, but are only dead carcasses lying within the Union. In either case, it is very plain that it requires the action of Congress to enable them to form a State government and send representatives to Congress. Nobody, I believe, pretends that with their old constitutions and frames of government they can be permitted to claim their old rights under the Constitution. They have torn their constitutional States into atoms, and built on their foundations fabrics of a totally different character. Dead men cannot raise themselves. Dead States cannot restore their own existence "as it was." Whose especial duty is it to do it? In whom does the Constitution place the power? Not in the judicial branch of Government, for it only adjudicates and does not prescribe laws. Not in the Executive, for he only executes and cannot make laws. Not in the Commander-in-Chief of the armies, for he can only hold them under military rule until the sovereign legislative power of the conqueror shall give them law.

There is fortunately no difficulty in solving the question. There are two provisions in the Constitution, under one of which the case must fall. The fourth article says:

"New States may be admitted by the Congress into this Union."

In my judgment this is the controlling provision in this case. Unless the law of nations is a dead letter, the late war between two acknowledged belligerents severed their original compacts, and broke all the ties that bound them together. The future condition of the conquered power depends on the will of the conqueror. They must come in as new States or remain as conquered provinces. Congress—the Senate and House of Representatives, with the concurrence of the President—is the only power that can act in the matter. But suppose, as some dreaming theorists imagine, that these States have never been out of the Union, but have only destroyed their State governments so as to be incapable of political action; then the fourth section of the fourth article applies, which says:

"The United States shall guaranty to every State in this Union a republican form of government."

Who is the United States? Not the judiciary; not the President; but the sovereign power of the people, exercised through their representatives in Congress, with the concurrence of the Executive. It means the political Government—the concurrent action of both branches of Congress and the Executive. The separate action of each amounts to nothing, either in admitting new States or guarantying republican governments to lapsed or outlawed States. Whence springs the preposterous idea that either the President, or the Senate, or the House of Representatives, acting separately, can determine the right of States to send members or Senators to the Congress of the Union?

To prove that they are and for four years have been out of the Union for all legal purposes, and being now conquered, subject to the absolute disposal of Congress, I will suggest a few ideas and adduce a few authorities. If the so-called "confederate States of America" were an independent belligerent, and were so acknowledged by the United States and by Europe, or had assumed and maintained an attitude which entitled them to be considered and treated as a belligerent, then, during such time, they were precisely in the condition of a foreign nation with whom we were at war; nor need their independence as a nation be acknowledged by us to produce that effect. In the able opinion delivered by that accomplished and loyal jurist, Mr. Justice Grier, in the prize cases, all the law on these points is collected and clearly stated. (2 Black, page 66.) Speaking of civil wars, and following Vattel, he says:

"When the party in rebellion occupy and hold in a hostile manner a certain portion of territory; have declared their independence; have cast off their allegiance; have organized armies; have commenced hostilities against their former sovereign, the world acknowledges them as belligerents, and the contest a war."

And

"The parties belligerent in a public war are independent nations. But it is not necessary, to constitute war, that both parties should be acknowledged as independent nations or foreign States. A war may exist where one of the belligerents claims sovereign rights as against the other."

The idea that the States could not and did not make war because the Constitution forbids it, and that this must be treated as a war of individuals, is a very injurious and groundless fallacy. Individuals cannot make war. They may commit murder, but that is no war. Communities, societies, States, make war, Phillimore says, (volume three, page 68:)

"War between private individuals who are members of a society cannot exist. The use of force in such a case is trespass and not war."

But why appeal to reason to prove that the seceded States made war as States, when the conclusive opinion of the Supreme Court is at hand? In the prize cases already cited, the Supreme Court say:

"Hence, in organizing this rebellion, they have acted as States claiming to be sovereign over all persons and property within their respective limits, and asserting a right to absolve their citizens from their allegiance to the Federal Government. Several of these States have combined to form a new confederacy, claiming to be acknowledged by the world as a sovereign State. Their right to do so is now being decided by wager of battle. The ports and territory of each of these States are held in hostility to the General Government. It is no loose, unorganized insurrection, having no defined boundary or possession. It has a boundary marked by lines of bayonets, and which can be crossed only by force. South of this line is enemies' territory, because it is claimed and held in possession by an organized hostile and belligerent power."

Again, the court say, what I have been astonished that any one should doubt:

"The proclamation of blockade is itself official and conclusive evidence to the court that a state of war existed."

Now, what was the legal result of such war?

"The conventions, the treaties, made with a nation are broken or annulled by a war arising between the contracting parties."—*Vattel*, 372; *Halleck*, 371, section 23.

If gentlemen suppose that this doctrine applies only to national and not to civil wars, I beg leave to refer them to Vattel, page 423. He says:

"A civil war breaks the bands of society and government, or at least suspends their force and effect; it produces in the nation two independent parties, who consider each other as enemies, and acknowledge no common judge. These two parties must therefore be considered as thenceforward constituting, at least for a time, two separate bodies; two distinct societies. They stand, therefore, in precisely the same predicament as two nations who engage in a contest, and being unable to come to an agreement, have recourse to arms."

At page 427:

"And when a nation becomes divided into two parties absolutely independent, and no longer acknowledge a common superior, the State is dissolved, and the war between the two parties stands on the same ground, in every respect, as a public war between two different nations."

But must the belligerent be acknowledged as an independent nation, as some contend? That is answered in the case referred to in 2 Black, as follows:

"It is not the less a civil war, with belligerent parties in hostile array, because it may be called an 'insurrection' by one side, and the insurgents be considered as rebels or traitors. It is not necessary that the independence of the revolted province or State be acknowledged in order to constitute it a party belligerent in a war, according to the law of nations."

This doctrine, so clearly established by publicists, and so distinctly stated by Mr. Justice Grier, has been frequently reiterated since by the Supreme Court of the United States. In Mr. Alexander's case (2 Wallace, 419) the present able Chief Justice, delivering the opinion of the court, says:

"We must be governed by the principle of public law so often announced from this bench as applicable to civil and international wars, that all the people of each State or district in insurrection against the United States must be regarded as enemies until by the action of the Legislature and Executive, or otherwise, that relation is thoroughly and permanently changed."

After such clear and repeated decisions it is something worse than ridiculous to hear men of respectable standing attempting to nullify the law of nations, and declare the Supreme Court of the United States in error, because, as the Constitution forbids it, the States could not go out of the Union in fact. A respectable gentleman was lately reciting this argument, when he suddenly stopped and said, "Did you hear of that atrocious murder committed in our town? A rebel deliberately murdered a Government official." The person addressed said, "I think you are mistaken." "How so? I saw it myself." "You are wrong, no murder was or could be committed, for the law forbids it."

The theory that the rebel States, for four years a separate power and without representation in Congress, were all the time here in the Union, is a good deal less ingenious and respectable than the metaphyscis of Berkeley, which proved that neither the world nor any human being was in existence. If this theory were simply ridiculous it could be forgiven; but its effect is deeply injurious to the stability of the nation. I cannot doubt that the late confederate States are out of the Union to all intents and purposes for which the conqueror may choose so to consider them.

But on the ground of estoppel, the United States have the clear right to elect to adjudge them out of the Union. They are estopped both by matter of record and matter *in pais.* One of the first resolutions passed by seceded South Carolina in January, 1861, is as follows:

> "*Resolved, unanimously,* That the separation of South Carolina from the Federal Union is final, and she has no further interest in the Constitution of the United States; and that the only appropriate negotiations between her and the Federal Government are as to their mutual relations as foreign States."

Similar resolutions appear upon all their State and confederate government records. The speeches of their members of congress, their generals and executive officers, and the answers of their government to our shameful sueings for peace, went upon the defiant ground that no terms would be offered or received except upon the prior acknowledgment of the entire and permanent independence of the confederate States. After this, to deny that we have a right to treat them as a conquered belligerent, severed from the Union in fact, is not argument but mockery. Whether it be our interest to do so is the only question hereafter and more deliberately to be considered.

But suppose these powerful but now subdued belligerents, instead of being out of the Union, are merely destroyed, and are now lying about, a dead corpse, or with animation so suspended as to be incapable of action, and wholly unable to heal themselves by any unaided movements of their own. Then they may fall under the provision of the Constitution which says "the United States shall guaranty to every State in the Union a republican form of government." Under that power can the judiciary, or the President, or the Commander-in-Chief of the Army, or the Senate or House of Representatives, acting separately, restore them to life and readmit them into the Union? I insist that if each acted separately, though the action of each was identical with the others, it would amount to nothing. Nothing but the joint action of the two Houses of Congress and the concurrence of the President could do it. If the Senate admitted their Senators, and the House their members, it would have no effect on the future action of Congress. The Fortieth Congress might reject both. Such is the ragged record of Congress for the last four years.

In Luther *vs.* Borden (7 Howard, 1–42) the Supreme Court say:

"Under this article of the Constitution [the one above cited] it rests with Congress to decide what government is the established one in a State. For as the United States guaranty to each State a republican government, Congress must necessarily decide what government is established in the State before it can determine whether it is republican or not."

Congress alone can do it. But Congress does not mean the Senate, or the House of Representatives, and President, all acting severally. Their joint action constitutes Congress. Hence a law of Congress must be passed before any new State can be admitted; or any dead ones revived. Until then no member can be lawfully admitted into either House. Hence it appears with how little knowledge of constitutional law each branch is urged to admit members separately from these destroyed States. The provision that "each House shall be the judge of the elections, returns, and qualifications of its own members," has not the most distant bearing on this question. Congress must create States and declare when they are entitled to be represented. Then each House must judge whether the members presenting themselves from a recognized State possess the requisite qualifications of age, residence, and citizenship; and whether the election and returns are according to law. The Houses, separately, can judge of nothing else. It seems amazing that any man of legal education could give it any larger meaning.

It is obvious from all this that the first duty of Congress is to pass a law declaring the condition of these outside or defunct States, and providing proper civil governments for them. Since the conquest they have been governed by martial law. Military rule is necessarily despotic, and ought not to exist longer than is absolutely necessary. As there are no symptoms that the people of these provinces will be prepared to participate in constitutional government for some years, I know of no arrangement so proper for them as territorial governments. There they can learn the principles of freedom and eat the fruit of foul rebellion. Under such governments, while electing members to the Territorial Legislatures, they will necessarily mingle with those to whom Congress shall extend the right of suffrage. In Territories Congress fixes the qualifications of electors; and I know of no better place nor better occasion for the conquered rebels and the conqueror to practice justice to all men, and accustom themselves to make and to obey equal laws.

As these fallen rebels cannot at their option reënter the heaven which they have disturbed, the garden of Eden which they have deserted, and flaming swords are set at the gates to secure their exclusion, it becomes important to the welfare of the nation to inquire when the doors shall be reopened for their admission.

According to my judgment they ought never to be recognized as capable of acting in the Union, or of being counted as valid States, until the Constitution shall have been so amended as to make it what its framers intended; and so as to secure perpetual ascendency to the party of the Union; and so as to render our republican Government firm and stable forever. The first of those amendments is to change the basis of representation among the States from Federal numbers to actual voters. Now all the colored freemen in the slave States, and three fifths of the slaves, are represented, though none of them have votes. The States have nineteen representatives of colored slaves. If the slaves are now free then they can add, for the other two fifths, thirteen more, making the slave representation thirty-two. I suppose the free blacks in those States will give at least five more, making the representation of non-voting people of color about thirty-seven. The whole number of representatives now from the slave States is seventy. Add the other two fifths and it will be eighty-three.

If the amendment prevails, and those States withhold the right of suffrage from persons of color, it will deduct about thirty-seven, leaving them but forty-six. With the basis unchanged, the eighty-three southern members, with the Democrats that will in the best times be elected from the North, will always give them a majority in Congress and in the Electoral College. They will at the very first election take posession of the White House and the halls of Congress. I need not depict the ruin that would follow. Assumption of the rebel debt or repudiation of the Federal debt would be sure to follow. The oppression of the freedmen; the reamendment of their State constitutions, and the reëstablishment of slavery would be the inevitable result. That they would scorn and disregard their present constitutions, forced upon them in the midst of martial law, would be both natural and just. No one who has any regard for freedom of elections can look upon those governments, forced upon them in duress, with any favor. If they should grant the right of suffrage to persons of color, I think there would always be Union white men enough in the South, aided by the blacks, to divide the representation, and thus continue the Republican ascendency. If they should refuse to thus alter their election laws it would reduce the representatives of the late slave States to about forty-five and render them powerless for evil.

It is plain that this amendment must be consummated before the defunct States are admitted to be capable of State action, or it never can be.

The proposed amendment to allow Congress to lay a duty on exports is precisely in the same situation. Its importance cannot well be overstated. It is very obvious that for many years the South will not pay much under our internal revenue laws. The only article on which we can raise any considerable amount is cotton. It will be grown largely at once. With ten cents a pound export duty it would be furnished cheaper to foreign markets than they could obtain it from any other part of the world. The late war has shown that. Two million bales exported, at five hundred pounds to the bale, would yield $100,000,000. This seems to be the chief revenue we shall ever derive from the South. Besides, it would be a protection to that amount to our domestic manufactures. Other proposed amendments—to make all laws uniform; to prohibit the assumption of the rebel debt—are of vital importance, and the only thing that can prevent the combined forces of copperheads and secessionists from legislating against the interests of the Union whenever they may obtain an accidental majority.

But this is not all that we ought to do before these inveterate rebels are invited to participate in our legislation. We have turned, or are about to turn, loose four million slaves without a hut to shelter them or a cent in their pockets. The infernal laws of slavery have prevented them from acquiring an education, understanding the commonest laws of contract, or of managing the ordinary business of life. This Congress is bound to provide for them until they can take care of themselves. If we do not furnish them with homesteads, and hedge them around with protective laws; if we leave them to the legislation of their late masters, we had better have left them in bondage. Their condition would be worse than that of our prisoners at Andersonville. If we fail in this great duty now, when we have the power, we shall deserve and receive the execration of history and of all future ages.

Two things are of vital importance.

1. So to establish a principle that none of the rebel States shall be counted in any of the amendments of the Constitution until they are duly admitted into the family of States by the law-making power of their conqueror. For more than six months the amendment of the Constitution abolishing slavery has been ratified by the Legislatures of three fourths of the States that acted on its passage by Congress, and which had Legislatures, or which were States capable of acting, or required to act, on the question.

I take no account of the aggregation of whitewashed rebels, who without any legal authority have assembled in the capitals of the late rebel States and simulated legislative bodies. Nor do I regard with any respect the cunning byplay into which they deluded the Secretary of State by frequent telegraphic announcements that "South Carolina had adopted the amendment;" "Alabama has adopted the amendment, being the twenty-seventh State," &c. This was intended to delude the people, and accustom Congress to hear repeated the names of these extinct States as if they were alive; when, in truth, they have now no more existence than the revolted cities of Latium, two thirds of whose people were colonized and their property confiscated, and their right of citizenship withdrawn by conquering and avenging Rome.

2. It is equally important to the stability of this Republic that it should now be solemnly decided what power can revive, recreate, and reinstate these provinces into the family of States, and invest them with the rights of American citizens. It is time that Congress should assert its sovereignty, and assume something of the dignity of a Roman senate. It is fortunate that the President invites Congress to take this manly attitude. After stating with great frankness in his able message his theory,

which, however, is found to be impracticable, and which I believe very few now consider tenable, he refers the whole matter to the judgment of Congress. If Congress should fail firmly and wisely to discharge that high duty it is not the fault of the President.

This Congress owes it to its own character to set the seal of reprobation upon a doctrine which is becoming too fashionable, and unless rebuked will be the recognized principle of our Government. Governor Perry and other provisional governors and orators proclaim that "this is the white man's Government." The whole copperhead party, pandering to the lowest prejudices of the ignorant, repeat the cuckoo cry, "This is the white man's Government." Demagogues of all parties, even some high in authority, gravely shout, "This is the white man's Government." What is implied by this? That one race of men are to have the exclusive right forever to rule this nation, and to exercise all acts of sovereignty, while all other races and nations and colors are to be their subjects, and have no voice in making the laws and choosing the rulers by whom they are to be governed. Wherein does this differ from slavery except in degree? Does not this contradict all the distinctive principles of the Declaration of Independence? When the great and good men promulgated that instrument, and pledged their lives and sacred honors to defend it, it was supposed to form an epoch in civil government. Before that time it was held that the right to rule was vested in families, dynasties, or races, not because of superior intelligence or virtue, but because of a divine right to enjoy exclusive privileges.

Our fathers repudiated the whole doctrine of the legal superiority of families or races, and proclaimed the equality of men before the law. Upon that they created a revolution and built the Republic. They were prevented by slavery from perfecting the superstructure whose foundation they had thus broadly laid. For the sake of the Union they consented to wait, but never relinquished the idea of its final completion. The time to which they looked forward with anxiety has come. It is our duty to complete their work. If this Republic is not now made to stand on their great principles, it has no honest foundation, and the Father of all men will still shake it to its center. If we have not yet been sufficiently scourged for our national sin to teach us to do justice to all God's creatures, without distinction of race or color, we must expect the still more heavy vengeance of an offended Father, still increasing his inflictions as he increased the severity of the plagues of Egypt until the tyrant consented to do justice. And when that tyrant repented of his reluctant consent, and attempted to re-enslave the people, as our southern tyrants are attempting to do now, he filled the Red sea with broken chariots and drowned horses, and strewed the shores with dead carcasses.

Mr. Chairman, I trust the Republican party will not be alarmed at what I am saying. I do not profess to speak their sentiments, nor must they be held responsible for them. I speak for myself, and take the responsibility, and will settle with my intelligent constituents.

This is not a "white man's Government," in the exclusive sense in which it is used. To say so is political blasphemy, for it violates the fundamental principles of our gospel of liberty. This is man's Government; the Government of all men alike; not that all men will have equal power and sway within it. Accidental circumstances, natural and acquired endowment and ability, will vary their fortunes. But equal rights to all the privileges of the Government is innate in every immortal being, no matter what the shape or color of the tabernacle which it inhabits.

If equal privileges were granted to all, I should not expect any but white men to be elected to office for long ages to come. The prejudice engendered by slavery would not soon permit merit to be preferred to color. But it would still be beneficial to the weaker races. In a country where political divisions will always exist, their power, joined with just white men, would greatly modify, if it did not entirely prevent, the injustice of majorities. Without the right of suffrage in the late slave States, (I do not speak of the free States,) I believe the slaves had far better been left in bondage. I see it stated that very distinguished advocates of the right of suffrage lately declared in this city that they do not expect to obtain it by congressional legislation, but only by administrative action, because, as one gallant gentleman said, the States had not been out of the Union. Then they will never get it. The President is far sounder than they. He sees that administrative action has nothing to do with it. If it ever is to come, it must be constitutional amendments or congressional action in the Territories, and in enabling acts.

How shameful that men of influence should mislead and miseducate the public mind! They proclaim, "This is the white man's Government," and the whole coil of copperheads echo the same sentiment, and upstart, jealous Republicans join the cry. Is it any wonder ignorant foreigners and illiterate natives should learn this doctrine, and be led to despise and maltreat a whole race of their fellow-men?

Sir, this doctrine of a white man's Government is as atrocious as the infamous sentiment that damned the late Chief Justice to everlasting fame; and, I fear, to everlasting fire.

SOJOURNER TRUTH

Speech at Meeting Commemorating Emancipation

Boston, January 1, 1871

WELL, chilern, I'm glad to see so many together. Ef I am eighty-three years old, I only count my age from de time dat I was 'mancipated. Then I 'gun ter live. God is a ful-fillin', an' my lost time dat I lost bein' a slave was made up. W'en I was a slave I hated de w'ite pepul. My mother said to me when I was to be sole from her, 'I want to tole ye dese tings dat you will allers know dat I have tole you, for dar will be a great many tings tole you after I sta't out ob dis life inter de world to come.' An' I say dis to you all, for here is a great many pepul dat when I step out ob dis existence, dat you will know what you heered ole Sojourn' Truth tell you. I was boun' a slave in the State of Noo Yo'k, Ulster County, 'mong de low Dutch. W'en I was ten years old, I couldn't speak a word of Inglish, an' hab no eddicati'n at all. Dere's wonder what dey has done fur me. As I tole you w'en I was sole, my master died, an' we was goin' to hab a auction. We was all brought up to be sole. My mother, my fader was very ole, my brudder younger 'en myself, an' my mother took my han'. Dey opened a canoby ob ebben, an' she sat down an' I an' my brudder sat down by her, en she says, 'Look up to de moon an' stars dat shine upon you father an' upon you mother when you sole far away, an' upon you brudders an' sisters, dat is sole away,' for dere was a great number ob us, an' was all sole away befor' my mem-brance. I asked her who had made de moon an' de stars, an' she says, 'God,' an' says I, Where is God? 'Oh!' says she, 'chile, he sits in de sky, an' he hears you w'en you ax him w'en you are away from us to make your marster an' misteress good, an' he will do it.'

"When we were sole, I did what my mother told me; I said, O God, my mother tole me ef I asked you to make my marster

19

an' misteress good, you'd do it, an' dey didn't get good. [Laughter.] Why, says I, God, mebbe you can't do it. Kill 'em. [Laughter and applause.] I didn't tink he could make dem good. Dat was de idee I had. After I made such wishes my conscience burned me. Then I wud say, O God, don't be mad. My marster make me wicked; an' I of'm thought how pepul can do such 'bominable wicked things an' dere conscience not burn dem. Now I only made wishes. I used to tell God this—I would say, 'Now, God, ef I was you, an' you was me [laughter], and you wanted any help I'd help ye;—why done you help me?' [Laughter and applause.] Well, ye see I was in want, an' I felt dat dere was no help. I know what it is to be taken in the barn an' tied up an' de blood drawed out ob yere bare back, an' I tell you it would make you think 'bout God. Yes, an' den I felt, O God, ef I was you an' you felt like I do, an' asked me for help I would help you—now why won't you help me? Trooly I done know but God has helped me. But I got no good marster ontil de las' time. I was sole, an' den I found one an' his name was Jesus. Oh, I tell ye, didn't I fine a good marster when I use to feel so bad, when I use to say, O God, how ken I libe? I'm sorely 'prest both widin and widout. W'en God gi' me dat marster he healed all de wounds up. My soul rejoiced. I used to hate de w'ite pepul so, an' I tell ye w'en de lobe come in me I had so much lobe I didn't know what to lobe. Den de w'ite pepul come, an' I thought dat lobe was too good fur dem. Den I said, Yea, God, I'll lobe ev'ybuddy an' de w'ite pepul too. Ever since dat, dat lobe has continued an' kep' me 'mong de w'ite pepul. Well, 'mancipation came; we all know; can't stop to go troo de hull. I go fur adgitatin'. But I believe dere is works belong wid adgitatin', too. On'y think ob it! Ain't it wonderful dat God gives lobe enough to de Ethiopins to lobe you?

"Now, here is de question dat I am here to-night to say. I been to Washin'ton, an' I fine out dis, dat de colud pepul dat is in Washin'tun libin on de gobernment dat de United Staas ort to gi' 'em lan' an' move 'em on it. Dey are libin on de gov'ment, an' dere is pepul takin' care of 'em costin' you so much, an' it don't benefit him 'tall. It degrades him wuss an' wuss. Therefo' I say dat these people, take an' put 'em in de West where you ken enrich 'em. I know de good pepul in de

South can't take care of de negroes as dey ort to, case de ribils won't let 'em. How much better will it be for to take them cu lud pepul an' give 'em land? We've airnt lan' enough for a home, an' it would be a benefit for you all an' God would bless de hull ob ye for doin' it. Dey say, Let 'em take keer of derselves. Why, you've taken dat all away from 'em. Ain't got nuffin lef'. Get dese culud pepul out of Washin'tun off ob de gov'ment, an' get de ole pepul out and build dem homes in de West, where dey can feed themselves, and dey would soon be abel to be a pepul among you. Dat is my commission. Now adgitate them pepul an' put 'em dere; learn 'em to read one part of de time an' learn 'em to work de udder part ob de time."

At this moment a member in the audience arose and left, greatly to the disturbance of the lady, who could with difficulty make herself heard.

"I'll hole on a while," she said. "Whoever is agoin' let him go. When you tell about work here, den you have to scud. [Laughter and applause.] I tell you I can't read a book, but I can read de people. [Applause.] I speak dese tings so dat when you have a paper come for you to sign, you ken sign it."

SUSAN B. ANTHONY

Is It a Crime for a Citizen of the United States to Vote?

Monroe County, N.Y., March–April 1873
Ontario County, N.Y., May–June 1873

FRIENDS AND FELLOW-CITIZENS: I stand before you to-night, under indictment for the alleged crime of having voted at the last Presidential election, without having a lawful right to vote. It shall be my work this evening to prove to you that in thus voting, I not only committed no crime, but, instead, simply exercised my *citizen's right*, guaranteed to me and all United States citizens by the National Constitution, beyond the power of any State to deny.

Our democratic-republican government is based on the idea of the natural right of every individual member thereof to a voice and a vote in making and executing the laws. We assert the province of government to be to secure the people in the enjoyment of their unalienable rights. We throw to the winds the old dogma that governments can give rights. Before governments were organized, no one denies that each individual possessed the right to protect his own life, liberty and property. And when 100 or 1,000,000 people enter into a free government, they do not barter away their natural rights; they simply pledge themselves to protect each other in the enjoyment of them, through prescribed judicial and legislative tribunals. They agree to abandon the methods of brute force in the adjustment of their differences, and adopt those of civilization.

Nor can you find a word in any of the grand documents left us by the fathers that assumes for government the power to create or to confer rights. The Declaration of Independence, the United States Constitution, the constitutions of the several states and the organic laws of the territories, all alike propose to protect the people in the exercise of their God-given rights. Not one of them pretends to bestow rights.

"All men are created equal, and endowed by their Creator with certain unalienable rights. Among these are life, liberty and the pursuit of happiness. That to secure these, governments are instituted among men, deriving their just powers from the consent of the governed."

Here is no shadow of government authority over rights, nor exclusion of any class from their full and equal enjoyment. Here is pronounced the right of all men, and "consequently," as the Quaker preacher said, "of all women," to a voice in the government. And here, in this very first paragraph of the declaration, is the assertion of the natural right of all to the ballot; for, how can "the consent of the governed" be given, if the right to vote be denied. Again:

"That whenever any form of government becomes destructive of these ends, it is the right of the people to alter or abolish it, and to institute a new government, laying its foundations on such principles, and organizing its powers in such forms as to them shall seem most likely to effect their safety and happiness."

Surely, the right of the whole people to vote is here clearly implied. For however destructive to their happiness this government might become, a disfranchised class could neither alter nor abolish it, nor institute a new one, except by the old brute force method of insurrection and rebellion. One-half of the people of this nation to-day are utterly powerless to blot from the statute books an unjust law, or to write there a new and a just one. The women, dissatisfied as they are with this form of government, that enforces taxation without representation,— that compels them to obey laws to which they have never given their consent,—that imprisons and hangs them without a trial by a jury of their peers, that robs them, in marriage, of the custody of their own persons, wages and children,—are this half of the people left wholly at the mercy of the other half, in direct violation of the spirit and letter of the declarations of the framers of this government, every one of which was based on the immutable principle of equal rights to all. By those declarations, kings, priests, popes, aristocrats, were all alike dethroned, and placed on a common level, politically, with the lowliest born subject or serf. By them, too, men, as such, were deprived of their divine right to rule, and placed on a political level with women. By the practice of those declarations all class and caste distinction will be abolished; and slave, serf, plebeian, wife, woman, all alike, bound from their subject position to the proud platform of equality.

The preamble of the federal constitution says:

"We, the people of the United States, in order to form a more perfect union, establish justice, insure *domestic* tranquility, provide for the common defence, promote the general welfare and secure the blessings of liberty to ourselves and our posterity, do ordain and establish this constitution for the United States of America."

It was we, the people, not we, the white male citizens, nor yet we, the male citizens; but we, the whole people, who formed this Union. And we formed it, not to give the blessings of liberty, but to secure them; not to the half of ourselves and the half of our posterity, but to the whole people—women as well as men. And it is downright mockery to talk to women of their enjoyment of the blessings of liberty while they are denied the use of the only means of securing them provided by this democratic-republican government—the ballot.

The early journals of Congress show that when the committee reported to that body the original articles of confederation, the very first article which became the subject of discussion was that respecting equality of suffrage. Article 4th said:

"The better to secure and perpetuate mutual friendship and intercourse between the people of the different States of this Union, the free inhabitants of each of the States, (paupers, vagabonds and fugitives from justice excepted,) shall be entitled to all the privileges and immunities of the free citizens of the several States."

Thus, at the very beginning, did the fathers see the necessity of the universal application of the great principle of equal rights to all—in order to produce the desired result—a harmonious union and a homogeneous people.

Luther Martin, attorney-general of Maryland, in his report to the Legislature of that State of the convention that framed the United States Constitution, said:

"Those who advocated the equality of suffrage took the matter up on the original principles of government: that the reason why each individual man in forming a State government should have an equal vote, is because each individual, before he enters into government, is equally free and equally independent."

James Madison said;

"Under every view of the subject, it seems indispensable that the mass of the citizens should not be without a voice in making the laws which they are to obey, and in choosing the magistrates who are to administer them." Also, "Let it be remembered, finally, that it has ever been the pride and the boast of America that the rights for which she contended were the rights of human nature."

And these assertions of the framers of the United States Constitution of the equal and natural rights of all the people to a voice in the government, have been affirmed and reaffirmed by the leading statesmen of the nation, throughout the entire history of our government.

Thaddeus Stevens, of Pennsylvania, said in 1866:

"I have made up my mind that the elective franchise is one of the inalienable rights meant to be secured by the declaration of independence."

B. Gratz Brown, of Missouri, in the three days' discussion in the United States Senate in 1866, on Senator Cowan's motion to strike "male" from the District of Columbia suffrage bill, said:

"Mr. President, I say here on the floor of the American Senate, I stand for universal suffrage; and as a matter of fundamental principle, do not recognize the right of society to limit it on any ground of race or sex. I will go farther and say, that I recognize the right of franchise as being intrinsically a natural right. I do not believe that society is authorized to impose any limitations upon it that do not spring out of the necessities of the social state itself. Sir, I have been shocked, in the course of this debate, to hear Senators declare this right only a conventional and political arrangement, a privilege yielded to you and me and others; not a right in any sense, only a concession! Mr. President, I do not hold my liberties by any such tenure. On the contrary, I believe that whenever you establish that doctrine, whenever you crystalize that idea in the public mind of this country, you ring the death-knell of American liberties."

Charles Sumner, in his brave protests against the fourteenth and fifteenth amendments, insisted that, so soon as by the thirteenth amendment the slaves became free men, the original powers of the United States Constitution guaranteed to them equal rights—the right to vote and to be voted for. In closing one of his great speeches he said;

"I do not hesitate to say that when the slaves of our country became 'citizens' they took their place in the body politic as a component part of the 'people,' entitled to equal rights, and under the protection of these two guardian principles: First— That all just governments stand on the consent of the governed; and second, that taxation without representation is tyranny; and these rights it is the duty of Congress to guarantee as essential to the idea of a Republic."

The preamble of the Constitution of the State of New York declares the same purpose. It says:

"We, the people of the State of New York, grateful to Almighty God for our freedom, in order to secure its blessings, do establish this Constitution."

Here is not the slightest intimation, either of receiving freedom from the United States Constitution, or of the State conferring the blessings of liberty upon the people; and the same is true of every one of the thirty-six State Constitutions. Each and all, alike declare rights God-given, and that to secure the people in the enjoyment of their inalienable rights, is their one and only object in ordaining and establishing government. And all of the State Constitutions are equally emphatic in their recognition of the ballot as the means of securing the people in the enjoyment of these rights.

Article 1 of the New York State Constitution says:

"No member of this State shall be disfranchised or deprived of the rights or privileges secured to any citizen thereof, unless by the law of the land, or the judgment of his peers."

And so carefully guarded is the citizen's right to vote, that the Constitution makes special mention of all who may be excluded. It says:

"Laws may be passed excluding from the right of suffrage all persons who have been or may be convicted of bribery, larceny or any infamous crime."

In naming the various employments that shall not affect the residence of voters—the 3d section of article 2d says "that being kept at any alms house, or other asylum, at public expense, nor being confined at any public prison, shall deprive a person of his residence," and hence his vote. Thus is the right of voting most sacredly hedged about. The only seeming permission in the New York State Constitution for the disfranchisement of women is in section 1st of article 2d, which says:

"Every male citizen of the age of twenty-one years, &c., shall be entitled to vote."

But I submit that in view of the explicit assertions of the equal right of the whole people, both in the preamble and previous article of the constitution, this omission of the adjective "female" in the second, should not be construed into a denial; but, instead, counted as of no effect. Mark the direct prohibition: "No member of this State shall be disfranchised, unless by the 'law of the land,' or the judgment of his peers." "The law of the land," is the United States Constitution: and there is no provision in that document that can be fairly construed into a permission to the States to deprive any class of their citizens of their right to vote. Hence New York can get no power from that source to disfranchise one entire half of her members. Nor has "the judgment of their peers" been pronounced against women exercising their right to vote; no disfranchised person is allowed to be judge or juror—and none but disfranchised persons can be women's peers; nor has the legislature passed laws excluding them on account of idiocy or lunacy; nor yet the courts convicted them of bribery, larceny, or any infamous crime. Clearly, then, there is no constitutional ground for the exclusion of women from the ballot-box in the State of New York. No barriers whatever stand to-day between women and the exercise of their right to vote save those of precedent and prejudice.

The clauses of the United States Constitution, cited by our opponents as giving power to the States to disfranchise any classes of citizens they shall please, are contained in sections 2d and 4th of article 1st. The second says:

"The House of Representatives shall be composed of

members chosen every second year by the people of the several States; and the electors in each State shall have the qualifications requisite for electors of the most numerous branch of the State Legislature."

This cannot be construed into a concession to the States of the power to destroy the right to become an elector, but simply to prescribe what shall be the qualifications, such as competency of intellect, maturity of age, length of residence, that shall be deemed necessary to enable them to make an intelligent choice of candidates. If, as our opponents assert, the last clause of this section makes it the duty of the United States to protect citizens in the several States against higher or different qualifications for electors for representatives in Congress, than for members of Assembly, then must the first clause make it equally imperative for the national government to interfere with the States, and forbid them from arbitrarily cutting off the right of one-half of the people to become electors altogether. Section 4th says:

"The times, places and manner of holding elections for Senators and Representatives shall be prescribed in each State by the Legislature thereof; but Congress may at any time, by law, make or alter such regulations, except as to the places of choosing Senators."

Here is conceded the power only to prescribe times, places and manner of holding the elections; and even with these Congress may interfere, with all excepting the mere place of choosing Senators. Thus you see, there is not the slightest permission in either section for the States to discriminate against the right of any class of citizens to vote. Surely, to regulate cannot be to annihilate! nor to qualify to wholly deprive. And to this principle every true Democrat and Republican said amen, when applied to black men by Senator Sumner in his great speeches for Equal Rights to all from 1865 to 1869; and when, in 1871, I asked that Senator to declare the power of the United States Constitution to protect women in their right to vote—as he had done for black men—he handed me a copy of all his speeches during that reconstruction period, and said:

"Miss Anthony, put 'sex' where I have 'race' or 'color,' and you have here the best and strongest argument I can make for woman. There is not a doubt but women have the constitutional right to vote, and I will never vote for a sixteenth amendment to guarantee it to them. I voted for both the fourteenth and fifteenth under protest; would never have done it but for the pressing emergency of that hour; would have insisted that the power of the original Constitution to protect all citizens in the equal enjoyment of their rights should have been vindicated through the courts. But the newly made freedmen had neither the intelligence, wealth nor time to wait that slow process. Women possess all these in an eminent degree, and I insist that they shall appeal to the courts, and through them establish the powers of our American *magna charta*, to protect every citizen of the Republic." But, friends, when in accordance with Senator Sumner's counsel, I went to the ballot-box, last November, and exercised my citizen's right to vote, the courts did not wait for me to appeal to them—they appealed to me, and indicted me on the charge of having voted illegally.

Senator Sumner, putting sex where he did color, said:

"Qualifications cannot be in their nature permanent or insurmountable. Sex cannot be a qualification any more than size, race, color, or previous condition of servitude. A permanent or insurmountable qualification is equivalent to a deprivation of the suffrage. In other words, it is the tyranny of taxation without representation, against which our revolutionary mothers, as well as fathers, rebelled."

For any State to make sex a qualification that must ever result in the disfranchisement of one entire half of the people, is to pass a bill of attainder, or an *ex post facto* law, and is therefore a violation of the supreme law of the land. By it, the blessings of liberty are forever withheld from women and their female posterity. To them, this government has no just powers derived from the consent of the governed. To them this government is not a democracy. It is not a republic. It is an odious aristocracy; a hateful obligarchy of sex. The most hateful aristocracy ever established on the face of the globe. An obligarchy of wealth, where the rich govern the poor; an obligarchy of learning, where the educated govern the ignorant; or even an obligarchy of race, where the Saxon rules the African, might be endured; but this obligarchy of sex, which makes father, brothers, husband, sons, the obligarchs over the mother and sisters, the wife and daughters of every household; which ordains all men sovereigns, all women subjects, carries dissension, discord and rebellion into every home of the nation. And this most odious aristocracy exists, too, in the face of Section 4, of Article 4, which says:

"The United States shall guarantee to every State in the Union a republican form of government."

What, I ask you, is the distinctive difference between the inhabitants of a monarchical and those of a republican form of government, save that in the monarchical the people are subjects, helpless, powerless, bound to obey laws made by superiors—while in the republican, the people are citizens, individual sovereigns, all clothed with equal power, to make and unmake both their laws and law makers, and the moment you deprive a person of his right to a voice in the government, you degrade him from the status of a citizen of the republic, to that of a subject, and it matters very little to him whether his monarch be an individual tyrant, as is the Czar of Russia, or a 15,000,000 headed monster, as here in the United States; he is a powerless subject, serf or slave; not a free and independent citizen in any sense.

But, it is urged, the use of the masculine pronouns he, his and him, in all the constitutions and laws, is proof that only men were meant to be included in their provisions. If you insist on this version of the letter of the law, we shall insist that you be consistent, and accept the other horn of the dilemma, which would compel you to exempt women from taxation for the support of the government, and from penalties for the violation of laws.

A year and a half ago I was at Walla Walla, Washington Territory. I saw there a theatrical company, called the "Pixley Sisters," playing before crowded houses, every night of the whole week of the territorial fair. The eldest of those three fatherless girls was scarce eighteen. Yet every night a United States officer stretched out his long fingers, and clutched six dollars of the proceeds of the exhibitions of those orphan girls, who, but a few years before, were half starvelings in the streets of Olympia, the capital of that far-off northwest territory. So the poor widow, who keeps a boarding house, manufactures shirts, or sells apples and peanuts on the street corners of our cities, is compelled to pay taxes from her scanty pittance. I would that the women of this republic, at once, resolve, never again to submit to taxation, until their right to vote be recognized.

Miss Sarah E. Wall, of Worcester, Mass., twenty years ago, took this position. For several years, the officers of the law distrained her property, and sold it to meet the necessary amount; still she persisted, and would not yield an iota, though every foot of her lands should be struck off under the hammer. And now, for several years, the assessor has left her name off the tax list, and the collector passed her by without a call.

Mrs. J. S. Weeden, of Viroqua, Wis., for the past six years, has refused to pay her taxes, though the annual assessment is $75.

Mrs. Ellen Van Valkenburg, of Santa Cruz, Cal., who sued the County Clerk for refusing to register her name, declares she will never pay another dollar of tax until allowed to vote; and all over the country, women property holders are waking up to the injustice of taxation without representation, and ere long will refuse, *en masse*, to submit to the imposition.

There is no she, or her, or hers, in the tax laws.

The statute of New York reads:

"Every person shall be assessed in the town or ward where *he* resides when the assessment is made, for the lands owned by *him*, &c." "Every collector shall call at least once on the person taxed, or at *his* usual place of residence, and shall demand payment of the taxes charged on *him*. If any one shall refuses to pay the tax imposed on *him*, the collector shall levy the same by distress and sale of *his* property."

The same is true of all the criminal laws:

"No person shall be compelled to be a witness against *himself*, &c."

The same with the law of May 31st, 1870, the 19th section of which I am charged with having violated; not only are all the pronouns in it masculine, but everybody knows that that particular section was intended expressly to hinder the rebels from voting. It reads "If any person shall knowingly vote without *his* having a lawful right," &c. Precisely so with all the papers served on me—the U.S. Marshal's warrant, the bail-bond, the petition for habeas corpus, the bill of indictment—not one of them had a feminine pronoun printed in it; but, to make them applicable to me, the Clerk of the Court made a little carat at the left of "he" and placed an "s" over it, thus making *she* out of *he*. Then the letters "i s" were scratched out, the little carat under and "e r" over, to make *her* out of *his*, and I insist if government officials may thus manipulate the pronouns to tax, fine, imprison and hang women, women may take the same liberty with them to secure to themselves their right to a voice in the government.

So long as any classes of men were denied their right to vote, the government made a show of consistency, by exempting them from taxation. When a property qualification of $250 was required of black men in New York, they were not compelled to pay taxes, so long as they were content to report themselves worth less than that sum; but the moment the black man died, and his property fell to his widow or daughter, the black woman's name would be put on the assessor's list, and she be compelled to pay taxes on the same property exempted to her husband. The same is true of ministers in New York. So long as the minister lives, he is exempted from taxation on $1,500 of property, but the moment the breath goes out of his body, his widow's name will go down on the assessor's list, and she will have to pay taxes on the $1,500. So much for the special legislation in favor of women.

In all the penalties and burdens of the government, (except the military,) women are reckoned as citizens, equally with men. Also, in all the privileges and immunities, save those of the jury box and ballot box, the two fundamental privileges on which rest all the others. The United States government not only taxes, fines, imprisons and hangs women, but it allows them to pre-empt lands, register ships, and take out passport and naturalization papers. Not only does the law permit single women and widows to the right of naturalization, but Section 2 says: "A married woman may be naturalized without the concurrence of her husband." (I wonder the fathers were not afraid of creating discord in the families of foreigners); and again: "When an alien, having complied with the law, and declared his intention to become a citizen, dies before he is actually naturalized, his widow and children shall be considered citizens, entitled to all rights and privileges as such, on taking the required oath." If a foreign born woman by becoming a naturalized citizen, is entitled to all the rights and privileges of citizenship, is not a native born woman, by her national citizenship, possessed of equal rights and privileges?

The question of the masculine pronouns, yes and nouns, too, has been settled by the United States Supreme Court, in the Case of *Silver versus Ladd*, December, 1868, in a decision as to whether a woman was entitled to lands, under the Oregon donation law of 1850. Elizabeth Cruthers, a widow, settled upon a claim, and received patents. She died, and her son was heir. He died. Then Messrs. Ladd & Nott took possession, under the general pre-emption law, December, 1861. The administrator, E. P. Silver, applied for a writ of ejectment at the land office in Oregon City. Both the Register and Receiver decided that an unmarried woman could not hold land under that law. The Commissioner of the General Land Office, at Washington, and the Secretary of the Interior, also gave adverse opinions. Here patents were issued to Ladd & Nott, and duly recorded. Then a suit was brought to set aside Ladd's patent, and it was carried through all the State Courts and the Supreme Court of Oregon, each, in turn, giving adverse decisions. At last, in the United States Supreme Court, Associate Justice Miller reversed the decisions of all the lower tribunals, and ordered the land back to the heirs of Mrs. Cruthers. The Court said:

"In construing a benevolent statute of the government, made for the benefit of its own citizens, inviting and encouraging them to settle on its distant public lands, the words 'single man,' and 'unmarried man' may, especially if aided by the context and other parts of the statute, be taken in a generic sense. Held, accordingly, that the Fourth Section of the Act of Congress, of September 27th, 1850, granting by way of donation, lands in Oregon Territory, to every white settler or occupant, American half-breed Indians included, embraced within the term *single man* an *unmarried woman*."

And the attorney, who carried this question to its final success, is now the United States senator elect from Oregon, Hon. J. H. Mitchell, in whom the cause of equal rights to women has an added power on the floor of the United States Senate.

Though the words persons, people, inhabitants, electors, citizens, are all used indiscriminately in the national and state constitutions, there was always a conflict of opinion, prior to the war, as to whether they were synonymous terms, as for instance:

"No *person* shall be a *representative* who shall not have been seven years a *citizen*, and who shall not, when elected, be an *inhabitant* of that state in which he is chosen. No *person* shall be a senator who shall not have been a *citizen* of the United States, and an *inhabitant* of that state in which he is chosen."

But, whatever room there was for a doubt, under the old regime, the adoption of the fourteenth amendment settled that question forever, in its first sentence: "All persons born or naturalized in the United States and subject to the jurisdiction thereof, are citizens of the United States and of the state wherein they reside."

And the second, settles the equal status of all persons—all citizens:

"No state shall make or enforce any law which shall abridge the privileges or immunities of citizens; nor shall any state deprive any person of life, liberty or property, without due process of law, nor deny to any person within its jurisdiction the equal protection of the laws."

The only question left to be settled, now, is: Are women persons? And I hardly believe any of our opponents will have the hardihood to say they are not. Being persons, then, women are citizens, and no state has a right to make any new law, or to enforce any old law, that shall abridge their privileges or immunities. Hence, every discrimination against women in the constitutions and laws of the several states, is to-day null and void, precisely as is every one against negroes.

Is the right to vote one of the privileges or immunities of citizens? I think the disfranchised ex-rebels, and the ex-state prisoners will all agree with me, that it is not only one of them, but the one without which all the others are nothing. Seek first the kingdom of the ballot, and all things else shall be given thee, is the political injunction.

Webster, Worcester and Bouvier all define citizen to be a person, in the United States, entitled to vote and hold office.

Prior to the adoption of the thirteenth amendment, by which slavery was forever abolished, and black men transformed from property to persons, the judicial opinions of the country had always been in harmony with these definitions. To be a person was to be a citizen, and to be a citizen was to be a voter.

Associate Justice Washington, in defining the privileges and immunities of the citizen, more than fifty years ago, said "they included all such privileges as were fundamental in their nature. And among them is the right to exercise the elective franchise, and to hold office."

Even the "Dred Scott" decision, pronounced by the abolitionists and republicans infamous, because it virtually declared "black men had no rights white men were bound to respect," gave this true and logical conclusion, that to be one of the people was to be a citizen and a voter.

Chief Judge Daniels said:

"There is not, it is believed, to be found in the theories of writers on government, or in any actual experiment heretofore tried, an exposition of the term citizen, which has not been considered as conferring the actual possession and enjoyment of the perfect right of acquisition and enjoyment of an entire equality of privileges, civil and political."

Associate Justice Taney said:

"The words 'people of the United States,' and 'citizens,' are synonymous terms, and mean the same thing. They both describe the political body, who, according to our republican institutions, form the sovereignty, and who hold the power and conduct the government, through their representatives. They are what we familiarly call the sovereign people, and every citizen is one of this people, and a constituent member of this sovereignty."

Thus does Judge Taney's decision, which was such a terrible ban to the black man, while he was a slave, now, that he is a person, no longer property, pronounce him a citizen, possessed of an entire equality of privileges, civil and political. And not only the black man, but the black woman, and all women as well.

And it was not until after the abolition of slavery, by which the negroes became free men, hence citizens, that the United States Attorney, General Bates, rendered a contrary opinion. He said:

"The constitution uses the word 'citizen' only to express the political quality, (not equality mark,) of the individual in his relation to the nation; to declare that he is a member of the body politic, and bound to it by the reciprocal obligations of allegiance on the one side, and protection on the other. The phrase, 'a citizen of the United States,' without addition or qualification, means neither more nor less than a member of the nation."

Then, to be a citizen of this republic, is no more than to be a subject of an empire. You and I, and all true and patriotic citizens must repudiate this base conclusion. We all know that American citizenship, without addition or qualification, means the possession of equal rights, civil and political. We all know that the crowning glory of every citizen of the United States is, that he can either give or withhold his vote from every law and every legislator under the government.

Did "I am a Roman citizen," mean nothing more than that I am a "member" of the body politic of the republic of Rome, bound to it by the reciprocal obligations of allegiance on the one side, and protection on the other? Ridiculously absurd question, you say. When you, young man, shall travel abroad, among the monarchies of the old world, and there proudly boast yourself an "American citizen," will you thereby declare yourself neither more nor less than a "member" of the American nation?

And this opinion of Attorney General Bates, that a black citizen was not a voter, made merely to suit the political exigency of the republican party, in that transition hour between emancipation and enfranchisement, was no less infamous, in spirit or purpose, than was the decision of Judge Taney, that a black man was not one of the people, rendered in the interest and at the behest of the old democratic party, in its darkest hour of subjection to the slave power. Nevertheless, all of the adverse arguments, adverse congressional reports and judicial opinions, thus far, have been based on this purely partisan, time-serving opinion of General Bates, that the normal condition of the citizen of the United States is that of disfranchisement. That only such classes of citizens as have had special legislative guarantee have a legal right to vote.

And if this decision of Attorney General Bates was infamous, as against black men, but yesterday plantation slaves, what shall we pronounce upon Judge Bingham, in the house of Representatives, and Carpenter, in the Senate of the United States, for citing it against the women of the entire nation, vast numbers of whom are the peers of those honorable gentlemen, themselves, in morals!! intellect, culture, wealth, family—paying taxes on large estates, and contributing equally with them and their sex, in every direction, to the growth, prosperity and well-being of the republic? And what shall be said of the judicial opinions of Judges Carter, Jameson, McKay and Sharswood, all based upon this aristocratic, monarchial idea, of the right of one class to govern another?

I am proud to mention the names of the two United States Judges who have given opinions honorable to our republican idea, and honorable to themselves—Judge Howe, of Wyoming Territory, and Judge Underwood, of Virginia.

The former gave it as his opinion a year ago, when the Legislature seemed likely to revoke the law enfranchising the women of that territory, that, in case they succeeded, the women would still possess the right to vote under the fourteenth amendment.

Judge Underwood, of Virginia, in noticing the recent decision of Judge Carter, of the Supreme Court of the District of Columbia, denying to women the right to vote, under the fourteenth and fifteenth amendment, says;

"If the people of the United States, by amendment of their constitution, could expunge, without any explanatory or assisting legislation, an adjective of five letters from all state and local constitutions, and thereby raise millions of our most ignorant fellow-citizens to all of the rights and privileges of electors, why should not the same people, by the same amendment, expunge an adjective of four letters from the same state and local constitutions, and thereby raise other millions of more educated and better informed citizens to equal rights and privileges, without explanatory or assisting legislation?"

If the fourteenth amendment does not secure to all citizens the right to vote, for what purpose was that grand old charter of the fathers lumbered with its unwieldy proportions? The republican party, and Judges Howard and Bingham, who drafted the document, pretended it was to do something for black men; and if that something was not to secure them in their right to vote and hold office, what could it have been? For, by the thirteenth amendment, black men had become people, and hence were entitled to all the privileges and immunities of the government, precisely as were the women of the country, and foreign men not naturalized. According to Associate Justice Washington, they already had the

"Protection of the government, the enjoyment of life and liberty, with the right to acquire and possess property of every kind, and to pursue and obtain happiness and safety, subject to such restraints as the government may justly prescribe for the general welfare of the whole; the right of a citizen of one state to pass through or to reside in any other state for the purpose of trade, agriculture, professional pursuit, or otherwise; to claim the benefit of the writ of habeas corpus, to institute and maintain actions of any kind in the courts of the state; to take, hold, and dispose of property, either real or personal, and an exemption from higher taxes or impositions than are paid by the other citizens of the state."

Thus, you see, those newly freed men were in possession of every possible right, privilege and immunity of the government, except that of suffrage, and hence, needed no constitutional amendment for any other purpose. What right, I ask you, has the Irishman the day after he receives his naturalization papers that he did not possess the day before, save the right to vote and hold office? And the Chinamen, now crowding our Pacific coast, are in precisely the same position. What privilege or immunity has California or Oregon the constitutional right to deny them, save that of the ballot? Clearly, then, if the fourteenth amendment was not to secure to black men their right to vote, it did nothing for them, since they possessed everything else before. But, if it was meant to be a prohibition of the states, to deny or abridge their right to vote—which I fully believe—then it did the same for all persons, white women included, born or naturalized in the United States; for the amendment does not say all male persons of African descent, but all persons are citizens.

The second section is simply a threat to punish the states, by reducing their representation on the floor of Congress, should they disfranchise any of their male citizens, on account of color, and does not allow of the inference that the states may disfranchise from any, or all other causes, nor in any wise weaken or invalidate the universal guarantee of the first section. What

rule of law or logic would allow the conclusion, that the prohibition of a crime to one person, on severe pains and penalties, was a sanction of that crime to any and all other persons
save that one?

But, however much the doctors of the law may disagree, as to
whether people and citizens, in the original constitution, were
one and the same, or whether the privileges and immunities in
the fourteenth amendment include the right of suffrage, the
question of the citizen's right to vote is settled forever by the
fifteenth amendment. "The citizen's right to vote shall not be
denied by the United States, nor any state thereof; on account
of race, color, or previous condition of servitude." How can
the state deny or abridge the right of the citizen, if the citizen
does not possess it? There is no escape from the conclusion,
that to vote is the citizen's right, and the specifications of race,
color, or previous condition of servitude can, in no way, impair
the force of the emphatic assertion, that the citizen's right to
vote shall not be denied or abridged.

The political strategy of the second section of the fourteenth
amendment, failing to coerce the rebel states into enfranchising
their negroes, and the necessities of the republican party demanding their votes throughout the South, to ensure the reelection of Grant in 1872, that party was compelled to place
this positive prohibition of the fifteenth amendment upon the
United States and all the states thereof.

If we once establish the false principle, that United States
citizenship does not carry with it the right to vote in every
state in this Union, there is no end to the petty freaks and cunning devices, that will be resorted to, to exclude one and another class of citizens from the right of suffrage.

It will not always be men combining to disfranchise all
women; native born men combining to abridge the rights of
all naturalized citizens, as in Rhode Island. It will not always
be the rich and educated who may combine to cut off the poor
and ignorant; but we may live to see the poor, hard-working,
uncultivated day laborers, foreign and native born, learning the
power of the ballot and their vast majority of numbers, combine and amend state constitutions so as to disfranchise the
Vanderbilts and A. T. Stewarts, the Conklings and Fentons. It
is a poor rule that won't work more ways than one. Establish

this precedent, admit the right to deny suffrage to the states, and there is no power to foresee the confusion, discord and disruption that may await us. There is, and can be, but one safe principle of government—equal rights to all. And any and every discrimination against any class, whether on account of color, race, nativity, sex, property, culture, can but imbitter and disaffect that class, and thereby endanger the safety of the whole people.

Clearly, then, the national government must not only define the rights of citizens, but it must stretch out its powerful hand and protect them in every state in this Union.

But if you will insist that the fifteenth amendment's emphatic interdiction against robbing United States citizens of their right to vote, "on account of race, color, or previous condition of servitude," is a recognition of the right, either of the United States, or any state, to rob citizens of that right, for any or all other reasons, I will prove to you that the class of citizens for which I now plead, and to which I belong, may be, and are, by all the principles of our government, and many of the laws of the states, included under the term "previous condition of servitude."

First.—The married women and their legal status. What is servitude? "The condition of a slave." What is a slave? "A person who is robbed of the proceeds of his labor; a person who is subject to the will of another."

By the law of Georgia, South Carolina, and all the states of the South, the negro had no right to the custody and control of his person. He belonged to his master. If he was disobedient, the master had the right to use correction. If the negro didn't like the correction, and attempted to run away, the master had a right to use coercion to bring him back.

By the law of every state in this Union to-day, North as well as South, the married woman has no right to the custody and control of her person. The wife belongs to her husband; and if she refuses obedience to his will, he may use moderate correction, and if she doesn't like his moderate correction, and attempts to leave his "bed and board," the husband may use moderate coercion to bring her back. The little word "moderate," you see, is the saving clause for the wife, and would doubtless be overstepped should her offended husband administer his correction with the "cat-o'-nine-tails," or accomplish his coercion with blood-hounds.

Again, the slave had no right to the earnings of his hands, they belonged to his master; no right to the custody of his children, they belonged to his master; no right to sue or be sued, or testify in the courts. If he committed a crime, it was the master who must sue or be sued.

In many of the states there has been special legislation, giving to married women the right to property inherited, or received by bequest, or earned by the pursuit of any avocation outside of the home; also, giving her the right to sue and be sued in matters pertaining to such separate property; but not a single state of this Union has ever secured the wife in the enjoyment of her right to the joint ownership of the joint earnings of the marriage copartnership. And since, in the nature of things, the vast majority of married women never earn a dollar, by work outside of their families, nor inherit a dollar from their fathers, it follows that from the day of their marriage to the day of the death of their husbands, not one of them ever has a dollar, except it shall please her husband to *let* her have it.

In some of the states, also, there have been laws passed giving to the mother a joint right with the father in the guardianship of the children. But twenty years ago, when our woman's rights movement commenced, by the laws of the State of New York, and all the states, the father had the sole custody and control of the children. No matter if he were a brutal, drunken libertine, he had the legal right, without the mother's consent, to apprentice her sons to rumsellers, or her daughters to brothel keepers. He could even will away an unborn child, to some other person than the mother. And in many of the states the law still prevails, and the mothers are still utterly powerless under the common law.

I doubt if there is, to-day, a State in this Union where a married woman can sue or be sued for slander of character, and until quite recently there was not one in which she could sue or be sued for injury of person. However damaging to the wife's reputation any slander may be, she is wholly powerless to institute legal proceedings against her accuser, unless her husband shall join with her; and how often have we heard of the husband conspiring with some outside barbarian to blast the good name of his wife? A married woman cannot testify in courts in cases of joint interest with her husband. A good farmer's wife near Earlville, Ill., who had all the rights she wanted, went to a dentist of the village and had a full set of false teeth, both upper and under. The dentist pronounced them an admirable fit, and the wife declared they gave her fits to wear them; that she could neither chew nor talk with them in her mouth. The dentist sued the husband; his counsel brought the wife as witness; the judge ruled her off the stand, saying "a married woman cannot be a witness in matters of joint interest between herself and her husband." Think of it, ye good wives, the false teeth in your mouths are joint interest with your husbands, about which you are legally incompetent to speak!! If in our frequent and shocking railroad accidents a married woman is injured in her person, in nearly all of the States, it is her husband who must sue the company, and it is to her husband that the damages, if there are any, will be awarded. In Ashfield, Mass., supposed to be the most advanced of any State in the Union in all things, humanitarian as well as intellectual, a married woman was severely injured by a defective sidewalk. Her husband sued the corporation and recovered $13,000 damages. And those $13,000 belong to him *bona fide*; and whenever that unfortunate wife wishes a dollar of it to supply her needs she must ask her husband for it; and if the man be of a narrow, selfish, niggardly nature, she will have to hear him say, every time, "What have you done, my dear, with the twenty-five cents I gave you yesterday?" Isn't such a position, I ask you, humiliating enough to be called "servitude?" That husband, as would any other husband, in nearly every State of this Union, sued and obtained damages for the loss of the services of his wife, precisely as the master, under the old slave regime, would have done, had his slave been thus injured, and precisely as he himself would have done had it been his ox, cow or horse instead of his wife.

There is an old saying that "a rose by any other name would smell as sweet," and I submit if the deprivation by law of the ownership of one's own person, wages, property, children, the denial of the right as an individual, to sue and be sued, and to testify in the courts, is not a condition of servitude most bitter and absolute, though under the sacred name of marriage?

Does any lawyer doubt my statement of the legal status of

married women? I will remind him of the fact that the old common law of England prevails in every State in this Union, except where the Legislature has enacted special laws annulling it. And I am ashamed that not one State has yet blotted from its statute books the old common law of marriage, by which Blackstone, summed up in the fewest words possible, is made to say, "husband and wife are one, and that one is the husband."

Thus may all married women, wives and widows, by the laws of the several States, be technically included in the fifteenth amendment's specification of "condition of servitude," present or previous. And not only married women, but I will also prove to you that by all the great fundamental principles of our free government, the entire womanhood of the nation is in a "condition of servitude" as surely as were our revolutionary fathers, when they rebelled against old King George. Women are taxed without representation, governed without their consent, tried, convicted and punished without a jury of their peers. And is all this tyranny any less humiliating and degrading to women under our democratic-republican government to-day than it was to men under their aristocratic, monarchical government one hundred years ago? There is not an utterance of old John Adams, John Hancock or Patrick Henry, but finds a living response in the soul of every intelligent, patriotic woman of the nation. Bring to me a common-sense woman property holder, and I will show you one whose soul is fired with all the indignation of 1776 every time the tax-gatherer presents himself at her door. You will not find one such but feels her condition of servitude as galling as did James Otis when he said:

"The very act of taxing exercised over those who are not represented appears to me to be depriving them of one of their most essential rights, and if continued, seems to be in effect an entire disfranchisement of every civil right. For, what one civil right is worth a rush after a man's property is subject to be taken from him at pleasure without his consent? If a man is not his own assessor in person, or by deputy, his liberty is gone, or he is wholly at the mercy of others."

What was the three-penny tax on tea, or the paltry tax on paper and sugar to which our revolutionary fathers were subjected, when compared with the taxation of the women of this Republic? The orphaned Pixley sisters, six dollars a day, and even the women, who are proclaiming the tyranny of our taxation without representation, from city to city throughout the country, are often compelled to pay a tax for the poor privilege of defending our rights. And again, to show that disfranchisement was precisely the slavery of which the fathers complained, allow me to cite to you old Ben. Franklin, who in those olden times was admitted to be good authority, not merely in domestic economy, but in political as well; he said:

"Every man of the commonalty, except infants, insane persons and criminals, is, of common right and the law of God, a freeman and entitled to the free enjoyment of liberty. That liberty or freedom consists in having an actual share in the appointment of those who are to frame the laws, and who are to be the guardians of every man's life, property and peace. For the all of one man is as dear to him as the all of another; and the poor man has an equal right, but more need to have representatives in the Legislature than the rich one. That they who have no voice or vote in the electing of representatives, do not enjoy liberty, but are absolutely enslaved to those who have votes and their representatives; for to be enslaved is to have governors whom other men have set over us, and to be subject to laws made by the representatives of others, without having had representatives of our own to give consent in our behalf."

Suppose I read it with the feminine gender:

"That women who have no voice nor vote in the electing of representatives, do not enjoy liberty, but are absolutely enslaved to men who have votes and their representatives; for to be enslaved is to have governors whom men have set over us, and to be subject to the laws made by the representatives of men, without having representatives of our own to give consent in our behalf."

And yet one more authority; that of Thomas Paine, than whom not one of the Revolutionary patriots more ably vindicated the principles upon which our government is founded:

"The right of voting for representatives is the primary right by which other rights are protected. To take away this right is to reduce man to a state of slavery; for slavery consists in being subject to the will of another; and he that has not a vote in the election of representatives is in this case. The proposal, therefore, to disfranchise any class of men is as criminal as the proposal to take away property."

Is anything further needed to prove woman's condition of servitude sufficiently orthodox to entitle her to the guaranties of the fifteenth amendment?

Is there a man who will not agree with me, that to talk of freedom without the ballot, is mockery—is slavery—to the women of this Republic, precisely as New England's orator Wendell Phillips, at the close of the late war, declared it to be to the newly emancipated black men?

I admit that prior to the rebellion, by common consent, the right to enslave, as well as to disfranchise both native and foreign born citizens, was conceded to the States. But the one grand principle, settled by the war and the reconstruction legislation, is the supremacy of national power to protect the citizens of the United States in their right to freedom and the elective franchise, against any and every interference on the part of the several States. And again and again, have the American people asserted the triumph of this principle, by their overwhelming majorities for Lincoln and Grant.

The one issue of the last two Presidential elections was, whether the fourteenth and fifteenth amendments should be considered the irrevocable will of the people; and the decision was, they shall be—and that it is not only the right, but the duty of the National Government to protect all United States citizens in the full enjoyment and free exercise of all their privileges and immunities against any attempt of any State to deny or abridge.

And in this conclusion Republicans and Democrats alike agree.

Senator Frelinghuysen said:

"The heresy of State rights has been completely buried in these amendments, that as amended, the Constitution confers not only national but State citizenship upon all persons born or naturalized within our limits."

The Call for the national Republican convention said:

"Equal suffrage has been engrafted on the national Constitution; the privileges and immunities of American citizenship have become a part of the organic law."

The national Republican platform said:

"Complete liberty and exact equality in the enjoyment of all civil, political and public rights, should be established and maintained throughout the Union by efficient and appropriate State and federal legislation."

If that means anything, it is that Congress should pass a law to require the States to protect women in their equal political rights, and that the States should enact laws making it the duty of inspectors of elections to receive women's votes on precisely the same conditions they do those of men.

Judge Stanley Mathews—a substantial Ohio democrat—in his preliminary speech at the Cincinnati convention, said most emphatically:

"The constitutional amendments have established the political equality of all citizens before the law."

President Grant, in his message to Congress March 30th, 1870, on the adoption of the fifteenth amendment, said:

"A measure which makes at once four millions of people voters, is indeed a measure of greater importance than any act of the kind from the foundation of the Government to the present time."

How could *four* millions negroes be made voters if *two* millions were not included?

The California State Republican convention said:

"Among the many practical and substantial triumphs of the principles achieved by the Republican party during the past twelve years, it enumerated with pride and pleasure, the prohibiting of any State from abridging the privileges of any citizen of the Republic, the declaring the civil and political equality of every citizen, and the establishing all these principles in the federal constitution by amendments thereto, as the permanent law."

Benjamin F. Butler, in a recent letter to me, said:

"I do not believe anybody in Congress doubts that the Constitution authorizes the right of women to vote, precisely as it authorizes trial by jury and many other like rights guaranteed to citizens."

And again, General Butler said:

"It is not laws we want; there are plenty of laws—good enough, too. Administrative ability to enforce law is the great want of the age, in this country especially. Everybody talks of law, law. If everybody would insist on the enforcement of law, the government would stand on a firmer basis, and questions would settle themselves."

And it is upon this just interpretation of the United States Constitution that our National Woman Suffrage Association which celebrates the twenty-fifth anniversary of the woman's rights movement in New York on the 6th of May next, has based all its arguments and action the past five years.

We no longer petition Legislature or Congress to give us the right to vote. We appeal to the women everywhere to exercise their too long neglected "citizen's right to vote." We appeal to the inspectors of election everywhere to receive the votes of all United States citizens as it is their duty to do. We appeal to United States commissioners and marshals to arrest the inspectors who reject the names and votes of United States citizens, as it is their duty to do, and leave those alone who, like our eighth ward inspectors, perform their duties faithfully and well.

We ask the juries to fail to return verdicts of "guilty" against honest, law-abiding, tax-paying United States citizens for offering their votes at our elections. Or against intelligent, worthy young men, inspectors of elections, for receiving and counting such citizens' votes.

We ask the judges to render true and unprejudiced opinions of the law, and wherever there is room for a doubt to give its benefit on the side of liberty and equal rights to women, remembering that "the true rule of interpretation under our national constitution, especially since its amendments, is that anything for human rights is constitutional, everything against human rights unconstitutional."

And it is on this line that we propose to fight our battle for the ballot—all peaceably, but nevertheless persistently through to complete triumph, when all United States citizens shall be recognized as equals before the law.

ROBERT BROWN ELLIOTT

Speech in Congress on the Civil Rights Bill

Washington, D.C., January 6, 1874

W HILE I am sincerely grateful for this high mark of courtesy that has been accorded to me by this House, it is a
matter of regret to me that it is necessary at this day that I
should rise in the presence of an American Congress to advocate a bill which simply asserts equal rights and equal public
privileges for all classes of American citizens. I regret, sir, that
the dark hue of my skin may lend a color to the imputation
that I am controlled by motives personal to myself in my advocacy of this great measure of national justice. Sir, the motive
that impels me is restricted by no such narrow boundary, but is
as broad as your Constitution. I advocate it, sir, because it is
right. The bill, however, not only appeals to your justice, but it
demands a response from your gratitude.

In the events that led to the achievement of American Independence the negro was not an inactive or unconcerned
spectator. He bore his part bravely upon many battle-fields,
although uncheered by that certain hope of political elevation
which victory would secure to the white man. The tall granite
shaft, which a grateful State has reared above its sons who fell
in defending Fort Griswold against the attack of Benedict
Arnold, bears the name of Jordan, Freeman, and other brave
men of the African race who there cemented with their blood
the corner-stone of the Republic. In the State which I have the
honor in part to represent the rifle of the black man rang out
against the troops of the British crown in the darkest days of
the American Revolution. Said General Greene, who has been
justly termed the Washington of the North, in a letter written
by him to Alexander Hamilton, on the 10th day of January,
1781, from the vicinity of Camden, South Carolina:

There is no such thing as national character or national sentiment. The inhabitants are numerous, but they would be rather formidable abroad than at home. There is a great spirit of enterprise among the black people, and those that come out as volunteers are not a little formidable to the enemy.

At the battle of New Orleans, under the immortal Jackson, a colored regiment held the extreme right of the American line unflinchingly, and drove back the British column that pressed upon them, at the point of the bayonet. So marked was their valor on that occasion that it evoked from their great commander the warmest encomiums, as will be seen from his dispatch announcing the brilliant victory.

As the gentleman from Kentucky, [Mr. BECK,] who seems to be the leading exponent on this floor of the party that is arrayed against the principle of this bill, has been pleased, in season and out of season, to cast odium upon the negro and to vaunt the chivalry of his State, I may be pardoned for calling attention to another portion of the same dispatch. Referring to the various regiments under his command, and their conduct on that field which terminated the second war of American Independence, General Jackson says:

At the very moment when the entire discomfiture of the enemy was looked for with a confidence amounting to certainty, the Kentucky re-enforcements, in whom so much reliance had been placed, ingloriously fled.

In quoting this indisputable piece of history, I do so only by way of admonition and not to question the well-attested gallantry of the true Kentuckian, and to suggest to the gentleman that it would be well that he should not flaunt his heraldry so proudly while he bears this bar-sinister on the military escutcheon of his State—a State which answered the call of the Republic in 1861, when treason thundered at the very gates of the capital, by coldly declaring her neutrality in the impending struggle. The negro, true to that patriotism and love of country that have ever characterized and marked his history on this continent, came to the aid of the Government in its efforts to maintain the Constitution. To that Government he now appeals;

that Constitution he now invokes for protection against outrage and unjust prejudices founded upon caste.

But, sir, we are told by the distinguished gentleman from
Georgia [Mr. STEPHENS] that Congress has no power under
the Constitution to pass such a law, and that the passage of
such an act is in direct contravention of the rights of the States.
I cannot assent to any such proposition. The constitution of a
free government ought always to be construed in favor of human rights. Indeed, the thirteenth, fourteenth, and fifteenth
amendments, in positive words, invest Congress with the power
to protect the citizen in his civil and political rights. Now, sir,
what are civil rights? Rights natural, modified by civil society.
Mr. Lieber says:

> By civil liberty is meant, not only the absence of individual re-
> straint, but liberty within the social system and political organism—a
> combination of principles and laws which acknowledge, protect, and
> favor the dignity of man.   *   *   *   Civil liberty is the result of
> man's two-fold character as an individual and social being, so soon as
> both are equally respected.—*Lieber on Civil Liberty*, page 25.

Alexander Hamilton, the right-hand man of Washington in
the perilous days of the then infant Republic, the great interpreter and expounder of the Constitution, says:

> Natural liberty is a gift of the beneficent Creator to the whole hu-
> man race; civil liberty is founded on it; civil liberty is only natural lib-
> erty modified and secured by civil society.—*Hamilton's History of the
> American Republic*, vol. 1, page 70.

In the French constitution of June, 1793, we find this grand
and noble declaration:

> Government is instituted to insure to man the free use of his natu-
> ral and inalienable rights. These rights are equality, liberty, security,
> property. All men are equal by nature and before the law.   *   *   *
> Law is the same for all, be it protective or penal. Freedom is the power
> by which man can do what does not interfere with the rights of
> another; its basis is nature, its standard is justice, its protection is law,
> its moral boundary is the maxim: "Do not unto others what you do
> not wish they should do unto you."

Are we then, sir, with the amendments to our Constitution
staring us in the face; with these grand truths of history before

our eyes; with innumerable wrongs daily inflicted upon five million citizens demanding redress, to commit this question to the diversity of State legislation? In the words of Hamilton—

Is it the interest of the Government to sacrifice individual rights to the preservation of the rights of an artificial being, called States? There can be no truer principle than this, that every individual of the community at large has an equal right to the protection of Government. Can this be a free Government if partial distinctions are tolerated or maintained?

The rights contended for in this bill are among "the sacred rights of mankind, which are not to be rummaged for among old parchments or musty records; they are written as with a sunbeam, in the whole volume of human nature, by the hand of the Divinity itself, and can never be erased or obscured by mortal power."

But the Slaughter-house cases!—the Slaughter-house cases!

The honorable gentleman from Kentucky, always swift to sustain the failing and dishonored cause of proscription, rushes forward and flaunts in our faces the decision of the Supreme Court of the United States in the Slaughter-house cases, and in that act he has been willingly aided by the gentleman from Georgia. Hitherto, in the contests which have marked the progress of the cause of equal civil rights, our opponents have appealed sometimes to custom, sometimes to prejudice, more often to pride of race, but they have never sought to shield themselves behind the Supreme Court. But now, for the first time, we are told that we are barred by a decision of that court, from which there is no appeal. If this be true we must stay our hands. The cause of equal civil rights must pause at the command of a power whose edicts must be obeyed till the fundamental law of our country is changed.

Has the honorable gentleman from Kentucky considered well the claim he now advances? If it were not disrespectful I would ask, has he ever read the decision which he now tells us is an insuperable barrier to the adoption of this great measure of justice?

In the consideration of this subject, has not the judgment of the gentleman from Georgia been warped by the ghost of the dead doctrines of State-rights? Has he been altogether free from prejudices engendered by long training in that school of politics that wellnigh destroyed this Government?

Mr. Speaker, I venture to say here in the presence of the gentleman from Kentucky, and the gentleman from Georgia, and in the presence of the whole country, that there is not a line or word, not a thought or dictum even, in the decision of the Supreme Court in the great Slaughter-house cases which casts a shadow of doubt on the right of Congress to pass the pending bill, or to adopt such other legislation as it may judge proper and necessary to secure perfect equality before the law to every citizen of the Republic. Sir, I protest against the dishonor now cast upon our Supreme Court by both the gentleman from Kentucky and the gentleman from Georgia. In other days, when the whole country was bowing beneath the yoke of slavery, when press, pulpit, platform, Congress, and courts felt the fatal power of the slave oligarchy, I remember a decision of that court which no American now reads without shame and humiliation. But those days are past. The Supreme Court of to-day is a tribunal as true to freedom as any department of this Government, and I am honored with the opportunity of repelling a deep disgrace which the gentleman from Kentucky, backed and sustained as he is by the gentleman from Georgia, seeks to put upon it.

What were these Slaughter-house cases? The gentleman should be aware that a decision of any court should be examined in the light of the exact question which is brought before it for decision. That is all that gives authority to any decision.

The State of Louisiana, by act of her Legislature, had conferred on certain persons the exclusive right to maintain stock-landings and slaughter-houses within the city of New Orleans, or the parishes of Orleans, Jefferson, and Saint Bernard, in that State. The corporation which was thereby chartered were invested with the sole and exclusive privilege of conducting and carrying on the live-stock, landing, and slaughter-house business within the limits designated.

The supreme court of Louisana sustained the validity of the act conferring these exclusive privileges, and the plaintiffs in error brought the case before the Supreme Court of the United States for review. The plaintiffs in error contended that the act in question was void, because, first, it established a monopoly which was in derogation of common right and in contravention of the common law; and, second, that the grant of such exclusive privileges was in violation of the thirteenth and fourteenth amendments of the Constitution of the United States.

It thus appears from a simple statement of the case that the question which was before the court was not whether a State law which denied to a particular portion of her citizens the rights conferred on her citizens generally, on account of race, color, or previous condition of servitude, was unconstitutional because in conflict with the recent amendments, but whether an act which conferred on certain citizens exclusive privileges for police purposes was in conflict therewith, because imposing an involuntary servitude forbidden by the thirteenth amendment, or abridging the rights and immunities of citizens of the United States, or denying the equal protection of the laws, prohibited by the fourteenth amendment.

On the part of the defendants in error it was maintained that the act was the exercise of the ordinary and unquestionable power of the State to make regulation for the health and comfort of society—the exercise of the police power of the State, defined by Chancellor Kent to be "the right to interdict unwholesome trades, slaughter-houses, operations offensive to the senses, the deposit of powder, the application of steam-power to propel cars, the building with combustible materials, and the burial of the dead in the midst of dense masses of population, on the general and rational principle that every person ought so to use his own property as not to injure his neighbors, and that private interests must be made subservient to the general interests of the community."

The decision of the Supreme Court is to be found in the 16th volume of Wallace's Reports, and was delivered by Associate Justice Miller. The court hold, first, that the act in question is a legitimate and warrantable exercise of the police power of the State in regulating the business of stock-landing and slaughtering in the city of New Orleans and the territory immediately contiguous. Having held this, the court proceeds to discuss the question whether the conferring of exclusive privileges, such as those conferred by the act in question, is the imposing of an involuntary servitude, the abridging of the rights and immunities of citizens of the United States, or the denial to any person within the jurisdiction of the State of the equal protection of the laws.

That the act is not the imposition of an involuntary servitude the court hold to be clear, and they next proceed to examine the remaining questions arising under the fourteenth amendment. Upon this question the court hold that the leading and comprehensive purpose of the thirteenth, fourteenth, and fifteenth amendments was to secure the complete freedom of the race, which, by the events of the war, had been wrested from the unwilling grasp of their owners. I know no finer or more just picture, albeit painted in the neutral tints of true judicial impartiality, of the motives and events which led to these amendments. Has the gentleman from Kentucky read these passages which I now quote? Or has the gentleman from Georgia considered well the force of the language therein used? Says the court on page 70:

The process of restoring to their proper relations with the Federal Government and with the other States those which had sided with the rebellion, undertaken under the proclamation of President Johnson in 1865, and before the assembling of Congress, developed the fact that, notwithstanding the formal recognition by those States of the abolition of slavery, the condition of the slave race would, without further protection of the Federal Government, be almost as bad as it was before. Among the first acts of legislation adopted by several of the States in the legislative bodies which claimed to be in their normal relations with the Federal Government, were laws which imposed upon the colored race onerous disabilities and burdens, and curtailed their rights in the pursuit of life, liberty, and property to such an extent that their freedom was of little value, while they had lost the protection which they had received from their former owners from motives both of interest and humanity.

They were in some States forbidden to appear in the towns in any other character than menial servants. They were required to reside on and cultivate the soil, without the right to purchase or own it. They were excluded from any occupations of gain, and were not permitted to give testimony in the courts in any case where a white man was a party. It was said that their lives were at the mercy of bad men, either because the laws for their protection were insufficient or were not enforced.

These circumstances, whatever of falsehood or misconception may have been mingled with their presentation, forced upon the statesmen who had conducted the Federal Government in safety through the crisis of the rebellion, and who supposed that by the thirteenth article of amendment they had secured the result of their labors, the conviction that something more was necessary in the way of constitutional protection to the unfortunate race who had suffered so much. They accordingly passed through Congress the proposition for the fourteenth amendment, and they declined to treat as restored to their full participation in the Government of the Union the States which had been in insurrection until they ratified that article by a formal vote of their legislative bodies.

Before we proceed to examine more critically the provisions of this amendment, on which the plaintiffs in error rely, let us complete and dismiss the history of the recent amendments, as that history relates to the general purpose which pervades them all. A few years' experience satisfied the thoughtful men who had been the authors of the other two amendments that, notwithstanding the restraints of those articles on the States and the laws passed under the additional powers granted to Congress, these were inadequate for the protection of life, liberty, and property, without which freedom to the slave was no boon. They were in all those States denied the right of suffrage. The laws were administered by the white man alone. It was urged that a race of men distinctively marked as was the negro, living in the midst of another and dominant race, could never be fully secured in their person and their property without the right of suffrage.

Hence the fifteenth amendment, which declares that "the right of a citizen of the United States to vote shall not be denied or abridged by any State on account of race, color, or previous condition of servitude." The negro having, by the fourteenth amendment, been declared to be a citizen of the United States, is thus made a voter in every State of the Union.

We repeat, then, in the light of this recapitulation of events almost too recent to be called history, but which are familiar to us all, and on the most casual examination of the language of these amendments, no one can fail to be impressed with the one pervading purpose found in them all, lying at the foundation of each, and without which none of them would have been even suggested: we mean the freedom of the slave race, the security and firm establishment of that freedom, and the protection of the newly-made freeman and citizen from the oppressions of those who had formerly exercised unlimited dominion over him. It is true that only the fifteenth amendment in terms mentions the negro by speaking of his color and his slavery. But it is just as true that each of the other articles was addressed to the grievances of that race, and designed to remedy them, as the fifteenth.

These amendments, one and all, are thus declared to have as their all-pervading design and end the security to the recently enslaved race, not only their nominal freedom, but their complete protection from those who had formerly exercised unlimited dominion over them. It is in this broad light that all these amendments must be read, the purpose to secure the perfect equality before the law of all citizens of the United States. What you give to one class you must give to all; what you deny to one class you shall deny to all, unless in the exercise of the common and universal police power of the State you find it needful to confer exclusive privileges on certain citizens, to be held and exercised still for the common good of all.

Such are the doctrines of the Slaughter-house cases—doctrines worthy of the Republic, worthy of the age, worthy of the great tribunal which thus loftily and impressively enunciates them. Do they—I put it to any man, be he lawyer or not; I put it to the gentleman from Georgia—do they give color even to the claim that this Congress may not now legislate against a plain discrimination made by State laws or State customs against that very race for whose complete freedom and protection these great amendments were elaborated and adopted? Is it pretended, I ask the honorable gentleman from Kentucky or the honorable gentleman from Georgia—is it pretended anywhere that the evils of which we complain, our exclusion from the public inn, from the saloon and table of the steamboat, from the sleeping-coach on the railway, from the right of sepulture in the public burial-ground, are an exercise of the police power of the State? Is such oppression and injustice nothing but the exercise by the State of the right to make regulations for the health, comfort, and security of all her citizens? Is it merely enacting that one man shall so use his own as not to injure another's? Are the colored race to be assimilated to an unwholesome trade or to combustible materials, to be interdicted, to be shut up within prescribed limits? Let the gentleman from Kentucky or the gentleman from Georgia answer. Let the country know to what extent even the audacious prejudice of the gentleman from Kentucky will drive him, and how far even the gentleman from Georgia will permit himself to be led captive by the unrighteous teachings of a false political faith.

If we are to be likened in legal view to "unwholesome trades," to "large and offensive collections of animals," to "noxious slaughter-houses," to "the offal and stench which attend on certain manufactures," let it be avowed. If that is still the doctrine of the political party to which the gentlemen belong, let it be put upon record. If State laws which deny us the common rights and privileges of other citizens, upon no possible or conceivable ground save one of prejudice, or of "taste," as the gentleman from Texas termed it, and as I suppose the gentlemen will prefer to call it, are to be placed under the protection of a decision which affirms the right of a State to regulate the police of her great cities, then the decision is in conflict with the bill before us. No man will dare maintain such a doctrine. It is as shocking to the legal mind as it is offensive to the heart and conscience of all who love justice or respect manhood. I am astonished that the gentleman from Kentucky or the gentleman from Georgia should have been so grossly misled as to rise here and assert that the decision of the Supreme Court in these cases was a denial to Congress of the power to legislate against discriminations on account of race, color, or previous condition of servitude, because that court has decided that exclusive privileges conferred for the common protection of the lives and health of the whole community are not in violation of the recent amendments. The only ground upon which the grant of exclusive privileges to a portion of the community is ever defended is that the substantial good of all is promoted; that in truth it is for the welfare of the whole community that certain persons should alone pursue certain occupations. It is not the special benefit conferred on the few that moves the legislature, but the ultimate and real benefit of all, even of those who are denied the right to pursue those specified occupations. Does the gentleman from Kentucky say that my good is promoted when I am excluded from the public inn? Is the health or safety of the community promoted? Doubtless his prejudice is gratified. Doubtless his democratic instincts are pleased; but will he or his able coadjutor say that such exclusion is a lawful exercise of the police power of the State, or that it is not a denial to me of the equal protection of the laws? They will not so say.

But each of these gentlemen quote at some length from the

decision of the court to show that the court recognizes a difference between citizenship of the United States and citizenship of the States. That is true, and no man here who supports this bill questions or overlooks the difference. There are privileges and immunities which belong to me as a citizen of the United States, and there are other privileges and immunities which belong to me as a citizen of my State. The former are under the protection of the Constitution and laws of the United States, and the latter are under the protection of the constitution and laws of my State. But what of that? Are the rights which I now claim—the right to enjoy the common public conveniences of travel on public highways, of rest and refreshment at public inns, of education in public schools, of burial in public cemeteries—rights which I hold as a citizen of the United States or of my State? Or, to state the question more exactly, is not the denial of such privileges to me a denial to me of the equal protection of the laws? For it is under this clause of the fourteenth amendment that we place the present bill, no State shall "deny to any person within its jurisdiction the equal protection of the laws." No matter, therefore, whether his rights are held under the United States or under his particular State, he is equally protected by this amendment. He is always and everywhere entitled to the equal protection of the laws. All discrimination is forbidden; and while the rights of citizens of a State as such are not defined or conferred by the Constitution of the United States, yet all discrimination, all denial of equality before the law, all denial of the equal protection of the laws, whether State or national laws, is forbidden.

The distinction between the two kinds of citizenship is clear, and the Supreme Court have clearly pointed out this distinction, but they have nowhere written a word or line which denies to Congress the power to prevent a denial of equality of rights, whether those rights exist by virtue of citizenship of the United States or of a State. Let honorable members mark well this distinction. There are rights which are conferred on us by the United States. There are other rights conferred on us by the States of which we are individually the citizens. The fourteenth amendment does not forbid a State to deny to all its citizens any of those rights which the State itself has conferred, with certain exceptions, which are pointed out in the decision which we are examining. What it does forbid is inequality, is discrimination, or, to use the words of the amendment itself, is the denial "to any person within its jurisdiction the equal protection of the laws." If a State denies to me rights which are common to all her other citizens, she violates this amendment, unless she can show, as was shown in the Slaughter-house cases, that she does it in the legitimate exercise of her police power. If she abridges the rights of all her citizens equally, unless those rights are specially guarded by the Constitution of the United States, she does not violate this amendment. This is not to put the rights which I hold by virtue of my citizenship of South Carolina under the protection of the national Government; it is not to blot out or overlook in the slightest particular the distinction between rights held under the United States and rights held under the States; but it seeks to secure equality, to prevent discrimination, to confer as complete and ample protection on the humblest as on the highest.

The gentleman from Kentucky, in the course of the speech to which I am now replying, made a reference to the State of Massachusetts which betrays again the confusion which exists in his mind on this precise point. He tells us that Massachusetts excludes from the ballot-box all who cannot read and write, and points to that fact as the exercise of a right which this bill would abridge or impair. The honorable gentleman from Massachusetts [Mr. DAWES] answered him truly and well, but I submit that he did not make the best reply. Why did he not ask the gentleman from Kentucky if Massachusetts had ever discriminated against any of her citizens on account of color, or race, or previous condition of servitude? When did Massachusetts sully her proud record by placing on her statute-book any law which admitted to the ballot the white man and shut out the black man? She has never done it; she will not do it; she cannot do it so long as we have a Supreme Court which reads the Constitution of our country with the eyes of justice; nor can Massachusetts or Kentucky deny to any man, on account of his race, color, or previous condition of servitude, that perfect equality of protection under the laws so long as Congress shall exercise the power to enforce, by appropriate legislation, the great and unquestionable securities embodied in the fourteenth amendment to the Constitution.

But, sir, a few words more as to the suffrage regulation of Massachusetts.

It is true that Massachusetts in 1857, finding that her illiterate population was being constantly augmented by the continual influx of ignorant emigrants, placed in her constitution the least possible limitation consistent with manhood suffrage to stay this tide of foreign ignorance. Its benefit has been fully demonstrated in the intelligent character of the voters of that honored Commonwealth, reflected so conspicuously in the able Representatives she has to-day upon this floor. But neither is the inference of the gentleman from Kentucky legitimate, nor do the statistics of the census of 1870, drawn from his own State, sustain his astounding assumption. According to the statistics we find the whole white population of that State is 1,098,692; the whole colored population 222,210. Of the whole white population who cannot write we find 201,077; of the whole colored population who cannot write, 126,048; giving us, as will be seen, 96,162 colored persons who can write to 897,615 white persons who can write. Now, the ratio of the colored population to the white is as 1 to 5, and the ratio of the illiterate colored population to the whole colored population is as 1 to 2; the ratio of the illiterate white population is to the whole white population as 1 is to 5. Reducing this, we have only a preponderance of three-tenths in favor of the whites as to literacy, notwithstanding the advantages which they have always enjoyed and do now enjoy of free-school privileges, and this, too, taking solely into account the single item of being unable to write; for with regard to the inability to read, there is no discrimination in the statistics between the white and colored population. There is, moreover, a peculiar felicity in these statistics with regard to the State of Kentucky, quoted so opportunely for me by the honorable gentleman; for I find that the population of that State, both with regard to its white and colored populations, bears the same relative rank in regard to the white and colored populations of the United States; and, therefore, while one negro would be disfranchised were the limitation of Massachusetts put in force, nearly three white men would at the same time be deprived of the right of suffrage—a consummation which I think would be far more acceptable to the colored people of that State than to the whites.

Now, sir, having spoken as to the intention of the prohibition imposed by Massachusetts, I may be pardoned for a slight inquiry as to the effect of this prohibition. First, it did not in any way abridge or curtail the exercise of the suffrage by any person who at that time enjoyed such right. Nor did it discriminate between the illiterate native and the illiterate foreigner. Being enacted for the good of the entire Commonwealth, like all just laws, its obligations fell equally and impartially upon all its citizens. And as a justification for such a measure, it is a fact too well known almost for mention here that Massachusetts had, from the beginning of her history, recognized the inestimable value of an educated ballot, by not only maintaining a system of free schools, but also enforcing an attendance thereupon, as one of the safeguards for the preservation of a real republican form of government. Recurring then, sir, to the possible contingency alluded to by the gentleman from Kentucky, should the State of Kentucky, having first established a system of common schools whose doors shall swing open freely to all, as contemplated by the provisions of this bill, adopt a provision similar to that of Massachusetts, no one would have cause justly to complain. And if in the coming years the result of such legislation should produce a constituency rivaling that of the old Bay State, no one would be more highly gratified than I.

Mr. Speaker, I have neither the time nor the inclination to notice the many illogical and forced conclusions, the numerous transfers of terms, or the vulgar insinuations which further incumber the argument of the gentleman from Kentucky. Reason and argument are worse than wasted upon those who meet every demand for political and civil liberty by such ribaldry as this—extracted from the speech of the gentleman from Kentucky:

I suppose there are gentlemen on this floor who would arrest, imprison, and fine a young woman in any State of the South if she were to refuse to marry a negro man on account of color, race, or previous condition of servitude, in the event of his making her a proposal of marriage, and her refusing on that ground. That would be depriving him of a right he had under the amendment, and Congress would be asked to take it up and say, "This insolent white woman must be taught to know that it is a misdemeanor to deny a man marriage because of race, color, or previous condition of servitude;" and Congress will be urged to say after a while that that sort of thing must be put a stop to, and your conventions of colored men will come here asking you to enforce that right.

Now, sir, recurring to the venerable and distinguished gentleman from Georgia, [Mr. STEPHENS,] who has added his remonstrance against the passage of this bill, permit me to say that I share in the feeling of high personal regard for that gentleman which pervades this House. His years, his ability, and his long experience in public affairs entitle him to the measure of consideration which has been accorded to him on this floor. But in this discussion I cannot and I will not forget that the welfare and rights of my whole race in this country are involved. When, therefore, the honorable gentleman from Georgia lends his voice and influence to defeat this measure, I do not shrink from saying that it is not from him that the American House of Representatives should take lessons in matters touching human rights or the joint relations of the State and national governments. While the honorable gentleman contented himself with harmless speculations in his study, or in the columns of a newspaper, we might well smile at the impotence of his efforts to turn back the advancing tide of opinion and progress; but, when he comes again upon this national arena, and throws himself with all his power and influence across the path which leads to the full enfranchisement of my race, I meet him only as an adversary; nor shall age or any other consideration restrain me from saying that he now offers this Government, which he has done his utmost to destroy, a very poor return for its magnanimous treatment, to come here and seek to continue, by the assertion of doctrines obnoxious to the true principles of our Government, the burdens and oppressions which rest upon five millions of his countrymen who never failed to lift their earnest prayers for the success of this Government when the gentleman was seeking to break up the Union of these States and to blot the American Republic from the galaxy of nations. [Loud applause.]

Sir, it is scarcely twelve years since that gentleman shocked the civilized world by announcing the birth of a government which rested on human slavery as its corner-stone. The progress of events has swept away that *pseudo*-government which rested on greed, pride, and tyranny; and the race whom he then ruthlessly spurned and trampled on are here to meet him in debate, and to demand that the rights which are enjoyed by their former oppressors—who vainly sought to overthrow a Government which they could not prostitute to the base uses of slavery— shall be accorded to those who even in the darkness of slavery kept their allegiance true to freedom and the Union. Sir, the gentleman from Georgia has learned much since 1861; but he is still a laggard. Let him put away entirely the false and fatal theories which have so greatly marred an otherwise enviable record. Let him accept, in its fullness and beneficence, the great doctrine that American citizenship carries with it every civil and political right which manhood can confer. Let him lend his influence, with all his masterly ability, to complete the proud structure of legislation which makes this nation worthy of the great declaration which heralded its birth, and he will have done that which will most nearly redeem his reputation in the eyes of the world, and best vindicate the wisdom of that policy which has permitted him to regain his seat upon this floor.

To the diatribe of the gentleman from Virginia, [Mr. HARRIS,] who spoke on yesterday, and who so far transcended the limits of decency and propriety as to announce upon this floor that his remarks were addressed to white men alone, I shall have no word of reply. Let him feel that a negro was not only too magnanimous to smite him in his weakness, but was even charitable enough to grant him the mercy of his silence. [Laughter and applause on the floor and in the galleries.] I shall, sir, leave to others less charitable the unenviable and fatiguing task of sifting out of that mass of chaff the few grains of sense that may, perchance, deserve notice. Assuring the gentleman that the negro in this country aims at a higher degree of intellect than that exhibited by him in this debate, I cheerfully commend him to the commiseration of all intelligent men the world over—black men as well as white men.

Sir, equality before the law is now the broad, universal, glorious rule and mandate of the Republic. No State can violate that. Kentucky and Georgia may crowd their statute-books with retrograde and barbarous legislation; they may rejoice in the odious eminence of their consistent hostility to all the great steps of human progress which have marked our national history since slavery tore down the stars and stripes on Fort Sumter; but, if Congress shall do its duty, if Congress shall enforce the great guarantees which the Supreme Court has declared to be the one pervading purpose of all the recent amendments, then their unwise and unenlightened conduct will fall with the same weight upon the gentlemen from those States who now lend their influence to defeat this bill, as upon the poorest slave who once had no rights which the honorable gentlemen were bound to respect.

But, sir, not only does the decision in the Slaughter-house cases contain nothing which suggests a doubt of the power of Congress to pass the pending bill, but it contains an express recognition and affirmance of such power. I quote now from page 81 of the volume:

"Nor shall any State deny to any person within its jurisdiction the equal protection of the laws."

In the light of the history of these amendments, and the pervading purpose of them, which we have already discussed, it is not difficult to give a meaning to this clause. The existence of laws in the States where the newly emancipated negroes resided, which discriminated with gross injustice and hardship against them as a class, was the evil to be remedied by this clause, and by it such laws are forbidden.

If, however, the States did not conform their laws to its requirements, then, by the fifth section of the article of amendment, Congress was authorized to enforce it by suitable legislation. We doubt very much whether any action of a State not directed by way of discrimination against the negroes as a class, or on account of their race, will ever be held to come within the purview of this provision. It is so clearly a provision for that race and that emergency, that a strong case would be necessary for its application to any other. But as it is a State that is to be dealt with, and not alone the validity of its laws, we may safely leave that matter until Congress shall have exercised its power, or some case of State oppression, by denial of equal justice in its courts shall have claimed a decision at our hands.

No language could convey a more complete assertion of the power of Congress over the subject embraced in the present bill than is here expressed. If the States do not conform to the requirements of this clause, if they continue to deny to any person within their jurisdiction the equal protection of the laws, or as the Supreme Court had said, "deny equal justice in its courts," then Congress is here said to have power to enforce the constitutional guarantee by appropriate legislation. That is the power which this bill now seeks to put in exercise. It proposes to enforce the constitutional guarantee against inequality and discrimination by appropriate legislation. It does not seek to confer new rights, nor to place rights conferred by State citizenship under the protection of the United States, but simply to prevent and forbid inequality and discrimination on account of race, color, or previous condition of servitude. Never was there a bill more completely within the constitutional power of Congress. Never was there a bill which appealed for support more strongly to that sense of justice and fair-play which has been said, and in the main with justice, to be a characteristic of the Anglo-Saxon race. The Constitution warrants it; the Supreme Court sanctions it; justice demands it.

Sir, I have replied to the extent of my ability to the arguments which have been presented by the opponents of this measure. I have replied also to some of the legal propositions advanced by gentlemen on the other side; and now that I am about to conclude, I am deeply sensible of the imperfect manner in which I have performed the task. Technically, this bill is to decide upon the civil status of the colored American citizen; a point disputed at the very formation of our present Government, when by a short-sighted policy, a policy repugnant to true republican government, one negro counted as three-fifths of a man. The logical result of this mistake of the framers of the Constitution strengthened the cancer of slavery, which finally spread its poisonous tentacles over the southern portion of the body-politic. To arrest its growth and save the nation we have passed through the harrowing operation of intestine war, dreaded at all times, resorted to at the last extremity, like the surgeon's knife, but absolutely necessary to extirpate the disease which threatened with the life of the nation the overthrow of civil and political liberty on this continent. In that dire extremity the members of the race which I have the honor in part to represent—the race which pleads for justice at your hands to-day, forgetful of their inhuman and brutalizing servitude at the South, their degradation and ostracism at the North —flew willingly and gallantly to the support of the national

Government. Their sufferings, assistance, privations, and trials in the swamps and in the rice-fields, their valor on the land and on the sea, is a part of the ever-glorious record which makes up the history of a nation preserved, and might, should I urge the claim, incline you to respect and guarantee their rights and privileges as citizens of our common Republic. But I remember that valor, devotion, and loyalty are not always rewarded according to their just deserts, and that after the battle some who have borne the brunt of the fray may, through neglect or contempt, be assigned to a subordinate place, while the enemies in war may be preferred to the sufferers.

The results of the war, as seen in reconstruction, have settled forever the political status of my race. The passage of this bill will determine the civil status, not only of the negro, but of any other class of citizens who may feel themselves discriminated against. It will form the cap-stone of that temple of liberty, begun on this continent under discouraging circumstances, carried on in spite of the sneers of monarchists and the cavils of pretended friends of freedom, until at last it stands in all its beautiful symmetry and proportions, a building the grandest which the world has ever seen, realizing the most sanguine expectations and the highest hopes of those who, in the name of equal, impartial, and universal liberty, laid the foundation stones.

The Holy Scriptures tell us of an humble hand-maiden who long, faithfully and patiently gleaned in the rich fields of her wealthy kinsman; and we are told further that at last, in spite of her humble antecedents, she found complete favor in his sight. For over two centuries our race has "reaped down your fields." The cries and woes which we have uttered have "entered into the ears of the Lord of Sabaoth," and we are at last politically free. The last vestiture only is needed—civil rights. Having gained this, we may, with hearts overflowing with gratitude, and thankful that our prayer has been granted, repeat the prayer of Ruth: "Entreat me not to leave thee, or to return from following after thee; for whither thou goest, I will go; and where thou lodgest, I will lodge; thy people shall be my people, and thy God my God; where thou diest, will I die, and there will I be buried; the Lord do so to me, and more also, if aught but death part thee and me." [Great applause.]

BENJAMIN F. BUTLER

Speech in Congress on the Civil Rights Bill

Washington, D.C., January 7, 1874

Now, Mr. Speaker, if these are rights, again let me ask, why should they not be given to all citizens of the United States, if we have the constitutional power so to do? If the States give them and execute them, then there will be no longer any need for this statute. It will not be enforced and will do no harm. Where a State will do its duty, there this statute will be inoperative. Where the State does not do its duty in this behalf, then the flag of the United States, and the power of the United States, and the judiciary of the United States, should protect the citizens against all unfriendly State legislation, or against the want of legislation. And I have the authority of the gentleman from Virginia [Mr. HARRIS] for saying "that no State has legislated on the subject."

And it is because of the very prejudice which has prevented such legislation that I claim the passage of the bill.

Is it a prejudice at all? Was there any objection in the South to consorting with the negro as a slave? O, no; your children and your servants' children played together; your children sucked the same mother with your servants' children; had the same nurse; and, unless tradition speaks falsely, sometimes had the same father. [Laughter and applause.]

Would you not ride in first-class cars with your negroes in the olden time? What negro servant, accompanying its mistress or master, and administering to his or her health, was ever denied a first-class passage in a first-class car in the South before the war? What negro girl, being the nurse or servant of a lady, was not allowed to sit by that lady and her child in a first-class car? What negro servant, accompanying a lady or a gentleman, was ever denied admittance to a first-class hotel? My friend from Tennessee, confirming this, told us that in the olden time the master and his slave always used to worship together in the same churches, but that now there are separate churches, and the negroes prefer to worship by themselves.

These are facts before the war? You talk about your prejudices against social equality! I put this question to the minds and consciences of every man of you. Who is the highest in the social scale, a slave or a freeman? You once associated with the slave in every relation of life. He has now become a freeman, and now you cannot associate with him; he has got up in the scale, and you cannot stomach him. Why is this? It is because he claims that as a right which you accorded him always freely as a boon. It is because the laws of your land, the Constitution of your country, gave all men equal rights in accordance with the fiat of God Almighty which has made some of them your equal in all things, and therefore he is no longer to be associated with or tolerated! This is not a prejudice against the negro or any personal objection to him—it is a political idea only.

I had, sir, to deal with this question early in the war, and I cannot better explain the operations of this kind of prejudice than by stating the exact fact which happened on board one of the boats upon Chesapeake Bay, between Baltimore and Fortress Monroe. A member of the Christian Commission went North after two school-teachers, and brought back two ladies, one of whom had some colored blood in her veins, but so much more white that it took a *connoisseur* to find the color. The women bought first-class tickets, and took their stateroom, sat down at the table, and paid for their supper. A Virginian, who was on board, being able to know a negro, from long use, whenever he saw one, smoked out the fact that one of them, a lady in dress, a lady in culture, a lady in manners, had some negro blood in her veins, and he complained to the clerk of the boat that he could not eat at the table in the saloon with her, and the clerk ordered her forward among the deck-hands and servants. The lady and her companion, frightened, ran to their state-room, and locked themselves in. The Virginian insisted on her being taken out of that. But a provost messenger on board was roused to his duty, and insisted that all that should be stopped. Next morning complaint was made to me as commanding general, and I sent for the clerk—an inoffensive old gentleman, who looked as if he would not harm anybody. I said, "What is all this?" He said, "I was only carrying out the rules of my boat." I said, "Do you not recognize the fact the war has made a difference in these things?" He answered, "Not in the rules of our boat." I asked, "What were the rules of your boat before the war? Could not a colored nurse go with the children of her mistress, and occupy a state-room with them?" "Yes, sir." "Could she come to the table with them?" "Yes, sir." "Which do you think, Mr. Clerk, is the highest in the social scale, a freeman or a slave?" "O, a freeman, General, of course." "Very well, Mr. Clerk; I think I can make a rule for your boat now that will be easy of enforcement. Do not go away and say that the commanding general says that the negro is as good as a white man. I am not going to say any such thing. But hereafter let this be your rule: Let no free person ever be deprived of any privileges on your boat that were ever accorded to a slave person. Do this, and there will be no trouble hereafter." And there was none.

That tells the whole story and covers the whole argument of prejudice. It is not a prejudice, gentlemen. You make a mistake. A prejudice is where you do not like the thing itself. We in the North had somewhat of this prejudice against the colored. You of the South had none. From the rarity, they were offensive to us. But we are getting used to the negro, and are getting free from our former mode of feeling and speaking on the subject. That was a prejudice. But you had not any such feeling of dislike or offensiveness at the South. Now I am getting over that feeling and you are getting it. And it is a political idea you are getting and not a prejudice at all. [Laughter.]

Now, sir, you will allow me to state how I got over my prejudices. I think the House got over theirs after the exhibition we had yesterday. I think no man will get up here and say he speaks only to white men again. He must at first show himself worthy before he can speak to some colored men in this House after what occurred yesterday. [Applause.]

I got over my prejudices from the exhibition of like high qualities in the negro, but in a different manner from that in which, I have no doubt, many a prejudice was removed against the negro in the House yesterday. In Louisiana, in 1862, when our arms were meeting with disasters before Richmond, I was in command of the city of New Orleans with a very few troops, and those daily diminishing by the diseases incident to the climate, with a larger number of confederate soldiers paroled in the city than I had troops. I called upon my Government for re-enforcemeuts, and they could not give me any, and I therefore called upon the colored men to enlist in defense of their country. I brought together the officers of two colored regiments that had been raised by the confederates for the defense of the city against us—but which disbanded when we came there because they would not fight against us, and staid at home when their white comrades ran away—and I said, "How soon can you enlist me one thousand men?" "In ten days, General," they answered; and when the thousand men were brought together in a large hall, I saw such a body of recruits as I never saw before. Why, sir, every one of them had on a clean shirt, a thing not often got in a body of a thousand recruits. [Laughter.] I put colored officers in command of them, and I organized them. But we all had our prejudice against them. I was told they would not fight. I raised another regiment, and by the time I got them organized, before I could test their fighting qualities in the field, the exigencies of the service required that I should be relieved from the command of that department.

I came into command again in Virginia in 1863. I there organized twenty-five regiments, with some that were sent to me, and disciplined them. Still all my brother officers of the Regular Army said my colored soldiers would not fight; and I felt it was necessary that they should fight to show that their race were capable of the duties of citizens; for one of the highest duties of citizens is to defend their own liberties and their country's flag and honor.

On the 29th of September, 1864, I was ordered by the Commanding General of the armies to cross the James River at two points and attack the enemy's line of works; one in the center of their line, Fort Harrison, the other a strong work guarding their left flank at New Market Heights; and there are men on this floor who will remember that day, I doubt not, as I do myself. I gave the center of the line to the white troops, the Eighteenth Corps, under General Ord, and they attacked one very strong work and carried it gallantly. I went myself with the colored troops to attack the enemy at New Market Heights; which was the key to the enemy's flank on the north side of James

River. That work was a redoubt built on the top of a hill of some considerable elevation; then running down into a marsh; in that marsh was a brook; then rising again to a plain which gently rolled away toward the river. On that plain, when the flash of dawn was breaking, I placed a column of three thousand colored troops, in close column by divisions, right in front, with guns at "right shoulder shift." I said, "That work must be taken by the weight of your column; no shot must be fired;" and to prevent their firing I had the caps taken from the nipples of their guns. Then I said, "Your cry, when you charge, will be, 'Remember Fort Pillow!'" and as the sun rose up in the heavens the order was given, "Forward," and they marched forward, steadily as if on parade —went down the hill, across the marsh, and as they got into the brook they came within range of the enemy's fire, which vigorously opened upon them. They broke a little as they forded the brook, and the column wavered. O, it was a moment of intensest anxiety, but they formed again, as they reached the firm ground, marching steadily on with closed ranks under the enemy's fire, until the head of the column reached the first line of abatis, some one hundred and fifty yards from the enemy's work. Then the ax-men ran to the front to cut away the heavy obstructions of defense, while one thousand men of the enemy, with their artillery concentrated, poured from the redoubt a heavy fire upon the head of the column hardly wider than the Clerk's desk. The ax-men went down under that murderous fire; other strong hands grasp the axes in their stead, and the abatis is cut away. Again, at double-quick, the column goes forward to within fifty yards of the fort, to meet there another line of abatis. The column halts, and there a very fire of hell is pouring upon them. The abatis resists and holds; the head of the column seems literally to melt away under the rain of shot and shell; the flags of the leading regiments go down, but a brave black hand seizes the colors; they are up again and wave their starry light over the storm of battle; again the ax-men fall, but strong hands and willing hearts seize the heavy, sharpened trees and drag them away, and the column rushes forward, and with a shout which now rings in my ear, go over that redoubt like a flash, and the enemy never stop running for four miles. [Applause on the floor and in the galleries.]

It became my painful duty, sir, to follow in the track of that charging column, and there, in a space not wider than the Clerk's desk and three hundred yards long, lay the dead bodies of five hundred and forty-three of my colored comrades, slain in defense of their country, who had laid down their lives to uphold its flag and its honor as a willing sacrifice; and as I rode along among them, guiding my horse this way and that way lest he should profane with his hoofs what seemed to me the sacred dead, and as I looked on their bronzed faces upturned in the shining sun to heaven as if in mute appeal against the wrongs of the country for which they had given their lives, and whose flag had only been to them a flag of stripes on which no star of glory had ever shone for them—feeling I had wronged them in the past and believing what was the future of my country to them—among my dead comrades there I swore to myself a solemn oath, "May my right hand forget its cunning and my tongue cleave to the roof of my month if I ever fail to defend the rights of these men who have given their blood for me and my country this day and for their race forever;" and, God helping me, I will keep that oath. [Great applause on the floor and in the galleries.]

From that hour all prejudice was gone, and an old-time States-right democrat became a lover of the negro race; and as long as their rights are not equal to the rights of other men under this Government I am with them against all comers, and when their rights are assured, as other men's rights are held sacred, then, I trust, we shall have what we sought to have, a united country North and South, white and black, under one glorious flag, for which we and our fathers have fought with an equal and not to be distinguished valor. [Applause.]

Now, Mr. Speaker, these men have fought for their country; one of their representatives has spoken, as few can speak on this floor, for his race; they have shown themselves our equals in battle; as citizens they are kind, quiet, temperate, laborious; they have shown that they know how to exercise the right of suffrage which we have given to them, for they always vote right; they vote the republican ticket, and all the powers of death and hell cannot persuade them to do otherwise. [Laughter.] They show that they knew better than their masters did,

,or they always knew how to be loyal. They have industry, they have temperance, they have all the good qualities of citizens, they have bravery, they have culture, they have power, they have eloquence. And who shall say that they shall not have what the Constitution gives them—equal rights? [Continued applause.]

FREDERICK DOUGLASS

Oration in Memory of Abraham Lincoln

Washington, D.C., April 14, 1876

FRIENDS AND FELLOW CITIZENS: I warmly congratulate
you upon the highly interesting object which has caused
you to assemble in such numbers and spirit as you have today. This occasion is in some respects remarkable. Wise and
thoughtful men of our race, who shall come after us, and study
the lessons of our history in the United States, who shall survey the long and dreary space over which we have traveled,
who shall count the links in the great chain of events by which
we have reached our present position, will make a note of this
occasion—they will think of it, and with a sense of manly pride
and complacency. I congratulate you also upon the very favorable circumstances in which we meet to-day. They are high,
inspiring and uncommon. They lend grace, glory and significance to the object for which we have met. Nowhere else in
this great country, with its uncounted towns and cities, uncounted wealth, and immeasurable territory extending from
sea to sea, could conditions be found more favorable to the
success of this occasion than here. We stand to-day at the national centre to perform something like a national act, an act
which is to go into history, and we are here where every pulsa-
tion of the national heart can be heard, felt and reciprocated.

A thousand wires, fed with thought and winged with lightning, put us in instantaneous communication with the loyal
and true men all over this country. Few facts could better illustrate the vast and wonderful change which has taken place in
our condition as a people, than the fact of our assembling here
for the purpose we have to-day. Harmless, beautiful, proper
and praiseworthy as this demonstration is, I cannot forget that
no such demonstration would have been tolerated here twenty
years ago. The spirit of slavery and barbarism, which still lingers
to blight and destroy in some dark and distant parts of our

country, would have made our assembling here to-day the signal and excuse for opening upon us all the flood-gates of wrath
and violence. That we are here in peace to-day is a compliment
and credit to American civilization, and a prophecy of still
greater national enlightenment and progress in the future. I
refer to the past not in malice, for this is no day for malice, but
simply to place more distinctly in front the gratifying and glorious change which has come both to our white fellow-citizens
and ourselves, and to congratulate all upon the contrast between now and then, the new dispensation of freedom with its
thousand blessings to both races, and the old dispensation of
slavery with its ten thousand evils to both races—white and
black. In view then, of the past, the present and the future, with
the long and dark history of our bondage behind us, and with
liberty, progress and enlightenment before us, I again congratulate you upon this auspicious day and hour.

Friends and fellow-citizens: The story of our presence here
is soon and easily told. We are here in the District of Columbia;
here in the city of Washington, the most luminous point of
American territory—a city recently transformed and made
beautiful in its body and in its spirit; we are here, in the place
where the ablest and best men of the country are sent to devise
the policy, enact the laws and shape the destiny of the Republic; we are here, with the stately pillars and majestic dome of the
Capitol of the nation looking down upon us; we are here, with
the broad earth freshly adorned with the foliage and flowers of
spring for our church, and all races, colors and conditions of
men for our congregation; in a word, we are here to express, as
best we may, by appropriate forms and ceremonies, our grateful sense of the vast, high and pre-eminent services rendered to
ourselves, to our race, to our country and to the whole world
by Abraham Lincoln.

The sentiment that brings us here to-day is one of the noblest
that can stir and thrill the human heart. It has crowned and
made glorious the high places of all civilized nations, with the
grandest and most enduring works of art, designed to illustrate
characters and perpetuate the memories of great public men.
It is the sentiment which from year to year adorns with fra-
grant and beautiful flowers the graves of our loyal, brave, and
patriotic soldiers who fell in defense of the Union and liberty.

It is the sentiment of gratitude and appreciation, which often, in the presence of many who hear me, has filled yonder heights of Arlington with the eloquence of eulogy and the sublime enthusiasm of poetry and song; a sentiment which can never die while the Republic lives. For the first time in the history of our people, and in the history of the whole American people, we join in this high worship and march conspicuously in the line of this time-honored custom. First things are always interesting, and this is one of our first things. It is the first time that, in this form and manner, we have sought to do honor to any American great man, however deserving and illustrious. I commend the fact to notice. Let it be told in every part of the Republic; let men of all parties and opinions hear it; let those who despise us, not less than those who respect us, know that now and here, in the spirit of liberty, loyalty, and gratitude, let it be known everywhere and by everybody who takes an interest in human progress and in the amelioration of the condition of mankind, that in the presence and with the approval of the members of the American House of Representatives, reflecting the general sentiment of the country; that in the presence of that august body, the American Senate, representing the highest intelligence and the calmest judgment of the country; in presence of the Supreme Court and Chief Justice of the United States, to whose decisions we all patriotically bow; in the presence and under the steady eye of the honored and trusted President of the United States, we, the colored people, newly emancipated and rejoicing in our blood-bought freedom, near the close of the first century in the life of this Republic, have now and here unveiled, set apart, and dedicated a monument of enduring granite and bronze, in every line, feature, and figure of which the men of this generation may read—and those of after-coming generations may read—something of the exalted character and great works of Abraham Lincoln, the first martyr President of the United States.

Fellow citizens: In what we have said and done to-day, and in what we may say and do hereafter, we disclaim everything like arrogance and assumption. We claim for ourselves no superior devotion to the character, history and memory of the illustrious name whose monument we have here dedicated to-day. We fully comprehend the relation of Abraham Lincoln, both to ourselves and the white people of the United States. Truth is proper and beautiful at all times and in all places, and it is never more proper and beautiful in any case than when speaking of a great public man whose example is likely to be commended for honor and imitation long after his departure to the solemn shades, the silent continents of eternity. It must be admitted, truth compels me to admit even here in the presence of the monument we have erected to his memory, Abraham Lincoln was not, in the fullest sense of the word, either our man or our model. In his interests, in his associations, in his habits of thought, and in his prejudices, he was a white man. He was preeminently the white man's President, entirely devoted to the welfare of white men. He was ready and willing at any time during the last years of his administration to deny, postpone and sacrifice the rights of humanity in the colored people, to promote the welfare of the white people of his country. In all his education and feelings he was an American of the Americans.

He came into the Presidential chair upon one principle alone, namely, opposition to the extension of slavery. His arguments in furtherance of this policy had their motive and mainspring in his patriotic devotion to the interest of his own race. To protect, defend and perpetuate slavery in the States where it existed, Abraham Lincoln was not less ready than any other President to draw the sword of the nation. He was ready to execute all the supposed constitutional guarantees of the Constitution in favor of the slave system anywhere inside the Slave States. He was willing to pursue, recapture, and send back the fugitive slave to his master, and to suppress a slave rising for liberty, though his guilty masters were already in arms against the Government. The race to which we belong were not the special objects of his consideration. Knowing this, I concede to you, my white fellow-citizens, a pre-eminence in this worship at once full and supreme. First, midst and last you and yours were the object of his deepest affection and his most earnest solicitude.

You are the children of Abraham Lincoln. We are at best only his step-children, children by adoption, children by force of circumstances and necessity. To you it especially belongs to sound his praises, to preserve and perpetuate his memory, to multiply his statues, to hang his pictures on your walls, and commend his example, for to you he was a great and glorious friend and benefactor. Instead of supplanting you at this altar we would exhort you to build high his monuments; let them be of the most costly material, of the most costly workmanship; let their forms be symmetrical, beautiful and perfect; let their bases be upon solid rocks, and their summits lean against the unchanging blue overhanging sky, and let them endure forever! But while in the abundance of your wealth and in the fullness of your just and patriotic devotion you do all this, we entreat you to despise not the humble offering we this day unveil to view: for while Abraham Lincoln saved for you a country, he delivered us from a bondage, according to Jefferson, one hour of which was worse than ages of the oppression your fathers rose in rebellion to oppose.

Fellow-citizens: Ours is a new-born zeal and devotion, a thing of the hour. The name of Abraham Lincoln was near and dear to our hearts in the darkest and most perilous hours of the Republic. We were no more ashamed of him when shrouded in clouds of darkness, of doubt and defeat than when crowned with victory, honor and glory. Our faith in him was often taxed and strained to the uttermost, but it never failed. When he tarried long in the mountain; when he strangely told us that we were the cause of the war; when he still more strangely told us to leave the land in which we were born; when he refused to employ our arms in defense of the Union; when, after accepting our services as colored soldiers, he refused to retaliate when we were murdered as colored prisoners; when he told us he would save the Union if he could with slavery; when he revoked the proclamation of emancipation of General Frémont; when he refused to remove the commander of the Army of the Potomac, who was more zealous in his efforts to protect slavery than suppress rebellion; when we saw this, and more, we were at times stunned, grieved and greatly bewildered; but our hearts believed while they ached and bled. Nor was this, even at that time, a blind and unreasoning superstition. Despite the mist and haze that surrounded him, despite the tumult, the hurry and confusion of the hour, we were able to take a comprehensive view of Abraham Lincoln, and to make reasonable allowance for the circumstances of his position. We saw him, measured him, and estimated him; not by stray utterances to injudicious and tedious delegations, who often tried his patience; not by isolated facts torn from their connection; not by any partial and imperfect glimpses, caught at inopportune moments; but by a broad survey, in the light of the stern logic of great events—and in view of that divinity which shapes our ends, rough hew them as we will, we came to the conclusion that the hour and the man of our redemption had met in the person of Abraham Lincoln. It mattered little to us what language he might employ upon special occasions; it mattered little to us, when we fully knew him, whether he was swift or slow in his movements; it was enough for us that Abraham Lincoln was at the head of a great movement, and was in living and earnest sympathy with that movement; which, in the nature of things, must go on till slavery should be utterly and forever abolished in the United States. When, therefore, it shall be asked what we have to do with the memory of Abraham Lincoln, or what Abraham Lincoln had to do with us, the answer is ready, full and complete. Though he loved Caesar less than Rome, though the Union was more to him than our freedom or our future, under his wise and beneficent rule we saw ourselves gradually lifted from the depths of slavery to the heights of liberty and manhood; under his wise and beneficent rule, and by measures approved and vigorously pressed by him, we saw that the handwriting of ages, in the form of prejudice and proscription, was rapidly fading away from the face of our whole country; under his rule, and in due time, about as soon after all as the country could tolerate the strange spectacle, we saw our brave sons and brothers laying off the rags of bondage, and being clothed all over in the blue uniforms of the soldiers of the United States; under his rule we saw two hundred thousand of our dark and dusky people responding to the call of Abraham Lincoln, and, with muskets on their shoulders and eagles on their buttons, timing their high footsteps to liberty and union under the national flag; under his rule we saw the independence of the black Republic of Hayti, the special object of slaveholding aversion and horror fully recognized, and her minister, a colored gentleman, duly received here in the city of Washington; under his rule we saw the internal slave trade which so long disgraced the nation abolished, and slavery abolished in the District of Columbia; under his rule we saw for the first time the law enforced against the foreign slave trade and the first slave-trader hanged, like any other pirate or murderer; under his rule and his inspiration we saw the Confederate States, based upon the idea that our race must be slaves, and slaves forever, battered to pieces and scattered to the four winds; under his rule, and in the fullness of time, we saw Abraham Lincoln, after giving the slaveholders three months of grace in which to save their hateful slave system, penning the immortal paper which, though special in its language, was general in its principles and effect, making slavery forever impossible in the United States. Though we waited long, we saw all this and more.

Can any colored man, or any white man friendly to the freedom of all men, ever forget the night which followed the first day of January, 1863? When the world was to see if Abraham Lincoln would prove to be as good as his word? I shall never forget that memorable night, when in a distant city I waited and watched at a public meeting, with three thousand others not less anxious than myself, for the word of deliverance which we have heard read to-day. Nor shall I ever forget the outburst of joy and thanksgiving that rent the air when the lightning brought to us the emancipation. In that happy hour we forgot all delay, and forgot all tardiness, forgot that the President had bribed the rebels to lay down their arms by a promise to withhold the bolt which would smite the slave system with destruction; and we were thenceforward willing to allow the President all the latitude of time, phraseology, and every honorable device that statesmanship might require for the achievement of a great and beneficent measure of liberty and progress.

Fellow-citizens, there is little necessity on this occasion to speak at length and critically of this great and good man, and of his high mission in the world. That ground has been fully occupied and completely covered both here and elsewhere. The whole field of fact and fancy has been gleaned and garnered. Any man can say things that are true of Abraham Lincoln, but no man can say anything new of Abraham Lincoln. His personal traits and public acts are better known to the American people than are those of any other man of his age. He was a mystery to no man who saw him and heard him. Though high in position, the humblest could approach him and feel at home in his presence. Though deep, he was transparent; though strong, he was gentle; though decided and pronounced in his convictions, he was tolerant towards those who differed from him, and patient under reproaches.

Even those who only knew him through his public utterances obtained a tolerably clear idea of his character and his personality. The image of the man went out with his words, and those who read him knew him. I have said that President Lincoln was a white man, and shared the prejudices common to his countrymen towards the colored race. Looking back to his times and to the condition of the country, this unfriendly feeling on his part may safely be set down as one element of his wonderful success in organizing the loyal American people for the tremendous conflict before them, and bringing them safely through that conflict. His great mission was to accomplish two things; first, to save his country from dismemberment and ruin, and second, to free his country from the great crime of slavery. To do one or the other, or both, he must have the earnest sympathy and the powerful cooperation of his loyal fellow-countrymen. Without this primary and essential condition to success, his efforts must have been vain and utterly fruitless. Had he put the abolition of slavery before the salvation of the Union, he would have inevitably driven from him a powerful class of the American people, and rendered resistance to rebellion impossible. Viewed from the genuine abolition ground, Mr. Lincoln seemed tardy, cold, dull, and indifferent: but measuring him by the sentiment of his country, a sentiment he was bound as a statesman to consult, he was swift, zealous, radical, and determined. Though Mr. Lincoln shared the prejudices of his white fellow-countrymen against the negro, it is hardly necessary to say that in his heart of hearts he loathed and hated slavery. He was willing while the South was loyal that it should have its pound of flesh, because he thought it was so nominated in the bond, but further than this no earthly power could make him go.

Fellow-citizens, whatever else in this world may be partial, unjust and uncertain, *time! time!* is impartial, just and certain in its actions. In the realm of mind, as well as in the realm of matter, it is a great worker, and often works wonders. The honest and comprehensive statesman, clearly discerning the needs of his country, and earnestly endeavoring to do his whole duty, though covered and blistered with reproaches, may safely leave his course to the silent judgment of time. Few great public men have ever been the victims of fiercer denunciation than Abraham Lincoln was during his administration. He was often wounded in the house of his friends. Reproaches came thick and fast upon him from within and from without, and from opposite quarters. He was assailed by abolitionists; he was assailed by slaveholders; he was assailed by men who were for peace at any price; he was assailed by those who were for a more vigorous prosecution of the war; he was assailed for not making the war an abolition war; and he was most bitterly assailed for making the war an abolition war.

But now behold the change; the judgment of the present hour is, that taking him for all in all, measuring the tremendous magnitude of the work before him, considering the necessary means to ends, and surveying the end from the beginning, infinite wisdom has seldom sent any man into the world better fitted for his mission than was Abraham Lincoln. His birth, his training, and his natural endowments, both mental and physical, were strongly in his favor. Born and reared among the lowly, a stranger to wealth and luxury, compelled to grapple single-handed with the flintiest hardships from tender youth to sturdy manhood, he grew strong in the manly and heroic qualities demanded by the great mission to which he was called by the votes of his countrymen. The hard condition of his early life, which would have depressed and broken down weaker men, only gave greater life, vigor and buoyancy to the heroic spirit of Abraham Lincoln. He was ready for any kind and any quality of work. What other young men dreaded in the shape of toil, he took hold of with the utmost cheerfulness.

> A spade, a rake, a hoe,
>   A pick-axe or a bill;
> A hook to reap, a scythe to mow,
>   A flail, or what you will.

All day long he could split heavy rails in the woods, and half the night long he could study his English grammar by the uncertain flare and glare of the light made by a pine knot. He was at home on the land with his axe, with his maul, with gluts and his wedges; and he was equally at home on water, with his oars, with his poles, with his planks and with his boathooks. And whether in his flatboat on the Mississippi river, or at the fireside of his frontier cabin, he was a man of work. A son of toil himself he was linked in brotherly sympathy with the sons of toil in every loyal part of the Republic. This very fact gave him tremendous power with the American people, and materially contributed not only to selecting him to the Presidency, but in sustaining his administration of the Government.

Upon his inauguration as President of the United States, an office even where assumed under the most favorable conditions, it is fitted to tax and strain the largest abilities, Abraham Lincoln was met by a tremendous pressure. He was called upon not merely to administer the Government, but to decide, in the face of terrible odds, the fate of the Republic. A formidable rebellion rose in his path before him; the Union was already practically dissolved. His country was torn and rent asunder at the centre. Hostile enemies were already organized against the Republic, armed with the munitions of war which the Republic had provided for its own defense. The tremendous question for him to decide was whether his country should survive the crisis and flourish or be dismembered and perish. His predecessor in office had already decided the question in favor of national dismemberment, by denying it the right of self-defense and self-preservation.

Happily for the country, happily for you and for me, the judgment of James Buchanan, the patrician, was not the judgment of Abraham Lincoln, the plebeian. He brought his strong common sense, sharpened in the school of adversity, to bear upon the question. He did not hesitate, he did not doubt, he did not falter, but at once resolved at whatever peril, at whatever cost, the union of the States should be preserved. A patriot himself, his faith was firm and unwavering in the patriotism of his countrymen. Timid men said before Mr. Lincoln's inauguration that we had seen the last President of the United States. A voice in influential quarters said let the Union slide. Some said that a Union maintained by the sword was worthless. Others said a rebellion of 8,000,000 cannot be suppressed. But in the midst of all this tumult and timidity, and against all this Abraham Lincoln was clear in his duty, and had an oath in heaven. He calmly and bravely heard the voice of doubt and fear all around him, but he had an oath in heaven, and there was not power enough on the earth to make this honest boat-man, backwoodsman and broad-handed splitter of rails evade or violate that sacred oath. He had not been schooled in the ethics of slavery; his plain life favored his love of truth. He had not been taught that treason and perjury were the proofs of honor and honesty. His moral training was against his saying one thing when he meant another. The trust which Abraham Lincoln had of himself and in the people was surprising and grand, but it was also enlightened and well founded. He knew the American people better than they knew themselves, and his truth was based upon his knowledge.

Had Abraham Lincoln died from any of the numerous ills to which flesh is heir; had he reached that good old age of which his vigorous constitution and his temperate habits gave prom-ise; had he been permitted to see the end of his great work; had the solemn curtain of death come down but gradually, we should still have been smitten with a heavy grief and treasured his name lovingly. But dying as he did die, by the red hand of violence; killed, assassinated, taken off without warning, not because of personal hate, for no man who knew Abraham Lin-coln could hate him, but because of his fidelity to Union and liberty, he is doubly dear to us, and will be precious forever.

Fellow-citizens, I end as I began, with congratulations. We have done a good work for our race to-day. In doing honor to the memory of our friend and liberator we have been doing highest honor to ourselves and those who come after us. We have been fastening ourselves to a name and fame imperishable and immortal. We have also been defending ourselves from a blighting slander. When now it shall be said that the colored man is soulless; that he has no appreciation of benefits or bene-factors; when the foul reproach of ingratitude is hurled at us, and it is attempted to scourge us beyond the range of human brotherhood, we may calmly point to the monument we have this day erected to the memory of Abraham Lincoln.

ROBERT G. INGERSOLL

Speech Nominating James G. Blaine

Cincinnati, June 15, 1876

MASSACHUSETTS may be satisfied with the loyalty of Benjamin H. Bristow; so am I; but if any man nominated by this convention can not carry the State of Massachusetts, I am not satisfied with the loyalty of that State. If the nominee of this convention can not carry the grand old Commonwealth of Massachusetts by seventy-five thousand majority, I would advise them to sell out Faneuil Hall as a Democratic headquarters. I would advise them to take from Bunker Hill that old monument of glory.

The Republicans of the United States demand as their leader in the great contest of 1876 a man of intelligence, a man of integrity, a man of well-known and approved political opinions. They demand a statesman; they demand a reformer after as well as before the election. They demand a politician in the highest, broadest and best sense—a man of superb moral courage. They demand a man acquainted with public affairs—with the wants of the people; with not only the requirements of the hour, but with the demands of the future. They demand a man broad enough to comprehend the relations of this government to the other nations of the earth. They demand a man well versed in the powers, duties, and prerogatives of each and every department of this government. They demand a man who will sacredly preserve the financial honor of the United States; one who knows enough to know that the national debt must be paid through the prosperity of this people; one who knows enough to know that all the financial theories in the world cannot redeem a single dollar; one who knows enough to know that all the money must be made, not by law, but by labor; one who knows enough to know that the people of the United States have the industry to make the money, and the honor to pay it over just as fast as they make it.

The Republicans of the United States demand a man who knows that prosperity and resumption, when they come, must come together; that when they come, they will come hand in hand through the golden harvest fields; hand in hand by the whirling spindles and the turning wheels; hand in hand past the open furnace doors; hand in hand by the flaming forges; hand in hand by the chimneys filled with eager fire, greeted and grasped by the countless sons of toil.

This money has to be dug out of the earth. You can not make it by passing resolutions in a political convention.

The Republicans of the United States want a man who knows that this government should protect every citizen, at home and abroad; who knows that any government that will not defend its defenders, and protect its protectors, is a disgrace to the map of the world. They demand a man who believes in the eternal separation and divorcement of church and school. They demand a man whose political reputation is spotless as a star; but they do not demand that their candidate shall have a certificate of moral character signed by a confederate congress. The man who has, in full, heaped and rounded measure, all these splendid qualifications, is the present grand and gallant leader of the Republican party—James G. Blaine.

Our country, crowned with the vast and marvelous achievements of its first century, asks for a man worthy of the past, and prophetic of her future; asks for a man who has the audacity of genius; asks for a man who is the grandest combination of heart, conscience and brain beneath her flag—such a man is James G. Blaine.

For the Republican host, led by this intrepid man, there can be no defeat.

This is a grand year—a year filled with the recollections of the Revolution; filled with proud and tender memories of the past; with the sacred legends of liberty—a year in which the sons of freedom will drink from the fountains of enthusiasm; a year in which the people call for a man who has preserved in Congress what our soldiers won upon the field; a year in which they call for the man who has torn from the throat of treason the tongue of slander—for the man who has snatched the mask of Democracy from the hideous face of rebellion; for the man who, like an intellectual athlete, has stood in the arena of debate and challenged all comers, and who is still a total stranger to defeat.

Like an armed warrior, like a plumed knight, James G. Blaine marched down the halls of the American Congress and threw his shining lance full and fair against the brazen foreheads of the defamers of his country and the maligners of his honor. For the Republican party to desert this gallant leader now, is as though an army should desert their general upon the field of battle.

James G. Blaine is now and has been for years the bearer of the sacred standard of the Republican party. I call it sacred, because no human being can stand beneath its folds without becoming and without remaining free.

Gentlemen of the convention, in the name of the great Republic, the only Republic that ever existed upon this earth; in the name of all her defenders and of all her supporters; in the name of all her soldiers living; in the name of all her soldiers dead upon the field of battle, and in the name of those who perished in the skeleton clutch of famine at Andersonville and Libby, whose sufferings he so vividly remembers, Illinois—Illinois nominates for the next President of this country, that prince of parliamentarians that leader of leaders—James G. Blaine.

CHIEF JOSEPH

Reply to General Howard

Bear Paw Mountains, Montana Territory, October 5, 1877

TELL General HOWARD I know his heart. What he told me before, I have it in my heart. I am tired of fighting. Our chiefs are killed; LOOKING-GLASS is dead, TA-HOOL-HOOL-SHUTE is dead. The old men are all dead. It is the young men who say "Yes" or "No." He who led on the young men is dead. It is cold, and we have no blankets; the little children are freezing to death. My people, some of them, have run away to the hills, and have no blankets, no food. No one knows where they are—perhaps freezing to death. I want to have time to look for my children, and see how many of them I can find. Maybe I shall find them among the dead. Hear me, my chiefs! I am tired; my heart is sick and sad. From where the sun now stands I will fight no more forever.

OLIVER WENDELL HOLMES, JR.

Memorial Day Address

Keene, N.H., May 30, 1884

NOT LONG AGO I heard a young man ask why people still kept up Memorial Day, and it set me thinking of the answer. Not the answer that you and I should give to each other—not the expression of those feelings that, so long as you and I live, will make this day sacred to memories of love and grief and heroic youth—but an answer which should command the assent of those who do not share our memories, and in which we of the North and our brethren of the South could join in perfect accord.

So far as this last is concerned, to be sure, there is no trouble. The soldiers who were doing their best to kill each other felt less of personal hostility, I am very certain, than some who were not imperiled by their mutual endeavors. I have heard more than one of those who had been gallant and distinguished officers on the Confederate side say that they had had no such feeling. I know that I and those whom I knew best had not. We believed that it was most desirable that the North should win; we believed in the principle that the Union is indissoluble; we, or many of us at least, also believed that the conflict was inevitable, and that slavery had lasted long enough. But we equally believed that those who stood against us held just as sacred convictions that were the opposite of ours, and we respected them as every man with a heart must respect those who give all for their belief. The experience of battle soon taught its lesson even to those who came into the field more bitterly disposed. You could not stand up day after day in those indecisive contests where overwhelming victory was impossible because neither side would run as they ought when beaten, without getting at last something of the same brotherhood for the enemy that the north pole of a magnet has for the south—each working in an opposite sense to the other, but each unable to get along without the other. As it was then, it is now. The soldiers of the war need no explanations; they can join in commemorating a soldier's death with feelings not different in kind, whether he fell toward them or by their side.

But Memorial Day may and ought to have a meaning also for those who do not share our memories. When men have instinctively agreed to celebrate an anniversary, it will be found that there is some thought or feeling behind it which is too large to be dependent upon associations alone. The Fourth of July, for instance, has still its serious aspect, although we should no longer think of rejoicing like children that we have escaped from an outgrown control, although we have achieved not only our national but our moral independence and know it far too profoundly to make a talk about it, and although an Englishman can join in the celebration without a scruple. For, stripped of the temporary associations which gave rise to it, it is now the moment when by common consent we pause to become conscious of our national life and to rejoice in it, to recall what our country has done for each of us and to ask ourselves what we can do for our country in return.

So to the indifferent inquirer who asks why Memorial Day is still kept up we may answer, It celebrates and solemnly reaffirms from year to year a national act of enthusiasm and faith. It embodies in the most impressive form our belief that to act with enthusiasm and faith is the condition of acting greatly. To fight out a war you must believe something and want something with all your might. So must you do to carry anything else to an end worth reaching. More than that, you must be willing to commit yourself to a course, perhaps a long and hard one, without being able to foresee exactly where you will come out. All that is required of you is that you should go somewhither as hard as ever you can. The rest belongs to fate. One may fall— at the beginning of the charge or at the top of the earthworks—but in no other way can he reach the rewards of victory.

When it was felt so deeply as it was on both sides that a man ought to take his part in the war unless some conscientious scruple or strong practical reason made it impossible, was that feeling simply the requirement of a local majority that their neighbors should agree with them? I think not: I think the feeling was right—in the South as in the North. I think that as life is action and passion, it is required of a man that he should share the passion and action of his time at peril of being judged not to have lived.

If this be so, the use of this day is obvious. It is true that I cannot argue a man into a desire. If he says to me, Why should I wish to know the secrets of philosophy? Why seek to decipher the hidden laws of creation that are graven upon the tablets of the rocks, or to unravel the history of civilization that is woven in the tissue of our jurisprudence, or to do any great work, either of speculation or of practical affairs? I cannot answer him; or, at least my answer is as little worth making for any effect it will have upon his wishes as if he asked, why should I eat this or drink that? You must begin by wanting to. But, although desire cannot be imparted by argument, it can be by contagion. Feeling begets feeling, and great feeling begets great feeling. We can hardly share the emotions that make this day to us the most sacred day of the year and embody them in ceremonial pomp without in some degree imparting them to those who come after us. I believe from the bottom of my heart that our memorial halls and statues and tablets, the tattered flags of our regiments gathered in the State-houses, and this day with its funeral march and decorated graves, are worth more to our young men by way of chastening and inspiration than the monuments of another hundred years of peaceful life could be.

But even if I am wrong, even if those, who come after us are to forget all that we hold dear, and the future is to teach and kindle its children in ways as yet unrevealed, it is enough for us that to us this day is dear and sacred.

Accidents may call up the events of the war. You see a battery of guns go by at a trot, and for a moment you are back at White Oak Swamp or Antietam or on the Jerusalem Road. You hear a few shots fired in the distance, and for an instant your heart stops as you say to yourself, The skirmishers are at it, and listen for the long roll of fire from the main line. You meet an old comrade after many years of absence; he recalls the moment when you were nearly surrounded by the enemy, and again there comes up to you that swift and cunning thinking on which once hung life or freedom—Shall I stand the best chance if I try the pistol or the saber on that man who means to stop me? Will he get his carbine free before I reach him, or can I kill him first? These and the thousand other events we have known are called up, I say, by accident, and, apart from accident, they lie forgotten.

But as surely as this day comes round we are in the presence of the dead. For one hour, twice a year at least—at the regimental dinner, where the ghosts sit at table more numerous than the living, and on this day when we decorate their graves— the dead come back and live with us.

I see them now, more than I can number, as once I saw them on this earth. They are the same bright figures, or their counterparts, that come also before your eyes; and when I speak of those who were my brothers the same words describe yours.

I see a fair-haired lad, a lieutenant, and a captain on whom life had begun somewhat to tell, but still young, sitting by the long mess-table in camp before the regiment left the State and wondering how many of those who gathered in our tent could hope to see the end of what was then beginning. For neither of them was that destiny reserved. I remember, as I awoke from my first long stupor in the hospital after the battle of Ball's Bluff, I heard the doctor say, "He was a beautiful boy," and I knew that one of those two speakers was no more. The other, after passing harmless through all the previous battles, went into Fredericksburg with strange premonition of the end and there met his fate.

I see another youthful lieutenant as I saw him in the Seven Days, when I looked down the line at Glendale. The officers were at the head of their companies. The advance was beginning. We caught each other's eye and saluted. When next I looked he was gone.

I see the brother of the last—the flame of genius and daring in his face—as he rode before us into the wood of Antietam, out of which came only dead and deadly wounded men. So, a little later, he rode to his death at the head of his cavalry in the Valley.

In the portraits of some of those who fell in the civil wars of England, Vandyke has fixed on canvas the type of those who stand before my memory. Young and gracious figures, somewhat remote and proud, but with a melancholy and sweet kindness. There is upon their faces the shadow of approaching fate and the glory of generous acceptance of it. I may say of them, as I once heard it said of two Frenchmen, relics of the *ancien régime*, "They were very gentle. They cared nothing for their lives." High breeding, romantic chivalry—we who have seen these men can never believe that the power of money or the enervation of pleasure has put an end to them. We know that life may still be lifted into poetry and lit with spiritual charm.

But the men, not less, perhaps even more, characteristic of New England, were the Puritans of our day—for the Puritan still lives in New England, thank God! and will live there so long as New England lives and keeps her old renown. New England is not dead yet. She still is mother of a race of conquerors. Stern men, little given to the expression of their feelings, sometimes careless of the graces, but fertile, tenacious, and knowing only duty. Each of you, as I do, thinks of a hundred such that he has known. I see one—grandson of a hard rider of the Revolution and bearer of his historic name—who was with us at Fair Oaks, and afterwards for five days and nights in front of the enemy the only sleep that he would take was what he could snatch sitting erect in his uniform and resting his back against a hut. He fell at Gettysburg.

His brother, a surgeon, who rode, as our surgeons so often did, wherever the troops would go, I saw kneeling in ministration to a wounded man just in rear of our line at Antietam, his horse's bridle round his arm—the next moment his ministrations were ended. His senior associate survived all the wounds and perils of the war, but, not yet through with duty as he understood it, fell in helping the helpless poor who were dying of cholera in a Western city.

I see another quiet figure of virtuous life and silent ways, not much heard of until our left was turned at Petersburg. He was in command of the regiment as he saw our comrades driven in. He threw back his left wing and the advancing tide of defeat was shattered against his iron wall. He saved an army corps from disaster, and then a round shot ended all for him.

There is one who on this day is always present to my mind. He entered the army at nineteen, a second lieutenant. In the Wilderness, already at the head of his regiment, he fell, using the moment that was left him of life to give all his little fortune to his soldiers. I saw him in camp, on the march, in action. I crossed debatable land with him when we were rejoining the army together. I observed him in every kind of duty, and never in all the time that I knew him did I see him fail to choose that alternative of conduct which was most disagreeable to himself. He was indeed a Puritan in all his virtues without the Puritan austerity; for, when duty was at an end, he who had been the master and leader became the chosen companion in every pleasure that a man might honestly enjoy. In action he was sublime. His few surviving companions will never forget the awful spectacle of his advance alone with his company in the streets of Fredericksburg. In less than sixty seconds he would become the focus of a hidden and annihilating fire from a semi-circle of houses. His first platoon had vanished under it in an instant, ten men falling dead by his side. He had quietly turned back to where the other half of his company was waiting, had given the order, "Second Platoon, forward!" and was again moving on, in obedience to superior command, to certain and useless death, when the order he was obeying was counter-manded. The end was distant only a few seconds; but if you had seen him with his indifferent carriage, and sword swinging from his finger like a cane, you would never have suspected that he was doing more than conducting a company drill on the camp parade ground. He was little more than a boy, but the grizzled corps commanders knew and admired him; and for us, who not only admired but loved, his death seemed to end a portion of our life also.

There is one grave and commanding presence that you all would recognize, for his life has become a part of our common history. Who does not remember the leader of the assault at the mine of Petersburg? the solitary horseman in front of Port Hudson, whom a foeman worthy of him bade his soldiers spare, from love and admiration of such gallant bearing? Who does not still hear the echo of those eloquent lips after the war teaching reconciliation and peace? I may not do more than al-lude to his death, fit ending of his life. All that the world has a right to know has been told by a beloved friend in a book wherein friendship has found no need to exaggerate facts that speak for themselves. I knew him; and I may even say I knew him well; yet, until that book appeared, I had not known the governing motive of his soul. I had admired him as a hero.

When I read, I learned to revere him as a saint. His strength was not in honor alone but in religion; and those who do not share his creed must see that it was on the wings of religious faith that he mounted above even valiant deeds into an empyrean of ideal life.

I have spoken of some of the men who were near to me among others very near and dear, not because their lives have become historic, but because their lives are the type of what every soldier has known and seen in his own company. In the great democracy of self-devotion private and general stand side by side. Unmarshaled save by their own deeds, the armies of the dead sweep before us, "wearing their wounds like stars." It is not because the men whom I have mentioned were my friends that I have spoken of them, but, I repeat, because they are types. I speak of those whom I have seen. But you all have known such; you, too, remember!

It is not of the dead alone that we think on this day. There are those still living whose sex forbade them to offer their lives, but who gave instead their happiness. Which of us has not been lifted above himself by the sight of one of those lovely, lonely women, around whom the wand of sorrow has traced its excluding circle—set apart, even when surrounded by loving friends who would fain bring back joy to their lives? I think of one whom the poor of a great city know as their benefactress and friend. I think of one who has lived not less greatly in the midst of her children, to whom she has taught such lessons as may not be heard elsewhere from mortal lips. The story of these and of their sisters we must pass in reverent silence. All that may be said has been said by one of their own sex:

> But when the days of golden dreams had perished,
> And even despair was powerless to destroy;
> Then did I learn how existence could be cherished,
> Strengthened, and fed without the aid of joy.
>
> Then did I check the tears of useless passion,
> Weaned my young soul from yearning after thine;
> Sternly denied its burning wish to hasten
> Down to that tomb already more than mine.

Comrades, some of the associations of this day are not only triumphant but joyful. Not all of those with whom we once stood shoulder to shoulder—not all of those whom we once loved and revered—are gone. On this day we still meet our companions in the freezing winter bivouacs and in those dreadful summer marches where every faculty of the soul seemed to depart one after another, leaving only a dumb animal power to set the teeth and to persist—a blind belief that somewhere and at last there was rest and water. On this day, at least, we still meet and rejoice in the closest tie which is possible between men—a tie which suffering has made indissoluble for better, for worse.

When we meet thus, when we do honor to the dead in terms that must sometimes embrace the living, we do not deceive ourselves. We attribute no special merit to a man for having served when all were serving. We know that if the armies of our war did anything worth remembering, the credit belongs not mainly to the individuals who did it, but to average human nature. We also know very well that we cannot live in associations with the past alone, and we admit that if we would be worthy of the past we must find new fields for action or thought and make for ourselves new careers.

But, nevertheless, the generation that carried on the war has been set apart by its experience. Through our great good fortune, in our youth our hearts were touched with fire. It was given to us to learn at the outset that life is a profound and passionate thing. While we are permitted to scorn nothing but indifference, and do not pretend to undervalue the worldly rewards of ambition, we have seen with our own eyes beyond and above the gold fields the snowy hights of honor, and it is for us to bear the report to those who come after us. But above all, we have learned that whether a man accepts from Fortune her spade, and will look downward and dig, or from Aspiration her axe and cord, and will scale the ice, the one and only success which it is his to command is to bring to his work a mighty heart.

Such hearts—ah me, how many!—were stilled twenty years ago; and to us who remain behind is left this day of memories. Every year—in the full tide of spring—at the hight of the symphony of flowers and love and life—there comes a pause, and through the silence we hear the lonely pipe of death. Year after year lovers wandering under the apple boughs and through the clover and deep grass are surprised with sudden tears as they see black veiled figures stealing through the morning to a soldier's grave. Year after year the comrades of the dead follow with public honor, procession and commemorative flags and funeral march—honor and grief from us who stand almost alone, and have seen the best and noblest of our generation pass away.

But grief is not the end of all. I seem to hear the funeral march become a pæan. I see beyond the forest the moving banners of a hidden column. Our dead brothers still live for us, and bid us think of life, not death—of life to which in their youth they lent the passion and glory of the spring. As I listen, the great chorus of life and joy begins again, and amid the awful orchestra of seen and unseen powers and destinies of good and evil our trumpets sound once more a note of daring, hope, and will.

GROVER CLEVELAND

Address at the Dedication of the Statue of Liberty

New York City, October 28, 1886

THE PEOPLE of the United States accept with gratitude from their brethren of the French Republic the grand and completed work of art we here inaugurate.

This token of the affection and consideration of the people of France demonstrates the kinship of republics, and conveys to us the assurance that in our efforts to commend to mankind the excellence of a government resting upon popular will, we still have beyond the American continent a steadfast ally.

We are not here to-day to bow before the representation of a fierce and warlike god, filled with wrath and vengeance, but we joyously contemplate instead our own deity keeping watch and ward before the open gates of America, and greater than all that have been celebrated in ancient song. Instead of grasping in her hand thunderbolts of terror and of death, she holds aloft the light which illumines the way to man's enfranchisement.

We will not forget that Liberty has here made her home; nor shall her chosen altar be neglected. Willing votaries will constantly keep alive its fires, and these shall gleam upon the shores of our sister republic in the east. Reflected thence and joined with answering rays, a stream of light shall pierce the darkness of ignorance and man's oppression, until Liberty enlightens the world.

ELIZABETH CADY STANTON

The Solitude of Self

Washington, D.C., January 18, 1892

MR. CHAIRMAN and gentlemen of the committee: We have been speaking before Committees of the Judiciary for the last twenty years, and we have gone over all the arguments in favor of a sixteenth amendment which are familiar to all you gentlemen; therefore, it will not be necessary that I should repeat them again.

The point I wish plainly to bring before you on this occasion is the individuality of each human soul; our Protestant idea, the right of individual conscience and judgment—our republican idea, individual citizenship. In discussing the rights of woman, we are to consider, first, what belongs to her as an individual, in a world of her own, the arbiter of her own destiny, an imaginary Robinson Crusoe with her woman Friday on a solitary island. Her rights under such circumstances are to use all her faculties for her own safety and happiness.

Secondly, if we consider her as a citizen, as a member of a great nation, she must have the same rights as all other members, according to the fundamental principals of our Government.

Thirdly, viewed as a woman, an equal factor in civilization, her rights and duties are still the same—individual happiness and development.

Fourthly, it is only the incidental relations of life, such as mother, wife, sister, daughter, that may involve some special duties and training. In the usual discussion in regard to woman's sphere, such men as Herbert Spencer, Frederic Harrison, and Grant Allen uniformly subordinate her rights and duties as an individual, as a citizen, as a woman, to the necessities of these incidental relations, some of which a large class of women may never assume. In discussing the sphere of man we do not decide his rights as an individual, as a citizen, as a man by his duties as a father, a husband, a brother, or a son, relations some of which he may never fill. Moreover he would be better fitted for these very relations and whatever special work he might choose to do to earn his bread by the complete development of all his faculties as an individual.

Just so with woman. The education that will fit her to discharge the duties in the largest sphere of human usefulness will best fit her for whatever special work she may be compelled to do.

The isolation of every human soul and the necessity of self-dependence must give each individual the right, to choose his own surroundings.

The strongest reason for giving woman all the opportunities for higher education, for the full development of her faculties, forces of mind and body; for giving her the most enlarged freedom of thought and action; a complete emancipation from all forms of bondage, of custom, dependence, superstition; from all the crippling influences of fear, is the solitude and personal responsibility of her own individual life. The strongest reason why we ask for woman a voice in the government under which she lives; in the religion she is asked to believe; equality in social life, where she is the chief factor; a place in the trades and professions, where she may earn her bread, is because of her birthright to self-sovereignty; because, as an individual, she must rely on herself. No matter how much women prefer to lean, to be protected and supported, nor how much men desire to have them do so, they must make the voyage of life alone, and for safety in an emergency they must know something of the laws of navigation. To guide our own craft, we must be captain, pilot, engineer; with chart and compass to stand at the wheel; to watch the wind and waves and know when to take in the sail, and to read the signs in the firmament over all. It matters not whether the solitary voyager is man or woman.

Nature having endowed them equally, leaves them to their own skill and judgment in the hour of danger, and, if not equal to the occasion, alike they perish.

To appreciate the importance of fitting every human soul for independent action, think for a moment of the immeasurable solitude of self. We come into the world alone, unlike all who have gone before us; we leave it alone under circumstances peculiar to ourselves. No mortal ever has been, no mortal ever will be like the soul just launched on the sea of life. There can never again be just such environments as make up the infancy, youth and manhood of this one. Nature never repeats herself, and the possibilities of one human soul will never be found in another. No one has ever found two blades of ribbon grass alike, and no one will ever find two human beings alike. Seeing, then, what must be the infinite diversity in human character, we can in a measure appreciate the loss to a nation when any large class of the people is uneducated and unrepresented in the government. We ask for the complete development of every individual, first, for his own benefit and happiness. In fitting out an army we give each soldier his own knap-sack, arms, pow-der, his blanket, cup, knife, fork and spoon. We provide alike for all their individual necessities, then each man bears his own burden.

Again we ask complete individual development for the gen-eral good; for the consensus of the competent on the whole round of human interests; on all questions of national life, and here each man must bear his share of the general burden. It is sad to see how soon friendless children are left to bear their own burdens before they can analize their feelings; before they can even tell their joys and sorrows, they are thrown on their own resources. The great lesson that nature seems to teach us at all ages is self-dependence, self-protection, self-support. What a touching instance of a child's solitude; of that hunger of heart for love and recognition, in the case of the little girl who helped to dress a christmas tree for the children of the family in which she served. On finding there was no present for herself she slipped away in the darkness and spent the night in an open field sitting on a stone, and when found in the morning was weeping as if her heart would break. No mortal will ever know the thoughts that passed through the mind of that friendless child in the long hours of that cold night, with only the silent stars to keep her company. The mention of her case in the daily papers moved many generous hearts to send her presents, but in the hours of her keenest sufferings she was thrown wholly on herself for consolation.

In youth our most bitter disappointments, our brightest

hopes and ambitions are known only to ourselves; even our friendship and love we never fully share with another; there is something of every passion in every situation we conceal. Even so in our triumphs and our defeats.

The successful candidate for Presidency and his opponent each have a solitude peculiarly his own, and good form forbids either to speak of his pleasure or regret. The solitude of the king on his throne and the prisoner in his cell differs in character and degree, but it is solitude nevertheless.

We ask no sympathy from others in the anxiety and agony of a broken friendship or shattered love. When death sunders our nearest ties, alone we sit in the shadows of our affliction. Alike mid the greatest triumphs and darkest tragedies of life we walk alone. On the divine heights of human attainments, eulogized and worshiped as a hero or saint, we stand alone. In ignorance, poverty, and vice, as a pauper or criminal, alone we starve or steal; alone we suffer the sneers and rebuffs of our fellows; alone we are hunted and hounded thro dark courts and alleys, in by-ways and highways; alone we stand in the judgment seat; alone in the prison cell we lament our crimes and misfortunes; alone we expiate them on the gallows. In hours like these we realize the awful solitude of individual life, its pains, its penalties, its responsibilities; hours in which the youngest and most helpless are thrown on their own resources for guidance and consolation. Seeing then that life must ever be a march and a battle, that each soldier must be equipped for his own protection, it is the height of cruelty to rob the individual of a single natural right.

To throw obstacles in the way of a complete education is like putting out the eyes; to deny the rights of property, like cutting off the hands. To deny political equality is to rob the ostracised of all self-respect; of credit in the market place; of recompense in the world of work; of a voice among those who make and administer the law; a choice in the jury before whom they are tried, and in the judge who decides their punishment. Shakespeare's play of Titus and Andronicus contains a terrible satire on woman's position in the nineteenth century—"Rude men" (the play tells us) "seized the king's daughter, cut out her tongue, cut off her hands, and then bade her go call for water and wash her hands." What a picture of woman's position. Robbed of her natural rights, handicapped by law and custom at every turn, yet compelled to fight her own battles, and in the emergencies of life to fall back on herself for protection.

The girl of sixteen, thrown on the world to support herself, to make her own place in society, to resist the temptations that surround her and maintain a spotless integrity, must do all this by native force or superior education. She does not acquire this power by being trained to trust others and distrust herself. If she wearies of the struggle, finding it hard work to swim upstream, and allows herself to drift with the current, she will find plenty of company, but not one to share her misery in the hour of her deepest humiliation. If she tries to retrieve her position, to conceal the past, her life is hedged about with fears lest willing hands should tear the veil from what she fain would hide. Young and friendless, she knows the bitter solitude of self.

How the little courtesies of life on the surface of society, deemed so important from man towards woman, fade into utter insignificance in view of the deeper tragedies in which she must play her part alone, where no human aid is possible.

The young wife and mother, at the head of some establishment with a kind husband to shield her from the adverse winds of life, with wealth, fortune and position, has a certain harbor of safety, secure against the ordinary ills of life. But to manage a household, have a desirable influence in society, keep her friends and the affections of her husband, train her children and servants well, she must have rare common sense, wisdom, diplomacy, and a knowledge of human nature. To do all this she needs the cardinal virtues and the strong points of character that the most successful statesman possesses.

An uneducated woman, trained to dependence, with no resources in herself must make a failure of any position in life. But society says women do not need a knowledge of the world; the liberal training that experience in public life must give, all the advantages of collegiate education; but when for the lack of all this, the woman's happiness is wrecked, alone she bears her humiliation; and the solitude of the weak and the ignorant is indeed pitiful. In the wild chase for the prizes of life they are ground to powder.

In age, when the pleasures of youth are passed, children grown up, married and gone, the hurry and bustle of life in a measure over, when the hands are weary of active service, when the old armchair and the fireside are the chosen resorts, then men and women alike must fall back on their own resources. If they cannot find companionship in books, if they have no interest in the vital questions of the hour, no interest in watching the consummation of reforms, with which they might have been identified, they soon pass into their dotage. The more fully the faculties of the mind are developed and kept in use, the longer the period of vigor and active interest in all around us continues. If from a lifelong participation in public affairs a woman feels responsible for the laws regulating our system of education, the discipline of our jails and prisons, the sanitary conditions of our private homes, public buildings, and thoroughfares, an interest in commerce, finance, our foreign relations, in any or all of these questions, her solitude will at least be respectable, and she will not be driven to gossip or scandal for entertainment.

The chief reason for opening to every soul the doors to the whole round of human duties and pleasures is the individual development thus attained, the resources thus provided under all circumstances to mitigate the solitude that at times must come to everyone. I once asked Prince Krapotkin, the Russian nihilist, how he endured his long years in prison, deprived of books, pen, ink, and paper. "Ah," he said, "I thought out many questions in which I had a deep interest. In the pursuit of an idea I took no note of time. When tired of solving knotty problems I recited all the beautiful passages in prose or verse I had ever learned. I became acquainted with myself and my own resources. I had a world of my own, a vast empire, that no Russian jailor or Czar could invade." Such is the value of liberal thought and broad culture when shut off from all human companionship, bringing comfort and sunshine within even the four walls of a prison cell.

As women ofttimes share a similar fate, should they not have all the consolation that the most liberal education can give? Their suffering in the prisons of St. Petersburg; in the long, weary marches to Siberia, and in the mines, working side by side with men, surely call for all the self-support that the most exalted sentiments of heroism can give. When suddenly roused at midnight, with the startling cry of "fire! fire!" to find the house over their heads in flames, do women wait for men to point the way to safety? And are the men, equally bewildered and half suffocated with smoke, in a position to more than try to save themselves?

At such times the most timid women have shown a courage and heroism in saving their husbands and children that has surprised everybody. Inasmuch, then, as woman shares equally the joys and sorrows of time and eternity, is it not the height of presumption in man to propose to represent her at the ballot box and the throne of grace, do her voting in the state, her praying in the church, and to assume the position of priest at the family altar.

Nothing strengthens the judgment and quickens the conscience like individual responsibility. Nothing adds such dignity to character as the recognition of one's self-sovereignty; the right to an equal place, every where conceded; a place earned by personal merit, not an artificial attainment, by inheritance, wealth, family, and position. Seeing, then that the responsibilities of life rests equally on man and woman, that their destiny is the same, they need the same preparation for time and eternity. The talk of sheltering woman from the fierce storms of life is the sheerest mockery, for they beat on her from every point of the compass, just as they do on man, and with more fatal results, for he has been trained to protect himself, to resist, to conquer. Such are the facts in human experience, the responsibilities of individual sovereignty. Rich and poor, intelligent and ignorant, wise and foolish, virtuous and vicious, man and woman, it is ever the same, each soul must depend wholly on itself.

Whatever the theories may be of woman's dependence on man, in the supreme moments of her life he can not bear her burdens. Alone she goes to the gates of death to give life to every man that is born into the world. No one can share her fears, no one can mitigate her pangs; and if her sorrow is greater than she can bear, alone she passes beyond the gates into the vast unknown.

From the mountain tops of Judea, long ago, a heavenly voice bade His disciples, "Bear ye one another's burdens," but humanity has not yet risen to that point of self-sacrifice, and if ever so willing, how few the burdens are that one soul can bear for another. In the highways of Palestine; in prayer and fasting on the solitary mountain top; in the Garden of Gethsemane; before the judgment seat of Pilate; betrayed by one of His trusted disciples at His last supper; in His agonies on the cross, even Jesus of Nazareth, in these last sad days on earth, felt the awful solitude of self. Deserted by man, in agony he cries, "My God! My God! why hast Thou forsaken me?" And so it ever must be in the conflicting scenes of life, in the long weary march, each one walks alone. We may have many friends, love, kindness, sympathy and charity to smooth our pathway in everyday life, but in the tragedies and triumphs of human experience each mortal stands alone.

But when all artificial trammels are removed, and women are recognized as individuals, responsible for their own environments, thoroughly educated for all the positions in life they may be called to fill; with all the resources in themselves that liberal thought and broad culture can give; guided by their own conscience and judgment; trained to self-protection by a healthy development of the muscular system and skill in the use of weapons of defense, and stimulated to self-support by the knowledge of the business world and the pleasure that pecuniary independence must ever give; when women are trained in this way they will, in a measure, be fitted for those hours of solitude that come alike to all, whether prepared or otherwise. As in our extremity we must depend on ourselves, the dictates of wisdom point to complete individual development.

In talking of education how shallow the argument that each class must be educated for the special work it proposes to do, and all those faculties not needed in this special walk must lie dormant and utterly wither for want of use, when, perhaps, these will be the very faculties needed in life's greatest emergencies. Some say, Where is the use of drilling girls in the languages, the sciences, in law, medicine, theology? As wives, mothers, housekeepers, cooks, they need a different curriculum from boys who are to fill all positions. The chief cooks in our great hotels and ocean steamers are men. In large cities men run the bakeries; they make our bread, cake and pies. They manage the laundries; they are now considered our best milliners and dressmakers. Because some men fill these departments of usefulness, shall we regulate the curriculum in Harvard and Yale to their present necessities? If not, why this talk in our best colleges of a curriculum for girls who are crowding into the trades and professions; teachers in all our public schools rapidly filling many lucrative and honorable positions in life? They are showing, too, their calmness and courage in the most trying hours of human experience.

You have probably all read in the daily papers of the terrible storm in the Bay of Biscay when a tidal wave made such havoc on the shore, wrecking vessels, unroofing houses and carrying destruction everywhere. Among other buildings the woman's prison was demolished. Those who escaped saw men struggling to reach the shore. They promptly by clasping hands made a chain of themselves and pushed out into the sea, again and again, at the risk of their lives until they had brought six men to shore, carried them to a shelter, and did all in their power for their comfort and protection.

What special school of training could have prepared these women for this sublime moment of their lives. In times like this humanity rises above all college curriculums and recognizes Nature as the greatest of all teachers in the hour of danger and death. Women are already the equals of men in the whole of realm of thought, in art, science, literature, and government. With telescopic vision they explore the starry firmament, and bring back the history of the planetary world. With chart and compass they pilot ships across the mighty deep, and with skillful finger send electric messages around the globe. In galleries of art the beauties of nature and the virtues of humanity are immortalized by them on their canvas and by their inspired touch dull blocks of marble are transformed into angels of light.

In music they speak again the language of Mendelssohn, Beethoven, Chopin, Schumann, and are worthy interpreters of their great thoughts. The poetry and novels of the century are theirs, and they have touched the keynote of reform in religion, politics, and social life. They fill the editor's and professor's chair, and plead at the bar of justice, walk the wards of the hospital, and speak from the pulpit and the platform; such is the type of womanhood that an enlightened public sentiment welcomes today, and such the triumph of the facts of life over the false theories of the past.

Is it, then, consistent to hold the developed woman of this day within the same narrow political limits as the dame with the spinning wheel and knitting needle occupied in the past? No! no! Machinery has taken the labors of woman as well as man on its tireless shoulders; the loom and the spinning wheel are but dreams of the past; the pen, the brush, the easel, the chisel, have taken their places, while the hopes and ambitions of women are essentially changed.

We see reason sufficient in the outer conditions of human being for individual liberty and development, but when we consider the self dependence of every human soul we see the need of courage, judgment, and the exercise of every faculty of mind and body, strengthened and developed by use, in woman as well as man.

Whatever may be said of man's protecting power in ordinary conditions, mid all the terrible disasters by land and sea, in the supreme moments of danger, alone, woman must ever meet the horrors of the situation; the Angel of Death even makes no royal pathway for her. Man's love and sympathy enter only into the sunshine of our lives. In that solemn solitude of self, that links us with the immeasurable and the eternal, each soul lives alone forever. A recent writer says:

I remember once, in crossing the Atlantic, to have gone upon the deck of the ship at midnight, when a dense black cloud enveloped the sky, and the great deep was roaring madly under the lashes of demoniac winds. My feeling was not of danger or fear (which is a base surrender of the immortal soul), but of utter desolation and loneliness; a little speck of life shut in by a tremendous darkness. Again I remember to have climbed the slopes of the Swiss Alps, up beyond the point where vegetation ceases, and the stunted conifers no longer struggle against the unfeeling blasts. Around me lay a huge confusion of rocks, out of which the gigantic ice peaks shot into the measureless blue of the heavens, and again my only feeling was the awful solitude.

And yet, there is a solitude, which each and every one of us has always carried with him, more inaccessible than the ice-cold mountains, more profound than the midnight sea; the solitude of self. Our inner being, which we call ourself, no eye nor touch of man or angel has ever pierced. It is more hidden than the caves of the gnome; the sacred adytum of the oracle; the hidden chamber of eleusinian mystery, for to it only omniscience is permitted to enter.

Such is individual life. Who, I ask you, can take, dare take, on himself the rights, the duties, the responsibilities of another human soul?

IDA B. WELLS

Lynch Law in All Its Phases

Boston, February 13, 1893

I AM before the American people to-day through no inclination of my own, but because of a deep-seated conviction that the country at large does not know the extent to which lynch law prevails in parts of the Republic, nor the conditions which force into exile those who speak the truth. I cannot believe that the apathy and indifference which so largely obtains regarding mob rule is other than the result of ignorance of the true situation. And yet, the observing and thoughtful must know that in one section, at least, of our common country, a government of the people, by the people, and for the people, means a government by the mob; where the land of the free and home of the brave means a land of lawlessness, murder and outrage; and where liberty of speech means the license of might to destroy the business and drive from home those who exercise this privilege contrary to the will of the mob. Repeated attacks on the life, liberty and happiness of any citizen or class of citizens are attacks on distinctive American institutions; such attacks imperiling as they do the foundation of government, law and order, merit the thoughtful consideration of far-sighted Americans; not from a standpoint of sentiment, not even so much from a standpoint of justice to a weak race, as from a desire to preserve our institutions.

The race problem or negro question, as it has been called, has been omnipresent and all-pervading since long before the Afro-American was raised from the degradation of the slave to the dignity of the citizen. It has never been settled because the right methods have not been employed in the solution. It is the Banquo's ghost of politics, religion, and sociology which will not down at the bidding of those who are tormented with its ubiquitous appearance on every occasion. Times without number, since invested with citizenship, the race has been in-dicted for ignorance, immorality and general worthlessness—declared guilty and executed by its self-constituted judges. The operations of law do not dispose of negroes fast enough, and lynching bees have become the favorite pastime of the South. As excuse for the same, a new cry, as false as it is foul, is raised in an effort to blast race character, a cry which has pro-claimed to the world that virtue and innocence are violated by Afro-Americans who must be killed like wild beasts to protect womanhood and childhood.

Born and reared in the South, I had never expected to live elsewhere. Until this past year I was one among those who be-lieved the condition of the masses gave large excuse for the hu-miliations and proscriptions under which we labored; that when wealth, education and character became more general among us,—the cause being removed—the effect would cease, and justice be accorded to all alike. I shared the general belief that good newspapers entering regularly the homes of our people in every state could do more to bring about this result than any agency. Preaching the doctrine of self-help, thrift and econ-omy every week, they would be the teachers to those who had been deprived of school advantages, yet were making history every day—and train to think for themselves our mental chil-dren of a larger growth. And so, three years ago last June, I be-came editor and part owner of the *Memphis Free Speech*. As editor, I had occasion to criticise the city School Board's em-ployment of inefficient teachers and poor school-buildings for Afro-American children. I was in the employ of that board at the time, and at the close of that school-term one year ago, was not re-elected to a position I had held in the city schools for seven years. Accepting the decision of the Board of Education, I set out to make a race newspaper pay—a thing which older and wiser heads said could not be done. But there were enough of our people in Memphis and surrounding territory to sup-port a paper, and I believed they would do so. With nine months hard work the circulation increased from 1,500 to 3,500; in twelve months it was on a good paying basis. Throughout the Mississippi Valley in Arkansas, Tennessee and Mississippi—on plantations and in towns, the demand for and interest in the paper increased among the masses. The newsboys who would not sell it on the trains, voluntarily testified that they had never known colored people to demand a paper so eagerly.

To make the paper a paying business I became advertising agent, solicitor, as well as editor, and was continually on the go. Wherever I went among the people, I gave them in church, school, public gatherings, and home, the benefit of my honest conviction that maintenance of character, money getting and education would finally solve our problem and that it depended on us to say how soon this would be brought about. This sentiment bore good fruit in Memphis. We had nice homes, representatives in almost every branch of business and profession, and refined society. We had learned that helping each other helped all, and every well-conducted business by Afro-Americans prospered. With all our proscription in theatres, hotels and on railroads, we had never had a lynching and did not believe we could have one. There had been lynchings and brutal outrages of all sorts in our own state and those adjoining us, but we had confidence and pride in our city and the majesty of its laws. So far in advance of other Southern cities was ours, we were content to endure the evils we had, to labor and to wait.

But there was a rude awakening. On the morning of March 9, the bodies of three of our best young men were found in an old field horribly shot to pieces. These young men had owned and operated the People's Grocery, situated at what was known as the Curve—a suburb made up almost entirely of colored people—about a mile from city limits. Thomas Moss, one of the oldest letter-carriers in the city, was president of the company, Calvin McDowell was manager and Will Stewart was a clerk. There were about ten other stockholders, all colored men. The young men were well known and popular and their business flourished, and that of Barrett, a white grocer who kept store there before the "People's Grocery" was established, went down. One day an officer came to the "People's Grocery" and inquired for a colored man who lived in the neighborhood, and for whom the officer had a warrant. Barrett was with him and when McDowell said he knew nothing as to the whereabouts of the man for whom they were searching, Barrett, not the officer, then accused McDowell of harboring the man, and McDowell gave the lie. Barrett drew his pistol and struck McDowell with it; thereupon McDowell, who was a tall, fine-looking six-footer, took Barrett's pistol from him, knocked him down and gave him a good thrashing, while Will Stewart, the clerk, kept the special officer at bay. Barrett went to town, swore out a warrant for their arrest on a charge of assault and battery. McDowell went before the Criminal Court, immediately gave bond and returned to his store. Barrett then threatened (to use his own words) that he was going to clean out the whole store. Knowing how anxious he was to destroy their business, these young men consulted a lawyer who told them they were justified in defending themselves if attacked, as they were a mile beyond city limits and police protection. They accordingly armed several of their friends—not to assail, but to resist the threatened Saturday night attack.

When they saw Barrett enter the front door and a half dozen men at the rear door at 11 o'clock that night, they supposed the attack was on and immediately fired into the crowd, wounding three men. These men, dressed in citizens' clothes, turned out to be deputies who claimed to be hunting another man for whom they had a warrant, and whom any one of them could have arrested without trouble. When these men found they had fired upon officers of the law, they threw away their firearms and submitted to arrest, confident they should establish their innocence of intent to fire upon officers of the law. The daily papers in flaming headlines roused the evil passions of the whites, denounced these poor boys in unmeasured terms, nor permitted them a word in their own defense.

The neighborhood of the Curve was searched next day, and about thirty persons were thrown into jail, charged with conspiracy. No communication was to be had with friends any of the three days these men were in jail; bail was refused and Thomas Moss was not allowed to eat the food his wife prepared for him. The judge is reported to have said, "Any one can see them after three days." They were seen after three days, but they were no longer able to respond to the greeting of friends. On Tuesday following the shooting at the grocery, the papers which had made much of the sufferings of the wounded deputies, and promised it would go hard with those who did the shooting, if they died, announced that the officers were all out of danger, and would recover. The friends of the prisoners breathed more easily and relaxed their vigilance. They felt that as the officers would not die, there was no danger that in the heat of passion the prisoners would meet violent death at the hands of the mob. Besides, we had such confidence in the law. But the law did not provide capital punishment for shooting which did not kill. So the mob did what the law could not be made to do, as a lesson to the Afro-American that he must not shoot a white man,—no matter what the provocation. The same night after the announcement was made in the papers that the officers would get well, the mob, in obedience to a plan known to every prominent white man in the city, went to the jail between two and three o'clock in the morning, dragged out these young men, hatless and shoeless, put them on the yard engine of the railroad which was in waiting just behind the jail, carried them a mile north of city limits and horribly shot them to death while the locomotive at a given signal let off steam and blew the whistle to deaden the sound of the firing.

"It was done by unknown men," said the jury, yet the *Appeal-Avalanche*, which goes to press at 3 a.m., had a two-column account of the lynching. The papers also told how McDowell got hold of the guns of the mob, and as his grasp could not be loosened, his hand was shattered with a pistol ball and all the lower part of his face was torn away. There were four pools of blood found and only three bodies. It was whispered that he, McDowell, killed one of the lynchers with his gun, and it is well known that a policeman who was seen on the street a few days previous to the lynching, died very suddenly the next day after.

"It was done by unknown parties," said the jury, yet the papers told how Tom Moss begged for his life, for the sake of his wife, his little daughter and his unborn infant. They also told us that his last words were, "If you will kill us, turn our faces to the West."

All this we learned too late to save these men, even if the law had not been in the hands of their murderers. When the colored people realized that the flower of our young manhood had been stolen away at night and murdered, there was a rush for firearms to avenge the wrong, but no house would sell a colored man a gun; the armory of the Tennessee Rifles, our only colored military company, and of which McDowell was a member, was broken into by order of the Criminal Court judge, and its guns taken. One hundred men and irresponsible boys from fifteen years and up were armed by order of the authorities and rushed out to the Curve, where it was reported that the colored people were massing, and at point of the bayonet dispersed these men who could do nothing but talk. The cigars, wines, etc., of the grocery stock were freely used by the mob, who possessed the place on pretence of dispersing the conspiracy. The money drawer was broken into and contents taken. The trunk of Calvin McDowell, who had a room in the store, was broken open, and his clothing, which was not good enough to take away, was thrown out and trampled on the floor.

These men were murdered, their stock was attached by creditors and sold for less than one-eighth of its cost to that same man Barrett, who is to-day running his grocery in the same place. He had indeed kept his word, and by aid of the authorities destroyed the People's Grocery Company root and branch. The relatives of Will Stewart and Calvin McDowell are bereft of their protectors. The baby daughter of Tom Moss, too young to express how she misses her father, toddles to the wardrobe, seizes the legs of the trousers of his letter-carrier uniform, hugs and kisses them with evident delight and stretches up her little hands to be taken up into the arms which will nevermore clasp his daughter's form. His wife holds Thomas Moss, Jr., in her arms, upon whose unconscious baby face the tears fall thick and fast when she is thinking of the sad fate of the father he will never see, and of the two helpless children who cling to her for the support she cannot give. Although these men were peaceable, law-abiding citizens of this country, we are told there can be no punishment for their murderers nor indemnity for their relatives.

I have no power to describe the feeling of horror that possessed every member of the race in Memphis when the truth dawned upon us that the protection of the law which we had so long enjoyed was no longer ours; all this had been destroyed in a night, and the barriers of the law had been thrown down, and the guardians of the public peace and confidence scoffed away into the shadows, and all authority given into the hands of the mob, and innocent men cut down as if they were brutes—the first feeling was one of utter dismay, then intense indignation. Vengeance was whispered from ear to ear, but sober reflection brought the conviction that it would be extreme folly to seek vengeance when such action meant certain death for the men, and horrible slaughter for the women and children, as one of the evening papers took care to remind us. The power of the State, country and city, the civil authorities and the strong arm of the military power were all on the side of the mob and of lawlessness. Few of our men possessed firearms, our only company's guns were confiscated, and the only white man who would sell a colored man a gun, was himself jailed, and his store closed. We were helpless in our great strength. It was our first object lesson in the doctrine of white supremacy; an illustration of the South's cardinal principle that no matter what the attainments, character or standing of an Afro-American, the laws of the South will not protect him against a white man.

There was only one thing we could do, and a great determination seized upon the people to follow the advice of the martyred Moss, and "turn our faces to the West," whose laws protect all alike. The *Free Speech* supported by our ministers and leading business men advised the people to leave a community whose laws did not protect them. Hundreds left on foot to walk four hundred miles between Memphis and Oklahoma. A Baptist minister went to the territory, built a church, and took his entire congregation out in less than a month. Another minister sold his church and took his flock to California, and still another has settled in Kansas. In two months, six thousand persons had left the city and every branch of business began to feel this silent resentment of the outrage, and failure of the authorities to punish the lynchers. There were a number of business failures and blocks of houses were for rent. The superintendent and treasurer of the street railway company called at the office of the *Free Speech*, to have us urge the colored people to ride again on the street cars. A real estate dealer said to a colored man who returned some property he had been buying on the installment plan: "I don't see what you 'niggers' are cutting up about. You got off light. We first intended to kill every one of those thirty-one 'niggers' in jail, but concluded to

let all go but the 'leaders.'" They did let all go to the penitentiary. These so-called rioters have since been tried in the Criminal Court for the conspiracy of defending their property, and
are now serving terms of three, eight, and fifteen years each in
the Tennessee State prison.

To restore the equilibrium and put a stop to the great financial loss, the next move was to get rid of the *Free Speech*,—the
disturbing element which kept the waters troubled; which
would not let the people forget, and in obedience to whose advice nearly six thousand persons had left the city. In casting
about for an excuse, the mob found it in the following editorial which appeared in the Memphis *Free Speech*,—May 21, 1892:
"Eight negroes lynched in one week. Since last issue of the
Free Speech one was lynched at Little Rock, Ark., where the citizens broke into the penitentiary and got their man; three near
Anniston, Ala., and one in New Orleans, all on the same
charge, the new alarm of assaulting white women—and three
near Clarksville, Ga., for killing a white man. The same program
of hanging—then shooting bullets into the lifeless bodies was
carried out to the letter. Nobody in this section of the country
believes the old threadbare lie that negro men rape white
women. If Southern white men are not careful they will overreach themselves, and public sentiment will have a reaction. A
conclusion will then be reached which will be very damaging
to the moral reputation of their women." Commenting on this,
The Daily Commercial of Wednesday following said: "Those
negroes who are attempting to make lynching of individuals of
their race a means for arousing the worst passions of their kind,
are playing with a dangerous sentiment. The negroes may as
well understand that there is no mercy for the negro rapist,
and little patience with his defenders. A negro organ printed in
this city in a recent issue publishes the following atrocious
paragraph: 'Nobody in this section believes the old threadbare
lie that negro men rape white women. If Southern white men
are not careful they will overreach themselves and public sentiment will have a reaction. A conclusion will be reached which
will be very damaging to the moral reputation of their women.'
The fact that a black scoundrel is allowed to live and utter such
loathsome and repulsive calumnies is a volume of evidence as
to the wonderful patience of Southern whites. There are some

things the Southern white man will not tolerate, and the ob-
scene intimation of the foregoing has brought the writer to
the very uttermost limit of public patience. We hope we have
said enough."

The Evening *Scimitar* of the same day copied this leading
editorial and added this comment: "Patience under such circumstances is not a virtue. If the negroes themselves do not
apply the remedy without delay, it will be the duty of those he
has attacked, to tie the wretch who utters these calumnies to a
stake at the intersection of Main and Madison streets, brand
him in the forehead with a hot iron and—"

Such open suggestions by the leading daily papers of the
progressive city of Memphis were acted upon by the leading
citizens and a meeting was held at the Cotton Exchange that
evening. *The Commercial* two days later had the following account of it:

ATROCIOUS BLACKGUARDISM.
There will be no Lynching and no Repetition of the Offense.

In its issue of Wednesday *The Commercial* reproduced and com-
mented upon an editorial which appeared a day or two before in a
negro organ known as the *Free Speech.* The article was so insufferably
and indecently slanderous that the whole city awoke to a feeling of intense resentment which came within an ace of culminating in one of
those occurrences whose details are so eagerly seized and so promi-
nently published by Northern newspapers. Conservative counsels,
however, prevailed, and no extreme measures were resorted to. On
Wednesday afternoon a meeting of citizens was held. It was not an assemblage of hoodlums or irresponsible fire-eaters, but solid, substantial business men who knew exactly what they were doing and who
were far more indignant at the villainous insult to the women of the
South than they would have been at any injury done themselves. This
meeting appointed a committee to seek the author of the infamous
editorial and warn him quietly that upon repetition of the offense he
would find some other part of the country a good deal safer and
pleasanter place of residence than this. The committee called on a negro preacher named Nightingale, but he disclaimed responsibility and
convinced the gentlemen that he had really sold out his paper to a
woman named Wells. This woman is not in Memphis at present. It
was finally learned that one Fleming, a negro who was driven out of
Crittenden Co. during the trouble there a few years ago, wrote the
paragraph. He had, however, heard of the meeting, and fled from a

fate which he feared was in store for him, and which he knew he deserved. His whereabouts could not be ascertained, and the committee so reported. Later on, a communication from Fleming to a prominent Republican politician, and that politician's reply were shown to one or two gentlemen. The former was an inquiry as to whether the writer might safely return to Memphis, the latter was an emphatic answer in the negative, and Fleming is still in hiding. Nothing further will be done in the matter. There will be no lynching, and it is very certain there will be no repetition of the outrage. If there should be—— Friday, May 25.

The only reason there was no lynching of Mr. Fleming who was business manager and half owner of the *Free Speech*, and who did not write the editorial, was because this same white Republican told him the committee was coming, and warned him not to trust them, but get out of the way. The committee scoured the city hunting him, and had to be content with Mr. Nightingale who was dragged to the meeting, shamefully abused (although it was known he had sold out his interest in the paper six months before). He was struck in the face and forced at the pistol's point to sign a letter which was written by them, in which he denied all knowledge of the editorial, denounced and condemned it as slander on white women. I do not censure Mr. Nightingale for his action because, having never been at the pistol's point myself, I do not feel that I am competent to sit in judgment on him, or say what I would do under such circumstances.

I had written that editorial with other matter for the week's paper before leaving home the Friday previous for the General Conference of the A.M.E. Church in Philadelphia. Conference adjourned Tuesday, and Thursday, May 25, at 3 p.m., I landed in New York City for a few days' stay before returning home, and there learned from the papers that my business manager had been driven away and the paper suspended. Telegraphing for news, I received telegrams and letters in return informing me that the trains were being watched, that I was to be dumped into the river and beaten, if not killed; it had been learned that I wrote the editorial and I was to be hanged in front of the court-house and my face bled if I returned, and I was implored by my friends to remain away. The creditors attacked the office in the meantime and the outfit was sold without more ado, thus destroying effectually that which it had taken years to build. One prominent insurance agent publicly declares he will make it his business to shoot me down on sight if I return to Memphis in twenty years, while a leading white lady has remarked that she was opposed to the lynching of those three men in March, but she did wish there was some way by which I could be gotten back and lynched.

I have been censured for writing that editorial, but when I think of the five men who were lynched that week for assault on white women and that not a week passes but some poor soul is violently ushered into eternity on this trumped-up charge, knowing the many things I do, and part of which I tried to tell in the *New York Age* of June 25, (and in the pamphlets I have with me) seeing that the whole race in the South was injured in the estimation of the world because of these false reports, I could no longer hold my peace, and I feel, yes, I am sure, that if it had to be done over again (provided no one else was the loser save myself) I would do and say the very same again.

The lawlessness here described is not confined to one locality. In the past ten years over a thousand colored men, women and children have been butchered, murdered and burnt in all parts of the South. The details of these horrible outrages seldom reach beyond the narrow world where they occur. Those who commit the murders write the reports, and hence these lasting blots upon the honor of a nation cause but a faint ripple on the outside world. They arouse no great indignation and call forth no adequate demand for justice. The victims were black, and the reports are so written as to make it appear that the helpless creatures deserved the fate which overtook them.

Not so with the Italian lynching of 1891. They were not black men, and three of them were not citizens of the Republic, but subjects of the King of Italy. The chief of police of New Orleans was shot and eleven Italians were arrested charged with the murder; they were tried and the jury disagreed; the good, law-abiding citizens of New Orleans thereupon took them from the jail and lynched them at high noon. A feeling of horror ran through the nation at this outrage. All Europe was amazed. The Italian government demanded thorough investigation and redress, and the Federal Government promised to give the matter the consideration which was its due. The diplomatic relations between the two countries became very much strained and for a while war talk was freely indulged. Here was a case where the power of the Federal Government to protect its own citizens and redeem its pledges to a friendly power was put to the test. When our State Department called upon the authorities of Louisiana for investigation of the crime and punishment of the criminals, the United States government was told that the crime was strictly within the authority of the State of Louisiana, and Louisiana would attend to it. After a farcical investigation, the usual verdict in such cases was rendered: "Death at the hands of parties unknown to the jury," the same verdict which has been pronounced over the bodies of over 1,000 colored persons! Our general government has thus admitted that it has no jurisdiction over the crimes committed at New Orleans upon citizens of the country, nor upon those citizens of a friendly power to whom the general government and not the state government has pledged protection. Not only has our general government made the confession that one of the states is greater than the Union, but the general government has paid $25,000 of the people's money to the King of Italy for the lynching of those three subjects, the evil-doing of one State, over which it has no control, but for whose lawlessness the whole country must pay. The principle involved in the treaty power of the government has not yet been settled to the satisfaction of foreign powers; but the principle involved in the right of State jurisdiction in such matters, was settled long ago by the decision of the United States Supreme Court.

I beg your patience while we look at another phase of the lynching mania. We have turned heretofore to the pages of ancient and mediæval history, to Roman tyranny, the Jesuitical Inquisition of Spain for the spectacle of a human being burnt to death. In the past ten years three instances, at least, have been furnished where men have literally been roasted to death to appease the fury of Southern mobs. The Texarkana instance of last year and the Paris, Texas, case of this month are the most recent as they are the most shocking and repulsive. Both were charged with crimes for which the laws provide adequate punishment. The Texarkana man, Ed Coy, was charged with assaulting a white woman. A mob pronounced him guilty, strapped him to a tree, chipped the flesh from his body, poured coal oil over him and the woman in the case set fire to him. The country looked on and in many cases applauded, because it was published that this man had violated the honor of a white woman, although he protested his innocence to the last. Judge Tourjee in the Chicago *Inter Ocean* of recent date says investigation has shown that Ed Coy had supported this woman, (who was known to be of bad character,) and her drunken husband for over a year previous to the burning.

The Paris, Texas, burning of Henry Smith, February 1st, has exceeded all the others in its horrible details. The man was drawn through the streets on a float, as the Roman generals used to parade their trophies of war, while the scaffold ten feet high, was being built, and irons were heated in the fire. He was bound on it, and red-hot irons began at his feet and slowly branded his body, while the mob howled with delight at his shrieks. Red hot irons were run down his throat and cooked his tongue; his eyes were burned out, and when he was at last unconscious, cotton seed hulls were placed under him, coal oil poured all over him, and a torch applied to the mass. When the flames burned away the ropes which bound Smith and scorched his flesh, he was brought back to sensibility—and burned and maimed and sightless as he was, he rolled off the platform and away from the fire. His half-cooked body was seized and trampled and thrown back into the flames while the mob of twenty thousand persons who came from all over the country howled with delight, and gathered up some buttons and ashes after all was over to preserve for relics. This man was charged with outraging and murdering a four-year-old white child, covering her body with brush, sleeping beside her through the night, then making his escape. If true, it was the deed of a madman, and should have been clearly proven so. The fact that no time for verification of the newspaper reports was given, is suspicious, especially when I remember that a negro was lynched in Indianola, Sharkey Co., Miss., last summer. The dispatches said it was because he had assaulted the sheriff's eight-year-old daughter. The girl was more than eighteen years old and was found by her father in this man's room, who was a servant on the place.

These incidents have been made the basis of this terrible

story because they overshadow all others of a like nature in cruelty and represent the legal phases of the whole question. They could be multiplied without number—and each outrival the other in the fiendish cruelty exercised, and the frequent awful lawlessness exhibited. The following table shows the number of black men lynched from January 1, 1882, to January 1, 1892: In 1882, 52; 1883, 39; 1884, 53; 1885, 77; 1886, 73; 1887, 70; 1888, 72; 1889, 95; 1890, 100; 1891, 169. Of these 728 black men who were murdered, 269 were charged with rape, 253 with murder, 44 with robbery, 37 with incendiarism, 32 with reasons unstated (it was not necessary to have a reason), 27 with race prejudice, 13 with quarreling with white men, 10 with making threats, 7 with rioting, 5 with miscegenation, 4 with burglary. One of the men lynched in 1891 was Will Lewis, who was lynched because "he was drunk and saucy to white folks." A woman who was one of the 73 victims in 1886, was hung in Jackson, Tenn., because the white woman for whom she cooked, died suddenly of poisoning. An examination showed arsenical poisoning. A search in the cook's room found rat poison. She was thrown into jail, and when the mob had worked itself up to the lynching pitch, she was dragged out, every stitch of clothing torn from her body, and was hung in the public court house square in sight of everybody. That white woman's husband has since died, in the insane asylum, a raving maniac, and his ravings have led to the conclusion that he, and not the cook, was the poisoner of his wife. A fifteen-year old colored girl was lynched last spring, at Rayville, La., on the same charge of poisoning. A woman was also lynched at Hollendale, Miss., last spring, charged with being an accomplice in the murder of her white paramour who had abused her. These were only two of the 159 persons lynched in the South from January 1, 1892, to January 1, 1893. Over a dozen black men have been lynched already since this new year set in, and the year is not yet two months old.

It will thus be seen that neither age, sex nor decency are spared. Although the impression has gone abroad that most of the lynchings take place because of assaults on white women only one-third of the number lynched in the past ten years have been charged with that offense, to say nothing of those who were not guilty of the charge. And according to law none of them were guilty until proven so. But the unsupported word of any white person for any cause is sufficient to cause a lynching. So bold have the lynchers become, masks are laid aside, the temples of justice and strongholds of law are invaded in broad daylight and prisoners taken out and lynched, while governors of states and officers of law stand by and see the work well done.

And yet this Christian nation, the flower of the nineteenth century civilization, says it can do nothing to stop this inhuman slaughter. The general government is willingly powerless to send troops to protect the lives of its black citizens, but the state governments are free to use state troops to shoot them down like cattle, when in desperation the black men attempt to defend themselves, and then tell the world that it was necessary to put down a "race war."

Persons unfamiliar with the condition of affairs in the Southern States do not credit the truth when it is told them. They cannot conceive how such a condition of affairs prevails so near them with steam power, telegraph wires and printing presses in daily and hourly touch with the localities where such disorder reigns. In a former generation the ancestors of these same people refused to believe that slavery was the "league with death and the covenant with hell." Wm. Lloyd Garrison declared it to be, until he was thrown into a dungeon in Baltimore, until the signal lights of Nat Turner lit the dull skies of Northampton County, and until sturdy old John Brown made his attack on Harper's Ferry. When freedom of speech was martyred in the person of Elijah Lovejoy at Alton, when the liberty of free-discussion in Senate of the Nation's Congress was struck down in the person of the fearless Charles Sumner, the Nation was at last convinced that slavery was not only a monster but a tyrant. That same tyrant is at work under a new name and guise. The lawlessness which has been here described is like unto that which prevailed under slavery. *The very same forces are at work now as then*. The attempt is being made to subject to a condition of civil and industrial dependence, those whom the Constitution declares to be free men. The events which have led up to the present wide-spread lawlessness in the South can be traced to the very first year Lee's conquered veterans marched from Appomatox to their homes in the Southland. They were conquered in war, but not in spirit. They believed as firmly as ever that it was their right to rule black men and dictate to the National Government. The Knights of White Liners, and the Ku Klux Klans were composed of veterans of the Confederate army who were determined to destroy the effect of all the slave had gained by the war. They finally accomplished their purpose in 1876. The right of the Afro-American to vote and hold office remains in the Federal Constitution, but is destroyed in the constitution of the Southern states. Having destroyed the citizenship of the man, they are now trying to destroy the manhood of the citizen. All their laws are shaped to this end,—school laws, railroad car regulations, those governing labor liens on crops,—every device is adopted to make slaves of free men and rob them of their wages. Whenever a malicious law is violated in any of its parts, any farmer, any railroad conductor, or merchant can call together a posse of his neighbors and punish even with death the black man who resists and the legal authorities sanction what is done by failing to prosecute and punish the murderers. The Repeal of the Civil Rights Law removed their last barrier and the black man's last bulwark and refuge. The rule of the mob is absolute.

Those who know this recital to be true, say there is nothing they can do—they cannot interfere and vainly hope by further concession to placate the imperious and dominating part of our country in which this lawlessness prevails. Because this country has been almost rent in twain by internal dissension, the other sections seem virtually to have agreed that the best way to heal the breach is to permit the taking away of civil, political, and even human rights, to stand by in silence and utter indifference while the South continues to wreak fiendish vengeance on the irresponsible cause. They pretend to believe that with all the machinery of law and government in its hands; with the jails and penitentiaries and convict farms filled with petty race criminals; with the well-known fact that no negro has ever been known to escape conviction and punishment for any crime in the South—still there are those who try to justify and condone the lynching of over a thousand black men in less than ten years—an average of one hundred a year. The public sentiment of the country, by its silence in press, pulpit and in public meetings has encouraged this state of affairs, and public

sentiment is stronger than law. With all the country's disposition to condone and temporize with the South and its methods; with its many instances of sacrificing principle to prejudice
for the sake of making friends and healing the breach made by
the late war; of going into this lawless country with capital to
build up its waste places and remaining silent in the presence
of outrage and wrong—the South is as vindictive and bitter as
ever. She is willing to make friends as long as she is permitted
to pursue unmolested and uncensured, her course of proscription, injustice, outrage and vituperation. The malignant mis-
representation of General Butler, the uniformly indecent and
abusive assault of this dead man whose only crime was a defence of his country, is a recent proof that the South has lost
none of its bitterness. The *Nashville American*, one of the
leading papers of one of the leading southern cities, gleefully
announced editorially that " 'The Beast is dead.' Early yesterday morning, acting under the devil's orders, the angel of
Death took Ben Butler and landed him in the lowest depths of
hell, and we pity even the devil the possession he has secured."
The men who wrote these editorials are without exception young
men who know nothing of slavery and scarcely anything of the
war. The bitterness and hatred have been instilled in and taught
them by their parents, and they are men who make and reflect
the sentiment of their section. The South spares nobody else's
feelings, and it seems a queer logic that when it comes to a
question of right, involving lives of citizens and the honor of
the government, the South's feelings must be respected and
spared.

   Do you ask the remedy? A public sentiment strong against
lawlessness must be aroused. Every individual can contribute to
this awakening. When a sentiment against lynch law as strong,
deep and mighty as that roused against slavery prevails, I have
no fear of the result. It should be already established as a fact
and not as a theory, that every human being must have a fair
trial for his life and liberty, no matter what the charge against
him. When a demand goes up from fearless and persistent reformers from press and pulpit, from industrial and moral associations that this shall be so from Maine to Texas and from
ocean to ocean, a way will be found to make it so.

   In deference to the few words of condemnation uttered at

the M. E. General Conference last year, and by other organizations, Governors Hogg of Texas, Northern of Georgia, and Tillman of South Carolina, have issued proclamations offering rewards for the apprehension of lynchers. These rewards have never been claimed, and these governors knew they would not be when offered. In many cases they knew the ringleaders of the mobs. The prosecuting attorney of Shelby County, Tenn., wrote Governor Buchanan to offer a reward for the arrest of the lynchers of three young men murdered in Memphis. Everybody in that city and state knew well that the letter was written for the sake of effect and the governor did not even offer the reward. But the country at large deluded itself with the belief that the officials of the South and the leading citizens condemned lynching. The lynchings go on in spite of offered rewards, and in face of Governor Hogg's vigorous talk, the second man was burnt alive in his state with the utmost deliberation and publicity. Since he sent a message to the legislature the mob found and hung Henry Smith's stepson, because he refused to tell where Smith was when they were hunting for him. Public sentiment which shall denounce these crimes in season and out; public sentiment which turns capital and immigration from a section given over to lawlessness; public sentiment which insists on the punishment of criminals and lynchers by law must be aroused.

It is no wonder in my mind that the party which stood for thirty years as the champion of human liberty and human rights, the party of great moral ideas, should suffer overwhelming defeat when it has proven recreant to its professions and abandoned a position it created; when although its followers were being outraged in every sense, it was afraid to stand for the right, and appeal to the American people to sustain them in it. It put aside the question of a free ballot and fair count to every citizen and gave its voice and influence for the protection of the coat instead of the man who wore it, for the product of labor instead of the laborer; for the seal of citizenship rather than the citizen, and insisted upon the evils of free trade instead of the sacredness of free speech. I am no politician but I believe if the Republican party had met the issues squarely for human rights instead of the tariff, it would have occupied a different position to-day. The voice of the people is the voice of God, and I long with all the intensity of my soul for the Garrison, Douglas, Sumner, Whittier and Phillips who shall rouse this nation to a demand that from Greenland's icy mountains to the coral reefs of the Southern seas, mob rule shall be put down and equal and exact justice be accorded to every citizen of whatever race, who finds a home within the borders of the land of the free and the home of the brave.

Then no longer will our national hymn be sounding brass and a tinkling cymbal, but every member of this great composite nation will be a living, harmonious illustration of the words, and all can honestly and gladly join in singing:

> My country! 'tis of thee,
> Sweet land of liberty
>   Of thee I sing.
> Land where our fathers died,
> Land of the Pilgrim's pride,
> From every mountain side
>   Freedom does ring.

JOHN PETER ALTGELD

Labor Day Address

Chicago, September 8, 1893

YOU ARE to be congratulated on the success of your celebration. Two great demonstrations in Chicago alone are
vying with each other in honoring Labor Day. These vast as-
semblages represent sturdy manhood and womanhood. They
represent honest toil of every kind, and they represent strong
patriotism and desirable citizenship. The law has set apart this
day in recognition of the nobility of labor, and as the Governor
of this great State, I have come to pay homage to that force
which lays the foundation of empires, which builds cities,
builds railroads, develops agriculture, supports schools, founds
industries, creates commerce, and moves the world. It is wisely
directed labor that has made our country the greatest ever
known, and has made Chicago the wonder of mankind. I say
wisely directed labor; for without wise direction labor is fruitless. The pointing out and the doing are inseparably connected.
More than this, ahead of the directing, there must go the genius which originates and conceives, the genius which takes the
risk and moves a league forward. All three are necessary to each
other. Weaken either, and there are clouds in the sky. Destroy
either, and the hammer of industry ceases to be heard. Glance
over this majestic city, see its workshops, its warehouses, its
commercial palaces, its office temples, and the thousand other
structures that show the possibilities of human achievement
and tell who did all this. You say the laboring men; yes, that is
correct; but I tell you that if the gods keep a record of our
doings, they have set down the men who originated all this,
and then dared to make a forward step in building, as among
the greatest of laborers. We are at present in the midst of a
great industrial and commercial depression. Industry is nearly
at a stand-still all over the earth. The consumptive power, or
rather the purchasing power, of the world has been interfered

with, producing not only a derangement but a paralysis, not only stopping further production, but preventing the proper distribution of what there is already created; so that we have the anomalous spectacle of abundant food products on the one hand, and hungry men without bread on the other. Abundant fabrics on the one hand, and industrious, frugal men going half clad on the other. Employer and employe are affected alike.

There are thousands of honest, industrious and frugal men who walk the streets all day in search of work, and even bread, and there are many hundreds of the most enterprising employers who sweat by day and walk the floor by night trying to devise means to keep the sheriff away from the establishment. You are not responsible for this condition. Men here and in Europe, who call themselves statesmen, have inaugurated policies of which this is a natural result. Considering the increase in population, the increase in the industries and commercial activity of the world, as well as the increased area over which business was done, there has in recent years been a practical reduction in the volume of the money of the world of from thirty-three to forty per cent., and there had of necessity to follow a shrinkage in the value of property to a corresponding extent. This has been going on for a number of years, and as it has progressed it has become harder and harder for the debtor to meet his obligations. For the value of his property kept falling while his debt did not fall. Consequently, every little while a lot of debtors, who could no longer stand the strain, succumbed. The result was that each time there was a flurry in financial circles. By degrees these failures became more frequent, until finally people who had money took alarm, and withdrew it from circulation. This precipitated a panic and with it a harvest of bankruptcy. No doubt there were secondary causes that contributed, but this one cause was sufficient to create the distress that we see. If for some years to come there should not be sufficient blood in the industrial and commercial world to make affairs healthy, then you must console yourselves with the thought that our country, with all the other great nations, has been placed on a narrow gold basis, and you will not be troubled with any of these cheap dollars that the big newspapers claim you did not want. The present depression, resulting from a lack of ready money in the world, shows how indispensable capital is to labor—all the wheels of industry stand still the moment it is withdrawn. It also shows that while the interests of the employer and the employe may be antagonistic on the subject of wages, they are the same in every other respect; neither can do anything without the other—certain it is that the employe cannot prosper unless the employer does. On the other hand, if the purchasing power of the employe is destroyed, the employer must soon be without a market for his goods. The great American market was due to the purchasing power of the laboring classes. If this should in the end be destroyed it will change entirely the character of our institutions. Whenever our laboring classes are reduced to a condition where they can buy only a few coarse articles of food and clothing, then our glory will have departed. Still another thing has been made more clear than before, and that is, that the employers, as a rule, are not great capitalists of the country. As a rule, they are enterprising men who borrow idle capital, and put it to some use, and whenever they are suddenly called on to pay up and are not able to borrow elsewhere, they are obliged to shut down.

There are many advanced thinkers who look forward to a new industrial system that shall be an improvement on the present, and under which the laborer shall come nearer getting his share of the benefits resulting from invention and machinery, than under the present system. All lovers of their kind would hail such a system with joy. But we are forced to say that it is not yet at hand. As we must have bread and must have clothing, we are obliged to cling to the old system for the present, and probably for a long time to come, until the foundations can be laid for a better one by intelligent progress. Classes, like individuals, have their bright and their dark days, and just now there seems to be a long dark day ahead of you. It will be a day of suffering and distress, and I must say to you there seems to be no way of escaping it, and I therefore counsel you to face it squarely and bear it with that heroism and fortitude with which an American citizen should face and bear calamity. It has been suggested that the State and different branches of government should furnish employment during the winter to idle men. Certainly everything that can be done in this line will be done, but I must warn you not to expect too much from this source.

The powers of government are so hedged about with constitutional provisions that much cannot be done. The State at
present has no work to do. The parks can employ only a few
men. The city has work for more men, but it is also limited in
its funds. The great drainage canal may, and probably will, give
employment to a considerable number of men, but, after all,
you must recognize that these things will be only in the nature
of makeshifts; only to tide over; only to keep men and their
families from starving. And on this point let me say it will be
the duty of all public officials to see to it that no man is permitted to starve on the soil of Illinois, and provision will be
made to that end. But all this is temporary. The laborer must
look to ways and means that are permanent for the improvement of his condition when the panic is over, and these measures must be along the line of and in harmony with the
institutions of this century, and must move by a gradual and
steady development. Nothing that is violently done is of permanent advantage to the working man. He can only prosper
when his labor is in demand, and his labor can be in demand
only when his employer prospers and there is nothing to interfere with consumption.

The world has been slow to accord labor its due. For thousands of years pillage, plunder and organized robbery, called
warfare, were honorable pursuits, and the man who toiled, in
order that all might live, was despised. In the flight of time, it
was but yesterday that the labor of the earth was driven with
the lash, and either sold on the block like cattle, or tied by an
invisible chain to the soil, and was forbidden to even wander
outside his parish. In the yesterday of time, even the employers
of labor were despised. The men who conducted great industries, who carried on commerce, who practiced the useful arts,
the men who made the earth habitable, were looked down
upon by a class that considered it honorable to rob the toiler
of his bread, a class which, while possessing the pride of the
eagle, had only the character of the vulture. Great has been the
development since then. This century brought upon its wings
higher ideas, more of truth and more of common sense, and it
announced to mankind that he is honorable who creates; that
he should be despised who can only consume; that he is the
benefactor of the race who gives it an additional thought, an

additional flower, an additional loaf of bread, an additional comfort; and he is a curse to his kind who tramples down what others build, or, without compensation, devours what others create. The century brought with it still greater things. Not only did it lift the employer to a position of honor, influence and power, but it tore away parish boundaries, it cut the chains of the serf, it burned the auction block, where the laborer and his children were sold; and it brought ideas; it taught the laboring man to extend his hand to his fellow-laborer; it taught him to organize, and not only to read but to investigate, to inquire, to discuss, to consider and to look ahead; so that to-day, the laborer and his cause, at least theoretically, command the homage of all civilized men, and the greatest States in christendom have set apart a day to be annually observed as a holiday in honor of labor.

The children of Israel were forty years in marching from the bondage of Egypt to the freer atmosphere of Palestine, and a halo of glory envelops their history. In the last forty years the children of Toil have made a forward march which is greater than any ever made in the wilderness. True, the land is not conquered. You have simply camped upon that higher plane where you can more clearly see the difficulties of the past, and where, in the end, you may hope for a higher justice and a happier condition for yourselves and your children, but a great deal remains to be done. In a sense, you are just out of the wilderness. You ask, along what lines, then, shall we proceed when the times get better in order to improve our condition? I answer, along lines which harmonize, not only with nature's laws, but with the laws of the land. Occupying, as I do, a position which makes me in a sense a conservator of all interests and classes, I desire to see the harmonious prosperity of all; and let me say to you that, until all the active interests of the land prosper again, there can be no general demand for your services, and consequently, no healthy prosperity. What I wish to point out is the absolute necessity of each class or interest being able to take care of itself in the fierce struggle for existence. You have not yet fully reached this state. In the industrial world, as well as in the political world, only those forces survive which can maintain themselves, and which are so concentrated that their influence is immediately and directly felt.

A scattered force, no matter how great, is of no account in the sharp contests of the age. This is an age of concentration. Everywhere there is concentration and combination of capital and of those factors which to-day rule the world. The formation of corporations has greatly accelerated this movement, and no matter what is said about it, whether we approve it or not, it is the characteristic feature of our civilization, and grows out of increased invention, the speedy communication between different parts of the world, and the great industrial generalship and enterprise of the time. It is questionable whether this tendency to combination could have been stopped in any way. It is certain, without this concentration of force, the gigantic achievements of our times would have been an impossibility. Combination and concentration are the masters of the age. Let the laborer learn from this and act accordingly. Fault-finding and idle complaint are useless. Great forces, like great rivers, cannot be stopped. You must be able to fight your own battles. For the laborer to stand single-handed before giant combinations of power means annihilation. The world gives only when it is obliged to, and respects only those who compel its respect.

Government was created by power and has always been controlled by power. Do not imagine that it is sufficient if you have justice and equity on your side, for the earth is covered with the graves of justice and equity that failed to receive recognition, because there was no influence or force to compel it, and it will be so until the millennium. Whenever you demonstrate that you are an active, concentrated power, moving along lawful lines, then you will be felt in government. Until then you will not. This is an age of law as well as of force, and no force succeeds that does not move along legal lines. The laboring men of the world always have been, and are to-day, the support and principal reliance of the government. They support its flags in time of war, and their hands earn the taxes in time of peace. Their voice is for fair play, and no great government was ever destroyed by the laboring classes. Treason and rebellion never originated with them, but always came from the opposite source. Early in our history there occurred what was called Shay's rebellion, but they were not wage-workers who created it. Then came the so-called whisky rebellion, created not by day laborers. During the war of 1812, a convention was held in the East which practically advocated a dissolution of the Union, but wage-workers were not among its members. The great rebellion of 1861 was not fomented by the laboring classes, but by those classes which ate the bread that others toiled for. It was a rebellion by those who had long been prominent as leaders, who largely controlled the wealth of the country, who boasted of aristocratic society, and many of whom had been educated at the expense of the country whose flag they fired on. While, on the other hand, the great armies which put down this rebellion and supported the flag were composed of men who had literally earned their bread by the sweat of their brows. It is true that at times a number of laborers, more or less ignorant, who thought they were being robbed of the fruits of their toil, have indulged in rioting; and, while they have always lost by it, and while they cannot be too severely condemned, yet they do not stand alone in this condemnation, for there have been many broadcloth mobs in this country and in different sections of it, whose actions were lawless and as disgraceful as that of any labor mob that ever assembled. I must congratulate organized labor upon its freedom from turbulence. Rioting is nearly always by an ignorant class outside of all organizations, and which, in most cases, was brought into the community by conscienceless men to defeat organized labor. There should be a law compelling a man who brings this class of people into our midst to give bond for their support and their good behavior, for at present they are simply a disturbing element. They threaten the peace of society and bring reproach on the cause of labor. The lesson I wish to impress upon you is that in business, in the industries, in government, everywhere, only those interests and forces survive that can maintain themselves along legal lines, and if you permanently improve your condition it must be by intelligently and patriotically standing together all over the country. Every plan must fail unless you do this.

At present you are to a great extent yet a scattered force, sufficiently powerful, if collected, to make yourselves heard and felt; to secure, not only a fair hearing, but a fair decision of all questions. Unite this power and you will be independent; leave it scattered and you will fail. Organization is the result of education as well as an educator. Let all the men of America who toil with their hands once stand together and no more complaints will be heard about unfair treatment. The progress of labor in the future must be along the line of patriotic association, not simply in localities, but everywhere. And let me caution you that every act of violence is a hindrance to your progress. There will be men among you ready to commit it. They are your enemies. There will be sneaks and Judas Iscariots in your ranks, who will for a mere pittance act as spies and try to incite some of the more hot-headed of your number to deeds of violence, in order that these reptiles may get the credit of exposing you. They are your enemies. Cast them out of your ranks. Remember that any permanent prosperity must be based upon intelligence and upon conditions which are permanent. And let me say to you again, in conclusion: This fall and this winter will be a trying time to you. The record of the laborers of the earth is one of patriotism. They have maintained the government, they have maintained the schools and churches, and it behooves you now to face the hardships that are upon you and see that your cause is not injured by grave indiscretions. Make the ignorant understand that government is strong and that life and property will be protected and law and order will be maintained, and that, while the day is dark now, the future will place the laborer in a more exalted position than he has ever occupied.

BOOKER T. WASHINGTON

Address at the Atlanta Exposition

September 18, 1895

M R. PRESIDENT AND GENTLEMEN OF THE BOARD OF
DIRECTORS AND CITIZENS: One-third of the population of the South is of the Negro race. No enterprise seeking
the material, civil, or moral welfare of this section can disregard
this element of our population and reach the highest success. I
but convey to you, Mr. President and Directors, the sentiment
of the masses of my race when I say that in no way have the
value and manhood of the American Negro been more fittingly
and generously recognized than by the managers of this magnificent Exposition at every stage of its progress. It is a recognition that will do more to cement the friendship of the two
races than any occurrence since the dawn of our freedom.

Not only this, but the opportunity here afforded will awaken
among us a new era of industrial progress. Ignorant and inexperienced, it is not strange that in the first years of our new life
we began at the top instead of at the bottom; that a seat in
Congress or the state legislature was more sought than real estate or industrial skill; that the political convention or stump
speaking had more attractions than starting a dairy farm or
truck garden.

A ship lost at sea for many days suddenly sighted a friendly
vessel. From the mast of the unfortunate vessel was seen a signal, "Water, water; we die of thirst!" The answer from the
friendly vessel at once came back, "Cast down your bucket
where you are." A second time the signal, "Water, water; send
us water!" ran up from the distressed vessel, and was answered,
"Cast down your bucket where you are." And a third and
fourth signal for water was answered, "Cast down your bucket
where you are." The captain of the distressed vessel, at last
heeding the injunction, cast down his bucket, and it came up
full of fresh, sparkling water from the mouth of the Amazon

River. To those of my race who depend on bettering their condition in a foreign land or who underestimate the importance of cultivating friendly relations with the Southern white man, who is their next-door neighbour, I would say: "Cast down your bucket where you are"—cast it down in making friends in every manly way of the people of all races by whom we are surrounded.

Cast it down in agriculture, mechanics, in commerce, in domestic service, and in the professions. And in this connection it is well to bear in mind that whatever other sins the South may be called to bear, when it comes to business, pure and simple, it is in the South that the Negro is given a man's chance in the commercial world, and in nothing is this Exposition more eloquent than in emphasizing this chance. Our greatest danger is that in the great leap from slavery to freedom we may overlook the fact that the masses of us are to live by the productions of our hands, and fail to keep in mind that we shall prosper in proportion as we learn to dignify and glorify common labour, and put brains and skill into the common occupations of life; shall prosper in proportion as we learn to draw the line between the superficial and the substantial, the ornamental gewgaws of life and the useful. No race can prosper till it learns that there is as much dignity in tilling a field as in writing a poem. It is at the bottom of life we must begin, and not at the top. Nor should we permit our grievances to overshadow our opportunities.

To those of the white race who look to the incoming of those of foreign birth and strange tongue and habits for the prosperity of the South, were I permitted I would repeat what I say to my own race, "Cast down your bucket where you are." Cast it down among the eight millions of Negroes whose habits you know, whose fidelity and love you have tested in days when to have proved treacherous meant the ruin of your firesides. Cast down your bucket among these people who have, without strikes and labour wars, tilled your fields, cleared your forests, builded your railroads and cities, and brought forth treasures from the bowels of the earth, and helped make possible this magnificent representation of the progress of the South. Casting down your bucket among my people, helping and encouraging them as you are doing on these grounds, and to education of head, hand, and heart, you will find that they will buy your surplus land, make blossom the waste places in your fields, and run your factories. While doing this, you can be sure in the future, as in the past, that you and your families will be surrounded by the most patient, faithful, law-abiding, and un-resentful people that the world has seen. As we have proved our loyalty to you in the past, in nursing your children, watching by the sick-bed of your mothers and fathers, and often fol-lowing them with tear-dimmed eyes to their graves, so in the future, in our humble way, we shall stand by you with a devo-tion that no foreigner can approach, ready to lay down our lives, if need be, in defense of yours, interlacing our industrial, commercial, civil, and religious life with yours in a way that shall make the interests of both races one. In all things that are purely social we can be as separate as the fingers, yet one as the hand in all things essential to mutual progress.

There is no defense or security for any of us except in the highest intelligence and development of all. If anywhere there are efforts tending to curtail the fullest growth of the Negro, let these efforts be turned into stimulating, encouraging, and making him the most useful and intelligent citizen. Effort or means so invested will pay a thousand per cent interest. These efforts will be twice blessed—"blessing him that gives and him that takes."

There is no escape through law of man or God from the inevitable:—

> "The laws of changeless justice bind
>   Oppressor with oppressed;
> And close as sin and suffering joined
>   We march to fate abreast."

Nearly sixteen millions of hands will aid you in pulling the load upward, or they will pull against you the load downward. We shall constitute one-third and more of the ignorance and crime of the South, or one-third its intelligence and progress; we shall contribute one-third to the business and industrial prosperity of the South, or we shall prove a veritable body of death, stagnating, depressing, retarding every effort to ad-vance the body politic.

Gentlemen of the Exposition, as we present to you our

humble effort at an exhibition of our progress, you must not expect overmuch. Starting thirty years ago with ownership here and there in a few quilts and pumpkins and chickens (gathered from miscellaneous sources), remember the path that has led from these to the inventions and production of agricultural implements, buggies, steam-engines, newspapers, books, statuary, carving, paintings, the management of drug stores and banks, has not been trodden without contact with thorns and thistles. While we take pride in what we exhibit as a result of our independent efforts, we do not for a moment forget that our part in this exhibition would fall far short of your expectations but for the constant help that has come to our educational life, not only from the Southern states, but especially from Northern philanthropists, who have made their gifts a constant stream of blessing and encouragement.

The wisest among my race understand that the agitation of questions of social equality is the extremest folly, and that progress in the enjoyment of all the privileges that will come to us must be the result of severe and constant struggle rather than of artificial forcing. No race that has anything to contribute to the markets of the world is long in any degree ostracized. It is important and right that all privileges of the law be ours, but it is vastly more important that we be prepared for the exercise of these privileges. The opportunity to earn a dollar in a factory just now is worth infinitely more than the opportunity to spend a dollar in an opera-house.

In conclusion, may I repeat that nothing in thirty years has given us more hope and encouragement, and drawn us so near to you of the white race, as this opportunity offered by the Exposition; and here bending, as it were, over the altar that represents the results of the struggles of your race and mine, both starting practically empty-handed three decades ago, I pledge that in your effort to work out the great and intricate problem which God has laid at the doors of the South, you shall have at all times the patient, sympathetic help of my race; only let this be constantly in mind, that, while from representations in these buildings of the product of field, of forest, of mine, of factory, letters, and art, much good will come, yet far above and beyond material benefits will be that higher good, that, let

us pray God, will come, in a blotting out of sectional differences and racial animosities and suspicions, in a determination
to administer absolute justice, in a willing obedience among all
classes to the mandates of law. This, coupled with our material
prosperity, will bring into our beloved South a new heaven and
a new earth.

WILLIAM JENNINGS BRYAN

Speech to the Democratic
National Convention

Chicago, July 9, 1896

M R. CHAIRMAN AND GENTLEMEN OF THE CONVENTION:
I would be presumptuous, indeed, to present myself
against the distinguished gentlemen to whom you have listened if this were a mere measuring of abilities; but this is not
a contest between persons. The humblest citizen in all the land,
when clad in the armor of a righteous cause, is stronger than
all the hosts of error. I come to speak to you in defense of a
cause as holy as the cause of liberty—the cause of humanity.

When this debate is concluded, a motion will be made to lay
upon the table the resolution offered in commendation of the
administration, and also the resolution offered in condemnation of the administration. We object to bringing this question
down to the level of persons. The individual is but an atom; he
is born, he acts, he dies; but principles are eternal; and this has
been a contest over a principle.

Never before in the history of this country has there been
witnessed such a contest as that through which we have just
passed. Never before in the history of American politics has a
great issue been fought out as this issue has been, by the voters
of a great party. On the fourth of March, 1895, a few Democrats, most of them members of Congress, issued an address to
the Democrats of the nation, asserting that the money question was the paramount issue of the hour; declaring that a
majority of the Democratic party had the right to control the
action of the party on this paramount issue; and concluding
with the request that the believers in the free coinage of silver
in the Democratic party should organize, take charge of, and
control the policy of the Democratic party. Three months later,
at Memphis, an organization was perfected, and the silver
Democrats went forth openly and courageously proclaiming

their belief, and declaring that, if successful, they would crystallize into a platform the declaration which they had made. Then began the conflict. With a zeal approaching the zeal which inspired the crusaders who followed Peter the Hermit, our silver Democrats went forth from victory unto victory until they are now assembled, not to discuss, not to debate, but to enter up the judgment already rendered by the plain people of this country. In this contest brother has been arrayed against brother, father against son. The warmest ties of love, acquaintance and association have been disregarded; old leaders have been cast aside when they have refused to give expression to the sentiments of those whom they would lead, and new leaders have sprung up to give direction to this cause of truth. Thus has the contest been waged, and we have assembled here under as binding and solemn instructions as were ever imposed upon representatives of the people.

We do not come as individuals. As individuals we might have been glad to compliment the gentleman from New York (Senator Hill), but we know that the people for whom we speak would never be willing to put him in a position where he could thwart the will of the Democratic party. I say it was not a question of persons; it was a question of principle, and it is not with gladness, my friends, that we find ourselves brought into conflict with those who are now arrayed on the other side.

The gentleman who preceded me (ex-Governor Russell) spoke of the State of Massachusetts; let me assure him that not one present in all this convention entertains the least hostility to the people of the State of Massachusetts, but we stand here representing people who are the equals, before the law, of the greatest citizens in the State of Massachusetts. When you (turning to the gold delegates) come before us and tell us that we are about to disturb your business interests, we reply that you have disturbed our business interests by your course.

We say to you that you have made the definition of a business man too limited in its application. The man who is employed for wages is as much a business man as his employer; the attorney in a country town is as much a business man as the corporation counsel in a great metropolis; the merchant at the cross-roads store is as much a business man as the merchant of New York; the farmer who goes forth in the morning and toils all day—who begins in the spring and toils all summer—and who by the application of brain and muscle to the natural resources of the country creates wealth, is as much a business man as the man who goes upon the board of trade and bets upon the price of grain; the miners who go down a thousand feet into the earth, or climb two thousand feet upon the cliffs, and bring forth from their hiding places the precious metals to be poured into the channels of trade are as much business men as the few financial magnates who, in a back room, corner the money of the world. We come to speak for this broader class of business men.

Ah, my friends, we say not one word against those who live upon the Atlantic coast, but the hardy pioneers who have braved all the dangers of the wilderness, who have made the desert to blossom as the rose—the pioneers away out there (pointing to the West), who rear their children near to Nature's heart, where they can mingle their voices with the voices of the birds—out there where they have erected schoolhouses for the education of their young, churches where they praise their Creator, and cemeteries where rest the ashes of their dead— these people, we say, are as deserving of the consideration of our party as any people in this country. It is for these that we speak. We do not come as aggressors. Our war is not a war of conquest; we are fighting in the defense of our homes, our families, and posterity. We have petitioned, and our petitions have been scorned; we have entreated, and our entreaties have been disregarded; we have begged, and they have mocked when our calamity came. We beg no longer; we entreat no more; we petition no more. We defy them.

The gentleman from Wisconsin has said that he fears a Robespierre. My friends, in this land of the free you need not fear that a tyrant will spring up from among the people. What we need is an Andrew Jackson to stand, as Jackson stood, against the encroachments of organized wealth.

They tell us that this platform was made to catch votes. We reply to them that changing conditions make new issues; that the principles upon which Democracy rests are as everlasting as the hills, but that they must be applied to new conditions as they arise. Conditions have arisen, and we are here to meet those conditions. They tell us that the income tax ought not to be brought in here; that it is a new idea. They criticise us for our criticism of the Supreme Court of the United States. My friends, we have not criticised; we have simply called attention to what you already know. If you want criticisms, read the dissenting opinions of the court. There you will find criticisms. They say that we passed an unconstitutional law; we deny it. The income tax law was not unconstitutional when it was passed; it was not unconstitutional when it went before the Supreme Court for the first time; it did not become unconstitutional until one of the judges changed his mind, and we cannot be expected to know when a judge will change his mind. The income tax is just. It simply intends to put the burdens of government justly upon the backs of the people. I am in favor of an income tax. When I find a man who is not willing to bear his share of the burdens of the government which protects him, I find a man who is unworthy to enjoy the blessings of a government like ours.

They say that we are opposing national bank currency; it is true. If you will read what Thomas Benton said, you will find he said that, in searching history, he could find but one parallel to Andrew Jackson; that was Cicero, who destroyed the conspiracy of Cataline and saved Rome. Benton said that Cicero only did for Rome what Jackson did for us when he destroyed the bank conspiracy and saved America. We say in our platform that we believe that the right to coin and issue money is a function of government. We believe it. We believe that it is a part of sovereignty, and can no more with safety be delegated to private individuals than we could afford to delegate to private individuals the power to make penal statutes or levy taxes. Mr. Jefferson, who was once regarded as good Democratic authority, seems to have differed in opinion from the gentleman who has addressed us on the part of the minority. Those who are opposed to this proposition tell us that the issue of paper money is a function of the bank, and that the Government ought to go out of the banking business. I stand with Jefferson rather than with them, and tell them, as he did, that the issue of money is a function of government, and that the banks ought to go out of the governing business.

They complain about the plank which declares against life tenure in office. They have tried to strain it to mean that which it does not mean. What we oppose by that plank is the life tenure which is being built up in Washington, and which excludes from participation in official benefits the humbler members of society.

Let me call your attention to two or three important things. The gentleman from New York says that he will propose an amendment to the platform providing that the proposed change in our monetary system shall not affect contracts already made. Let me remind you that there is no intention of affecting those contracts which according to present laws are made payable in gold; but if he means to say that we cannot change our monetary system without protecting those who have loaned money before the change was made, I desire to ask him where, in law or in morals, he can find justification for not protecting the debtors when the act of 1873 was passed, if he now insists that we must protect the creditors.

He says he will also propose an amendment which will provide for the suspension of free coinage if we fail to maintain the parity within a year. We reply that when we advocate a policy which we believe will be successful, we are not compelled to raise a doubt as to our own sincerity by suggesting what we shall do if we fail. I ask him, if he would apply his logic to us, why he does not apply it to himself. He says he wants this country to try to secure an international agreement. Why does he not tell us what he is going to do if he fails to secure an international agreement? There is more reason for him to do that than there is for us to provide against the failure to maintain the parity. Our opponents have tried for twenty years to secure an international agreement, and those are waiting for it most patiently who do not want it at all.

And now, my friends, let me come to the paramount issue. If they ask us why it is that we say more on the money question than we say upon the tariff question, I reply that, if protection has slain its thousands, the gold standard has slain its tens of thousands. If they ask us why we do not embody in our platform all the things that we believe in, we reply that when we have restored the money of the Constitution all other necessary reforms will be possible; but that until this is done there is no other reform that can be accomplished.

Why is it that within three months such a change has come

over the country? Three months ago, when it was confidently asserted that those who believe in the gold standard would frame our platform and nominate our candidates, even the advocates of the gold standard did not think that we could elect a president. And they had good reason for their doubt, because there is scarcely a State here today asking for the gold standard which is not in the absolute control of the Republican party. But note the change. Mr. McKinley was nominated at St. Louis upon a platform which declared for the maintenance of the gold standard until it can be changed into bimetallism by international agreement. Mr. McKinley was the most popular man among the Republicans, and three months ago everybody in the Republican party prophesied his election. How is today? Why, the man who was once pleased to think that he looked like Napoleon—that man shudders today when he remembers that he was nominated on the anniversary of the battle of Waterloo. Not only that, but as he listens he can hear with ever-increasing distinctness the sound of the waves as they beat upon the lonely shores of St. Helena.

Why this change? Ah, my friends, is not the reason for the change evident to any one who will look at the matter? No private character, however pure, no personal popularity, however great, can protect from the avenging wrath of an indignant people a man who will declare that he is in favor of fastening the gold standard upon this country, or who is willing to surrender the right of self-government and place the legislative control of our affairs in the hands of foreign potentates and powers.

We go forth confident that we shall win. Why? Because upon the paramount issue of this campaign there is not a spot of ground upon which the enemy will dare to challenge battle. If they tell us that the gold standard is a good thing, we shall point to their platform and tell them that their platform pledges the party to get rid of the gold standard and substitute bimetallism. If the gold standard is a good thing, why try to get rid of it? I call your attention to the fact that some of the very people who are in this convention today and who tell us that we ought to declare in favor of international bimetallism—thereby declaring that the gold standard is wrong and that the principle of bimetallism is better—these very people four months ago were open and avowed advocates of the gold standard, and were then telling us that we could not legislate two metals together, even with the aid of all the world. If the gold standard is a good thing, we ought to declare in favor of its retention and not in favor of abandoning it; and if the gold standard is a bad thing why should we wait until other nations are willing to help us to let go? Here is the line of battle, and we care not upon which issue they force the fight; we are prepared to meet them on either issue or on both. If they tell us that the gold standard is the standard of civilization, we reply to them that this, the most enlightened of all the nations of the earth, has never declared for a gold standard and that both the great parties this year are declaring against it. If the gold standard is the standard of civilization, why, my friends, should we not have it? If they come to meet us on that issue we can present the history of our nation. More than that; we can tell them that they will search the pages of history in vain to find a single instance where the common people of any land have ever declared themselves in favor of the gold standard. They can find where the holders of fixed investments have declared for a gold standard, but not where the masses have.

Mr. Carlisle said in 1878 that this was a struggle between "the idle holders of idle capital" and "the struggling masses, who produce the wealth and pay the taxes of the country;" and, my friends, the question we are to decide is: Upon which side will the Democratic party fight; upon the side of "the idle holders of idle capital" or upon the side of "the struggling masses?" That is the question which the party must answer first, and then it must be answered by each individual hereafter. The sympathies of the Democratic party, as shown by the platform, are on the side of the struggling masses who have ever been the foundation of the Democratic party. There are two ideas of government. There are those who believe that, if you will only legislate to make the well-to-do prosperous, their prosperity will leak through on those below. The Democratic idea, however, has been that if you legislate to make the masses prosperous, their prosperity will find its way up through every class which rests upon them.

You come to us and tell us that the great cities are in favor of the gold standard; we reply that the great cities rest upon our broad and fertile prairies. Burn down your cities and leave our farms, and your cities will spring up again as if by magic; but destroy our farms and the grass will grow in the streets of every city in the country.

My friends, we declare that this nation is able to legislate for its own people on every question, without waiting for the aid or consent of any other nation on earth; and upon that issue we expect to carry every State in the Union. I shall not slander the inhabitants of the fair State of Massachusetts nor the inhabitants of the State of New York by saying that, when they are confronted with the proposition, they will declare that this nation is not able to attend to its own business. It is the issue of 1776 over again. Our ancestors, when but three millions in number, had the courage to declare their political independence of every other nation; shall we, their descendants, when we have grown to seventy millions, declare that we are less independent than our forefathers? No, my friends, that will never be the verdict of our people. Therefore, we care not upon what lines the battle is fought. If they say bimetallism is good, but that we cannot have it until other nations help us, we reply that, instead of having a gold standard because England has, we will restore bimetallism, and then let England have bimetallism because the United States has it. If they dare to come out in the open field and defend the gold standard as a good thing, we will fight them to the uttermost. Having behind us the producing masses of this nation and the world, supported by the commercial interests, the laboring interests, and the toilers everywhere, we will answer their demand for a gold standard by saying to them: You shall not press down upon the brow of labor this crown of thorns, you shall not crucify mankind upon a cross of gold.

THEODORE ROOSEVELT

The Strenuous Life

Chicago, April 10, 1899

I N SPEAKING to you, men of the greatest city of the West, men of the State which gave to the country Lincoln and Grant, men who preëminently and distinctly embody all that is most American in the American character, I wish to preach, not the doctrine of ignoble ease, but the doctrine of the strenuous life, the life of toil and effort, of labor and strife; to preach that highest form of success which comes, not to the man who desires mere easy peace, but to the man who does not shrink from danger, from hardship, or from bitter toil, and who out of these wins the splendid ultimate triumph.

A life of slothful ease, a life of that peace which springs merely from lack either of desire or of power to strive after great things, is as little worthy of a nation as of an individual. I ask only that what every self-respecting American demands from himself and from his sons shall be demanded of the American nation as a whole. Who among you would teach your boys that ease, that peace, is to be the first consideration in their eyes—to be the ultimate goal after which they strive? You men of Chicago have made this city great, you men of Illinois have done your share, and more than your share, in making America great, because you neither preach nor practise such a doctrine. You work yourselves, and you bring up your sons to work. If you are rich and are worth your salt, you will teach your sons that though they may have leisure, it is not to be spent in idleness; for wisely used leisure merely means that those who possess it, being free from the necessity of working for their livelihood, are all the more bound to carry on some kind of non-remunerative work in science, in letters, in art, in exploration, in historical research— work of the type we most need in this country, the successful carrying out of which reflects most honor upon the nation. We do not admire the man of timid peace. We admire the man who embodies victorious effort; the man who never wrongs his neighbor, who is prompt to help a friend, but who has those virile qualities necessary to win in the stern strife of actual life. It is hard to fail, but it is worse never to have tried to succeed. In this life we get nothing save by effort. Freedom from effort in the present merely means that there has been stored up effort in the past. A man can be freed from the necessity of work only by the fact that he or his fathers before him have worked to good purpose. If the freedom thus purchased is used aright, and the man still does actual work, though of a different kind, whether as a writer or a general, whether in the field of politics or in the field of exploration and adventure, he shows he deserves his good fortune. But if he treats this period of freedom from the need of actual labor as a period, not of preparation, but of mere enjoyment, even though perhaps not of vicious enjoyment, he shows that he is simply a cumberer of the earth's surface, and he surely unfits himself to hold his own with his fellows if the need to do so should again arise. A mere life of ease is not in the end a very satisfactory life, and, above all, it is a life which ultimately unfits those who follow it for serious work in the world.

In the last analysis a healthy state can exist only when the men and women who make it up lead clean, vigorous, healthy lives; when the children are so trained that they shall endeavor, not to shirk difficulties, but to overcome them; not to seek ease, but to know how to wrest triumph from toil and risk. The man must be glad to do a man's work, to dare and endure and to labor; to keep himself, and to keep those dependent upon him. The woman must be the housewife, the helpmeet of the homemaker, the wise and fearless mother of many healthy children. In one of Daudet's powerful and melancholy books he speaks of "the fear of maternity, the haunting terror of the young wife of the present day." When such words can be truthfully written of a nation, that nation is rotten to the heart's core. When men fear work or fear righteous war, when women fear motherhood, they tremble on the brink of doom; and well it is that they should vanish from the earth, where they are fit subjects for the scorn of all men and women who are themselves strong and brave and high-minded.

As it is with the individual, so it is with the nation. It is a base untruth to say that happy is the nation that has no history. Thrice happy is the nation that has a glorious history. Far better it is to dare mighty things, to win glorious triumphs, even though checkered by failure, than to take rank with those poor spirits who neither enjoy much nor suffer much, because they live in the gray twilight that knows not victory nor defeat. If in 1861 the men who loved the Union had believed that peace was the end of all things, and war and strife the worst of all things, and had acted up to their belief, we would have saved hundreds of thousands of lives, we would have saved hundreds of millions of dollars. Moreover, besides saving all the blood and treasure we then lavished, we would have prevented the heartbreak of many women, the dissolution of many homes, and we would have spared the country those months of gloom and shame when it seemed as if our armies marched only to defeat. We could have avoided all this suffering simply by shrinking from strife. And if we had thus avoided it, we would have shown that we were weaklings, and that we were unfit to stand among the great nations of the earth. Thank God for the iron in the blood of our fathers, the men who upheld the wisdom of Lincoln, and bore sword or rifle in the armies of Grant! Let us, the children of the men who proved themselves equal to the mighty days, let us, the children of the men who carried the great Civil War to a triumphant conclusion, praise the God of our fathers that the ignoble counsels of peace were rejected; that the suffering and loss, the blackness of sorrow and despair, were unflinchingly faced, and the years of strife endured; for in the end the slave was freed, the Union restored, and the mighty American republic placed once more as a helmeted queen among nations.

We of this generation do not have to face a task such as that our fathers faced, but we have our tasks, and woe to us if we fail to perform them! We cannot, if we would, play the part of China, and be content to rot by inches in ignoble ease within our borders, taking no interest in what goes on beyond them, sunk in a scrambling commercialism; heedless of the higher life, the life of aspiration, of toil and risk, busying ourselves only with the wants of our bodies for the day, until suddenly we should find, beyond a shadow of question, what China has already found, that in this world the nation that has trained itself to a career of unwarlike and isolated ease is bound, in the end, to go down before other nations which have not lost the manly and adventurous qualities. If we are to be a really great people, we must strive in good faith to play a great part in the world. We cannot avoid meeting great issues. All that we can determine for ourselves is whether we shall meet them well or ill. In 1898 we could not help being brought face to face with the problem of war with Spain. All we could decide was whether we should shrink like cowards from the contest, or enter into it as beseemed a brave and high-spirited people; and, once in, whether failure or success should crown our banners. So it is now. We cannot avoid the responsibilities that confront us in Hawaii, Cuba, Porto Rico, and the Philippines. All we can decide is whether we shall meet them in a way that will redound to the national credit, or whether we shall make of our dealings with these new problems a dark and shameful page in our history. To refuse to deal with them at all merely amounts to dealing with them badly. We have a given problem to solve. If we undertake the solution, there is, of course, always danger that we may not solve it aright; but to refuse to undertake the solution simply renders it certain that we cannot possibly solve it aright. The timid man, the lazy man, the man who distrusts his country, the over-civilized man, who has lost the great fighting, masterful virtues, the ignorant man, and the man of dull mind, whose soul is incapable of feeling the mighty lift that thrills "stern men with empires in their brains"—all these, of course, shrink from seeing the nation undertake its new duties; shrink from seeing us build a navy and an army adequate to our needs; shrink from seeing us do our share of the world's work, by bringing order out of chaos in the great, fair tropic islands from which the valor of our soldiers and sailors has driven the Spanish flag. These are the men who fear the strenuous life, who fear the only national life which is really worth leading. They believe in that cloistered life which saps the hardy virtues in a nation, as it saps them in the individual; or else they are wedded to that base spirit of gain and greed which recognizes in commercialism the be-all and end-all of national life, instead of realizing that, though an indispensable element, it is, after all, but one of the many elements that go to make up true national greatness. No country can long endure if its foundations are not laid deep in the material prosperity which comes from thrift, from business energy and enterprise, from hard, un-sparing effort in the fields of industrial activity; but neither was any nation ever yet truly great if it relied upon material pros-perity alone. All honor must be paid to the architects of our material prosperity, to the great captains of industry who have built our factories and our railroads, to the strong men who toil for wealth with brain or hand; for great is the debt of the nation to these and their kind. But our debt is yet greater to the men whose highest type is to be found in a statesman like Lincoln, a soldier like Grant. They showed by their lives that they recognized the law of work, the law of strife; they toiled to win a competence for themselves and those dependent upon them; but they recognized that there were yet other and even loftier duties—duties to the nation and duties to the race.

We cannot sit huddled within our own borders and avow ourselves merely an assemblage of well-to-do hucksters who care nothing for what happens beyond. Such a policy would defeat even its own end; for as the nations grow to have ever wider and wider interests, and are brought into closer and closer contact, if we are to hold our own in the struggle for naval and commercial supremacy, we must build up our power without our own borders. We must build the isthmian canal, and we must grasp the points of vantage which will enable us to have our say in deciding the destiny of the oceans of the East and the West.

So much for the commercial side. From the standpoint of international honor the argument is even stronger. The guns that thundered off Manila and Santiago left us echoes of glory, but they also left us a legacy of duty. If we drove out a mediæ-val tyranny only to make room for savage anarchy, we had better not have begun the task at all. It is worse than idle to say that we have no duty to perform, and can leave to their fates the is-lands we have conquered. Such a course would be the course of infamy. It would be followed at once by utter chaos in the wretched islands themselves. Some stronger, manlier power would have to step in and do the work, and we would have shown ourselves weaklings, unable to carry to successful com-pletion the labors that great and high-spirited nations are eager to undertake.

The work must be done; we cannot escape our responsibil-

ity; and if we are worth our salt, we shall be glad of the chance
to do the work—glad of the chance to show ourselves equal to
one of the great tasks set modern civilization. But let us not
deceive ourselves as to the importance of the task. Let us not
be misled by vainglory into underestimating the strain it will
put on our powers. Above all, let us, as we value our own self-
respect, face the responsibilities with proper seriousness, courage, and high resolve. We must demand the highest order of
integrity and ability in our public men who are to grapple with
these new problems. We must hold to a rigid accountability
those public servants who show unfaithfulness to the interests
of the nation or inability to rise to the high level of the new demands upon our strength and our resources.

Of course we must remember not to judge any public servant
by any one act, and especially should we beware of attacking
the men who are merely the occasions and not the causes of
disaster. Let me illustrate what I mean by the army and the
navy. If twenty years ago we had gone to war, we should have
found the navy as absolutely unprepared as the army. At that
time our ships could not have encountered with success the
fleets of Spain any more than nowadays we can put untrained
soldiers, no matter how brave, who are armed with archaic
black-powder weapons, against well-drilled regulars armed
with the highest type of modern repeating rifle. But in the early
eighties the attention of the nation became directed to our
naval needs. Congress most wisely made a series of appropriations to build up a new navy, and under a succession of able
and patriotic secretaries, of both political parties, the navy was
gradually built up, until its material became equal to its splendid personnel, with the result that in the summer of 1898 it
leaped to its proper place as one of the most brilliant and formidable fighting navies in the entire world. We rightly pay all
honor to the men controlling the navy at the time it won these
great deeds, honor to Secretary Long and Admiral Dewey, to
the captains who handled the ships in action, to the daring
lieutenants who braved death in the smaller craft, and to the
heads of bureaus at Washington who saw that the ships were
so commanded, so armed, so equipped, so well engined, as to
insure the best results. But let us also keep ever in mind that all
of this would not have availed if it had not been for the wisdom

of the men who during the preceding fifteen years had built up
the navy. Keep in mind the secretaries of the navy during those
years; keep in mind the senators and congressmen who by their
votes gave the money necessary to build and to armor the ships,
to construct the great guns, and to train the crews; remember
also those who actually did build the ships, the armor, and the
guns; and remember the admirals and captains who handled
battle-ship, cruiser, and torpedo-boat on the high seas, alone
and in squadrons, developing the seamanship, the gunnery, and
the power of acting together, which their successors utilized so
gloriously at Manila and off Santiago. And, gentlemen, remember the converse, too. Remember that justice has two
sides. Be just to those who built up the navy, and, for the sake
of the future of the country, keep in mind those who opposed
its building up. Read the "Congressional Record." Find out
the senators and congressmen who opposed the grants for
building the new ships; who opposed the purchase of armor,
without which the ships were worthless; who opposed any adequate maintenance for the Navy Department, and strove to
cut down the number of men necessary to man our fleets. The
men who did these things were one and all working to bring
disaster on the country. They have no share in the glory of
Manila, in the honor of Santiago. They have no cause to feel
proud of the valor of our sea-captains, of the renown of our
flag. Their motives may or may not have been good, but their
acts were heavily fraught with evil. They did ill for the national
honor, and we won in spite of their sinister opposition.

Now, apply all this to our public men of to-day. Our army has
never been built up as it should be built up. I shall not discuss
with an audience like this the puerile suggestion that a nation
of seventy millions of freemen is in danger of losing its liberties
from the existence of an army of one hundred thousand men,
three fourths of whom will be employed in certain foreign islands, in certain coast fortresses, and on Indian reservations.
No man of good sense and stout heart can take such a proposition seriously. If we are such weaklings as the proposition implies, then we are unworthy of freedom in any event. To no
body of men in the United States is the country so much in-
debted as to the splendid officers and enlisted men of the regular army and navy. There is no body from which the country

has less to fear, and none of which it should be prouder, none which it should be more anxious to upbuild.

Our army needs complete reorganization,—not merely enlarging,—and the reorganization can only come as the result of legislation. A proper general staff should be established, and the positions of ordnance, commissary, and quartermaster officers should be filled by detail from the line. Above all, the army must be given the chance to exercise in large bodies. Never again should we see, as we saw in the Spanish war, major generals in command of divisions who had never before commanded three companies together in the field. Yet, incredible to relate, Congress has shown a queer inability to learn some of the lessons of the war. There were large bodies of men in both branches who opposed the declaration of war, who opposed the ratification of peace, who opposed the upbuilding of the army, and who even opposed the purchase of armor at a reasonable price for the battle-ships and cruisers, thereby putting an absolute stop to the building of any new fighting-ships for the navy. If, during the years to come, any disaster should befall our arms, afloat or ashore, and thereby any shame come to the United States, remember that the blame will lie upon the men whose names appear upon the roll-calls of Congress on the wrong side of these great questions. On them will lie the burden of any loss of our soldiers and sailors, of any dishonor to the flag; and upon you and the people of this country will lie the blame if you do not repudiate, in no unmistakable way, what these men have done. The blame will not rest upon the untrained commander of untried troops, upon the civil officers of a department the organization of which has been left utterly inadequate, or upon the admiral with an insufficient number of ships; but upon the public men who have so lamentably failed in forethought as to refuse to remedy these evils long in advance, and upon the nation that stands behind those public men.

So, at the present hour, no small share of the responsibility for the blood shed in the Philippines, the blood of our brothers, and the blood of their wild and ignorant foes, lies at the thresholds of those who so long delayed the adoption of the treaty of peace, and of those who by their worse than foolish words deliberately invited a savage people to plunge into a war fraught with sure disaster for them—a war, too, in which our own brave men who follow the flag must pay with their blood for the silly, mock humanitarianism of the prattlers who sit at home in peace.

The army and the navy are the sword and the shield which this nation must carry if she is to do her duty among the nations of the earth—if she is not to stand merely as the China of the western hemisphere. Our proper conduct toward the tropic islands we have wrested from Spain is merely the form which our duty has taken at the moment. Of course we are bound to handle the affairs of our own household well. We must see that there is civic honesty, civic cleanliness, civic good sense in our home administration of city, State, and nation. We must strive for honesty in office, for honesty toward the creditors of the nation and of the individual; for the widest freedom of individual initiative where possible, and for the wisest control of individual initiative where it is hostile to the welfare of the many. But because we set our own household in order we are not thereby excused from playing our part in the great affairs of the world. A man's first duty is to his own home, but he is not thereby excused from doing his duty to the State; for if he fails in this second duty it is under the penalty of ceasing to be a free-man. In the same way, while a nation's first duty is within its own borders, it is not thereby absolved from facing its duties in the world as a whole; and if it refuses to do so, it merely forfeits its right to struggle for a place among the peoples that shape the destiny of mankind.

In the West Indies and the Philippines alike we are confronted by most difficult problems. It is cowardly to shrink from solving them in the proper way; for solved they must be, if not by us, then by some stronger and more manful race. If we are too weak, too selfish, or too foolish to solve them, some bolder and abler people must undertake the solution. Personally, I am far too firm a believer in the greatness of my country and the power of my countrymen to admit for one moment that we shall ever be driven to the ignoble alternative.

The problems are different for the different islands. Porto Rico is not large enough to stand alone. We must govern it wisely and well, primarily in the interest of its own people. Cuba is, in my judgment, entitled ultimately to settle for itself whether it shall be an independent state or an integral portion of the mightiest of republics. But until order and stable liberty are secured, we must remain in the island to insure them, and infinite tact, judgment, moderation, and courage must be shown by our military and civil representatives in keeping the island pacified, in relentlessly stamping out brigandage, in protecting all alike, and yet in showing proper recognition to the men who have fought for Cuban liberty. The Philippines offer a yet graver problem. Their population includes half-caste and native Christians, warlike Moslems, and wild pagans. Many of their people are utterly unfit for self-government, and show no signs of becoming fit. Others may in time become fit but at present can only take part in self-government under a wise supervision, at once firm and beneficent. We have driven Spanish tyranny from the islands. If we now let it be replaced by savage anarchy, our work has been for harm and not for good. I have scant patience with those who fear to undertake the task of governing the Philippines, and who openly avow that they do fear to undertake it, or that they shrink from it because of the expense and trouble; but I have even scanter patience with those who make a pretense of humanitarianism to hide and cover their timidity, and who cant about "liberty" and the "consent of the governed," in order to excuse themselves for their unwillingness to play the part of men. Their doctrines, if carried out, would make it incumbent upon us to leave the Apaches of Arizona to work out their own salvation, and to decline to interfere in a single Indian reservation. Their doctrines condemn your forefathers and mine for ever having settled in these United States.

England's rule in India and Egypt has been of great benefit to England, for it has trained up generations of men accustomed to look at the larger and loftier side of public life. It has been of even greater benefit to India and Egypt. And finally, and most of all, it has advanced the cause of civilization. So, if we do our duty aright in the Philippines, we will add to that national renown which is the highest and finest part of national life, will greatly benefit the people of the Philippine Islands, and, above all, we will play our part well in the great work of uplifting mankind. But to do this work, keep ever in mind that we must show in a very high degree the qualities of courage, of honesty, and of good judgment. Resistance must be stamped out. The first and all-important work to be done is to establish the supremacy of our flag. We must put down armed resistance before we can accomplish anything else, and there should be no parleying, no faltering, in dealing with our foe. As for those in our own country who encourage the foe, we can afford contemptuously to disregard them; but it must be remembered that their utterances are not saved from being treasonable merely by the fact that they are despicable.

When once we have put down armed resistance, when once our rule is acknowledged, then an even more difficult task will begin, for then we must see to it that the islands are administered with absolute honesty and with good judgment. If we let the public service of the islands be turned into the prey of the spoils politician, we shall have begun to tread the path which Spain trod to her own destruction. We must send out there only good and able men, chosen for their fitness, and not because of their partizan service, and these men must not only administer impartial justice to the natives and serve their own government with honesty and fidelity, but must show the utmost tact and firmness, remembering that, with such people as those with whom we are to deal, weakness is the greatest of crimes, and that next to weakness comes lack of consideration for their principles and prejudices.

I preach to you, then, my countrymen, that our country calls not for the life of ease but for the life of strenuous endeavor. The twentieth century looms before us big with the fate of many nations. If we stand idly by, if we seek merely swollen, slothful ease and ignoble peace, if we shrink from the hard contests where men must win at hazard of their lives and at the risk of all they hold dear, then the bolder and stronger peoples will pass us by, and will win for themselves the domination of the world. Let us therefore boldly face the life of strife, resolute to do our duty well and manfully; resolute to uphold righteousness by deed and by word; resolute to be both honest and brave, to serve high ideals, yet to use practical methods. Above all, let us shrink from no strife, moral or physical, within or without the nation, provided we are certain that the strife is justified, for it is only through strife, through hard and dangerous endeavor, that we shall ultimately win the goal of true national greatness.

CARL SCHURZ

The Policy of Imperialism

Chicago, October 17, 1899

MORE than eight months ago I had the honor of addressing the citizens of Chicago on the subject of American imperialism, meaning the policy of annexing to this Republic distant countries and alien populations that will not fit into our democratic system of government. I discussed at that time mainly the baneful effect that the pursuit of an imperialistic policy would produce upon our political institutions. After long silence, during which I have carefully reviewed my own opinions, as well as those of others in the light of the best information I could obtain, I shall now approach the same subject from another point of view.

We all know that the popular mind is much disturbed by the Philippine war, and that, however highly we admire the bravery of our soldiers, nobody professes to be proud of the war itself. There are few Americans who do not frankly admit their regret that this war should ever have happened. I think I risk nothing when I say that it is not merely the bungling conduct of military operations, but a serious trouble of conscience, that disturbs the American heart about this war, and that this trouble of conscience will not be allayed by a more successful military campaign, just as fifty years ago the trouble of conscience about slavery could not be allayed by any compromise.

Many people now, as the slavery compromisers did then, try to ease their minds by saying: "Well, we are in it, and now we must do the best we can." In spite of the obvious futility of this cry in some respects, I will accept it with the one proviso, that we make an honest effort to ascertain what really is *the best* we can do. To this end let us first clearly remember what has happened.

In April, 1898, we went to war with Spain for the avowed purpose of liberating the people of Cuba, who had long been struggling for freedom and independence. Our object in that war was clearly and emphatically proclaimed by a solemn resolution of Congress repudiating all intention of annexation on our part, and declaring that the Cuban people "are, and of right ought to be, free and independent." This solemn declaration was made to do justice to the spirit of the American people, who were indeed willing to wage a war of liberation, but would not have consented to a war of conquest. It was also to propitiate the opinion of mankind for our action. President McKinley also declared with equal solemnity that annexation by force could not be thought of, because, according to our code of morals, it would be "criminal aggression."

Can it justly be pretended that these declarations referred only to the island of Cuba? What would the American people, what would the world, have said if Congress had resolved that the Cuban people were indeed rightfully entitled to freedom and independence, but that as to the people of other Spanish colonies we recognized no such right; and if President McKinley had declared that the forcible annexation of Cuba would be criminal, but that the forcible annexation of other Spanish colonies would be a righteous act? A general outburst of protest from our own people, and of derision and contempt from the whole world, would have been the answer. No, there can be no cavil—that war was proclaimed to all mankind to be a war of liberation, and not of conquest, and even now our very imperialists are still boasting that the war was prompted by the most unselfish and generous purposes, and that those insult us who do not believe it.

In the course of that war Commodore Dewey, by a brilliant feat of arms, destroyed the Spanish fleet in the harbor of Manila. This did not change the heralded character of the war— certainly not in Dewey's own opinion. The Filipinos, constituting the strongest and foremost tribe of the population of the archipelago, had long been fighting for freedom and independence, just as the Cubans had. The great mass of the other islanders sympathized with them. They fought for the same cause as the Cubans, and they fought against the same enemy— the same enemy against whom we were waging our war of humanity and liberation. They had the same title to freedom and independence which we recognized as "of right" in the

Cubans—nay, more; for, as Admiral Dewey telegraphed to our Government, "they are far superior in their intelligence, and more capable of self-government, than the natives of Cuba." The Admiral adds: "I am familiar with both races, and further intercourse with them has confirmed me in this opinion."

Indeed, the mendacious stories spread by our imperialists, which represent those people as barbarians, their doings as mere "savagery" and their chiefs as no better than "cut-throats," have been refuted by such a mass of authoritative testimony, coming in part from men who are themselves imperialists, that their authors should hide their heads in shame; for surely it is not the part of really brave men to calumniate their victims before sacrificing them. We need not praise the Filipinos as in every way the equals of the "embattled farmers" of Lexington and Concord, and Aguinaldo as the peer of Washington; but there is an overwhelming abundance of testimony—some of it unwilling—that the Filipinos are fully the equals, and even the superiors, of the Cubans and the Mexicans. As to Aguinaldo, Admiral Dewey is credited with saying that he is controlled by men abler than himself. The same could be said of more than one of our Presidents. Moreover, it would prove that those are greatly mistaken who predict that the Filipino uprising would collapse were Aguinaldo captured or killed. The old slander that Aguinaldo had sold out the revolutionary movement for a bribe of $400,000 has been so thoroughly exploded by the best authority that it requires uncommon audacity to repeat it. (See 55th Cong., 3d session, *Senate Doc.* 62, Part 1, page 421.)

Now let us see what has happened. Two months before the beginning of our Spanish war, our Consul at Manila reported to the State Department: "Conditions here and in Cuba are practically alike. War exists, battles are of almost daily occurrence. The crown forces (Spanish) have not been able to dislodge a rebel army within ten miles of Manila. A republic is organized here as in Cuba." When, two months later, our war of liberation and humanity began, Commodore Dewey was at Hong Kong with his ships. He received orders to attack and destroy the Spanish fleet in those waters. It was then that our Consul-General at Singapore informed our State Department that he had conferred with General Aguinaldo, then at Singapore, as to the coöperation of the Philippine insurgents, and that he had telegraphed to Commodore Dewey that Aguinaldo was willing to come to Hong Kong to arrange with Dewey for "general coöperation, if desired"; whereupon Dewey promptly answered: "Tell Aguinaldo come soon as possible." The meeting was had. Dewey sailed to Manila to destroy the Spanish fleet, and Aguinaldo was taken to the seat of war on a vessel of the United States. His forces received a supply of arms through Commodore Dewey, and did faithfully and effectively coöperate with our forces against the Spaniards, so effectively, indeed, that soon afterwards by their efforts the Spaniards had lost the whole country, except a few garrisons in which they were practically blockaded.

Now, what were the relations between the Philippine insurgents and this Republic? There is some dispute as to certain agreements, including a promise of Philippine independence, said to have been made between Aguinaldo and our Consul-General at Singapore before Aguinaldo proceeded to coöperate with Dewey. But I lay no stress upon this point. I will let only the record of facts speak. Of these facts the first, of highest importance, is that Aguinaldo was "desired," that is, invited, by officers of the United States to coöperate with our forces. The second is that the Filipino Junta in Hong Kong immediately after these conferences appealed to their countrymen to receive the American fleet, about to sail for Manila, as friends, by a proclamation which had these words: "Compatriots, divine Providence is about to place independence within our reach. The Americans, not from any mercenary motives, but for the sake of humanity, have considered it opportune to extend their protecting mantle to our beloved country. Where you see the American flag flying, assemble in mass. They are our redeemers." With this faith his followers gave Aguinaldo a rapturous greeting upon his arrival at Cavité, where he proclaimed his government and organized his army under Dewey's eyes.

The arrival of our land forces did not at first change these relations. Brigadier-General Thomas M. Anderson, commanding, wrote to Aguinaldo, July 4th, as follows:

General, I have the honor to inform you that the United States of America, whose land forces I have the honor to command in this vicinity, being at war with the kingdom of Spain, has entire sympathy and most friendly sentiments for the native people of the Philippine Islands. For these reasons I desire to have the most amicable relations with you, and to have you and your people coöperate with us in military operations against the Spanish forces, etc.

Aguinaldo responded cordially, and an extended correspondence followed, special services being asked for by the party of the first part, being rendered by the second and duly acknowledged by the first. All this went on pleasantly until the capture of Manila, in which Aguinaldo effectively coöperated by fighting the Spaniards outside, taking many prisoners from them, and hemming them in. The services they rendered by taking thousands of Spanish prisoners, by harassing the Spaniards in the trenches and by completely blockading Manila on the land side, were amply testified to by our own officers. Aguinaldo was also active on the sea. He had ships which our commanders permitted to pass in and out of Manila Bay, under the flag of the Philippine Republic, on their expeditions against other provinces.

Now, whether there was or not any formal compact of alliance signed and sealed, no candid man who has studied the official documents will deny that in point of fact the Filipinos, having been desired and invited to do so, were, before the capture of Manila, acting, and were practically recognized, as our allies, and that as such they did effective service, which we accepted and profited by. This is an indisputable fact, proved by the record.

It is an equally indisputable fact that during that period the Filipino government constantly and publicly, so that nobody could plead ignorance of it or misunderstand it, informed the world that their object was the achievement of national independence, and that they believed the Americans had come in good faith to help them accomplish that end, as in the case of Cuba. It was weeks after various proclamations and other public utterances of Aguinaldo to that effect that the correspondence between him and General Anderson, which I have quoted, took place, and that the useful services of the Filipinos as our practical allies were accepted. It is, further, an indisputable fact that during this period our Government did not inform the Filipinos that their fond expectations as to our

recognition of their independence were mistaken. Our
Secretary of State did, indeed, on June 16th write to Mr. Pratt,
our Consul-General at Singapore, that our Government knew
the Philippine insurgents, not indeed as patriots struggling for
liberty, and who, like the Cubans, "are and of right ought to
be free and independent," but merely as "discontented and re-
bellious subjects of Spain," who, if we occupied their country
in consequence of the war, would have to yield us due "obedience." And other officers of our Government were instructed
not to make any promises to the Filipinos as to the future. But
the Filipinos themselves were not so informed. They were left
to believe that, while fighting in coöperation with the American forces, they were fighting for their own independence.
They could not imagine that the Government of the great
American Republic, while boasting of having gone to war with
Spain under the banner of liberation and humanity in behalf of
Cuba, was capable of secretly plotting to turn that war into
one for the conquest and subjugation of the Philippines. Thus
the Filipinos went faithfully and bravely on doing for us the
service of allies, of brothers in arms, far from dreaming that
the same troops with whom they had been asked to coöperate
would soon be employed by the great apostle of liberation and
humanity to slaughter them for no other reason than that they,
the Filipinos, continued to stand up for their own freedom and
independence.

But just that was to happen. As soon as Manila was taken and
we had no further use for our Filipino allies, they were ordered
to fall back and back from the city and its suburbs. Our military commanders treated the Filipinos' country as if it were our
own. When Aguinaldo sent one of his aides-de-camp to General
Merritt with a request for an interview, General Merritt was
"too busy." When our peace negotiations with Spain began,
and representatives of the Filipinos asked for audience to so-
licit consideration of the rights and wishes of their people, the
doors were slammed in their faces, in Washington as well as in
Paris. And behind those doors the scheme was hatched to deprive the Philippine Islanders of independence from foreign
rule, and to make them the subjects of another foreign ruler;
and that foreign ruler their late ally, this great Republic which

had grandly proclaimed to the world that its war against Spain was not a war of conquest, but a war of liberation and humanity.

Behind those doors which were tightly closed to the people of the Philippines, a treaty was made with Spain, by the direction of President McKinley, which provided for the cession of the Philippine Islands by Spain to the United States for a consideration of $20,000,000. It has been said that this sum was not purchase-money, but a compensation for improvements made by Spain, or a *solatium* to sweeten the pill of cession, or what not. But, stripped of all cloudy verbiage, it was really purchase-money, the sale being made by Spain under duress. Thus Spain sold, and the United States bought, what was called the sovereignty of Spain over the Philippine Islands and their people.

Now look at the circumstances under which that "cession" was made. Spain had lost the possession of the country, except a few isolated and helpless little garrisons, most of which were effectively blockaded by the Filipinos. The American forces occupied Cavité and the harbor and city of Manila, and nothing more. The bulk of the country was occupied and possessed by the people thereof, over whom Spain had, in point of fact, ceased to exercise any sovereignty, the Spanish power having been driven out or destroyed by the Filipino insurrection, while the United States had not acquired, beyond Cavité and Manila, any authority of whatever name by military occupation, nor by recognition on the part of the people. Aguinaldo's army surrounded Manila on the land side, and his government claimed organized control over fifteen provinces. That government was established at Malolos not far from Manila; and a very respectable government, it was. According to Mr. Barrett, our late Minister in Siam, himself an ardent imperialist, who had seen it, it had a well-organized Executive, divided into several departments, ably conducted, and a popular Assembly, a Congress, which would favorably compare with the Parliament of Japan—an infinitely better government than the insurrectionary government of Cuba ever was.

It is said that Aguinaldo's government was in operation among only a part of the people of the islands. This is true. But it is also certain that it was recognized and supported by an immeasurably larger part of the people than Spanish sovereignty, which had practically ceased to exist, and than American rule, which was confined to a harbor and a city, and which was carried on by the exercise of military force under what was substantially martial law over a people that constituted about one-twentieth of the whole population of the islands. Thus, having brought but a very small fraction of the country and its people under our military control, we bought by that treaty the sovereignty over the whole from a Power which had practically lost that sovereignty, and therefore did no longer possess it; and we contemptuously disdained to consult the existing native government, which actually did control a large part of the country and people, and which had been our ally in the war with Spain. The sovereignty we thus acquired may well be defined as Abraham Lincoln once defined the "popular sovereignty" of Senator Douglas's doctrine—as being like a soup made by boiling the shadow of the breastbone of a pigeon that had been starved to death.

No wonder that treaty found opposition in the Senate. Virulent abuse was heaped upon the "statesman who would oppose the ratification of a peace treaty." A peace treaty? This was no peace treaty at all. It was a treaty with half a dozen bloody wars in its belly. It was, in the first place, an open and brutal declaration of war against our allies, the Filipinos, who struggled for freedom and independence from foreign rule. Every man not totally blind could see that. For such a treaty the true friends of peace could, of course, not vote.

But more. Even before that treaty had been assented to by the Senate, that is, even before that ghastly shadow of our Philippine sovereignty had obtained any legal sanction, President McKinley assumed of his own motion the sovereignty of the Philippine Islands by his famous "benevolent assimilation" order of December 21, 1898, through which our military commander at Manila was directed forthwith to extend the military government of the United States over the whole archipelago, and by which the Filipinos were notified that, if they refused to submit, they would be compelled by force of arms. Having bravely fought for their freedom and independence from one foreign rule, they did refuse to submit to another foreign rule, and then the slaughter of our late allies began—

the slaughter by American arms of a once friendly and confiding people. And this slaughter has been going on ever since.

This is a grim story. Two years ago the prediction of such a possibility would have been regarded as a hideous nightmare, as the offspring of a diseased imagination. But to-day it is a true tale—a plain recital of facts taken from the official records. These things have actually been done in these last two years by and under the Administration of William McKinley. This is our Philippine war as it stands. Is it a wonder that the American people should be troubled in their consciences? But let us not be too swift in our judgment on the conduct of those in power over us. Let us hear what they have to say in defense of it.

It is pretended that we had a right to the possession of the Philippines, and that self-respect demanded us to enforce that right. What kind of right was it? The right of conquest? Had we really acquired that country by armed conquest, which, as President McKinley has told us, is, according to the American code of morals, "criminal aggression"? But if we had thrown aside our code of morals, we had then not conquered more than the bay and city of Manila. The rest of the country was controlled, if by anybody, by the Filipinos. Or was it the right of possession by treaty? I have already shown that the President ordered the enforcement of our sovereignty over the archipelago before the treaty had by ratification gained legal effect, and also that, in making that treaty, we had bought something called sovereignty which Spain had ceased to possess and could therefore not sell and deliver. But let me bring the matter home to you by a familiar example.

Imagine that in our revolutionary times, France, being at war with England, had brought to this country a fleet and an army, and had, without any definite compact to that effect, coöperated as an ally with our revolutionary forces, permitting all the while the Americans to believe that she did this without any mercenary motive, and that, in case of victory, the American colonies would be free and independent. Imagine then that, after the British surrendered at Yorktown, the King of France had extorted from the British King a treaty ceding, for a consideration of $20,000,000, the sovereignty over the American colonies to France, and that thereupon the King of France had coolly notified the Continental Congress and General

Washington that they had to give up their idea of National independence, and to surrender unconditionally to the sovereignty of France, wherefor the French King promised them "benevolent assimilation." Imagine, further, that upon the protest of the Americans that Great Britain, having lost everything in the colonies except New York City and a few other little posts, had no sovereignty to cede, the French King answered that he had bought the Americans at $5 a head, and that if they refused to submit he would give them benevolent assimilation in the shape of bullets. Can there be any doubt that the Continental Congress and General Washington would have retorted that, no matter what the French King might have bought, Great Britain had no sovereignty left to sell; that least of all would the Americans permit themselves to be sold; that the French, in so treating their American allies after such high-sounding professions of friendship and generosity, were a lot of mean, treacherous, contemptible hypocrites, and that the Americans would rather die than submit to such wolves in sheep's clothing? And will any patriotic American now deny that, whatever quibbles of international law about possible cessions of a lost sovereignty might be invented, such conduct of the French would have been simply a shame and that the Americans of that time would have eternally disgraced themselves if they had failed to resist unto death? How, then, can the same patriotic American demand that the Filipinos should surrender and accept American sovereignty under circumstances exactly parallel? And that parallel will not be shaken by any learned international law technicalities, which do not touch the moral element of the subject.

It is also pretended that, whatever our rights, the Filipinos were the original aggressors in the pending fight, and that our troops found themselves compelled to defend their flag against assault. What are the facts? One evening early in February last some Filipino soldiers entered the American lines without, however, attacking anybody. An American sentry fired, killing one of the Filipinos. Then a desultory firing began at the outposts. It spread until it assumed the proportions of an extensive engagement in which a large number of Filipinos were killed. It is a well-established fact that this engagement could not have been a premeditated affair on the part of the Filipinos, as many of their officers, including Aguinaldo's private secretary, were at the time in the theaters and cafés of Manila. It is further well known that the next day Aguinaldo sent an officer, General Torres, under a flag of truce to General Otis to declare that the fighting had not been authorized by Aguinaldo, but had begun accidentally; that Aguinaldo wished to have it stopped, and proposed to that end the establishment of a neutral zone between the two armies, such as might be agreeable to General Otis; whereupon General Otis curtly answered that the fighting, having once begun, must go on to the grim end. Who was it that really wanted the fight?

But far more important than all this is the fact that President McKinley's "benevolent assimilation" order, which even before the ratification of the treaty demanded that the Philippine Islanders should unconditionally surrender to American sovereignty, in default whereof our military forces would compel them, was really the President's declaration of war against the Filipinos insisting upon independence, however you may quibble about it. When an armed man enters my house under some questionable pretext, and tells me that I must yield to him unconditional control of the premises or he will knock me down—who is the aggressor, no matter who strikes the first blow? No case of aggression can be clearer, shuffle and prevaricate as you will.

Let us recapitulate. We go to war with Spain in behalf of an oppressed colony of hers. We solemnly proclaim this to be a war—not of conquest—God forbid!—but of liberation and humanity. We invade the Spanish colony of the Philippines, destroy the Spanish fleet, and invite the coöperation of the Filipino insurgents against Spain. We accept their effective aid as allies, all the while permitting them to believe that, in case of victory, they will be free and independent. By active fighting they get control of a large part of the interior country, from which Spain is virtually ousted. When we have captured Manila and have no further use for our Filipino allies, our President directs that, behind their backs, a treaty be made with Spain transferring their country to us; and even before that treaty is ratified, he tells them that, in place of the Spaniards, they must accept us as their masters, and that if they do not, they will be compelled by force of arms. They refuse, and we shoot them down; and, as President McKinley said at Pittsburgh, we shall continue to shoot them down "without useless parley."

I have recited these things in studiously sober and dry matter-of-fact language, without oratorical ornament or appeal. I ask you now what epithet can you find justly to characterize such a course? Happily, you need not search for one, for President McKinley himself has furnished the best when, in a virtuous moment, he said that annexation by force should not be thought of, for, according to the American code of morals, it would be "criminal aggression." Yes, "criminal" is the word. Have you ever heard of any aggression more clearly criminal than this? And in this case there is an element of peculiarly repulsive meanness and treachery. I pity the American who can behold this spectacle without the profoundest shame, contrition and resentment. Is it a wonder, I repeat, that the American people, in whose name this has been done, should be troubled in their consciences?

To justify, or rather to excuse, such things, nothing but a plea of the extremest necessity will avail. Did such a necessity exist? In a sort of helpless way the defenders of this policy ask: "What else could the President have done under the circumstances?" This question is simply childish. If he thought he could not order Commodore Dewey away from Manila after the execution of the order to destroy the Spanish fleet, he could have told the people of the Philippine Islands that this was, on our part, a war not of conquest, but of liberation and humanity; that we sympathized with their desire for freedom and independence, and that we would treat them as we had specifically promised to treat the Cuban people in furthering the establishment of an independent government. And this task would have been much easier than in the case of Cuba, since, according to Admiral Dewey's repeatedly emphatic testimony, the Filipinos were much better fitted for such a government.

Our ingenious Postmaster-General has told us that the President could not have done that because he had no warrant for it, since he did not know whether the American people would wish to keep the Philippine Islands. But what warrant, then, had the President for putting before the Filipinos, by his "benevolent assimilation order," the alternative of submission to our sovereignty or war? Had he any assurance that the American people willed that? If such was his dream, there may be a rude awakening in store for him. But I say that for assenting to the aspiration of the Filipinos to freedom and independence he would have had the fullest possible warrant in the spirit of our institutions and in the resolution of Congress stamping our war against Spain as a war of liberation and humanity. And such a course would surely have been approved by the American people, except perhaps some Jingoes bent upon wild adventure, and some syndicates of speculators unscrupulous in their greed of gain.

There are also some who, with the mysterious mien of a superior sense of responsibility, tell us that the President could not have acted otherwise, because Dewey's victory devolved upon us some grave international or other obligations which would have been disregarded had the President failed to claim sovereignty over the Philippines. What? Did not the destruction of Cervera's fleet and the taking of Santiago devolve the same obligations upon us with regard to Cuba? And who has ever asserted that therefore Cuba must be put under our sovereignty? And did ever anybody pretend that our victories in Mexico fifty years ago imposed upon us international or other obligations which compelled us to assume sovereignty over the Mexican Republic after we had conquered it much more than we have conquered the Philippines? Does not, in the light of history, this obligation-dodge appear as a hollow mockery?

An equally helpless plea is it, that the President could not treat with Aguinaldo and his followers because they did not represent the whole population of the islands. But having an established government and an army of some 25,000 or 30,000 men, and in that army men from various tribes, they represented at least something. They represented at least a large part of the population and a strong nucleus of a national organization. And, as we have to confess that in the Philippines there is no active opposition to the Filipino government except that which we ourselves manage to excite, it may be assumed that they represent the sympathy of practically the whole people.

But, pray, what do we represent there? At first, while the islanders confided in us as their liberators, we represented their hope for freedom and independence. Since we have betrayed that hope and have begun to slaughter them, we represent, as a

brute force bent upon subjugating them, only their bitter hatred and detestation. We have managed to turn virtually that
whole people, who at first greeted us with childlike trust as their
beloved deliverers, into deadly enemies. For it is a notorious
fact that those we regard as *amigos* to-day will to-morrow stand
in the ranks of our foes. We have not a true friend left among
the islanders unless it be some speculators and the Sultan of
Sulu with his harem and his slaves, whose support we have
bought with a stipend like that which the Republic in its feeble
infancy paid to the pirates of the Barbary States. And even his
friendship will hardly last long. Yes, it is a terrible fact that in
one year we have made them hate us more, perhaps, than they
hated even their Spanish oppressors, who were at least less foreign to them, and that the manner in which we are treating
them has caused many, if not most, of the Filipinos to wish
that they had patiently suffered Spanish tyranny rather than be
"liberated" by us.

Thus it appears that we who represent in the Philippines no
popular element at all, but are unpopular in the extreme, cannot enter into relations with an established government for the
pretended reason that it does not represent *all* the people, while
it does represent a very important part of them, and would
probably soon represent them all if we did not constantly
throw obstacles in its way—aye, if we did not seek to extinguish it in blood. Was there ever a false pretense more glaring?

But the ghastliest argument of all in defense of the President's course is that he had to extend American sovereignty
over the whole archipelago even before the ratification of the
treaty, and that he was, and is now, obliged to shoot down the
Filipinos, to the end of "restoring order" and "preventing anarchy" in the islands. We are to understand that if our strong
armed hand did not restrain them from doing as they pleased—
that is, if they were left free and independent—they would
quickly begin to cut one another's or other people's throats,
and to ravish and destroy one another's or other people's property. We may reasonably assume that if this were sure to be the
upshot of their being left free and independent, they would
have shown some such tendency where they have actually held
sway under their own revolutionary government.

Now for the facts. We have the reports of two naval officers

and of two members of the signal corps who travelled extensively behind Aguinaldo's lines through the country controlled
by his government. And what did they find? Quiet and orderly
rural or municipal communities, in all appearance well organized and governed, full of enthusiasm for their liberty and independence, which they thought secured by the expulsion of
the Spaniards, and for their leader Aguinaldo, and at the time—
it was before President McKinley had ordered the subjugation
of the islands—also for the Americans, whom, with childlike
confidence, they still believed friendly to their freedom from
all foreign rule. We may be sure that if any anarchical disturbances had happened among them, our imperialists would have
eagerly made report. But there has been nothing at all equivalent to such things of our own as the famous "battle of Virden" in Illinois, or the race troubles in our own States, or the
numerous lynchings we have witnessed with shame and alarm
in various parts of our Republic. The only rumors of so-called
"anarchy" have come through a British consul on the island of
Borneo, who writes that bloody broils are occurring in some
of the southernmost regions of the Philippine archipelago, and
that the Americans are wanted there. But the Americans are
engaged in killing orderly Filipinos—Filipino soldiers of just
that Filipino government which, on its part, would probably
soon restore order in the troubled places, if it had not to defend itself against the "criminal aggression" of the Americans.

The imperialists wish us to believe that in the Philippines
there is bloody disorder wherever our troops are *not*. In fact,
after the Filipinos had expelled the Spaniards from the interior
of their country, bloody disorders began there only when our
troops appeared. Here is an example. In December last the city
of Iloilo, the second city in commercial importance in the
Philippines, was evacuated by the Spaniards and occupied by
the Filipinos. General M. P. Miller of our Army was sent in command of an expedition to take possession of it. As he has publicly stated, when he appeared with his ships and soldiers before
the city he "received a letter from the business people of Iloilo,
principally foreigners, stating that good order was being maintained, life and property being protected, and requesting him
not to attack at present." But soon afterwards he received
peremptory orders to attack, and did so; and then the killing

and the burning of houses and other work of devastation
began. Can it be said that our troops had to go there to "restore
order" and prevent bloodshed and devastation? No, order and
safety existed there, and it was only with our troops that the
bloodshed and devastation came which otherwise might not
have occurred.

I am far from meaning to picture the Philippine Islanders as
paragons of virtue and gentle conduct. But I challenge the imperialists to show me any instances of bloody disturbance or
other savagery among them sufficient to create any necessity
for our armed interference to "restore order" or to "save them
from anarchy." I ask and demand an answer: Is it not true that,
even if there has been such a disorderly tendency, it would
have required a long time for it to kill one-tenth as many human beings as we have killed and to cause one-tenth as much
devastation as we have caused by our assaults upon them? Is it
not true that, instead of being obliged to "restore order," we
have carried riot and death and desolation into peaceful communities whose only offense was not that they did not maintain order and safety among themselves, but that they refused
to accept us as their rulers? And here is the rub.

In the vocabulary of our imperialists "order" means, above
all, submission to their will. Any other kind of order, be it ever
so peaceful and safe, must be suppressed with a bloody hand.
This "order" is the kind that has been demanded by the despot
since the world had a history. Its language has already become
dangerously familiar to us—a familiarity which cannot cease
too soon.

From all these points of view, therefore, the Philippine war
was as unnecessary as it is unjust. A wanton, wicked and abom-
inable war—so it is called by untold thousands of American
citizens, and so it is at heart felt to be, I have no doubt, by an
immense majority of the American people. Aye, as such it is
cursed by many of our very soldiers whom our Government
orders to shoot down innocent people. And who will deny that
this war would certainly have been avoided had the President
remained true to the National pledge that the war against Spain
should be a war of liberation and humanity and not of conquest? Can there be any doubt that, if the assurance had honestly been given and carried out, we might have had, for the

mere asking, all the coaling-stations, and facilities for commercial and industrial enterprise, and freedom for the establishment of schools and churches we might reasonably desire? And what have we now? After eight months of slaughter and devastation, squandered treasure and shame, an indefinite prospect of more and more slaughter, devastation, squandered treasure and shame.

But, we are asked, since we have to deal with a situation not as it might have been, but as it is, what do we propose to do now? We may fairly turn about and say, since not we, but you, have got the country into this frightful mess, what have you to propose? Well, and what is the answer? "No useless parley! More soldiers! More guns! More blood! More devastation! Kill, kill, kill! And when we have killed enough, so that further resistance stops, then we shall see." Translated from smooth phrase into plain English, this is the program. Let us examine it with candor and coolness.

What is the ultimate purpose of this policy? To be perfectly fair, I will assume that the true spirit of American imperialism is represented not by the extremists who want to subjugate the Philippine Islanders at any cost and then exploit the islands to the best advantage of the conquerors, but by the more humane persons who say that we must establish our sovereignty over them to make them happy, to prepare them for self-government, and even recognize their right to complete independence as soon as they show themselves fit for it.

Let me ask these well-meaning citizens a simple question. If you think that the American people may ultimately consent to the independence of those islanders as matter of right and good policy, why do you insist upon killing them now? You answer: Because they refuse to recognize our sovereignty. Why do they so refuse? Because they think themselves entitled to independence, and are willing to fight and die for it. But if you insist upon continuing to shoot them down for this reason, does not that mean that you want to kill them for demanding the identical thing which you yourself think that you may ultimately find it just and proper to grant them? Would not every drop of blood shed in such a guilty sport cry to Heaven? For you must not forget that establishing our sovereignty in the Philippines means the going on with the work of slaughter and devastation to the grim end, and nobody can tell where that end will be. To kill men in a just war and in obedience to imperative necessity is one thing. To kill men for demanding what you yourself may ultimately have to approve, is another. How can such killing adopted as a policy be countenanced by a man of conscience and humane feelings? And yet, such killing without useless parley is the policy proposed to us.

We are told that we must trust President McKinley and his advisers to bring us out "all right." I should be glad to be able to do so; but I cannot forget that they have got us in all wrong. And here we have to consider a point of immense importance, which I solemnly urge upon the attention of the American people.

It is one of the fundamental principles of our system of democratic government that only the Congress has the power to declare war. What does this signify? That a declaration of war, the initiation of an armed conflict between this Nation and some other Power—the most solemn and responsible act a nation can perform, involving as it does the lives and fortunes of an uncounted number of human beings—shall not be at the discretion of the Executive branch of the Government, but shall depend upon the authority of the legislative representatives of the people—in other words, that, as much as the machinery of government may make such a thing possible, the deliberate will of the people Constitutionally expressed shall determine the awful question of peace or war.

It is true there may be circumstances of foreign aggression or similar emergencies to precipitate an armed conflict without there being a possibility of consulting the popular will beforehand. But, such exceptional cases notwithstanding, the Constitutional principle remains that the question of peace or war is essentially one which the popular will is to decide, and that no possibility should be lost to secure upon it the expression of the popular will through its legislative organs. Whenever such a possibility is wilfully withheld or neglected, and a war has been brought upon the country without every available means being employed thus to consult the popular will upon that question, the spirit of the Constitution is flagrantly violated in one of its most essential principles.

We are now engaged in a war with the Filipinos. You may

quibble about it as you will, call it by whatever name you will—it *is* a war; and a war of conquest on our part at that—a war of barefaced, cynical conquest. Now, I ask any fairminded man whether the President, before beginning that war, or while carrying it on, has ever taken any proper steps to get from the Congress, the representatives of the people, any proper authority for making that war. He issued his famous "benevolent assimilation" order, directing the Army to bring the whole Philippine archipelago as promptly as possible under the military government of the United States, on December 21, 1898, while Congress was in session, and before the treaty with Spain, transferring her shadowy sovereignty over the islands, had acquired any force of law by the assent of the Senate. That was substantially a declaration of war against the Filipinos asserting their independence. He took this step of his own motion. To be sure, he has constantly been telling us that "the whole subject is with Congress," and that "Congress shall direct." But when did he, while Congress was in session, lay a full statement before that body and ask its direction? Why did he not, before he proclaimed that the slaughter must go on without useless parley, call Congress together to consult the popular will in Constitutional form? Why, even in these days, while "swinging around the circle," the President and his Secretaries are speaking of the principal thing, the permanent annexation of the Philippines, not as a question still to be determined, but as a thing done—concluded by the Executive, implying that Congress will have simply to regulate the details.

Now you may bring ever so many arguments to show that the President had *technically* a right to act as he did, and your reasoning may be ever so plausible—yet the great fact remains that the President did not seek and obtain authority from Congress as to the war to be made, and the policy to be pursued, and that he acted upon his own motion. And this autocratic conduct is vastly aggravated by the other fact that in this democratic Republic, the government of which should be that of an intelligent and well-informed public opinion, a censorship of news has been instituted, which is purposely and systematically seeking to keep the American people in ignorance of the true state of things at the seat of war, and by all sorts of deceitful tricks to deprive them of the knowledge required for the formation of a correct judgment. And this censorship was practised not only in Manila, but directly by the Administration in Washington. Here is a specimen performance revealed by a member of Congress in a public speech; the War Department gave out a despatch from Manila, as follows: "Volunteers willing to remain." The Congressman went to the War Department and asked for the original, which read: "Volunteers unwilling to reënlist, but willing to remain until transports arrive." You will admit that such distortion of official news is a downright swindle upon the people. Does not this give strong color to the charge of the war correspondents that the news is systematically and confessedly so doctored by the officials that it may "help the Administration"?

Those are, therefore, by no means wrong who call this "the President's war." And a war so brought about and so conducted the American people are asked to approve and encourage, simply because "we are in it"—that is, because the President of his own motion has got us into it. Have you considered what this means?

Every man of public experience knows how powerful and seductive precedent is as an argument in the interpretation of laws and of constitutional provisions, or in justification of governmental practices. When a thing, no matter how questionable, has once been done by the government, and approved, or even acquiesced in, by the people, that act will surely be used as a justification of its being done again. In nothing is the authority of precedent more dangerous than in defending usurpations of governmental power. And it is remarkable how prone the public mind is, especially under the influence of party spirit, to accept precedent as a warrant for such usurpations, which, judged upon their own merits, would be sternly condemned. And every such precedent is apt to bring forth a worse one. It is in this way that the most indispensable bulwarks of free government, and of public peace and security, may be undermined. To meet such dangers the American people should, if ever, remember the old saying that "eternal vigilance is the price of liberty."

I am not here as a partisan, but as an American citizen anxious for the future of the Republic. And I cannot too earnestly admonish the American people, if they value the fundamental principles of their government, and their own security and that of their children, for a moment to throw aside all partisan bias and soberly to consider what kind of a precedent they would set, if they consented to, and by consenting approved, the President's management of the Philippine business merely because "we are in it." We cannot expect all our future Presidents to be models of public virtue and wisdom, as George Washington was. Imagine now in the Presidential office a man well-meaning but, it may be, short-sighted and pliable, and under the influence of so-called "friends" who are greedy and reckless speculators, and who would not scruple to push him into warlike complications in order to get great opportunities for profit; or a man of that inordinate ambition which intoxicates the mind and befogs the conscience; or a man of extreme partisan spirit, who honestly believes the victory of his party to be necessary for the salvation of the universe, and may think that a foreign broil would serve the chances of his party; or a man of an uncontrollable combativeness of temperament which might run away with his sense of responsibility—and that we shall have such men in the Presidential chair is by no means unlikely with our loose way of selecting candidates for the Presidency. Imagine, then, a future President belonging to either of these classes to have before him the precedent of Mr. McKinley's management of the Philippine business, sanctioned by the approval or only the acquiescence of the people, and to feel himself permitted—nay, even encouraged—to say to himself that, as this precedent shows, he may plunge the country into warlike conflicts of his own motion, without asking leave of Congress, with only some legal technicalities to cover his usurpation, or, even without such, and that he may, by a machinery of deception called a war-censorship, keep the people in the dark about what is going on; and that into however bad a mess he may have got the country, he may count upon the people, as soon as a drop of blood has been shed, to uphold the usurpation and to cry down everybody who opposes it as a "traitor," and all this because "we are in it"! Can you conceive a more baneful precedent, a more prolific source of danger to the peace and security of the country? Can any sane man deny that it will be all the more prolific of evil if in this way we drift into a foreign policy full of temptation for dangerous adventure?

I say, therefore, that, if we have the future of the Republic at heart, we must not only not uphold the Administration in its course, because "we are in it," but just because we are in it, have been got into it in such a way, the American people should stamp the Administration's proceedings with a verdict of disapproval so clear and emphatic, and "get out of it" in such a fashion, that this will be a solemn warning to future Presidents instead of a seductive precedent.

What, then, to accomplish this end is to be done? Of course, we, as we are here, can only advise. But by calling forth expressions of the popular will by various means of public demonstration, and, if need be, at the polls, we can make that advice so strong that those in power will hardly disregard it. We have often been taunted with having no positive policy to propose. But such a policy has more than once been proposed and I can only repeat it.

In the first place, let it be well understood that those are egregiously mistaken who think that if by a strong military effort the Philippine war be stopped, everything will be right and no more question about it. No, the American trouble of conscience will not be appeased, and the question will be as big and virulent as ever, unless the close of the war be promptly followed by an assurance to the islanders of their freedom and independence, which assurance, if given now, would surely end the war without more fighting.

We propose, therefore, that it be given now. Let there be at once an armistice between our forces and the Filipinos. Let the Philippine Islanders at the same time be told that the American people will be glad to see them establish an independent government, and to aid them in that task as far as may be necessary; that, if the different tribes composing the population of the Philippines are disposed, as at least most of them, if not all, are likely to be, to attach themselves in some way to the government already existing under the Presidency of Aguinaldo, we shall cheerfully accept that solution of the question, and even, if required, lend our good offices to bring it about; and that meanwhile we shall deem it our duty to protect them against interference from other foreign Powers—in other words, that with regard to them we mean honestly to live up to the righteous principles with the profession of which we commended to the world our Spanish war.

And then let us have in the Philippines, to carry out this program, not a small politician, nor a meddlesome martinet, but a statesman of large mind and genuine sympathy who will not merely deal in sanctimonious cant and oily promises with a string to them, but who will prove *by his acts* that he and we are honest; who will keep in mind that their government is not merely to suit us, but to suit them; that it should not be measured by standards which we ourselves have not been able to reach, but be a government of their own, adapted to their own conditions and notions—whether it be a true republic, like ours, or better, or a dictatorship like that of Porfirio Diaz, in Mexico, or an oligarchy like the one maintained by us in Hawaii, or even something like the boss rule we are tolerating in New York and Pennsylvania.

Those who talk so much about "fitting a people for self-government" often forget that no people were ever made "fit" for self-government by being kept in the leading-strings of a foreign Power. You learn to walk by doing your own crawling and stumbling. Self-government is learned only by exercising it upon one's own responsibility. Of course there will be mistakes, and troubles and disorders. We have had and now have these, too—at the beginning our persecution of the Tories, our flounderings before the Constitution was formed, our Shays's rebellion, our whisky war and various failures and disturbances—among them a civil war that cost us a loss of life and treasure horrible to think of, and the murder of two Presidents. But who will say that on account of these things some foreign Power should have kept the American people in leading-strings to teach them to govern themselves? If the Philippine Islanders do as well as the Mexicans, who have worked their way, since we let them alone after our war of 1847, through many disorders, to an orderly government, who will have a right to find fault with the result? Those who seek to impose upon them an unreasonable standard of excellence in self-government do not seriously wish to let them govern themselves at all. You may take it as a general rule that he who wants to reign over others is solemnly convinced that they are quite unable to govern themselves.

Now, what objection is there to the policy dictated by our fundamental principles and our good faith? I hear the angry cry: "What? Surrender to Aguinaldo? Will not the world ridicule and despise us for such a confession of our incompetency to deal with so feeble a foe? What will become of our prestige?" No, we shall not surrender to Aguinaldo. In giving up a criminal aggression, we shall surrender only to our own consciences, to our own sense of right and justice, to our own understanding of our own true interests and to the vital principles of our own Republic. Nobody will laugh at us whose good opinion we have reason to cherish. There will, of course, be an outcry of disappointment in England. But from whom will it come? From such men as James Bryce or John Morley or any one of those true friends of this Republic who understand and admire and wish to perpetuate and spread the fundamental principles of its vitality? No, not from them. But the outcry will come from those in England who long to see us entangled in complications apt to make this American Republic dependent upon British aid and thus subservient to British interests. They, indeed, will be quite angry. But the less we mind their displeasure as well as their flattery, the better for the safety as well as the honor of our country.

The true friends of this Republic in England, and, indeed, all over the world, who are now grieving to see us go astray, will rejoice, and their hearts will be uplifted with new confidence in our honesty, in our wisdom and in the virtue of democratic institutions when they behold the American people throwing aside all the puerilities of false pride, and returning to the path of their true duty. The world knows how strong we are. It knows full well that if the American people chose to put forth their strength, they could quickly overcome a foe infinitely more powerful than the Filipinos, and that, if we, possessing the strength of the giant, do not use the giant's strength against this feeble foe, it is from the noblest of motives—our love of liberty, our sense of justice and our respect for the rights of others—the respect of the strong for the rights of the weak. The moral prestige which, in fact, we have lost, will be restored, while our prestige of physical prowess and power will certainly not be lessened by showing that we have not only soldiers, guns, ships and money, but also a conscience.

Therefore, the cry is childish, that, unless we take and keep the Philippines, some other Power will promptly grab them. Many a time this cry has been raised to stampede the American people into a policy of annexation—in the San Domingo case, twenty-eight years ago, and more recently in the case of Hawaii—and in neither case was there the slightest danger—not that there were no foreign Powers that would have liked to have those islands, but because they could not have taken them without the risk of grave consequences. Now the old bugbear must do service again. Why should not American diplomacy set about to secure the consent of the Powers most nearly concerned to an agreement to make the Philippine Islands neutral territory, as Belgium and Switzerland are in Europe? Because some of those Powers would like to have the Philippines themselves? Well, are there not among the European Powers some that would like to have Belgium or Switzerland? Certainly; and just because there are several watching each other, the neutrality of those two countries is guaranteed. But even if such an agreement could not be obtained, we may be sure that there is no foreign Power that would lightly risk a serious quarrel with the United States, if this Republic, for the protection of the Philippine Islanders in their effort to build up an independent government, said to the world: "Hands off!" So much for those who think that somebody else might be wicked enough to grab the Philippine Islands, and that, therefore, we must be wicked enough to do the grabbing ourselves.

There are some American citizens who take of this question a purely commercial view. I declare I am ardently in favor of the greatest possible expansion of our trade, and I am happy to say that, according to official statistics, our foreign commerce, in spite of all hindrances raised against it, is now expanding tremendously, owing to the simple rule that the nation offering the best goods at proportionately the lowest prices will have the markets. It will have them without armies, without war fleets, without bloody conquests, without colonies. I confess I am not in sympathy with those, if there be such men among us, who would sacrifice our National honor and the high ideals of the Republic, and who would inflict upon our people the burdens and the demoralizing influences of militarism for a mere matter of dollars and cents. They are among the most dangerous enemies of the public welfare. But as to the annexation of the Philippines, I will, for argument's sake, adopt even their point of view for a moment and ask: Will it pay?

Now, it may well be that the annexation of the Philippines would pay a speculative syndicate of wealthy capitalists, without at the same time paying the American people at large. As to people of our race, tropical countries like the Philippines may be fields of profit for rich men who can hire others to work for them, but not for those who have to work for themselves. Taking a general view of the Philippines as a commercial market for us, I need not again argue against the barbarous notion that in order to have a profitable trade with a country we must own it. If that were true, we should never have had any foreign commerce at all. Neither need I prove that it is very bad policy, when you wish to build up a profitable trade, to ruin your customer first, as you would ruin the Philippines by a protracted war. It is equally needless to show to any well-informed person that the profits of the trade with the islands themselves can never amount to the cost of making and maintaining the conquest of the Philippines.

But there is another point of real importance. Many imperialists admit that our trade with the Philippines themselves will not nearly be worth its cost; but they say that we must have the Philippines as a foothold, a sort of power station, for the expansion of our trade on the Asiatic continent, especially in China. Admitting this, for argument's sake, I ask what kind of a foothold we should really need. Coaling-stations and docks for our fleet, and facilities for the establishment of commercial houses and depots. That is all. And now I ask further, whether we could not easily have had these things if we had, instead of making war upon the Filipinos, favored the independence of the islands. Everybody knows that we could. We might have those things now for the mere asking, if we stopped the war and came to a friendly understanding with the Filipinos to-morrow.

But now suppose we fight on and subjugate the Filipinos and annex the islands—what then? We shall then have of coaling-stations and commercial facilities no more than we would have had in the other case; but the islanders will hate us as their bloody oppressors, and be our bitter and revengeful enemies for generations to come. You may say that this will be of no commercial importance. Let us see. It is by no means impossible, nor even improbable, that, if we are once in the way of extending our commerce with guns behind it, we may get into hot trouble with one or more of our competitors for that Asiatic trade. What then? Then our enemies need only land some Filipino refugees whom we have driven out of their country, and some cargoes of guns and ammunition on the islands, and we shall soon—all the more if we depend on native troops— have a fire in our rear which will oblige us to fight the whole old fight over again. The present subjugation of the Philippines will, therefore, not only not be a help to the expansion of our Asiatic trade, but rather a constant danger and a clog to our feet.

And here a word by the way. A year ago I predicted in an article published in the *Century Magazine*, that if we turned our war of liberation into a war of conquest, our American sister republics south of us would become distrustful of our intentions with regard to them, and soon begin to form combinations against us, eventually even with European Powers. The newspapers have of late been alive with vague rumors of that sort, so much so that a prominent journal of imperialistic tendency has found it necessary most earnestly to admonish the President, in his next message, to give to the republics south of us the strongest possible assurances of our friendship and good faith. Suppose he does—who will believe him after we have turned our loudly heralded war of liberation into a land-grabbing game—a "criminal aggression"? Nobody will have the slightest trust in our words, be they ever so fair. Drop your conquests, and no assurances of good faith will be required. Keep your conquests, and no such assurances will avail. Our southern neighbors, no less than the Filipinos, will then inevitably distrust our professions, fear our greed and become our secret or open enemies. And who can be foolish enough to believe that this will strengthen our power and help our commerce?

It is useless to say that the subjugated Philippine Islanders will become our friends if we give them good government. However good that government may be, it will, to them, be foreign rule, and foreign rule especially hateful when begun by broken faith, cemented by streams of innocent blood and erected upon the ruins of devastated homes. The American will be and remain to them more a foreigner, an unsympathetic foreigner, than the Spaniard ever was. Let us indulge in no delusion about this. People of our race are but too much inclined to have little tenderness for the rights of what we regard as inferior races, especially those of darker skin. It is of ominous significance that to so many of our soldiers the Filipinos were only "niggers," and that they likened their fights against them to the "shooting of rabbits." And how much good government have we to give them? Are you not aware that our first imperialistic Administration is also the first that, since the enactment of the civil service law, has widened the gates again for a new foray of spoils politics in the public service? What assurance have we that the Philippines, far away from public observation, will not be simply a pasture for needy politicians and for speculating syndicates to grow fat on, without much scruple as to the rights of the despised "natives"? Has it not been so with the British in India, although the British monarchy is much better fitted for imperial rule than our democratic Republic can ever be? True, in the course of time the government of India has been much improved, but it required more than a century of slaughter, robbery, devastation, disastrous blundering, insurrection and renewed bloody subjugation to evolve what there is of good government in India now. And have the populations of India ever become the friends of England? Does not England at heart tremble to-day lest some hostile foreign Power come close enough to throw a firebrand into that fearful mass of explosives?

I ask you, therefore, in all soberness, leaving all higher considerations of justice, morality and principle aside, whether, from a mere business point of view, the killing policy of subjugation is not a colossal, stupid blunder, and whether it would not have been, and would now be, infinitely more sensible to win the confidence and cultivate the friendship of the islanders by recognizing them as of right entitled to their freedom and independence, as we have recognized the Cubans, and thus to obtain from their friendship and gratitude, for the mere asking, all the coaling-stations and commercial facilities we require, instead of getting those things by fighting at an immense cost of blood and treasure, with a probability of having to fight for them again? I put this question to every business man who is not a fool or a reckless speculator. Can there be any doubt of the answer?

A word now on a special point: There are some very estimable men among us who think that even if we concede to the islanders their independence, we should at least keep the city of Manila. I think differently, not from a mere impulse of generosity, but from an entirely practical point of view. Manila is the traditional, if not the natural capital of the archipelago. To recognize the independence of the Philippine Islanders, and at the same time to keep from them Manila, would mean as much as to recognize the independence of Cuba and to keep Havana. It would mean to withhold from the islanders their metropolis, that in which they naturally take the greatest pride, that which they legitimately most desire to have, and which, if withheld from them, they would most ardently wish to get back. The withholding of Manila would inevitably leave a sting in their hearts which would never cease to rankle, and might, under critical circumstances, give us as much trouble as the withholding of independence itself. If we wish them to be our friends, we should not do things by halves, but enable them to be our friends without reserve. And I maintain that, commercially as well as politically speaking, the true friendship of the Philippine Islanders will, as to our position in the East, be worth far more to us than the possession of Manila. We can certainly find other points which will give us similar commercial as well as naval advantages without exciting any hostile feeling.

Although I have by no means exhausted this vast subject, discussing only a few phases of it, I have said enough, I think, to show that this policy of conquest is, from the point of view of public morals, in truth "criminal aggression"—made doubly criminal by the treacherous character of it; and that from the point of view of material interest it is a blunder—a criminal blunder, and a blundering crime. I have addressed myself to your reason by sober argument, without any appeal to prejudice or passion. Might we not ask our opponents to answer these arguments, if they can, with equally sober reasoning, instead of merely assailing us with their wild cries of "treason" and "lack of patriotism," and what not? Or do they really feel their cause to be so weak that they depend for its support on their assortment of inarticulate shouts and nebulous phrases?

Here are our "manifest destiny" men who tell us that, whether it be right or not, we must take and keep the Philippines because "destiny" so wills it. We have heard this cry of manifest destiny before, especially when, a half century ago, the slave-power demanded the annexation of Cuba and Central America to strengthen the slave-power. The cry of destiny is most vociferously put forward by those who want to do a wicked thing and to shift the responsibility. The destiny of a free people lies in its intelligent will and its moral strength. When it pleads destiny, it pleads "the baby act." Nay, worse; the cry of destiny is apt to be the refuge of evil intent and of moral cowardice.

Here are our "burden" men, who piously turn up their eyes and tell us, with a melancholy sigh, that all this conquest business may be very irksome, but that a mysterious Providence has put it as a "burden" upon us, which, however sorrowfully, we must bear; that this burden consists in our duty to take care of the poor people of the Philippines; and that in order to take proper care of them we must exercise sovereignty over them; and that if they refuse to accept our sovereignty, we must— alas! alas!—kill them, which makes the burden very solemn and sad.

But cheer up, brethren! We may avoid that mournful way of taking care of them by killing them, if we simply recognize their right to take care of themselves, and gently aid them in doing so. Besides, you may be as much mistaken about the decrees of Providence as before our civil war the Southern Methodist bishops were who solemnly insisted that Providence willed the negroes to remain in slavery.

Next there are our "flag" men, who insist that we must kill the Filipinos fighting for their independence to protect the honor of the stars and stripes. I agree that the honor of our flag sorely needs protection. We have to protect it against desecration by those who are making it an emblem of that hypocrisy which seeks to cover a war of conquest and subjugation with a cloak of humanity and religion; an emblem of that greed which would treat a matter involving our National honor, the integrity of our institutions and the peace and character of the Republic as a mere question of dollars and cents; an emblem of that vulgar lust of war and conquest which recklessly tramples upon right and justice and all our higher ideals; an emblem of the imperialistic ambitions which mock the noblest part of our history and stamp the greatest National heroes of our past as hypocrites or fools. These are the dangers threatening the honor of our flag, against which it needs protection, and that protection we are striving to give it.

Now, a last word to those of our fellow-citizens who feel and recognize as we do that the Philippine war of subjugation is wrong and cruel, and that we ought to recognize the independence of those people, but who insist that, having begun that war, we must continue it until the submission of the Filipinos is complete. I detest, but I can understand, the Jingo whose moral sense is obscured by intoxicating dreams of wild adventure and conquest, and to whom bloodshed and devastation have become a reckless sport. I detest even more, but still I can understand, the cruel logic of those to whom everything is a matter of dollars and cents and whose greed of gain will walk coolly over slaughtered populations. But I must confess I cannot understand the reasoning of those who have moral sense enough to recognize that this war is criminal aggression—who must say to themselves that every drop of blood shed in it by friend or foe is blood wantonly and wickedly shed, and that every act of devastation is barbarous cruelty inflicted upon an innocent people—but who still maintain that we must go on killing, and devastating, and driving our brave soldiers into a fight which they themselves are cursing, because we have once begun it. This I cannot understand. Do they not consider that in such a war, which they themselves condemn as wanton and iniquitous, the more complete our success, the greater will be our disgrace?

What do they fear for the Republic if, before having fully consummated this criminal aggression, we stop to give a people struggling for their freedom what is due them? Will this Republic be less powerful? It will be as strong as ever, nay, stronger, for it will have saved the resources of its power from useless squandering and transformed vindictive enemies into friends. Will it be less respected? Nay, more, for it will have demonstrated its honesty at the sacrifice of false pride. Is this the first time that a powerful nation desisted from the subjugation of a weaker adversary? Have we not the example of England before us, who, after a seven-year war against the American colonists, recognized their independence? Indeed, the example of England teaches us a double lesson. England did not, by recognizing American independence, lose her position in the world and her chances of future greatness; on the contrary, she grew in strength. And secondly, England would have retained, or won anew, the friendship of the Americans, if she had recognized American independence more promptly, before appearing to have been forced to do so by humiliating defeats. Will our friends who are for Philippine independence, but also for continuing to kill those who fight for it, take these two lessons to heart?

Some of them say that we have here to fulfill some of the disagreeable duties of patriotism. Patriotism! Who were the true patriots of England at the time of the American Revolution— King George and Lord North, who insisted upon subjugation; or Lord Chatham and Edmund Burke, who stood up for American rights and American liberty?

Who were the true patriots of France when, recently, that ghastly farce of a military trial was enacted to sacrifice an innocent man for the honor of the French army and the prestige of the French Republic—who were the true French patriots, those who insisted that the hideous crime of an unjust condemnation must be persisted in, or those who bravely defied the cry of "traitor!" and struggled to undo the wrong, and thus to restore the French Republic to the path of justice and to the esteem of the world? Who are the true patriots in America to-day—those who drag our Republic, once so proud of its high principles and ideals, through the mire of broken pledges, vulgar ambitions and vanities and criminal aggressions—those who do violence to their own moral sense by insisting that, like the Dreyfus iniquity, a criminal course once begun must be persisted in, or those who, fearless of the demagogue clamor, strive to make the flag of the Republic once more what it once was— the flag of justice, liberty and true civilization, and to lift up the American people among the nations of the earth to the proud position of *the* people that have a conscience and obey it?

The country has these days highly and deservedly honored Admiral Dewey as a National hero. Who are his true friends—those who would desecrate Dewey's splendid achievement at Manila by making it the starting-point of criminal aggression, and thus the opening of a most disgraceful and inevitably disastrous chapter of American history, to be remembered with sorrow, or those who strive so to shape the results of that brilliant feat of arms that it may stand in history not as a part of a treacherous conquest, but as a true victory of American good faith in an honest war of liberation and humanity—to be proud of for all time, as Dewey himself no doubt meant it to be?

I know the imperialists will say that I have been pleading here for Aguinaldo and his Filipinos against our Republic. No—not for the Filipinos merely, although as one of those who have grown gray in the struggle for free and honest government, I would never be ashamed to plead for the cause of freedom and independence, even when its banner is carried by dusky and feeble hands. But I am pleading for more. I am pleading for the cause of American honor and self-respect, American interests, American democracy—aye, for the cause of the American people against an administration of our public affairs which has wantonly plunged this country into an iniquitous war; which has disgraced the Republic by a scandalous breach of faith to a people struggling for their freedom whom we had used as allies; which has been systematically seeking to deceive and mislead the public mind by the manufacture of false news; which has struck at the very foundation of our Constitutional government by an Executive usurpation of the war-power; which makes sport of the great principles and high ideals that have been and should ever remain the guiding star of our course; and which, unless stopped in time, will transform this government of the people, for the people and by the people into an imperial government cynically calling itself republican—a government in which the noisy worship of arrogant might will drown the voice of right; which will impose upon the people a burdensome and demoralizing militarism, and which will be driven into a policy of wild and rapacious adventure by the unscrupulous greed of the exploiter—a policy always fatal to democracy.

I plead the cause of the American people against all this, and I here declare my profound conviction that if this administration of our affairs were submitted for judgment to a popular vote on a clear issue, it would be condemned by an overwhelming majority.

I confidently trust that the American people will prove themselves too clear-headed not to appreciate the vital difference between the expansion of the Republic and its free institutions over contiguous territory and kindred populations, which we all gladly welcome if accomplished peaceably and honorably—and imperialism which reaches out for distant lands to be ruled as subject provinces; too intelligent not to perceive that our very first step on the road of imperialism has been a betrayal of the fundamental principles of democracy, followed by disaster and disgrace; too enlightened not to understand that a monarchy may do such things and still remain a strong monarchy, while a democracy cannot do them and still remain a democracy; too wise not to detect the false pride or the dangerous ambitions or the selfish schemes which so often hide themselves under that deceptive cry of mock patriotism: "Our country, right or wrong!" They will not fail to recognize that our dignity, our free institutions and the peace and welfare of this and coming generations of Americans will be secure only as we cling to the watchword of *true* patriotism: "Our country—when right to be kept right; when wrong to be put right."

THEODORE ROOSEVELT

The Man with the Muck-Rake

Washington, D.C., April 14, 1906

O VER a century ago Washington laid the corner-stone of the Capitol in what was then little more than a tract of wooded wilderness here beside the Potomac. We now find it necessary to provide by great additional buildings for the business of the government. This growth in the need for the housing of the government is but a proof and example of the way in which the nation has grown and the sphere of action of the National Government has grown. We now administer the affairs of a nation in which the extraordinary growth of population has been outstripped by the growth of wealth and the growth in complex interests. The material problems that face us to-day are not such as they were in Washington's time, but the underlying facts of human nature are the same now as they were then. Under altered external form we war with the same tendencies toward evil that were evident in Washington's time, and are helped by the same tendencies for good. It is about some of these that I wish to say a word to-day.

In Bunyan's "Pilgrim's Progress" you may recall the description of the Man with the Muck-rake, the man who could look no way but downward, with the muck-rake in his hand; who was offered a celestial crown for his muck-rake, but who would neither look up nor regard the crown he was offered, but continued to rake to himself the filth of the floor.

In "Pilgrim's Progress" the Man with the Muck-rake is set forth as the example of him whose vision is fixed on carnal instead of on spiritual things. Yet he also typifies the man who in this life consistently refuses to see aught that is lofty, and fixes his eyes with solemn intentness only on that which is vile and debasing. Now, it is very necessary that we should not flinch from seeing what is vile and debasing. There is filth on the floor, and it must be scraped up with the muck-rake; and there are times and places where this service is the most needed of all the services that can be performed. But the man who never does anything else, who never thinks or speaks or writes, save of his feats with the muck-rake, speedily becomes, not a help to society, not an incitement to good, but one of the most potent forces for evil.

There are, in the body politic, economic and social, many and grave evils, and there is urgent necessity for the sternest war upon them. There should be relentless exposure of and attack upon every evil man whether politician or business man, every evil practice, whether in politics, in business, or in social life. I hail as a benefactor every writer or speaker, every man who, on the platform, or in book, magazine, or newspaper, with merciless severity makes such attack, provided always that he in his turn remembers that the attack is of use only if it is absolutely truthful. The liar is no whit better than the thief, and if his mendacity takes the form of slander, he may be worse than most thieves. It puts a premium upon knavery untruthfully to attack an honest man, or even with hysterical exaggeration to assail a bad man with untruth. An epidemic of indiscriminate assault upon character does not good, but very great harm. The soul of every scoundrel is gladdened whenever an honest man is assailed, or even when a scoundrel is untruthfully assailed.

Now, it is easy to twist out of shape what I have just said, easy to affect to misunderstand it, and, if it is slurred over in repetition, not difficult really to misunderstand it. Some persons are sincerely incapable of understanding that to denounce mudslinging does not mean the indorsement of whitewashing; and both the interested individuals who need whitewashing, and those others who practise mud-slinging, like to encourage such confusion of ideas. One of the chief counts against those who make indiscriminate assault upon men in business or men in public life, is that they invite a reaction which is sure to tell powerfully in favor of the unscrupulous scoundrel who really ought to be attacked, who ought to be exposed, who ought, if possible, to be put in the penitentiary. If Aristides is praised overmuch as just, people get tired of hearing it; and overcensure of the unjust finally and from similar reasons results in their favor.

Any excess is almost sure to invite a reaction; and, unfortunately, the reaction, instead of taking the form of punishment of those guilty of the excess, is very apt to take the form either of punishment of the unoffending or of giving immunity, and even strength, to offenders. The effort to make financial or political profit out of the destruction of character can only result in public calamity. Gross and reckless assaults on character, whether on the stump or in newspaper, magazine, or book, create a morbid and vicious public sentiment, and at the same time act as a profound deterrent to able men of normal sensitiveness and tend to prevent them from entering the public service at any price. As an instance in point, I may mention that one serious difficulty encountered in getting the right type of men to dig the Panama Canal is the certainty that they will be exposed, both without, and, I am sorry to say, sometimes within, Congress, to utterly reckless assaults on their character and capacity.

At the risk of repetition let me say again that my plea is, not for immunity to but for the most unsparing exposure of the politician who betrays his trust, of the big business man who makes or spends his fortune in illegitimate or corrupt ways. There should be a resolute effort to hunt every such man out of the position he has disgraced. Expose the crime, and hunt down the criminal; but remember that even in the case of crime, if it is attacked in sensational, lurid, and untruthful fashion, the attack may do more damage to the public mind than the crime itself. It is because I feel that there should be no rest in the endless war against the forces of evil that I ask that the war be conducted with sanity as well as with resolution. The men with the muck-rakes are often indispensable to the well-being of society; but only if they know when to stop raking the muck, and to look upward to the celestial crown above them, to the crown of worthy endeavor. There are beautiful things above and roundabout them; and if they gradually grow to feel that the whole world is nothing but muck, their power of usefulness is gone. If the whole picture is painted black there remains no hue whereby to single out the rascals for distinction from their fellows. Such painting finally induces a kind of moral color-blindness; and people affected by it come to the conclusion that no man is really black, and no man really white, but they are all gray. In other words, they neither believe in the truth of the attack, nor in the honesty of the man who is attacked; they grow as suspicious of the accusation as of the offense; it becomes well-nigh hopeless to stir them either to wrath against wrong-doing or to enthusiasm for what is right; and such a mental attitude in the public gives hope to every knave, and is the despair of honest men.

To assail the great and admitted evils of our political and industrial life with such crude and sweeping generalizations as to include decent men in the general condemnation means the searing of the public conscience. There results a general attitude either of cynical belief in and indifference to public corruption or else of a distrustful inability to discriminate between the good and the bad. Either attitude is fraught with untold damage to the country as a whole. The fool who has not sense to discriminate between what is good and what is bad is well-nigh as dangerous as the man who does discriminate and yet chooses the bad. There is nothing more distressing to every good patriot, to every good American, than the hard, scoffing spirit which treats the allegation of dishonesty in a public man as a cause for laughter. Such laughter is worse than the crackling of thorns under a pot, for it denotes not merely the vacant mind, but the heart in which high emotions have been choked before they could grow to fruition.

There is any amount of good in the world, and there never was a time when loftier and more disinterested work for the betterment of mankind was being done than now. The forces that tend for evil are great and terrible, but the forces of truth and love and courage and honesty and generosity and sympathy are also stronger than ever before. It is a foolish and timid, no less than a wicked, thing to blink the fact that the forces of evil are strong, but it is even worse to fail to take into account the strength of the forces that tell for good. Hysterical sensationalism is the very poorest weapon wherewith to fight for lasting righteousness. The men who with stern sobriety and truth assail the many evils of our time, whether in the public press, or in magazines, or in books, are the leaders and allies of all engaged in the work for social and political betterment. But if they give good reason for distrust of what they say, if they chill the ardor of those who demand truth as a primary virtue, they thereby betray the good cause, and play into the hands of the very men against whom they are nominally at war.

In his "Ecclesiastical Polity" that fine old Elizabethan divine, Bishop Hooker, wrote:

"He that goeth about to persuade a multitude that they are not so well governed as they ought to be, shall never want attentive and favorable hearers; because they know the manifold defects whereunto every kind of regimen is subject, but the secret lets and difficulties, which in public proceedings are innumerable and inevitable, they have not ordinarily the judgment to consider."

This truth should be kept constantly in mind by every free people desiring to preserve the sanity and poise indispensable to the permanent success of self-government. Yet, on the other hand, it is vital not to permit this spirit of sanity and self-command to degenerate into mere mental stagnation. Bad though a state of hysterical excitement is, and evil though the results are which come from the violent oscillations such excitement invariably produces, yet a sodden acquiescence in evil is even worse. At this moment we are passing through a period of great unrest—social, political, and industrial unrest. It is of the utmost importance for our future that this should prove to be not the unrest of mere rebelliousness against life, of mere dissatisfaction with the inevitable inequality of conditions, but the unrest of a resolute and eager ambition to secure the betterment of the individual and the nation. So far as this movement of agitation throughout the country takes the form of a fierce discontent with evil, of a determination to punish the authors of evil, whether in industry or politics, the feeling is to be heartily welcomed as a sign of healthy life.

If, on the other hand, it turns into a mere crusade of appetite against appetite, of a contest between the brutal greed of the "have-nots" and the brutal greed of the "haves," then it has no significance for good, but only for evil. If it seeks to establish a line of cleavage, not along the line which divides good men from bad, but along that other line, running at right angles thereto, which divides those who are well off from those who are less well off, then it will be fraught with immeasurable harm to the body politic.

We can no more and no less afford to condone evil in the man of capital than evil in the man of no capital. The wealthy man who exults because there is a failure of justice in the effort to bring some trust magnate to an account for his misdeeds is as bad as, and no worse than, the so-called labor leader who clamorously strives to excite a foul class feeling on behalf of some other labor leader who is implicated in murder. One attitude is as bad as the other, and no worse; in each case the accused is entitled to exact justice; and in neither case is there need of action by others which can be construed into an expression of sympathy for crime.

It is a prime necessity that if the present unrest is to result in permanent good the emotion shall be translated into action, and that the action shall be marked by honesty, sanity, and self-restraint. There is mighty little good in a mere spasm of reform. The reform that counts is that which comes through steady, continuous growth; violent emotionalism leads to exhaustion.

It is important to this people to grapple with the problems connected with the amassing of enormous fortunes, and the use of those fortunes, both corporate and individual, in business. We should discriminate in the sharpest way between fortunes well-won and fortunes ill-won; between those gained as an incident to performing great services to the community as a whole, and those gained in evil fashion by keeping just within the limits of mere law-honesty. Of course no amount of charity in spending such fortunes in any way compensates for misconduct in making them. As a matter of personal conviction, and without pretending to discuss the details or formulate the system, I feel that we shall ultimately have to consider the adoption of some such scheme as that of a progressive tax on all fortunes, beyond a certain amount either given in life or devised or bequeathed upon death to any individual—a tax so framed as to put it out of the power of the owner of one of these enormous fortunes to hand on more than a certain amount to any one individual; the tax, of course, to be imposed by the National and not the State Government. Such taxation should, of course, be aimed merely at the inheritance or transmission in their entirety of those fortunes swollen beyond all healthy limits.

Again, the National Government must in some form exercise supervision over corporations engaged in interstate business—and all large corporations are engaged in interstate business—whether by license or otherwise, so as to permit us to deal with the far-reaching evils of overcapitalization. This year we are making a beginning in the direction of serious effort to settle some of these economic problems by the railway-rate legislation. Such legislation, if so framed, as I am sure it will be, as to secure definite and tangible results, will amount to something of itself; and it will amount to a great deal more in so far as it is taken as a first step in the direction of a policy of superintendence and control over corporate wealth engaged in interstate commerce, this superintendence and control not to be exercised in a spirit of malevolence toward the men who have created the wealth, but with the firm purpose both to do justice to them and to see that they in their turn do justice to the public at large.

The first requisite in the public servants who are to deal in this shape with corporations, whether as legislators or as executives, is honesty. This honesty can be no respecter of persons. There can be no such thing as unilateral honesty. The danger is not really from corrupt corporations; it springs from the corruption itself, whether exercised for or against corporations.

The eighth commandment reads: "Thou shalt not steal." It does not read: "Thou shalt not steal from the rich man." It does not read: "Thou shalt not steal from the poor man." It reads simply and plainly: "Thou shalt not steal." No good whatever will come from that warped and mock morality which denounces the misdeeds of men of wealth and forgets the misdeeds practised at their expense; which denounces bribery, but blinds itself to blackmail; which foams with rage if a corporation secures favors by improper methods, and merely leers with hideous mirth if the corporation is itself wronged. The only public servant who can be trusted honestly to protect the rights of the public against the misdeed of a corporation is that public man who will just as surely protect the corporation itself from wrongful aggression. If a public man is willing to yield to popular clamor and do wrong to the men of wealth or to rich corporations, it may be set down as certain that if the opportunity comes he will secretly and furtively do wrong to the public in the interest of a corporation.

But, in addition to honesty, we need sanity. No honesty will make a public man useful if that man is timid or foolish, if he is a hot-headed zealot or an impracticable visionary. As we strive for reform we find that it is not at all merely the case of a long up-hill pull. On the contrary, there is almost as much of breeching work as of collar work; to depend only on traces means that there will soon be a runaway and an upset. The men of wealth who to-day are trying to prevent the regulation and control of their business in the interest of the public by the proper government authorities will not succeed, in my judgment, in checking the progress of the movement. But if they did succeed they would find that they had sown the wind and would surely reap the whirlwind, for they would ultimately provoke the violent excesses which accompany a reform coming by convulsion instead of by steady and natural growth.

On the other hand, the wild preachers of unrest and discontent, the wild agitators against the entire existing order, the men who act crookedly, whether because of sinister design or from mere puzzle-headedness, the men who preach destruction without proposing any substitute for what they intend to destroy, or who propose a substitute which would be far worse than the existing evils—all these men are the most dangerous opponents of real reform. If they get their way they will lead the people into a deeper pit than any into which they could fall under the present system. If they fail to get their way they will still do incalculable harm by provoking the kind of reaction which, in its revolt against the senseless evil of their teaching, would enthrone more securely than ever the very evils which their misguided followers believe they are attacking.

More important than aught else is the development of the broadest sympathy of man for man. The welfare of the wage-worker, the welfare of the tiller of the soil, upon these depend the welfare of the entire country; their good is not to be sought in pulling down others; but their good must be the prime object of all our statesmanship.

Materially we must strive to secure a broader economic opportunity for all men, so that each shall have a better chance to show the stuff of which he is made. Spiritually and ethically we must strive to bring about clean living and right thinking. We appreciate that the things of the body are important; but we appreciate also that the things of the soul are immeasurably more important. The foundation-stone of national life is, and ever must be, the high individual character of the average citizen.

MARY CHURCH TERRELL

What It Means to be Colored in the Capital of the United States

Washington, D.C., October 10, 1906

WASHINGTON, D.C., has been called "The Colored Man's Paradise." Whether this sobriquet was given to the national capital in bitter irony by a member of the handicapped race, as he reviewed some of his own persecutions and rebuffs, or whether it was given immediately after the war by an ex-slave-holder who for the first time in his life saw colored people walking about like freemen, minus the overseer and his whip, history saith not. It is certain that it would be difficult to find a worse misnomer for Washington than "The Colored Man's Paradise" if so prosaic a consideration as veracity is to determine the appropriateness of a name.

For fifteen years I have resided in Washington, and while it was far from being a paradise for colored people, when I first touched these shores, it has been doing its level best ever since to make conditions for us intolerable. As a colored woman I might enter Washington any night, a stranger in a strange land, and walk miles without finding a place to lay my head. Unless I happened to know colored people who live here or ran across a chance acquaintance who could recommend a colored boarding-house to me, I should be obliged to spend the entire night wandering about. Indians, Chinamen, Filipinos, Japanese and representatives of any other dark race can find hotel accommodations, if they can pay for them. The colored man alone is thrust out of the hotels of the national capital like a leper.

As a colored woman I may walk from the Capitol to the White House, ravenously hungry and abundantly supplied with money with which to purchase a meal, without finding a single restaurant in which I would be permitted to take a morsel of food, if it was patronized by white people, unless I were willing to sit behind a screen. As a colored woman I cannot visit the tomb of the Father of this country, which owes its very existence to the love of freedom in the human heart and which stands for equal opportunity to all, without being forced to sit in the Jim Crow section of an electric car which starts from the very heart of the city—midway between the Capitol and the White House. If I refuse thus to be humiliated, I am cast into jail and forced to pay a fine for violating the Virginia laws. Every hour in the day Jim Crow cars filled with colored people, many of whom are intelligent and well to do, enter and leave the national capital.

As a colored woman I may enter more than one white church in Washington without receiving that welcome which as a human being I have a right to expect in the sanctuary of God. Sometimes the color blindness of the usher takes on that peculiar form which prevents a dark face from making any impression whatsoever upon his retina, so that it is impossible for him to see colored people at all. If he is not so afflicted, after keeping a colored man or woman waiting a long time, he will ungraciously show these dusky Christians who have had the temerity to thrust themselves into a temple where only the fair of face are expected to worship God to a seat in the rear, which is named in honor of a certain personage, well known in this country, and commonly called Jim Crow.

Unless I am willing to engage in a few menial occupations, in which the pay for my services would be very poor, there is no way for me to earn an honest living, if I am not a trained nurse or a dressmaker or can secure a position as teacher in the public schools, which is exceedingly difficult to do. It matters not what my intellectual attainments may be or how great is the need of the services of a competent person, if I try to enter many of the numerous vocations in which my white sisters are allowed to engage, the door is shut in my face.

From one Washington theater I am excluded altogether. In the remainder certain seats are set aside for colored people, and it is almost impossible to secure others. I once telephoned to the ticket seller just before a matinee and asked if a neat-appearing colored nurse would be allowed to sit in the parquet with her little white charge, and the answer rushed quickly and positively thru the receiver—NO. When I remonstrated a bit and told him that in some of the theaters colored nurses were allowed to sit with the white children for whom they cared, the ticket seller told me that in Washington it was very poor policy to employ colored nurses, for they were excluded from many places where white girls would be allowed to take children for pleasure.

If I possess artistic talent, there is not a single art school of repute which will admit me. A few years ago a colored woman who possessed great talent submitted some drawings to the Corcoran Art School, of Washington, which were accepted by the committee of awards, who sent her a ticket entitling her to a course in this school. But when the committee discovered that the young woman was colored, they declined to admit her, and told her that if they had suspected that her drawings had been made by a colored woman, they would not have examined them at all. The efforts of Frederick Douglass and a lawyer of great repute who took a keen interest in the affair were unavailing. In order to cultivate her talent this young woman was forced to leave her comfortable home in Washington and incur the expense of going to New York. Having entered the Woman's Art School of Cooper Union, she graduated with honor, and then went to Paris to continue her studies, where she achieved signal success and was complimented by some of the greatest living artists in France.

With the exception of the Catholic University, there is not a single white college in the national capital to which colored people are admitted, no matter how great their ability, how lofty their ambition, how unexceptionable their character or how great their thirst for knowledge may be.

A few years ago the Columbian Law School admitted colored students, but in deference to the Southern white students the authorities have decided to exclude them altogether.

Some time ago a young woman who had already attracted some attention in the literary world by her volume of short stories answered an advertisement which appeared in a Washington newspaper, which called for the services of a skilled stenographer and expert typewriter. It is unnecessary to state the reasons why a young woman whose literary ability was so great as that possessed by the one referred to should decide to earn money in this way. The applicants were requested to send specimens of their work and answer certain questions concerning their experience and their speed before they called in person. In reply to her application the young colored woman, who, by the way, is very fair and attractive indeed, received a letter from the firm stating that her references and experience were the most satisfactory that had been sent and requesting her to call. When she presented herself there was some doubt in the mind of the man to whom she was directed concerning her racial pedigree, so he asked her point-blank whether she was colored or white. When she confessed the truth the merchant expressed great sorrow and deep regret that he could not avail himself of the services of so competent a person, but frankly admitted that employing a colored woman in his establishment in any except a menial position was simply out of the question.

Another young friend had an experience which, for some reasons, was still more disheartening and bitter than the one just mentioned. In order to secure lucrative employment she left Washington and went to New York. There she worked her way up in one of the largest dry goods stores till she was placed as saleswoman in the cloak department. Tired of being separated from her family, she decided to return to Washington, feeling sure that, with her experience and her fine recommendation from the New York firm, she could easily secure employment. Nor was she overconfident, for the proprietor of one of the largest dry goods stores in her native city was glad to secure the services of a young woman who brought such hearty credentials from New York. She had not been in this store very long, however, before she called upon me one day and asked me to intercede with the proprietor in her behalf, saying that she had been discharged that afternoon because it had been discovered that she was colored. When I called upon my young friend's employer he made no effort to avoid the issue, as I feared he would. He did not say he had discharged the young saleswoman because she had not given satisfaction, as he might easily have done. On the contrary, he admitted without the slightest hesitation that the young woman he had just discharged was one of the best clerks he had ever had. In the cloak department, where she had been assigned, she had been a brilliant success, he said. "But I cannot keep Miss Smith in my employ," he concluded. "Are you not master of your own store?" I ventured to inquire. The proprietor of this store was a Jew, and I felt that it was particularly cruel, unnatural and cold-blooded for the representative of one oppressed and persecuted race to deal so harshly and unjustly with a member of another. I had intended to make this point when I decided to intercede for my young friend, but when I thought how a reference to the persecution of his own race would wound his feelings, the words froze on my lips. "When I first heard your friend was colored," he explained, "I did not believe it and said so to the clerks who made the statement. Finally, the girls who had been most pronounced in their opposition to working in a store with a colored girl came to me in a body and threatened to strike. 'Strike away,' said I, 'your places will be easily filled.' Then they started on another tack. Delegation after delegation began to file down to my office, some of the women my very best customers, to protest against my employing a colored girl. Moreover, they threatened to boycott my store if I did not discharge her at once. Then it became a question of bread and butter and I yielded to the inevitable—that's all. Now," said he, concluding, "if I lived in a great, cosmopolitan city like New York, I should do as I pleased, and refuse to discharge a girl simply because she was colored." But I thought of a similar incident that happened in New York. I remembered that a colored woman, as fair as a lily and as beautiful as a Madonna, who was the head saleswoman in a large department store in New York, had been discharged, after she had held this position for years, when the proprietor accidentally discovered that a fatal drop of African blood was percolating somewhere thru her veins.

Not only can colored women secure no employment in the Washington stores, department and otherwise, except as menials, and such positions, of course, are few, but even as customers they are not infrequently treated with discourtesy both by the clerks and the proprietor himself. Following the trend of the times, the senior partner of the largest and best department store in Washington, who originally hailed from Boston, once the home of William Lloyd Garrison, Wendell Phillips, and Charles Sumner, if my memory serves me right, decided to open a restaurant in his store. Tired and hungry after her morning's shopping a colored school teacher, whose relation to her African progenitors is so remote as scarcely to be dis-

cernible to the naked eye, took a seat at one of the tables in the
restaurant of this Boston store. After sitting unnoticed a long
time the colored teacher asked a waiter who passed her by if she
would not take her order. She was quickly informed that colored people could not be served in that restaurant and was
obliged to leave in confusion and shame, much to the amusement of the waiters and the guests who had noticed the incident. Shortly after that a teacher in Howard University, one of
the best schools for colored youth in the country, was similarly
insulted in the restaurant of the same store.

In one of the Washington theaters from which colored
people are excluded altogether, members of the race have been
viciously assaulted several times, for the proprietor well knows
that colored people have no redress for such discriminations
against them in the District courts. Not long ago a colored clerk
in one of the departments who looks more like his paternal ancestors who fought for the lost cause than his grandmothers
who were the victims of the peculiar institution, bought a ticket
for the parquet of this theater in which colored people are
nowhere welcome, for himself and mother, whose complexion
is a bit swarthy. The usher refused to allow the young man to
take the seats for which his tickets called and tried to snatch
from him the coupons. A scuffle ensued and both mother and
son were ejected by force. A suit was brought against the proprietor and the damages awarded the injured man and his
mother amounted to the munificent sum of one cent. One of
the teachers in the Colored High School received similar treatment in the same theater.

Not long ago one of my little daughter's bosom friends fig-
ured in one of the most pathetic instances of which I have ever
heard. A gentleman who is very fond of children promised to
take six little girls in his neighborhood to a matinee. It happened that he himself and five of his little friends were so fair
that they easily passed muster, as they stood in judgment before
the ticket seller and the ticket taker. Three of the little girls were
sisters, two of whom were very fair and the other a bit brown.
Just as this little girl, who happened to be last in the procession, went by the ticket taker, that argus-eyed sophisticated
gentleman detected something which caused a deep, dark
frown to mantle his brow and he did not allow her to pass. "I

guess you have made a mistake," he called to the host of this theater party. "Those little girls," pointing to the fair ones, "may be admitted, but this one," designating the brown one, "can't." But the colored man was quite equal to the emergency. Fairly frothing at the mouth with anger, he asked the ticket taker what he meant, what he was trying to insinuate about that particular little girl. "Do you mean to tell me," he shouted in rage, "that I must go clear to the Philippine Islands to bring this child to the United States and then I can't take her to the theater in the National Capital?" The little ruse succeeded brilliantly, as he knew it would. "Beg your pardon," said the ticket taker, "don't know what I was thinking about. Of course she can go in."

"What was the matter with me this afternoon? mother," asked the little brown girl innocently, when she mentioned the affair at home. "Why did the man at the theater let my two sisters and the other girls in and try to keep me out?" In relating this incident, the child's mother told me her little girl's question, which showed such blissful ignorance of the depressing, cruel conditions which confronted her, completely unnerved her for a time.

Altho white and colored teachers are under the same Board of Education and the system for the children of both races is said to be uniform, prejudice against the colored teachers in the public schools is manifested in a variety of ways. From 1870 to 1900 there was a colored superintendent at the head of the colored schools. During all that time the directors of the cooking, sewing, physical culture, manual training, music and art departments were colored people. Six years ago a change was inaugurated. The colored superintendent was legislated out of office and the directorships, without a single exception, were taken from colored teachers and given to the whites. There was no complaint about the work done by the colored directors, no more than is heard about every officer in every school. The directors of the art and physical culture departments were particularly fine. Now, no matter how competent or superior the colored teachers in our public schools may be, they know that they can never rise to the height of a directorship, can never hope to be more than an assistant and receive the meager salary therefor, unless the present regime is radically changed.

Not long ago one of the most distinguished kindergartners in the country came to deliver a course of lectures in Washington. The colored teachers were eager to attend, but they could not buy the coveted privilege for love or money. When they appealed to the director of kindergartens, they were told that the expert kindergartner had come to Washington under the auspices of private individuals, so that she could not possibly have them admitted. Realizing what a loss colored teachers had sustained in being deprived of the information and inspiration which these lectures afforded, one of the white teachers volunteered to repeat them as best she could for the benefit of her colored co-laborers for half the price she herself had paid, and the proposition was eagerly accepted by some.

Strenuous efforts are being made to run Jim Crow street cars in the national capital. "Resolved, that a Jim Crow law should be adopted and enforced in the District of Columbia," was the subject of a discussion engaged in last January by the Columbian Debating Society of the George Washington University in our national capital, and the decision was rendered in favor of the affirmative. Representative Heflin, of Alabama, who introduced a bill providing for Jim Crow street cars in the District of Columbia last winter, has just received a letter from the president of the East Brookland Citizens' Association "indorsing the movement for separate street cars and sincerely hoping that you will be successful in getting this enacted into a law as soon as possible." Brookland is a suburb of Washington.

The colored laborer's path to a decent livelihood is by no means smooth. Into some of the trades unions here he is admitted, while from others he is excluded altogether. By the union men this is denied, altho I am personally acquainted with skilled workmen who tell me they are not admitted into the unions because they are colored. But even when they are allowed to join the unions they frequently derive little benefit, owing to certain tricks of the trade. When the word passes round that help is needed and colored laborers apply, they are often told by the union officials that they have secured all the men they needed, because the places are reserved for white men, until they have been provided with jobs, and colored men must remain idle, unless the supply of white men is too small.

I am personally acquainted with one of the most skilful laborers in the hardware business in Washington. For thirty years he has been working for the same firm. He told me he could not join the union, and that his employer had been almost forced to discharge him, because the union men threatened to boycott his store if he did not. If another man could have been found at the time to take his place he would have lost his job, he said. When no other human being can bring a refractory chimney or stove to its senses, this colored man is called upon as the court of last appeal. If he fails to subdue it, it is pronounced a hopeless case at once. And yet this expert workman receives much less for his services than do white men who cannot compare with him in skill.

And so I might go on citing instance after instance to show the variety of ways in which our people are sacrificed on the altar of prejudice in the Capital of the United States and how almost insurmountable are the obstacles which block his path to success. Early in life many a colored youth is so appalled by the helplessness and the hopelessness of his situation in this country that, in a sort of stoical despair he resigns himself to his fate. "What is the good of our trying to acquire an education? We can't all be preachers, teachers, doctors and lawyers. Besides those professions, there is almost nothing for colored people to do but engage in the most menial occupations, and we do not need an education for that." More than once such remarks, uttered by young men and women in our public schools who possess brilliant intellects, have wrung my heart.

It is impossible for any white person in the United States, no matter how sympathetic and broad, to realize what life would mean to him if his incentive to effort were suddenly snatched away. To the lack of incentive to effort, which is the awful shadow under which we live, may be traced the wreck and ruin of scores of colored youth. And surely nowhere in the world do oppression and persecution based solely on the color of the skin appear more hateful and hideous than in the capital of the United States, because the chasm between the principles upon which this Government was founded, in which it still professes to believe, and those which are daily practiced under the protection of the flag, yawns so wide and deep.

THEODORE ROOSEVELT

The New Nationalism

Osawatomie, Kansas, August 31, 1910

WE COME here to-day to commemorate one of the epoch-making events of the long struggle for the rights of man —the long struggle for the uplift of humanity. Our country— this great Republic—means nothing unless it means the triumph of a real democracy, the triumph of popular government, and, in the long run, of an economic system under which each man shall be guaranteed the opportunity to show the best that there is in him. That is why the history of America is now the central feature of the history of the world; for the world has set its face hopefully toward our democracy; and, O my fellow citizens, each one of you carries on your shoulders not only the burden of doing well for the sake of your own country, but the burden of doing well and of seeing that this nation does well for the sake of mankind.

There have been two great crises in our country's history: first, when it was formed, and then, again, when it was perpetuated; and, in the second of these great crises—in the time of stress and strain which culminated in the Civil War, on the outcome of which depended the justification of what had been done earlier, you men of the Grand Army, you men who fought through the Civil War, not only did you justify your generation, not only did you render life worth living for our generation, but you justified the wisdom of Washington and Washington's colleagues. If this Republic had been founded by them only to be split asunder into fragments when the strain came, then the judgment of the world would have been that Washington's work was not worth doing. It was you who crowned Washington's work, as you carried to achievement the high purpose of Abraham Lincoln.

Now, with this second period of our history the name of John Brown will be forever associated; and Kansas was the theatre upon which the first act of the second of our great national life dramas was played. It was the result of the struggle in Kansas which determined that our country should be in deed as well as in name devoted to both union and freedom; that the great experiment of democratic government on a national scale should succeed and not fail. In name we had the Declaration of Independence in 1776; but we gave the lie by our acts to the words of the Declaration of Independence until 1865; and words count for nothing except in so far as they represent acts. This is true everywhere; but, O my friends, it should be truest of all in political life. A broken promise is bad enough in private life. It is worse in the field of politics. No man is worth his salt in public life who makes on the stump a pledge which he does not keep after election; and, if he makes such a pledge and does not keep it, hunt him out of public life. I care for the great deeds of the past chiefly as spurs to drive us onward in the present. I speak of the men of the past partly that they may be honored by our praise of them, but more that they may serve as examples for the future.

It was a heroic struggle; and, as is inevitable with all such struggles, it had also a dark and terrible side. Very much was done of good, and much also of evil; and, as was inevitable in such a period of revolution, often the same man did both good and evil. For our great good fortune as a nation, we, the people of the United States as a whole, can now afford to forget the evil, or, at least, to remember it without bitterness, and to fix our eyes with pride only on the good that was accomplished. Even in ordinary times there are very few of us who do not see the problems of life as through a glass, darkly; and when the glass is clouded by the murk of furious popular passion, the vision of the best and the bravest is dimmed. Looking back, we are all of us now able to do justice to the valor and the disinterestedness and the love of the right, as to each it was given to see the right, shown both by the men of the North and the men of the South in that contest which was finally decided by the attitude of the West. We can admire the heroic valor, the sincerity, the self-devotion shown alike by the men who wore the blue and the men who wore the gray; and our sadness that such men should have had to fight one another is tempered by the glad knowledge that ever hereafter their descendants shall be found fighting side by side, struggling in peace as well as in war for the uplift of their common country, all alike resolute to raise to the highest pitch of honor and usefulness the nation to which they all belong. As for the veterans of the Grand Army of the Republic, they deserve honor and recognition such as is paid to no other citizens of the Republic; for to them the republic owes its all; for to them it owes its very existence. It is because of what you and your comrades did in the dark years that we of to-day walk, each of us, head erect, and proud that we belong, not to one of a dozen little squabbling contemptible commonwealths, but to the mightiest nation upon which the sun shines.

I do not speak of this struggle of the past merely from the historic standpoint. Our interest is primarily in the application to-day of the lessons taught by the contest of half a century ago. It is of little use for us to pay lip-loyalty to the mighty men of the past unless we sincerely endeavor to apply to the problems of the present precisely the qualities which in other crises enabled the men of that day to meet those crises. It is half melancholy and half amusing to see the way in which well-meaning people gather to do honor to the men who, in company with John Brown, and under the lead of Abraham Lincoln, faced and solved the great problems of the nineteenth century, while, at the same time, these same good people nervously shrink from, or frantically denounce, those who are trying to meet the problems of the twentieth century in the spirit which was accountable for the successful solution of the problems of Lincoln's time.

Of that generation of men to whom we owe so much, the man to whom we owe most is, of course, Lincoln. Part of our debt to him is because he forecast our present struggle and saw the way out. He said:

"I hold that while man exists it is his duty to improve not only his own condition, but to assist in ameliorating mankind."

And again:

"Labor is prior to, and independent of, capital. Capital is only the fruit of labor, and could never have existed if labor had not first existed. Labor is the superior of capital, and deserves much the higher consideration."

If that remark was original with me, I should be even more

strongly denounced as a Communist agitator than I shall be anyhow. It is Lincoln's. I am only quoting it; and that is one side; that is the side the capitalist should hear. Now, let the working man hear his side.

"Capital has its rights, which are as worthy of protection as any other rights. . . . Nor should this lead to a war upon the owners of property. Property is the fruit of labor; . . . property is desirable; is a positive good in the world."

And then comes a thoroughly Lincolnlike sentence:

"Let not him who is houseless pull down the house of another, but let him work diligently and build one for himself, thus by example assuring that his own shall be safe from violence when built."

It seems to me that, in these words, Lincoln took substantially the attitude that we ought to take; he showed the proper sense of proportion in his relative estimates of capital and labor, of human rights and property rights. Above all, in this speech, as in many others, he taught a lesson in wise kindliness and charity; an indispensable lesson to us of to-day. But this wise kindliness and charity never weakened his arm or numbed his heart. We cannot afford weakly to blind ourselves to the actual conflict which faces us to-day. The issue is joined, and we must fight or fail.

In every wise struggle for human betterment one of the main objects, and often the only object, has been to achieve in large measure equality of opportunity. In the struggle for this great end, nations rise from barbarism to civilization, and through it people press forward from one stage of enlightenment to the next. One of the chief factors in progress is the destruction of special privilege. The essence of any struggle for healthy liberty has always been, and must always be, to take from some one man or class of men the right to enjoy power, or wealth, or position, or immunity, which has not been earned by service to his or their fellows. That is what you fought for in the Civil War, and that is what we strive for now.

At many stages in the advance of humanity, this conflict between the men who possess more than they have earned and the men who have earned more than they possess is the central condition of progress. In our day it appears as the struggle of freemen to gain and hold the right of self-government as against the special interests, who twist the methods of free government into machinery for defeating the popular will. At every stage, and under all circumstances, the essence of the struggle is to equalize opportunity, destroy privilege, and give to the life and citizenship of every individual the highest possible value both to himself and to the commonwealth. That is nothing new. All I ask in civil life is what you fought for in the Civil War. I ask that civil life be carried on according to the spirit in which the army was carried on. You never get perfect justice, but the effort in handling the army was to bring to the front the men who could do the job. Nobody grudged promotion to Grant, or Sherman, or Thomas, or Sheridan, because they earned it. The only complaint was when a man got promotion which he did not earn.

Practical equality of opportunity for all citizens, when we achieve it, will have two great results. First, every man will have a fair chance to make of himself all that in him lies; to reach the highest point to which his capacities, unassisted by special privilege of his own and unhampered by the special privilege of others, can carry him, and to get for himself and his family substantially what he has earned. Second, equality of opportunity means that the commonwealth will get from every citizen the highest service of which he is capable. No man who carries the burden of the special privileges of another can give to the commonwealth that service to which it is fairly entitled.

I stand for the square deal. But when I say that I am for the square deal, I mean not merely that I stand for fair play under the present rules of the game, but that I stand for having those rules changed so as to work for a more substantial equality of opportunity and of reward for equally good service. One word of warning, which, I think, is hardly necessary in Kansas. When I say I want a square deal for the poor man, I do not mean that I want a square deal for the man who remains poor because he has not got the energy to work for himself. If a man who has had a chance will not make good, then he has got to quit. And you men of the Grand Army, you want justice for the brave man who fought, and punishment for the coward who shirked his work. Is not that so?

Now, this means that our government, National and State, must be freed from the sinister influence or control of special interests. Exactly as the special interests of cotton and slavery threatened our political integrity before the Civil War, so now the great special business interests too often control and corrupt the men and methods of government for their own profit. We must drive the special interests out of politics. That is one of our tasks to-day. Every special interest is entitled to justice— full, fair, and complete—and, now, mind you, if there were any attempt by mob-violence to plunder and work harm to the special interest, whatever it may be, that I most dislike, and the wealthy man, whomsoever he may be, for whom I have the greatest contempt, I would fight for him, and you would if you were worth your salt. He should have justice. For every special interest is entitled to justice, but not one is entitled to a vote in Congress, to a voice on the bench, or to representation in any public office. The Constitution guarantees protection to property, and we must make that promise good. But it does not give the right of suffrage to any corporation.

The true friend of property, the true conservative, is he who insists that property shall be the servant and not the master of the commonwealth; who insists that the creature of man's making shall be the servant and not the master of the man who made it. The citizens of the United States must effectively control the mighty commercial forces which they have themselves called into being.

There can be no effective control of corporations while their political activity remains. To put an end to it will be neither a short nor an easy task, but it can be done.

We must have complete and effective publicity of corporate affairs, so that the people may know beyond peradventure whether the corporations obey the law and whether their management entities them to the confidence of the public. It is necessary that laws should be passed to prohibit the use of corporate funds directly or indirectly for political purposes; it is still more necessary that such laws should be thoroughly enforced. Corporate expenditures for political purposes, and especially such expenditures by public-service corporations, have supplied one of the principal sources of corruption in our political affairs.

It has become entirely clear that we must have government supervision of the capitalization, not only of public-service corporations, including, particularly, railways, but of all corporations doing an interstate business. I do not wish to see the nation forced into the ownership of the railways if it can possibly be avoided, and the only alternative is thoroughgoing and effective regulation, which shall be based on a full knowledge of all the facts, including a physical valuation of property. This physical valuation is not needed, or, at least, is very rarely needed, for fixing rates; but it is needed as the basis of honest capitalization.

We have come to recognize that franchises should never be granted except for a limited time, and never without proper provision for compensation to the public. It is my personal belief that the same kind and degree of control and supervision which should be exercised over public-service corporations should be extended also to combinations which control necessaries of life, such as meat, oil, and coal, or which deal in them on an important scale. I have no doubt that the ordinary man who has control of them is much like ourselves. I have no doubt he would like to do well, but I want to have enough supervision to help him realize that desire to do well.

I believe that the officers, and, especially, the directors, of corporations should be held personally responsible when any corporation breaks the law.

Combinations in industry are the result of an imperative economic law which cannot be repealed by political legislation. The effort at prohibiting all combination has substantially failed. The way out lies, not in attempting to prevent such combinations, but in completely controlling them in the interest of the public welfare. For that purpose the Federal Bureau of Corporations is an agency of first importance. Its powers, and, therefore, its efficiency, as well as that of the Interstate Commerce Commission, should be largely increased. We have a right to expect from the Bureau of Corporations and from the Interstate Commerce Commission a very high grade of public service. We should be as sure of the proper conduct of the interstate railways and the proper management of interstate business as we are now sure of the conduct and management of the national banks, and we should have as effective supervision in one case as in the other. The Hepburn Act, and the amendment to the act in the shape in which it finally passed

Congress at the last session, represent a long step in advance, and we must go yet further.

There is a wide-spread belief among our people that, under the methods of making tariffs which have hitherto obtained, the special interests are too influential. Probably this is true of both the big special interests and the little special interests. These methods have put a premium on selfishness, and, naturally, the selfish big interests have gotten more than their smaller, though equally selfish, brothers. The duty of Congress is to provide a method by which the interest of the whole people shall be all that receives consideration. To this end there must be an expert tariff commission, wholly removed from the possibility of political pressure or of improper business influence. Such a commission can find the real difference between cost of production, which is mainly the difference of labor cost here and abroad. As fast as its recommendations are made, I believe in revising one schedule at a time. A general revision of the tariff almost inevitably leads to log-rolling and the subordination of the general public interest to local and special interests.

The absence of effective State, and, especially, national, restraint upon unfair money-getting has tended to create a small class of enormously wealthy and economically powerful men, whose chief object is to hold and increase their power. The prime need is to change the conditions which enable these men to accumulate power which it is not for the general welfare that they should hold or exercise. We grudge no man a fortune which represents his own power and sagacity, when exercised with entire regard to the welfare of his fellows. Again, comrades over there, take the lesson from your own experience. Not only did you not grudge, but you gloried in the promotion of the great generals who gained their promotion by leading the army to victory. So it is with us. We grudge no man a fortune in civil life if it is honorably obtained and well used. It is not even enough that it should have been gained without doing damage to the community. We should permit it to be gained only so long as the gaining represents benefit to the community. This, I know, implies a policy of a far more active governmental interference with social and economic conditions in this country than we have yet had, but I think we have got to face the fact that such an increase in governmental control is now necessary.

No man should receive a dollar unless that dollar has been fairly earned. Every dollar received should represent a dollar's worth of service rendered—not gambling in stocks, but service rendered. The really big fortune, the swollen fortune, by the mere fact of its size acquires qualities which differentiate it in kind as well as in degree from what is possessed by men of relatively small means. Therefore, I believe in a graduated income tax on big fortunes, and in another tax which is far more easily collected and far more effective—a graduated inheritance tax on big fortunes, properly safeguarded against evasion and increasing rapidly in amount with the size of the estate.

The people of the United States suffer from periodical financial panics to a degree substantially unknown among the other nations which approach us in financial strength. There is no reason why we should suffer what they escape. It is of profound importance that our financial system should be promptly investigated, and so thoroughly and effectively revised as to make it certain that hereafter our currency will no longer fail at critical times to meet our needs

It is hardly necessary for me to repeat that I believe in an efficient army and a navy large enough to secure for us abroad that respect which is the surest guaranty of peace. A word of special warning to my fellow citizens who are as progressive as I hope I am. I want them to keep up their interest in our internal affairs; and I want them also continually to remember Uncle Sam's interests abroad. Justice and fair dealing among nations rest upon principles identical with those which control justice and fair dealing among the individuals of which nations are composed, with the vital exception that each nation must do its own part in international police work. If you get into trouble here, you can call for the police; but if Uncle Sam gets into trouble, he has got to be his own policeman, and I want to see him strong enough to encourage the peaceful aspirations of other peoples in connection with us. I believe in national friendships and heartiest good-will to all nations; but national friendships, like those between men, must be founded on respect as well as on liking, on forbearance as well as upon trust. I should be heartily ashamed of any American who did not try to make the American Government act as justly toward the other nations in international relations as he himself would act toward any individual in private relations. I should be heartily ashamed to see us wrong a weaker power, and I should hang my head forever if we tamely suffered wrong from a stronger power.

Of conservation I shall speak more at length elsewhere. Conservation means development as much as it does protection. I recognize the right and duty of this generation to develop and use the natural resources of our land; but I do not recognize the right to waste them, or to rob, by wasteful use, the generations that come after us. I ask nothing of the nation except that it so behave as each farmer here behaves with reference to his own children. That farmer is a poor creature who skins the land and leaves it worthless to his children. The farmer is a good farmer who, having enabled the land to support himself and to provide for the education of his children, leaves it to them a little better than he found it himself. I believe the same thing of a nation.

Moreover, I believe that the natural resources must be used for the benefit of all our people, and not monopolized for the benefit of the few, and here again is another case in which I am accused of taking a revolutionary attitude. People forget now that one hundred years ago there were public men of good character who advocated the nation selling its public lands in great quantities, so that the nation could get the most money out of it, and giving it to the men who could cultivate it for their own uses. We took the proper democratic ground that the land should be granted in small sections to the men who were actually to till it and live on it. Now, with the water-power, with the forests, with the mines, we are brought face to face with the fact that there are many people who will go with us in conserving the resources only if they are to be allowed to exploit them for their benefit. That is one of the fundamental reasons why the special interests should be driven out of politics. Of all the questions which can come before this nation, short of the actual preservation of its existence in a great war, there is none which compares in importance with the great central task of leaving this land even a better land for our descendants than it is for us, and training them into a better race to inhabit the land and pass it on. Conservation is a great moral issue, for it involves the patriotic duty of insuring the safety and continuance of the nation. Let me add that the health and vitality of our people are at least as well worth conserving as their forests, waters, lands, and minerals, and in this great work the national government must bear a most important part.

I have spoken elsewhere also of the great task which lies before the farmers of the country to get for themselves and their wives and children not only the benefits of better farming, but also those of better business methods and better conditions of life on the farm. The burden of this great task will fall, as it should, mainly upon the great organizations of the farmers themselves. I am glad it will, for I believe they are all well able to handle it. In particular, there are strong reasons why the Departments of Agriculture of the various States, the United States Department of Agriculture, and the agricultural colleges and experiment stations should extend their work to cover all phases of farm life, instead of limiting themselves, as they have far too often limited themselves in the past, solely to the question of the production of crops. And now a special word to the farmer. I want to see him make the farm as fine a farm as it can be made; and let him remember to see that the improvement goes on indoors as well as out; let him remember that the farmer's wife should have her share of thought and attention just as much as the farmer himself.

Nothing is more true than that excess of every kind is followed by reaction; a fact which should be pondered by reformer and reactionary alike. We are face to face with new conceptions of the relations of property to human welfare, chiefly because certain advocates of the rights of property as against the rights of men have been pushing their claims too far. The man who wrongly holds that every human right is secondary to his profit must now give way to the advocate of human welfare, who rightly maintains that every man holds his property subject to the general right of the community to regulate its use to whatever degree the public welfare may require it.

But I think we may go still further. The right to regulate the use of wealth in the public interest is universally admitted. Let us admit also the right to regulate the terms and conditions of labor, which is the chief element of wealth, directly in the interest of the common good. The fundamental thing to do for every man is to give him a chance to reach a place in which he will make the greatest possible contribution to the public welfare. Understand what I say there. Give him a chance, not push him up if he will not be pushed. Help any man who stumbles; if he lies down, it is a poor job to try to carry him; but if he is a worthy man, try your best to see that he gets a chance to show the worth that is in him. No man can be a good citizen unless he has a wage more than sufficient to cover the bare cost of living, and hours of labor short enough so that after his day's work is done he will have time and energy to bear his share in the management of the community, to help in carrying the general load. We keep countless men from being good citizens by the conditions of life with which we surround them. We need comprehensive workmen's compensation acts, both State and national laws to regulate child labor and work for women, and, especially, we need in our common schools not merely education in book-learning, but also practical training for daily life and work. We need to enforce better sanitary conditions for our workers and to extend the use of safety appliances for our workers in industry and commerce, both within and between the States. Also, friends, in the interest of the working man himself we need to set our faces like flint against mob-violence just as against corporate greed; against violence and injustice and lawlessness by wage-workers just as much as against lawless cunning and greed and selfish arrogance of employers. If I could ask but one thing of my fellow countrymen, my request would be that, whenever they go in for reform, they remember the two sides, and that they always exact justice from one side as much as from the other. I have small use for the public servant who can always see and denounce the corruption of the capitalist, but who cannot persuade himself, especially before election, to say a word about lawless mob-violence. And I have equally small use for the man, be he a judge on the bench, or editor of a great paper, or wealthy and influential private citizen, who can see clearly enough and denounce the lawlessness of mob-violence, but whose eyes are closed so that he is blind when the question is one of corruption in business on a gigantic scale. Also remember what I said about excess in reformer and reactionary alike. If the reactionary man, who thinks of nothing but the rights of property, could have his way, he would bring about a revolution; and one of my chief fears in connection with progress comes because I do not want to see our people, for lack of proper leadership, compelled to follow men whose intentions are excellent, but whose eyes are a little too wild to make it really safe to trust them. Here in Kansas there is one paper which habitually denounces me as the tool of Wall Street, and at the same time frantically repudiates the statement that I am a Socialist on the ground that that is an unwarranted slander of the Socialists.

National efficiency has many factors. It is a necessary result of the principle of conservation widely applied. In the end it will determine our failure or success as a nation. National efficiency has to do, not only with natural resources and with men, but it is equally concerned with institutions. The State must be made efficient for the work which concerns only the people of the State; and the nation for that which concerns all the people. There must remain no neutral ground to serve as a refuge for lawbreakers, and especially for lawbreakers of great wealth, who can hire the vulpine legal cunning which will teach them how to avoid both jurisdictions. It is a misfortune when the national legislature fails to do its duty in providing a national remedy, so that the only national activity is the purely negative activity of the judiciary in forbidding the State to exercise power in the premises.

I do not ask for overcentralization; but I do ask that we work in a spirit of broad and far-reaching nationalism when we work for what concerns our people as a whole. We are all Americans. Our common interests are as broad as the continent. I speak to you here in Kansas exactly as I would speak in New York or Georgia, for the most vital problems are those which affect us all alike. The National Government belongs to the whole American people, and where the whole American people are interested, that interest can be guarded effectively only by the National Government. The betterment which we seek must be accomplished, I believe, mainly through the National Government.

The American people are right in demanding that New Nationalism, without which we cannot hope to deal with new problems. The New Nationalism puts the national need before sectional or personal advantage. It is impatient of the utter confusion that results from local legislatures attempting to treat national issues as local issues. It is still more impatient of the impotence which springs from overdivision of governmental powers, the impotence which makes it possible for local selfishness or for legal cunning, hired by wealthy special interests, to bring national activities to a deadlock. This New Nationalism regards the executive power as the steward of the public welfare. It demands of the judiciary that it shall be interested primarily in human welfare rather than in property, just as it demands that the representative body shall represent all the people rather than any one class or section of the people.

I believe in shaping the ends of government to protect property as well as human welfare. Normally, and in the long run, the ends are the same; but whenever the alternative must be faced, I am for men and not for property, as you were in the Civil War. I am far from underestimating the importance of dividends; but I rank dividends below human character. Again, I do not have any sympathy with the reformer who says be does not care for dividends. Of course, economic welfare is necessary, for a man must pull his own weight and be able to support his family. I know well that the reformers must not bring upon the people economic ruin, or the reforms themselves will go down in the ruin. But we must be ready to face temporary disaster, whether or not brought on by those who will war against us to the knife. Those who oppose all reform will do well to remember that ruin in its worst form is inevitable if our national life brings us nothing better than swollen fortunes for the few and the triumph in both politics and business of a sordid and selfish materialism.

If our political institutions were perfect, they would absolutely prevent the political domination of money in any part of our affairs. We need to make our political representatives more quickly and sensitively responsive to the people whose servants they are. More direct action by the people in their own affairs under proper safeguards is vitally necessary. The direct primary is a step in this direction, if it is associated with a corrupt-practices act effective to prevent the advantage of the man willing recklessly and unscrupulously to spend money over his more honest competitor. It is particularly important that all moneys received or expended for campaign purposes should be publicly accounted for, not only after election, but before election as well. Political action must be made simpler, easier, and freer from confusion for every citizen. I believe that the prompt removal of unfaithful or incompetent public servants should be made easy and sure in whatever way experience shall show to be most expedient in any given class of cases.

One of the fundamental necessities in a representative government such as ours is to make certain that the men to whom the people delegate their power shall serve the people by whom they are elected, and not the special interests. I believe that every national officer, elected or appointed, should be forbidden to perform any service or receive any compensation, directly or indirectly, from interstate corporations; and a similar provision could not fail to be useful within the States.

The object of government is the welfare of the people. The material progress and prosperity of a nation are desirable chiefly so far as they lead to the moral and material welfare of all good citizens. Just in proportion as the average man and woman are honest, capable of sound judgment and high ideals, active in public affairs—but, first of all, sound in their home life, and the father and mother of healthy children whom they bring up well—just so far, and no farther, we may count our civilization a success. We must have—I believe we have already —a genuine and permanent moral awakening, without which no wisdom of legislation or administration really means anything; and, on the other hand, we must try to secure the social and economic legislation without which any improvement due to purely moral agitation is necessarily evanescent. Let me again illustrate by a reference to the Grand Army. You could not have won simply as a disorderly and disorganized mob. You needed generals; you needed careful administration of the most advanced type; and a good commissary—the cracker line. You well remember that success was necessary in many different lines in order to bring about general success. You had to have the administration at Washington good, just as you had to have the administration in the field; and you had to have the work of the generals good. You could not have triumphed without that administration and leadership; but it would all have been worthless if the average soldier had not had the right stuff in him. He had to have the right stuff in him, or you could not get it out of him. In the last analysis, therefore, vitally necessary though it was to have the right kind of organization and the right kind of generalship, it was even more vitally necessary that the average soldier should have the fighting edge, the right character. So it is in our civil life. No matter how honest and decent we are in our private lives, if we do not have the right kind of law and the right kind of administration of the law, we cannot go forward as a nation. That is imperative; but it must be an addition to, and not a substitution for, the qualities that make us good citizens. In the last analysis, the most important elements in any man's career must be the sum of those qualities which, in the aggregate, we speak of as character. If he has not got it, then no law that the wit of man can devise, no administration of the law by the boldest and strongest executive, will avail to help him. We must have the right kind of character—character that makes a man, first of all, a good man in the home, a good father, a good husband—that makes a man a good neighbor. You must have that, and, then, in addition, you must have the kind of law and the kind of administration of the law which will give to those qualities in the private citizen the best possible chance for development. The prime problem of our nation is to get the right type of good citizenship, and, to get it, we must have progress, and our public men must be genuinely progressive.

JOHN JAY CHAPMAN

Speech at Prayer Meeting

Coatesville, Pennsylvania, August 18, 1912

W E ARE MET to commemorate the anniversary of one of the most dreadful crimes in history—not for the purpose of condemning it, but to repent of our share in it. We do not start any agitation with regard to that particular crime. I understand that an attempt to prosecute the chief criminals has been made, and has entirely failed; because the whole community, and in a sense our whole people, are really involved in the guilt. The failure of the prosecution in this case, in all such cases, is only a proof of the magnitude of the guilt, and of the awful fact that everyone shares in it.

I will tell you why I am here; I will tell you what happened to me. When I read in the newspapers of August 14, a year ago, about the burning alive of a human being, and of how a few desperate, fiend-minded men had been permitted to torture a man chained to an iron bedstead, burning alive, thrust back by pitchforks when he struggled out of it, while around about stood hundreds of well-dressed American citizens, both from the vicinity and from afar, coming on foot and in wagons, assembling on telephone call, as if by magic, silent, whether from terror or indifference, fascinated and impotent, hundreds of persons watching this awful sight and making no attempt to stay the wickedness, and no one man among them all who was inspired to risk his life in an attempt to stop it, no one man to name the name of Christ, of humanity, of government! As I read the newspaper accounts of the scene enacted here in Coatesville a year ago, I seemed to get a glimpse into the unconscious soul of this country. I saw a seldom revealed picture of the American heart and of the American nature. I seemed to be looking into the heart of the criminal—a cold thing, an awful thing.

I said to myself, "I shall forget this, we shall all forget it; but it will be there. What I have seen is not an illusion. It is the truth. I have seen death in the heart of this people." For to look at the agony of a fellow-being and remain aloof means death in the heart of the onlooker. Religious fanaticism has sometimes lifted men to the frenzy of such cruelty, political passion has sometimes done it, personal hatred might do it, the excitement of the amphitheater in the degenerate days of Roman luxury could do it. But here an audience chosen by chance in America has stood spellbound through an improvised *auto-da-fé*, irregular, illegal, having no religious significance, not sanctioned by custom, having no immediate provocation, the audience standing by merely in cold dislike.

I saw during one moment something beyond all argument in the depth of its significance. You might call it the paralysis of the nerves about the heart in a people habitually and unconsciously given over to selfish aims, an ignorant people who knew not what spectacle they were providing, or what part they were playing in a judgment-play which history was exhibiting on that day.

No theories about the race problem, no statistics, legislation, or mere educational endeavor, can quite meet the lack which that day revealed in the American people. For what we saw was death. The people stood like blighted things, like ghosts about Acheron, waiting for someone or something to determine their destiny for them.

Whatever life itself is, that thing must be replenished in us. The opposite of hate is love, the opposite of cold is heat; what we need is the love of God and reverence for human nature. For one moment I knew that I had seen our true need; and I was afraid that I should forget it and that I should go about framing arguments and agitations and starting schemes of education, when the need was deeper than education. And I became filled with one idea, that I must not forget what I had seen, and that I must do something to remember it. And I am here to-day chiefly that I may remember that vision. It seems fitting to come to this town where the crime occurred and hold a prayer-meeting, so that our hearts may be turned to God through whom mercy may flow into us.

Let me say one thing more about the whole matter. The subject we are dealing with is not local. The act, to be sure, took place at Coatesville and everyone looked to Coatesville to follow it up. Some months ago I asked a friend who lives not far from here something about this case, and about the expected prosecutions, and he replied to me: "It wasn't in my county," and that made me wonder whose county it was in. And it seemed to be in my county. I live on the Hudson River; but I knew that this great wickedness that happened in Coatesville is not the wickedness of Coatesville nor of to-day. It is the wickedness of all America and of three hundred years—the wickedness of the slave trade. All of us are tinctured by it. No special place, no special persons, are to blame. A nation cannot practice a course of inhuman crime for three hundred years and then suddenly throw off the effects of it. Less than fifty years ago domestic slavery was abolished among us; and in one way and another the marks of that vice are in our faces. There is no country in Europe where the Coatesville tragedy or anything remotely like it could have been enacted, probably no country in the world.

On the day of the calamity, those people in the automobiles came by the hundred and watched the torture, and passers-by came in a great multitude and watched it—and did nothing. On the next morning the newspapers spread the news and spread the paralysis until the whole country seemed to be helplessly watching this awful murder, as awful as anything ever done on the earth; and the whole of our people seemed to be looking on helplessly, not able to respond, not knowing what to do next. That spectacle has been in my mind.

The trouble has come down to us out of the past. The only reason that slavery is wrong is that it is cruel and makes men cruel and leaves them cruel. Someone may say that you and I cannot repent because we did not do the act. But we are involved in it. We are still looking on. Do you not see that this whole event is merely the last parable, the most vivid, the most terrible illustration that ever was given by man or imagined by a Jewish prophet, of the relation between good and evil in this world, and of the relation of men to one another?

This whole matter has been an historic episode; but it is a part, not only of our national history, but of the personal history of each one of us. With the great disease (slavery) came the climax (the war), and after the climax gradually began the cure, and in the process of cure comes now the knowledge of what the evil was. I say that our need is new life, and that books and resolutions will not save us, but only such disposition in our hearts and souls as will enable the new life, love, force, hope, virtue, which surround us always, to enter into us.

This is the discovery that each man must make for himself— the discovery that what he really stands in need of he cannot get for himself, but must wait till God gives it to him. I have felt the impulse to come here to-day to testify to this truth.

The occasion is not small; the occasion looks back on three centuries and embraces a hemisphere. Yet the occasion is small compared with the truth it leads us to. For this truth touches all ages and affects every soul in the world.

WOODROW WILSON

First Inaugural Address

Washington, D.C., March 4, 1913

THERE has been a change of government. It began two
years ago, when the House of Representatives became
Democratic by a decisive majority. It has now been completed.
The Senate about to assemble will also be Democratic. The
offices of President and Vice President have been put into
the hands of Democrats. What does the change mean? That is
the question that is uppermost in our minds today. That is the
question I am going to try to answer, in order, if I may, to interpret the occasion.

It means much more than the mere success of a party. The
success of a party means little except when the nation is using
that party for a large and definite purpose. No one can mistake
the purpose for which the nation now seeks to use the Democratic party. It seeks to use it to interpret a change in its own
plans and point of view. Some old things with which we had
grown familiar, and which had begun to creep into the very
habit of our thought and of our lives, have altered their aspect
as we have latterly looked critically upon them, with fresh,
awakened eyes; have dropped their disguises and shown themselves alien and sinister. Some new things, as we look frankly
upon them, willing to comprehend their real character, have
come to assume the aspect of things long believed in and familiar, stuff of our own convictions. We have been refreshed
by a new insight into our own life.

We see that in many things that life is very great. It is incomparably great in its material aspects, in its body of wealth,
in the diversity and sweep of its energy, in the industries which
have been conceived and built up by the genius of individual
men and the limitless enterprise of groups of men. It is great,
also, very great, in its moral force. Nowhere else in the world
have noble men and women exhibited in more striking forms

the beauty and the energy of sympathy and helpfulness and counsel in their efforts to rectify wrong, alleviate suffering, and set the weak in the way of strength and hope. We have built up, moreover, a great system of government, which has stood through a long age as in many respects a model for those who seek to set liberty upon foundations that will endure against fortuitous change, against storm and accident. Our life contains every great thing, and contains it in rich abundance.

But the evil has come with the good, and much fine gold has been corroded. With riches has come inexcusable waste. We have squandered a great part of what we might have used, and have not stopped to conserve the exceeding bounty of nature without which our genius for enterprise would have been worthless and impotent, scorning to be careful, shamefully prodigal as well as admirably efficient. We have been proud of our industrial achievements, but we have not hitherto stopped thoughtfully enough to count the human cost, the cost of lives snuffed out, of energies overtaxed and broken, the fearful physical and spiritual cost to the men and women and children upon whom the dead weight and burden of it all has fallen pitilessly the years through. The groans and agony of it all had not yet reached our ears, the solemn, moving undertone of our life, coming up out of the mines and factories and out of every home where the struggle had its intimate and familiar seat. With the great government went many deep secret things which we too long delayed to look into and scrutinize with candid, fearless eyes. The great government we loved has too often been made use of for private and selfish purposes, and those who used it had forgotten the people.

At last a vision has been vouchsafed us of our life as a whole. We see the bad with the good, the debased and decadent with the sound and vital. With this vision we approach new affairs. Our duty is to cleanse, to reconsider, to restore, to correct the evil without impairing the good, to purify and humanize every process of our common life without weakening or sentimentalizing it. There has been something crude and heartless and unfeeling in our haste to succeed and be great. Our thought has been "Let every man look out for himself; let every generation look out for itself," while we reared giant machinery which made it impossible that any but those who stood at the levers of control should have a chance to look out for themselves. We had not forgotten our morals. We remembered well enough that we had set up a polity which was meant to serve the humblest as well as the most powerful, with an eye single to the standards of justice and fair play, and remembered it with pride. But we were very heedless and in a hurry to be great.

We have come now to the sober second thought. The scales of heedlessness have fallen from our eyes. We have made up our minds to square every process of our national life again with the standards we so proudly set up at the beginning and have always carried at our hearts. Our work is a work of restoration.

We have itemized with some degree of particularity the things that ought to be altered, and here are some of the chief items: A tariff which cuts us off from our proper part in the commerce of the world, violates the just principles of taxation, and makes the government a facile instrument in the hands of private interests; a banking and currency system based upon the necessity of the government to sell its bonds fifty years ago and perfectly adapted to concentrating cash and restricting credits; an industrial system which, take it on all its sides, financial as well as administrative, holds capital in leading strings, restricts the liberties and limits the opportunities of labor, and exploits without renewing or conserving the natural resources of the country; a body of agricultural activities never yet given the efficiency of great business undertakings or served as it should be through the instrumentality of science taken directly to the farm, or afforded the facilities of credit best suited to its practical needs; watercourses undeveloped, waste places unreclaimed, forests untended, fast disappearing without plan or prospect of renewal, unregarded waste heaps at every mine. We have studied as perhaps no other nation has the most effective means of production, but we have not studied cost or economy as we should either as organizers of industry, as statesmen, or as individuals.

Nor have we studied and perfected the means by which government may be put at the service of humanity, in safeguarding the health of the nation, the health of its men and its women and its children, as well as their rights in the struggle for existence. This is no sentimental duty. The firm basis of government is justice, not pity. These are matters of justice. There can be no equality of opportunity, the first essential of justice in the body politic, if men and women and children be not shielded in their lives, their very vitality, from the consequences of great industrial and social processes which they cannot alter, control, or singly cope with. Society must see to it that it does not itself crush or weaken or damage its own constituent parts. The first duty of law is to keep sound the society it serves. Sanitary laws, pure food laws, and laws determining conditions of labor which individuals are powerless to determine for themselves are intimate parts of the very business of justice and legal efficiency.

These are some of the things we ought to do, and not leave the others undone, the old-fashioned, never to be neglected, fundamental safeguarding of property and of individual right. This is the high enterprise of the new day: to lift everything that concerns our life as a nation to the light that shines from the hearth-fire of every man's conscience and vision of the right. It is inconceivable that we should do this as partisans; it is inconceivable we should do it in ignorance of the facts as they are or in blind haste. We shall restore, not destroy. We shall deal with our economic system as it is and as it may be modified, not as it might be if we had a clean sheet of paper to write upon; and step by step we shall make it what it should be, in the spirit of those who question their own wisdom and seek counsel and knowledge, not shallow self-satisfaction or the excitement of excursions whither they cannot tell. Justice, and only justice, shall always be our motto.

And yet it will be no cool process of mere science. The nation has been deeply stirred, stirred by a solemn passion, stirred by the knowledge of wrong, of ideals lost, of government too often debauched and made an instrument of evil. The feelings with which we face this new age of right and opportunity sweep across our heartstrings like some air out of God's own presence, where justice and mercy are reconciled and the judge and the brother are one. We know our task to be no mere task of politics but a task which shall search us through and through, whether we be able to understand our time and the need of our people, whether we be indeed their spokesmen and interpreters, whether we have the pure heart to comprehend and the rectified will to choose our high course of action.

This is not a day of triumph; it is a day of dedication. Here muster, not the forces of party, but the forces of humanity. Men's hearts wait upon us, men's lives hang in the balance; men's hopes call upon us to say what we will do. Who shall live up to the great trust? Who dares fail to try? I summon all honest men, all patriotic, all forward-looking men, to my side. God helping me, I will not fail them, if they will but counsel and sustain me!

WOODROW WILSON

Address to Congress on War with Gemany

Washington, D.C., April 2, 1917

GENTLEMEN OF THE CONGRESS: I have called the Congress into extraordinary session because there are serious, very serious, choices of policy to be made, and made immediately, which it was neither right nor constitutionally permissible that I should assume the responsibility of making.

On the third of February last I officially laid before you the extraordinary announcement of the Imperial German Government that on and after the first day of February it was its purpose to put aside all restraints of law or of humanity and use its submarines to sink every vessel that sought to approach either the ports of Great Britain and Ireland or the western coasts of Europe or any of the ports controlled by the enemies of Germany within the Mediterranean. That had seemed to be the object of the German submarine warfare earlier in the war, but since April of last year the Imperial Government had somewhat restrained the commanders of its undersea craft in conformity with its promise then given to us that passenger boats should not be sunk and that due warning would be given to all other vessels which its submarines might seek to destroy, when no resistance was offered or escape attempted, and care taken that their crews were given at least a fair chance to save their lives in their open boats. The precautions taken were meagre and haphazard enough, as was proved in distressing instance after instance in the progress of the cruel and unmanly business, but a certain degree of restraint was observed. The new policy has swept every restriction aside. Vessels of every kind, whatever their flag, their character, their cargo, their destination, their errand, have been ruthlessly sent to the bottom without warning and without thought of help or mercy for those on board, the vessels of friendly neutrals along with those of belligerents. Even hospital ships and ships carrying relief to the sorely bereaved and stricken people of Belgium, though the latter were provided with safe conduct through the proscribed areas by the German Government itself and were distinguished by unmistakable marks of identity, have been sunk with the same reckless lack of compassion or of principle.

I was for a little while unable to believe that such things would in fact be done by any government that had hitherto subscribed to the humane practices of civilized nations. International law had its origin in the attempt to set up some law which would be respected and observed upon the seas, where no nation had right of dominion and where lay the free highways of the world. By painful stage after stage has that law been built up, with meagre enough results, indeed, after all was accomplished that could be accomplished, but always with a clear view, at least, of what the heart and conscience of mankind demanded. This minimum of right the German Government has swept aside under the plea of retaliation and necessity and because it had no weapons which it could use at sea except these which it is impossible to employ as it is employing them without throwing to the winds all scruples of humanity or of respect for the understandings that were supposed to underlie the intercourse of the world. I am not now thinking of the loss of property involved, immense and serious as that is, but only of the wanton and wholesale destruction of the lives of noncombatants, men, women, and children, engaged in pursuits which have always, even in the darkest periods of modern history, been deemed innocent and legitimate. Property can be paid for; the lives of peaceful and innocent people cannot be. The present German submarine warfare against commerce is a warfare against mankind.

It is a war against all nations. American ships have been sunk, American lives taken, in ways which it has stirred us very deeply to learn of, but the ships and people of other neutral and friendly nations have been sunk and overwhelmed in the waters in the same way. There has been no discrimination. The challenge is to all mankind. Each nation must decide for itself how it will meet it. The choice we make for ourselves must be made with a moderation of counsel and a temperateness of judgment befitting our character and our motives as a nation. We must put excited feeling away. Our motive will not be revenge or the victorious assertion of the physical might of the nation, but only the vindication of right, of human right, of which we are only a single champion.

When I addressed the Congress on the twenty-sixth of February last I thought that it would suffice to assert our neutral rights with aims, our right to use the seas against unlawful interference, our right to keep our people safe against unlawful violence. But armed neutrality, it now appears, is impracticable. Because submarines are in effect outlaws when used as the German submarines have been used against merchant shipping, it is impossible to defend ships against their attacks as the law of nations has assumed that merchantmen would defend themselves against privateers or cruisers, visible craft giving chase upon the open sea. It is common prudence in such circumstances, grim necessity, indeed, to endeavour to destroy them before they have shown their own intention. They must be dealt with upon sight, if dealt with at all. The German Government denies the right of neutrals to use arms at all within the areas of the sea which it has proscribed, even in the defense of rights which no modern publicist has ever before questioned their right to defend. The intimation is conveyed that the armed guards which we have placed on our merchant ships will be treated as beyond the pale of law and subject to be dealt with as pirates would be. Armed neutrality is ineffectual enough at best; in such circumstances and in the face of such pretensions it is worse than ineffectual: it is likely only to produce what it was meant to prevent; it is practically certain to draw us into the war without either the rights or the effectiveness of belligerents. There is one choice we cannot make, we are incapable of making: we will not choose the path of submission and suffer the most sacred rights of our nation and our people to be ignored or violated. The wrongs against which we now array ourselves are no common wrongs; they cut to the very roots of human life.

With a profound sense of the solemn and even tragical character of the step I am taking and of the grave responsibilities which it involves, but in unhesitating obedience to what I deem my constitutional duty, I advise that the Congress declare the recent course of the Imperial German Government to be in fact nothing less than war against the government and people of the United States; that it formally accept the status of belligerent which has thus been thrust upon it; and that it take immediate steps not only to put the country in a more thorough state of defense but also to exert all its power and employ all its resources to bring the Government of the German Empire to terms and end the war.

What this will involve is clear. It will involve the utmost practicable cooperation in counsel and action with the governments now at war with Germany, and, as incident to that, the extension to those governments of the most liberal financial credits, in order that our resources may so far as possible be added to theirs. It will involve the organization and mobilization of all the material resources of the country to supply the materials of war and serve the incidental needs of the nation in the most abundant and yet the most economical and efficient way possible. It will involve the immediate full equipment of the navy in all respects but particularly in supplying it with the best means of dealing with the enemy's submarines. It will involve the immediate addition to the armed forces of the United States already provided for by law in case of war at least five hundred thousand men, who should, in my opinion, be chosen upon the principle of universal liability to service, and also the authorization of subsequent additional increments of equal force so soon as they may be needed and can be handled in training. It will involve also, of course, the granting of adequate credits to the Government, sustained, I hope, so far as they can equitably be sustained by the present generation, by well conceived taxation.

I say sustained so far as may be equitable by taxation because it seems to me that it would be most unwise to base the credits which will now be necessary entirely on money borrowed. It is our duty, I most respectfully urge, to protect our people so far as we may against the very serious hardships and evils which would be likely to arise out of the inflation which would be produced by vast loans.

In carrying out the measures by which these things are to be accomplished we should keep constantly in mind the wisdom of interfering as little as possible in our own preparation and in the equipment of our own military forces with the duty,—for it will be a very practical duty,—of supplying the nations already at war with Germany with the materials which they can obtain only from us or by our assistance. They are in the field and we should help them in every way to be effective there.

I shall take the liberty of suggesting, through the several executive departments of the Government, for the consideration of your committees, measures for the accomplishment of the several objects I have mentioned. I hope that it will be your pleasure to deal with them as having been framed after very careful thought by the branch of the Government upon which the responsibility of conducting the war and safeguarding the nation will most directly fall.

While we do these things, these deeply momentous things, let us be very clear, and make very clear to all the world what our motives and our objects are. My own thought has not been driven from its habitual and normal course by the unhappy events of the last two months, and I do not believe that the thought of the nation has been altered or clouded by them. I have exactly the same things in mind now that I had in mind when I addressed the Senate on the twenty-second of January last; the same that I had in mind when I addressed the Congress on the third of February and on the twenty-sixth of February. Our object now, as then, is to vindicate the principles of peace and justice in the life of the world as against selfish and autocratic power and to set up amongst the really free and self-governed peoples of the world such a concert of purpose and of action as will henceforth ensure the observance of those principles. Neutrality is no longer feasible or desirable where the peace of the world is involved and the freedom of its peoples, and the menace to that peace and freedom lies in the existence of autocratic governments backed by organized force which is controlled wholly by their will, not by the will of their people. We have seen the last of neutrality in such circumstances. We are at the beginning of an age in which it will be insisted that the same standards of conduct and of responsibility for wrong done shall be observed among nations and their governments that are observed among the individual citizens of civilized states.

We have no quarrel with the German people. We have no feeling towards them but one of sympathy and friendship. It was not upon their impulse that their government acted in entering this war. It was not with their previous knowledge or approval. It was a war determined upon as wars used to be determined upon in the old, unhappy days when peoples were nowhere consulted by their rulers and wars were provoked and waged in the interest of dynasties or of little groups of ambitious men who were accustomed to use their fellow men as pawns and tools. Self-governed nations do not fill their neighbour states with spies or set the course of intrigue to bring about some critical posture of affairs which will give them an opportunity to strike and make conquest. Such designs can be successfully worked out only under cover and where no one has the right to ask questions. Cunningly contrived plans of deception or aggression, carried, it may be, from generation to generation, can be worked out and kept from the light only within the privacy of courts or behind the carefully guarded confidences of a narrow and privileged class. They are happily impossible where public opinion commands and insists upon full information concerning all the nation's affairs.

A steadfast concert for peace can never be maintained except by a partnership of democratic nations. No autocratic government could be trusted to keep faith within it or observe its covenants. It must be a league of honour, a partnership of opinion. Intrigue would eat its vitals away; the plottings of inner circles who could plan what they would and render account to no one would be a corruption seated at its very heart. Only free peoples can hold their purpose and their honour steady to a common end and prefer the interests of mankind to any narrow interest of their own.

Does not every American feel that assurance has been added to our hope for the future peace of the world by the wonderful and heartening things that have been happening within the last few weeks in Russia? Russia was known by those who knew it best to have been always in fact democratic at heart, in all the vital habits of her thought, in all the intimate relationships of her people that spoke their natural instinct, their habitual attitude towards life. The autocracy that crowned the summit of her political structure, long as it had stood and terrible as was the reality of its power, was not in fact Russian in origin, character, or purpose; and now it has been shaken off and the great, generous Russian people have been added in all their naive

majesty and might to the forces that are fighting for freedom
in the world, for justice, and for peace. Here is a fit partner for
a League of Honour.

One of the things that has served to convince us that the
Prussian autocracy was not and could never be our friend is
that from the very outset of the present war it has filled our
unsuspecting communities and even our offices of government
with spies and set criminal intrigues everywhere afoot against
our national unity of counsel, our peace within and without,
our industries and our commerce. Indeed it is now evident
that its spies were here even before the war began; and it is unhappily not a matter of conjecture but a fact proved in our
courts of justice that the intrigues which have more than once
come perilously near to disturbing the peace and dislocating
the industries of the country have been carried on at the insti-
gation, with the support, and even under the personal direction of official agents of the Imperial Government accredited
to the Government of the United States. Even in checking
these things and trying to extirpate them we have sought to
put the most generous interpretation possible upon them because we knew that their source lay, not in any hostile feeling
or purpose of the German people towards us (who were, no
doubt as ignorant of them as we ourselves were), but only in
the selfish designs of a Government that did what it pleased
and told its people nothing. But they have played their part in
serving to convince us at last that that Government entertains
no real friendship for us and means to act against our peace
and security at its convenience. That it means to stir up enemies against us at our very doors the intercepted note to the
German Minister at Mexico City is eloquent evidence.

We are accepting this challenge of hostile purpose because
we know that in such a government, following such methods,
we can never have a friend; and that in the presence of its organized power, always lying in wait to accomplish we know
not what purpose, there can be no assured security for the
democratic governments of the world. We are now about to
accept gauge of battle with this natural foe to liberty and shall,
if necessary, spend the whole force of the nation to check and
nullify its pretensions and its power. We are glad, now that we
see the facts with no veil of false pretence about them, to fight

thus for the ultimate peace of the world and for the liberation of its peoples, the German peoples included: for the rights of nations great and small and the privilege of men everywhere to choose their way of life and of obedience. The world must be made safe for democracy. Its peace must be planted upon the tested foundations of political liberty. We have no selfish ends to serve. We desire no conquest, no dominion. We seek no indemnities for ourselves, no material compensation for the sacrifices we shall freely make. We are but one of the champions of the rights of mankind. We shall be satisfied when those rights have been made as secure as the faith and the freedom of nations can make them.

Just because we fight without rancour and without selfish object, seeking nothing for ourselves but what we shall wish to share with all free peoples, we shall, I feel confident, conduct our operations as belligerents without passion and ourselves observe with proud punctilio the principles of right and of fair play we profess to be fighting for.

I have said nothing of the governments allied with the Imperial Government of Germany because they have not made war upon us or challenged us to defend our right and our honour. The Austro-Hungarian Government has, indeed, avowed its unqualified endorsement and acceptance of the reckless and lawless submarine warfare adopted now without disguise by the Imperial German Government, and it has therefore not been possible for this Government to receive Count Tarnowski, the Ambassador recently accredited to this Government by the Imperial and Royal Government of Austria-Hungary; but that Government has not actually engaged in warfare against citizens of the United States on the seas, and I take the liberty, for the present at least, of postponing a discussion of our relations with the authorities at Vienna. We enter this war only where we are clearly forced into it because there are no other means of defending our rights.

It will be all the easier for us to conduct ourselves as belligerents in a high spirit of right and fairness because we act without animus, not in enmity towards a people or with the desire to bring any injury or disadvantage upon them, but only in armed opposition to an irresponsible government which has thrown aside all considerations of humanity and of right and is running amuck. We are, let me say again, the sincere friends of the German people, and shall desire nothing so much as the early re-establishment of intimate relations of mutual advantage between us,—however hard it may be for them, for the time being, to believe that this is spoken from our hearts. We have borne with their present government through all these bitter months because of that friendship,—exercising a patience and forbearance which would otherwise have been impossible. We shall, happily, still have an opportunity to prove that friendship in our daily attitude and actions towards the millions of men and women of German birth and native sympathy who live amongst us and share our life, and we shall be proud to prove it towards all who are in fact loyal to their neighbours and to the Government in the hour of test. They are, most of them, as true and loyal Americans as if they had never known any other fealty or allegiance. They will be prompt to stand with us in rebuking and restraining the few who may be of a different mind and purpose. If there should be disloyalty, it will be dealt with with a firm hand of stern repression; but, if it lifts its head at all, it will lift it only here and there and without countenance except from a lawless and malignant few.

It is a distressing and oppressive duty, Gentlemen of the Congress, which I have performed in thus addressing you. There are, it may be, many months of fiery trial and sacrifice ahead of us. It is a fearful thing to lead this great peaceful people into war, into the most terrible and disastrous of all wars, civilization itself seeming to be in the balance. But the right is more precious than peace, and we shall fight for the things which we have always carried nearest our hearts,—for democracy, for the right of those who submit to authority to have a voice in their own governments, for the rights and liberties of small nations, for a universal dominion of right by such a concert of free peoples as shall bring peace and safety to all nations and make the world itself at last free. To such a task we can dedicate our lives and our fortunes, everything that we are and everything that we have, with the pride of those who know that the day has come when America is privileged to spend her blood and her might for the principles that gave her birth and happiness and the peace which she has treasured. God helping her, she can do no other.

ROBERT M. LA FOLLETTE, SR.

Speech in the Senate
on Free Speech in Wartime

Washington, D.C., October 6, 1917

MR. PRESIDENT, I rise to a question of personal privilege. I have no intention of taking the time of the Senate with a review of the events which led to our entrance into the war except in so far as they bear upon the question of personal privilege to which I am addressing myself.

Six members of the Senate and fifty members, of the House voted against the declaration of war. Immediately there was let loose upon those senators and representatives a flood of invective and abuse from newspapers and individuals who had been clamoring for war, unequaled, I believe, in the history of civilized society.

Prior to the declaration of war every man who had ventured to oppose our entrance into it had been condemned as a coward or worse, and even the president had by no means been immune from these attacks.

Since the declaration of war the triumphant war press has pursued those senators and representatives who voted against war with malicious falsehood and recklessly libelous attacks, going to the extreme limit of charging them with treason against their country.

This campaign of libel and character assassination directed against the members of Congress who opposed our entrance into the war has been continued down to the present hour, and I have upon my desk newspaper clippings, some of them libels upon me alone, some directed as well against other senators who voted in opposition to the declaration of war.

One of these newspaper reports most widely circulated represents a federal judge in the state of Texas as saying, in a charge to a grand jury—I read the article as it appeared in the newspaper and the headline with which it is introduced:

DISTRICT JUDGE WOULD LIKE TO TAKE SHOT
AT TRAITORS IN CONGRESS

[By Associated Press leased wire]

Houston, Tex., *October 1, 1917.*

Judge Waller T. Burns, of the United States district court, in charging a Federal grand jury at the beginning of the October term to-day, after calling by name Senators STONE of Missouri, HARD-WICK of Georgia, VARDAMAN of Mississippi, GRONNA of North Dakota, GORE of Oklahoma, and LA FOLLETTE of Wisconsin, said:

If I had a wish, I would wish that you men had jurisdiction to re-turn bills of indictment against these men. They ought to be tried promptly and fairly, and I believe this court could administer the law fairly; but I have a conviction, as strong as life, that this country should stand them up against an adobe wall to-morrow and give them what they deserve. If any man deserves death, it is a traitor. I wish that I could pay for the ammunition. I would like to attend the execution, and if I were in the firing squad I would not want to be the marksman who had the blank shell.

The above clipping, Mr. President, was sent to me by another federal judge, who wrote upon the margin of the clipping that it occurred to him that the conduct of this judge might very properly be the subject of investigation. He inclosed with the clipping a letter, from which I quote the following:

I have been greatly depressed by the brutal and unjust attacks that great business interests have organized against you. It is a time when all the spirits of evil are turned loose. The Kaisers of high finance, who have been developing hatred of you for a generation because you have fought against them and for the common good, see this oppor-tunity to turn the war patriotism into an engine of attack. They are using it everywhere, and it is a day when lovers of democracy, not only in the world, but here in the United States, need to go apart on the mountain and spend the night in fasting and prayer. I still have faith that the forces of good on this earth will be found to be greater than the forces of evil, but we all need resolution. I hope you will have the grace to keep your center of gravity on the inside of you and to keep a spirit that is unclouded by hatred. It is a time for the words, "with malice toward none and charity for all." It is the office of great service to be a shield to the good man's character against malice. Be-fore this fight is over you will have a new revelation that such a shield is yours.

If this newspaper clipping were a single or exceptional instance of lawless defamation, I should not trouble the Senate with a reference to it. But, Mr. President, it is not.

In this mass of newspaper clippings which I have here upon my desk, and which I shall not trouble the Senate to read unless it is desired, and which represent but a small part of the accumulation clipped from the daily press of the country in the last three months, I find other senators, as well as myself, accused of the highest crimes of which any man can be guilty—treason and disloyalty—and, sir, accused not only with no evidence to support the accusation, but without the suggestion that such evidence anywhere exists. It is not claimed that senators who opposed the declaration of war have since that time acted with any concerted purpose either regarding war measures or any others. They have voted according to their individual opinions, have often been opposed to each other on bills which have come before the Senate since the declaration of war, and, according to my recollection, have never all voted together since that time upon any single proposition upon which the Senate has been divided.

I am aware, Mr. President, that in pursuance of this general campaign of vilification and attempted intimidation, requests from various individuals and certain organizations have been submitted to the Senate for my expulsion from this body, and that such requests have been referred to and considered by one of the committees of the Senate.

If I alone had been made the victim of these attacks, I should not take one moment of the Senate's time for their consideration, and I believe that other senators who have been unjustly and unfairly assailed, as I have been, hold the same attitude upon this that I do. *Neither the clamor of the mob nor the voice of power will ever turn me by the breadth of a hair from the course I mark out for myself, guided by such knowledge as I can obtain and controlled and directed by a solemn conviction of right and duty.*

But, sir, it is not alone members of Congress that the war party in this country has sought to intimidate. The mandate seems to have gone forth to the sovereign people of this country that they must be silent while those things are being done by their government which most vitally concern their well-being, their happiness, and their lives. Today and for weeks past honest and law-abiding citizens of this country are being terrorized and outraged in their rights by those sworn to uphold the laws and protect the rights of the people. I have in my possession numerous affidavits establishing the fact that people are being unlawfully arrested, thrown into jail, held incommunicado for days, only to be eventually discharged without even having been taken into court, because they have committed no crime. Private residences are being invaded, loyal citizens of undoubted integrity and probity arrested, cross-examined, and the most sacred constitutional rights guaranteed to every American citizen are being violated.

It appears to be the purpose of those conducting this campaign to throw the country into a state of terror, to coerce public opinion, to stifle criticism, and suppress discussion of the great issues involved in this war.

I think all men recognize that in time of war the citizen must surrender some rights for the common good which he is entitled to enjoy in time of peace. *But, sir, the right to control their own government according to constitutional forms is not one of the rights that the citizens of this country are called upon to surrender in time of war.*

Rather in time of war the citizen must be more alert to the preservation of his right to control his government. He must be most watchful of the encroachment of the military upon the civil power. He must beware of those precedents in support of arbitrary action by administrative officials, which excused on the plea of necessity in wartime, become the fixed rule when the necessity has passed and normal conditions have been restored.

More than all, the citizen and his representative in Congress in time of war must maintain his right of free speech. More than in times of peace it is necessary that the channels for free public discussion of governmental policies shall be open and unclogged. I believe, Mr. President, that I am now touching upon the most important question in this country today—and that is the right of the citizens of this country and their representatives in Congress to discuss in an orderly way frankly and publicly and without fear, from the platform and through the press, every important phase of this war; its causes, the manner in which it should be conducted, and the terms upon which peace should be made. The belief which is becoming widespread in this land that this most fundamental right is being denied to the citizens of this country is a fact the tremendous significance of which, those in authority have not yet begun to appreciate. I am contending, Mr. President, for the great fundamental right of the sovereign people of this country to make their voice heard and have that voice heeded upon the great questions arising out of this war, including not only how the war shall be prosecuted but the conditions upon which it may be terminated with a due regard for the rights and the honor of this nation and the interests of humanity.

I am contending for this right because the exercise of it is necessary to the welfare, to the existence, of this government, to the successful conduct of this war, and to a peace which shall be enduring and for the best interest of this country.

Suppose success attends the attempt to stifle all discussion of the issues of this war, all discussion of the terms upon which it should be concluded, all discussion of the objects and purposes to be accomplished by it, and concede the demand of the war-mad press and war extremists that they monopolize the right of public utterance upon these questions unchallenged, what think you would be the consequences to this country not only during the war but after the war?

RIGHT OF PEOPLE TO DISCUSS WAR ISSUES

Mr. President, our government, above all others, is founded on the right of the people freely to discuss all matters pertaining to their government, in war not less than in peace, for in this government the people are the rulers in war no less than in peace. It is true, sir, that members of the House of Representatives are elected for two years, the president for four years, and the members of the Senate for six years, and during their temporary official terms these officers constitute what is called the government. But back of them always is the controlling sovereign power of the people, and when the people can make their will known, the faithful officer will obey that will. Though the right of the people to express their will by ballot is suspended during the term of office of the elected official, nevertheless the duty of the official to obey the popular will continues throughout his entire term of office. How can that popular will express itself between elections except by meetings, by speeches, by publications, by petitions, and by addresses to the representatives of the people? Any man who seeks to set a limit upon those rights, whether in war or peace, aims a blow at the most vital part of our government. And then as the time for election approaches and the official is called to account for his stewardship—not a day, not a week, not a month, before the election, but a year or more before it, if the people choose— they must have the right to the freest possible discussion of every question upon which their representative has acted, of the merits of every measure he has supported or opposed, of every vote he has cast and every speech that he has made. And before this great fundamental right every other must, if necessary, give way, for in no other manner can representative government be preserved.

Mr. President, what I am saying has been exemplified in the lives and public discussion of the ablest statesmen of this country, whose memories we most revere and whose deeds we most justly commemorate. I shall presently ask the attention of the Senate to the views of some of these men upon the subject we are now considering.

Closely related to this subject of the right of the citizen to discuss war is that of the constitutional power and duty of the Congress to declare the purposes and objects of any war in which our country may be engaged. The authorities which I shall cite cover both the right of the people to discuss the war in all its phases and the right and the duty of the people's representatives in Congress to declare the purposes and objects of the war. For the sake of brevity, I shall present these quotations together at this point instead of submitting them separately.

DISCUSSION BY AMERICAN STATESMEN

Henry Clay, in a memorable address at Lexington, Kentucky, on the 13th day of November, 1847, during the Mexican War, took a strong position in behalf of the right of the people to freely discuss every question relating to the war, even though the discussion involved a strong condemnation of the war policy of the executive. He also declared it to be not only the right but the duty of the Congress to declare the objects of the war. As a part of that address he presented certain resolutions embodying his views on these subjects. These resolutions were adopted at that meeting by the people present, and were adopted at many other mass meetings throughout the country during the continuance of the Mexican War.

For introducing in this body some time ago a resolution asserting the right of Congress to declare the purposes of the present war, I have, as the newspaper clippings here will show, been denounced as a traitor and my conduct characterized as treasonable.

As bearing directly upon the conduct for which I have been so criticized and condemned, I invite your attention to the language of Henry Clay in the address I have mentioned.

He said:

But the havoc of war is in progress and the no less deplorable havoc of an inhospitable and pestilential climate. Without indulging in an unnecessary retrospect and useless reproaches on the past, all hearts and heads should unite in the patriotic endeavor to bring it to a satisfactory close. Is there no way that this can be done? Must we blindly continue the conflict without any visible object or any prospect of a definite termination? This is the important subject upon which I desire to consult and to commune with you. Who in this free government is to decide upon the objects of a war at its commencement or at any time during its existence? Does the power belong to collective wisdom of the nation in Congress assembled, or is it vested solely in a single functionary of the government?

A declaration of war is the highest and most awful exercise of sovereignty. The convention which framed our federal Constitution had learned from the pages of history that it had been often and greatly abused. It had seen that war had often been commenced upon the most trifling pretexts; that it had been frequently waged to establish or exclude a dynasty; to snatch a crown from the head of one potentate and place it upon the head of another; that it had often been prosecuted to promote alien and other interests than those of the nation whose chief had proclaimed it, as in the case of English wars for Hanoverian interests; and, in short, that such a vast and tremendous power ought not to be confided to the perilous exercise of one single man. The convention therefore resolved to guard the warmaking power against those great abuses, of which, in the hands of a monarch, it was so susceptible. And the security against those abuses which its wisdom devised was to vest the war-making power in the Congress of the United States, being the immediate representatives of the people and the states. So apprehensive and jealous was the convention of its abuse in any other hands that it interdicted the exercise of the power to any state in the Union without the consent of Congress. Congress, then, in our system of government, is the sole depository of that tremendous power.

Mr. President, it is impossible for me to quote as extensively from this address as I should like to do and still keep within the compass of the time that I have set down for myself; but the whole of the address is accessible to every senator here, together with all of the discussion which followed it over the country, and in these times it would seem to me worthy of the review of senators and of newspaper editors and of those who have duties to discharge in connection with this great crisis that is upon the world.

I quote further:

The Constitution provides that Congress shall have power to declare war and grant letters of marque and reprisal, to make rules concerning captures on land and water, to raise and support armies, and provide and maintain a navy, and to make rules for the government of the land and naval forces. Thus we perceive that the principal power, in regard to war, with all its auxiliary attendants, is granted to Congress. Whenever called upon to determine upon the solemn question of peace or war, Congress must consider and deliberate and decide upon the motives, objects, and causes of the war.

If that be true, is it treason for a senator upon this floor to offer a resolution dealing with that question?

I quote further from Mr. Clay:

And, if a war be commenced without any previous declaration of its objects, as in the case of the existing war with Mexico, Congress must necessarily possess the authority, at any time, to declare for what purposes it shall be further prosecuted. If we suppose Congress does not possess the controlling authority attributed to it, if it be contended that a war having been once commenced, the president of the United States may direct it to the accomplishment of any object he pleases, without consulting and without any regard to the will of Congress, the convention will have utterly failed in guarding the nation against the abuses and ambition of a single individual. Either Congress or the president must have the right of determining upon the objects for which a war shall be prosecuted. There is no other alternative. If the president possess it and may prosecute it for objects against the will of

Congress, where is the difference between our free government and that of any other nation which may be governed by an absolute czar, emperor, or king?

In closing his address, Mr. Clay said:

I conclude, therefore, Mr. President and fellow citizens, with entire confidence, that Congress has the right, either at the beginning or during the prosecution of any war, to decide the objects and purposes for which it was proclaimed or for which it ought to be continued. And I think it is the duty of Congress, by some deliberate and authentic act, to declare for what objects the present war shall be longer prosecuted. I suppose the president would not hesitate to regulate his conduct by the pronounced will of Congress and to employ the force and the diplomatic power of the nation to execute that will. But if the president should decline or refuse to do so and, in contempt of the supreme authority of Congress, should persevere in waging the war for other objects than those proclaimed by Congress, then it would be the imperative duty of that body to vindicate its authority by the most stringent and effectual and appropriate measures. And if, on the contrary, the enemy should refuse to conclude a treaty containing stipulations securing the objects designated by Congress, it would become the duty of the whole government to prosecute the war with all the national energy until those objects were attained by a treaty of peace. There can be no insuperable difficulty in Congress making such an authoritative declaration. Let It resolve, simply, that the war shall or shall not be a war of conquest; and, if a war of conquest, what is to be conquered. Should a resolution pass disclaiming the design of conquest, peace would follow in less than sixty days, if the president would conform to his constitutional duty.

Mr. Clay as a part of that speech presented certain resolutions which were unanimously adopted by the meeting and which declared that the power to determine the purposes of the war rested with Congress, and then proceeded clearly to state the purposes, and the only purposes, for which the war should be prosecuted.

The last of these resolutions is so pertinent to the present discussion that I invite your attention to it at this time. It is as follows:

Resolved, That we invite our fellow citizens of the United States who are anxious for the restoration of the blessings of peace, or, if the existing war shall continue to be prosecuted, are desirous that its purposes and objects shall be defined and known, who are anxious to avert present and future perils and dangers, with which it may be fraught, and who are also anxious to produce contentment and satisfaction at home, and to elevate the national character abroad, to assemble together in their respective communities, and to express their views, feelings, and opinions.

Abraham Lincoln was a member of Congress at the time of the Mexican War. He strongly opposed the war while it was in progress and severely criticized President Polk on the floor of the House because he did not state in his message when peace might be expected.

In the course of his speech Lincoln said:

At its beginning, Gen. Scott was by this same president driven into disfavor, if not disgrace, for intimating that peace could not be conquered in less than three or four months. But now, at the end of twenty months . . . this same president gives a long message, without showing us that as to the end he himself has even an imaginary conception. As I have said, he knows not where he is. He is a bewildered, confounded, and miserably perplexed man. God grant he may be able to show there is not something about his conscience more painful than his mental perplexity.

Writing to a friend who had objected to his opposition to Polk in relation to this power of the president in war, Lincoln said:

The provision of the Constitution giving the warmaking power to Congress was dictated, as I understand it, by the following reasons: kings had always been involving and impoverishing their people in wars, pretending generally, if not always, that the good of the people was the object. This our convention understood to be the most oppressive of all kingly oppressions, and they resolved to so frame the Constitution that no man should hold the power of bringing this oppression upon us. But your view destroys the whole matter and places our president where kings have always stood.

I now quote from the speech of Charles Sumner, delivered at Tremont Temple, Boston, November 5, 1846.

John A. Andrew, who was the great war governor of Massachusetts, as I remember, presided at this public meeting, which was in support of the independent nomination of Dr. I. G. Howe as Representative in Congress. Mr. Sumner was followed by Hon. Charles Francis Adams, who also delivered an address at this meeting.

This is the view of Mr. Sumner on the Mexican War, which was then in progress, as expressed by him on this occasion:

> The Mexican War is an enormity born of slavery. . . . Base in object, atrocious in beginning, immoral in all its influences, vainly prodigal of treasure and life, it is a war of infamy, which must blot the pages of our history.

In closing his eloquent and powerful address, he said:

> Even if we seem to fail in this election we shall not fail in reality. The influence of this effort will help to awaken and organize that powerful public opinion by which this war will at last be arrested. Hang out, fellow citizens, the white banner of peace; let the citizens of Boston rally about it; and may it be borne forward by an enlightened, conscientious people, aroused to condemnation of this murderous war, until Mexico, now wet with blood unjustly shed, shall repose undisturbed beneath its folds.

Contrast this position taken by Charles Summer at Tremont Temple with that of the secretary of the treasury, Mr. McAdoo. He is now touring the country with all the prestige of his great financial mission and the authority of his high place in the administration. I quote the language of the authorized report of his speech before the Bankers' Association of West Virginia, September 21, 1917. According to daily press reports he is making substantially the same denunciation in all his addresses:

> America intends that those well-meaning but misguided people who talk inopportunely of peace when there can be no peace until the cancer which has rotted civilization in Europe is extinguished and destroyed forever shall be silenced. I want to say here and now and with due deliberation that every pacifist speech in this country made at this inopportune and improper time is in effect traitorous.

In these times we had better turn the marble bust of Charles Sumner to the wall. It ill becomes those who tamely surrender the right of free speech to look upon that strong, noble, patriotic face.

Mr. President, Daniel Webster, then in the zenith of his power, and with the experience and knowledge of his long life and great public service in many capacities, to add weight to his

words, spoke at Faneuil Hall, November 6, 1846, in opposition
to the Mexican War. He said:

> Mr. Chairman, I wish to speak with all soberness in this respect,
> and I would say nothing here tonight which I would not say in my
> place in Congress or before the whole world. The question now is,
> *For what purposes and to what ends is this present war to be prosecuted?*

What will you say to the stature of the statesmanship that
imputes treason to his country to a member of this body who
introduces a resolution having no other import than that?

Webster saw no reason why the purposes of the war in which
his country was engaged should not be discussed in Congress
or out of Congress by the people's representatives or by the
people themselves.

After referring to Mexico as a weak and distracted country
he proceeded:

> *It is time for us to know what are the objects and designs of our*
> *government*
> It is not the habit of the American people, nor natural to their
> character, to consider the expense of a war which they deem just and
> necessary.—

Not only just, but necessary—

> but it is their habit and belongs to their character to inquire into the
> justice and necessity of a war in which it is proposed to involve them.

Mr. Webster discussed the Mexican War at Springfield, Mass.,
September 29, 1847, and again, while the war was in progress,
he did not hesitate to express his disapproval in plain language.

Many battles had been fought and won, and our victorious
armies were in the field, on foreign soil.

Sir, free speech had not been suppressed. The right of the
people to assemble and to state their grievances was still an attribute of American freedom. Mr. Webster said:

> We are, in my opinion, in a most unnecessary and therefore a most
> unjustifiable war.

Whoever expects to whip men, free men, in this country into
a position where they are to be denied the right to exercise the
same freedom of speech and discussion that Webster exercised
in that speech little understand the value which the average cit-

izen of this country places upon the liberty guaranteed to him by the Constitution. Sir, until the sacrifices of every battlefield consecrated to the establishment of representative government and of constitutional freedom shall be obliterated from the pages of history and forgotten of men, the plain citizenship of this country will jealously guard that liberty and that freedom and will not surrender it.

To return to my text. Mr. Webster said:

> We are, in my opinion, in a most unnecessary and therefore a most unjustifiable war. I hope we are nearing the close of it. I attend carefully and anxiously to every rumor and every breeze that brings to us any report that the effusion of blood, caused, in my judgment, by a rash and unjustifiable proceeding on the part of the government, may cease.

He makes the charge that the war was begun under false pretexts, as follows:

> Now, sir, the law of nations instructs us that there are wars of pretexts. The history of the world proves that there have been, and we are not now without proof that there are, wars waged on pretexts; that is, on pretenses, where the cause assigned is not the true cause. That I believe on my conscience is the true character of the war now waged against Mexico. I believe it to be a war of pretexts; a war in which the true motive is not distinctly avowed, but in which pretenses, afterthoughts, evasions, and other methods are employed to put a case before the community which is not the true case.

Think you Mr. Webster was not within his constitutional rights in thus criticizing the character of the war, its origin, and the reasons which were given from time to time in justification of it?

Mr. Webster discusses at length what he considers some of the false pretexts of the war. Later on he says:

> Sir, men there are whom we see, and whom we hear speak of the duty of extending our free institutions over the whole world if possible. We owe it to benevolence, they think, to confer the blessings we enjoy on every other people. But while I trust that liberty and free civil institutions, as we have experienced them, may ultimately spread over the globe, I am by no means sure that all people are fit for them; nor am I desirous of imposing, or forcing, our peculiar forms upon any nation that does not wish to embrace them.

Taking up the subject that war does now exist, Mr. Webster asks:

What is our duty? I say for one, that I suppose it to be true—I hope it to be true—that a majority of the next House of Representatives will be Whigs; will be opposed to the war. I think we have heard from the East and the West, the North and the South, some things that make that pretty clear. Suppose it to be so. What then? Well, sir, I say for one, and at once, that unless the president of the United States shall make out a case which shall show to Congress that the aim and object for which the war is now prosecuted is no purpose not connected with the safety of the Union and the just rights of the American people, then Congress ought to pass resolutions against the prosecution of the war, and grant no further supplies. I would speak here with caution and all just limitation. It must be admitted to be the clear intent of the Constitution that no foreign war should exist without the assent of Congress. This was meant as a restraint on the executive power. But, if, when a war has once begun, the president may continue it as long as he pleases, free of all control of Congress, then it is clear that the war power is substantially in his own single hand. Nothing will be done by a wise Congress hastily or rashly, nothing that partakes of the nature of violence or recklessness; a high and delicate regard must, of course, be had for the honor and credit of the nation; but, after all, if the war should become odious to the people, if they shall disapprove the objects for which it appears to be prosecuted, then it will be the bounden duty of their representatives in Congress to demand of the president a full statement of his objects and purposes. And if these purposes shall appear to them not to be founded in the public good, or not consistent with the honor and character of the country, then it will be their duty to put an end to it by the exercise of their constitutional authority. If this be not so, then the whole balance of the Constitution is overthrown, and all just restraint on the executive power, in a matter of the highest concern to the peace and happiness of the country, entirely destroyed. If we do not maintain this doctrine; if it is not so—if Congress, in whom the warmaking power is expressly made to reside, is to have no voice in the declaration or continuance of war; if it is not to judge of the propriety of beginning or carrying it on—then we depart at once, and broadly, from the Constitution.

Mr. Webster concluded his speech in these memorable words:

We may be tossed upon an ocean where we can see no land—nor, perhaps, the sun or stars. But there is a chart and a compass for us to study, to consult, and to obey. That chart is the Constitution of the country. That compass is an honest, single-eyed purpose to preserve the institutions and the liberty with which God has blessed us.

In 1847 Senator Tom Corwin made a memorable speech in the Senate on the Mexican War. It was one of the ablest addresses made by that very able statesman, and one of the great contributions to the discussion of the subject we are now considering. At the time of Senator Corwin's address the majority in Congress were supporting the president. The people up to that time had had no chance to express their views at an election. After referring to the doctrine then preached by the dominant faction of the Senate, that after war is declared it must be prosecuted to the bitter end as the president may direct, until one side or the other is hopelessly beaten and devastated by the conflict, with one man—the president—in sole command of the destinies of the Nation, Mr. Corwin said:

> With these doctrines for our guide, I will thank any senator to furnish me with any means of escaping from the prosecution of this or any other war for an hundred years to come if it please the president who shall be, to continue it so long. Tell me, ye who contend that being in war duty demands of Congress for its prosecution all the money and every able bodied man in America to carry it on if need be, who also contend that it is the right of the president without the control of Congress to march your embodied hosts to Monterey, to Yucatan, to Mexico, to Panama, to China, and that under penalty of death to the officer who disobeys him; tell me, I demand it of you, tell me, tell the American people, tell the nations of Christendom what is the difference between your American democracy and the most odious, most hateful despotism that merciful God has ever allowed a nation to be afflicted with since government on earth began? You may call this free government, but it is such freedom, and no other as of old was established at Babylon, at Susa, at Bactriana, or Persepolis. Its parallel is scarcely to be found when thus falsely understood in any, even the worst, forms of civil polity in modern times. Sir, it is not so; such is not your Constitution; it is something else, something other and better than this.

Lincoln, Webster, Clay, Sumner—what a galaxy of names in American history! They all believed and asserted and advocated in the midst of war that it was the right—the constitutional right—and the patriotic duty of American citizens, after the declaration of war and while the war was in progress, to discuss the issues of the war and to criticize the policies employed in its prosecution and to work for the election of representatives opposed to prolonging war.

The right of Lincoln, Webster, Clay, Sumner to oppose the Mexican War, criticize its conduct, advocate its conclusion on a just basis, is exactly the same right and privilege as that possessed by every representative in Congress and by each and every American citizen in our land today in respect to the war in which we are now engaged. Their arguments as to the power of Congress to shape the war policy and their opposition to what they believed to be the usurpation of power on the part of the executive are potent so long as the Constitution remains the law of the land.

English history, like our own, shows that it has ever been the right of the citizen to criticize and, when he thought necessary, to condemn the war policy of his government.

DISCUSSION BY ENGLISH STATESMEN

John Bright consistently fought the Crimean War with all the power of his great personality and noble mind; he fought it inch by inch and step by step from the floor of the English Parliament. After his death Gladstone, although he had been a part of the ministry that Bright had opposed because of the Crimean War, selected this as the theme for his eulogy of the great statesman, as best portraying his high character and great service to the English people.

Lloyd George aggressively opposed the Boer War. Speaking in the House of Commons July 25, 1900, in reply to the prime minister, he said:

> He has led us into two blunders. The first was the war. But worse than the war is the change that has been effected in the purpose for which we are prosecuting the war. We went into the war for equal rights; we are prosecuting it for annexation. . . . You entered into these two Republics for philanthropic purposes and remained to commit burglary. . . . A war of annexation, however, against a proud people must be a war of extermination, and that is, unfortunately, what it seems we are now committing ourselves to—burning homesteads and turning men and women out of their homes.

I am citing this language, Mr. President, as showing the length to which statesmen have gone in opposing wars which have been conducted by their governments and the latitude that has been accorded them.

. . . The right honorable gentleman has made up his mind that this war shall produce electioneering capital to his own side. He is in a great hurry to go to the country before the facts are known. He wants to have the judgment of the people in the very height and excitement of the fever. He wants a verdict before the pleadings are closed and before "discovery" has been obtained. He does not want the documents to come, but he wants to have the judgment of the country upon censured news, suppressed dispatches, and unpaid bills.

In a speech delivered October 23, 1901, Lloyd George charged that the English Army had burned villages, blown up farmhouses, swept away the cattle, burned thousands of tons of grain, destroyed all agricultural implements, all the mills, the irrigation works, and left the territory "a blackened devastated wilderness." He said:

In June the death rate among the children in the Orange River Colony camps was at the rate of 192 per thousand per annum, and in Transvaal 233 per thousand per annum. In July the figures were 220 and 336 per thousand per annum, respectively. In August they had risen to 250 and 468, and in September to 442 in Orange River Colony and to 457 in the Transvaal. These are truly appalling figures. It means that at that rate in two years' time there would not be a little child left in the whole of these two new territories. The worst of it is that I can not resist the conclusion that their lives could have been saved had it not been that these camps had been deliberately chosen for military purposes. In the few camps near the coast there is hardly any mortality at all—

Observe that here is a criticism of the military policies of his government—

and if the children had been removed from the Orange River Colony and the Transvaal to the seacoasts, where they could have been easily fed and clothed and cared for, their lives might be saved; but as long as they were kept up in the north there was a terrible inducement offered to the Boer commanders not to attack the lines of communication. . . . If I were to despair for the future of this country it would not be because of trade competition from either America or Germany, or the ineffectiveness of its army, or anything that might happen to its ships; but rather because it used its great, hulking strength to torture a little child. Had it not been that his ministry had shown distinct symptoms of softening of the brain, I would call the torpor and indifference they are showing in face of all this, criminal. It is a maddening horror, and it will haunt the Empire to its dying hour. What wonder is it that Europe should mock and hiss at us? Let any honest Britisher fearlessly search his heart and answer this question: Is there any ground for the reproach flung at us by the civilized world that, having failed to crush the men, we have now taken to killing babes?

Mr. President, while we were struggling for our independence the Duke of Grafton, in the House of Lords, October 26, 1775, speaking against voting thanks to British officers and soldiers, after the battles of Lexington and Bunker Hill, declared:

I pledge myself to your lordships and my country that if necessity should require it and my health otherwise permit it, I mean to come down to this House in a litter in order to express my full and hearty disapproval of the measures now pursued, and, as I understand from the noble lords in office, meant to be pursued.

On the same occasion, Mr. Fox said:

I could not consent to the bloody consequences of so silly a contest, about so silly an object, conducted in the silliest manner that history or observation had ever furnished an instance of, and from which we are likely to derive poverty, misery, disgrace, defeat, and ruin.

In the House of Commons, May 14, 1777, Mr. Burke is reported in the parliamentary debates against the war on the American colonies, as saying he was, and ever would be, ready to support a just war, whether against subjects or alien enemies, but where justice or color of justice was wanting he would ever be the first to oppose it.

Lord Chatham, November 18, 1777, spoke as follows regarding the war between England and the American colonies:

I would sell my shirt off my back to assist in proper measures, properly and wisely conducted, but I would not part with a single shilling to the present ministers. Their plans are founded in destruction and disgrace. It is, my lords, a ruinous and destructive war; it is full of danger: it teems with disgrace and must end in ruin. . . . If I were an American, as I am an Englishman, while a foreign troop was landed in my country I never would lay down my arms! Never! Never! Never!

Mr. President, I have made these quotations from some of the leading statesmen of England to show that the principle of free speech was no new doctrine born of the Constitution of the United States. Our Constitution merely declared the principle. It did not create it. It is a heritage of English-speaking peoples, which has been won by incalculable sacrifice, and which they must preserve so long as they hope to live as free men. I say without fear of contradiction that there has never been a time for more than a century and a half when the right of free speech and free press and the right of the people to peaceably assemble for public discussion have been so violated among English-speaking people as they are violated today throughout the United States. Today, in the land we have been wont to call the free United States, governors, mayors, and policemen are preventing or breaking up peaceable meetings called to discuss the questions growing out of this war, and judges and courts with some notable and worthy exceptions, are failing to protect the citizens in their rights.

It is no answer to say that when the war is over the citizen may once more resume his rights and feel some security in his liberty and his person. As I have already tried to point out, now is precisely the time when the country needs the counsel of all its citizens. In time of war even more than in time of peace, whether citizens happen to agree with the ruling administration or not, these precious fundamental personal rights—free speech, free press, and right of assemblage so explicitly and emphatically guaranteed by the Constitution should be maintained inviolable. There is no rebellion in the land, no martial law, no courts are closed, no legal processes suspended, and there is no threat even of invasion.

But more than this, if every preparation for war can be made the excuse for destroying free speech and a free press and the right of the people to assemble together for peaceful discussion, then we may well despair of ever again finding ourselves for a long period in a state of peace. With the possessions we already have in remote parts of the world, with the obligations we seem almost certain to assume as a result of the present war, a war can be made any time overnight and the destruction of personal rights now occurring will be pointed to then as precedents for a still further invasion of the rights of the citizen. This is the road which all free governments have heretofore traveled to their destruction, and how far we have progressed along it is shown when we compare the standard of liberty of Lincoln, Clay, and Webster with the standard of the present day.

This leads me, Mr. President, to the next thought to which I desire to invite the attention of the Senate, and that is the power of Congress to declare the purpose and objects of the war, and the failure of Congress to exercise that power in the present crisis.

POWER OF CONGRESS TO DECLARE OBJECTS OF WAR

For the mere assertion of that right, in the form of a resolution to be considered and discussed—which I introduced August 11, 1917—I have been denounced throughout this broad land as a traitor to my country.

Mr. President, we are in a war the awful consequences of which no man can foresee, which, in my judgment, could have been avoided if the Congress had exercised its constitutional power to influence and direct the foreign policy of this country.

On the 8th day of February, 1915, I introduced in the Senate a resolution authorizing the president to invite the representatives of the neutral nations of the world to assemble and consider, among other things, whether it would not be possible to lay out lanes of travel upon the high seas and through proper negotiation with the belligerent powers have those lanes recognized as neutral territory, through which the commerce of neutral nations might pass. This, together with other provisions, constituted a resolution, as I shall always regard it, of most vital and supreme importance in the world crisis, and one that should have been considered and acted upon by Congress.

I believe, sir, that had some such action been taken the history of the world would not be written at this hour in the blood of more than one-half of the nations of the earth, with the remaining nations in danger of becoming involved.

I believe that had Congress exercised the power in this respect, which I contend it possesses, we could and probably would have avoided the present war.

Mr. President, I believe that if we are to extricate ourselves from this war and restore this country to an honorable and lasting peace, the Congress must exercise in full the war powers intrusted to it by the Constitution. I have already called your attention sufficiently, no doubt, to the opinions upon this subject expressed by some of the greatest lawyers and statesmen of the country, and I now venture to ask your attention to a little closer examination of the subject viewed in the light of distinctly legal authorities and principles.

CONSTITUTIONAL PROVISIONS INVOLVED

Section 8, Article I, of the Constitution provides:

> The Congress shall have power to lay and collect taxes, duties, imposts, and excise to pay the debts and provide for the common defense and general welfare of the United States.

In this first sentence we find that no war can be prosecuted without the consent of the Congress. No war can be prosecuted without money. There is no power to raise the money for war except the power of Congress. From this provision alone it must follow absolutely and without qualification that the duty of determining whether a war shall be prosecuted or not, whether the people's money shall be expended for the purpose of war or not rests upon the Congress, and with that power goes necessarily the power to determine the purposes of the war, for if the Congress does not approve the purposes of the war, it may refuse to lay the tax upon the people to prosecute it.

Again, section 8 further provides that Congress shall have power—

> To declare war, grant letters of marque and reprisal, and make rules concerning captures on land and water;
>
> To raise and support armies, but no appropriation of money to that use shall be for a longer term than two years;
>
> To provide and maintain a Navy;
>
> To make rules for the government and regulation of the land and naval forces;

To provide for calling forth the militia to execute the laws of the Union, suppress insurrection, and repel invasion;

To provide for organizing, arming, and disciplining the militia, and for governing such part of them as may be employed in the service of the United States, reserving to the States, respectively, the appointment of the officers and the authority of training the militia according to the discipline prescribed by Congress.

In the foregoing grants of power, which are as complete as language can make them, there is no mention of the president. Nothing is omitted from the powers conferred upon the Congress. Even the power to make the rules for the government and the regulation of all the national forces, both on land and on the sea, is vested in the Congress.

Then, not content with this, to make certain that no question could possibly arise, the framers of the Constitution declared that Congress shall have power—

To make all laws which shall be necessary and proper for carrying into execution the foregoing powers, and all other powers vested by this Constitution in the Government of the United States, or in any department or officer thereof.

We all know from the debates which took place in the constitutional convention why it was that the Constitution was so framed as to vest in the Congress the entire warmaking power. The framers of the Constitution knew that to give to one man that power meant danger to the rights and liberties of the people. They knew that it mattered not whether you call the man king or emperor, czar or president, to put into his hands the power of making war or peace meant despotism. It meant that the people would be called upon to wage wars in which they had no interest or to which they might even be opposed. It meant secret diplomacy and secret treaties. It meant that in those things, most vital to the lives and welfare of the people, they would have nothing to say. The framers of the Constitution believed that they had guarded against this in the language I have quoted. They placed the entire control of this subject in the hands of the Congress. And it was assumed that debate would be free and open, that many men representing all the sections of the country would freely, frankly, and calmly exchange their views, unafraid of the power of the executive, uninfluenced by anything except their own convictions, and a desire to obey the will of the people expressed in a constitutional manner.

Another reason for giving this power to the Congress was that the Congress, particularly the House of Representatives, was assumed to be directly responsible to the people and would most nearly represent their views. The term of office for a representative was fixed at only two years. One-third of the Senate would be elected each two years. It was believed that this close relation to the people would insure a fair representation of the popular will in the action which the Congress might take. Moreover, if the Congress for any reason was unfaithful to its trust and declared a war which the people did not desire to support or to continue, they could in two years at most retire from office their unfaithful representatives and return others who would terminate the war. It is true that within two years much harm could be done by an unwise declaration of war, especially a war of aggression, where men were sent abroad. The framers of the Constitution made no provision for such a condition, for they apparently never contemplated that such a condition would arise.

Moreover, under the system of voluntary enlistment, which was the only system of raising an army for use outside the country of which the framers of the Constitution had any idea, the people could force a settlement of any war to which they were opposed by the simple means of not volunteering to fight it.

The only power relating to war with which the executive was intrusted was that of acting as commander in chief of the army and navy and of the militia when called into actual service. This provision is found in section 2 of Article II, and is as follows:

> The President shall be Commander in Chief of the Army and Navy of the United States and of the militia of the several States when called into the actual service of the United States.

Here is found the sum total of the president's war powers. After the army is raised he becomes the general in command. His function is purely military. He is the general in command of the entire army, just as there is a general in command of a certain field of operation. The authority of each is confined strictly to the field of military service. The Congress must raise and support and equip and maintain the army which the president is to command. Until the army is raised the president has no military authority over any of the persons that may compose it. He cannot enlist a man, or provide a uniform, or a single gun, or pound of powder. The country may be invaded from all sides and except for the command of the regular army, the president, as commander in chief of the army, is as powerless as any citizen to stem the tide of the invasion. In such case his only resort would be to the militia, as provided in the Constitution. Thus completely did the fathers of the Constitution strip the executive of military power.

It may be said that the duty of the president to enforce the laws of the country carries with it by implication control over the military forces for that purpose, and that the decision as to when the laws are violated, and the manner in which they should be redressed rests with the president. This whole matter was considered in the famous case of *Ex parte Milligan* (4 Wall., 2). The question of enforcing the laws of the United States, however, does not arise in the present discussion. *The laws of the United States have no effect outside the territory of the United States.* Our army in France or our navy on the high seas may be engaged in worthy enterprises, but they are not enforcing the laws of the United States, and the president derives from his constitutional obligation to enforce the laws of the country no power to determine the purposes of the present war.

The only remaining provision of the Constitution to be considered on the subject is that provision of Article II, section 2, which provides that the president—

Shall have power by and with the consent of the Senate to make treaties, *providing two-thirds of the Senate present concur.*

This is the same section of the Constitution which provides that the president "shall nominate, and by and with the advice and consent of the Senate, shall appoint ambassadors, other public ministers, consuls, judges of the Supreme Court," and so forth.

Observe, the president under this constitutional provision gets no authority to declare the purposes and objects of any war in which the country may be engaged. It is true that a treaty of peace cannot be executed except the president and the Senate concur in its execution. If a president should refuse to agree to terms of peace which were proposed, for instance, by a resolution of Congress, and accepted by the parliament of an enemy nation against the will, we will say, of an emperor, the war would simply stop, if the two parliaments agreed and exercised their powers respectively to withhold supplies; and the formal execution of a treaty of peace would be postponed until the people could select another president. It is devoutly to be hoped that such a situation will never arise, and it is hardly conceivable that it should arise with both an executive and a Senate anxious, respectively, to discharge the constitutional duties of their office. But if it should arise, under the Constitution, the final authority and the power to ultimately control is vested by the Constitution in the Congress. The president can no more make a treaty of peace without the approval not only of the Senate but of two-thirds of the senators present than he can appoint a judge of the Supreme Court without the concurrence of the Senate. A decent regard for the duties of the president, as well as the duties of the senators, and the consideration of the interests of the people, whose servants both the senators and the president are, requires that the negotiations which lead up to the making of peace should be participated in equally by the senators and by the president. For senators to take any other position is to shirk a plain duty; is to avoid an obligation imposed upon them by the spirit and letter of the Constitution and by the solemn oath of office each has taken.

PRECEDENTS AND AUTHORITIES

As might be expected from the plain language of the Constitution, the precedents and authorities are all one way. I shall not attempt to present them all here, but only refer to those which have peculiar application to the present situation.

Watson, in his work on the Constitution, Volume II, page 915, says:

The authority of the President over the Army and Navy to command and control is only subject to the restrictions of Congress to make rules for the government and regulation of the land and naval forces. . . . Neither can impair or invade the authority of the other. . . . The powers of the President (under the war clause) are only those which may be called "military."

The same author on the same and succeeding page points out that the president as commander in chief of the army may direct the military force in such a way as to most effectively injure the enemy. He may even direct an invasion of enemy territory. But, says the author, this can be done "temporarily, however, only until Congress has defined what the permanent policy of the country is to be."

How, then, can the president declare the purposes of the war to be, to extend permanently the territory of an ally or secure for an ally damages either in the form of money or new territory?

Mr. KING. Mr. President, will the senator yield for a question?

Mr. LA FOLLETTE. I prefer not to yield, if the senator will permit me to continue. I can hardly get through within the time allotted, and I am certain to be diverted if I begin to yield.

Mr. KING. I just wanted to ask the senator whether he thinks the president of the United States has contravened any constitutional powers conferred upon him thus far in the prosecution of the war?

Mr. LA FOLLETTE. Well, sir, I am discussing the constitutional question here, and senators must make their own application.

Pomeroy, in his *Introduction to the Constitutional Law of the United States* (9th edition, 1886, p. 373), says:

The organic law nowhere prescribes or limits the causes for which hostilities may be waged against a foreign country. *The causes of war it leaves to the discretion and judgment of the legislature.*

In other words, it is for Congress to determine what we are fighting for. The president, as commander in chief of the army, is to determine the best method of carrying on the fight. But since the purposes of the war must determine what are the best methods of conducting it, the primary duty at all times rests upon Congress to declare either in the declaration of war or subsequently what the objects are which it is expected to accomplish by the war.

In Elliot's *Debates* (supplement 2d edition, 1866, p. 439, vol. 5), it is said:

There is a material difference between the cases of making *war* and making *peace*. It should be more easy to get out of war than into it.

In the same volume, at page 140, we find:

Mr. Sherman said he considered the executive magistracy as nothing more than an institution for carrying the will of the legislature into effect.

Story, in his work on the Constitution (5th edition, 1891, p. 92), says:

The history of republics has but too fatally proved that they are too ambitious of military fame and conquest and too easily devoted to the interests of demagogues, who flatter their pride and *betray their interests*. It should, therefore, be difficult in a republic to *declare war, but not to make peace*. The representatives of the people are to lay the taxes to support a war, and therefore have a right to be consulted as to its propriety and necessity.

I commend this language to those gentlemen, both in and out of public office, who condemn as treasonable all efforts, either by the people or by their representatives in Congress, to discuss terms of peace or who even venture to suggest that a peace is not desirable until such time as the president, acting solely on his own responsibility, shall declare for peace. It is a strange doctrine we hear these days that the mass of the people, who pay in money, misery, and blood all the costs of this war, out of which a favored few profit so largely, may not freely and publicly discuss terms of peace. I believe that I have shown that such an odious and tyrannical doctrine has never been held by the men who have stood for liberty and representative government in this country.

Ordronaux, in his work on Constitutional Legislation, says:

This power (the war-making power) the Constitution has lodged in Congress, as the political department of the Government, and more immediate representative of the will of the people. (P. 495).

On page 496, the same author points out that—

The general power to declare war, and the consequent right to conduct it as long as the public interests may seem to require—

is vested in Congress.

The right to determine when and upon what terms the public interests require that war shall cease must therefore necessarily vest in Congress.

I have already referred to the fact that Lincoln, Webster, Clay, Sumner, Corwin, and others, all contended and declared in the midst of war that it was the right—the constitutional right—and the patriotic duty of American citizens, after the declaration of war, as well as before the declaration of war, and while the war was in progress, to discuss the issues of the war, to criticize the policies employed in its prosecution, and to work for the election of representatives pledged to carry out the will of the people respecting the war.

Let me call your attention to what James Madison, who became the fourth president of the United States, said on the subject in a speech at the Constitutional Convention, June 29, 1787:

A standing military force, with an overgrown Executive, will not long be safe companions to liberty. The means of defense against foreign dangers have always been the instrument of tyranny at home. Among the Romans it was a standing maxim to excite war whenever a revolt was apprehended. Throughout all Europe the armies kept up under the pretense of defending have enslaved the people. It is perhaps questionable whether the best concerted system of absolute power in Europe could maintain itself in a situation where no alarms of external danger could tame the people to the domestic yoke.

I now invite your attention to some of the precedents established by Congress showing that it has exercised almost from the time of the first Congress substantially the powers I am urging it should assert now.

CONGRESSIONAL PRECEDENTS

Many of the precedents to which I shall now briefly refer will be found in *Hinds' Precedents*, volume 2, chapter 49. My authority for the others are the records of Congress itself as contained in the *Congressional Globe* and *Congressional Record*.

In 1811 the House originated and the Senate agreed to a res-olution as follows:

> Taking into view the present state of the world, the peculiar situa-tion of Spain and of her American Provinces, and the intimate relations of the territory eastward of the River Perdido, adjoining the United States, to their security and tranquility: Therefore
> *Resolved, etc.*, That the United States can not see with indifference any part of the Spanish Provinces adjoining the said States eastward of the River Perdido pass from the hands of Spain into those of any other foreign power.

In 1821 Mr. Clay introduced the following resolution, which passed the House:

> *Resolved*, That the House of Representatives participates with the people of the United States in the deep interest which they feel for the success of the Spanish Provinces of South America, which are strug-gling to establish their liberty and independence, and that it will give its constitutional support to the President of the United States when-ever he may deem it expedient to recognize the sovereignty and inde-pendence of any of the said Provinces.

In 1825 there was a long debate in the House relating to an unconditional appropriation for the expenses of the ministers to the Panama Congress. According to Mr. Hinds' summary of this debate, the opposition to the amendment, led by Mr. Web-ster, was that—

> While the House had an undoubted right to express its general opinion in regard to questions of foreign policy, in this case it was proposed to decide what should be discussed by the particular minis-ters already appointed. If such instructions might be furnished by the House in this case they might be furnished in all, thus usurping the power of the Executive.

James Buchanan and John Forsyth, who argued in favor of the amendment, "contended that it did not amount to an in-struction to diplomatic agents, but was a proper expression of opinion by the House. The House has always exercised the right of expressing its opinion on great questions, either for-eign or domestic, and such expressions were never thought to be an improper interference with the Executive."

In April, 1864, the House originated and passed a resolution declaring that—

It did not accord with the policy of the United States to acknowledge a monarchical government erected on the ruins of any republican government in America under the auspices of any European power.

On May 23 the House passed a resolution requesting the president to communicate any explanation given by the government of the United States to France respecting the sense and bearing of the joint resolution relative to Mexico.

The president transmitted the correspondence to the House.

The correspondence disclosed that Secretary Seward had transmitted a copy of the resolution to our minister to France, with the explanation that—

This is a practical and purely executive question, and the decision of its constitutionality belongs not to the House of Representatives or even to Congress but to the President of the United States.

After a protracted struggle, evidently accompanied with much feeling, the House of Representatives adopted the following resolution, which had been reported by Mr. Henry Winter Davis from the Committee on Foreign Affairs:

Resolved, That Congress has a constitutional right to an authoritative voice in declaring and prescribing the foreign policy of the United States as well in the recognition of new powers as in other matters, and it is the constitutional duty of the president to respect that policy no less in diplomatic negotiations than *in the use of the national force when authorized by law.*

It will be observed from the language last read that it was assumed as a matter of course that Congress had an authoritative voice as to the use of the national forces to be made in time of war, and that it was the constitutional duty of the president to respect the policy of the Congress in that regard, and Mr. Davis in the resolution just read argued that it was the duty of the president to respect the authority of Congress in diplomatic negotiations even as he must respect it when the Congress determined the policy of the government in the use of the national forces. The portion of the resolution I have just read was adopted by a vote of 119 to 8. The balance of the resolution was adopted by a smaller majority, and was as follows:

And the propriety of any declaration of foreign policy by Congress is sufficiently proved by the vote which pronounces it, and such proposition, while pending and undetermined is not a fit topic of diplomatic explanation with any foreign power.

The joint resolution of 1898 declaring the intervention of the United States to remedy conditions existing in the island of Cuba is recent history and familiar to all. This resolution embodied a clear declaration of foreign policy regarding Cuba as well as a declaration of war. It passed both branches of Congress and was signed by the president.

After reading the abhorrent conditions existing in Cuba it reads as follows:

Resolved, etc., First. That the people of the island of Cuba are, and of right ought to be, free and independent.

Second. That it is the duty of the United States to demand, and the government of the United States does hereby demand, that the government of Spain at once relinquish its authority and government in the island of Cuba and withdraw its land and naval forces from Cuba and Cuban waters.

Third. That the president of the United States be, and he hereby is, directed and empowered to use the entire land and naval forces of the United States, and to call into the actual service of the United States the militia of the several states, to such extent as may be necessary to carry these resolutions into effect.

Fourth. That the United States hereby disclaims any disposition or intention to exercise sovereignty, jurisdiction, or control over said island except for the pacification thereof, and asserts its determination, when that is accomplished, to leave the government and control of the island to its people.

On April 28, 1904, a joint resolution was passed by both houses of Congress in the following terms:

That it is the sense of the Congress of the United States that it is desirable in the interests of uniformity of action by maritime states in time of war, that the president endeavor to bring about an understanding among the principal maritime powers, with a view to incorporating into the permanent law of civilized nations the principle of the exemption of all private property at sea, not contraband of war, from capture or destruction by belligerents.

Here it will be observed that the Congress proposed by

resolution to direct the president as to the policy of exempting from capture private property at sea, not contraband of war, in not only one war merely but in all wars, providing that other maritime powers could be brought to adopt the same policy. So far as I am aware, there is an unbroken line of precedents by Congress upon this subject down to the time of the present administration. It is true that in 1846 President Polk, without consulting Congress, assumed to send the army of the United States into territory the title of which was in dispute between the United States and Mexico, thereby precipitating bloodshed and the Mexican War. But it is also true that this act was con- demned as unconstitutional by the great constitutional lawyers of the country, and Abraham Lincoln, when he became a mem- ber of the next Congress, voted for and supported the resolu- tion, called the Ashmun amendment, which passed the House of Representatives, declaring that the Mexican War had been—

Unnecessarily and unconstitutionally begun by the President of the United States. (See Schouler's History of the United States, vol. 5, p. 83. See also Lincoln's speech in the House of Representatives, Jan. 12, 1848.)

That the full significance of this resolution was appreciated by the House of Representatives is shown by the speech of Mr. Venable, representative from North Carolina, and a warm sup- porter of President Polk, made in the House, January 12, 1848, where referring to this resolution he says:

Eighty-five members of this House sustained that amendment (re- ferring to the Ashmun amendment) and it now constitutes one of our recorded acts. I will not here stop to inquire as to the moral effect upon the Mexican people and the Mexican Government which will result to us from such a vote in the midst of a war. I suppose gentle- men have fully weighed this matter. Neither will I now inquire how much such a vote will strengthen our credit or facilitate the govern- ment in furnishing the necessary supply of troops. . . .

They [referring to his fellow members in the House of Represen- tatives] have said by their votes that the president has violated the Constitution in the most flagrant manner; that every drop of blood which has been shed, every bone which now whitens the plains of Mexico, every heart-wringing agony which has been produced must be placed to his account who has so flagitiously violated the Constitution and involved the nation in the horrors of war. This the majority of this House have declared on oath. The grand inquest of the nation have asserted the fact and fixed it on their records, and I here demand of them to impeach the president.

That Mr. Lincoln was in no manner deterred from the discharge of his duty as he saw it is evidenced by the fact that on the day following the speech of Representative Venable, Lincoln replied with one of the ablest speeches of his career, the opening sentences of which I desire to quote. He said:

> Some, if not all, the gentlemen of the other side of the House, who have addressed the committee within the last two days, have spoken rather complainingly, if I have rightly understood them, of the vote given a week or ten days ago, declaring that the war with Mexico was unnecessarily and unconstitutionally commenced by the President. I admit that such a vote should not be given in mere party wantonness and that the one given is justly censurable, if it have no other or better foundation. I am one of those who joined in that vote; and I did so under my best impression of the truth of the case.

Lincoln then proceeded to demonstrate the truth of the charge as he regarded it. Evidently he did not think that patriotism in war more than in peace required the suppression of the truth respecting anything pertaining to the conduct of the war.

And yet today, Mr. President, for merely suggesting a possible disagreement with the administration on any measure submitted, or the offering of amendments to increase the tax upon incomes, or on war profits, is "treason to our country and an effort to serve the enemy."

Since the Constitution vests in Congress the supreme power to determine when and for what purpose the country will engage in war and the objects to attain which the war will be prosecuted, it seems to me to be an evasion of a solemn duty on the part of the Congress not to exercise that power at this critical time in the nation's affairs. The Congress can no more avoid its responsibility in this matter than it can in any other. As the nation's purposes in conducting this war are of supreme importance to the country, it is the supreme duty of Congress to exercise the function conferred upon it by the Constitution of guiding the foreign policy of the nation in the present crisis.

A minor duty may be evaded by Congress, a minor responsibility avoided without disaster resulting, but on this momentous question there can be no evasion, no shirking of duty of the Congress, without subverting our form of government. If our Constitution is to be changed so as to give the president the power to determine the purposes for which this Nation will engage in war, and the conditions on which it will make peace, then let that change be made deliberately by an amendment to the Constitution proposed and adopted in a constitutional manner. It would be bad enough if the Constitution clothed the president with any such power, but to exercise such power without constitutional authority can not long be tolerated if even the forms of free government are to remain. We all know that no amendment to the Constitution giving the president the powers suggested would be adopted by the people. We know that if such an amendment were to be proposed it would be overwhelmingly defeated.

The universal conviction of those who yet believe in the rights of the people is that the first step toward the prevention of war and the establishment of peace, permanent peace, is to give the people who must bear the brunt of war's awful burden more to say about it. The masses will understand that it was the evil of a one-man power exercised in a half dozen nations through the malevolent influences of a system of secret diplomacy that plunged the helpless peoples of Europe into the awful war that has been raging with increasing horror and fury ever since it began and that now threatens to engulf the world before it stops.

No conviction is stronger with the people today than that there should be no future wars except in case of actual invasion, unless supported by a referendum, a plebiscite, a vote of ratification upon the declaration of war before it shall become effective.

And because there is no clearness of understanding, no unity of opinion in this country on the part of the people as to the conditions upon which we are prosecuting this war or what the specific objects are upon the attainment of which the present administration would be willing to conclude a peace, it becomes still more imperative each day that Congress should assert its constitutional power to define and declare the objects of this war which will afford the basis for a conference and for the establishment of permanent peace. The president has asked the German people to speak for themselves on this great world issue; why should not the American people voice their convictions through their chosen representatives in Congress?

Ever since new Russia appeared upon the map she has been holding out her hands to free America to come to her support in declaring for a clear understanding of the objects to be attained to secure peace. Shall we let this most remarkable revolution the world has ever witnessed appeal to us in vain?

We have been six months at war. We have incurred financial obligations and made expenditures of money in amounts already so large that the human mind cannot comprehend them. The government has drafted from the peaceful occupations of civil life a million of our finest young men—and more will be taken if necessary—to be transported four thousand miles over the sea, with their equipment and supplies, to the trenches of Europe.

The first chill winds of autumn remind us that another winter is at hand. The imagination is paralyzed at the thought of the human misery, the indescribable suffering, which the winter months, with their cold and sleet and ice and snow, must bring to the war-swept lands, not alone to the soldiers at the front but to the noncombatants at home.

To such excesses of cruelty has this war descended that each nation is now, as a part of its strategy, planning to starve the women and children of the enemy countries. Each warring nation is carrying out the unspeakable plan of starving noncombatants. Each nurses the hope that it may break the spirit of the men of the enemy country at the front by starving the wives and babes at home, and woe be it that we have become partners in this awful business and are even cutting off food shipments from neutral countries in order to force them to help starve women and children of the country against whom we have declared war.

There may be some necessity overpowering enough to justify these things, but the people of America should demand to know what results are expected to satisfy the sacrifice of all that civilization holds dear upon the bloody altar of a conflict which employs such desperate methods of warfare.

The question is, are we to sacrifice millions of our young men—the very promise of the land—and spend billions and more billions, and pile up the cost of living until we starve—and for what? Shall the fearfully overburdened people of this country continue to bear the brunt of a prolonged war for any objects not openly stated and defined?

The answer, sir, rests in my judgment, with the Congress, whose duty it is to declare our specific purposes in the present war and to state the objects upon the attainment of which we will make peace.

CAMPAIGN SHOULD BE MADE ON CONSTITUTIONAL LINES

And, sir, this is the ground on which I stand. I maintain that Congress has the right and the duty to declare the objects of the war and the people have the right and the obligation to discuss it.

American citizens may hold all shades of opinion as to the war; one citizen may glory in it, another may deplore it, each has the same right to voice his judgment. An American citizen may think and say that we are not justified in prosecuting this war for the purpose of dictating the form of government which shall be maintained by our enemy or our ally, and not be subject to punishment at law. He may pray aloud that our boys shall not be sent to fight and die on European battlefields for the annexation of territory or the maintenance of trade agreements and be within his legal rights. He may express the hope that an early peace may be secured on the terms set forth by the new Russia and by President Wilson in his speech of January 22, 1917, and he cannot lawfully be sent to jail for the expression of his convictions.

It is the citizen's duty to obey the law until it is repealed or declared unconstitutional. But he has the inalienable right to fight what he deems an obnoxious law or a wrong policy in the courts and at the ballot box.

It is the suppressed emotion of the masses that breeds revolution.

If the American people are to carry on this great war, if

public opinion is to be enlightened and intelligent, there must be free discussion.

Congress, as well as the people of the United States, entered the war in great confusion of mind and under feverish excitement. The president's leadership was followed in the faith that he had some big, unrevealed plan by which peace that would exalt him before all the world would soon be achieved.

Gradually, reluctantly, Congress and the country are beginning to perceive that we are in this terrific world conflict, not only to *right* our wrongs, not only to *aid* the allies, not only to *share* its awful death toll and its fearful tax burden, but, perhaps, to *bear the brunt* of the war.

And so I say, if we are to forestall the danger of being drawn into years of war, perhaps finally to maintain imperialism and exploitation, the people must unite in a campaign along constitutional lines for free discussion of the policy of the war and its conclusion on a just basis.

Permit me, sir, this word in conclusion. It is said by many persons for whose opinions I have profound respect and whose motives I know to be sincere that "we are in this war and must go through to the end." That is true. But it is not true that we must go through to the end to *accomplish an undisclosed purpose, or to reach an unknown goal.*

I believe that whatever there is of honest difference of opinion concerning this war, arises precisely at this point.

There is, and of course can be, no real difference of opinion concerning the duty of the citizen to discharge to the last limit whatever obligation the war lays upon him.

Our young men are being taken by the hundreds of thousands for the purpose of waging this war on the Continent of Europe, possibly Asia or Africa, or anywhere else that they may be ordered. Nothing must be left undone for their protection. They must have the best army, ammunition, and equipment that money can buy. They must have the best training and the best officers which this great country can provide. The dependents and relatives they leave at home must be provided for, not meagerly, but generously so far as money can provide for them.

I have done some of the hardest work of my life during the last few weeks on the revenue bill to raise the largest possible amount of money from surplus incomes and war profits for this war and upon other measures to provide for the protection of the soldiers and their families. That I was not able to accomplish more along this line is a great disappointment to me. I did all that I could, and I shall continue to fight with all the power at my command until wealth is made to bear more of the burden of this war than has been laid upon it by the present Congress. Concerning these matters there can be no difference of opinion. We have not yet been able to muster the forces to conscript wealth, as we have conscripted men, but no one has ever been able to advance even a plausible argument for not doing so.

No, Mr. President; it is on the other point suggested where honest differences of opinion may arise. Shall we ask the people of this country to shut their eyes and take the entire war program on faith? There are no doubt many honest and well-meaning persons who are willing to answer that question in the affirmative rather than risk the dissensions which they fear may follow a free discussion of the issues of this war. With that position I do not—I cannot agree. Have the people no intelligent contribution to make to the solution of the problems of this war? I believe that they have, and that in this matter, as in so many others, they may be wiser than their leaders, and that if left free to discuss the issues of the war they will find the correct settlement of these issues.

But it is said that Germany will fight with greater determination if her people believe that we are not in perfect agreement. Mr. President, that is the same worn-out pretext which has been used for three years to keep the plain people of Europe engaged in killing each other in this war. And, sir, as applied to this country, at least, it is a pretext with nothing to support it.

The way to paralyze the German arm, to weaken the German military force, in my opinion, is to declare our objects in this war, and show by that declaration to the German people that we are not seeking to dictate a form of government to Germany or to render more secure England's domination of the seas.

A declaration of our purposes in this war, so far from strengthening our enemy, I believe would immeasurably weaken her, for it would no longer be possible to misrepresent our purposes to the German people. Such a course on our part, so far from endangering the life of a single one of our boys, I believe would result in saving the lives of hundreds of thousands of them by bringing about an earlier and more lasting peace by intelligent negotiation, instead of securing a peace by the complete exhaustion of one or the other of the belligerents.

Such a course would also immeasurably, I believe, strengthen our military force in this country, because when the objects of this war are clearly stated and the people approve of those objects they will give to the war a popular support it will never otherwise receive.

Then, again, honest dealing with the entente allies, as well as with our own people, requires a clear statement of our objects in this war. If we do not expect to support the entente allies in the dreams of conquest we know some of them entertain, then in all fairness to them that fact should be stated now. If we do expect to support them in their plans for conquest, and aggrandizement, then our people are entitled to know that vitally important fact before this war proceeds further. Common honesty and fair dealing with the people of this country and with the nations by whose side we are fighting, as well as a sound military policy at home, requires the fullest and freest discussion before the people of every issue involved in this great war and that a plan and specific declaration of our purposes in the war be speedily made by the Congress of the United States.

CARRIE CHAPMAN CATT

Address to Woman Suffrage Convention

Washington, D.C., December 1917

AN ADDRESS TO THE CONGRESS OF THE
UNITED STATES

WOMAN SUFFRAGE is inevitable. Suffragists knew it before November 6, 1917; opponents afterward. Three distinct causes make it inevitable.

1. *The history of our country.* Ours is a nation born of revolution; of rebellion against a system of government so securely entrenched in the customs and traditions of human society that in 1776 it seemed impregnable. From the beginning of things nations had been ruled by kings and for kings, while the people served and paid the cost. The American Revolutionists boldly proclaimed the heresies:

"*Taxation without representation is tyranny.*"

"*Governments derive their just powers from the consent of the governed.*"

The Colonists won and the nation which was established as a result of their victory has held unfailingly that these two fundamental principles of democratic government are not only the spiritual source of our national existence but have been our chief historic pride and at all times the sheet anchor of our liberties.

Eighty years after the Revolution Abraham Lincoln welded those two maxims into a new one:

"*Ours is a government of the people, by the people and for the people.*"

Fifty years more passed and the President of the United States, Woodrow Wilson, in a mighty crisis of the nation, proclaimed to the world:

"*We are fighting for the things which we have always carried nearest our hearts—for democracy, for the right of those who submit to authority to have a voice in their own government.*"

All the way between these immortal aphorisms political leaders have declared unabated faith in their truth. Not one American has arisen to question their logic in the one hundred and forty-one years of our national existence. However stupidly our country may have evaded the logical application at times, it has never swerved from its devotion to the theory of democracy as expressed by those two axioms.

Not only has it unceasingly upheld the THEORY but it has carried these theories into PRACTICE whenever men made application.

Certain denominations of Protestants, Catholics, Jews, non-land holders, workingmen, Negroes, Indians, were at one time disfranchised in all, or in part, of our country. Class by class they have been admitted to the electorate. Political motives may have played their part in some instances but the only reason given by historians for their enfranchisement is the unassailability of the logic of these maxims of the Declaration.

Meantime the United States opened wide its gates to men of all the nations of earth. By the combination of naturalization granted the foreigner after a five-years' residence by our national government and the uniform provision of the State constitutions which extends the vote to *male citizens*, it has been the custom in our country for three generations that any male immigrant, accepted by the national government as a citizen, automatically becomes a voter in any State in which he chooses to reside, subject only to the minor qualifications prescribed by the State. Justifiable exceptions to the general principle might have been entered. Men just emerging from slavery, untrained to think or act for themselves and in most cases wholly illiterate, were not asked to qualify for voting citizenship. Not even as a measure of national caution has the vote ever been withheld from immigrants until they have learned our language, earned a certificate of fitness from our schools or given definite evidence of loyalty to our country. When such questions have been raised, political leaders have replied: "What! Tax men and in return give them no vote; compel men to obey the authority of a government to which they may not give consent! Never. That is un-American." So, it happens that men of all nations and all races, except the Mongolian, may secure citizenship and automatically become voters in any State in the

Union, and even the Mongolian born in this country is a citizen and has the vote. With such a history behind it, how can our nation escape the logic it has never failed to follow, when its last unenfranchised class calls for the vote? Behold our Uncle Sam floating the banner with one hand, "Taxation without representation is tyranny," and with the other seizing the billions of dollars paid in taxes by women to whom he refuses "representation." Behold him again, welcoming the boys of twenty-one and the newly-made immigrant citizen to "a voice in their own government" while he denies that fundamental right of democracy to thousands of women public school teachers from whom many of these men learn all they know of citizenship and patriotism, to women college presidents, to women who preach in our pulpits, interpret law in our courts, preside over our hospitals, write books and magazines and serve in every uplifting moral and social enterprise.

Is there a single man who can justify such inequality of treatment, such outrageous discriminations? Not one.

Woman suffrage became an assured fact when the Declaration of Independence was written. It matters not at all whether Thomas Jefferson and his compatriots thought of women when they wrote that immortal document. They conceived and voiced a principle greater than any man. "A Power not of themselves which makes for righteousness" gave them the vision and they proclaimed truisms as immutable as the multiplication table, as changeless as time. The Hon. Champ Clark announced that he had been a woman suffragist ever since he "got the hang of the Declaration of Independence." So it must be with every other American. The amazing thing is that it has required so long a time for a people, most of whom know how to read, "to get the hang of it." Indeed, so inevitable does our history make woman suffrage that any citizen, political party, Congress or Legislature that now blocks its coming by so much as a single day, contributes to the indefensible inconsistency which threatens to make our nation a jest among the onward moving peoples of the world.

2. *The suffrage for women already established in the United States makes woman suffrage for the nation inevitable.* When Elihu Root, as President of the American Society of International Law, at the eleventh annual meeting in Washington,

April 26, 1917, said, "The world cannot be half democratic and half autocratic. It must be all democratic or all Prussian. There can be no compromise," he voiced a general truth. Precisely the same intuition has already taught the blindest and most hostile foe of woman suffrage that our nation cannot long continue a condition under which government in half its territory rests upon the consent of half the people and in the other half upon the consent of all the people; a condition which grants representation to the taxed in half its territory and denies it in the other half; a condition which permits women in some States to share in the election of the President, Senators and Representatives and denies them that privilege in others. It is too obvious to require demonstration that woman suffrage, now covering half our territory, will eventually be ordained in all the nation. No one will deny it; the only question left is when and how will it be completely established.

3. *The leadership of the United States in world democracy compels the enfranchisement of its own women.*

The maxims of the Declaration were once called "fundamental principles of government." They are now called "American principles" or even "Americanisms." They have become the slogans of every movement toward political liberty the world around; of every effort to widen the suffrage for men or women in any land. Not a people, race or class striving for freedom is there, anywhere in the world, that has not made our axioms the chief weapon of the struggle. More, all men and women the world around, with far-sighted vision into the verities of things, know that the world tragedy of our day is not now being waged over the assassination of an Archduke, nor commercial competition, nor national ambitions, nor the freedom of the seas—it is a death grapple between the forces which deny and those which uphold the truths of the Declaration of Independence.

Our "Americanisms" have become the issue of the great war!

Every day the conviction grows deeper that a world humanity will emerge from the war, demanding political liberty and accepting nothing less. In that new struggle there is little doubt that men and women will demand and attain political liberty together. To-day they are fighting the world's battle for Democracy together. Men and women are paying the frightful cost of war and bearing its sad and sickening sorrows together. To-morrow they will share its rewards together in democracies which make no discriminations on account of sex.

These are new times and, as an earnest of its sincerity in the battle for democracy, the government of Great Britain has not only pledged votes to its disfranchised men and to its women, but the measure passed the House of Commons in June, 1917, by a vote of 7 to 1 and will be sent to the House of Lords in December with the assurances of Premier Lloyd George that it will shortly become a national law. The measure will apply to England, Scotland, Ireland, Wales and all the smaller British islands.

Canada, too, has enfranchised the women of all its provinces stretching from the Pacific Coast to Northern New York, and the Premier has predicted votes for all Canadian women before the next national election.

Russia, whose opposing forces have made a sad farce of the new liberty, is nevertheless pledged to a democracy which shall include women. It must be remembered that no people ever passed from absolute autocracy into a smoothly running democracy with ready-made constitution and a full set of statutes to cover all conditions. Russia is no exception. She must have time to work out her destiny. Except those maxims of democracy put forth by our own country, it is interesting to note that the only one worthy of immortality is the slogan of the women of New Russia, *"Without the participation of women, suffrage is not universal."*

France has pledged votes to its women as certainly as a Republic can. Italian men have declared woman suffrage an imperative issue when the war is over and have asked its consideration before. The city of Prague (Bohemia) has appointed a Commission to report a new municipal suffrage plan which shall include women. Even autocratic Germany has debated the question in the Imperial Reichstag.

In the words of Premier Lloyd George: "There are times in history when the world spins along its destined course so leisurely that for centuries it seems to be at a standstill. Then come awful times when it rushes along at so giddy a pace that the track of centuries is covered in a single year. These are the times in which we now live."

It is true; democracy, votes for men and votes for women, making slow but certain progress in 1914, have suddenly become established facts in many lands in 1917. Already our one-time Mother Country has become the standard bearer of our Americanisims, the principles she once denied, and—cynical fact—Great Britain, not the United States, is now leading the world on to the coming democracy. Any man who has red American blood in his veins, any man who has gloried in our history and has rejoiced that our land was the leader of world democracy, will share with us the humbled national pride that our country has so long delayed action upon this question that another country has beaten us in what we thought was our especial world mission.

Is it not clear that American history makes woman suffrage inevitable? That full suffrage in twelve States makes its coming in all forty-eight States inevitable? That the spread of democracy over the world, including votes for the women of many countries, in each case based upon the principles our Republic gave to the world, compels action by our nation? Is it not clear that the world expects such action and fails to understand its delay?

In the face of these facts we ask you, Senators and Members of the House of Representatives of the United States, is not the immediate enfranchisement of the women of our nation the duty of the hour?

Why hesitate? Not an inch of solid ground is left for the feet of the opponent. The world's war has killed, buried and pronounced the obsequies upon the hard worked "war argument." Mr. Asquith, erstwhile champion anti-suffragist of the world, has said so and the British Parliament has confirmed it by its enfranchisement of British women. The million and fifteen thousand women of New York who signed a declaration that they wanted the vote, plus the heavy vote of women in every State and country where women have the franchise, have finally and completely disposed of the familiar "they don't want it" argument. Thousands of women annually emerging from the schools and colleges have closed the debate upon the one-time serious "they don't know enough" argument. The statistics of police courts and prisons have laid the ghost of the "too bad to vote" argument. The woman who demanded the book and verse in the Bible which gave men the vote, declaring that the next verse gave it to women, brought the "Bible argument" to a sudden end. The testimony of thousands of reputable citizens of our own suffrage States and of all other suffrage lands that woman suffrage has brought no harm and much positive good, and the absence of reputable citizens who deny these facts, has closed the "women only double the vote" argument. The increasing number of women wage-earners, many supporting families and some supporting hubands, has thrown out the "women are represented" argument. One by one these pet misgivings have been relegated to the scrap heap of all rejected, cast-off prejudices. Not an argument is left. The case against woman suffrage, carefully prepared by the combined wit, skill and wisdom of opponents, including some men of high repute, during sixty years, has been closed. The jury of the New York electorate heard it all, weighed the evidence and pronounced it "incompetent, irrelevant and immaterial." Historians tell us that the battle of Gettysburg brought our Civil War to an end, although the fighting went on a year longer, because the people who directed it did not see that the end had come. Had their sight been clearer, a year's casualties of human life, desolated homes, high taxes and bitterness of spirit, might have been avoided. The battle of New York is the Gettysburg of the woman suffrage movement. There are those too blind to see that the end has come, and others, unrelenting and unreasoning, who stubbornly deny that the end has come although they know it. These can compel the women of the nation to keep a standing suffrage army, to finance it, to fight on until these blind and stubborn ones are gathered to their fathers and men with clearer vision come to take their places, but the casualties will be sex antagonism, party antagonism, bitterness, resentment, contempt, hate and the things which grow out of a rankling grievance autocratically denied redress. These things are not mentioned in the spirit of threat, but merely to voice well known principles of historical psychology.

Benjamin Franklin once said "The cost of war is not paid at the time, the bills come afterwards." So too the nation, refusing justice when justice is due, finds the costs accumulating and the bills presented at unexpected and embarrassing times. Think it over.

If enfranchisement is to be given to women now, how is it to be done? Shall it be by amendment of State constitutions or by amendment of the Federal Constitution? There are no other ways. The first sends the question from the Legislature by referendum to all male voters of the State; the other sends the question from Congress to the Legislatures of the several States.

We elect the Federal method. There are three reasons why we make this choice and three reasons why we reject the State method. We choose the Federal method (1) because it is the quickest process and justice demands immediate action. If passed by the Sixty-fifth Congress, as it should be, the amendment will go to forty-one Legislatures in 1919, and when thirty-six have ratified it, will become national law. In 1869 Wyoming led the way and 1919 will round out half a century of the most self-sacrificing struggle any class ever made for the vote. It is enough. The British women's suffrage army will be mustered out at the end of their half century of similiar endeavor. Surely men of the land of George Washington will not require a longer time than those of the land of George the Third to discover that taxation without representation is tyranny no matter whether it be men or women who are taxed! We may justly expect American men to be as willing to grant to the women of the United States as generous consideration as those of Great Britain have done.

(2) Every other country dignifies woman suffrage as a national question. Even Canada and Australia, composed of self-governing states like our own, so regard it. Were the precedent not established our own national government has taken a step which makes the treatment of woman suffrage as a national question imperative. For the first time in our history Congress has imposed a direct tax upon women and has thus deliberately violated the most fundamental and sacred principle of our government, since it offers no compensating "representation" for the tax it imposes. Unless reparation is made it becomes the same kind of tyrant as was George the Third. When the exemption for unmarried persons under the Income Tax was reduced to $1,000, the Congress laid the tax upon thousands of wage-earning women—teachers, doctors, lawyers, bookkeepers, secretaries and the proprietors of many businesses. Such women

are earning their incomes under hard conditions of economic inequalities largely due to their disfranchisment. Many of these, while fighting their own economic battle, have been contributors to the campaign for suffrage that they might bring easier conditions for all women. Now those contributions will be deflected from suffrage treasuries into government funds through taxation. Women realize the dire need of huge government resources at this time and will make no protest against the tax, but it must be understood, and understood clearly, that the protest is there just the same and that women income taxpayers with few exceptions harbor a genuine grievance against the government of the United States. The national government is guilty of the violation of the principle that the tax and the vote are inseparable; it alone can make amends. Two ways are open: exempt the women from the Income Tax or grant them the vote—there can be no compromise. To shift responsibility from Congress to the States is to invite the scorn of every human being who has learned to reason. A Congress which creates the law and has the power to violate a world-acknowledged axiom of just government can also command the law and the power to make reparation to those it has wronged by the violation. To you, the Congress of the United States, we must and do look for this act of primary justice.

(3) If the entire forty-eight States should severally enfranchise women, their political status would still be inferior to that of men, since no provision for national protection in their right to vote would exist. The women of California or New York are not wholly enfranchised, for the national government has not denied the States the right to deprive them of the vote. This protection can come only by Federal action. Therefore, since women will eventually be forced to demand Congressional action in order to equalize the rights of men and women, why not take such action now and thus shorten and ease the process? When such submission is secured, as it will be, forty-eight simultaneous State ratification campaigns will he necessary. By the State method thirty-six States would be obliged to have individual campaigns, and those would still have to be followed by the forty-eight additional campaigns to secure the final protection in their right to vote by the national government. We propose to conserve money, time and woman's strength by the

elimination of the thirty-six State campaigns as unnecessary at this stage of the progress of the woman suffrage movement.

The three reasons why we object to the State amendment process are: (1) The constitutions of many States contain such difficult provisions for amending that it is practically impossible to carry an amendment at the polls. Several States require a majority of all the votes cast at an election to insure the passage of an amendment. As the number of persons voting on amendments is usually considerably smaller than the number voting for the head of the ticket, the effect of such provision is that a majority of those men who do not vote at all on the amendment are counted as voting against it. For example, imagine a State casting 100,000 votes for Governor and 80,000 on a woman suffrage amendment. That proportion would be a usual one. Now suppose there were 45,000 votes in favor and 35,000 against woman suffrage. The amendment would have been carried by 10,000 majority in a State which requires only a majority of the votes cast on the amendment, as in the State of New York. If, however, the State requires a majority of the votes cast at the election, the amendment would be lost by 10,000 majority. The men who were either too ignorant, too indifferent or too careless to vote on the question would have de feated it. Such constitutions have rarely been amended and then only on some non-controversial question which the dominant powers have agreed to support with the full strength of their "machines."

New Mexico, for example, requires three-fourths of those voting at an election, including two-thirds from each county. New Mexico is surrounded by suffrage States but the women who live there probably can secure enfranchisement only by federal action. The Indiana constitution provides that a majority of all voters is necessary to carry an amendment; thus the courts may decide that registered voters who did not go to the polls at all may be counted in the number, a majority of whom it is necessary to secure. The constitution cannot be amended. The courts have declared that the constitution prohibits the Legislature from granting suffrage to women. What then can the women of Indiana do? They have no other hope than the Federal Amendment. Several State constitutions stipulate that a definite period of time must elapse before an amendment defeated at the polls can again be submitted. New York has no such provision and the second campaign of 1917 immediately followed the first in 1915; but Pennsylvania and New Jersey, both voting on the question in 1915, cannot vote on it again before 1920. New Hampshire has no provision for the submission of an amendment by the Legislature at all. A Constitutional Convention alone has the right to submit an amendment, and such conventions can not be called oftener than once in seven years. The constitutional complications in many of the States are numerous, varied and difficult to overcome.

All careful investigators must arrive at the same conclusion that the only hope for the enfranchisement of the women of several States is through Congressional action. Since this is true, we hold it unnecessary to force women to pass through any more referenda campaigns. The hazards of the State constitutional provisions which women are expected to overcome in order to get the vote, as compared with the easy process by which the vote is fairly thrust upon foreigners who choose to make their residence among us, is so offensive an outrage to one's sense of justice that a woman's rebellion would surely have been fomented long ago had women not known that the discrimination visited upon them was without deliberate intent. The continuation of this condition is, however, the direct responsibility now of every man who occupies a position authorized to right the wrong. You are such men, Honorable Senators and Representatives. To you we appeal to remove a grievance more insulting than any nation in the wide world has put upon its women.

2. The second reason why we object to the State process is far more serious and important than the first. It is because the statutory laws governing elections are so inadequate and defective as to vouchsafe little or no protection to a referendum in most States. The need for such protection seems to have been universally overlooked by the lawmakers. Bipartisan election boards offer efficient machinery whereby the representatives of one political party may check any irregularities of the other. The interests of all political parties in an election are further protected by partisan watchers. None of these provisions is available to those interested in a referendum. In most States women may not serve as watchers and no political party as-

sumes responsibility for a non-partisan question. In the State of New York women may serve as watchers. They did so serve in 1915 and in 1917; nearly every one in the more than 5,000 polling places was covered by efficiently trained women watchers. The women believe that this fact had much to do with the favorable result.

In twenty-four States there is no law providing for a recount on a referendum. Voters may be bribed, colonized, repeated and the law provides for no possible redress. In some States corrupt voters may be arrested, tried and punished, but that does not remove their votes from the total vote cast nor in any way change the results. When questions which are supported by men's organizations go to referendum, such as prohibition, men interested may secure posts as election officials or party watchers and thus be in position to guard the purity of the election. This privilege is not open to women.

That corrupt influences have exerted their full power against woman suffrage, we know well. I have myself seen blocks of men marched to the polling booth and paid money in plain sight, both men and bribers flaunting the fact boldly that they were "beating the —— women." I have myself seen men who could not speak a word of English, nor write their names in any language, driven to the polls like sheep to vote against woman suffrage and no law at the time could punish them for the misuse of the vote so cheaply extended to them, nor change the result.

It is our sincere belief based upon evidence which has been completely convincing to us that woman suffrage amendments in several States have been won on referendum, but that the returns were juggled and the amendment counted out. We have given to such campaigns our money, our time, our strength, our very lives. We have believed the amendment carried and yet have seen our cause announced as lost. We are tired of playing the State campaign game with "the political dice loaded and the cards stacked" against us before we begin. The position of such an amendment is precisely like that of the defendant in a case brought before an inexperienced judge. After having heard the plaintiff, he untactfully remarked that he would listen to the defendant's remarks but he was bound to tell him in advance that he proposed to give the verdict to the plaintiff. From this lower court, often unscrupulous in its unfairness, we appeal to the higher, the Congress and the Legislatures of the United States.

3. The third reason why we object to the State method is even more weighty than either or both of the others. It is because the State method fixes responsibility upon no one. The Legislatures pass the question on to the voters and have no further interest in it. The political parties, not knowing how the election may decide the matter, are loth to espouse the cause of woman suffrage, lest if it loses, they will have alienated from their respective parties the support of enemies of woman suffrage.

Contributors to campaign funds have at times stipulated the return service of the party machinery to defeat woman suffrage, and as such contributors are wily enough to make certain of their protection, they often contribute to both dominant parties. Thousands of men in every State have become so accustomed to accept party nominations and platforms as their unquestioned guide that they refuse to act upon a political question without instruction from their leaders. When the leaders pass the word along the line to defeat a woman suffrage amendment, it is impossible to carry it. It is not submitted to an electorate of thinking voters whose reason must be convinced, but to such voters, plus political "machines" skillfully organized, servilely obedient, who have their plans laid to defeat the question at the polls even before it leaves the Legislature. From a condition where no one is responsible for the procedure of the amendment through the hazards of an election, where every enemy may effectively hide his enmity and the methods employed behind the barriers of constitutions and election laws, we appeal to a method which will bring our cause into the open where every person or party, friend or foe involved in the campaign, may be held responsible to the public. We appeal from the method which has kept the women of this country disfranchised a quarter of a century after their enfranchisement was due, to the method by which the vote has been granted to the men and women of other lands. We do so with the certain assurance that every believer in fair play, regardless of party fealties, will approve our decision.

These are the three reasons why we elect the federal method, and the three reasons why we reject the State method. We are so familiar with the objections Congressional opponents urge against suffrage by the federal method that we know those objections also, curiously, number three.

Objection No. 1. *War time is not the proper time to consider this question.* Two neutral countries, Iceland and Denmark, and three beligerent countries, Canada, Russia and Great Britain, have enfranchised their women during war time and they have been engaged in war for three and a half years. That which is a proper time for such countries is surely proper enough for us.

More, it is not our fault, you will admit, that this question is still unsettled in 1917. If our urgent advice had been taken it would have been disposed of twenty-five years ago and our nation would now be proudly leading the world to democracy instead of following in third place. Had Congress "got the hang of the Declaration of Independence" then, more men today would know the definition of democracy than do and more men would understand what a world's war "to make the world safe for democracy" means.

In 1866 an Address to Congress was adopted by a Suffrage Convention held in New York and presented to Congress later by Susan B. Anthony and Elizabeth Cady Stanton. They protested against the enfranchisement of Negro men while women remained disfranchised and asked for Congressional action. That was fifty-one years ago. In 1878 the Federal Suffrage Amendment now pending was introduced in Congress at the request of the National Woman Suffrage Association and has been reintroduced in each succeeding Congress.

The representatives of this Association have appeared before the Committees of every Congress since 1878 to urge its passage. The women who made the first appeal, brave, splendid souls, have long since passed into the Beyond, and every one died knowing that the country she loved and served classified her as a political pariah. Every Congress has seen the Committee Rooms packed with anxious women yearning for the declaration of their nation that they were no longer to be classed with idiots, criminals and paupers. Every State has sent its quota of woman to those Committees. Among them have been the daughters of Presidents, Governors, Chief Justices, Speakers of the House, leaders of political parties and leaders of great movements. List the women of the last century whose names will pass into history among the immortals and scarcely one is there who has not appeared before your committees— Susan B. Anthony, Elizabeth Cady Stanton, Lucy Stone, Mary A. Livermore, Lillie Devereux Blake, Julia Ward Howe, Harriet Beecher Stowe, Frances Willard, Clara Barton and hundreds more. There are hundreds of women in the suffrage convention now sitting who have paid out more money in railroad fare to come to Washington in order to persuade men that "women are people" than all the men in the entire country ever paid to get a vote.

Perhaps you think our pleas in those Committee Rooms were poor attempts at logic. Ah, one chairman of the committee long ago said to a fellow member: "There is no man living or dead who could answer the arguments of those women," and then he added, "but I'd rather see my wife dead in her coffin than going to vote." Yet, there are those of you who have said that women are illogical and sentimental! Since Congress has already had fifty-one years of peace in which to deal with the question of woman suffrage, we hold that a further postponement is unwarranted.

Objection No. 2. *A vote on this question by Congress and the Legislatures is undemocratic; it should go to the "people" of the States.* You are wrong, gentlemen, as your reason will quickly tell you, if you will reflect a moment. When a State submits a constitutional amendment to male voters, it does a legal, constitutional thing, but when that amendment chiefly concerns one-half the people of the State and the law permits the other half to settle it, the wildest stretch of the imagination could not describe the process as democratic. Democracy means "the rule of people," and, let me repeat, women are people. No State referendum goes to the people; it goes to the male voters. Such referenda can never be democratic. Were the question of woman suffrage to be submitted to a vote of both sexes, the action would be democratic, but in that case it would not be legal nor constitutional.

Male voters have never been named by any constitution or statute as the representatives of women; we therefore decline to accept them in that capacity. The nearest approach to representation allowed voteless women are the members of Congress and the Legislatures. These members are apportioned among the several States upon the basis of population and not upon the basis of numbers of voters. Therefore every Congressman theoretically represents the women of his constituency as well as the male voters. He is theoretically responsible to them and they may properly go to him for redress of such grievances as fall within his jurisdiction. More, every member of Congress not only represents the small constituency confined to his district, but all the people of the country, since his vote upon national questions affects them all. Women, whether voters or non-voters, may properly claim members of Congress as the only substitution for representation provided by the constitution. We apply to you, therefore, to correct a grievous wrong which your constitutional jurisdiction gives you authority to set right.

Objection No. 3. *States Rights.* You pronounce it unfair that thirty-six States should determine who may vote in the remaining twelve; that possible Republican Northern States should decide who may vote in Democratic Southern States. It is no more unfair than that some counties within a State should decide who may vote in the remaining counties; no more unfair than that the Democratic city of New York should enfranchise the women of the Republican cities of Albany and Rochester, as it has just done.

Forty-eight States will have the opportunity to ratify the Federal Amendment and every State, therefore, will have its opportunity to enfranchise its own women in this manner. If any State fails to do it, we may agree that that State would probably not enfranchise its own women by the State method; but if it would not so enfranchise them that State is behind the times and is holding our country up to the scorn of the nations. It has failed to catch the vision and the spirit of Democracy sweeping over the world. This nation cannot, must not, wait for any State, so ignorant, so backward. That State more than all others needs woman suffrage to shake its dry bones, to bring political questions into the home and set discussion going. It needs education, action, stimulation to prevent atrophy. In after years posterity will utter grateful thanks that there was a method which could throw a bit of modernity into it from the outside.

It is urged that the women of some such States do not want the vote. Of course if the thought of an entire State is antiquated, its women will share the general stagnation, but there is no State where there is not a large number of women who are working, and working hard, for the vote. The vote is permissive, a liberty extended. It is never a burden laid upon the individual, since there is no obligation to exercise the right. On the other hand, the refusal to permit those who want the vote to have and to use it is oppression, tyranny—and no other words describe the condition. When, therefore, men within a State are so ungenerous or unprogressive or stubborn as to continue the denial of the vote to the women who want it, men on the outside should have no scruples in constituting themselves the liberators of those women.

Despite these truths there are among you those who still harbor honest misgivings. Please remember that woman suffrage is coming; you know it is. In this connection, have you ever thought that the women of your own families who may tell you now that they do not want the vote are going to realize some day that there is something insincere in your protestations of chivalry, protection and "you are too good to vote, my dear," and are going to discover that the trust, respect, and frank acknowledgment of equality which men of other States have given their women are something infinitely higher and nobler than you have ever offered them? Have you thought that you may now bestow upon them a liberty that they may not yet realize they need, but that tomorrow they may storm your castle and demand? Do you suppose that any woman in the land is going to be content with unenfranchisement when she once comprehends that men of other countries have given women the vote? Do you not see that when that time comes to her she is going to ask why you, her husband, her father, who were so placed, perhaps, that you could observe the progress of world affairs, did not see the coming change of custom and save her from the humiliation of having to beg for that which women in other countries are already enjoying? Have you known that no more potent influence has aroused the sheltered and consequently narrow-visioned woman into a realization that she wanted to be a part of an enfranchised class than the manner in which men treat enfranchised women? There is no patronizing "I am holier than thou" air, but the equality of "fellow citizens." One never sees that relation between men and women except where women vote. Some day that woman who doesn't know the world is moving on and leaving her behind will see and know these things. What will she say and do then? What will you do for her now?

There are many well known men in Great Britain who frankly confess that their desire to give British women the vote is founded upon their sense of gratitude for the loyal and remarkable war service women have performed. They speak of suffrage as a reward. For years women have asked the vote as a recognition of the incontrovertible fact that they are responsible, intelligent citizens of the country and because its denial has been an outrageous discrimination against their sex. British women will receive their enfranchisement with joyous appreciation but the joy will be lessened and the appreciation tempered by the perfect understanding that "vote as a reward" is only an escape from the uncomfortable corner into which the unanswerable logic of the women had driven the government. Mutual respect between those who give and those who receive the vote would have been promoted had the inevitable duty not been deferred. We hope American men will be wiser.

Many of you have admitted that "State's Rights" is less a principle than a tradition—a tradition, however, which we all know is rooted deep in the memory of bitter and, let us say, regrettable incidents of history. But the past is gone. We are living in the present and facing the future. Other men of other lands have thrown aside traditions as tenderly revered as yours in response to the higher call of Justice, Progress and Democracy. Can you, too, not rise to this same call of duty? Is any good to be served by continuing one injustice in order to resent another injustice? We are one nation and those of us who live now and make our appeal to you are like yourselves not of the generation whose differences created the conditions which entrenched the tradition of State's Rights. We ask you, our representatives, to right the wrong done us by the law of our land as the men of other lands have done.

Our nation, is in the extreme crisis of its existence and men should search their very souls to find just and reasonable causes for every thought and act. If you, making this search shall find

"State's Rights" a sufficient cause to lead you to vote "no" on the Federal Suffrage Amendment, then, with all the gentleness which should accompany the reference to a sacred memory, let us tell you that your cause will bear neither the test of time nor critical analysis, and that your vote will compel your children to apologize for your act.

Already your vote has forwarded some of the measures which are far more distinctly State's Rights questions than the fundamental demand for equal human rights. Among such questions are the regulation of child labor, the eight-hour law, the white slave traffic, moving pictures, questionable literature, food supply, clothing supply, prohibition. All of these acts are in the direction of the restraint of "personal liberty" in the supposed interest of the public good. Every instinct of justice, every principle of logic and ethics is shocked at the reasoning which grants Congress the right to curtail personal liberty but no right to extend it. "Necessity knows no law" may seem to you sufficient authority to tax the incomes of women, to demand exhausting amounts of volunteer military service, to commandeer women for public work and in other ways to restrain their liberty as war measures. But by the same token the grant of more liberty may properly be conferred as a war measure. If other lands have been brave enough to extend suffrage to women in war time, our own country, the mother of democracy, surely will not hesitate. We are told that a million or more American men will be on European battlefields ere many months. For every man who goes, there is one loyal woman and proably more who would vote to support to the utmost that man's cause. The disloyal men will be here to vote. Suffrage for women now as a war measure means suffrage for the loyal forces, for those who know what it means "to fight to keep the world safe for democracy."

The framers of the Constitution gave unquestioned authority to Congress to act upon woman suffrage. Why not use that authority and use it now to do the big, noble, just thing of catching pace with other natons on this question of democracy? The world and posterity will honor you for it.

In conclusion, we know, and you know that we know, that it has been the aim of both dominant parties to postpone woman suffrage as long as possible. A few men in each party have always fought with us fearlessly, but the party machines have evaded, avoided, tricked and buffeted this question from Congress to Legislatures, from Legislatures to political conventions. I confess to you that many of us have a deep and abiding distrust of all existing political parties—they have tricked us so often and in such unscrupulous fashion that our doubts are natural. Some of you are leaders of those parties and all are members. Your parties we also know have a distrust and suspicion of new women voters. Let us counsel together. Women suffrage is inevitable—you know it. The political parties will go on—we know it. Shall we then be enemies or friends? Can party leaders in twelve States really obtain the loyal support of women voters when those women know that the same party is ordering the defeat of amendments in States where campaigns are pending, or delaying action in Congress on the Federal Amendment? Gentlemen, we ask you to put yourselves in our places. What would you do? Would you keep on spending your money and your lives on a slow, laborious, clumsy State method, or would you use the votes you have won to complete your campaign on behalf of suffrage for all women in the nation? Would you be content to keep a standing army of women, told off for the special work of educating men in the meaning of democracy; would you raise and spend millions of dollars in the process; would you give up every other thing in life you hold dear in order to keep State campaigns going for another possible quarter of a century? Would you do this and see the women of other countries leaving you behind, or would you make "a hard pull, a long pull and a pull altogether" and finish the task at once? You know you would choose the latter. We make the same choice.

Do you realize that in no other country in the world with democratic tendencies is suffrage so completely denied as in a considerable number of our own States? There are 13 black States where no suffrage for women exists, and 14 others where suffrage for women is more limited than in many foreign countries.

Do you realize that no class of men in our own or in any other land have been compelled to ask their inferiors for the ballot?

Do you realize that when you ask women to take their cause to State referendum you compel them to do this; that you drive women of education, refinement, achievement, to beg men who cannot read for their political freedom?

Do you realize that such anomalies as a College President asking her janitor to give her a vote are overstraining the patience and driving women to desperation?

Do you realize that women in increasing numbers indignantly resent the long delay in their enfranchisement?

Your party platforms have pledged woman suffrage. Then why not be honest, frank friends of our cause, adopt it in reality as your own, make it a party program and "fight with us"? As a party measure—a measure of all parties—why not put the amendment through Congress and the Legislatures? We shall all be better friends, we shall have a happier nation, we women will be free to support loyally the party of our choice and we shall be far prouder of our history.

"There is one thing mightier than kings and armies"—aye, than Congresses and political parties—"the power of an idea when its time has come to move." The time for woman suffrage has come. The woman's hour has struck. If parties prefer to postpone action longer and thus do battle with this idea, they challenge the inevitable. The idea will not perish; the party which opposes it may. Every delay, every trick, every political dishonesty from now on will antagonize the women of the land more and more, and when the party or parties which have so delayed woman suffrage finally let it come, their sincerity will be doubted and their appeal to the new voters will be met with suspicion. This is the psychology of the situation. Can you afford the risk? Think it over.

We know you will meet opposition. There are a few "woman haters" left, a few "old males of the tribe," as Vance Thompson calls them, whose duty they believe it to be to keep women in the places they have carefully picked out for them. Treitschke, made world famous by war literature, said some years ago: "Germany, which knows all about Germany and France, knows far better what is good for Alsace-Lorraine than that miserable people can possibly know." A few American Treitschkes we have who know better than women what is good for them. There are women, too, with "slave souls" and "clinging vines" for backbones. There are female dolls and male dandies. But the world does not wait for such as these, nor does Liberty pause to heed the plaint of men and women with a grouch. She does not wait for those who have a special interest to serve, nor a selfish reason for depriving other people of freedom. Holding her torch aloft, Liberty is pointing the way onward and upward and saying to America, "Come."

To you the supporters of our cause, in Senate and House, and the number is large, the suffragists of the nation express their grateful thanks. This address is not meant for you. We are more truly appreciative of all you have done than any words can express. We ask you to make a last, hard fight for the amendment during the present session. Since last we asked a vote on this amendment your position has been fortified by the addition to suffrage territory of Great Britain, Canada and New York.

Some of you have been too indifferent to give more than casual attention to this question. It is worthy of your immediate consideration—a question big enough to engage the attention of our Allies in war time, is too big a question for you to neglect.

Some of you have grown old in party service. Are you willing that those who take your places by and by shall blame you for having failed to keep pace with the world and thus having lost for them a party advantage? Is there any real gain for you, for your party, for the nation by delay? Do you want to drive the progressive men and women out of your party?

Some of you hold to the doctrine of State's rights, as applying to woman suffrage. Adherence to that theory will keep the United States far behind all other democratic nations in action upon this question. *A theory which prevents a nation from keeping up with the trend of world progress cannot be justified.*

Gentlemen, we hereby petition you, our only designated representatives, to redress our grievances by the immediate passage of the Federal Suffrage Amendment and to use your influence to secure its ratification in your own state, in order that the women of our nation may be endowed with political freedom before the next presidential election, and that our nation may resume its world leadership in democracy.

Woman suffrage is coming—you know it. Will you, Honorable Senators and Members of the House of Representatives, help or hinder it?

EUGENE V. DEBS

Speech to the Court

Cleveland, September 14, 1918

YOUR HONOR, years ago I recognized my kinship with all living beings, and I made up my mind that I was not one bit better than the meanest of earth. I said then, I say now, that while there is a lower class I am in it; while there is a criminal element, I am of it; while there is a soul in prison, I am not free.

If the law under which I have been convicted is a good law, then there is no reason why sentence should not be pronounced upon me. I listened to all that was said in this court in support and justification of this law, but my mind remains unchanged. I look upon it as a despotic enactment in flagrant conflict with democratic principles and with the spirit of free institutions.

I have no fault to find with this court or with the trial. Everything in connection with this case has been conducted upon a dignified plane, and in a respectful and decent spirit—with just one exception. Your Honor, my sainted mother inspired me with a reverence for womanhood that amounts to worship. I can think with disrespect of no woman, and I can think with respect of no man who can. I resent the manner in which the names of two noble women were bandied with in this court. The levity and the wantonness in this instance were absolutely inexcusable. When I think of what was said in this connection, I feel that when I pass a woman, even though it be a sister of the street, I should take off my hat and apologize to her for being a man

Your Honor, I have stated in this court that I am opposed to the form of our present government; that I am opposed to the social system in which we live; that I believed in the change of both—but by perfectly peaceable and orderly means.

Let me call your attention to the fact this morning that in this system five per cent of our people own and control two-thirds of our wealth; sixty-five per cent. of the people, embracing the working class who produce all wealth, have but five per cent to show for it.

Standing here this morning, I recall my boyhood. At fourteen, I went to work in the railroad shops; at sixteen, I was firing a freight engine on a railroad. I remember all the hardships, all the privations, of that earlier day, and from that time until now, my heart has been with the working class. I could have been in Congress long ago. I have preferred to go to prison. The choice has been deliberately made. I could not have done otherwise. I have no regret.

In the struggle—the unceasing struggle—between the toilers and producers and their exploiters, I have tried, as best I might, to serve those among whom I was born, with whom I expect to share my lot until the end of my days.

I am thinking this morning of the men in the mills and factories; I am thinking of the women who, for a paltry wage, are compelled to work out their lives; of the little children who, in this system, are robbed of their childhood, and in their early, tender years, are seized in the remorseless grasp of Mammon, and forced into the industrial dungeons, there to feed the machines while they themselves are being starved body and soul. I can see them dwarfed, diseased, stunted, their little lives broken, and their hopes blasted, because in this high noon of our twentieth century civilization money is still so much more important than human life. Gold is god and rules in the affairs of men.

The little girls, and there are a million of them in this country —this the most favored land beneath the bending skies, a land in which we have vast areas of rich and fertile soil, material resources in inexhaustible abundance, the most marvelous productive machinery on earth, millions of eager workers ready to apply their labor to that machinery to produce an abundance for every man, woman and child—and if there are still many millions of our people who are the victims of poverty, whose life is a ceaseless struggle all the way from youth to age, until at last death comes to their rescue and stills the aching heart, and lulls the victim to dreamless sleep, it is not the fault of the Almighty, it can't be charged to nature; it is due entirely to an outgrown social system that ought to be abolished not only in the interest of the working class, but in a higher interest of all humanity.

When I think of these little children—the girls that are in the textile mills of all description in the East, in the cotton factories of the South—when I think of them at work in a vitiated atmosphere, when I think of them at work when they ought to be at play or at school, when I think that when they do grow up, if they live long enough to approach the marriage state, they are unfit for it. Their nerves are worn out, their tissue is exhausted, their vitality is spent. They have been fed to industry. Their lives have been coined into gold. Their offspring are born tired. That is why there are so many failures in our modern life.

Your Honor, the five per cent of the people that I have made reference to constitute that element that absolutely rules our country. They privately own all our public necessities. They wear no crowns; they wield no scepters; they sit upon no thrones; and yet they are our economic masters and our political rulers. They control this government and all of its institutions. They control the courts.

And, Your Honor, if you will permit me, I wish to make just one correction. It was stated here that I had charged that all federal judges were crooks. The charge is absolutely untrue. I did say that all federal judges are appointed through the influence and power of the capitalist class and not the working class. If that statement is not true, I am more than willing to retract it.

The five per cent of our people who own and control all the sources of wealth, all of the nation's industries, all of the means of our common life, it is they who declare war; it is they who make peace; it is they who control our destiny. And so long as this is true, we can make no just claim to being a democratic government—a self-governing people.

I believe, Your Honor, in common with all Socialists, that this nation ought to own and control its industries. I believe, as all Socialists do, that all things that are jointly needed and used ought to be jointly owned—that industry, the basis of life, instead of being the private property of the few and operated for their enrichment, ought to be the common property of all, democratically administered in the interest of all.

John D. Rockefeller has to-day an income of sixty million dollars a year, five million dollars a month, two hundred thousand dollars a day. He does not produce a penny of it. I make no attack upon Mr. Rockefeller personally. I do not in the least dislike him. If he were in need and it were in my power to serve him, I should serve him as gladly as I would any other human being. I have no quarrel with Mr. Rockefeller personally, nor with any other capitalist. I am simply opposing a social order in which it is possible for one man who does absolutely nothing that is useful to amass a fortune of hundreds of millions of dollars, while millions of men and women who work all of the days of their lives secure barely enough for an existence.

This order of things cannot always endure. I have registered my protest against it. I recognize the feebleness of my effort, but, fortunately, I am not alone. There are multiplied thousands of others who, like myself, have come to realize that before we may truly enjoy the blessings of civilized life, we must reorganize society upon a mutual and coöperative basis; and to this end we have organized a great economic and political movement that is spread over the face of all the earth.

There are to-day upwards of sixty million Socialists, loyal, devoted, adherents to this cause, regardless of nationality, race, creed, color or sex. They are all making common cause. They are all spreading the propaganda of the new social order. They are waiting, watching and working through all the weary hours of the day and night. They are still in the minority. They have learned how to be patient and abide their time. They feel— they know, indeed,—that the time is coming, in spite of all opposition, all persecution, when this emancipating gospel will spread among all the peoples, and when this minority will become the triumphant majority, and sweeping into power, inaugurate the greatest change in history.

In that day we will have the universal commonwealth—not the destruction of the nation, but, on the contrary, the harmonious coöperation of every nation with every other nation on earth. In that day war will curse this earth no more.

I have been accused, Your Honor, of being an enemy of the soldier. I hope I am laying no flattering unction to my soul when I say that I don't believe the soldier has a more sympathetic friend than I am. If I had my way there would be no soldiers. But I realize the sacrifices they are making, Your Honor. I can think of them. I can feel for them. I can sympathize with them. That is one of the reasons why I have been doing what little has been in my power to bring about a condition of affairs in this country worthy of the sacrifices they have made and that they are now making in its behalf.

Your Honor, in a local paper yesterday there was some editorial exultation about my prospective imprisonment. I do not resent it in the least. I can understand it perfectly. In the same paper there appears an editorial this morning that has in it a hint of the wrong to which I have been trying to call attention.

Reading: "A senator of the United States receives a salary of $7500—$45,000 for the six years for which he is elected. One of the candidates for senator from a state adjoining Ohio is reported to have spent through his committee $150,000 to secure the nomination. For advertising he spent $35,000; for printing $30,000; for traveling expenses $10,000 and the rest in ways known to political managers.

"The theory is that public office is as open to a poor man as to a rich man. One may easily imagine, however, how slight a chance one of ordinary resources would have in a contest against this man who was willing to spend more than three times his six years' salary merely to secure a nomination. Were these conditions to hold in every state, the senate would soon become again what it was once held to be—a rich men's club.

"Campaign expenditures have been the subject of much restrictive legislation in recent years, but it has not always reached the mark. The authors of primary reform have accomplished some of the things they set out to do, but they have not yet taken the bank roll out of politics."

They never will take it out of politics, they never can take it out of politics in this system.

Your Honor, I wish to make acknowledgment of my thanks to the counsel for the defense. They have not only defended me with exceptional legal ability, but with a personal attachment and devotion of which I am deeply sensible, and which I can never forget.

Your Honor, I ask no mercy, I plead for no immunity. I realize that finally the right must prevail. I never more clearly comprehended than now the great struggle between the powers of greed on the one hand and upon the other the rising hosts of freedom. I can see the dawn of a better day of humanity. The people are awakening. In due course of time they will come into their own.

When the mariner, sailing over tropic seas, looks for relief from his weary watch, he turns his eyes toward the Southern Cross, burning luridly above the tempest-vexed ocean. As the midnight approaches, the Southern Cross begins to bend, and the whirling worlds change their places, and with starry finger-points the Almighty marks the passage of Time upon the dial of the universe; and though no bell may beat the glad tidings, the look-out knows that the midnight is passing—that relief and rest are close at hand.

Let the people take heart and hope everywhere, for the cross is bending, the midnight is passing, and joy cometh with the morning.

> "He is true to God who is true to man.
> Wherever wrong is done
> To the humblest and the weakest
> 'Neath the all-beholding sun,
> That wrong is also done to us,
> And they are slaves most base
> Whose love of right is for themselves
> And not for all the race."

Your Honor, I thank you, and I thank all of this court for their courtesy, for their kindness, which I shall remember always.

I am prepared to receive your sentence.

WOODROW WILSON

Address to the Senate on the League of Nations

Washington, D.C., July 10, 1919

GENTLEMEN OF THE SENATE: The treaty of peace with Germany was signed at Versailles on the twenty-eighth of June. I avail myself of the earliest opportunity to lay the treaty before you for ratification and to inform you with regard to the work of the Conference by which that treaty was formulated.

The treaty constitutes nothing less than a world settlement. It would not be possible for me either to summarize or to construe its manifold provisions in an address which must of necessity be something less than a treatise. My services and all the information I possess will be at your disposal and at the disposal of your Committee on Foreign Relations at any time, either informally or in session, as you may prefer; and I hope that you will not hesitate to make use of them. I shall at this time, prior to your own study of the document, attempt only a general characterization of its scope and purpose.

In one sense, no doubt, there is no need that I should report to you what was attempted and done at Paris. You have been daily cognizant of what was going on there,—of the problems with which the Peace Conference had to deal and of the difficulty of laying down straight lines of settlement anywhere on a field on which the old lines of international relationship, and the new alike, followed so intricate a pattern and were for the most part cut so deep by historical circumstances which dominated action even where it would have been best to ignore or reverse them. The cross currents of politics and of interest must have been evident to you. It would be presuming in me to attempt to explain the questions which arose or the many diverse elements that entered into them. I shall attempt something less ambitious than that and more clearly suggested by my duty to report to the Congress the part it seemed necessary for my colleagues and me to play as the representatives of the Government of the United States.

That part was dictated by the role America had played in the war and by the expectations that had been created in the minds of the peoples with whom we had associated ourselves in that great struggle.

The United States entered the war upon a different footing from every other nation except our associates on this side of the sea. We entered it, not because our material interests were directly threatened or because any special treaty obligations to which we were parties had been violated, but only because we saw the supremacy, and even the validity, of right everywhere put in jeopardy and free government likely to be everywhere imperiled by the intolerable aggression of a power which respected neither right nor obligation and whose very system of government flouted the rights of the citizens as against the autocratic authority of his governors. And in the settlements of the peace we have sought no special reparation for ourselves, but only the restoration of right and the assurance of liberty everywhere that the effects of the settlement were to be felt. We entered the war as the disinterested champions of right and we interested ourselves in the terms of the peace in no other capacity.

The hopes of the nations allied against the central powers were at a very low ebb when our soldiers began to pour across the sea. There was everywhere amongst them, except in their stoutest spirits, a sombre foreboding of disaster. The war ended in November, eight months ago, but you have only to recall what was feared in midsummer last, four short months before the armistice, to realize what it was that our timely aid accomplished alike for their morale and their physical safety. That first, never-to-be-forgotten action at Château-Thierry had already taken place. Our redoubtable soldiers and marines had already closed the gap the enemy had succeeded in opening for their advance upon Paris,—had already turned the tide of battle back towards the frontiers of France and begun the rout that was to save Europe and the world. Thereafter the Germans were to be always forced back, back, were never to thrust successfully forward again. And yet there was no confident hope. Anxious men and women, leading spirits of France, attended the celebration of the fourth of July last year in Paris out of generous courtesy,—with no heart for festivity, little zest for hope. But they came away with something new at their hearts: they have themselves told us so. The mere sight of our men,—of their vigour, of the confidence that showed itself in every movement of their stalwart figures and every turn of their swinging march, in their steady comprehending eyes and easy discipline, in the indomitable air that added spirit to everything they did,— made everyone who saw them that memorable day realize that something had happened that was much more than a mere incident in the fighting, something very different from the mere arrival of fresh troops. A great moral force had flung itself into the struggle. The fine physical force of those spirited men spoke of something more than bodily vigour. They carried the great ideals of a free people at their hearts and with that vision were unconquerable. Their very presence brought reassurance; their fighting made victory certain.

They were recognized as crusaders, and as their thousands swelled to millions their strength was seen to mean salvation. And they were fit men to carry such a hope and make good the assurance it forecast. Finer men never went into battle; and their officers were worthy of them. This is not the occasion upon which to utter a eulogy of the armies America sent to France, but perhaps, since I am speaking of their mission, I may speak also of the pride I shared with every American who saw or dealt with them there. They were the sort of men America would wish to be represented by, the sort of men every American would wish to claim as fellow countrymen and comrades in a great cause. They were terrible in battle, and gentle and helpful out of it, remembering the mothers and the sisters, the wives and the little children at home. They were free men under arms, not forgetting their ideals of duty in the midst of tasks of violence. I am proud to have had the privilege of being associated with them and of calling myself their leader.

But I speak now of what they meant to the men by whose sides they fought and to the people with whom they mingled with such utter simplicity, as friends who asked only to be of service. They were for all the visible embodiment of America. What they did made America and all that she stood for a living reality in the thoughts not only of the people of France but also of tens of millions of men and women throughout all the toiling nations of a world standing everywhere in peril of its freedom and of the loss of everything it held dear, in deadly fear that its bonds were never to be loosed, its hopes forever to be mocked and disappointed.

And the compulsion of what they stood for was upon us who represented America at the peace table. It was our duty to see to it that every decision we took part in contributed, so far as we were able to influence it, to quiet the fears and realize the hopes of the peoples who had been living in that shadow, the nations that had come by our assistance to their freedom. It was our duty to do everything that it was within our power to do to make the triumph of freedom and of right a lasting triumph in the assurance of which men might everywhere live without fear.

Old entanglements of every kind stood in the way,— promises which Governments had made to one another in the days when might and right were confused and the power of the victor was without restraint. Engagements which contemplated any dispositions of territory, any extensions of sovereignty that might seem to be to the interest of those who had the power to insist upon them, had been entered into without thought of what the peoples concerned might wish or profit by; and these could not always be honourably brushed aside. It was not easy to graft the new order of ideas on the old, and some of the fruits of the grafting may, I fear, for a time be bitter. But, with very few exceptions, the men who sat with us at the peace table desired as sincerely as we did to get away from the bad influences, the illegitimate purposes, the demoralizing ambitions, the international counsels and expedients out of which the sinister designs of Germany had sprung as a natural growth.

It had been our privilege to formulate the principles which were accepted as the basis of the peace, but they had been accepted, not because we had come in to hasten and assure the victory and insisted upon them, but because they were readily acceded to as the principles to which honourable and enlightened minds everywhere had been bred. They spoke the conscience of the world as well as the conscience of America, and I am happy to pay my tribute of respect and gratitude to the able, forward-looking men with whom it was my privilege to cooperate for their unfailing spirit of cooperation, their constant effort to accommodate the interests they represented to the principles we were all agreed upon. The difficulties, which were many, lay in the circumstances, not often in the men. Almost without exception the men who led had caught the true and full vision of the problem of peace as an indivisible whole, a problem, not of mere adjustments of interest, but of justice and right action.

The atmosphere in which the Conference worked seemed created, not by the ambitions of strong governments, but by the hopes and aspirations of small nations and of peoples hitherto under bondage to the power that victory had shattered and destroyed. Two great empires had been forced into political bankruptcy, and we were the receivers. Our task was not only to make peace with the central empires and remedy the wrongs their armies had done. The central empires had lived in open violation of many of the very rights for which the war had been fought, dominating alien peoples over whom they had no natural right to rule, enforcing, not obedience, but veritable bondage, exploiting those who were weak for the benefit of those who were masters and overlords only by force of arms. There could be no peace until the whole order of central Europe was set right.

That meant that new nations were to be created,—Poland, Czecho-Slovakia, Hungary itself. No part of ancient Poland had ever in any true sense become a part of Germany, or of Austria, or of Russia. Bohemia was alien in every thought and hope to the monarchy of which she had so long been an artificial part; and the uneasy partnership between Austria and Hungary had been one rather of interest than of kinship or sympathy. The Slavs whom Austria had chosen to force into her empire on the south were kept to their obedience by nothing but fear. Their hearts were with their kinsmen in the Balkans. These were all arrangements of power, not arrangements of natural union or association. It was the imperative task of those who would make peace and make it intelligently to establish a new order which would rest upon the free choice of peoples rather than upon the arbitrary authority of Hapsburgs or Hohenzollerns.

More than that, great populations bound by sympathy and actual kin to Rumania were also linked against their will to the conglomerate Austro-Hungarian monarchy or to other alien sovereignties, and it was part of the task of peace to make a new Rumania as well as a new Slavic state clustering about Serbia.

And no natural frontiers could be found to these new fields of adjustment and redemption. It was necessary to look constantly forward to other related tasks. The German colonies were to be disposed of. They had not been governed; they had been exploited merely, without thought of the interest or even the ordinary human rights of their inhabitants.

The Turkish Empire, moreover, had fallen apart, as the Austro-Hungarian had. It had never had any real unity. It had been held together only by pitiless, inhuman force. Its people cried aloud for release, for succour from unspeakable distress, for all that the new day of hope seemed at last to bring within its dawn. Peoples hitherto in utter darkness were to be led out into the same light and given at last a helping hand. Undeveloped peoples and peoples ready for recognition but not yet ready to assume the full responsibilities of statehood were to be given adequate guarantees of friendly protection, guidance, and assistance.

And out of the execution of these great enterprises of liberty sprang opportunities to attempt what statesmen had never found the way before to do; an opportunity to throw safeguards about the rights of racial, national, and religious minorities by solemn international covenant; an opportunity to limit and regulate military establishments where they were most likely to be mischievous; an opportunity to effect a complete and systematic internationalization of waterways and railways which were necessary to the free economic life of more than one nation and to clear many of the normal channels of commerce of unfair obstructions of law or of privilege; and the very welcome opportunity to secure for labour the concerted protection of definite international pledges of principle and practice.

These were not tasks which the Conference looked about it to find and went out of its way to perform. They were thrust upon it by circumstances which could not be overlooked. The war had created them. In all quarters of the world old established relationships had been disturbed or broken and affairs were at loose ends, needing to be mended or united again, but could not be made what they were before. They had to be set right by applying some uniform principle of justice or enlightened expediency. And they could not be adjusted by merely prescribing in a treaty what should be done. New states were to be set up which could not hope to live through their first period of weakness without assured support by the great nations that had consented to their creation and won for them their independence. Ill governed colonies could not be put in the hands of governments which were to act as trustees for their people and not as their masters if there was to be no common authority among the nations to which they were to be responsible in the execution of their trust. Future international conventions with regard to the control of waterways, with regard to illicit traffic of many kinds, in arms or in deadly drugs, or with regard to the adjustment of many varying international administrative arrangements could not be assured if the treaty were to provide no permanent common international agency, if its execution in such matters was to be left to the slow and uncertain processes of cooperation by ordinary methods of negotiation. If the Peace Conference itself was to be the end of cooperative authority and common counsel among the governments to which the world was looking to enforce justice and give pledges of an enduring settlement, regions like the Saar basin could not be put under a temporary administrative regime which did not involve a transfer of political sovereignty and which contemplated a final determination of its political connections by popular vote to be taken at a distant date; no free city like Dantzig could be created which was, under elaborate international guarantees, to accept exceptional obligations with regard to the use of its port and exceptional relations with a State of which it was not to form a part; properly safeguarded plebiscites could not be provided for where populations were at some future date to make choice what sovereignty they would live under; no certain and uniform method of arbitration could be secured for the settlement of anticipated difficulties of final decision with regard to many matters dealt with in the treaty itself; the long-continued supervision of the task of reparation which Germany was to undertake to complete within the next generation might entirely break down; the reconsideration and revision of administrative arrangements and restrictions which the treaty prescribed but which it was recognized might not prove of lasting advantage or entirely fair if too long enforced would be impracticable. The promises governments were making to one another about the way in which labour was to be dealt with, by law not only but in fact as well, would remain a mere humane thesis if there was to be no common tribunal of opinion and judgment to which liberal statesmen could resort for the influences which alone might secure their redemption. A league of free nations had become a practical necessity. Examine the treaty of peace and you will find that everywhere throughout its manifold provisions its framers have felt obliged to turn to the League of Nations as an indispensable instrumentality for the maintenance of the new order it has been their purpose to set up in the world,—the world of civilized men.

That there should be a league of nations to steady the counsels and maintain the peaceful understandings of the world, to make, not treaties alone, but the accepted principles of international law as well, the actual rule of conduct among the governments of the world, had been one of the agreements accepted from the first as the basis of peace with the central powers. The statesmen of all the belligerent countries were agreed that such a league must be created to sustain the settlements that were to be effected. But at first I think there was a feeling among some of them that, while it must be attempted, the formulation of such a league was perhaps a counsel of perfection which practical men, long experienced in the world of affairs, must agree to very cautiously and with many misgivings. It was only as the difficult work of arranging an all but universal adjustment of the world's affairs advanced from day to day from one stage of conference to another that it became evident to them that what they were seeking would be little more than something written upon paper, to be interpreted and applied by such methods as the chances of politics might make available if they did not provide a means of common counsel which all were obliged to accept, a common authority whose decisions would be recognized as decisions which all must respect.

And so the most practical, the most skeptical among them

turned more and more to the League as the authority through which international action was to be secured, the authority without which, as they had come to see it, it would be difficult to give assured effect either to this treaty or to any other international understanding upon which they were to depend for the maintenance of peace. The fact that the Covenant of the League was the first substantive part of the treaty to be worked out and agreed upon, while all else was in solution, helped to make the formulation of the rest easier. The Conference was, after all, not to be ephemeral. The concert of nations was to continue, under a definite Covenant which had been agreed upon and which all were convinced was workable. They could go forward with confidence to make arrangements intended to be permanent. The most practical of the conferees were at last the most ready to refer to the League of Nations the superintendence of all interests which did not admit of immediate determination, of all administrative problems which were to require a continuing oversight. What had seemed a counsel of perfection had come to seem a plain counsel of necessity. The League of Nations was the practical statesman's hope of success in many of the most difficult things he was attempting.

And it had validated itself in the thought of every member of the Conference as something much bigger, much greater every way, than a mere instrument for carrying out the provisions of a particular treaty. It was universally recognized that all the peoples of the world demanded of the Conference that it should create such a continuing concert of free nations as would make wars of aggression and spoliation such as this that has just ended forever impossible. A cry had gone out from every home in every stricken land from which sons and brothers and fathers had gone forth to the great sacrifice that such a sacrifice should never again be exacted. It was manifest why it had been exacted. It had been exacted because one nation desired dominion and other nations had known no means of defence except armaments and alliances. War had lain at the heart of every arrangement of the Europe,—of every arrangement of the world,—that preceded the war. Restive peoples had been told that fleets and armies, which they toiled to sustain, meant peace; and they now knew that they had been lied to: that fleets and armies had been maintained to promote national ambi-

tions and meant war. They knew that no old policy meant anything else but force, force,—always force. And they knew that
it was intolerable. Every true heart in the world, and every enlightened judgment demanded that, at whatever cost of independent action, every government that took thought for its
people or for justice or for ordered freedom should lend itself
to a new purpose and utterly destroy the old order of international politics. Statesmen might see difficulties, but the
people could see none and could brook no denial. A war in
which they had been bled white to beat the terror that lay concealed in every Balance of Power must not end in a mere victory of arms and a new balance. The monster that had resorted
to arms must be put in chains that could not be broken. The
united power of free nations must put a stop to aggression,
and the world must be given peace. If there was not the will or
the intelligence to accomplish that now, there must be another
and a final war and the world must be swept clean of every
power that could renew the terror. The League of Nations was
not merely an instrument to adjust and remedy old wrongs
under a new treaty of peace; it was the only hope for mankind.
Again and again had the demon of war been cast out of the
house of the peoples and the house swept clean by a treaty of
peace; only to prepare a time when he would enter in again with
spirits worse than himself. The house must now be given a ten-
ant who could hold it against all such. Convenient, indeed indispensable, as statesmen found the newly planned League of
Nations to be for the execution of present plans of peace and
reparation, they saw it in a new aspect before their work was
finished. They saw it as the main object of the peace, as the
only thing that could complete it or make it worth while. They
saw it as the hope of the world, and that hope they did not dare
to disappoint. Shall we or any other free people hesitate to accept this great duty? Dare we reject it and break the heart of the
world?

And so the result of the Conference of Peace, so far as Germany is concerned, stands complete. The difficulties encountered were very many. Sometimes they seemed insuperable.
It was impossible to accommodate the interests of so great a
body of nations,—interests which directly or indirectly affected
almost every nation in the world,—without many minor

compromises. The treaty, as a result, is not exactly what we would have written. It is probably not what any one of the national delegations would have written. But results were worked out which on the whole bear test. I think that it will be found that the compromises which were accepted as inevitable nowhere cut to the heart of any principle. The work of the Conference squares, as a whole, with the principles agreed upon as the basis of the peace as well as with the practical possibilities of the international situations which had to be faced and dealt with as facts.

I shall presently have occasion to lay before you a special treaty with France, whose object is the temporary protection of France from unprovoked aggression by the Power with whom this treaty of peace has been negotiated. Its terms link it with this treaty. I take the liberty, however, of reserving it for special explication on another occasion.

The rôle which America was to play in the Conference seemed determined, as I have said, before my colleagues and I got to Paris,—determined by the universal expectations of the nations whose representatives, drawn from all quarters of the globe, we were to deal with. It was universally recognized that America had entered the war to promote no private or peculiar interest of her own but only as the champion of rights which she was glad to share with free men and lovers of justice everywhere. We had formulated the principles upon which the settlement was to be made,—the principles upon which the armistice had been agreed to and the parleys of peace undertaken,—and no one doubted that our desire was to see the treaty of peace formulated along the actual lines of those principles,—and desired nothing else. We were welcomed as disinterested friends. We were resorted to as arbiters in many a difficult matter. It was recognized that our material aid would be indispensable in the days to come, when industry and credit would have to be brought back to their normal operation again and communities beaten to the ground assisted to their feet once more, and it was taken for granted, I am proud to say, that we would play the helpful friend in these things as in all others without prejudice or favour. We were generously accepted as the unaffected champions of what was right. It was a very responsible rôle to play; but I am happy to report that the fine group of Americans who helped with their expert advice in each part of the varied settlements sought in every translation to justify the high confidence reposed in them.

And that confidence, it seems to me, is the measure of our opportunity and of our duty in the days to come, in which the new hope of the peoples of the world is to be fulfilled or disappointed. The fact that America is the friend of the nations, whether they be rivals or associates, is no new fact: it is only the discovery of it by the rest of the world that is new.

America may be said to have just reached her majority as a world power. It was almost exactly twenty-one years ago that the results of the war with Spain put us unexpectedly in possession of rich islands on the other side of the world and brought us into association with other governments in the control of the West Indies. It was regarded as a sinister and ominous thing by the statesmen of more than one European chancellery that we should have extended our power beyond the confines of our continental dominions. They were accustomed to think of new neighbours as a new menace, of rivals as watchful enemies. There were persons amongst us at home who looked with deep disapproval and avowed anxiety on such extensions of our national authority over distant islands and over peoples whom they feared we might exploit, not serve and assist. But we have not exploited them. And our dominion has been a menace to no other nation. We redeemed our honour to the utmost in our dealings with Cuba. She is weak but absolutely free; and it is her trust in us that makes her free. Weak peoples everywhere stand ready to give us any authority among them that will assure them a like friendly oversight and direction. They know that there is no ground for fear in receiving us as their mentors and guides. Our isolation was ended twenty years ago; and now fear of us is ended also, our counsel and association sought after and desired. There can be no question of our ceasing to be a world power. The only question is whether we can refuse the moral leadership that is offered us, whether we shall accept or reject the confidence of the world.

The war and the Conference of Peace now sitting in Paris seem to me to have answered that question. Our participation in the war established our position among the nations and nothing but our own mistaken action can alter it. It was not an accident or a matter of sudden choice that we are no longer isolated and devoted to a policy which has only our own interest and advantage for its object. It was our duty to go in, if we were indeed the champions of liberty and of right. We answered to the call of duty in a way so spirited, so utterly without thought of what we spent of blood or treasure, so effective, so worthy of the admiration of true men everywhere, so wrought out of the stuff of all that was heroic, that the whole world saw at last, in the flesh, in noble action, a great ideal asserted and vindicated, by a nation they had deemed material and now found to be compact of the spiritual forces that must free men of every nation from every unworthy bondage. It is thus that a new role and a new responsibility have come to this great nation that we honour and which we would all wish to lift to yet higher levels of service and achievement.

The stage is set, the destiny disclosed. It has come about by no plan of our conceiving, but by the hand of God who led us into this way. We cannot turn back. We can only go forward, with lifted eyes and freshened spirit, to follow the vision. It was of this that we dreamed at our birth. America shall in truth show the way. The light streams upon the path ahead, and nowhere else.

HENRY CABOT LODGE

Speech in the Senate on the League of Nations

Washington, D.C., August 12, 1919

MR. PRESIDENT, in the Essays of Elia, one of the most delightful is that entitled "Popular Fallacies." There is one very popular fallacy, however, which Lamb did not include in his list, and that is the common saying that history repeats itself. Universal negatives are always dangerous, but if there is anything which is fairly certain, it is that history never exactly repeats itself. Popular fallacies, nevertheless, generally have some basis, and this saying springs from the undoubted truth that mankind from generation to generation is constantly repeating itself. We have an excellent illustration of this fact in the proposed experiment now before us, of making arrangements to secure the permanent peace of the world. To assure the peace of the world by a combination of the nations is no new idea. Leaving out the leagues of antiquity and of mediæval times and going back no further than the treaty of Utrecht, at the beginning of the eighteenth century, we find that at that period a project of a treaty to establish perpetual peace was brought forward in 1713 by the Abbé de Saint-Pierre. The treaty of Utrecht was to be the basis of an international system. A European league or Christian republic was to be set up, under which the members were to renounce the right of making war against each other and submit their disputes for arbitration to a central tribunal of the allies, the decisions of which were to be enforced by a common armament. I need not point out the resemblance between this theory and that which underlies the present league of nations. It was widely discussed during the eighteenth century, receiving much support in public opinion; and Voltaire said that the nations of Europe, united by ties of religion, institutions, and culture, were really but a single family. The idea remained in an academic condition until 1791, when under the pressure of the French Revolution Count

Kaunitz sent out a circular letter in the name of Leopold, of Austria, urging that it was the duty of all the powers to make common cause for the purpose of "preserving public peace, tranquillity of States, the inviolability of possession, and the faith of treaties," which has a very familiar sound. Napoleon had a scheme of his own for consolidating the Great European peoples and establishing a central assembly, but the Napoleonic idea differed from that of the eighteenth century, as one would expect. A single great personality dominated and hovered over all. In 1804 the Emperor Alexander took up the question and urged a general treaty for the formation of a European confederation. "Why could one not submit to it," the Emperor asked, "the positive rights of nations, assure the privilege of neutrality, insert the obligation of never beginning war until all the resources which the mediation of a third party could offer have been exhausted, until the grievances have by this means been brought to light, and an effort to remove them has been made? On principles such as these one could proceed to a general pacification, and give birth to a league of which the stipulations would form, so to speak, a new code of the law of nations, while those who should try to infringe it would risk bringing upon themselves the forces of the new union."

The Emperor, moved by more immediately alluring visions, put aside this scheme at the treaty of Tilsit and then decided that peace could best be restored to the world by having two all-powerful emperors, one of the east and one of the west. After the Moscow campaign, however, he returned to his early dream. Under the influence of the Baroness von Krudener he became a devotee of a certain mystic pietism which for some time guided his public acts, and I think it may be fairly said that his liberal and popular ideas of that period, however vague and uncertain, were sufficiently genuine. Based upon the treaties of alliance against France, those of Chaumont and of Vienna, was the final treaty of Paris, of November 20, 1815. In the preamble the signatories, who were Great Britain, Austria, Russia, and Prussia, stated that it is the purpose of the ensuing treaty and their desire "to employ all their means to prevent the general tranquillity—the object of the wishes of mankind and the constant end of their efforts—from being again disturbed; desirous, moreover, to draw closer the ties which unite them for the common interests of their people, have resolved to give to the principles solemnly laid down in the treaties of Chaumont of March 1, 1814, and of Vienna of March 25, 1815, the application the most analogous to the present state of affairs, and to fix beforehand by a solemn treaty the principles which they propose to follow, in order to guarantee Europe from dangers by which she may still be menaced."

Then follow five articles which are devoted to an agreement to hold France in control and checks, based largely on other more detailed agreements. But in article 6 it is said:

"To facilitate and to secure the execution of the present treaty, and to consolidate the connections which at the present moment so closely unite the four sovereigns for the happiness of the world, the high contracting parties have agreed to renew their meeting at fixed periods, either under the immediate auspices of the sovereigns themselves, or by their respective ministers, for the purpose of consulting upon their common interests, and for the consideration of the measures which at each of those periods shall be considered the most salutary for the repose and prosperity of nations and for the maintenance of the peace of Europe."

Certainly nothing could be more ingenuous or more praiseworthy than the purposes of the alliance then formed, and yet it was this very combination of powers which was destined to grow into what has been known, and we might add cursed, throughout history as the Holy Alliance.

As early as 1818 it had become apparent that upon this innocent statement might be built an alliance which was to be used to suppress the rights of nationalities and every attempt of any oppressed people to secure their freedom. Lord Castlereagh was a Tory of the Tories, but at that time, only three years after the treaty of Paris, when the representatives of the alliance met at Aix-la-Chapelle, he began to suspect that this new European system was wholly inconsistent with the liberties to which Englishmen of all types were devoted. At the succeeding meetings, at Troppau and Laibach, his suspicion was confirmed, and England began to draw away from her partners. He had indeed determined to break with the alliance before the Congress of Verona, but his death threw the question into the hands of George Canning, who stands forth as the man who separated Great Britain from the combination of the continental powers. The attitude of England, which was defined in a memorandum where it was said that nothing could be more injurious to the idea of government generally than the belief that their force was collectively to be prostituted to the support of an established power without any consideration of the extent to which it was to be abused, led to a compromise in 1818 in which it was declared that it was the intention of the five powers, France being invited to adhere, "to maintain the intimate union, strengthened by the ties of Christian brotherhood, contracted by the sovereigns; to pronounce the object of this union to be the preservation of peace on the basis of respect for treaties." Admirable and gentle words these, setting forth purposes which all men must approve.

In 1820 the British Government stated that they were prepared to fulfill all treaty obligations, but that if it was desired "to extend the alliance, so as to include all objects, present and future, foreseen and unforeseen, it would change its character to such an extent and carry us so far that we should see in it an additional motive for adhering to our course at the risk of seeing the alliance move away from us, without our having quitted it." The Czar Alexander abandoned his Liberal theories and threw himself into the arms of Metternich, as mean a tyrant as history can show, whose sinister designs probably caused as much misery and oppression in the years which followed as have ever been evolved by one man of second-rate abilities. The three powers, Russia, Austria, and Prussia, then put out a famous protocol in which it was said that the "States which have undergone a change of government due to revolution, the results of which threaten other States, *ipso facto* cease to be members of the European alliance and remain excluded from it until their situation gives guaranties for legal order and stability. If, owing to such alterations, immediate danger threatens other States, the powers bind themselves, by peaceful means, or, if need be, by arms, to bring back the guilty State into the bosom of the great alliance." To this point had the innocent and laudable declaration of the treaty of Paris already developed. In 1822 England broke away, and Canning made no secret of his pleasure at the breach. In a letter to the British minister at St. Petersburg he said:

"So things are getting back to a wholesome state again. Every nation for itself, and God for us all. The time for Areopagus, and the like of that, is gone by."

He also said, in the same year, 1823:

"What is the influence we have had in the counsels of the alliance, and which Prince Metternich exhorts us to be so careful not to throw away? We protested at Laibach; we remonstrated at Verona. Our protest was treated as waste paper; our remonstrances mingled with the air. Our influence, if it is to be maintained abroad, must be secured in the source of strength at home; and the sources of that strength are in sympathy between the people and the Government; in the union of the public sentiment with the public counsels; in the reciprocal confidence and cooperation of the House of Commons and the Crown."

These words of Canning are as applicable and as weighty now as when they were uttered and as worthy of consideration.

The Holy Alliance, thus developed by the three continental powers and accepted by France under the Bourbons, proceeded to restore the inquisition in Spain, to establish the Neapolitan Bourbons, who for 40 years were to subject the people of southern Italy to one of the most detestable tyrannies ever known, and proposed further to interfere against the colonies in South America which had revolted from Spain and to have their case submitted to a congress of the powers. It was then that Canning made his famous statement, "We have called a new world into existence to redress the balance of the old." It was at this point also that the United States intervened. The famous message of Monroe, sent to Congress on December 2, 1823, put an end to any danger of European influence in the American Continents. A distinguished English historian, Mr. William Alison Phillips, says:

"The attitude of the United States effectually prevented the attempt to extend the dictatorship of the alliance beyond the bounds of Europe, in itself a great service to mankind."

In 1825 Great Britain recognized the South American Republics. So far as the New World was concerned the Holy Alliance had failed. It was deprived of the support of France by the revolution of 1830, but it continued to exist under the guidance of Metternich and its last exploit was in 1849, when the Emperor Nicholas sent a Russian army into Hungary to crush out the struggle of Kossuth for freedom and independence.

I have taken the trouble to trace in the merest outline the development of the Holy Alliance, so hostile and dangerous to human freedom, because I think it carries with it a lesson for us at the present moment, showing as it does what may come from general propositions and declarations of purposes in which all the world agrees. Turn to the preamble of the covenant of the league of nations now before us, which states the object of the league. It is formed "in order to promote international cooperation and to achieve international peace and security by the acceptance of obligations not to resort to war, by the prescription of open, just, and honorable relations between nations, by the firm establishment of the under-standings of international laws as the actual rule of conduct among governments and by the maintenance of justice and a scrupulous respect for all treaty obligations in the dealings of organized peoples with one another."

No one would contest the loftiness or the benevolence of these purposes. Brave words, indeed! They do not differ essentially from the preamble of the treaty of Paris, from which sprang the Holy Alliance. But the covenant of this league contains a provision which I do not find in the treaty of Paris, and which is as follows:

"The assembly may deal at its meetings with any matter within the sphere of action of the league or affecting the peace of the world."

There is no such sweeping or far-reaching provision as that in the treaty of Paris, and yet able men developed from that treaty the Holy Alliance, which England, and later France were forced to abandon and which, for 35 years, was an unmitigated curse to the world. England broke from the Holy Alliance and the breach began three years after it was formed, because English statesmen saw that it was intended to turn the alliance— and this league is an alliance—into a means of repressing internal revolutions or insurrections. There was nothing in the treaty of Paris which warranted such action, but in this covenant of the league of nations the authority is clearly given in the third paragraph of article 3, where it is said:

"The assembly may deal at its meetings with any matter within the sphere of action of the league or affecting the peace of the world."

No revolutionary movement, no internal conflict of any magnitude can fail to affect the peace of the world. The French Revolution, which was wholly internal at the beginning, affected the peace of the world to such an extent that it brought on a world war which lasted some 25 years. Can anyone say that our Civil War did not affect the peace of the world? At this very moment, who would deny that the condition of Russia, with internal conflicts raging in all parts of that great Empire, does not affect the peace of the world and therefore come properly within the jurisdiction of the league. "Any matter affecting the peace of the world" is a very broad statement which could be made to justify almost any interference on the part of the league with the internal affairs of other countries. That this fair and obvious interpretation is the one given to it abroad is made perfectly apparent in the direct and vigorous statement of M. Clemenceau in his letter to Mr. Paderewski, in which he takes the ground in behalf of the Jews and other nationalities in Poland that they should be protected, and where he says that the associated powers would feel themselves bound to secure guaranties in Poland "of certain essential rights which will afford to the inhabitants the necessary protection, whatever changes may take place in the internal constitution of the Polish Republic." He contemplates and defends interference with the internal affairs of Poland—among other things—in behalf of a complete religious freedom, a purpose with which we all deeply sympathize. These promises of the French prime minister are embodied in effective clauses in the treaties with Germany and with Poland and deal with the internal affairs of nations, and their execution is intrusted to the "principal allied and associated powers"; that is, to the United States, Great Britain, France, Italy, and Japan. This is a practical demonstration of what can be done under article 3 and under article 11 of the league covenant, and the authority which permits interference in behalf of religious freedom, an admirable object, is easily extended to the repression of internal disturbances which may well prove a less admirable purpose. If Europe desires such an alliance or league with a power of this kind, so be it. I have no objection, provided they do not interfere with the American Continents or force us against our will but bound by a moral obligation into all the quarrels of Europe. If England, abandoning the policy of Canning, desires to be a member of a league which has such powers as this, I have not a word to say. But I object in the strongest possible way to having the United States agree, directly or indirectly, to be controlled by a league which may at any time, and perfectly lawfully and in accordance with the terms of the covenant, be drawn in to deal with internal conflicts in other countries, no matter what those conflicts may be. We should never permit the United States to be involved in any internal conflict in another country, except by the will of her people expressed through the Congress which represents them.

With regard to wars of external aggression on a member of the league the case is perfectly clear. There can be no genuine dispute whatever about the meaning of the first clause of article 10. In the first place, it differs from every other obligation in being individual and placed upon each nation without the intervention of the league. Each nation for itself promises to respect and preserve as against external aggression the boundaries and the political independence of every member of the league. Of the right of the United States to give such a guaranty I have never had the slightest doubt, and the elaborate arguments which have been made here and the learning which has been displayed about our treaty with Granada, now Colombia, and with Panama, were not necessary for me, because, I repeat, there can be no doubt of our right to give a guaranty to another nation that we will protect its boundaries and independence. The point I wish to make is that the pledge is an individual pledge. We have, for example, given guaranties to Panama and for obvious and sufficient reasons. The application of that guaranty would not be in the slightest degree affected by 10 or 20 other nations giving the same pledge if Panama, when in danger, appealed to us to fulfill our obligation. We should be bound to do so without the slightest reference to the other guarantors. In article 10 the United States is bound on the appeal of any member of the league not only to respect but to preserve its independence and its boundaries, and that pledge if we give it, must be fulfilled.

There is to me no distinction whatever in a treaty between what some persons are pleased to call legal and moral obligations. A treaty rests and must rest, except where it is imposed under duress and securities and hostages are taken for its fulfillment, upon moral obligations. No doubt a great power im possible of coercion can cast aside a moral obligation if it sees fit and escape from the performance of the duty which it promises. The pathway of dishonor is always open. I, for one, however, cannot conceive of voting for a clause of which I disapprove because I know it can be escaped in that way. Whatever the United States agrees to, by that agreement she must abide. Nothing could so surely destroy all prospects of the world's peace as to have any powerful nation refuse to carry out an obligation, direct or indirect, because it rests only on moral grounds. Whatever we promise we must carry out to the full, "without mental reservation or purpose of evasion." To me any other attitude is inconceivable. Without the most absolute and minute good faith in carrying out a treaty to which we have agreed, without ever resorting to doubtful interpretations or to the plea that it is only a moral obligation, treaties are worthless. The greatest foundation of peace is the scrupulous observance of every promise, express or implied, of every pledge, whether it can be described as legal or moral. No vote should be given to any clause in any treaty or to any treaty except in this spirit and with this understanding.

I return, then, to the first clause of article 10. It is, I repeat, an individual obligation. It requires no action on the part of the league, except that in the second sentence the authorities of the league are to have the power to advise as to the means to be employed in order to fulfill the purpose of the first sentence. But that is a detail of execution, and I consider that we are morally and in honor bound to accept and act upon that advice. The broad fact remains that if any member of the league suffering from external aggression should appeal directly to the United States for support the United States would be bound to give that support in its own capacity and without reference to the action of other powers because the United States itself is bound, and I hope the day will never come when the United States will not carry out its promises. If that day should come, and the United States or any other great country should refuse, no matter how specious the reasons, to fulfill both in letter and spirit every obligation in this covenant, the United States would be dishonored and the league would crumble into dust, leaving behind it a legacy of wars. If China should rise up and attack Japan in an effort to undo the great wrong of the cession of the control of Shantung to that power, we should be bound under the terms of article 10 to sustain Japan against China, and a guaranty of that sort is never involved except when the question has passed beyond the stage of negotiation and has become a question for the application of force. I do not like the prospect. It shall not come into existence by any vote of mine.

Article 11 carries this danger still further, for it says:

"Any war or threat of war, whether immediately affecting any of the members of the league or not, is hereby declared a matter of concern to the whole league, and the league shall take any action that shall be deemed wise and effectual to safeguard the peace of nations."

"Any war or threat of war"—that means both external aggression and internal disturbance, as I have already pointed out in dealing with article 3. "Any action" covers military action, because it covers action of any sort or kind. Let me take an example, not an imaginary case, but one which may have been overlooked because most people have not the slightest idea where or what a King of the Hedjaz is. The following dispatch appeared recently in the newspapers:

"HEDJAZ AGAINST BEDOUINS.
"The forces of Emir Abdullah recently suffered a grave defeat, the Wahabis attacking and capturing Kurma, east of Mecca. Ibn Savond is believed to be working in harmony with the Wahabis. A squadron of the royal air force was ordered recently to go to the assistance of King Hussein."

Hussein I take to be the Sultan of Hedjaz. He is being attacked by the Bedouins, as they are known to us, although I fancy the general knowledge about the Wahabis and Ibn Savond and Emir Abdullah is slight and the names mean but little to the American people. Nevertheless, here is a case of a member of the league—for the King of Hedjaz is such a member in good and regular standing and signed the treaty by his representatives, Mr. Rustem Haidar and Mr. Abdul Havi Aouni.

Under article 10, if King Hussein appealed to us for aid and protection against external aggression affecting his independence and the boundaries of his Kingdom, we should be bound to give that aid and protection and to send American soldiers to Arabia. It is not relevant to say that this is unlikely to occur; that Great Britain is quite able to take care of King Hussein, who is her fair creation, reminding one a little of the Mosquito King, a monarch once developed by Great Britain on the Mosquito Coast of Central America. The fact that we should not be called upon does not alter the right which the King of Hedjaz possesses to demand the sending of American troops to Arabia in order to preserve his independence against the assaults of the Wahabis or Bedouins. I am unwilling to give that right to King Hussein, and this illustrates the point which is to me the most objectionable in the league as it stands; the right of other powers to call out American troops and American ships to go to any part of the world, an obligation we are bound to fulfill under the terms of this treaty. I know the answer well— that of course they could not be sent without action by Congress. Congress would have no choice if acting in good faith, and if under article 10 any member of the league summoned us, or if under article 11 the league itself summoned us, we should be bound in honor and morally to obey. There would be no escape except by a breach of faith, and legislation by Congress under those circumstances would be a mockery of independent action. Is it too much to ask that provision should be made that American troops and American ships should never be sent anywhere or ordered to take part in any conflict except after the deliberate action of the American people, expressed according to the Constitution through their chosen representatives in Congress?

Let me now briefly point out the insuperable difficulty which I find in article 15. It begins: "If there should arise between members of the league any dispute likely to lead to a rupture." "Any dispute" covers every possible dispute. It therefore covers a dispute over tariff duties and over immigration. Suppose we have a dispute with Japan or with some European country as to immigration. I put aside tariff duties as less important than immigration. This is not an imaginary case. Of late years there has probably been more international discussion and negotiation about questions growing out of immigration laws than any other one subject. It comes within the definition of "any dispute" at the beginning of article 15. In the eighth paragraph of that article it is said that "if the dispute between the parties is claimed by one of them, and is found by the council to arise out of a matter which, by international law, is solely within the domestic jurisdiction of that party, the council shall so report and shall make no recommendation as to its settlement." That is one of the statements, of which there are several in this treaty, where words are used which it is difficult to believe their authors could have written down in seriousness. They seem to have been put in for the same purpose as what is known in natural history as protective coloring. Protective coloring is intended so to merge the animal, the bird, or the insect in its background that it will be indistinguishable from its surroundings and difficult, if not impossible, to find the elusive and hidden bird, animal, or insect. Protective coloring here is used in the form of words to give an impression that we are perfectly safe upon immigration and tariffs, for example, because questions which international law holds to be solely within domestic jurisdiction are not to have any recommendation from the council, but the dangers are there just the same, like the cunningly colored insect on the tree or the young bird crouching motionless upon the sand. The words and the coloring are alike intended to deceive. I wish somebody would point out to me those provisions of international law which make a list of questions which are hard and fast within the domestic jurisdiction. No such distinction can be applied to tariff duties or immigration, nor indeed finally and conclusively to any subject. Have we not seen the school laws of California, most domestic of subjects, rise to the dignity of a grave international dispute? No doubt both import duties and immigration are primarily domestic questions, but they both constantly involve and will continue to involve international effects. Like the protective coloration, this paragraph is wholly worthless unless it is successful in screening from the observer the existence of the animal, insect, or bird which it is desired to conceal. It fails to do so and the real object is detected. But even if this bit of deception was omitted—and so far as the question of immigration or tariff questions are concerned it might as well be—the ninth paragraph brings the important point clearly to the front. Immigration, which is the example I took, cannot escape the action of the league by any claim of domestic juris diction; it has too many international aspects.

Article 9 says:

"The council may, in any case under this article, refer the dispute to the assembly."

We have our dispute as to immigration with Japan or with one of the Balkan States, let us say. The council has the power to refer the dispute to the assembly. Moreover the dispute shall be so referred at the request of either party to the dispute, provided that such request be made within 14 days after the submission of the dispute to the council. So that Japan or the Balkan States, for example, with which we may easily have the dispute, ask that it be referred to the assembly and the immigration question between the United States and Jugoslavia or Japan as the case may be, goes to the assembly. The United States and Japan or Jugoslavia are excluded from voting and the provision of article 12, relating to the action and powers of the council apply to the action and powers of the assembly provided, as set forth in article 15, that a report made by the assembly "if concurred in by the representatives of those members of the league represented on the council and of a majority of the other members of the league, exclusive in each case of the representatives of the parties to the dispute, shall have the same force as a report by the council concurred in by all the members thereof other than the representatives of one or more of the parties to the dispute." This course of procedure having been pursued, we find the question of immigration between the United States and Japan is before the assembly for decision. The representatives of the council, except the delegates of the United States and of Japan or Jugoslavia, must all vote unanimously upon it as I understand it, but a majority of the entire assembly, where the council will have only seven votes, will decide. Can anyone say beforehand what the decision of that assembly will be, in which the United States and Jugoslavia or Japan will have no vote? The question in one case may affect immigration from every country in Europe, although the dispute exists only for one, and in the other the whole matter of Asiatic immigration is involved. Is it too fanciful to think that it might be decided against us? For my purpose it matters not whether it is decided for or against us. An immigration dispute or a dispute over tariff duties, met by the procedure set forth in article 15, comes before the assembly of delegates for a decision by what is practically a majority vote of the entire assembly. That is something to which I do not find myself able to give my assent. So far as immigration is concerned, and also so far as tariff duties, although less important, are concerned, I deny the jurisdiction. There should be no possibility of other nations deciding who shall come into the United States, or under what conditions they shall enter. The right to say who shall come into a country is one of the very highest attributes of sovereignty. If a nation cannot say without appeal who shall come within its gates and become a part of its citizenship it has ceased to be a sovereign nation. It has become a tributary and a subject nation, and it makes no difference whether it is subject to a league or to a conqueror.

If other nations are willing to subject themselves to such a domination, the United States, to which many immigrants have come and many more will come, ought never to submit to it for a moment. They tell us that so far as Asiatic emigration is concerned there is not the slightest danger that that will ever be forced upon us by the league, because Australia and Canada and New Zealand are equally opposed to it. I think it highly improbable that it would be forced upon us under those conditions, but it is by no means impossible. It is true the United States has one vote and that England, if you count the King of the Hedjaz, has seven—in all eight—votes; yet it might not be impossible for Japan and China and Siam to rally enough other votes to defeat us; but whether we are protected in that way or not does not matter. The very offering of that explanation accepts the jurisdiction of the league, and personally, I cannot consent to putting the protection of my country and of her workingmen against undesirable immigration, out of our own hands. We and we alone must say who shall come into the United States and become citizens of this Republic, and no one else should have any power to utter one word in regard to it.

Article 21 says:

"Nothing in this covenant shall be deemed to affect the validity of international engagements, such as treaties of arbitration or regional understandings like the Monroe doctrine for securing the maintenance of peace."

The provision did not appear in the first draft of the covenant, and when the President explained the second draft of the convention in the peace conference he said:

"Article 21 is new."

And that was all he said. No one can question the truth of the remark, but I trust I shall not be considered disrespectful if I say that it was not an illuminating statement. The article was new, but the fact of its novelty, which the President declared, was known to everyone who had taken the trouble to read the two documents. We were not left, however, without a fitting explanation. The British delegation took it upon themselves to explain article 21 at some length, and this is what they said:

"Article 21 makes it clear that the covenant is not intended to abrogate or weaken any other agreements, so long as they are consistent with its own terms, into which members of the league may have entered or may hereafter enter for the assurance of peace. Such agreements would include special treaties for compulsory arbitration and military conventions that are genuinely defensive.

"The Monroe doctrine and similar understandings are put in the same category. They have shown themselves in history to be not instruments of national ambition, but guarantees of peace. The origin of the Monroe doctrine is well known. It was proclaimed in 1823 to prevent America from becoming a theater for intrigues of European absolutism. At first a principle of American foreign policy, it has become an international understanding, and it is not illegitimate for the people of the United States to say that the covenant should recognize that fact.

"In its essence it is consistent with the spirit of the covenant, and, indeed, the principles of the league, as expressed in article 10, represent the extension to the whole world of the principles of the doctrine, while, should any dispute as to the meaning of the latter ever arise between the American and European powers, the league is there to settle it."

The explanation of Great Britain received the assent of France.

"It seems to me monumentally paradoxical and a trifle infantile—"

Says M. Lausanne, editor of the *Matin* and a chief spokesman for M. Clemenceau—

"to pretend the contrary.

"When the executive council of the league of nations fixes the 'reasonable limits of the armament of Peru'; when it shall demand information concerning the naval program of Brazil (art. 7 of the covenant); when it shall tell Argentina what shall be the measure of the 'contribution to the armed forces to protect the signature of the social covenant' (art. 16); when it shall demand the immediate registration of the treaty between the United States and Canada at the seat of the league, it will control, whether it wills or not, the destinies of America.

"And when the American States shall be obliged to take a hand in every war or menace of war in Europe (art. 11) they will necessarily fall afoul of the fundamental principle laid down by Monroe.

"*   *   *   If the league takes in the world, then Europe must mix in the affairs of America; if only Europe is included, then America will violate of necessity her own doctrine by intermixing in the affairs of Europe."

It has seemed to me that the British delegation traveled a little out of the precincts of the peace conference when they undertook to explain the Monroe doctrine and tell the United States what it was and what it was not proposed to do with it under the new article. That, however, is merely a matter of taste and judgment. Their statement that the Monroe doctrine under this article, if any question arose in regard to it, would be passed upon and interpreted by the league of nations is absolutely correct. There is no doubt that this is what the article means. Great Britain so stated it, and no American authority, whether friendly or unfriendly to the league, has dared to question it. I have wondered a little why it was left to the British delegation to explain that article, which so nearly concerns the United States, but that was merely a fugitive thought upon which I will not dwell. The statement of M. Lausanne is equally explicit and truthful, but he makes one mistake. He says, in substance, that if we are to meddle in Europe, Europe cannot be excluded from the Americas. He overlooks the fact that the Monroe doctrine also says:

"Our policy in regard to Europe, which was adopted at an early stage of the wars which have so long agitated that quarter of the globe, nevertheless remains the same, which is not to interfere in the internal concerns of any of the powers."

The Monroe doctrine was the corollary of Washington's neutrality policy and of his injunction against permanent alliances. It reiterates and reaffirms the principle. We do not seek to meddle in the affairs of Europe and keep Europe out of the Americas. It is as important to keep the United States out of European affairs as to keep Europe out of the American Continents. Let us maintain the Monroe doctrine, then, in its entirety, and not only preserve our own safety, but in this way best promote the real peace of the world. Whenever the preservation of freedom and civilization and the overthrow of a menacing world conqueror summon us we shall respond fully and nobly, as we did in 1917. He who doubts that we could do so has little faith in America. But let it be our own act and not done reluctantly by the coercion of other nations, at the bidding or by the permission of other countries.

Let me now deal with the article itself. We have here some protective coloration again. The Monroe doctrine is described as a "regional understanding" whatever that may mean. The boundaries between the States of the Union, I suppose, are "regional understandings," if anyone chooses to apply to them that somewhat swollen phraseology. But the Monroe doctrine is no more a regional understanding than it is an "international engagement." The Monroe doctrine was a policy declared by President Monroe. Its immediate purpose was to shut out Europe from interfering with the South American Republics, which the Holy Alliance designed to do. It was stated broadly, however, as we all know, and went much further than that. It was, as I have just said, the corollary of Washington's declaration against our interfering in European questions. It was so regarded by Jefferson at the time and by John Quincy Adams, who formulated it, and by President Monroe, who declared it. It rested firmly on the great law of self-preservation, which is the basic principle of every independent State.

It is not necessary to trace its history or to point out the extensions which it has received or its universal acceptance by all

American statesmen without regard to party. All Americans have always been for it. They may not have known its details or read all the many discussions in regard to it, but they knew that it was an American doctrine and that, broadly stated, it meant the exclusion of Europe from interference with American affairs and from any attempt to colonize or set up new States within the boundaries of the American Continent. I repeat it was purely an American doctrine, a purely American policy, designed and wisely designed for our defense. It has never been an "international engagement." No nation has ever formally recognized it. It has been the subject of reservation at international conventions by American delegates. It has never been a "regional understanding" or an understanding of any kind with anybody. It was the declaration of the United States of America, in their own behalf, supported by their own power. They brought it into being, and its life was predicated on the force which the United States could place behind it. Unless the United States could sustain it it would die. The United States has supported it. It has lived—strong, efficient, respected. It is now proposed to kill it by a provision in a treaty for a league of nations.

The instant that the United States, who declared, interpreted, and sustained the doctrine, ceases to be the sole judge of what it means, that instant the Monroe doctrine ceases and disappears from history and from the face of the earth. I think it is just as undesirable to have Europe interfere in American affairs now as Mr. Monroe thought it was in 1823, and equally undesirable that we should be compelled to involve ourselves in all the wars and brawls of Europe. The Monroe doctrine has made for peace. Without the Monroe doctrine we should have had many a struggle with European powers to save ourselves from possible assault and certainly from the necessity of becoming a great military power, always under arms and always ready to resist invasion from States in our near neighborhood. In the interests of the peace of the world it is now proposed to wipe away this American policy, which has been a bulwark and a barrier for peace. With one exception it has always been successful, and then success was only delayed. When we were torn by civil war France saw fit to enter Mexico and endeavored to establish an empire there. When our hands were once free the empire perished, and with it the unhappy tool of the third Napoleon. If the United States had not been rent by civil war no such attempt would have been made, and nothing better illustrates the value to the cause of peace of the Monroe doctrine. Why, in the name of peace, should we extinguish it? Why, in the name of peace, should we be called upon to leave the interpretation of the Monroe doctrine to other nations? It is an American policy. It is our own. It has guarded us well, and I, for one, can never find consent in my heart to destroy it by a clause in a treaty and hand over its body for dissection to the nations of Europe. If we need authority to demonstrate what the Monroe doctrine has meant to the United States we cannot do better than quote the words of Grover Cleveland, who directed Mr. Olney to notify the world that "to-day the United States is practically sovereign on this continent, and its fiat is law to which it confines its interposition." Theodore Roosevelt, in the last article written before his death, warned us, his countrymen, that we are "in honor bound to keep ourselves so prepared that the Monroe doctrine shall be accepted as immutable international law." Grover Cleveland was a Democrat and Theodore Roosevelt was a Republican, but they were both Americans, and it is the American spirit which has carried this country always to victory and which should govern us to-day, and not the international spirit which would in the name of peace hand the United States over bound hand and foot to obey the fiat of other powers.

Another point in this covenant where change must be made in order to protect the safety of the United States in the future is in article 1, where withdrawal is provided for. This provision was an attempt to meet the very general objection to the first draft of the league, that there was no means of getting out of it without denouncing the treaty; that is, there was no arrangement for the withdrawal of any nation. As it now stands it reads that—

"Any member of the league may, after two years' notice of its intention to do so, withdraw from the league, provided that all its international obligations, and all its obligations under this covenant shall have been fulfilled at the time of its withdrawal."

The right of withdrawal is given by this clause, although the time for notice, two years, is altogether too long. Six months or a year would be found, I think, in most treaties to be the normal period fixed for notice of withdrawal. But whatever virtue there may be in the right thus conferred is completely nullified by the proviso. The right of withdrawal cannot be exercised until all the international obligations and all the obligations of the withdrawing nations have been fulfilled. The league alone can decide whether "all international obligations and all obligations under this covenant" have been fulfilled, and this would require, under the provisions of the league, a unanimous vote so that any nation desiring to withdraw could not do so, even on the two years' notice, if one nation voted that the obligations had not been fulfilled. Remember that this gives the league not only power to review all our obligations under the covenant but all our treaties with all nations for every one of those is an "international obligation."

Are we deliberately to put ourselves in fetters and be examined by the league of nations as to whether we have kept faith with Cuba or Panama before we can be permitted to leave the league? This seems to me humiliating to say the least. The right of withdrawal, if it is to be of any value whatever, must be absolute, because otherwise a nation desiring to withdraw could be held in the league by objections from other nations until the very act which induces the nation to withdraw had been completed; until the withdrawing nation had been forced to send troops to take part in a war with which it had no concern and upon which it did not desire to enter. It seems to me vital to the safety of the United States not only that this provision should be eliminated and the right to withdraw made absolute but that the period of withdrawal should be much reduced. As it stands it is practically no better in this respect than the first league draft which contained no provision for withdrawal at all, because the proviso here inserted so incumbers it that every nation to all intents and purposes must remain a member of the league indefinitely unless all the other members are willing that it should retire. Such a provision as this, ostensibly framed to meet the objection, has the defect which other similar gestures to give an impression of meeting objections have, that it apparently keeps the promise to the ear but most certainly breaks it to the hope.

I have dwelt only upon those points which seem to me most dangerous. There are, of course, many others, but these points, in the interest not only of the safety of the United States but of the maintenance of the treaty and the peace of the world, should be dealt with here before it is too late. Once in the league the chance of amendment is so slight that it is not worth considering. Any analysis of the provisions of this league covenant, however, brings out in startling relief one great fact. Whatever may be said, it is not a league of peace; it is an alliance, dominated at the present moment by five great powers, really by three, and it has all the marks of an alliance. The development of international law is neglected. The court which is to decide disputes brought before it fills but a small place. The conditions for which this league really provides with the utmost care are political conditions, not judicial questions, to be reached by the executive council and the assembly, purely political bodies without any trace of a judicial character about them. Such being its machinery, the control being in the hands of political appointees whose votes will be controlled by interest and expedience, it exhibits that most marked characteristic of an alliance—that its decisions are to be carried out by force. Those articles upon which the whole structure rests are articles which provide for the use of force; that is, for war. This league to enforce peace does a great deal for enforcement and very little for peace. It makes more essential provisions looking to war than to peace, for the settlement of disputes.

Article 10 I have already discussed. There is no question that the preservation of a State against external aggression can contemplate nothing but war. In article 11, again, the league is authorized to take any action which may be necessary to safeguard the peace of the world. "Any action" includes war. We also have specific provisions for a boycott, which is a form of economic warfare. The use of troops might be avoided but the enforcement of a boycott would require blockades in all probability, and certainly a boycott in its essence is simply an effort to starve a people into submission, to ruin their trade, and, in the case of nations which are not self-supporting, to cut off their food supply. The misery and suffering caused by such a measure as this may easily rival that caused by actual war. Article 16 embodies the boycott and also, in the last paragraph, provides explicitly for war. We are told that the word "recommends" has no binding force; it constitutes a moral obligation, that is all. But it means that if we, for example, should refuse to accept the recommendation, we should nullify the operation of article 16 and, to that extent, of the league. It seems to me that to attempt to relieve us of clearly imposed duties by saying that the word "recommend" is not binding is an escape of which no nation regarding the sanctity of treaties and its own honor would care to avail itself. The provisions of article 16 are extended to States outside the league who refuse to obey its command to come in and submit themselves to its jurisdiction; another provision for war.

Taken altogether, these provisions for war present what to my mind is the gravest objection to this league in its present form. We are told that of course nothing will be done in the way of warlike acts without the assent of Congress. If that is true, let us say so in the covenant. But as it stands there is no doubt whatever in my mind that American troops and American ships may be ordered to any part of the world by nations other than the United States, and that is a proposition to which I for one can never assent. It must be made perfectly clear that no American soldiers, not even a corporal's guard, that no American sailors, not even the crew of a submarine, can ever be engaged in war or ordered anywhere except by the constitutional authorities of the United States. To Congress is granted by the Constitution the right to declare war, and nothing that would take the troops out of the country at the bidding or demand of other nations should ever be permitted except through congressional action. The lives of Americans must never be sacrificed except by the will of the American people expressed through their chosen Representatives in Congress. This is a point upon which no doubt can be permitted. American soldiers and American sailors have never failed the country when the country called upon them. They went in their hundreds of thousands into the war just closed. They went to die for the great cause of freedom and of civilization. They went at their country's bidding and because their country summoned them to service. We were late in entering the war. We made no preparation as we ought to have done, for the ordeal which was clearly coming upon us; but we went and we turned the wavering scale. It was done by the American soldier, the American sailor, and the spirit and energy of the American people. They overrode all obstacles and all shortcomings on the part of the administration or of Congress, and gave to their country a great place in the great victory. It was the first time we had been called upon to rescue the civilized world. Did we fail? On the contrary, we succeeded, we succeeded largely and nobly, and we did it without any command from any league of nations. When the emergency came we met it and we were able to meet it because we had built up on this continent the greatest and most powerful nation in the world, built it up under our own policies, in our own way, and one great element of our strength was the fact that we had held aloof and had not thrust ourselves into European quarrels; that we had no selfish interest to serve. We made great sacrifices. We have done splendid work. I believe that we do not require to be told by foreign nations when we shall do work which freedom and civilization require. I think we can move to victory much better under our own command than under the command of others. Let us unite with the world to promote the peaceable settlement of all international disputes. Let us try to develop international law. Let us associate ourselves with the other nations for these purposes. But let us retain in our own hands and in our own control the lives of the youth of the land. Let no American be sent into battle except by the constituted authorities of his own country and by the will of the people of the United States.

Those of us, Mr. President, who are either wholly opposed to the league or who are trying to preserve the independence and the safety of the United States by changing the terms of the league and who are endeavoring to make the league, if we are to be a member of it, less certain to promote war instead of peace, have been reproached with selfishness in our outlook and with a desire to keep our country in a state of isolation. So far as the question of isolation goes, it is impossible to isolate the United States. I well remember the time, 20 years ago, when eminent Senators and other distinguished gentlemen who were opposing the Philippines and shrieking about imperialism, sneered at the statement made by some of us, that the United States had become a world power. I think no one now would question that the Spanish War marked the entrance of the United States into world affairs to a degree which had never obtained before. It was both an inevitable and an irrevocable step, and our entrance into the war with Germany certainly showed once and for all that the United States was not unmindful of its world responsibilities. We may set aside all this empty talk about isolation. Nobody expects to isolate the United States or to make it a hermit Nation, which is a sheer absurdity. But there is a wide difference between taking a suitable part and bearing a due responsibility in world affairs and plunging the United States into every controversy and conflict on the face of the globe. By meddling in all the differences which may arise among any portion or fragment of humankind we simply fritter away our influence and injure ourselves to no good purpose. We shall be of far more value to the world and its peace by occupying, so far as possible, the situation which we have occupied for the last 20 years and by adhering to the policy of Washington and Hamilton, of Jefferson and Monroe, under which we have risen to our present greatness and prosperity. The fact that we have been separated by our geographical situation and by our consistent policy from the broils of Europe has made us more than any one thing capable of performing the great work which we performed in the war against Germany, and our disinterestedness is of far more value to the world than our eternal meddling in every possible dispute could ever be.

Now, as to our selfishness. I have no desire to boast that we are better than our neighbors, but the fact remains that this Nation in making peace with Germany had not a single selfish or individual interest to serve. All we asked was that Germany should be rendered incapable of again breaking forth, with all the horrors incident to German warfare, upon an unoffending world, and that demand was shared by every free nation and indeed by humanity itself. For ourselves we asked absolutely nothing. We have not asked any government or governments to guarantee our boundaries or our political independence. We have no fear in regard to either. We have sought no territory, no privileges, no advantages, for ourselves. That is the fact. It is apparent on the face of the treaty. I do not mean to reflect upon a single one of the powers with which we have been associated in the war against Germany, but there is not one of them which has not sought individual advantages for their own national benefit. I do not criticize their desires at all. The services and sacrifices of England and France and Belgium and Italy are beyond estimate and beyond praise. I am glad they should have what they desire for their own welfare and safety. But they all receive under the peace territorial and commercial benefits. We are asked to give, and we in no way seek to take. Surely it is not too much to insist that when we are offered nothing but the opportunity to give and to aid others we should have the right to say what sacrifices we shall make and what the magnitude of our gifts shall be. In the prosecution of the war we gave unstintedly American lives and American treasure. When the war closed we had 3,000,000 men under arms. We were turning the country into a vast workshop for war. We advanced ten billions to our allies. We refused no assistance that we could possibly render. All the great energy and power of the Republic were put at the service of the good cause. We have not been ungenerous. We have been devoted to the cause of freedom, humanity, and civilization everywhere. Now we are asked, in the making of peace, to sacrifice our sovereignty in important respects, to involve ourselves almost without limit in the affairs of other nations, and to yield up policies and rights which we have maintained throughout our history. We are asked to incur liabilities to an unlimited extent and furnish assets at the same time which no man can measure. I think it is not only our right but our duty to determine how far we shall go. Not only must we look carefully to see where we are being led into endless disputes and entanglements, but we must not forget that we have in this country millions of people of foreign birth and parentage.

Our one great object is to make all these people Americans so that we may call on them to place America first and serve America as they have done in the war just closed. We cannot Americanize them if we are continually thrusting them back into the quarrels and difficulties of the countries from which they came to us. We shall fill this land with political disputes about the troubles and quarrels of other countries. We shall have a large portion of our people voting not on American questions and not on what concerns the United States but dividing on issues which concern foreign countries alone. That is an unwholesome and perilous condition to force upon this country. We must avoid it. We ought to reduce to the lowest possible point the foreign questions in which we involve ourselves. Never forget that this league is primarily—I might say overwhelmingly—a political organization, and I object strongly to having the politics of the United States turn upon disputes where deep feeling is aroused but in which we have no direct interest. It will all tend to delay the Americanization of our great population, and it is more important not only to the United States but to the peace of the world to make all these people good Americans than it is to determine that some piece of territory should belong to one European country rather than to another. For this reason I wish to limit strictly our interference in the affairs of Europe and of Africa. We have interests of our own in Asia and in the Pacific which we must guard upon our own account, but the less we undertake to play the part of umpire and thrust ourselves into European conflicts the better for the United States and for the world.

It has been reiterated here on this floor, and reiterated to the point of weariness, that in every treaty there is some sacrifice of sovereignty. That is not a universal truth by any means, but it is true of some treaties and it is a platitude which does not require reiteration. The question and the only question before us here is how much of our sovereignty we are justified in sacrificing. In what I have already said about other nations putting us into war I have covered one point of sovereignty which ought never to be yielded, the power to send American soldiers and sailors everywhere, which ought never to be taken from the American people or impaired in the slightest degree. Let us beware how we palter with our independence. We have not reached the great position from which we were able to come down into the field of battle and help to save the world from tyranny by being guided by others. Our vast power has all been built up and gathered together by ourselves alone. We forced our way upward from the days of the Revolution, through a world often hostile and always indifferent. We owe no debt to anyone except to France in that Revolution, and those policies and those rights on which our power has been founded should never be lessened or weakened. It will be no service to the world to do so and it will be of intolerable injury to the

United States. We will do our share. We are ready and anxious to help in all ways to preserve the world's peace. But we can do it best by not crippling ourselves.

I am as anxious as any human being can be to have the United States render every possible service to the civilization and the peace of mankind, but I am certain we can do it best by not putting ourselves in leading strings or subjecting our policies and our sovereignty to other nations. The independence of the United States is not only more precious to ourselves but to the world than any single possession. Look at the United States to-day. We have made mistakes in the past. We have had short-comings. We shall make mistakes in the future and fall short of our own best hopes. But none the less is there any country to-day on the face of the earth which can compare with this in ordered liberty, in peace, and in the largest freedom? I feel that I can say this without being accused of undue boastfulness, for it is the simple fact, and in making this treaty and taking on these obligations all that we do is in a spirit of unselfishness and in a desire for the good of mankind. But it is well to remember that we are dealing with nations every one of which has a direct individual interest to serve and there is grave danger in an unshared idealism. Contrast the United States with any country on the face of the earth to-day and ask yourself whether the situation of the United States is not the best to be found. I will go as far as anyone in world service, but the first step to world service is the maintenance of the United States. You may call me selfish if you will, conservative or reactionary, or use any other harsh adjective you see fit to apply, but an American I was born, an American I have remained all my life. I can never be anything else but an American, and I must think of the United States first, and when I think of the United States first in an arrangement like this I am thinking of what is best for the world, for if the United States fails the best hopes of mankind fail with it. I have never had but one allegiance—I cannot divide it now. I have loved but one flag and I cannot share that devotion and give affection to the mongrel banner invented for a league. Internationalism, illustrated by the Bolshevik and by the men to whom all countries are alike provided they can make money out of them, is to me repulsive. National I must remain, and in that way I, like all other Americans, can render the amplest service to the world. The United States is the world's best hope, but if you fetter her in the interests and quarrels of other nations, if you tangle her in the intrigues of Europe, you will destroy her power for good and endanger her very existence. Leave her to march freely through the centuries to come as in the years that have gone. Strong, generous, and confident, she has nobly served mankind. Beware how you trifle with your marvelous inheritance, this great land of ordered liberty, for if we stumble and fall, freedom and civilization everywhere will go down in ruin.

We are told that we shall "break the heart of the world" if we do not take this league just as it stands. I fear that the hearts of the vast majority of mankind would beat on strongly and steadily and without any quickening if the league were to perish altogether. If it should be effectively and beneficently changed the people who would lie awake in sorrow for a single night could be easily gathered in one not very large room, but those who would draw a long breath of relief would reach to millions.

We hear much of visions and I trust we shall continue to have visions and dream dreams of a fairer future for the race. But visions are one thing and visionaries are another, and the mechanical appliances of the rhetorician designed to give a picture of a present which does not exist and of a future which no man can predict are as unreal and shortlived as the steam or canvas clouds, the angels suspended on wires, and the artificial lights of the stage. They pass with the moment of effect and are shabby and tawdry in the daylight. Let us at least be real. Washington's entire honesty of mind and his fearless look into the face of all facts are qualities which can never go out of fashion and which we should all do well to imitate.

Ideals have been thrust upon us as an argument for the league until the healthy mind, which rejects cant, revolts from them. Are ideals confined to this deformed experiment upon a noble purpose, tainted as it is with bargains, and tied to a peace treaty which might have been disposed of long ago to the great benefit of the world if it had not been compelled to carry this rider on its back? "*Post equitem sedet atra cura,*" Horace tells us, but no blacker care ever sat behind any rider than we shall find in this covenant of doubtful and disputed inter-pretation as it now perches upon the treaty of peace.

No doubt many excellent and patriotic people see a coming fulfillment of noble ideals in the words "league for peace." We all respect and share these aspirations and desires, but some of us see no hope, but rather defeat, for them in this murky cove-nant. For we, too, have our ideals, even if we differ from those who have tried to establish a monopoly of idealism. Our first ideal is our country, and we see her in the future, as in the past, giving service to all her people and to the world. Our ideal of the future is that she should continue to render that service of her own free will. She has great problems of her own to solve, very grim and perilous problems, and a right solution, if we can attain to it, would largely benefit mankind. We would have our country strong to resist a peril from the West, as she has flung back the German menace from the East. We would not have our politics distracted and embittered by the dissensions of other lands. We would not have our country's vigor ex-hausted or her moral force abated by everlasting meddling and muddling in every quarrel, great and small, which afflicts the world. Our ideal is to make her ever stronger and better and finer, because in that way alone, as we believe, can she be of the greatest service to the world's peace and to the welfare of mankind. [Prolonged applause in the galleries.]

HERBERT HOOVER

"Rugged Individualism" Speech

New York City, October 22, 1928

THIS CAMPAIGN now draws near a close. The platforms of the two parties defining principles and offering solutions of various national problems have been presented and are being earnestly considered by our people.

After four months' debate it is not the Republican Party which finds reason for abandonment of any of the principles it has laid down or of the views it has expressed for solution of the problems before the country. The principles to which it adheres are rooted deeply in the foundations of our national life. The solutions which it proposes are based on experience with government and on a consciousness that it may have the responsibility for placing those solutions in action.

In my acceptance speech I endeavored to outline the spirit and ideals by which I would be guided in carrying that platform into administration. Tonight, I will not deal with the multitude of issues which have been already well canvassed. I intend rather to discuss some of those more fundamental principles and ideals upon which I believe the government of the United States should be conducted.

The Republican Party has ever been a party of progress. I do not need to review its seventy years of constructive history. It has always reflected the spirit of the American people. Never has it done more for the advancement of fundamental progress than during the past seven and one-half years since we took over the government amidst the ruin left by war.

It detracts nothing from the character and energy of the American people, it minimizes in no degree the quality of their accomplishments to say that the policies of the Republican Party have played a large part in recuperation from the war and the building of the magnificent progress which shows upon every hand today. I say with emphasis that without the wise policies which the Republican Party has brought into action during this period, no such progress would have been possible.

The first responsibility of the Republican administration was to renew the march of progress from its collapse by the war. That task involved the restoration of confidence in the future and the liberation and stimulation of the constructive energies of our people. It discharged that task. There is not a person within the sound of my voice who does not know the profound progress which our country has made in this period. Every man and woman knows that American comfort, hope, and confidence for the future are immeasurably higher this day than they were seven and one-half years ago.

It is not my purpose to enter upon a detailed recital of the great constructive measures of the past seven and one-half years by which this has been brought about. It is sufficient to remind you of the restoration of employment to the millions who walked your streets in idleness; to remind you of the creation of the budget system; the reduction of six billions of national debt which gave the powerful impulse of that vast sum returned to industry and commerce; the four sequent reductions of taxes and thereby the lift to the living of every family; the enactment of adequate protective tariff and immigration laws which have safeguarded our workers and farmers from floods of goods and labor from foreign countries; the creation of credit facilities and many other aids to agriculture; the building up of foreign trade; the care of veterans; the development of aviation, of radio, of our inland waterways, of our highways; the expansion of scientific research, of welfare activities; the making of safer highways, safer mines, better homes; the spread of outdoor recreation; the improvement in public health and the care of children; and a score of other progressive actions.

Nor do I need to remind you that government today deals with an economic and social system vastly more intricate and delicately adjusted than ever before. That system now must be kept in perfect tune if we would maintain uninterrupted employment and the high standards of living of our people. The government has come to touch this delicate web at a thousand points. Yearly the relations of government to national prosperity become more and more intimate. Only through keen vision and helpful co-operation by the government has stability in business and stability in employment been maintained during this past seven and one-half years. There always are some localities, some industries, and some individuals who do not share the prevailing prosperity. The task of government is to lessen these inequalities.

Never has there been a period when the Federal Government has given such aid and impulse to the progress of our people, not alone to economic progress but to the development of those agencies which make for moral and spiritual progress.

But in addition to this great record of contributions of the Republican Party to progress, there has been a further fundamental contribution—a contribution underlying and sustaining all the others—and that is the resistance of the Republican Party to every attempt to inject the government into business in competition with its citizens.

After the war, when the Republican Party assumed administration of the country, we were faced with the problem of determination of the very nature of our national life. During one hundred and fifty years we have builded up a form of self-government and a social system which is peculiarly our own. It differs essentially from all others in the world. It is the American system. It is just as definite and positive a political and social system as has ever been developed on earth. It is founded upon a particular conception of self-government in which decentralized local responsibility is the very base. Further than this, it is founded upon the conception that only through ordered liberty, freedom, and equal opportunity to the individual will his initiative and enterprise spur on the march of progress. And in our insistence upon equality of opportunity has our system advanced beyond all the world.

During the war we necessarily turned to the government to solve every difficult economic problem. The government having absorbed every energy of our people for war, there was no other solution. For the preservation of the state the Federal Government became a centralized despotism which undertook unprecedented responsibilities, assumed autocratic powers, and took over the business of citizens. To a large degree we regimented our whole people temporarily into a socialistic state. However justified in time of war, if continued in peace-time it would destroy not only our American system but with it our progress and freedom as well.

When the war closed, the most vital of all issues both in our own country and throughout the world was whether governments should continue their war-time ownership and operation of many instrumentalities of production and distribution. We were challenged with a peace-time choice between the American system of rugged individualism and a European philosophy of diametrically opposed doctrines—doctrines of paternalism and state socialism. The acceptance of these ideas would have meant the destruction of self-government through centralization of government. It would have meant the undermining of the individual initiative and enterprise through which our people have grown to unparalleled greatness.

The Republican Party from the beginning resolutely turned its face away from these ideas and these war practices. A Republican Congress co-operated with the Democratic administration to demobilize many of our war activities. At that time the two parties were in accord upon that point. When the Republican Party came into full power it went at once resolutely back to our fundamental conception of the state and the rights and responsibilities of the individual. Thereby it restored confidence and hope in the American people, it freed and stimulated enterprise, it restored the government to its position as an umpire instead of a player in the economic game. For these reasons the American people have gone forward in progress while the rest of the world has halted, and some countries have even gone backward. If anyone will study the causes of retarded recuperation in Europe, he will find much of it due to stifling of private initiative on one hand, and overloading of the government with business on the other.

There has been revived in this campaign, however, a series of proposals which, if adopted, would be a long step toward the abandonment of our American system and a surrender to the destructive operation of governmental conduct of commercial business. Because the country is faced with difficulty and doubt over certain national problems—that is, prohibition, farm relief, and electrical power—our opponents propose that we must thrust government a long way into the businesses which give rise to these problems. In effect, they abandon the tenets of their own party and turn to state socialism as a solution for the difficulties presented by all three. It is proposed that we shall change from prohibition to the state purchase and sale of liquor. If their agricultural relief program means anything, it means that the government shall directly or indirectly buy and sell and fix prices of agricultural products. And we are to go into the hydro-electric power business. In other words, we are confronted with a huge program of government in business.

There is, therefore, submitted to the American people a question of fundamental principle. That is: shall we depart from the principles of our American political and economic system, upon which we have advanced beyond all the rest of the world, in order to adopt methods based on principles destructive of its very foundations? And I wish to emphasize the seriousness of these proposals. I wish to make my position clear; for this goes to the very roots of American life and progress.

I should like to state to you the effect that this projection of government in business would have upon our system of self-government and our economic system. That effect would reach to the daily life of every man and woman. It would impair the very basis of liberty and freedom not only for those left outside the fold of expanded bureaucracy but for those embraced within it.

Let us first see the effect upon self-government. When the Federal Government undertakes to go into commercial business it must at once set up the organization and administration of that business, and it immediately finds itself in a labyrinth, every alley of which leads to the destruction of self-government.

Commercial business requires a concentration of responsibility. Self-government requires decentralization and many checks and balances to safeguard liberty. Our government to succeed in business would need become in effect a despotism. There at once begins the destruction of self-government.

The first problem of the government about to adventure in commercial business is to determine a method of administration. It must secure leadership and direction. Shall this leadership be chosen by political agencies or shall we make it elective? The hard practical fact is that leadership in business must come through the sheer rise in ability and character. That rise can only take place in the free atmosphere of competition.

Competition is closed by bureaucracy. Political agencies are feeble channels through which to select able leaders to conduct commercial business.

Government, in order to avoid the possible incompetence, corruption, and tyranny of too great authority in individuals entrusted with commercial business, inevitably turns to boards and commissions. To make sure that there are checks and balances, each member of such boards and commissions must have equal authority. Each has his separate responsibility to the public, and at once we have the conflict of ideas and the lack of decision which would ruin any commercial business. It has contributed greatly to the demoralization of our shipping business. Moreover, these commissions must be representative of different sections and different political parties, so that at once we have an entire blight upon coordinated action within their ranks which destroys any possibility of effective administration.

Moreover, our legislative bodies cannot in fact delegate their full authority to commissions or to individuals for the conduct of matters vital to the American people; for if we would preserve government by the people we must preserve the authority of our legislators in the activities of our government.

Thus every time the Federal Government goes into a commercial business, five hundred and thirty-one Senators and Congressmen become the actual board of directors of that business. Every time a state government goes into business one or two hundred state senators and legislators become the actual directors of that business. Even if they were supermen and if there were no politics in the United States, no body of such numbers could competently direct commercial activities; for that requires initiative, instant decision, and action. It took Congress six years of constant discussion to even decide what the method of administration of Muscle Shoals should be.

When the Federal Government undertakes to go into business, the state governments are at once deprived of control and taxation of that business; when a state government undertakes to go into business, it at once deprives the municipalities of taxation and control of that business. Municipalities, being local and close to the people, can, at times, succeed in business where federal and state governments must fail. We have trouble enough with log-rolling in legislative bodies today. It originates naturally from desires of citizens to advance their particular section or to secure some necessary service. It would be multiplied a thousandfold were the federal and state governments in these businesses.

The effect upon our economic progress would be even worse. Business progressiveness is dependent on competition. New methods and new ideas are the outgrowth of the spirit of adventure, of individual initiative, and of individual enterprise. Without adventure there is no progress. No government administration can rightly take chances with taxpayers' money.

There is no better example of the practical incompetence of government to conduct business than the history of our railways. During the war the government found it necessary to operate the railways. That operation continued until after the war. In the year before being freed from government operation they were not able to meet the demands for transportation. Eight years later we find them under private enterprise transporting fifteen per cent more goods and meeting every demand for service. Rates have been reduced by fifteen per cent and net earnings increased from less than one per cent on their valuation to about five per cent. Wages of employees have improved by thirteen per cent. The wages of railway employees are today one hundred and twenty-one per cent above pre-war, while the wages of government employees are today only sixty-five per cent above pre-war. That should be a sufficient commentary upon the efficiency of government operation.

Let us now examine this question from the point of view of the person who may get a government job and is admitted into the new bureaucracy. Upon that subject let me quote from a speech of that great leader of labor, Samuel Gompers, delivered in Montreal in 1920, a few years before his death. He said:

"I believe there is no man to whom I would take second position in my loyalty to the Republic of the United States, and yet I would not give it more power over the individual citizenship of our country. . . . .

"It is a question of whether it shall be government ownership or private ownership under control. . . . . If I were in the minority of one in this convention, I would want to cast my vote so that the men of labor shall not willingly enslave themselves to government authority in their industrial effort for freedom. . . . .

"Let the future tell the story of who is right or who is wrong; who has stood for freedom and who has been willing to submit their fate industrially to the government."

I would amplify Mr. Gompers' statement. The great body of government employees which would be created by the proposals of our opponents would either comprise a political machine at the disposal of the party in power, or, alternatively, to prevent this, the government by stringent civil-service rules must debar its employees from their full political rights as free men. It must limit them in the liberty to bargain for their own wages, for no government employee can strike against his government and thus against the whole people. It makes a legislative body with all its political currents their final employer and master. Their bargaining does not rest upon economic need or economic strength but on political potence.

But what of those who are outside the bureaucracy? What is the effect upon their lives?

The area of enterprise and opportunity for them to strive and rise is at once limited.

The government in commercial business does not tolerate amongst its customers the freedom of competitive reprisals to which private business is subject. Bureaucracy does not tolerate the spirit of independence; it spreads the spirit of submission into our daily life and penetrates the temper of our people not with the habit of powerful resistance to wrong but with the habit of timid acceptance of irresistible might.

Bureaucracy is ever desirous of spreading its influence and its power. You cannot extend the mastery of the government over the daily working life of a people without at the same time making it the master of the people's souls and thoughts. Every expansion of government in business means that government in order to protect itself from the political consequences of its errors and wrongs is driven irresistibly without peace to greater and greater control of the nation's press and platform. Free speech does not live many hours after free industry and free commerce die.

It is a false liberalism that interprets itself into the government operation of commercial business. Every step of bureaucratizing of the business of our country poisons the very roots of liberalism—that is, political equality, free speech, free assembly, free press, and equality of opportunity. It is the road not to more liberty, but to less liberty. Liberalism should be found not striving to spread bureaucracy but striving to set bounds to it. True liberalism seeks all legitimate freedom first in the confident belief that without such freedom the pursuit of all other blessings and benefits is vain. That belief is the foundation of all American progress, political as well as economic.

Liberalism is a force truly of the spirit, a force proceeding from the deep realization that economic freedom cannot be sacrificed if political freedom is to be preserved. Even if governmental conduct of business could give us more efficiency instead of less efficiency, the fundamental objection to it would remain unaltered and unabated. It would destroy political equality. It would increase rather than decrease abuse and corruption. It would stifle initiative and invention. It would undermine the development of leadership. It would cramp and cripple the mental and spiritual energies of our people. It would extinguish equality and opportunity. It would dry up the spirit of liberty and progress. For these reasons primarily it must be resisted. For a hundred and fifty years liberalism has found its true spirit in the American system, not in the European systems.

I do not wish to be misunderstood in this statement. I am defining a general policy. It does not mean that our government is to part with one iota of its national resources without complete protection to the public interest. I have already stated that where the government is engaged in public works for purposes of flood control, of navigation, of irrigation, of scientific research or national defense, or in pioneering a new art, it will at times necessarily produce power or commodities as a by-product. But they must be a by-product of the major purpose, not the major purpose itself.

Nor do I wish to be misinterpreted as believing that the United States is free-for-all and devil-take-the-hindmost. The very essence of equality of opportunity and of American individualism is that there shall be no domination by any group or combination in this republic, whether it be business or political. On the contrary, it demands economic justice as well as political and social justice. It is no system of laissez faire.

I feel deeply on this subject because during the war I had some practical experience with governmental operation and control. I have witnessed not only at home but abroad the many failures of government in business. I have seen its tyrannies, its injustices, its destructions of self-government, its undermining of the very instincts which carry our people forward to progress. I have witnessed the lack of advance, the lowered standards of living, the depressed spirits of people working under such a system. My objection is based not upon theory or upon a failure to recognize wrong or abuse, but I know the adoption of such methods would strike at the very roots of American life and would destroy the very basis of American progress.

Our people have the right to know whether we can continue to solve our great problems without abandonment of our American system. I know we can. We have demonstrated that our system is responsive enough to meet any new and intricate development in our economic and business life. We have demonstrated that we can meet any economic problem and still maintain our democracy as master in its own house, and that we can at the same time preserve equality of opportunity and individual freedom.

In the last fifty years we have discovered that mass production will produce articles for us at half the cost they required previously. We have seen the resultant growth of large units of production and distribution. This is big business. Many businesses must be bigger, for our tools are bigger, our country is bigger. We now build a single dynamo of a hundred thousand horsepower. Even fifteen years ago that would have been a big business all by itself. Yet today advance in production requires that we set ten of these units together in a row.

The American people from bitter experience have a rightful fear that great business units might be used to dominate our industrial life and by illegal and unethical practices destroy equality of opportunity.

Years ago the Republican administration established the principle that such evils could be corrected by regulation. It developed methods by which abuses could be prevented while the full value of industrial progress could be retained for the public. It insisted upon the principle that when great public utilities were clothed with the security of partial monopoly, whether it be railways, power plants, telephones, or what not, then there must be the fullest and most complete control of rates, services, and finances by government or local agencies. It declared that these businesses must be conducted with glass pockets.

As to our great manufacturing and distributing industries, the Republican Party insisted upon the enactment of laws that not only would maintain competition but would destroy conspiracies to destroy the smaller units or dominate and limit the equality of opportunity amongst our people.

One of the great problems of government is to determine to what extent the government shall regulate and control commerce and industry and how much it shall leave it alone. No system is perfect. We have had many abuses in the private conduct of business. That every good citizen resents. It is just as important that business keep out of government as that government keep out of business.

Nor am I setting up the contention that our institutions are perfect. No human ideal is ever perfectly attained, since humanity itself is not perfect.

The wisdom of our forefathers in their conception that progress can only be attained as the sum of the accomplishment of free individuals has been reinforced by all of the great leaders of the country since that day. Jackson, Lincoln, Cleveland, McKinley, Roosevelt, Wilson, and Coolidge have stood unalterably for these principles.

And what have been the results of our American system? Our country has become the land of opportunity to those born without inheritance, not merely because of the wealth of its resources and industry but because of this freedom of initiative and enterprise. Russia has natural resources equal to ours. Her people are equally industrious, but she has not had the blessings of one hundred and fifty years of our form of government and of our social system.

By adherence to the principles of decentralized self-government, ordered liberty, equal opportunity, and freedom to the individual, our American experiment in human welfare has yielded a degree of well-being unparalleled in all the world. It has come nearer to the abolition of poverty, to the abolition of fear of want, than humanity has ever reached before. Progress of the past seven years is the proof of it. This alone furnishes the answer to our opponents, who ask us to introduce destructive elements into the system by which this has been accomplished.

Let us see what this system has done for us in our recent years of difficult and trying reconstruction and then solemnly ask ourselves if we now wish to abandon it.

As a nation we came out of the war with great losses. We made no profits from it. The apparent increases in wages were at that time fictitious. We were poorer as a nation when we emerged from the war. Yet during these last eight years we have recovered from these losses and increased our national income by over one-third, even if we discount the inflation of the dollar. That there has been a wide diffusion of our gain in wealth and income is marked by a hundred proofs. I know of no better test of the improved conditions of the average family than the combined increase in assets of life and industrial insurance, building and loan associations, and savings deposits. These are the savings banks of the average man. These agencies alone have in seven years increased by nearly one hundred per cent to the gigantic sum of over fifty billions of dollars, or nearly one-sixth of our whole national wealth. We have increased in home ownership, we have expanded the investments of the average man.

In addition to these evidences of larger savings, our people are steadily increasing their spending for higher standards of living. Today there are almost nine automobiles for each ten families, where seven and one-half years ago only enough automobiles were running to average less than four for each ten families. The slogan of progress is changing from the full dinner pail to the full garage. Our people have more to eat, better things to wear, and better homes. We have even gained in elbow room, for the increase of residential floor space is over twenty-five per cent, with less than ten per cent increase in our number of people. Wages have increased, the cost of living has decreased. The job of every man and woman has been made more secure. We have in this short period decreased the fear of poverty, the fear of unemployment, the fear of old age; and these are fears that are the greatest calamities of humankind.

All this progress means far more than increased creature comforts. It finds a thousand interpretations into a greater and fuller life. A score of new helps save the drudgery of the home. In seven years we have added seventy per cent to the electric power at the elbows of our workers and further promoted them from carriers of burdens to directors of machines. We have steadily reduced the sweat in human labor. Our hours of labor are lessened; our leisure has increased. We have expanded our parks and playgrounds. We have nearly doubled our attendance at games. We pour into outdoor recreation in every direction. The visitors at our national parks have trebled and we have so increased the number of sportsmen fishing in our streams and lakes that the longer time between bites is becoming a political issue. In these seven and one-half years the radio has brought music and laughter, education and political discussion to almost every fireside.

Springing from our prosperity with its greater freedom, its vast endowment of scientific research, and the greater resources with which to care for public health, we have according to our insurance actuaries during this short period since the war lengthened the average span of life by nearly eight years. We have reduced infant mortality, we have vastly decreased the days of illness and suffering in the life of every man and woman. We have improved the facilities for the care of the crippled and helpless and deranged.

From our increasing resources we have expanded our educational system in eight years from an outlay of twelve hundred millions to twenty-seven hundred millions of dollars. The education of our youth has become almost our largest and certainly our most important activity. From our greater income and thus our ability to free youth from toil we have increased the attendance in our grade schools by fourteen per cent, in our high schools by eighty per cent, and in our institutions of higher learning by ninety-five per cent. Today we have more youth in these institutions of higher learning twice over than all the rest of the world put together. We have made notable progress in literature, in art, and in public taste.

We have made progress in the leadership of every branch of American life. Never in our history was the leadership in our economic life more distinguished in its abilities than today, and it has grown greatly in its consciousness of public responsibility. Leadership in our professions and in moral and spiritual affairs of our country was never of a higher order. And our magnificent educational system is bringing forward a host of recruits for the succession to this leadership.

I do not need to recite more figures and more evidence. I cannot believe that the American people wish to abandon or in any way to weaken the principles of economic freedom and self-government which have been maintained by the Republican Party and which have produced results so amazing and so stimulating to the spiritual as well as to the material advance of the nation.

Your city has been an outstanding beneficiary of this great progress and of these safeguarded principles. With its suburbs it has, during the last seven and one-half years, grown by over a million and a half of people until it has become the largest metropolitan district of all the world. Here you have made abundant opportunity not only for the youth of the land but for the immigrant from foreign shores. This city is the commercial center of the United States. It is the commercial agent of the American people. It is a great organism of specialized skill and leadership in finance, industry, and commerce which reaches every spot in our country. Its progress and its beauty are the pride of the whole American people. It leads our nation in its benevolences to charity, to education, and to scientific research. It is the center of art, music, literature, and drama. It has come to have a more potent voice than any other city in the United States.

But when all is said and done, the very life, progress, and prosperity of this city is wholly dependent on the prosperity of the 115,000,000 people who dwell in our mountains and valleys across the three thousand miles to the Pacific Ocean. Every activity of this city is sensitive to every evil and every favorable tide that sweeps this great nation of ours. Be there a slackening of industry in any place, it affects New York far more than any other part of the country. In a time of depression one-quarter of all the unemployed in the United States can be numbered in this city. In a time of prosperity the citizens of the great interior of our country pour into your city for business and entertainment at the rate of one hundred and fifty thousand a day. In fact, so much is this city the reflex of the varied interests of our country that the concern of every one of your citizens for national stability, for national prosperity, for national progress, for preservation of our American system is far greater than that of any other single part of our country.

We still have great problems if we would achieve the full economic advancement of our country. In these past few years some groups in our country have lagged behind others in the march of progress. I refer more particularly to those engaged in the textile, coal, and agricultural industries. We can assist in solving these problems by co-operation of our government. To the agricultural industry we shall need to advance initial capital to assist them to stabilize their industry. But this proposal implies that they shall conduct it themselves, and not the government. It is in the interest of our cities that we shall bring agriculture and all industries into full stability and prosperity. I know you will gladly co-operate in the faith that in the common prosperity of our country lies its future.

In bringing this address to a conclusion I should like to restate to you some of the fundamental things I have endeavored to bring out.

The foundations of progress and prosperity are dependent as never before upon the wise policies of government, for government now touches at a thousand points the intricate web of economic and social life.

Under administration by the Republican Party in the last seven and one-half years our country as a whole has made unparalleled progress and this has been in generous part reflected to this great city. Prosperity is no idle expression. It is a job for every worker; it is the safety and the safeguard of every business and every home. A continuation of the policies of the Republican Party is fundamentally necessary to the further advancement of this progress and to the further building up of this prosperity.

I have dwelt at some length on the principles of relationship between the government and business. I make no apologies for dealing with this subject. The first necessity of any nation is the smooth functioning of the vast business machinery for employment, feeding, clothing, housing, and providing luxuries and comforts to a people. Unless these basic elements are properly organized and function, there can be no progress in business, in education, literature, music, or art. There can be no advance in the fundamental ideals of a people. A people cannot make progress in poverty.

I have endeavored to present to you that the greatness of America has grown out of a political and social system and a method of control of economic forces distinctly its own—our American system—which has carried this great experiment in human welfare farther than ever before in all history. We are nearer today to the ideal of the abolition of poverty and fear from the lives of men and women than ever before in any land. And I again repeat that the departure from our American system by injecting principles destructive to it which our opponents propose will jeopardize the very liberty and freedom of our people, will destroy equality of opportunity not alone to ourselves but to our children.

To me the foundation of American life rests upon the home and the family. I read into these great economic forces, these intricate and delicate relations of the government with business and with our political and social life, but one supreme end—that we reinforce the ties that bind together the millions of our families, that we strengthen the security, the happiness, and the independence of every home.

My conception of America is a land where men and women may walk in ordered freedom in the independent conduct of their occupations; where they may enjoy the advantages of wealth, not concentrated in the hands of the few but spread through the lives of all; where they build and safeguard their homes, and give to their children the fullest advantages and opportunities of American life; where every man shall be respected in the faith that his conscience and his heart direct him to follow; where a contented and happy people, secure in their liberties, free from poverty and fear, shall have the leisure and impulse to seek a fuller life.

Some may ask where all this may lead beyond mere material progress. It leads to a release of the energies of men and women from the dull drudgery of life to a wider vision and a higher hope. It leads to the opportunity for greater and greater service, not alone from man to man in our own land, but from our country to the whole world. It leads to an America, healthy in body, healthy in spirit, unfettered, youthful, eager—with a vision searching beyond the farthest horizons, with an open mind, sympathetic and generous. It is to these higher ideals and for these purposes that I pledge myself and the Republican Party.

FRANKLIN D. ROOSEVELT

Speech to the Democratic National Convention

Chicago, July 2, 1932

CHAIRMAN WALSH, my friends of the Democratic National Convention of 1932:

I appreciate your willingness after these six arduous days to remain here, for I know well the sleepless hours which you and I have had. I regret that I am late, but I have no control over the winds of Heaven and could only be thankful for my Navy training.

The appearance before a National Convention of its nominee for President, to be formally notified of his selection, is unprecedented and unusual, but these are unprecedented and unusual times. I have started out on the tasks that lie ahead by breaking the absurd traditions that the candidate should remain in professed ignorance of what has happened for weeks until he is formally notified of that event many weeks later.

My friends, may this be the symbol of my intention to be honest and to avoid all hypocrisy or sham, to avoid all silly shutting of the eyes to the truth in this campaign. You have nominated me and I know it, and I am here to thank you for the honor.

Let it also be symbolic that in so doing I broke traditions. Let it be from now on the task of our Party to break foolish traditions. We will break foolish traditions and leave it to the Republican leadership, far more skilled in that art, to break promises.

Let us now and here highly resolve to resume the country's interrupted march along the path of real progress, of real justice, of real equality for all of our citizens, great and small. Our indomitable leader in that interrupted march is no longer with us, but there still survives today his spirit. Many of his captains, thank God, are still with us, to give us wise counsel. Let us feel that in everything we do there still lives with us, if not the body, the great indomitable, unquenchable, progressive soul of our Commander-in-Chief, Woodrow Wilson.

I have many things on which I want to make my position clear at the earliest possible moment in this campaign. That admirable document, the platform which you have adopted, is clear. I accept it 100 percent.

And you can accept my pledge that I will leave no doubt or ambiguity on where I stand on any question of moment in this campaign.

As we enter this new battle, let us keep always present with us some of the ideals of the Party: The fact that the Democratic Party by tradition and by the continuing logic of history, past and present, is the bearer of liberalism and of progress and at the same time of safety to our institutions. And if this appeal fails, remember well, my friends, that a resentment against the failure of Republican leadership—and note well that in this campaign I shall not use the words "Republican Party," but I shall use, day in and day out, the words, "Republican leadership"—the failure of Republican leaders to solve our troubles may degenerate into unreasoning radicalism.

The great social phenomenon of this depression, unlike others before it, is that it has produced but a few of the disorderly manifestations that too often attend upon such times.

Wild radicalism has made few converts, and the greatest tribute that I can pay to my countrymen is that in these days of crushing want there persists an orderly and hopeful spirit on the part of the millions of our people who have suffered so much. To fail to offer them a new chance is not only to betray their hopes but to misunderstand their patience.

To meet by reaction that danger of radicalism is to invite disaster. Reaction is no barrier to the radical. It is a challenge, a provocation. The way to meet that danger is to offer a workable program of reconstruction, and the party to offer it is the party with clean hands.

This, and this only, is a proper protection against blind reaction on the one hand and an improvised, hit-or-miss, irresponsible opportunism on the other.

There are two ways of viewing the Government's duty in matters affecting economic and social life. The first sees to it that a favored few are helped and hopes that some of their prosperity will leak through, sift through, to labor, to the farmer, to the small business man. That theory belongs to the party of Toryism, and I had hoped that most of the Tories left this country in 1776.

But it is not and never will be the theory of the Democratic Party. This is no time for fear, for reaction or for timidity. Here and now I invite those nominal Republicans who find that their conscience cannot be squared with the groping and the failure of their party leaders to join hands with us; here and now, in equal measure, I warn those nominal Democrats who squint at the future with their faces turned toward the past, and who feel no responsibility to the demands of the new time, that they are out of step with their Party.

Yes, the people of this country want a genuine choice this year, not a choice between two names for the same reactionary doctrine. Ours must be a party of liberal thought, of planned action, of enlightened international outlook, and of the greatest good to the greatest number of our citizens.

Now it is inevitable—and the choice is that of the times—it is inevitable that the main issue of this campaign should revolve about the clear fact of our economic condition, a depression so deep that it is without precedent in modern history. It will not do merely to state, as do Republican leaders to explain their broken promises of continued inaction, that the depression is worldwide. That was not their explanation of the apparent prosperity of 1928. The people will not forget the claim made by them then that prosperity was only a domestic product manufactured by a Republican President and a Republican Congress. If they claim paternity for the one they cannot deny paternity for the other.

I cannot take up all the problems today. I want to touch on a few that are vital. Let us look a little at the recent history and the simple economics, the kind of economics that you and I and the average man and woman talk.

In the years before 1929 we know that this country had completed a vast cycle of building and inflation; for ten years we expanded on the theory of repairing the wastes of the War, but actually expanding far beyond that, and also beyond our natural and normal growth. Now it is worth remembering, and the cold figures of finance prove it, that during that time there was little or no drop in the prices that the consumer had to pay, although those same figures proved that the cost of production fell very greatly; corporate profit resulting from this period was enormous; at the same time little of that profit was devoted to the reduction of prices. The consumer was forgotten. Very little of it went into increased wages; the worker was forgotten, and by no means an adequate proportion was even paid out in dividends—the stock-holder was forgotten.

And, incidentally, very little of it was taken by taxation to the beneficent Government of those years.

What was the result? Enormous corporate surpluses piled up—the most stupendous in history. Where, under the spell of delirious speculation, did those surpluses go? Let us talk economics that the figures prove and that we can understand. Why, they went chiefly in two directions: first, into new and unnecessary plants which now stand stark and idle; and second, into the call-money market of Wall Street, either directly by the corporations, or indirectly through the banks. Those are the facts. Why blink at them?

Then came the crash. You know the story. Surpluses invested in unnecessary plants became idle. Men lost their jobs; purchasing power dried up; banks became frightened and started calling loans. Those who had money were afraid to part with it. Credit contracted. Industry stopped. Commerce declined, and unemployment mounted.

And there we are today.

Translate that into human terms. See how the events of the past three years have come home to specific groups of people: first, the group dependent on industry; second, the group dependent on agriculture; third, and made up in large part of members of the first two groups, the people who are called "small investors and depositors." In fact, the strongest possible tie between the first two groups, agriculture and industry, is the fact that the savings and to a degree the security of both are tied together in that third group—the credit structure of the Nation.

Never in history have the interests of all the people been so united in a single economic problem. Picture to yourself, for instance, the great groups of property owned by millions of our citizens, represented by credits issued in the form of bonds and mortgages—Government bonds of all kinds, Federal, State, county, municipal; bonds of industrial companies, of utility companies; mortgages on real estate in farms and cities, and finally the vast investments of the Nation in the railroads. What is the measure of the security of each of those groups? We know well that in our complicated, interrelated credit structure if any one of these credit groups collapses they may all collapse. Danger to one is danger to all.

How, I ask, has the present Administration in Washington treated the interrelationship of these credit groups? The answer is clear: It has not recognized that interrelationship existed at all. Why, the Nation asks, has Washington failed to understand that all of these groups, each and every one, the top of the pyramid and the bottom of the pyramid, must be considered together, that each and every one of them is dependent on every other; each and every one of them affecting the whole financial fabric?

Statesmanship and vision, my friends, require relief to all at the same time.

Just one word or two on taxes, the taxes that all of us pay toward the cost of Government of all kinds.

I know something of taxes. For three long years I have been going up and down this country preaching that Government —Federal and State and local—costs too much. I shall not stop that preaching. As an immediate program of action we must abolish useless offices. We must eliminate unnecessary functions of Government—functions, in fact, that are not definitely essential to the continuance of Government. We must merge, we must consolidate subdivisions of Government, and, like the private citizen, give up luxuries which we can no longer afford.

By our example at Washington itself, we shall have the opportunity of pointing the way of economy to local government, for let us remember well that out of every tax dollar in the average State in this Nation, 40 cents enter the treasury in Washington, D.C., 10 or 12 cents only go to the State capitals, and 48 cents are consumed by the costs of local government in counties and cities and towns.

I propose to you, my friends, and through you, that

Government of all kinds, big and little, be made solvent and that the example be set by the President of the United States and his Cabinet.

And talking about setting a definite example, I congratulate this convention for having had the courage fearlessly to write into its declaration of principles what an overwhelming majority here assembled really thinks about the 18th Amendment. This convention wants repeal. Your candidate wants repeal. And I am confident that the United States of America wants repeal.

Two years ago the platform on which I ran for Governor the second time contained substantially the same provision. The overwhelming sentiment of the people of my State, as shown by the vote of that year, extends, I know, to the people of many of the other States. I say to you now that from this date on the 18th Amendment is doomed. When that happens, we as Democrats must and will, rightly and morally, enable the States to protect themselves against the importation of intoxicating liquor where such importation may violate their State laws. We must rightly and morally prevent the return of the saloon.

To go back to this dry subject of finance, because it all ties in together—the 18th Amendment has something to do with finance, too—in a comprehensive planning for the reconstruction of the great credit groups, including Government credit, I list an important place for that prize statement of principle in the platform here adopted calling for the letting in of the light of day on issues of securities, foreign and domestic, which are offered for sale to the investing public.

My friends, you and I as common-sense citizens know that it would help to protect the savings of the country from the dishonesty of crooks and from the lack of honor of some men in high financial places. Publicity is the enemy of crookedness.

And now one word about unemployment, and incidentally about agriculture. I have favored the use of certain types of public works as a further emergency means of stimulating employment and the issuance of bonds to pay for such public works, but I have pointed out that no economic end is served if we merely build without building for a necessary purpose. Such works, of course, should insofar as possible be self-sustaining if they are to be financed by the issuing of bonds. So as to spread the points of all kinds as widely as possible, we must take definite steps to shorten the working day and the working week.

Let us use common sense and business sense. Just as one example, we know that a very hopeful and immediate means of relief, both for the unemployed and for agriculture, will come from a wide plan of the converting of many millions of acres of marginal and unused land into timberland through reforestation. There are tens of millions of acres east of the Mississippi River alone in abandoned farms, in cut-over land, now growing up in worthless brush. Why, every European Nation has a definite land policy, and has had one for generations. We have none. Having none, we face a future of soil erosion and timber famine. It is clear that economic foresight and immediate employment march hand in hand in the call for the reforestation of these vast areas.

In so doing, employment can be given to a million men. That is the kind of public work that is self-sustaining, and therefore capable of being financed by the issuance of bonds which are made secure by the fact that the growth of tremendous crops will provide adequate security for the investment.

Yes, I have a very definite program for providing employment by that means. I have done it, and I am doing it today in the State of New York. I know that the Democratic Party can do it successfully in the Nation. That will put men to work, and that is an example of the action that we are going to have.

Now as a further aid to agriculture, we know perfectly well—but have we come out and said so clearly and distinctly?—we should repeal immediately those provisions of law that compel the Federal Government to go into the market to purchase, to sell, to speculate in farm products in a futile attempt to reduce farm surpluses. And they are the people who are talking of keeping Government out of business. The practical way to help the farmer is by an arrangement that will, in addition to lightening some of the impoverishing burdens from his back, do something toward the reduction of the surpluses of staple commodities that hang on the market. It should be our aim to add to the world prices of staple products the amount of a reasonable tariff protection, to give agriculture the same protection that industry has today.

And in exchange for this immediately increased return I am

sure that the farmers of this Nation would agree ultimately to such planning of their production as would reduce the surpluses and make it unnecessary in later years to depend on dumping those surpluses abroad in order to support domestic prices. That result has been accomplished in other Nations; why not in America, too?

Farm leaders and farm economists, generally, agree that a plan based on that principle is a desirable first step in the reconstruction of agriculture. It does not in itself furnish a complete program, but it will serve in great measure in the long run to remove the pall of a surplus without the continued perpetual threat of world dumping. Final voluntary reduction of surplus is a part of our objective, but the long continuance and the present burden of existing surpluses make it necessary to repair great damage of the present by immediate emergency measures.

Such a plan as that, my friends, does not cost the Government any money, nor does it keep the Government in business or in speculation.

As to the actual wording of a bill, I believe that the Democratic Party stands ready to be guided by whatever the responsible farm groups themselves agree on. That is a principle that is sound; and again I ask for action.

One more word about the farmer, and I know that every delegate in this hall who lives in the city knows why I lay emphasis on the farmer. It is because one-half of our population, over 50,000,000 people, are dependent on agriculture; and, my friends, if those 50,000,000 people have no money, no cash, to buy what is produced in the city, the city suffers to an equal or greater extent.

That is why we are going to make the voters understand this year that this Nation is not merely a Nation of independence, but it is, if we are to survive, bound to be a Nation of interdependence—town and city, and North and South, East and West. That is our goal, and that goal will be understood by the people of this country no matter where they live.

Yes, the purchasing power of that half of our population dependent on agriculture is gone. Farm mortgages reach nearly ten billions of dollars today and interest charges on that alone are $560,000,000 a year. But that is not all. The tax burden caused by extravagant and inefficient local government is an additional factor. Our most immediate concern should be to reduce the interest burden on these mortgages.

Rediscounting of farm mortgages under salutary restrictions must be expanded and should, in the future, be conditioned on the reduction of interest rates. Amortization payments, maturities should likewise in this crisis be extended before rediscount is permitted where the mortgagor is sorely pressed. That, my friends, is another example of practical, immediate relief: Action.

I aim to do the same thing, and it can be done, for the small home-owner in our cities and villages. We can lighten his burden and develop his purchasing power. Take away, my friends, that spectre of too high an interest rate. Take away that spectre of the due date just a short time away. Save homes; save homes for thousands of self respecting families, and drive out that spectre of insecurity from our midst.

Out of all the tons of printed paper, out of all the hours of oratory, the recriminations, the defenses, the happy-thought plans in Washington and in every State, there emerges one great, simple, crystal-pure fact that during the past ten years a Nation of 120,000,000 people has been led by the Republican leaders to erect an impregnable barbed wire entanglement around its borders through the instrumentality of tariffs which have isolated us from all the other human beings in all the rest of the round world. I accept that admirable tariff statement in the platform of this convention. It would protect American business and American labor. By our acts of the past we have invited and received the retaliation of other Nations. I propose an invitation to them to forget the past, to sit at the table with us, as friends, and to plan with us for the restoration of the trade of the world.

Go into the home of the business man. He knows what the tariff has done for him. Go into the home of the factory worker. He knows why goods do not move. Go into the home of the farmer. He knows how the tariff has helped to ruin him.

At last our eyes are open. At last the American people are ready to acknowledge that Republican leadership was wrong and that the Democracy is right.

My program, of which I can only touch on these points, is

based upon this simple moral principle: the welfare and the soundness of a Nation depend first upon what the great mass of the people wish and need; and second, whether or not they are getting it.

What do the people of America want more than anything else? To my mind, they want two things: work, with all the moral and spiritual values that go with it; and with work, a reasonable measure of security—security for themselves and for their wives and children. Work and security—these are more than words. They are more than facts. They are the spiritual values, the true goal toward which our efforts of reconstruction should lead. These are the values that this program is intended to gain; these are the values we have failed to achieve by the leadership we now have.

Our Republican leaders tell us economic laws—sacred, inviolable, unchangeable—cause panics which no one could prevent. But while they prate of economic laws, men and women are starving. We must lay hold of the fact that economic laws are not made by nature. They are made by human beings.

Yes, when—not if—when we get the chance, the Federal Government will assume bold leadership in distress relief. For years Washington has alternated between putting its head in the sand and saying there is no large number of destitute people in our midst who need food and clothing, and then saying the States should take care of them, if there are. Instead of planning two and a half years ago to do what they are now trying to do, they kept putting it off from day to day, week to week, and month to month, until the conscience of America demanded action.

I say that while primary responsibility for relief rests with localities now, as ever, yet the Federal Government has always had and still has a continuing responsibility for the broader public welfare. It will soon fulfill that responsibility.

And now, just a few words about our plans for the next four months. By coming here instead of waiting for a formal notification, I have made it clear that I believe we should eliminate expensive ceremonies and that we should set in motion at once, tonight, my friends, the necessary machinery for an adequate presentation of the issues to the electorate of the Nation.

I myself have important duties as Governor of a great State, duties which in these times are more arduous and more grave than at any previous period. Yet I feel confident that I shall be able to make a number of short visits to several parts of the Nation. My trips will have as their first objective the study at first hand, from the lips of men and women of all parties and all occupations, of the actual conditions and needs of every part of an interdependent country.

One word more: Out of every crisis, every tribulation, every disaster, mankind rises with some share of greater knowledge, of higher decency, of purer purpose. Today we shall have come through a period of loose thinking, descending morals, an era of selfishness, among individual men and women and among Nations. Blame not Governments alone for this. Blame ourselves in equal share. Let us be frank in acknowledgment of the truth that many amongst us have made obeisance to Mammon, that the profits of speculation, the easy road without toil, have lured us from the old barricades. To return to higher standards we must abandon the false prophets and seek new leaders of our own choosing.

Never before in modern history have the essential differences between the two major American parties stood out in such striking contrast as they do today. Republican leaders not only have failed in material things, they have failed in national vision, because in disaster they have held out no hope, they have pointed out no path for the people below to climb back to places of security and of safety in our American life.

Throughout the Nation, men and women, forgotten in the political philosophy of the Government of the last years look to us here for guidance and for more equitable opportunity to share in the distribution of national wealth.

On the farms, in the large metropolitan areas, in the smaller cities and in the villages, millions of our citizens cherish the hope that their old standards of living and of thought have not gone forever. Those millions cannot and shall not hope in vain.

I pledge you, I pledge myself, to a new deal for the American people. Let us all here assembled constitute ourselves prophets of a new order of competence and of courage. This is more than a political campaign; it is a call to arms. Give me your help, not to win votes alone, but to win in this crusade to restore America to its own people.

FRANKLIN D. ROOSEVELT

Speech to the Commonwealth Club

San Francisco, September 23, 1932

M^{Y FRIENDS:}
I count it a privilege to be invited to address the Commonwealth Club. It has stood in the life of this city and State, and it is perhaps accurate to add, the Nation, as a group of citizen leaders interested in fundamental problems of Government, and chiefly concerned with achievement of progress in Government through non-partisan means. The privilege of addressing you, therefore, in the heat of a political campaign, is great. I want to respond to your courtesy in terms consistent with your policy.

I want to speak not of politics but of Government. I want to speak not of parties, but of universal principles. They are not political, except in that larger sense in which a great American once expressed a definition of politics, that nothing in all of human life is foreign to the science of politics.

I do want to give you, however, a recollection of a long life spent for a large part in public office. Some of my conclusions and observations have been deeply accentuated in these past few weeks. I have traveled far—from Albany to the Golden Gate. I have seen many people, and heard many things, and today, when in a sense my journey has reached the half-way mark, I am glad of the opportunity to discuss with you what it all means to me.

Sometimes, my friends, particularly in years such as these, the hand of discouragement falls upon us. It seems that things are in a rut, fixed, settled, that the world has grown old and tired and very much out of joint. This is the mood of depression, of dire and weary depression.

But then we look around us in America, and everything tells us that we are wrong. America is new. It is in the process of change and development. It has the great potentialities of youth, and particularly is this true of the great West, and of this coast, and of California.

I would not have you feel that I regard this as in any sense a new community. I have traveled in many parts of the world, but never have I felt the arresting thought of the change and development more than here, where the old, mystic East would seem to be near to us, where the currents of life and thought and commerce of the whole world meet us. This factor alone is sufficient to cause man to stop and think of the deeper meaning of things, when he stands in this community.

But more than that, I appreciate that the membership of this club consists of men who are thinking in terms beyond the immediate present, beyond their own immediate tasks, beyond their own individual interests. I want to invite you, therefore, to consider with me in the large, some of the relationships of Government and economic life that go deeply into our daily lives, our happiness, our future and our security.

The issue of Government has always been whether individual men and women will have to serve some system of Government or economics, or whether a system of Government and economics exists to serve individual men and women. This question has persistently dominated the discussion of Government for many generations. On questions relating to these things men have differed, and for time immemorial it is probable that honest men will continue to differ.

The final word belongs to no man; yet we can still believe in change and in progress. Democracy, as a dear old friend of mine in Indiana, Meredith Nicholson, has called it, is a quest, a never-ending seeking for better things, and in the seeking for these things and the striving for them, there are many roads to follow. But, if we map the course of these roads, we find that there are only two general directions.

When we look about us, we are likely to forget how hard people have worked to win the privilege of Government. The growth of the national Governments of Europe was a struggle for the development of a centralized force in the Nation, strong enough to impose peace upon ruling barons. In many instances the victory of the central Government, the creation of a strong central Government, was a haven of refuge to the individual. The people preferred the master far away to the exploitation and cruelty of the smaller master near at hand.

But the creators of national Government were perforce ruthless men. They were often cruel in their methods, but they did strive steadily toward something that society needed and very much wanted, a strong central State able to keep the peace, to stamp out civil war, to put the unruly nobleman in his place, and to permit the bulk of individuals to live safely. The man of ruthless force had his place in developing a pioneer country, just as he did in fixing the power of the central Government in the development of Nations. Society paid him well for his services and its development. When the development among the Nations of Europe, however, had been completed, ambition and ruthlessness, having served their term, tended to overstep their mark.

There came a growing feeling that Government was conducted for the benefit of a few who thrived unduly at the expense of all. The people sought a balancing—a limiting force. There came gradually, through town councils, trade guilds, national parliaments, by constitution and by popular participation and control, limitations on arbitrary power.

Another factor that tended to limit the power of those who ruled, was the rise of the ethical conception that a ruler bore a responsibility for the welfare of his subjects.

The American colonies were born in this struggle. The American Revolution was a turning point in it. After the Revolution the struggle continued and shaped itself in the public life of the country. There were those who because they had seen the confusion which attended the years of war for American independence surrendered to the belief that popular Government was essentially dangerous and essentially unworkable. They were honest people, my friends, and we cannot deny that their experience had warranted some measure of fear. The most brilliant, honest and able exponent of this point of view was Hamilton. He was too impatient of slow-moving methods. Fundamentally he believed that the safety of the republic lay in the autocratic strength of its Government, that the destiny of individuals was to serve that Government, and that fundamentally a great and strong group of central institutions, guided by a small group of able and public spirited citizens, could best direct all Government.

But Mr. Jefferson, in the summer of 1776, after drafting the Declaration of Independence turned his mind to the same problem and took a different view. He did not deceive himself with outward forms. Government to him was a means to an end, not an end in itself; it might be either a refuge and a help or a threat and a danger, depending on the circumstances. We find him carefully analyzing the society for which he was to organize a Government. "We have no paupers. The great mass of our population is of laborers, our rich who cannot live without labor, either manual or professional, being few and of moderate wealth. Most of the laboring class possess property, cultivate their own lands, have families and from the demand for their labor, are enabled to exact from the rich and the competent such prices as enable them to feed abundantly, clothe above mere decency, to labor moderately and raise their families."

These people, he considered, had two sets of rights, those of "personal competency" and those involved in acquiring and possessing property. By "personal competency" he meant the right of free thinking, freedom of forming and expressing opinions, and freedom of personal living, each man according to his own lights. To insure the first set of rights, a Government must so order its functions as not to interfere with the individual. But even Jefferson realized that the exercise of the property rights might so interfere with the rights of the individual that the Government, without whose assistance the property rights could not exist, must intervene, not to destroy individualism, but to protect it.

You are familiar with the great political duel which followed; and how Hamilton, and his friends, building toward a dominant centralized power were at length defeated in the great election of 1800, by Mr. Jefferson's party. Out of that duel came the two parties, Republican and Democratic, as we know them today.

So began, in American political life, the new day, the day of the individual against the system, the day in which individualism was made the great watchword of American life. The happiest of economic conditions made that day long and splendid. On the Western frontier, land was substantially free. No one, who did not shirk the task of earning a living, was entirely without opportunity to do so. Depressions could, and did, come and go; but they could not alter the fundamental fact that most of the people lived partly by selling their labor and partly by extracting their livelihood from the soil, so that starvation and dislocation were practically impossible. At the very worst there was always the possibility of climbing into a covered wagon and moving west where the untilled prairies afforded a haven for men to whom the East did not provide a place. So great were our natural resources that we could offer this relief not only to our own people, but to the distressed of all the world; we could invite immigration from Europe, and welcome it with open arms. Traditionally, when a depression came a new section of land was opened in the West; and even our temporary misfortune served our manifest destiny.

It was in the middle of the nineteenth century that a new force was released and a new dream created. The force was what is called the industrial revolution, the advance of steam and machinery and the rise of the forerunners of the modern industrial plant. The dream was the dream of an economic machine, able to raise the standard of living for everyone; to bring luxury within the reach of the humblest; to annihilate distance by steam power and later by electricity, and to release everyone from the drudgery of the heaviest manual toil. It was to be expected that this would necessarily affect Government. Heretofore, Government had merely been called upon to produce conditions within which people could live happily, labor peacefully, and rest secure. Now it was called upon to aid in the consummation of this new dream. There was, however, a shadow over the dream. To be made real, it required use of the talents of men of tremendous will and tremendous ambition, since by no other force could the problems of financing and engineering and new developments be brought to a consummation.

So manifest were the advantages of the machine age, however, that the United States fearlessly, cheerfully, and, I think, rightly, accepted the bitter with the sweet. It was thought that no price was too high to pay for the advantages which we could draw from a finished industrial system. The history of the last half century is accordingly in large measure a history of a group of financial Titans, whose methods were not scrutinized with too much care, and who were honored in proportion as they produced the results, irrespective of the means they used. The financiers who pushed the railroads to the Pacific were always ruthless, often wasteful, and frequently corrupt; but they did build railroads, and we have them today. It has been estimated that the American investor paid for the American railway system more than three times over in the process; but despite this fact the net advantage was to the United States. As long as we had free land; as long as population was growing by leaps and bounds; as long as our industrial plants were insufficient to supply our own needs, society chose to give the ambitious man free play and unlimited reward provided only that he produced the economic plant so much desired.

During this period of expansion, there was equal opportunity for all and the business of Government was not to interfere but to assist in the development of industry. This was done at the request of business men themselves. The tariff was originally imposed for the purpose of "fostering our infant industry," a phrase I think the older among you will remember as a political issue not so long ago. The railroads were subsidized, sometimes by grants of money, oftener by grants of land; some of the most valuable oil lands in the United States were granted to assist the financing of the railroad which pushed through the Southwest. A nascent merchant marine was assisted by grants of money, or by mail subsidies, so that our steam shipping might ply the seven seas. Some of my friends tell me that they do not want the Government in business. With this I agree; but I wonder whether they realize the implications of the past. For while it has been American doctrine that the Government must not go into business in competition with private enterprises, still it has been traditional, particularly in Republican administrations, for business urgently to ask the Government to put at private disposal all kinds of Government assistance. The same man who tells you that he does not want to see the Government interfere in business—and he means it, and has plenty of good reasons for saying so—is the first to go to Washington and ask the Government for a prohibitory tariff on his product. When things get just bad enough, as they did two years ago, he will go with equal speed to the United States Government and ask for a loan; and the Reconstruction

Finance Corporation is the outcome of it. Each group has sought protection from the Government for its own special interests, without realizing that the function of Government must be to favor no small group at the expense of its duty to protect the rights of personal freedom and of private property of all its citizens.

In retrospect we can now see that the turn of the tide came with the turn of the century. We were reaching our last frontier; there was no more free land and our industrial combinations had become great uncontrolled and irresponsible units of power within the State. Clear-sighted men saw with fear the danger that opportunity would no longer be equal; that the growing corporation, like the feudal baron of old, might threaten the economic freedom of individuals to earn a living. In that hour, our anti-trust laws were born. The cry was raised against the great corporations. Theodore Roosevelt, the first great Republican Progressive, fought a Presidential campaign on the issue of "trust busting" and talked freely about malefactors of great wealth. If the Government had a policy it was rather to turn the clock back, to destroy the large combinations and to return to the time when every man owned his individual small business.

This was impossible; Theodore Roosevelt, abandoning the idea of "trust busting," was forced to work out a difference between "good" trusts and "bad" trusts. The Supreme Court set forth the famous "rule of reason" by which it seems to have meant that a concentration of industrial power was permissible if the method by which it got its power, and the use it made of that power, were reasonable.

Woodrow Wilson, elected in 1912, saw the situation more clearly. Where Jefferson had feared the encroachment of political power on the lives of individuals, Wilson knew that the new power was financial. He saw, in the highly centralized economic system, the despot of the twentieth century, on whom great masses of individuals relied for their safety and their livelihood, and whose irresponsibility and greed (if they were not controlled) would reduce them to starvation and penury. The concentration of financial power had not proceeded so far in 1912 as it has today; but it had grown far enough for Mr. Wilson to realize fully its implications. It is interesting, now, to read his speeches. What is called "radical" today (and I have reason to know whereof I speak) is mild compared to the campaign of Mr. Wilson. "No man can deny," he said, "that the lines of endeavor have more and more narrowed and stiffened; no man who knows anything about the development of industry in this country can have failed to observe that the larger kinds of credit are more and more difficult to obtain unless you obtain them upon terms of uniting your efforts with those who already control the industry of the country, and nobody can fail to observe that every man who tries to set himself up in competition with any process of manufacture which has taken place under the control of large combinations of capital will presently find himself either squeezed out or obliged to sell and allow himself to be absorbed." Had there been no World War—had Mr. Wilson been able to devote eight years to domestic instead of to international affairs—we might have had a wholly different situation at the present time. However, the then distant roar of European cannon, growing ever louder, forced him to abandon the study of this issue. The problem he saw so clearly is left with us as a legacy; and no one of us on either side of the political controversy can deny that it is a matter of grave concern to the Government.

A glance at the situation today only too clearly indicates that equality of opportunity as we have known it no longer exists. Our industrial plant is built; the problem just now is whether under existing conditions it is not overbuilt. Our last frontier has long since been reached, and there is practically no more free land. More than half of our people do not live on the farms or on lands and cannot derive a living by cultivating their own property. There is no safety valve in the form of a Western prairie to which those thrown out of work by the Eastern economic machines can go for a new start. We are not able to invite the immigration from Europe to share our endless plenty. We are now providing a drab living for our own people.

Our system of constantly rising tariffs has at last reacted against us to the point of closing our Canadian frontier on the north, our European markets on the east, many of our Latin-American markets to the south, and a goodly proportion of our Pacific markets on the west, through the retaliatory tariffs of those countries. It has forced many of our great industrial institutions which exported their surplus production to such countries, to establish plants in such countries, within the tariff walls. This has resulted in the reduction of the operation of their American plants, and opportunity for employment.

Just as freedom to farm has ceased, so also the opportunity in business has narrowed. It still is true that men can start small enterprises, trusting to native shrewdness and ability to keep abreast of competitors; but area after area has been preempted altogether by the great corporations, and even in the fields which still have no great concerns, the small man starts under a handicap. The unfeeling statistics of the past three decades show that the independent business man is running a losing race. Perhaps he is forced to the wall; perhaps he cannot command credit; perhaps he is "squeezed out," in Mr. Wilson's words, by highly organized corporate competitors, as your corner grocery man can tell you. Recently a careful study was made of the concentration of business in the United States. It showed that our economic life was dominated by some six hundred odd corporations who controlled two-thirds of American industry. Ten million small business men divided the other third. More striking still, it appeared that if the process of concentration goes on at the same rate, at the end of another century we shall have all American industry controlled by a dozen corporations, and run by perhaps a hundred men. Put plainly, we are steering a steady course toward economic oligarchy, if we are not there already.

Clearly, all this calls for a re-appraisal of values. A mere builder of more industrial plants, a creator of more railroad systems, an organizer of more corporations, is as likely to be a danger as a help. The day of the great promoter or the financial Titan, to whom we granted anything if only he would build, or develop, is over. Our task now is not discovery or exploitation of natural resources, or necessarily producing more goods. It is the soberer, less dramatic business of administering resources and plants already in hand, of seeking to reestablish foreign markets for our surplus production, of meeting the problem of underconsumption, of adjusting production to consumption, of distributing wealth and products more equitably, of adapting existing economic organizations to the service of the people. The day of enlightened administration has come.

Just as in older times the central Government was first a haven of refuge, and then a threat, so now in a closer economic system the central and ambitious financial unit is no longer a servant of national desire, but a danger. I would draw the parallel one step farther. We did not think because national Government had become a threat in the 18th century that therefore we should abandon the principle of national Government. Nor today should we abandon the principle of strong economic units called corporations, merely because their power is susceptible of easy abuse. In other times we dealt with the problem of an unduly ambitious central Government by modifying it gradually into a constitutional democratic Government. So today we are modifying and controlling our economic units.

As I see it, the task of Government in its relation to business is to assist the development of an economic declaration of rights, an economic constitutional order. This is the common task of statesman and business man. It is the minimum requirement of a more permanently safe order of things.

Happily, the times indicate that to create such an order not only is the proper policy of Government, but it is the only line of safety for our economic structures as well. We know, now, that these economic units cannot exist unless prosperity is uniform, that is, unless purchasing power is well distributed throughout every group in the Nation. That is why even the most selfish of corporations for its own interest would be glad to see wages restored and unemployment ended and to bring the Western farmer back to his accustomed level of prosperity and to assure a permanent safety to both groups. That is why some enlightened industries themselves endeavor to limit the freedom of action of each man and business group within the industry in the common interest of all; why business men everywhere are asking a form of organization which will bring the scheme of things into balance, even though it may in some measure qualify the freedom of action of individual units within the business.

The exposition need not further be elaborated. It is brief and incomplete, but you will be able to expand it in terms of your own business or occupation without difficulty. I think everyone who has actually entered the economic struggle—which means everyone who was not born to safe wealth—knows in his own experience and his own life that we have now to apply the earlier concepts of American Government to the conditions of today.

The Declaration of Independence discusses the problem of Government in terms of a contract. Government is a relation of give and take, a contract, perforce, if we would follow the thinking out of which it grew. Under such a contract rulers were accorded power, and the people consented to that power on consideration that they be accorded certain rights. The task of statesmanship has always been the re-definition of these rights in terms of a changing and growing social order. New conditions impose new requirements upon Government and those who conduct Government.

I held, for example, in proceedings before me as Governor, the purpose of which was the removal of the Sheriff of New York, that under modern conditions it was not enough for a public official merely to evade the legal terms of official wrong-doing. He owed a positive duty as well. I said in substance that if he had acquired large sums of money, he was when accused required to explain the sources of such wealth. To that extent this wealth was colored with a public interest. I said that in financial matters, public servants should, even beyond private citizens, be held to a stern and uncompromising rectitude.

I feel that we are coming to a view through the drift of our legislation and our public thinking in the past quarter century that private economic power is, to enlarge an old phrase, a public trust as well. I hold that continued enjoyment of that power by any individual or group must depend upon the fulfillment of that trust. The men who have reached the summit of American business life know this best; happily, many of these urge the binding quality of this greater social contract.

The terms of that contract are as old as the Republic, and as new as the new economic order.

Every man has a right to life; and this means that he has also a right to make a comfortable living. He may by sloth or crime decline to exercise that right; but it may not be denied him. We have no actual famine or dearth; our industrial and agricultural mechanism can produce enough and to spare. Our Government formal and informal, political and economic, owes to everyone an avenue to possess himself of a portion of that plenty sufficient for his needs, through his own work.

Every man has a right to his own property; which means a right to be assured, to the fullest extent attainable, in the safety of his savings. By no other means can men carry the burdens of those parts of life which, in the nature of things, afford no chance of labor; childhood, sickness, old age. In all thought of property, this right is paramount; all other property rights must yield to it. If, in accord with this principle, we must restrict the operations of the speculator, the manipulator, even the financier, I believe we must accept the restriction as needful, not to hamper individualism but to protect it.

These two requirements must be satisfied, in the main, by the individuals who claim and hold control of the great industrial and financial combinations which dominate so large a part of our industrial life. They have undertaken to be, not business men, but princes of property. I am not prepared to say that the system which produces them is wrong. I am very clear that they must fearlessly and competently assume the responsibility which goes with the power. So many enlightened business men know this that the statement would be little more than a platitude, were it not for an added implication.

This implication is, briefly, that the responsible heads of finance and industry instead of acting each for himself, must work together to achieve the common end. They must, where necessary, sacrifice this or that private advantage; and in reciprocal self-denial must seek a general advantage. It is here that formal Government—political Government, if you chose—comes in. Whenever in the pursuit of this objective the lone wolf, the unethical competitor, the reckless promoter, the Ishmael or Insull whose hand is against every man's, declines to join in achieving an end recognized as being for the public welfare, and threatens to drag the industry back to a state of anarchy, the Government may properly be asked to apply restraint. Likewise, should the group ever use its collective power contrary to the public welfare, the Government must be swift to enter and protect the public interest.

The Government should assume the function of economic

regulation only as a last resort, to be tried only when private initiative, inspired by high responsibility, with such assistance and balance as Government can give, has finally failed. As yet there has been no final failure, because there has been no attempt; and I decline to assume that this Nation is unable to meet the situation.

The final term of the high contract was for liberty and the pursuit of happiness. We have learned a great deal of both in the past century. We know that individual liberty and individual happiness mean nothing unless both are ordered in the sense that one man's meat is not another man's poison. We know that the old "rights of personal competency," the right to read, to think, to speak, to choose and live a mode of life, must be respected at all hazards. We know that liberty to do anything which deprives others of those elemental rights is outside the protection of any compact; and that Government in this regard is the maintenance of a balance, within which every individual may have a place if he will take it; in which every individual may find safety if he wishes it; in which every individual may attain such power as his ability permits, consistent with his assuming the accompanying responsibility.

All this is a long, slow talk. Nothing is more striking than the simple innocence of the men who insist, whenever an objective is present, on the prompt production of a patent scheme guaranteed to produce a result. Human endeavor is not so simple as that. Government includes the art of formulating a policy, and using the political technique to attain so much of that policy as will receive general support; persuading, leading, sacrificing, teaching always, because the greatest duty of a statesman is to educate. But in the matters of which I have spoken, we are learning rapidly, in a severe school. The lessons so learned must not be forgotten, even, in the mental lethargy of a speculative upturn. We must build toward the time when a major depression cannot occur again; and if this means sacrificing the easy profits of inflationist booms, then let them go; and good riddance.

Faith in America, faith in our tradition of personal responsibility, faith in our institutions, faith in ourselves demand that we recognize the new terms of the old social contract. We shall fulfill them, as we fulfilled the obligation of the apparent Utopia which Jefferson imagined for us in 1776, and which Jefferson, Roosevelt and Wilson sought to bring to realization. We must do so, lest a rising tide of misery, engendered by our common failure, engulf us all. But failure is not an American habit; and in the strength of great hope we must all shoulder our common load.

FRANKLIN D. ROOSEVELT

First Inaugural Address

Washington, D.C., March 4, 1933

I AM CERTAIN that my fellow Americans expect that on my induction into the Presidency I will address them with a candor and a decision which the present situation of our Nation impels. This is preeminently the time to speak the truth, the whole truth, frankly and boldly. Nor need we shrink from honestly facing conditions in our country today. This great Nation will endure as it has endured, will revive and will prosper. So, first of all, let me assert my firm belief that the only thing we have to fear is fear itself—nameless, unreasoning, unjustified terror which paralyzes needed efforts to convert retreat into advance. In every dark hour of our national life a leadership of frankness and vigor has met with that understanding and support of the people themselves which is essential to victory. I am convinced that you will again give that support to leadership in these critical days.

In such a spirit on my part and on yours we face our common difficulties. They concern, thank God, only material things. Values have shrunken to fantastic levels; taxes have risen; our ability to pay has fallen; government of all kinds is faced by serious curtailment of income; the means of exchange are frozen in the currents of trade; the withered leaves of industrial enterprise lie on every side; farmers find no markets for their produce; the savings of many years in thousands of families are gone.

More important, a host of unemployed citizens face the grim problem of existence, and an equally great number toil with little return. Only a foolish optimist can deny the dark realities of the moment.

Yet our distress comes from no failure of substance. We are stricken by no plague of locusts. Compared with the perils which our forefathers conquered because they believed and were not afraid, we have still much to be thankful for. Nature still offers her bounty and human efforts have multiplied it. Plenty is at our doorstep, but a generous use of it languishes in the very sight of the supply. Primarily this is because rulers of the exchange of mankind's goods have failed through their own stubbornness and their own incompetence, have admitted their failure, and have abdicated. Practices of the unscrupulous money changers stand indicted in the court of public opinion, rejected by the hearts and minds of men.

True they have tried, but their efforts have been cast in the pattern of an outworn tradition. Faced by failure of credit they have proposed only the lending of more money. Stripped of the lure of profit by which to induce our people to follow their false leadership, they have resorted to exhortations, pleading tearfully for restored confidence. They know only the rules of a generation of self-seekers. They have no vision, and when there is no vision the people perish.

The money changers have fled from their high seats in the temple of our civilization. We may now restore that temple to the ancient truths. The measure of the restoration lies in the extent to which we apply social values more noble than mere monetary profit.

Happiness lies not in the mere possession of money; it lies in the joy of achievement, in the thrill of creative effort. The joy and moral stimulation of work no longer must be forgotten in the mad chase of evanescent profits. These dark days will be worth all they cost us if they teach us that our true destiny is not to be ministered unto but to minister to ourselves and to our fellow men.

Recognition of the falsity of material wealth as the standard of success goes hand in hand with the abandonment of the false belief that public office and high political position are to be valued only by the standards of pride of place and personal profit; and there must be an end to a conduct in banking and in business which too often has given to a sacred trust the likeness of callous and selfish wrongdoing. Small wonder that confidence languishes, for it thrives only on honesty, on honor, on the sacredness of obligations, on faithful protection, on unselfish performance; without them it cannot live.

Restoration calls, however, not for changes in ethics alone. This Nation asks for action, and action now.

Our greatest primary task is to put people to work. This is no unsolvable problem if we face it wisely and courageously. It can be accomplished in part by direct recruiting by the Government itself, treating the task as we would treat the emergency of a war, but at the same time, through this employment, accomplishing greatly needed projects to stimulate and reorganize the use of our natural resources.

Hand in hand with this we must frankly recognize the overbalance of population in our industrial centers and, by engaging on a national scale in a redistribution, endeavor to provide a better use of the land for those best fitted for the land. The task can be helped by definite efforts to raise the values of agricultural products and with this the power to purchase the output of our cities. It can be helped by preventing realistically the tragedy of the growing loss through foreclosure of our small homes and our farms. It can be helped by insistence that the Federal, State, and local governments act forthwith on the demand that their cost be drastically reduced. It can be helped by the unifying of relief activities which today are often scattered, uneconomical, and unequal. It can be helped by national planning for and supervision of all forms of transportation and of communications and other utilities which have a definitely public character. There are many ways in which it can be helped, but it can never be helped merely by talking about it. We must act and act quickly.

Finally, in our progress toward a resumption of work we require two safeguards against a return of the evils of the old order: there must be a strict supervision of all banking and credits and investments, so that there will be an end to speculation with other people's money; and there must be provision for an adequate but sound currency.

These are the lines of attack. I shall presently urge upon a new Congress, in special session, detailed measures for their fulfillment, and I shall seek the immediate assistance of the several States.

Through this program of action we address ourselves to putting our own national house in order and making income balance outgo. Our international trade relations, though vastly important, are in point of time and necessity secondary to the establishment of a sound national economy. I favor as a practical policy the putting of first things first. I shall spare no effort to restore world trade by international economic readjustment, but the emergency at home cannot wait on that accomplishment.

The basic thought that guides these specific means of national recovery is not narrowly nationalistic. It is the insistence, as a first consideration, upon the interdependence of the various elements in and parts of the United States—a recognition of the old and permanently important manifestation of the American spirit of the pioneer. It is the way to recovery. It is the immediate way. It is the strongest assurance that the recovery will endure.

In the field of world policy I would dedicate this Nation to the policy of the good neighbor—the neighbor who resolutely respects himself and, because he does so, respects the rights of others—the neighbor who respects his obligations and respects the sanctity of his agreements in and with a world of neighbors.

If I read the temper of our people correctly, we now realize as we have never realized before our interdependence on each other; that we cannot merely take but we must give as well; that if we are to go forward, we must move as a trained and loyal army willing to sacrifice for the good of a common discipline, because without such discipline no progress is made, no leadership becomes effective. We are, I know, ready and willing to submit our lives and property to such discipline, because it makes possible a leadership which aims at a larger good. This I propose to offer, pledging that the larger purposes will bind upon us all as a sacred obligation with a unity of duty hitherto evoked only in time of armed strife.

With this pledge taken, I assume unhesitatingly the leadership of this great army of our people dedicated to a disciplined attack upon our common problems.

Action in this image and to this end is feasible under the form of government which we have inherited from our ancestors. Our Constitution is so simple and practical that it is possible always to meet extraordinary needs by changes in emphasis and arrangement without loss of essential form. That is why our constitutional system has proved itself the most superbly enduring political mechanism the modern world has produced. It has met every stress of vast expansion of territory, of foreign wars, of bitter internal strife, of world relations.

It is to be hoped that the normal balance of Executive and legislative authority may be wholly adequate to meet the unprecedented task before us. But it may be that an unprecedented demand and need for undelayed action may call for temporary departure from that normal balance of public procedure.

I am prepared under my constitutional duty to recommend the measures that a stricken Nation in the midst of a stricken world may require. These measures, or such other measures as the Congress may build out of its experience and wisdom, I shall seek, within my constitutional authority, to bring to speedy adoption.

But in the event that the Congress shall fail to take one of these two courses, and in the event that the national emergency is still critical, I shall not evade the clear course of duty that will then confront me. I shall ask the Congress for the one remaining instrument to meet the crisis—broad Executive power to wage a war against the emergency, as great as the power that would be given to me if we were in fact invaded by a foreign foe.

For the trust reposed in me I will return the courage and the devotion that befit the time. I can do no less.

We face the arduous days that lie before us in the warm courage of national unity; with the clear consciousness of seeking old and precious moral values; with the clean satisfaction that comes from the stern performance of duty by old and young alike. We aim at the assurance of a rounded and permanent national life.

We do not distrust the future of essential democracy. The people of the United States have not failed. In their need they have registered a mandate that they want direct, vigorous action. They have asked for discipline and direction under leadership. They have made me the present instrument of their wishes. In the spirit of the gift I take it.

In this dedication of a Nation we humbly ask the blessing of God. May He protect each and every one of us. May He guide me in the days to come.

HUEY LONG

Every Man a King

Washington, D.C., February 23, 1934

Is THAT a right of life, when the young children of this country are being reared into a sphere which is more owned by twelve men than it is by 120 million people?

Ladies and gentlemen, I have only thirty minutes in which to speak to you this evening, and I, therefore, will not be able to discuss in detail so much as I can write when I have all of the time and space that is allowed me for the subjects, but I will undertake to sketch them very briefly without manuscript or preparation, so that you can understand them so well as I can tell them to you tonight.

I contend, my friends, that we have no difficult problem to solve in America, and that is the view of nearly everyone with whom I have discussed the matter here in Washington and elsewhere throughout the United States—that we have no very difficult problem to solve.

It is not the difficulty of the problem which we have; it is the fact that the rich people of this country—and by rich people I mean the superrich—will not allow us to solve the problems, or rather the one little problem that is afflicting this country, because in order to cure all of our woes it is necessary to scale down the big fortunes, that we may scatter the wealth to be shared by all of the people.

We have a marvelous love for this Government of ours; in fact, it is almost a religion, and it is well that it should be, because we have a splendid form of government and we have a splendid set of laws. We have everything here that we need, except that we have neglected the fundamentals upon which the American Government was principally predicated.

How many of you remember the first thing that the Declaration of Independence said? It said, "We hold these truths to be self-evident, that there are certain inalienable rights for the people, and among them are life, liberty, and the pursuit of happiness"; and it said, further, "We hold the view that all men are created equal."

Now, what did they mean by that? Did they mean, my friends, to say that all men were created equal and that that meant that any one man was born to inherit $10 billion and that another child was to be born to inherit nothing?

Did that mean, my friends, that someone would come into this world without having had an opportunity, of course, to have hit one lick of work, should be born with more than it and all of its children and children's children could ever dispose of, but that another one would have to be born into a life of starvation?

That was not the meaning of the Declaration of Independence when it said that all men are created equal or "That we hold that all men are created equal."

Nor was it the meaning of the Declaration of Independence when it said that they held that there were certain rights that were inalienable—the right of life, liberty, and the pursuit of happiness.

Is that right of life, my friends, when the young children of this country are being reared into a sphere which is more owned by 12 men than it is by 120 million people?

Is that, my friends, giving them a fair shake of the dice or anything like the inalienable right of life, liberty, and the pursuit of happiness, or anything resembling the fact that all people are created equal; when we have today in America thousands and hundreds of thousands and millions of children on the verge of starvation in a land that is overflowing with too much to eat and too much to wear?

I do not think you will contend that, and I do not think for a moment that they will contend it.

Now let us see if we cannot return this Government to the Declaration of Independence and see if we are going to do anything regarding it. Why should we hesitate or why should we quibble or why should we quarrel with one another to find out what the difficulty is, when we know what the Lord told us what the difficulty is, and Moses wrote it out so a blind man could see it, then Jesus told us all about it, and it was later written in the Book of James, where everyone could read it?

I refer to the Scriptures, now, my friends, and give you what it says not for the purpose of convincing you of the wisdom of myself, not for the purpose, ladies and gentlemen, of convincing you of the fact that I am quoting the Scripture means that I am to be more believed than someone else; but I quote you the Scripture, or rather refer you to the Scripture, because whatever you see there you may rely upon will never be disproved so long as you or your children or anyone may live; and you may further depend upon the fact that not one historical fact that the Bible has ever contained has ever yet been disproved by any scientific discovery or by reason of anything that has been disclosed to man through his own individual mind or through the wisdom of the Lord which the Lord has allowed him to have.

But the Scripture says, ladies and gentlemen, that no country can survive, or for a country to survive it is necessary that we keep the wealth scattered among the people, that nothing should be held permanently by any one person, and that fifty years seems to be the year of jubilee in which all property would be scattered about and returned to the sources from which it originally came, and every seventh year debt should be remitted.

Those two things the Almighty said to be necessary—I should say He knew to be necessary, or else He would not have so prescribed that the property would be kept among the general run of the people, and that everyone would continue to share in it; so that no one man would get half of it and hand it down to a son, who takes half of what was left, and that son hand it down to another one, who would take half of what was left, until, like a snowball going downhill, all of the snow was off of the ground except what the snowball had.

I believe that was the judgment and the view and the law of the Lord, that we would have to distribute wealth ever so often, in order that there could not be people starving to death in a land of plenty, as there is in America today.

We have in America today more wealth, more goods, more food, more clothing, more houses than we have ever had. We have everything in abundance here.

We have the farm problem, my friends, because we have too much cotton, because we have too much wheat, and have too much corn, and too much potatoes.

We have a home-loan problem because we have too many houses, and yet nobody can buy them and live in them.

We have trouble, my friends, in the country, because we have too much money owing, the greatest indebtedness that has ever been given to civilization, where it has been shown that we are incapable of distributing the actual things that are here, because the people have not money enough to supply themselves with them, and because the greed of a few men is such that they think it is necessary that they own everything, and their pleasure consists in the starvation of the masses, and in their possessing things they cannot use, and their children cannot use, but who bask in the splendor of sunlight and wealth, casting darkness and despair and impressing it on everyone else.

"So, therefore", said the Lord, in effect, "if you see these things that now have occurred and exist in this and other countries, there must be a constant scattering of wealth in any country if this country is to survive."

"Then", said the Lord, in effect, "every seventh year there shall be a remission of debts; there will be no debts after seven years." That was the law.

Now, let us take America today. We have in America today, ladies and gentlemen, $272,000,000,000 of debt. Two hundred and seventy-two thousand millions of dollars of debts are owed by the various people of this country today. Why, my friends, that cannot be paid. It is not possible for that kind of debt to be paid.

The entire currency of the United States is only $6 billion. That is all of the money that we have got in America today. All the actual money you have got in all of your banks, all that you have got in the Government Treasury, is $6 billion; and if you took all that money and paid it out today you would still owe $266 billion; and if you took all that money and paid again you would still owe $260 billion; and if you took it, my friends, twenty times and paid it you would still owe $150 billion.

You would have to have forty-five times the entire money supply of the United States today to pay the debts of the people of America and then they would just have to start out from scratch, without a dime to go on with.

So, my friends, it is impossible to pay all of these debts, and you might as well find out that it cannot be done. The United States Supreme Court has definitely found out that it could not be done, because, in a Minnesota case, it held that when a State has postponed the evil day of collecting a debt it was a valid and constitutional exercise of legislative power.

Now, ladies and gentlemen, if I may proceed to give you some other words that I think you can understand—I am not going to belabor you by quoting tonight—I am going to tell you what the wise men of all ages and all times, down even to the present day, have all said: That you must keep the wealth of the country scattered, and you must limit the amount that any one man can own. You cannot let any man own $300 billion or $400 billion. If you do, one man can own all of the wealth that the United States has in it.

Now, my friends, if you were off on an island where there were 100 lunches, you could not let one man eat up the hundred lunches, or take the hundred lunches and not let anybody else eat any of them. If you did, there would not be anything else for the balance of the people to consume.

So, we have in America today, my friends, a condition by which about 10 men dominate the means of activity in at least 85 percent of the activities that you own. They either own directly everything or they have got some kind of mortgage on it, with a very small percentage to be excepted. They own the banks, they own the steel mills, they own the railroads, they own the bonds, they own the mortgages, they own the stores, and they have chained the country from one end to the other until there is not any kind of business that a small, independent man could go into today and make a living, and there is not any kind of business that an independent man can go into and make any money to buy an automobile with; and they have finally and gradually and steadily eliminated everybody from the fields in which there is a living to be made, and still they have got little enough sense to think they ought to be able to get more business out of it anyway.

If you reduce a man to the point where he is starving to death and bleeding and dying, how do you expect that man to get hold of any money to spend with you? It is not possible.

Then, ladies and gentlemen, how do you expect people to live, when the wherewith cannot be had by the people?

In the beginning I quoted from the Scriptures. I hope you will understand that I am not quoting Scripture to you to convince you of my goodness personally, because that is a thing between me and my Maker, that is something as to how I stand with my Maker and as to how you stand with your Maker. That is not concerned with this issue, except and unless there are those of you who would be so good as to pray for the souls of some of us. But the Lord gave his law, and in the Book of James they said so, that the rich should weep and howl for the miseries that had come upon them; and, therefore, it was written that when the rich hold goods they could not use and could not consume, you will inflict punishment on them, and nothing but days of woe ahead of them.

Then we have heard of the great Greek philosopher, Socrates, and the greater Greek philosopher, Plato, and we have read the dialog between Plato and Socrates, in which one said that great riches brought on great poverty, and would be destructive of a country. Read what they said. Read what Plato said; that you must not let any one man be too poor, and you must not let any one man be too rich; that the same mill that grinds out the extra rich is the mill that will grind out the extra poor, because, in order that the extra rich can become so affluent, they must necessarily take more of what ordinarily would belong to the average man.

It is a very simple process of mathematics that you do not have to study, and that no one is going to discuss with you.

So that was the view of Socrates and Plato. That was the view of the English statesmen. That was the view of American statesmen. That was the view of American statesmen like Daniel Webster, Thomas Jefferson, Abraham Lincoln, William Jennings Bryan, and Theodore Roosevelt, and even as late as Herbert Hoover and Franklin D. Roosevelt.

Both of these men, Mr. Hoover and Mr. Roosevelt, came out and said there had to be a decentralization of wealth, but neither one of them did anything about it. But, nevertheless, they recognized the principle. The fact that neither one of them ever did anything about it is their own problem that I am not undertaking to criticize; but had Mr. Hoover carried out what he says ought to be done, he would be retiring from the President's office, very probably, three years from now, instead of one year ago; and had Mr. Roosevelt proceeded along the lines that he stated were necessary for the decentralization of wealth, he would have gone, my friends, a long way already, and within a few months he would have probably reached a solution of all of the problems that afflict this country today.

But I wish to warn you now that nothing that has been done up to this date has taken one dime away from these big-fortune holders; they own just as much as they did, and probably a little bit more; they hold just as many of the debts of the common people as they ever held, and probably a little bit more; and unless we, my friends, are going to give the people of this country a fair shake of the dice, by which they will all get something out of the funds of this land, there is not a chance on the topside of this God's eternal earth by which we can rescue this country and rescue the people of this country.

It is necessary to save the Government of the country, but is much more necessary to save the people of America. We love this country. We love this Government. It is a religion, I say. It is a kind of religion people have read of when women, in the name of religion, would take their infant babes and throw them into the burning flame, where they would be instantly devoured by the all-consuming fire, in days gone by; and there probably are some people of the world even today, who, in the name of religion, throw their own babes to destruction; but in the name of our good Government people today are seeing their own children hungry, tired, half-naked, lifting their tear-dimmed eyes into the sad faces of their fathers and mothers, who cannot give them food and clothing they both needed, and which is necessary to sustain them, and that goes on day after day, and night after night, when day gets into darkness and blackness, knowing those children would arise in the morning without being fed, and probably go to bed at night without being fed.

Yet in the name of our Government, and all alone, those people undertake and strive as hard as they can to keep a good government alive, and how long they can stand that no one knows. If I were in their place tonight, the place where millions are, I hope that I would have what I might say—I cannot give you the word to express the kind of fortitude they have; that is the word—I hope that I might have the fortitude to praise and honor my Government that had allowed me here in this land, where there is too much to eat and too much to wear, to starve in order that a handful of men can have so much more than they can ever eat or they can ever wear.

Now, we have organized a society, and we call it share-our-wealth society, a society with the motto "Every man a king."

Every man a king, so there would be no such thing as a man or woman who did not have the necessities of life, who would not be dependent upon the whims and caprices and ipsi dixit of the financial martyrs for a living. What do we propose by this society? We propose to limit the wealth of big men in the country. There is an average of $15,000 in wealth to every family in America. That is right here today.

We do not propose to divide it up equally. We do not propose a division of wealth, but we propose to limit poverty that we will allow to be inflicted upon any man's family. We will not say we are going to try to guarantee any equality, or $15,000 to families. No; but we do say that one third of the average is low enough for any one family to hold, that there should be a guaranty of a family wealth of around $5,000; enough for a home, an automobile, a radio, and the ordinary conveniences, and the opportunity to educate their children; a fair share of the income of this land thereafter to that family so there will be no such thing as merely the select to have those things, and so there will be no such thing as a family living in poverty and distress.

We have to limit fortunes. Our present plan is that we will allow no one man to own more than $50 million. We think that with that limit we will be able to carry out the balance of the program. It may be necessary that we limit it to less than $50 million. It may be necessary, in working out of the plans, that no man's fortune would be more than $10 million or $15 million. But be that as it may, it will still be more than any one man, or any one man and his children and their children, will be able to spend in their lifetimes; and it is not necessary or reasonable to have wealth piled up beyond that point where we cannot prevent poverty among the masses.

Another thing we propose is an old-age pension of $30 a month for everyone that is 60 years old. Now, we do not give this pension to a man making $1,000 a year, and we do not give it to him if he has $10,000 in property, but outside of that we do.

We will limit hours of work. There is not any necessity of having overproduction. I think all you have got to do, ladies and gentlemen, is just limit the hours of work to such an extent as people will work only so long as is necessary to produce enough for all of the people to have what they need. Why, ladies and gentlemen, let us say that all of these labor-saving devices reduce hours down to where you do not have to work but four hours a day; that is enough for these people, and then praise be the name of the Lord, if it gets that good. Let it be good and not a curse, and then we will have 5 hours a day and five days a week, or even less than that, and we might give a man a whole month off during a year, or give him two months; and we might do what other countries have seen fit to do, and what I did in Louisiana, by having schools by which adults could go back and learn the things that have been discovered since they went to school.

We will not have any trouble taking care of the agricultural situation. All you have to do is balance your production with your consumption. You simply have to abandon a particular crop that you have too much of, and all you have to do is store the surplus for the next year, and the Government will take it over. When you have good crops in the area in which the crops that have been planted are sufficient for another year, put in your public works in the particular year when you do not need to raise any more, and by that means you get everybody employed. When the Government has enough of any particular crop to take care of all of the people, that will be all that is necessary; and in order to do all of this, our taxation is going to be to take the billion-dollar fortunes and strip them down to frying size, not to exceed $50 million and if it is necessary to come to $10 million, we will come to $10 million. We have worked the proposition out to guarantee a limit upon property (and no man will own less than one third the average), and guarantee a reduction of fortunes and a reduction of hours to spread wealth throughout this country. We would care for the old people above 60 and take them away from this thriving industry and give them a chance to enjoy the necessities and live in ease, and thereby lift from the market the labor which would probably create a surplus of commodities.

Those are the things we propose to do. "Every man a king."

Every man to eat when there is something to eat; all to wear
something when there is something to wear. That makes us all
a sovereign.

You cannot solve these things through these various and
sundry alphabetical codes. You can have the NRA and PWA
and CWA and the UUG and GIN and any other kind of "dad-
gummed" lettered code. You can wait until doomsday and see
twenty-five more alphabets, but that is not going to solve this
proposition. Why hide? Why quibble? You know what the
trouble is. The man that says he does not know what the trouble is is just hiding his face to keep from seeing the sunlight.

God told you what the trouble was. The philosophers told
you what the trouble was; and when you have a country where
one man owns more than 100,000 people, or a million people,
and when you have a country where there are four men, as in
America, that have got more control over things than all the
130 million people together, you know what the trouble is.

We had these great incomes in this country; but the farmer,
who plowed from sunup to sundown, who labored here from
sunup to sundown for six days a week, wound up at the end of
the time with practically nothing.

And we ought to take care of the veterans of the wars in this
program. That is a small matter. Suppose it does cost a billion
dollars a year—that means that the money will be scattered
throughout this country. We ought to pay them a bonus. We
can do it. We ought to take care of every single one of the sick
and disabled veterans. I do not care whether a man got sick on
the battlefield or did not; every man that wore the uniform of
this country is entitled to be taken care of, and there is money
enough to do it; and we need to spread the wealth of the
country, which you did not do in what you call the NRA.

If the NRA has done any good, I can put it all in my eye
without having it hurt. All I can see that the NRA has done is
to put the little man out of business—the little merchant in his
store, the little Dago that is running a fruit stand, or the Greek
shoe-shining stand, who has to take hold of a code of 275 pages
and study it with a spirit level and compass and looking-glass;
he has to hire a Philadelphia lawyer to tell him what is in the
code; and by the time he learns what the code is, he is in jail or
out of business; and they have got a chain code system that has

already put him out of business. The NRA is not worth any-thing, and I said so when they put it through.

Now, my friends, we have got to hit the root with the ax. Centralized power in the hands of a few, with centralized credit in the hands of a few, is the trouble.

Get together in your community tonight or tomorrow and organize one of our share-our-wealth societies. If you do not understand it, write me and let me send you the platform; let me give you the proof of it.

This is Huey P. Long talking, United States Senator, Wash-ington, D.C. Write me and let me send you the data on this proposition. Enroll with us. Let us make known to the people what we are going to do. I will send you a button, if I have got enough of them left. We have got a little button that some of our friends designed, with our message around the rim of the button, and in the center "Every man a king." Many thousands of them are meeting through the United States, and every day we are getting hundreds and hundreds of letters. Share-our-wealth societies are now being organized, and people have it within their power to relieve themselves from this terrible situation.

Look at what the Mayo brothers announced this week, these greatest scientists of all the world today, who are entitled to have more money than all the Morgans and the Rockefellers, or anyone else, and yet the Mayos turn back their big fortunes to be used for treating the sick, and said they did not want to lay up fortunes in this earth, but wanted to turn them back where they would do some good; but the other big capitalists are not willing to do that, are not willing to do what these men, 10 times more worthy, have already done, and it is going to take a law to require them to do it.

Organize your share-our-wealth society and get your people to meet with you, and make known your wishes to your Sena-tors and Representatives in Congress.

Now, my friends, I am going to stop. I thank you for this opportunity to talk to you. I am having to talk under the aus-pices and by the grace and permission of the National Broad-casting System tonight, and they are letting me talk free. If I had the money, and I wish I had the money, I would like to talk to you more often on this line, but I have not got it, and I cannot expect these people to give it to me free except on some rare instance. But, my friends, I hope to have the opportunity to talk with you, and I am writing to you, and I hope that you will get up and help in the work, because the resolutions and bills are before Congress, and we hope to have your help in getting together and organizing your share-our-wealth society.

Now, that I have but a minute left, I want to say that I suppose my family is listening in on the radio in New Orleans, and I will say to my wife and three children that I am entirely well and hope to be home before many more days, and I hope they have listened to my speech tonight, and I wish them and all of their neighbors and friends everything good that may be had.

I thank you, my friends, for your kind attention, and I hope you will enroll with us, take care of your own work in the work of this Government, and share or help in our share-our-wealth society.

I thank you.

FRANKLIN D. ROOSEVELT

Speech to the Democratic National Convention

Philadelphia, June 27, 1936

SENATOR ROBINSON, MEMBERS OF THE DEMOCRATIC CONVENTION, MY FRIENDS:

Here, and in every community throughout the land, we are met at a time of great moment to the future of the Nation. It is an occasion to be dedicated to the simple and sincere expression of an attitude toward problems, the determination of which will profoundly affect America.

I come not only as a leader of a party, not only as a candidate for high office, but as one upon whom many critical hours have imposed and still impose a grave responsibility.

For the sympathy, help and confidence with which Americans have sustained me in my task I am grateful. For their loyalty I salute the members of our great party, in and out of political life in every part of the Union. I salute those of other parties, especially those in the Congress of the United States who on so many occasions have put partisanship aside. I thank the Governors of the several States, their Legislatures, their State and local officials who participated unselfishly and regardless of party in our efforts to achieve recovery and destroy abuses. Above all I thank the millions of Americans who have borne disaster bravely and have dared to smile through the storm.

America will not forget these recent years, will not forget that the rescue was not a mere party task. It was the concern of all of us. In our strength we rose together, rallied our energies together, applied the old rules of common sense, and together survived.

In those days we feared fear. That was why we fought fear. And today, my friends, we have won against the most dangerous of our foes. We have conquered fear.

But I cannot, with candor, tell you that all is well with the world. Clouds of suspicion, tides of ill-will and intolerance gather darkly in many places. In our own land we enjoy indeed a fullness of life greater than that of most Nations. But the rush of modern civilization itself has raised for us new difficulties, new problems which must be solved if we are to preserve to the United States the political and economic freedom for which Washington and Jefferson planned and fought.

Philadelphia is a good city in which to write American history. This is fitting ground on which to reaffirm the faith of our fathers; to pledge ourselves to restore to the people a wider freedom; to give to 1936 as the founders gave to 1776—an American way of life.

That very word freedom, in itself and of necessity, suggests freedom from some restraining power. In 1776 we sought freedom from the tyranny of a political autocracy—from the eighteenth century royalists who held special privileges from the crown. It was to perpetuate their privilege that they governed without the consent of the governed; that they denied the right of free assembly and free speech; that they restricted the worship of God; that they put the average man's property and the average man's life in pawn to the mercenaries of dynastic power; that they regimented the people.

And so it was to win freedom from the tyranny of political autocracy that the American Revolution was fought. That victory gave the business of governing into the hands of the average man, who won the right with his neighbors to make and order his own destiny through his own Government. Political tyranny was wiped out at Philadelphia on July 4, 1776.

Since that struggle, however, man's inventive genius released new forces in our land which reordered the lives of our people. The age of machinery, of railroads; of steam and electricity; the telegraph and the radio; mass production, mass distribution— all of these combined to bring forward a new civilization and with it a new problem for those who sought to remain free.

For out of this modern civilization economic royalists carved new dynasties. New kingdoms were built upon concentration of control over material things. Through new uses of corporations, banks and securities, new machinery of industry and agriculture, of labor and capital—all undreamed of by the fathers—the whole structure of modern life was impressed into this royal service.

There was no place among this royalty for our many thousands of small business men and merchants who sought to make a worthy use of the American system of initiative and profit. They were no more free than the worker or the farmer. Even honest and progressive-minded men of wealth, aware of their obligation to their generation, could never know just where they fitted into this dynastic scheme of things.

It was natural and perhaps human that the privileged princes of these new economic dynasties, thirsting for power, reached out for control over Government itself. They created a new despotism and wrapped it in the robes of legal sanction. In its service new mercenaries sought to regiment the people, their labor, and their property. And as a result the average man once more confronts the problem that faced the Minute Man.

The hours men and women worked, the wages they received, the conditions of their labor—these had passed beyond the control of the people, and were imposed by this new industrial dictatorship. The savings of the average family, the capital of the small business man, the investments set aside for old age—other people's money—these were tools which the new economic royalty used to dig itself in.

Those who tilled the soil no longer reaped the rewards which were their right. The small measure of their gains was decreed by men in distant cities.

Throughout the Nation, opportunity was limited by monopoly. Individual initiative was crushed in the cogs of a great machine. The field open for free business was more and more restricted. Private enterprise, indeed, became too private. It became privileged enterprise, not free enterprise.

An old English judge once said: "Necessitous men are not free men." Liberty requires opportunity to make a living—a living decent according to the standard of the time, a living which gives man not only enough to live by, but something to live for.

For too many of us the political equality we once had won was meaningless in the face of economic inequality. A small group had concentrated into their own hands an almost complete control over other people's property, other people's money, other people's labor—other people's lives. For too many of us life was no longer free; liberty no longer real; men could no longer follow the pursuit of happiness.

Against economic tyranny such as this, the American citizen could appeal only to the organized power of Government. The collapse of 1929 showed up the despotism for what it was. The election of 1932 was the people's mandate to end it. Under that mandate it is being ended.

The royalists of the economic order have conceded that political freedom was the business of the Government, but they have maintained that economic slavery was nobody's business. They granted that the Government could protect the citizen in his right to vote, but they denied that the Government could do anything to protect the citizen in his right to work and his right to live.

Today we stand committed to the proposition that freedom is no half-and-half affair. If the average citizen is guaranteed equal opportunity in the polling place, he must have equal opportunity in the market place.

These economic royalists complain that we seek to overthrow the institutions of America. What they really complain of is that we seek to take away their power. Our allegiance to American institutions requires the overthrow of this kind of power. In vain they seek to hide behind the Flag and the Constitution. In their blindness they forget what the Flag and the Constitution stand for. Now, as always, they stand for democracy, not tyranny; for freedom, not subjection; and against a dictatorship by mob rule and the overprivileged alike.

The brave and clear platform adopted by this Convention, to which I heartily subscribe, sets forth that Government in a modern civilization has certain inescapable obligations to its citizens, among which are protection of the family and the home, the establishment of a democracy of opportunity, and aid to those overtaken by disaster.

But the resolute enemy within our gates is ever ready to beat down our words unless in greater courage we will fight for them.

For more than three years we have fought for them. This

Convention, in every word and deed, has pledged that that fight will go on.

The defeats and victories of these years have given to us as a people a new understanding of our Government and of ourselves. Never since the early days of the New England town meeting have the affairs of Government been so widely discussed and so clearly appreciated. It has been brought home to us that the only effective guide for the safety of this most worldly of worlds, the greatest guide of all, is moral principle.

We do not see faith, hope and charity as unattainable ideals, but we use them as stout supports of a Nation fighting the fight for freedom in a modern civilization.

Faith—in the soundness of democracy in the midst of dictatorships.

Hope—renewed because we know so well the progress we have made.

Charity—in the true spirit of that grand old word. For charity literally translated from the original means love, the love that understands, that does not merely share the wealth of the giver, but in true sympathy and wisdom helps men to help themselves.

We seek not merely to make Government a mechanical implement, but to give it the vibrant personal character that is the very embodiment of human charity.

We are poor indeed if this Nation cannot afford to lift from every recess of American life the dread fear of the unemployed that they are not needed in the world. We cannot afford to accumulate a deficit in the books of human fortitude.

In the place of the palace of privilege we seek to build a temple out of faith and hope and charity.

It is a sobering thing, my friends, to be a servant of this great cause. We try in our daily work to remember that the cause belongs not to us, but to the people. The standard is not in the hands of you and me alone. It is carried by America. We seek daily to profit from experience, to learn to do better as our task proceeds.

Governments can err, Presidents do make mistakes, but the immortal Dante tells us that divine justice weighs the sins of the cold-blooded and the sins of the warm-hearted in different scales.

Better the occasional faults of a Government that lives in a spirit of charity than the consistent omissions of a Government frozen in the ice of its own indifference.

There is a mysterious cycle in human events. To some generations much is given. Of other generations much is expected. This generation of Americans has a rendezvous with destiny.

In this world of ours in other lands, there are some people, who, in times past, have lived and fought for freedom, and seem to have grown too weary to carry on the fight. They have sold their heritage of freedom for the illusion of a living. They have yielded their democracy.

I believe in my heart that only our success can stir their ancient hope. They begin to know that here in America we are waging a great and successful war. It is not alone a war against want and destitution and economic demoralization. It is more than that; it is a war for the survival of democracy. We are fighting to save a great and precious form of government for ourselves and for the world.

I accept the commission you have tendered me. I join with you. I am enlisted for the duration of the war.

FRANKLIN D. ROOSEVELT

Second Inaugural Address

Washington, D.C., January 20, 1937

WHEN four years ago we met to inaugurate a President, the Republic, single-minded in anxiety, stood in spirit here. We dedicated ourselves to the fulfillment of a vision—to speed the time when there would be for all the people that security and peace essential to the pursuit of happiness. We of the Republic pledged ourselves to drive from the temple of our ancient faith those who had profaned it; to end by action, tireless and unafraid, the stagnation and despair of that day. We did those first things first.

Our covenant with ourselves did not stop there. Instinctively we recognized a deeper need—the need to find through government the instrument of our united purpose to solve for the individual the ever-rising problems of a complex civilization. Repeated attempts at their solution without the aid of government had left us baffled and bewildered. For, without that aid, we had been unable to create those moral controls over the services of science which are necessary to make science a useful servant instead of a ruthless master of mankind. To do this we knew that we must find practical controls over blind economic forces and blindly selfish men.

We of the Republic sensed the truth that democratic government has innate capacity to protect its people against disasters once considered inevitable, to solve problems once considered unsolvable. We would not admit that we could not find a way to master economic epidemics just as, after centuries of fatalistic suffering, we had found a way to master epidemics of disease. We refused to leave the problems of our common welfare to be solved by the winds of chance and the hurricanes of disaster.

In this we Americans were discovering no wholly new truth;

we were writing a new chapter in our book of self-government.

This year marks the one hundred and fiftieth anniversary of the Constitutional Convention which made us a nation. At that Convention our forefathers found the way out of the chaos which followed the Revolutionary War; they created a strong government with powers of united action sufficient then and now to solve problems utterly beyond individual or local solution. A century and a half ago they established the Federal Government in order to promote the general welfare and secure the blessings of liberty to the American people.

Today we invoke those same powers of government to achieve the same objectives.

Four years of new experience have not belied our historic instinct. They hold out the clear hope that government within communities, government within the separate States, and government of the United States can do the things the times require, without yielding its democracy. Our tasks in the last four years did not force democracy to take a holiday.

Nearly all of us recognize that as intricacies of human relationships increase, so power to govern them also must increase—power to stop evil; power to do good. The essential democracy of our Nation and the safety of our people depend not upon the absence of power, but upon lodging it with those whom the people can change or continue at stated intervals through an honest and free system of elections. The Constitution of 1787 did not make our democracy impotent.

In fact, in these last four years, we have made the exercise of all power more democratic; for we have begun to bring private autocratic powers into their proper subordination to the public's government. The legend that they were invincible—above and beyond the processes of a democracy—has been shattered. They have been challenged and beaten.

Our progress out of the depression is obvious. But that is not all that you and I mean by the new order of things. Our pledge was not merely to do a patchwork job with second-hand materials. By using the new materials of social justice we have undertaken to erect on the old foundations a more enduring structure for the better use of future generations.

In that purpose we have been helped by achievements of

mind and spirit. Old truths have been relearned; untruths have been unlearned. We have always known that heedless self-interest was bad morals; we know now that it is bad economics. Out of the collapse of a prosperity whose builders boasted their practicality has come the conviction that in the long run economic morality pays. We are beginning to wipe out the line that divides the practical from the ideal; and in so doing we are fashioning an instrument of unimagined power for the establishment of a morally better world.

This new understanding undermines the old admiration of worldly success as such. We are beginning to abandon our tolerance of the abuse of power by those who betray for profit the elementary decencies of life.

In this process evil things formerly accepted will not be so easily condoned. Hard-headedness will not so easily excuse hard-heartedness. We are moving toward an era of good feeling. But we realize that there can be no era of good feeling save among men of good will.

For these reasons I am justified in believing that the greatest change we have witnessed has been the change in the moral climate of America.

Among men of good will, science and democracy together offer an ever-richer life and ever larger satisfaction to the individual. With this change in our moral climate and our rediscovered ability to improve our economic order, we have set our feet upon the road of enduring progress.

Shall we pause now and turn our back upon the road that lies ahead? Shall we call this the promised land? Or, shall we continue on our way? For "each age is a dream that is dying, or one that is coming to birth."

Many voices are heard as we face a great decision. Comfort says, "Tarry a while." Opportunism says, "This is a good spot." Timidity asks, "How difficult is the road ahead?"

True, we have come far from the days of stagnation and despair. Vitality has been preserved. Courage and confidence have been restored. Mental and moral horizons have been extended.

But our present gains were won under the pressure of more than ordinary circumstance. Advance became imperative under the goad of fear and suffering. The times were on the side of progress.

To hold to progress today, however, is more difficult. Dulled conscience, irresponsibility, and ruthless self-interest already reappear. Such symptoms of prosperity may become portents of disaster! Prosperity already tests the persistence of our progressive purpose.

Let us ask again: Have we reached the goal of our vision of that fourth day of March, 1933? Have we found our happy valley?

I see a great nation, upon a great continent, blessed with a great wealth of natural resources. Its hundred and thirty million people are at peace among themselves; they are making their country a good neighbor among the nations. I see a United States which can demonstrate that, under democratic methods of government, national wealth can be translated into a spreading volume of human comforts hitherto unknown, and the lowest standard of living can be raised far above the level of mere subsistence.

But here is the challenge to our democracy: In this nation I see tens of millions of its citizens—a substantial part of its whole population—who at this very moment are denied the greater part of what the very lowest standards of today call the necessities of life.

I see millions of families trying to live on incomes so meager that the pall of family disaster hangs over them day by day.

I see millions whose daily lives in city and on farm continue under conditions labeled indecent by a so-called polite society half a century ago.

I see millions denied education, recreation, and the opportunity to better their lot and the lot of their children.

I see millions lacking the means to buy the products of farm and factory and by their poverty denying work and productiveness to many other millions.

I see one-third of a nation ill-housed, ill-clad, ill-nourished.

It is not in despair that I paint you that picture. I paint it for you in hope—because the Nation, seeing and understanding the injustice in it, proposes to paint it out. We are determined to make every American citizen the subject of his country's interest and concern; and we will never regard any faithful, law-abiding group within our borders as superfluous. The test of our progress is not whether we add more to the abundance of those who have much; it is whether we provide enough for those who have too little.

If I know aught of the spirit and purpose of our Nation, we will not listen to Comfort, Opportunism, and Timidity. We will carry on.

Overwhelmingly, we of the Republic are men and women of good will; men and women who have more than warm hearts of dedication; men and women who have cool heads and willing hands of practical purpose as well. They will insist that every agency of popular government use effective instruments to carry out their will.

Government is competent when all who compose it work as trustees for the whole people. It can make constant progress when it keeps abreast of all the facts. It can obtain justified support and legitimate criticism when the people receive true information of all that government does.

If I know aught of the will of our people, they will demand that these conditions of effective government shall be created and maintained. They will demand a nation uncorrupted by cancers of injustice and, therefore, strong among the nations in its example of the will to peace.

Today we reconsecrate our country to long-cherished ideals in a suddenly changed civilization. In every land there are always at work forces that drive men apart and forces that draw men together. In our personal ambitions we are individualists. But in our seeking for economic and political progress as a nation, we all go up, or else we all go down, as one people.

To maintain a democracy of effort requires a vast amount of patience in dealing with differing methods, a vast amount of humility. But out of the confusion of many voices rises an understanding of dominant public need. Then political leadership can voice common ideals, and aid in their realization.

In taking again the oath of office as President of the United States, I assume the solemn obligation of leading the American people forward along the road over which they have chosen to advance.

While this duty rests upon me I shall do my utmost to speak their purpose and to do their will, seeking Divine guidance to help us each and every one to give light to them that sit in darkness and to guide our feet into the way of peace.

FRANKLIN D. ROOSEVELT

"Arsenal of Democracy" Fireside Chat

Washington, D.C., December 29, 1940

MY FRIENDS:
This not a fireside chat on war. It is a talk on national security; because the nub of the whole purpose of your President is to keep you now, and your children later, and your grandchildren much later, out of a last-ditch war for the preservation of American independence and all the things that American independence means to you and to me and to ours.

Tonight, in the presence of a world crisis, my mind goes back eight years to a night in the midst of a domestic crisis. It was a time when the wheels of American industry were grinding to a full stop, when the whole banking system of our country had ceased to function.

I well remember that while I sat in my study in the White House, preparing to talk with the people of the United States, I had before my eyes the picture of all those Americans with whom I was talking. I saw the workmen in the mills, the mines, the factories; the girl behind the counter; the small shopkeeper; the farmer doing his spring plowing; the widows and the old men wondering about their life's savings.

I tried to convey to the great mass of American people what the banking crisis meant to them in their daily lives.

Tonight, I want to do the same thing, with the same people, in this new crisis which faces America.

We met the issue of 1933 with courage and realism.

We face this new crisis—this new threat to the security of our nation—with the same courage and realism.

Never before since Jamestown and Plymouth Rock has our American civilization been in such danger as now.

For, on September 27, 1940, by an agreement signed in Berlin, three powerful nations, two in Europe and one in Asia, joined themselves together in the threat that if the United

States of America interfered with or blocked the expansion program of these three nations—a program aimed at world control—they would unite in ultimate action against the United States.

The Nazi masters of Germany have made it clear that they intend not only to dominate all life and thought in their own country, but also to enslave the whole of Europe, and then to use the resources of Europe to dominate the rest of the world.

It was only three weeks ago their leader stated this: "There are two worlds that stand opposed to each other." And then in defiant reply to his opponents, he said this: "Others are correct when they say: With this world we cannot ever reconcile ourselves. . . . I can beat any other power in the world." So said the leader of the Nazis.

In other words, the Axis not merely admits but *proclaims* that there can be no ultimate peace between their philosophy of government and our philosophy of government.

In view of the nature of this undeniable threat, it can be asserted, properly and categorically, that the United States has no right or reason to encourage talk of peace, until the day shall come when there is a clear intention on the part of the aggressor nations to abandon all thought of dominating or conquering the world.

At this moment, the forces of the states that are leagued against all peoples who live in freedom, are being held away from our shores. The Germans and the Italians are being blocked on the other side of the Atlantic by the British, and by the Greeks, and by thousands of soldiers and sailors who were able to escape from subjugated countries. In Asia, the Japanese are being engaged by the Chinese nation in another great defense.

In the Pacific Ocean is our fleet.

Some of our people like to believe that wars in Europe and in Asia are of no concern to us. But it is a matter of most vital concern to us that European and Asiatic war-makers should not gain control of the oceans which lead to this hemisphere.

One hundred and seventeen years ago the Monroe Doctrine was conceived by our Government as a measure of defense in the face of a threat against this hemisphere by an alliance in Continental Europe. Thereafter, we stood on guard in the

Atlantic, with the British as neighbors. There was no treaty. There was no "unwritten agreement."

And yet, there was the feeling, proven correct by history, that we as neighbors could settle any disputes in peaceful fashion. The fact is that during the whole of this time the Western Hemisphere has remained free from aggression from Europe or from Asia.

Does anyone seriously believe that we need to fear attack anywhere in the Americas while a free Britain remains our most powerful naval neighbor in the Atlantic? Does anyone seriously believe, on the other hand, that we could rest easy if the Axis powers were our neighbors there?

If Great Britain goes down, the Axis powers will control the continents of Europe, Asia, Africa, Australasia, and the high seas—and they will be in a position to bring enormous military and naval resources against this hemisphere. It is no exaggeration to say that all of us, in all the Americas, would be living at the point of a gun—a gun loaded with explosive bullets, economic as well as military.

We should enter upon a new and terrible era in which the whole world, our hemisphere included, would be run by threats of brute force. To survive in such a world, we would have to convert ourselves permanently into a militaristic power on the basis of war economy.

Some of us like to believe that even if Great Britain falls, we are still safe, because of the broad expanse of the Atlantic and of the Pacific.

But the width of those oceans is not what it was in the days of clipper ships. At one point between Africa and Brazil the distance is less than from Washington to Denver, Colorado— five hours for the latest type of bomber. And at the North end of the Pacific Ocean America and Asia almost touch each other.

Even today we have planes that could fly from the British Isles to New England and back again without refueling. And remember that the range of the modern bomber is ever being increased.

During the past week many people in all parts of the nation have told me what they wanted me to say tonight. Almost all of them expressed a courageous desire to hear the plain truth about the gravity of the situation. One telegram, however, expressed the attitude of the small minority who want to see no evil and hear no evil, even though they know in their hearts that evil exists. That telegram begged me not to tell again of the ease with which our American cities could be bombed by any hostile power which had gained bases in this Western Hemisphere. The gist of that telegram was: "Please, Mr. President, don't frighten us by telling us the facts."

Frankly and definitely there is danger ahead—danger against which we must prepare. But we well know that we cannot escape danger, or the fear of danger, by crawling into bed and pulling the covers over our heads.

Some nations of Europe were bound by solemn non-intervention pacts with Germany. Other nations were assured by Germany that they need *never* fear invasion. Non-intervention pact or not, the fact remains that they *were* attacked, overrun and thrown into the modern form of slavery at an hour's notice, or even without any notice at all. As an exiled leader of one of these nations said to me the other day—"The notice was a minus quantity. It was given to my Government two hours after German troops had poured into my country in a hundred places."

The fate of these nations tells us what it means to live at the point of a Nazi gun.

The Nazis have justified such actions by various pious frauds. One of these frauds is the claim that they are occupying a nation for the purpose of "restoring order." Another is that they are occupying or controlling a nation on the excuse that they are "protecting it" against the aggression of somebody else.

For example, Germany has said that she was occupying Belgium to save the Belgians from the British. Would she then hesitate to say to any South American country, "We are occupying you to protect you from aggression by the United States"?

Belgium today is being used as an invasion base against Britain, now fighting for its life. Any South American country, in Nazi hands, would always constitute a jumping-off place for German attack on any one of the other Republics of this hemisphere.

Analyze for yourselves the future of two other places even

nearer to Germany if the Nazis won. Could Ireland hold out? Would Irish freedom be permitted as an amazing pet exception in an unfree world? Or the Islands of the Azores which still fly the flag of Portugal after five centuries? You and I think of Hawaii as an outpost of defense in the Pacific. And yet, the Azores are closer to our shores in the Atlantic than Hawaii is on the other side.

There are those who say that the Axis powers would never have any desire to attack the Western Hemisphere. That is the same dangerous form of wishful thinking which has destroyed the powers of resistance of so many conquered peoples. The plain facts are that the Nazis have proclaimed, time and again, that all other races are their inferiors and therefore subject to their orders. And most important of all, the vast resources and wealth of this American Hemisphere constitute the most tempting loot in all the round world.

Let us no longer blind ourselves to the undeniable fact that the evil forces which have crushed and undermined and corrupted so many others are already within our own gates. Your Government knows much about them and every day is ferreting them out.

Their secret emissaries are active in our own and in neighboring countries. They seek to stir up suspicion and dissension to cause internal strife. They try to turn capital against labor, and vice versa. They try to reawaken long slumbering racial and religious enmities which should have no place in this country. They are active in every group that promotes intolerance. They exploit for their own ends our natural abhorrence of war. These trouble-breeders have but one purpose. It is to divide our people into hostile groups and to destroy our unity and shatter our will to defend ourselves.

There are also American citizens, many of them in high places, who, unwittingly in most cases, are aiding and abetting the work of these agents. I do not charge these American citizens with being foreign agents. But I do charge them with doing exactly the kind of work that the dictators want done in the United States.

These people not only believe that we can save our own skins by shutting our eyes to the fate of other nations. Some of them go much further than that. They say that we can and should become the friends and even the partners of the Axis powers. Some of them even suggest that we should imitate the methods of the dictatorships. Americans never can and never will do that.

The experience of the past two years has proven beyond doubt that no nation can appease the Nazis. No man can tame a tiger into a kitten by stroking it. There can be no appeasement with ruthlessness. There can be no reasoning with an incendiary bomb. We know now that a nation can have peace with the Nazis only at the price of total surrender.

Even the people of Italy have been forced to become accomplices of the Nazis; but at this moment they do not know how soon they will be embraced to death by their allies.

The American appeasers ignore the warning to be found in the fate of Austria, Czechoslovakia, Poland, Norway, Belgium, the Netherlands, Denmark, and France. They tell you that the Axis powers are going to win anyway; that all this bloodshed in the world could be saved; that the United States might just as well throw its influence into the scale of a dictated peace, and get the best out of it that we can.

They call it a "negotiated peace." Nonsense! Is it a negotiated peace if a gang of outlaws surrounds your community and on threat of extermination makes you pay tribute to save your own skins?

Such a dictated peace would be no peace at all. It would be only another armistice, leading to the most gigantic armament race and the most devastating trade wars in all history. And in these contests the Americas would offer the only real resistance to the Axis powers.

With all their vaunted efficiency, with all their parade of pious purpose in this war, there are still in their background the concentration camp and the servants of God in chains.

The history of recent years proves that shootings and chains and concentration camps are not simply the transient tools but the very altars of modern dictatorships. They may talk of a "new order" in the world, but what they have in mind is only a revival of the oldest and the worst tyranny. In that there is no liberty, no religion, no hope.

The proposed "new order" is the very opposite of a United States of Europe or a United States of Asia. It is not a

Government based upon the consent of the governed. It is not a union of ordinary, self-respecting men and women to protect themselves and their freedom and their dignity from oppression. It is an unholy alliance of power and pelf to dominate and enslave the human race.

The British people and their allies today are conducting an active war against this unholy alliance. Our own future security is greatly dependent on the outcome of that fight. Our ability to "keep out of war" is going to be affected by that outcome.

Thinking in terms of today and tomorrow, I make the direct statement to the American people that there is far less chance of the United States getting into war, if we do all we can now to support the nations defending themselves against attack by the Axis than if we acquiesce in their defeat, submit tamely to an Axis victory, and wait our turn to be the object of attack in another war later on.

If we are to be completely honest with ourselves, we must admit that there is risk in any course we may take. But I deeply believe that the great majority of our people agree that the course that I advocate involves the least risk now and the greatest hope for world peace in the future.

The people of Europe who are defending themselves do not ask us to do their fighting. They ask us for the implements of war, the planes, the tanks, the guns, the freighters which will enable them to fight for their liberty and for our security. Emphatically we must get these weapons to them in sufficient volume and quickly enough, so that we and our children will be saved the agony and suffering of war which others have had to endure.

Let not the defeatists tell us that it is too late. It will never be earlier. Tomorrow will be later than today.

Certain facts are self-evident.

In a military sense Great Britain and the British Empire are today the spearhead of resistance to world conquest. They are putting up a fight which will live forever in the story of human gallantry.

There is no demand for sending an American Expeditionary Force outside our own borders. There is no intention by any member of your Government to send such a force. You can, therefore, nail any talk about sending armies to Europe as deliberate untruth.

Our national policy is not directed toward war. Its sole purpose is to keep war away from our country and our people.

Democracy's fight against world conquest is being greatly aided, and must be more greatly aided, by the rearmament of the United States and by sending every ounce and every ton of munitions and supplies that we can possibly spare to help the defenders who are in the front lines. It is no more unneutral for us to do that than it is for Sweden, Russia and other nations near Germany, to send steel and ore and oil and other war materials into Germany every day in the week.

We are planning our own defense with the utmost urgency; and in its vast scale we must integrate the war needs of Britain and the other free nations which are resisting aggression.

This is not a matter of sentiment or of controversial personal opinion. It is a matter of realistic, practical military policy, based on the advice of our military experts who are in close touch with existing warfare. These military and naval experts and the members of the Congress and the Administration have a single-minded purpose—the defense of the United States.

This nation is making a great effort to produce everything that is necessary in this emergency—and with all possible speed. This great effort requires great sacrifice.

I would ask no one to defend a democracy which in turn would not defend everyone in the nation against want and privation. The strength of this nation shall not be diluted by the failure of the Government to protect the economic well-being of its citizens.

If our capacity to produce is limited by machines, it must ever be remembered that these machines are operated by the skill and the stamina of the workers. As the Government is determined to protect the rights of the workers, so the nation has a right to expect that the men who man the machines will discharge their full responsibilities to the urgent needs of defense.

The worker possesses the same human dignity and is entitled to the same security of position as the engineer or the manager or the owner. For the workers provide the human power that turns out the destroyers, the airplanes and the tanks.

The nation expects our defense industries to continue operation without interruption by strikes or lock-outs. It expects and insists that management and workers will reconcile their differences by voluntary or legal means, to continue to produce the supplies that are so sorely needed.

And on the economic side of our great defense program, we are, as you know, bending every effort to maintain stability of prices and with that the stability of the cost of living.

Nine days ago I announced the setting up of a more effective organization to direct our gigantic efforts to increase the production of munitions. The appropriation of vast sums of money and a well coordinated executive direction of our defense efforts are not in themselves enough. Guns, planes, ships and many other things have to be built in the factories and arsenals of America. They have to be produced by workers and managers and engineers with the aid of machines which in turn have to be built by hundreds of thousands of workers throughout the land.

In this great work there has been splendid cooperation between the Government and industry and labor; and I am very thankful.

American industrial genius, unmatched throughout the world in the solution of production problems, has been called upon to bring its resources and its talents into action. Manufacturers of watches, farm implements, linotypes, cash registers, automobiles, sewing machines, lawn mowers and locomotives are now making fuses, bomb packing crates, telescope mounts, shells, pistols and tanks.

But all our present efforts are not enough. We must have more ships, more guns, more planes—more of everything. This can only be accomplished if we discard the notion of "business as usual." This job cannot be done merely by superimposing on the existing productive facilities the added requirements of the nation for defense.

Our defense efforts must not be blocked by those who fear the future consequences of surplus plant capacity. The possible consequences of failure of our defense efforts now are much more to be feared.

After the present needs of our defenses are past, a proper

handling of the country's peace-time needs will require all the new productive capacity—if not more.

No pessimistic policy about the future of America shall delay the immediate expansion of those industries essential to defense. We need them.

I want to make it clear that it is the purpose of the nation to build now with all possible speed every machine, every arsenal, every factory that we need to manufacture our defense material. We have the men—the skill—the wealth—and above all, the will.

I am confident that if and when production of consumer or luxury goods in certain industries requires the use of machines and raw materials that are essential for defense purposes, then such production must yield, and will gladly yield, to our primary and compelling purpose.

I appeal to the owners of plants—to the managers—to the workers—to our own Government employees—to put every ounce of effort into producing these munitions swiftly and without stint. With this appeal I give you the pledge that all of us who are officers of your Government will devote ourselves to the same whole-hearted extent to the great task that lies ahead.

As planes and ships and guns and shells are produced, your Government, with its defense experts, can then determine how best to use them to defend this hemisphere. The decision as to how much shall be sent abroad and how much shall remain at home must be made on the basis of our over-all military necessities.

We must be the great arsenal of democracy. For us this is an emergency as serious as war itself. We must apply ourselves to our task with the same resolution, the same sense of urgency, the same spirit of patriotism and sacrifice as we would show were we at war.

We have furnished the British great material support and we will furnish far more in the future.

There will be no "bottlenecks" in our determination to aid Great Britain. No dictator, no combination of dictators, will weaken that determination by threats of how they will construe that determination.

The British have received invaluable military support from the heroic Greek army, and from the forces of all the governments in exile. Their strength is growing. It is the strength of men and women who value their freedom more highly than they value their lives.

I believe that the Axis powers are not going to win this war. I base that belief on the latest and best information.

We have no excuse for defeatism. We have every good reason for hope—hope for peace, hope for the defense of our civilization and for the building of a better civilization in the future.

I have the profound conviction that the American people are now determined to put forth a mightier effort than they have ever yet made to increase our production of all the implements of defense, to meet the threat to our democratic faith.

As President of the United States I call for that national effort. I call for it in the name of this nation which we love and honor and which we are privileged and proud to serve. I call upon our people with absolute confidence that our common cause will greatly succeed.

FRANKLIN D. ROOSEVELT

Eighth Annual Address to Congress

Washington, D.C., January 6, 1941

Mr. President, Mr. Speaker, Members of the Seventy-seventh Congress:

I address you, the Members of the Seventy-seventh Congress, at a moment unprecedented in the history of the Union. I use the word "unprecedented," because at no previous time has American security been as seriously threatened from without as it is today.

Since the permanent formation of our Government under the Constitution, in 1789, most of the periods of crisis in our history have related to our domestic affairs. Fortunately, only one of these—the four-year War Between the States—ever threatened our national unity. Today, thank God, one hundred and thirty million Americans, in forty-eight States, have forgotten points of the compass in our national unity.

It is true that prior to 1914 the United States often had been disturbed by events in other Continents. We had even engaged in two wars with European nations and in a number of undeclared wars in the West Indies, in the Mediterranean and in the Pacific for the maintenance of American rights and for the principles of peaceful commerce. But in no case had a serious threat been raised against our national safety or our continued independence.

What I seek to convey is the historic truth that the United States as a nation has at all times maintained clear, definite opposition, to any attempt to lock us in behind an ancient Chinese wall while the procession of civilization went past. Today, thinking of our children and of their children, we oppose enforced isolation for ourselves or for any other part of the Americas.

That determination of ours, extending over all these years,

was proved, for example, during the quarter century of wars following the French Revolution.

While the Napoleonic struggles did threaten interests of the United States because of the French foothold in the West Indies and in Louisiana, and while we engaged in the War of 1812 to vindicate our right to peaceful trade, it is nevertheless clear that neither France nor Great Britain, nor any other nation, was aiming at domination of the whole world.

In like fashion from 1815 to 1914—ninety-nine years—no single war in Europe or in Asia constituted a real threat against our future or against the future of any other American nation.

Except in the Maximilian interlude in Mexico, no foreign power sought to establish itself in this Hemisphere; and the strength of the British fleet in the Atlantic has been a friendly strength. It is still a friendly strength.

Even when the World War broke out in 1914, it seemed to contain only small threat of danger to our own American future. But, as time went on, the American people began to visualize what the downfall of democratic nations might mean to our own democracy.

We need not overemphasize imperfections in the Peace of Versailles. We need not harp on failure of the democracies to deal with problems of world reconstruction. We should remember that the Peace of 1919 was far less unjust than the kind of "pacification" which began even before Munich, and which is being carried on under the new order of tyranny that seeks to spread over every continent today. The American people have unalterably set their faces against that tyranny.

Every realist knows that the democratic way of life is at this moment being directly assailed in every part of the world—assailed either by arms, or by secret spreading of poisonous propaganda by those who seek to destroy unity and promote discord in nations that are still at peace.

During sixteen long months this assault has blotted out the whole pattern of democratic life in an appalling number of independent nations, great and small. The assailants are still on the march, threatening other nations, great and small.

Therefore, as your President, performing my constitutional duty to "give to the Congress information of the state of the Union," I find it, unhappily, necessary to report that the future and the safety of our country and of our democracy are overwhelmingly involved in events far beyond our borders.

Armed defense of democratic existence is now being gallantly waged in four continents. If that defense fails, all the population and all the resources of Europe, Asia, Africa and Australasia will be dominated by the conquerors. Let us remember that the total of those populations and their resources in those four continents greatly exceeds the sum total of the population and the resources of the whole of the Western Hemisphere—many times over.

In times like these it is immature—and incidentally, untrue —for anybody to brag that an unprepared America, singlehanded, and with one hand tied behind its back, can hold off the whole world.

No realistic American can expect from a dictator's peace international generosity, or return of true independence, or world disarmament, or freedom of expression, or freedom of religion—or even good business.

Such a peace would bring no security for us or for our neighbors. "Those, who would give up essential liberty to purchase a little temporary safety, deserve neither liberty nor safety."

As a nation, we may take pride in the fact that we are softhearted; but we cannot afford to be soft-headed.

We must always be wary of those who with sounding brass and a tinkling cymbal preach the "ism" of appeasement.

We must especially beware of that small group of selfish men who would clip the wings of the American eagle in order to feather their own nests.

I have recently pointed out how quickly the tempo of modern warfare could bring into our very midst the physical attack which we must eventually expect if the dictator nations win this war.

There is much loose talk of our immunity from immediate and direct invasion from across the seas. Obviously, as long as the British Navy retains its power, no such danger exists. Even if there were no British Navy, it is not probable that any enemy would be stupid enough to attack us by landing troops in the United States from across thousands of miles of ocean, until it had acquired strategic bases from which to operate.

But we learn much from the lessons of the past years in Europe—particularly the lesson of Norway, whose essential seaports were captured by treachery and surprise built up over a series of years.

The first phase of the invasion of this Hemisphere would not be the landing of regular troops. The necessary strategic points would be occupied by secret agents and their dupes—and great numbers of them are already here, and in Latin America.

As long as the aggressor nations maintain the offensive, they—not we—will choose the time and the place and the method of their attack.

That is why the future of all the American Republics is today in serious danger.

That is why this Annual Message to the Congress is unique in our history.

That is why every member of the Executive Branch of the Government and every member of the Congress faces great responsibility and great accountability.

The need of the moment is that our actions and our policy should be devoted primarily—almost exclusively—to meeting this foreign peril. For all our domestic problems are now a part of the great emergency.

Just as our national policy in internal affairs has been based upon a decent respect for the rights and the dignity of all our fellow men within our gates, so our national policy in foreign affairs has been based on a decent respect for the rights and dignity of all nations, large and small. And the justice of morality must and will win in the end.

Our national policy is this:

First, by an impressive expression of the public will and without regard to partisanship, we are committed to all-inclusive national defense.

Second, by an impressive expression of the public will and without regard to partisanship, we are committed to full support of all those resolute peoples, everywhere, who are resisting aggression and are thereby keeping war away from our Hemisphere. By this support, we express our determination that the democratic cause shall prevail; and we strengthen the defense and the security of our own nation.

Third, by an impressive expression of the public will and without regard to partisanship, we are committed to the proposition that principles of morality and considerations for our own security will never permit us to acquiesce in a peace dictated by aggressors and sponsored by appeasers. We know that enduring peace cannot be bought at the cost of other people's freedom.

In the recent national election there was no substantial difference between the two great parties in respect to that national policy. No issue was fought out on this line before the American electorate. Today it is abundantly evident that American citizens everywhere are demanding and supporting speedy and complete action in recognition of obvious danger.

Therefore, the immediate need is a swift and driving increase in our armament production.

Leaders of industry and labor have responded to our summons. Goals of speed have been set. In some cases these goals are being reached ahead of time; in some cases we are on schedule; in other cases there are slight but not serious delays; and in some cases—and I am sorry to say very important cases—we are all concerned by the slowness of the accomplishment of our plans.

The Army and Navy, however, have made substantial progress during the past year. Actual experience is improving and speeding up our methods of production with every passing day. And today's best is not good enough for tomorrow.

I am not satisfied with the progress thus far made. The men in charge of the program represent the best in training, in ability, and in patriotism. They are not satisfied with the progress thus far made. None of us will be satisfied until the job is done.

No matter whether the original goal was set too high or too low, our objective is quicker and better results.

To give you two illustrations:

We are behind schedule in turning out finished airplanes; we are working day and night to solve the innumerable problems and to catch up.

We are ahead of schedule in building warships but we are working to get even further ahead of that schedule.

To change a whole nation from a basis of peacetime production of implements of peace to a basis of wartime production of implements of war is no small task. And the greatest difficulty comes at the beginning of the program, when new tools, new plant facilities, new assembly lines, and new ship ways must first be constructed before the actual matériel begins to flow steadily and speedily from them.

The Congress, of course, must rightly keep itself informed at all times of the progress of the program. However, there is certain information, as the Congress itself will readily recognize, which, in the interests of our own security and those of the nations that we are supporting, must of needs be kept in confidence.

New circumstances are constantly begetting new needs for our safety. I shall ask this Congress for greatly increased new appropriations and authorizations to carry on what we have begun.

I also ask this Congress for authority and for funds sufficient to manufacture additional munitions and war supplies of many kinds, to be turned over to those nations which are now in actual war with aggressor nations.

Our most useful and immediate role is to act as an arsenal for them as well as for ourselves. They do not need man power, but they do need billions of dollars worth of the weapons of defense.

The time is near when they will not be able to pay for them all in ready cash. We cannot, and we will not, tell them that they must surrender, merely because of present inability to pay for the weapons which we know they must have.

I do not recommend that we make them a loan of dollars with which to pay for these weapons—a loan to be repaid in dollars.

I recommend that we make it possible for those nations to continue to obtain war materials in the United States, fitting their orders into our own program. Nearly all their matériel would, if the time ever came, be useful for our own defense.

Taking counsel of expert military and naval authorities, considering what is best for our own security, we are free to decide how much should be kept here and how much should be sent abroad to our friends who by their determined and heroic resistance are giving us time in which to make ready our own defense.

For what we send abroad, we shall be repaid within a reasonable time following the close of hostilities, in similar materials, or, at our option, in other goods of many kinds, which they can produce and which we need.

Let us say to the democracies: "We Americans are vitally concerned in your defense of freedom. We are putting forth our energies, our resources and our organizing powers to give you the strength to regain and maintain a free world. We shall send you, in ever-increasing numbers, ships, planes, tanks, guns. This is our purpose and our pledge."

In fulfillment of this purpose we will not be intimidated by the threats of dictators that they will regard as a breach of international law or as an act of war our aid to the democracies which dare to resist their aggression. Such aid is not an act of war, even if a dictator should unilaterally proclaim it so to be.

When the dictators, if the dictators, are ready to make war upon us, they will not wait for an act of war on our part. They did not wait for Norway or Belgium or the Netherlands to commit an act of war.

Their only interest is in a new one-way international law, which lacks mutuality in its observance, and, therefore, becomes an instrument of oppression.

The happiness of future generations of Americans may well depend upon how effective and how immediate we can make our aid felt. No one can tell the exact character of the emergency situations that we may be called upon to meet. The Nation's hands must not be tied when the Nation's life is in danger.

We must all prepare to make the sacrifices that the emergency—almost as serious as war itself—demands. Whatever stands in the way of speed and efficiency in defense preparations must give way to the national need.

A free nation has the right to expect full cooperation from all groups. A free nation has the right to look to the leaders of business, of labor, and of agriculture to take the lead in stimulating effort, not among other groups but within their own groups.

The best way of dealing with the few slackers or trouble makers in our midst is, first, to shame them by patriotic example, and, if that fails, to use the sovereignty of Government to save Government.

As men do not live by bread alone, they do not fight by armaments alone. Those who man our defenses, and those behind them who build our defenses, must have the stamina and the courage which come from unshakable belief in the manner of life which they are defending. The mighty action that we are calling for cannot be based on a disregard of all things worth fighting for.

The Nation takes great satisfaction and much strength from the things which have been done to make its people conscious of their individual stake in the preservation of democratic life in America. Those things have toughened the fibre of our people, have renewed their faith and strengthened their devotion to the institutions we make ready to protect.

Certainly this is no time for any of us to stop thinking about the social and economic problems which are the root cause of the social revolution which is today a supreme factor in the world.

For there is nothing mysterious about the foundations of a healthy and strong democracy. The basic things expected by our people of their political and economic systems are simple. They are:

Equality of opportunity for youth and for others.

Jobs for those who can work.

Security for those who need it.

The ending of special privilege for the few.

The preservation of civil liberties for all.

The enjoyment of the fruits of scientific progress in a wider and constantly rising standard of living.

These are the simple, basic things that must never be lost sight of in the turmoil and unbelievable complexity of our modern world. The inner and abiding strength of our economic and political systems is dependent upon the degree to which they fulfill these expectations.

Many subjects connected with our social economy call for immediate improvement.

As examples:

We should bring more citizens under the coverage of old-age pensions and unemployment insurance.

We should widen the opportunities for adequate medical care.

We should plan a better system by which persons deserving or needing gainful employment may obtain it.

I have called for personal sacrifice. I am assured of the willingness of almost all Americans to respond to that call.

A part of the sacrifice means the payment of more money in taxes. In my Budget Message I shall recommend that a greater portion of this great defense program be paid for from taxation than we are paying today. No person should try, or be allowed, to get rich out of this program; and the principle of tax payments in accordance with ability to pay should be constantly before our eyes to guide our legislation.

If the Congress maintains these principles, the voters, putting patriotism ahead of pocketbooks, will give you their applause.

In the future days, which we seek to make secure, we look forward to a world founded upon four essential human freedoms.

The first is freedom of speech and expression— everywhere in the world.

The second is freedom of every person to worship God in his own way—everywhere in the world.

The third is freedom from want—which, translated into world terms, means economic understandings which will secure to every nation a healthy peacetime life for its inhabitants— everywhere in the world.

The fourth is freedom from fear—which, translated into world terms, means a world-wide reduction of armaments to such a point and in such a thorough fashion that no nation will be in a position to commit an act of physical aggression against any neighbor—anywhere in the world.

That is no vision of a distant millennium. It is a definite basis for a kind of world attainable in our own time and generation. That kind of world is the very antithesis of the so-called new order of tyranny which the dictators seek to create with the crash of a bomb.

To that new order we oppose the greater conception—the moral order. A good society is able to face schemes of world domination and foreign revolutions alike without fear.

Since the beginning of our American history, we have been engaged in change—in a perpetual peaceful revolution—a revolution which goes on steadily, quietly adjusting itself to changing conditions—without the concentration camp or the quick-lime in the ditch. The world order which we seek is the cooperation of free countries, working together in a friendly, civilized society.

This nation has placed its destiny in the hands and heads and hearts of its millions of free men and women; and its faith in freedom under the guidance of God. Freedom means the supremacy of human rights everywhere. Our support goes to those who struggle to gain those rights or keep them. Our strength is our unity of purpose.

To that high concept there can be no end save victory.

FRANKLIN D. ROOSEVELT

Address to Congress on War with Japan

Washington, D.C., December 8, 1941

M R. VICE PRESIDENT, AND MR. SPEAKER, AND MEMBERS OF THE SENATE AND HOUSE OF REPRESENTATIVES:
Yesterday, December 7, 1941—a date which will live in infamy— the United States of America was suddenly and deliberately attacked by naval and air forces of the Empire of Japan.

The United States was at peace with that Nation and, at the solicitation of Japan, was still in conversation with its Government and its Emperor looking toward the maintenance of peace in the Pacific. Indeed, one hour after Japanese air squadrons had commenced bombing in the American Island of Oahu, the Japanese Ambassador to the United States and his colleague delivered to our Secretary of State a formal reply to a recent American message. And while this reply stated that it seemed useless to continue the existing diplomatic negotiations, it contained no threat or hint of war or of armed attack.

It will be recorded that the distance of Hawaii from Japan makes it obvious that the attack was deliberately planned many days or even weeks ago. During the intervening time the Japanese Government has deliberately sought to deceive the United States by false statements and expressions of hope for continued peace.

The attack yesterday on the Hawaiian Islands has caused severe damage to American naval and military forces. I regret to tell you that very many American lives have been lost. In addition American ships have been reported torpedoed on the high seas between San Francisco and Honolulu.

Yesterday the Japanese Government also launched an attack against Malaya.

Last night Japanese forces attacked Hong Kong.

Last night Japanese forces attacked Guam.

Last night Japanese forces attacked the Philippine Islands.

Last night the Japanese attacked Wake Island.

And this morning the Japanese attacked Midway Island.

Japan has, therefore, undertaken a surprise offensive extending throughout the Pacific area. The facts of yesterday and to-day speak for themselves. The people of the United States have already formed their opinions and well understand the implications to the very life and safety of our Nation.

As Commander in Chief of the Army and Navy I have directed that all measures be taken for our defense.

But always will our whole Nation remember the character of the onslaught against us.

No matter how long it may take us to overcome this premeditated invasion, the American people in their righteous might will win through to absolute victory.

I believe that I interpret the will of the Congress and of the people when I assert that we will not only defend ourselves to the uttermost but will make it very certain that this form of treachery shall never again endanger us.

Hostilities exist. There is no blinking at the fact that our people, our territory, and our interests are in grave danger.

With confidence in our armed forces—with the unbounding determination of our people—we will gain the inevitable triumph—so help us God.

I ask that the Congress declare that since the unprovoked and dastardly attack by Japan on Sunday, December 7, 1941, a state of war has existed between the United States and the Japanese Empire.

GEORGE S. PATTON

Speech to Third Army Troops

England, Spring 1944

B E SEATED.
 Men, this stuff we hear about America wanting to stay out of the war, not wanting to fight, is a lot of bullshit. Americans love to fight—traditionally. All real Americans love the sting and clash of battle. When you were kids, you all admired the champion marble player; the fastest runner; the big league ball players; the toughest boxers. Americans love a winner and will not tolerate a loser. Americans despise cowards. Americans play to win—all the time. I wouldn't give a hoot in hell for a man who lost and laughed. That's why Americans have never lost, not ever will lose a war, for the very thought of losing is hateful to an American.

You are not all going to die. Only two percent of you here today would die in a major battle. Death must not be feared. Every man is frightened at first in battle. If he says he isn't, he's a goddamn liar. Some men are cowards, yes! But they fight just the same, or get the hell shamed out of them watching men who do fight who are just as scared. The real hero is the man who fights even though he is scared. Some get over their fright in a minute under fire, some take an hour. For some it takes days. But the real man never lets fear of death overpower his honor, his sense of duty to this country and his innate manhood.

All through your army career you men have bitched about "This chickenshit drilling." That is all for a purpose. Drilling and discipline must be maintained in any army if for only one reason—INSTANT OBEDIENCE TO ORDERS AND TO CREATE CONSTANT ALERTNESS. I don't give a damn for a man who is not always on his toes. You men are veterans or you wouldn't be here. You are ready. A man to continue breathing must be alert at all times. If not, sometime a German son-of-a-bitch will sneak up behind him and beat him to death with a sock full of shit.

There are 400 neatly marked graves somewhere in Sicily all because one man went to sleep on his job—but they were German graves for we caught the bastard asleep before his officers did. An Army is a team. Lives, sleeps, eats, fights as a team. This individual heroic stuff is a lot of crap. The bilious bastards who wrote that kind of stuff for the *Saturday Evening Post* don't know any more about real fighting, under fire, than they do about fucking. We have the best food, the finest equipment, the best spirit and the best fighting men in the world. Why, by God, I actually pity these poor sons-of-bitches we are going up against. By God, I do!

My men don't surrender. I don't want to hear of any soldier under my command being captured unless he is hit. Even if you are hit, you can still fight. That's not just bullshit, either. The kind of man I want under me is like the lieutenant in Libya, who, with a Lugar against his chest, jerked off his helmet, swept the gun aside with one hand and busted hell out of the Boche with the helmet. Then he jumped on the gun and went out and killed another German: All this with a bullet through his lung. That's a man for you.

All real heroes are not story book combat fighters either. Every man in the army plays a vital part. Every little job is essential. Don't ever let down, thinking your role is unimportant. Every man has a job to do. Every man is a link in the great chain. What if every truck driver decided that he didn't like the whine of the shells overhead, turned yellow and jumped headlong into the ditch? He could say to himself, "They won't miss me—just one in thousands." What if every man said that? Where in hell would we be now? No, thank God, Americans don't say that! Every man does his job; every man serves the whole. Every department, every unit, is important to the vast scheme of things. The Ordnance men are needed to supply the guns, the Quartermaster to bring up the food and clothes to us—for where we're going there isn't a hell of a lot to steal. Every last man in the mess hall, even the one who heats the water to keep us from getting the GI shits has a job to do. Even the chaplain is important, for if we get killed and if he is not there to bury us we'd all go to hell.

Each man must not only think of himself, but of his buddy fighting beside him. We don't want yellow cowards in this army. They should all be killed off like flies. If not they will go back home after the war and breed more cowards. The brave men will breed brave men. Kill off the goddamn cowards and we'll have a nation of brave men.

One of the bravest men I ever saw in the African campaign was the fellow I saw on top of a telegraph pole in the midst of furious fire while we were plowing toward Tunis. I stopped and asked what the hell he was doing up there at that time. He answered, "Fixing the wire, sir." "Isn't it a little unhealthy right now?," I asked. "Yes sir, but this goddamn wire's got to be fixed." There was a real soldier. There was a man who devoted all he had to his duty, no matter how great the odds, no matter how seemingly insignificant his duty might appear at the time.

You should have seen those trucks on the road to Gabes. The drivers were magnificent. All day and all night they rolled over those son-of-a-bitching roads, never stopping, never faltering from their course, with shells bursting around them all the time. We got through on good old American guts. Many of these men drove over forty consecutive hours. These weren't combat men. But they were soldiers with a job to do. They did it—and in a whale of a way they did it. They were part of a team. Without them the fight would have been lost. All the links in the chain pulled together and that chain became unbreakable.

Don't forget, you don't know I'm here. No word of the fact is to be mentioned in any letters. The world is not supposed to know what the hell became of me. I'm not supposed to be commanding this Army. I'm not even supposed to be in England. Let the first bastards to find out be the goddamn Germans. Someday I want them to raise up on their hind legs and howl, "Jesus Christ, it's the goddamn Third Army and that son-of-a-bitch Patton again."

We want to get the hell over there. We want to get over there and clear the goddamn thing up. You can't win a war lying down. The quicker we clean up this goddamn mess, the quicker we can take a jaunt against the purple pissing Japs and clean their nest out too, before the Marines get all the goddamn credit.

Sure, we all want to be home. We want this thing over with. The quickest way to get it over is to get the bastards. The quicker they are whipped, the quicker we go home. The shortest way home is through Berlin. When a man is lying in a shell hole, if he just stays there all day, a Boche will get him eventually, and the hell with that idea. The hell with taking it. My men don't dig foxholes. I don't want them to. Foxholes only slow up an offensive. Keep moving. And don't give the enemy time to dig one. We'll win this war but we'll win it only by fighting and by showing the Germans we've got more guts than they have.

There is one great thing you men will all be able to say when you go home. You may thank God for it. Thank God, that at least, thirty years from now, when you are sitting around the fireside with your grandson on your knees, and he asks you what you did in the great war, you won't have to cough and say, "I shoveled shit in Louisiana."

DWIGHT D. EISENHOWER

Address to the Allied Expeditionary Forces

England, June 6, 1944

SOLDIERS, SAILORS, AND AIRMEN OF THE ALLIED EXPEDITIONARY FORCES!: You are about to embark upon the Great Crusade, toward which we have striven these many months. The eyes of the world are upon you. The hopes and prayers of liberty-loving people everywhere march with you. In company with our brave Allies and brothers-in-arms on other Fronts you will bring about the destruction of the German war machine, the elimination of Nazi tyranny over oppressed peoples of Europe, and security for ourselves in a free world.

Your task will not be an easy one. Your enemy is well trained, well equipped and battle-hardened. He will fight savagely.

But this is the year 1944! Much has happened since the Nazi triumphs of 1940–41. The United Nations have inflicted upon the Germans great defeats, in open battle, man-to man. Our air offensive has seriously reduced their strength in the air and their capacity to wage war on the ground. Our Home Fronts have given us an overwhelming superiority in weapons and munitions of war, and placed at our disposal great reserves of trained fighting men. The tide has turned! The free men of the world are marching together to Victory!

I have full confidence in your courage, devotion to duty and skill in battle. We will accept nothing less than full victory!

Good Luck! And let us all beseech the blessing of Almighty God upon this great and noble undertaking.

HARRY S. TRUMAN

Statement on the Atomic Bomb

Washington, D.C., August 6, 1945

SIXTEEN HOURS AGO an American airplane dropped one bomb on Hiroshima, an important Japanese Army base. That bomb had more power than 20,000 tons of T.N.T. It had more than two thousand times the blast power of the British "Grand Slam" which is the largest bomb ever yet used in the history of warfare.

The Japanese began the war from the air at Pearl Harbor. They have been repaid many fold. And the end is not yet. With this bomb we have now added a new and revolutionary increase in destruction to supplement the growing power of our armed forces. In their present form these bombs are now in production and even more powerful forms are in development.

It is an atomic bomb. It is a harnessing of the basic power of the universe. The force from which the sun draws its power has been loosed against those who brought war to the Far East.

Before 1939, it was the accepted belief of scientists that it was theoretically possible to release atomic energy. But no one knew any practical method of doing it. By 1942, however, we knew that the Germans were working feverishly to find a way to add atomic energy to the other engines of war with which they hoped to enslave the world. But they failed. We may be grateful to Providence that the Germans got the V-1's and V-2's late and in limited quantities and even more grateful that they did not get the atomic bomb at all.

The battle of the laboratories held fateful risks for us as well as the battles of the air, land and sea, and we have now won the battle of the laboratories as we have won the other battles.

Beginning in 1940, before Pearl Harbor, scientific knowledge useful in war was pooled between the United States and Great Britain, and many priceless helps to our victories have come from that arrangement. Under that general policy the research on the atomic bomb was begun. With American and British scientists working together we entered the race of discovery against the Germans.

The United States had available the large number of scientists of distinction in the many needed areas of knowledge. It had the tremendous industrial and financial resources necessary for the project and they could be devoted to it without undue impairment of other vital war work. In the United States substantial new work and the production plants, on which a ~~~~~~~~~~~~~~~ly been made, would be out of reach of enemy bombing, while at that time Britain was exposed to constant air attack and was still threatened with the possibility of invasion. For these reasons Prime Minister Churchill and President Roosevelt agreed that it was wise to carry on the project here. We now have two great plants and many lesser works devoted to the production of atomic power. Employment during peak construction numbered 125,000 and over 65,000 individuals are even now engaged in operating the plants. Many have worked there for two and a half years. Few know what they have been producing. They see great quantities of material going in and they see nothing coming out of these plants, for the physical size of the explosive charge is exceedingly small. We have spent two billion dollars on the greatest scientific gamble in history—and won.

But the greatest marvel is not the size of the enterprise, its secrecy, nor its cost, but the achievement of scientific brains in putting together infinitely complex pieces of knowledge held by many men in different fields of science into a workable plan. And hardly less marvelous has been the capacity of industry to design, and of labor to operate, the machines and methods to do things never done before so that the brain child of many minds came forth in physical shape and performed as it was supposed to do. Both science and industry worked under the direction of the United States Army, which achieved a unique success in managing so diverse a problem in the advancement of knowledge in an amazingly short time. It is doubtful if such another combination could be got together in the world. What has been done is the greatest achievement of organized science in history. It was done under high pressure and without failure.

We are now prepared to obliterate more rapidly and completely every productive enterprise the Japanese have above ground in any city. We shall destroy their docks, their factories, and their communications. Let there be no mistake; we shall completely destroy Japan's power to make war.

It was to spare the Japanese people from utter destruction that the ultimatum of July 26 was issued at Potsdam. Their leaders promptly rejected that ultimatum. If they do not now accept our terms they may expect a rain of ruin from the air, the like of which has never been seen on this earth. Behind this air attack will folow sea and land forces in such numbers and power as they have not yet seen and with the fighting skill of which they are already well aware.

The Secretary of War, who has kept in personal touch with all phases of the project, will immediately make public a statement giving further details.

His statement will give facts concerning the sites at Oak Ridge near Knoxville, Tennessee, and at Richland near Pasco, Washington, and an installation near Santa Fe, New Mexico. Although the workers at the sites have been making materials to be used in producing the greatest destructive force in history they have not themselves been in danger beyond that of many other occupations, for the utmost care has been taken of their safety.

The fact that we can release atomic energy ushers in a new era in man's understanding of nature's forces. Atomic energy may in the future supplement the power that now comes from coal, oil, and falling water, but at present it cannot be produced on a basis to compete with them commercially. Before that comes there must be a long period of intensive research.

It has never been the habit of the scientists of this country or the policy of this Government to withhold from the world scientific knowledge. Normally, therefore, everything about the work with atomic energy would be made public.

But under present circumstances it is not intended to divulge the technical processes of production or all the military applications, pending further examination of possible methods of protecting us and the rest of the world from the danger of sudden destruction.

I shall recommend that the Congress of the United States

consider promptly the establishment of an appropriate commission to control the production and use of atomic power
within the United States. I shall give further consideration and
make further recommendations to the Congress as to how
atomic power can become a powerful and forceful influence
towards the maintenance of world peace.

J. ROBERT OPPENHEIMER

Speech to Los Alamos Scientists

Los Alamos, N.M., November 2, 1945

I AM GRATEFUL to the Executive Committee for this chance to talk to you. I should like to talk tonight—if some of you have long memories perhaps you will regard it as justified—as a fellow scientist, and at least as a fellow worrier about the fix we are in. I do not have anything very radical to say, or anything that will strike most of you with a great flash of enlightenment. I don't have anything to say that will be of an immense encouragement. In some ways I would have liked to talk to you at an earlier date—but I couldn't talk to you as a Director. I could not talk, and will not tonight talk, too much about the practical political problems which are involved. There is one good reason for that—I don't know very much about practical politics. And there is another reason, which has to some extent restrained me in the past. As you know, some of us have been asked to be technical advisors to the Secretary of War, and through him to the President. In the course of this we have naturally discussed things that were on our minds and have been made, often very willingly, the recipient of confidences; it is not possible to speak in detail about what Mr. A thinks and Mr. B doesn't think, or what is going to happen next week, without violating these confidences. I don't think that's important. I think there are issues which are quite simple and quite deep, and which involve us as a group of scientists—involve us more, perhaps than any other group in the world. I think that it can only help to look a little at what our situation is—at what has happened to us—and that this must give us some honesty, some insight, which will be a source of strength in what may be the not-too-easy days ahead. I would like to take it as deep and serious as I know how, and then perhaps come to more immediate questions in the course of the discussion later. I want anyone who feels like it to ask me a question

458

and if I can't answer it, as will often be the case, I will just have to say so.

What has happened to us—it is really rather major, it is so major that I think in some ways one returns to the greatest developments of the twentieth century, to the discovery of relativity, and to the whole development of atomic theory and its interpretation in terms of complementarity, for analogy. These things, as you know, forced us to re-consider the relations between science and common sense. They forced on us the recognition that the fact that we were in the habit of talking a certain language and using certain concepts did not necessarily imply that there was anything in the real world to correspond to these. They forced us to be prepared for the inadequacy of the ways in which human beings attempted to deal with reality, for that reality. In some ways I think these virtues, which scientists quite reluctantly were forced to learn by the nature of the world they were studying, may be useful even today in preparing us for somewhat more radical views of what the issues are than would be natural or easy for people who had not been through this experience.

But the real impact of the creation of the atomic bomb and atomic weapons—to understand that one has to look further back, look, I think, to the times when physical science was growing in the days of the renaissance, and when the threat that science offered was felt so deeply throughout the Christian world. The analogy is, of course, not perfect. You may even wish to think of the days in the last century when the theories of evolution seemed a threat to the values by which men lived. The analogy is not perfect because there is nothing in atomic weapons—there is certainly nothing that we have done here or in the physics or chemistry that immediately preceded our work here—in which any revolutionary ideas were involved. I don't think that the conceptions of nuclear fission have strained any man's attempts to understand them, and I don't feel that any of us have really learned in a deep sense very much from following this up. It is in a quite different way. It is not an idea—it is a development and a reality—but it has in common with the early days of physical science the fact that the very existence of science is threatened, and its value is threatened. This is the point that I would like to speak a little about.

I think that it hardly needs to be said why the impact is so strong. There are three reasons: one is the extraordinary speed with which things which were right on the frontier of science were translated into terms where they affected many living people, and potentially all people. Another is the fact, quite accidental in many ways, and connected with the speed, that scientists themselves played such a large part, not merely in providing the foundation for atomic weapons, but in actually making them. In this we are certainly closer to it than any other group. The third is that the thing we made—partly because of the technical nature of the problem, partly because we worked hard, partly because we had good breaks—really arrived in the world with such a shattering reality and suddenness that there was no opportunity for the edges to be worn off.

In considering what the situation of science is, it may be helpful to think a little of what people said and felt of their motives in coming into this job. One always has to worry that what people say of their motives is not adequate. Many people said different things, and most of them, I think, had some validity. There was in the first place the great concern that our enemy might develop these weapons before we did, and the feeling—at least, in the early days, the very strong feeling—that without atomic weapons it might be very difficult, it might be an impossible, it might be an incredibly long thing to win the war. These things wore off a little as it became clear that the war would be won in any case. Some people, I think, were motivated by curiosity, and rightly so; and some by a sense of adventure, and rightly so. Others had more political arguments and said, "Well, we know that atomic weapons are in principle possible, and it is not right that the threat of their unrealized possibility should hang over the world. It is right that the world should know what can be done in their field and deal with it." And the people added to that that it was a time when all over the world men would be particularly ripe and open for dealing with this problem because of the immediacy of the evils of war, because of the universal cry from everyone that one could not go through this thing again, even a war without atomic bombs. And there was finally, and I think rightly, the feeling that there was probably no place in the world where the development of atomic weapons would have a better chance of leading to a reasonable solution, and a smaller chance of leading to disaster, than within the United States. I believe all these things that people said are true, and I think I said them all myself at one time or another.

But when you come right down to it the reason that we did this job is because it was an organic necessity. If you are a scientist you cannot stop such a thing. If you are a scientist you believe that it is good to find out how the world works; that it is good to find out what the realities are; that it is good to turn over to mankind at large the greatest possible power to control the world and to deal with it according to its lights and its values.

There has been a lot of talk about the evil of secrecy, of concealment, of control, of security. Some of that talk has been on a rather low plane, limited really to saying that it is difficult or inconvenient to work in a world where you are not free to do what you want. I think that the talk has been justified, and that the almost unanimous resistance of scientists to the imposition of control and secrecy is a justified position, but I think that the reason for it may lie a little deeper. I think that it comes from the fact that secrecy strikes at the very root of what science is, and what it is for. It is not possible to be a scientist unless you believe that it is good to learn. It is not good to be a scientist, and it is not possible, unless you think that it is of the highest value to share your knowledge, to share it with anyone who is interested. It is not possible to be a scientist unless you believe that the knowledge of the world, and the power which this gives, is a thing which is of intrinsic value to humanity, and that you are using it to help in the spread of knowledge, and are willing to take the consequences. And, therefore, I think that this resistance which we feel and see all around us to anything which is an attempt to treat science of the future as though it were rather a dangerous thing, a thing that must be watched and managed, is resisted not because of its inconvenience—I think we are in a position where we must be willing to take any inconvenience—but resisted because it is based on a philosophy incompatible with that by which we live, and have learned to live in the past.

There are many people who try to wiggle out of this. They say the real importance of atomic energy does not lie in the weapons that have been made; the real importance lies in all the great benefits which atomic energy, which the various radiations, will bring to mankind. There may be some truth in this. I am sure that there is truth in it, because there has never in the past been a new field opened up where the real fruits of it have not been invisible at the beginning. I have a very high confidence that the fruits—the so-called peacetime applications—of atomic energy will have in them all that we think, and more. There are others who try to escape the immediacy of this situation by saying that, after all, war has always been very terrible; after all, weapons have always gotten worse and worse; that this is just another weapon and it doesn't create a great change; that they are not so bad; bombings have been bad in this war and this is not a change in that—it just adds a little to the effectiveness of bombing; that some sort of protection will be found. I think that these efforts to diffuse and weaken the nature of the crisis make it only more dangerous. I think it is for us to accept it as a very grave crisis, to realize that these atomic weapons which we have started to make are very terrible, that they involve a change, that they are not just a slight modification: to accept this, and to accept with it the necessity for those transformations in the world which will make it possible to integrate these developments into human life.

As scientists I think we have perhaps a little greater ability to accept change, and accept radical change, because of our experiences in the pursuit of science. And that may help us—that, and the fact that we have lived with it—to be of some use in understanding these problems.

It is clear to me that wars have changed. It is clear to me that if these first bombs—the bomb that was dropped on Nagasaki —that if these can destroy ten square miles, then that is really quite something. It is clear to me that they are going to be very cheap if anyone wants to make them; it is clear to me that this is a situation where a quantitative change, and a change in which the advantage of aggression compared to defense—of attack compared to defense—is shifted, where this quantitative change has all the character of a change in quality, of a change in the nature of the world. I know that whereas wars have become intolerable, and the question would have been raised and would have been pursued after this war, more ardently

than after the last, of whether there was not some method by which they could be averted. But I think the advent of the atomic bomb and the facts which will get around that they are not too hard to make—that they will be universal if people wish to make them universal, that they will not constitute a real drain on the economy of any strong nation, and that their power of destruction will grow and is already incomparably greater than that of any other weapon—I think these things create a new situation, so new that there is some danger, even some danger in believing, that what we have is a new argument for arrangements, for hopes, that existed before this development took place. By that I mean that much as I like to hear advocates of a world federation, or advocates of a United Nations organization, who have been talking of these things for years— much as I like to hear them say that here is a new argument, I think that they are in part missing the point, because the point is not that atomic weapons constitute a new argument. There have always been good arguments. The point is that atomic weapons constitute also a field, a new field, and a new opportunity for realizing preconditions. I think when people talk of the fact that this is not only a great peril, but a great hope, this is what they should mean. I do not think they should mean the unknown, though sure, value of industrial and scientific virtues of atomic energy, but rather the simple fact that in this field, because it is a threat, because it is a peril, and because it has certain special characteristics, to which I will return, there exists a possibility of realizing, of beginning to realize, those changes which are needed if there is to be any peace.

Those are very far-reaching changes. They are changes in the relations between nations, not only in spirit, not only in law, but also in conception and feeling. I don't know which of these is prior; they must all work together, and only the gradual interaction of one on the other can make a reality. I don't agree with those who say the first step is to have a structure of international law. I don't agree with those who say the only thing is to have friendly feelings. All of these things will be involved. I think it is true to say that atomic weapons are a peril which affect everyone in the world, and in that sense a completely common problem, as common a problem as it was for the Allies to defeat the Nazis. I think that in order to handle

this common problem there must be a complete sense of community responsibility. I do not think that one may expect that people will contribute to the solution of the problem until they are aware of their ability to take part in the solution. I think that it is a field in which the implementation of such a common responsibility has certain decisive advantages. It is a new field, in which the position of vested interests in various parts of the world is very much less serious than in others. It is serious in this country, and that is one of our problems. It is a new field, in which the role of science has been so great that it is to my mind hardly thinkable that the international traditions of science, and the fraternity of scientists, should not play a constructive part. It is a new field, in which just the novelty and the special characteristics of the technical operations should enable one to establish a community of interest which might almost be regarded as a pilot plant for a new type of international collaboration. I speak of it as a pilot plant because it is quite clear that the control of atomic weapons cannot be in itself the unique end of such operation. The only unique end can be a world that is united, and a world in which war will not occur. But those things don't happen overnight, and in this field it would seem that one could get started, and get started without meeting those insuperable obstacles which history has so often placed in the way of any effort of cooperation. Now, this is not an easy thing, and the point I want to make, the one point I want to hammer home, is what an enormous change in spirit is involved. There are things which we hold very dear, and I think rightly hold very dear, I would say that the word democracy perhaps stood for some of them as well as any other word. There are many parts of the world in which there is no democracy. There are other things which we hold dear, and which we rightly should. And when I speak of a new spirit in international affairs I mean that even to these deepest of things which we cherish, and for which Americans have been willing to die—and certainly most of us would be willing to die—even in these deepest things, we realize that there is something more profound than that; namely, the common bond with other men everywhere. It is only if you do that that this makes sense; because if you approach the problem and say, "We know what is right and we would like to use the atomic bomb to persuade

you to agree with us," then you are in a very weak position and you will not succeed, because under those conditions you will not succeed in delegating responsibility for the survival of men. It is a purely unilateral statement; you will find yourselves attempting by force of arms to prevent a disaster.

I want to express the utmost sympathy with the people who have to grapple with this problem and in the strongest terms to urge you not to underestimate its difficulty. I can think of an analogy, and I hope it is not a completely good analogy: in the days in the first half of the nineteenth century there were many people, mostly in the North, but some in the South, who thought that there was no evil on earth more degrading than human slavery, and nothing that they would more willingly devote their lives to than its eradication. Always when I was young I wondered why it was that when Lincoln was President he did not declare that the war against the South, when it broke out, was a war that slavery should be abolished, that this was the central point, the rallying point, of that war. Lincoln was severely criticized by many of the Abolitionists as you know, by many then called radicals, because he seemed to be waging a war which did not hit the thing that was most important. But Lincoln realized, and I have only in the last months come to appreciate the depth and wisdom of it, that beyond the issue of slavery was the issue of the community of the people of the country, and the issue of the Union. I hope that today this will not be an issue calling for war; but I wanted to remind you that in order to preserve the Union Lincoln had to subordinate the immediate problem of the eradication of slavery, and trust—and I think if he had had his way it would have gone so—to the conflict of these ideas in a united people to eradicate it.

These are somewhat general remarks and it may be appropriate to say one or two things that are a little more programmatic, that are not quite so hard to get one's hands on. That is, what sort of agreement between nations would be a reasonable start. I don't know the answer to this, and I am very sure that no a priori answer should be given, that it is something that is going to take constant working out. But I think it is a thing where it will not hurt to have some reasonably concrete proposal. And I would go a step further and say of even such

questions as the great question of secrecy—which perplexes scientists and other people—that even this was not a suitable subject for unilateral action. If atomic energy is to be treated as an international problem, as I think it must be, if it is to be treated on the basis of an international responsibility and an international common concern, the problems of secrecy are also international problems. I don't mean by that that our present classifications and our present, in many cases inevitably ridiculous, procedures should be maintained. I mean that the fundamental problem of how to treat this peril ought not to be treated unilaterally by the United States, or by the United States in conjunction with Great Britain.

The first thing I would say about any proposals is that they ought to be regarded as interim proposals, and that whenever they are made it be understood and agreed that within a year or two years—whatever seems a reasonable time—they will be reconsidered and the problems which have arisen, and the new developments which have occurred, will cause a rewriting. I think the only point is that there should be a few things in these proposals which will work in the right direction, and that the things should be accepted without forcing all of the changes, which we know must ultimately occur, upon people who will not be ready for them. This is anyone's guess, but it would seem to me that if you took these four points, it might work: first, that we are dealing with an interim solution, so recognized. Second, that the nations participating in the arrangement would have a joint atomic energy commission, operating under the most broad directives from the different states, but with a power which only they had, and which was not subject to review by the heads of State, to go ahead with those constructive applications of atomic energy which we would all like to see developed—energy sources, and the innumerable research tools which are immediate possibilities. Third, that there would be not merely the possibility of exchange of scientists and students; that very, very concrete machinery more or less forcing such exchange should be established, so that we would be quite sure that the fraternity of scientists would be strengthened and that the bonds on which so much of the future depends would have some reinforcement and some scope. And fourth, I would say that no bombs be made. I don't know

whether these proposals are good ones, and I think that any-one in this group would have his own proposals. But I mention them as very simple things, which I don't believe solve the problem, and which I want to make clear are not the ultimate or even a touch of the ultimate, but which I think ought to be started right away; which I believe—though I know very little of this—may very well be acceptable to any of the nations that wish to become partners with us in this great undertaking.

One of the questions which you will want to hear more about, and which I can only partly hope to succeed in answering, is to what extent such views—essentially the view that the life of science is threatened, the life of the world is threatened, and that only by a profound revision of what it is that constitutes a thing worth fighting for and a thing worth living for can this crisis be met—to what extent these views are held by other men. They are certainly not held universally by scientists; but I think they are in agreement with all of the expressed opinions of this group, and I know that many of my friends here see pretty much eye to eye. I would speak especially of Bohr, who was here so much during the difficult days, who had many discussions with us, and who helped us reach the conclusion that it was not only a desirable solution, but that it was the unique solution, that there were no other alternatives.

I would say that among scientists there are certain centrifu-gal tendencies which seem to me a little dangerous, but not very. One of them is the attempt to try, in this imperilled world, in which the very function of science is threatened, to make convenient arrangements for the continuance of science, and to pay very little attention to the preconditions which give sense to it. Another is the tendency to say we must have a free science and a strong science, because this will make us a strong nation and enable us to fight better wars. It seems to me that this is a profound mistake, and I don't like to hear it. The third is even odder, and it is to say, "Oh give the bombs to the United Nations for police purposes, and let us get back to physics and chemistry." I think none of these are really held very widely, but they show that there are people who are desperately trying to avoid what I think is the most difficult problem. One must expect these false solutions, and overeasy solutions, and these are three which pop up from time to time.

As far as I can tell in the world outside there are many people just as quick to see the gravity of the situation, and to understand it in terms not so different from those I have tried to outline. It is not only among scientists that there are wise people and foolish people. I have had occasion in the last few months to meet people who had to do with the Government —the legislative branches, the administrative branches, and even the judicial branches, and I have found many in whom an understanding of what this problem is, and of the general lines along which it can be solved, is very clear. I would especially mention the former Secretary of War, Mr. Stimson, who, perhaps as much as any man, seemed to appreciate how hopeless and how impractical it was to attack this problem on a superficial level, and whose devotion to the development of atomic weapons was in large measure governed by his understanding of the hope that lay in it that there would be a new world. I know this is a surprise, because most people think that the War Department has as its unique function the making of war. The Secretary of War has other functions.

I think this is another question of importance: that is, what views will be held on these matters in other countries. I think it is important to realize that even those who are well informed in this country have been slow to understand, slow to believe that the bombs would work, and then slow to understand that their working would present such profound problems. We have certain interests in playing up the bomb, not only we here locally, but all over the country, because we made them, and our pride is involved. I think that in other lands it may be even more difficult for an appreciation of the magnitude of the thing to take hold. For this reason, I'm not sure that the greatest opportunities for progress do not lie somewhat further in the future than I had for a long time thought.

There have been two or three official statements by the President which defined, as nearly as their in some measure inevitable contradictions made possible, the official policy of the Government. And I think that one must not be entirely discouraged by the fact that there are contradictions, because the contradictions show that the problem is being understood as a difficult one, is temporarily being regarded as an insoluble one. Certainly you will notice, especially in the message to Congress, many indications of a sympathy with, and an understanding of, the views which this group holds, and which I have discussed briefly tonight. I think all of us were encouraged at the phrase "too revolutionary to consider in the framework of old ideas." That's about what we all think. I think all of us were encouraged by the sense of urgency that was frequently and emphatically stressed. I think all of us must be encouraged by the recognition, the official recognition by the Government of the importance—of the overriding importance—of the free exchange of scientific ideas and scientific information between all countries of the world. It would certainly be ridiculous to regard this as a final end, but I think that it would also be a very dangerous thing not to realize that it is a precondition. I am myself somewhat discouraged by the limitation of the objective to the elimination of atomic weapons, and I have seen many articles—probably you have, too—in which this is interpreted as follows: "Let us get international agreement to outlaw atomic weapons and then let us go back to having a good, clean war." This is certainly not a very good way of looking at it. I think, to say it again, that if one solves the problem presented by the atomic bomb, one will have made a pilot plant for solution of the problem of ending war.

But what is surely the thing which must have troubled you, and which troubled me, in the official statements was the insistent note of unilateral responsibility for the handling of atomic weapons. However good the motives of this country are—I am not going to argue with the President's description of what the motives and the aims are—we are 140 million people, and there are two billion people living on earth. We must understand that whatever our commitments to our own views and ideas, and however confident we are that in the course of time they will tend to prevail, our absolute—our completely absolute —commitment to them, in denial of the views and ideas of other people, cannot be the basis of any kind of agreement.

As I have said, I had for a long time the feeling of the most extreme urgency, and I think maybe there was something right about that. There was a period immediately after the first use of the bomb when it seemed most natural that a clear statement of policy, and the initial steps of implementing it, should have been made; and it would be wrong for me not to admit that something may have been lost, and that there may be tragedy in that loss. But I think the plain fact is that in the actual world, and with the actual people in it, it has taken time, and it may take longer, to understand what this is all about. And I am not sure, as I have said before, that in other lands it won't take longer than it does in this country. As it is now, our only course is to see what we can do to bring about an understanding on a level deep enough to make a solution practicable, and to do that without undue delay.

One may think that the views suggested in the President's Navy Day speech are not entirely encouraging, that many men who are more versed than we in the practical art of statesmanship have seen more hope in a radical view, which may at first sight seem visionary, than in an approach on a more conventional level.

I don't have very much more to say. There are a few things which scientists perhaps should remember, that I don't think I need to remind us of; but I will, anyway. One is that they are very often called upon to give technical information in one way or another, and I think one cannot be too careful to be honest. And it is very difficult, not because one tells lies, but because so often questions are put in a form which makes it very hard to give an answer which is not misleading. I think we will be in a very weak position unless we maintain at its highest the scrupulousness which is traditional for us in sticking to the truth, and in distinguishing between what we know to be true from what we hope may be true.

The second thing I think it right to speak of is this: it is everywhere felt that the fraternity between us and scientists in other countries may be one of the most helpful things for the future; yet it is apparent that even in this country not all of us who are scientists are in agreement. There is no harm in that; such disagreement is healthy. But we must not lose the sense of fraternity because of it; we must not lose our fundamental confidence in our fellow scientists.

I think that we have no hope at all if we yield in our belief in the value of science, in the good that it can be to the world to know about reality, about nature, to attain a gradually greater and greater control of nature, to learn, to teach, to understand. I think that if we lose our faith in this we stop being scientists, we sell out our heritage, we lose what we have most of value for this time of crisis.

But there is another thing: we are not only scientists; we are men, too. We cannot forget our dependence on our fellow men. I mean not only our material dependence, without which no science would be possible, and without which we could not work; I mean also our deep moral dependence, in that the value of science must lie in the world of men, that all our roots lie there. These are the strongest bonds in the world, stronger than those even that bind us to one another, these are the deepest bonds—that bind us to our fellow men.

GEORGE C. MARSHALL

Speech at Harvard University

Cambridge, Massachusetts, June 5, 1947

PRESIDENT DR. CONANT, MEMBERS OF THE BOARD OF OVERSEERS, LADIES AND GENTLEMEN: I am profoundly grateful and touched by the great distinction and honor, a great compliment, accorded me by the authorities of Harvard this morning. I am overwhelmed as a matter of fact and I am rather fearful of my inability to maintain such a high rating as you have been generous enough to accord to me. In these historic and lovely surroundings, this perfect day and this very wonderful assembly, it is a tremendously impressive thing to an individual in my position. But to speak more seriously:

I need not tell you that the world situation is very serious. That must be apparent to all intelligent people. I think one difficulty is that the problem is one of such enormous complexity that the very mass of facts presented to the public by press and radio make it exceedingly difficult for the man in the street to reach a clear appraisement of the situation. Furthermore, the people of this country are distant from the troubled areas of the earth and it is hard for them to comprehend the plight and consequent reactions of the long-suffering peoples of Europe and the effect of those reactions on their governments in connections with our efforts to promote peace in the world.

In considering the requirements for the rehabilitation of Europe, the physical loss of life, the visible destructions of cities, factories, mines and railroads was correctly estimated, but it has become obvious during recent months that this visible destruction was probably less serious than the dislocation of the entire fabric of European economy. For the past ten years conditions have been highly abnormal. The feverish preparation for war and the more feverish maintenance of the war effort engulfed all aspects of national economies. Machinery has fallen into disrepair or is entirely obsolete. Under the arbitrary and

destructive Nazi rule, virtually every possible enterprise was
geared into the German war machine. Long-standing commercial ties, private institutions, banks, insurance companies and
shipping companies disappeared, through loss of capital, ab-
sorption through nationalization or by simple destruction. In
many countries, confidence in the local currency has been
severely shaken. The breakdown of the business structure of
Europe during the war was complete. Recovery has been seriously retarded by the fact that two years after the close of hostilities a peace settlement with Germany and Austria has not
been agreed upon. But even given a more prompt solution of
these difficult problems, the rehabilitation of the economic
structure of Europe quite evidently will require a much longer
time and greater effort than had been foreseen.

There is a phase of this matter which is both interesting and
serious. The farmer has always produced the foodstuffs to exchange with the city dweller for the other necessities of life.
This division of labor is the basis of modern civilization. At the
present time it is threatened with breakdown. The town and
city industries are not producing adequate goods to exchange
with the food-producing farmer. Raw materials and fuel are in
short supply. Machinery, as I have said, is lacking or worn out.
The farmer or the peasant cannot find the goods for sale which
he desires to purchase. So the sale of his farm produce for
money which he cannot use seems to him an unprofitable trans-
action. He, therefore, has withdrawn many fields from crop
cultivation and is using them for grazing. He feeds more grain
to stock and finds for himself and his family an ample supply of
food, however short he may be on clothing and the other ordinary gadgets of civilization. Meanwhile people in the cities
are short of food and fuel and in some places approaching starvation limits. So the governments are forced to use their foreign money and credits to procure these necessities abroad.
This process exhausts funds which are urgently needed for reconstruction. Thus a very serious situation is rapidly developing which bodes no good for the world. The modern system
of the division of labor upon which the exchange of products
is based is in danger of breaking down.

The truth of the matter is that Europe's requirements for
the next three or four years of foreign food and other essential

products—principally from America—are so much greater than her present ability to pay that she must have substantial additional help, or face economic, social and political deterioration of a very grave character.

The remedy seems to lie in breaking the vicious circle and restoring the confidence of the people of Europe and the economic future of their own countries and of Europe as a whole. The manufacturer and the farmer throughout wide areas must be able and willing to exchange their products for currencies the continuing value of which is not open to question.

Aside from the demoralizing effect on the world at large and the possibilities of disturbances arising as a result of the desperation of the people concerned, the consequences to the economy of the United States should be apparent to all. It is logical that the United States should do whatever it is able to do to assist in the return of normal economic health in the world, without which there can be no political stability and no assured peace. Our policy is directed not against any country or doctrine but against hunger, poverty, desperation and chaos. Its purpose should be the revival of a working economy in the world so as to permit the emergence of political and social conditions in which free institutions can exist. Such assistance, I am convinced, must not be on a piecemeal basis as various crises develop. Any assistance that this Government may render in the future should provide a cure rather than a mere palliative. Any government that is willing to assist in the task of recovery will find full cooperation, I am sure, on the part of the United States Government. Any government which maneuvers to block the recovery of other countries cannot expect help from us. (*Applause*) Furthermore, governments, political parties or groups which seek to perpetuate human misery in order to profit therefrom politically or otherwise will encounter the opposition of the United States. (*Applause*)

It is already evident that, before the United States Government can proceed much further in its efforts to alleviate the situation and help start the European world on its way to recovery, there must be some agreement among the countries of Europe as to the requirements of the situation and the part those countries themselves will take in order to give proper effect to whatever action might be undertaken by this Government. It would be neither fitting nor efficacious for our Government to undertake to draw up unilaterally a program designed to place Europe on its feet economically. This is the business of the Europeans. The initiative, I think, must come from Europe. The role of this country should consist of friendly aid in the drafting of a European program and of later support of such a program so far as it may be practical for us to do so. The program should be a joint one, agreed to by a number, if not all European nations.

An essential part of any successful action on the part of the United States is an understanding on the part of the people of America of the character of the problem and the remedies to be applied. Political passion and prejudice should have no part. With foresight, and a willingness on the part of our people to face up to the vast responsibilities which history has clearly placed upon our country, the difficulties I have outlined can and will be overcome. I am sorry that on each occasion I have said something publicly in regard to our international situation, I have been forced by the necessities of the case to enter into rather technical discussions. But to my mind it is of vast importance that our people reach some general understanding of what the complications really are rather than react from a passion or a prejudice or an emotion of the moment. As I said more formally a moment ago, we are remote from the scene of these troubles. It is virtually impossible at this distance merely by reading or listening or even seeing photographs and motion pictures to grasp at all the real significance of the situation. Yet the whole world's future hangs on a proper judgment, it hangs, I think, to a large extent on the realization of the American people of just what are the very dominant factors, what are the reactions of the people, what are the justifications of those reactions, what are the sufferings, what is needed, what can best be done, what must be done. Thank you very much.

HUBERT H. HUMPHREY

Speech to the Democratic National Convention

Philadelphia, July 14, 1948

M R. CHAIRMAN, fellow Democrats, fellow Americans, I realize that in speaking in behalf of the minority report on civil rights as presented by Congressman Biemiller of Wisconsin, that I am dealing with a charged issue, with an issue which has been confused by emotionalism on all sides of the fence. I realize that there are those here—friends and colleagues of mine, many of them who feel just as deeply and keenly as I do about this issue, and who are yet in complete disagreement with me. My respect and admiration for these men and their views was great when I came to this convention. It is now far greater because of the sincerity, the courtesy, and the forthrightness with which many of them have argued in our prolonged discussions in the platform committee. Because of this very great respect, and because of my profound belief that we have a challenging task to do here, because good conscience demands it, decent morality demands it, I feel I must rise at this time to support a report, the minority report, a report that spells out our democracy. A report that the people of this country can and will understand and a report that they will enthusiastically acclaim on the great issue of civil rights.

Now let me say this at the outset, that this proposal is made for no single region, our proposal is made for no single class, for no single racial or religious group in mind. All of the regions of this country, all of the states have shared in our precious heritage of American freedom. All the states and all the regions have seen at least some of the infringements of that freedom. All people, get this, all people, white and black, all groups, all racial groups have been the victims at times in this nation of, let me say, vicious discrimination.

The masterly statement of our keynote speaker, the distinguished United States Senator from Kentucky, Alben Barkley, made that point with great force. Speaking of the founder of our party, Thomas Jefferson, he said this, and I quote;

He did not proclaim that all the white, or the black, or the red, or the yellow men are equal: that all Christian or Jewish men are equal: that all protestant and catholic men are equal: that all rich and poor men are equal: that all good and bad men are equal. What he declared was that all men are equal; and the equality which he proclaimed was the equality in the right to enjoy the blessings of free government in which they may participate and to which they have given their support.

Now these words of Senator Barkley are appropriate to this convention, appropriate to this convention of the oldest, the most truly progressive political party in America. From the time of Thomas Jefferson, the time when that immortal American doctrine of individual rights, under just and fairly administered laws, the Democratic Party has tried hard to secure expanding freedom for all citizens. Oh yes, I know other political parties may have talked more about civil rights, but the Democratic Party has surely done more about civil rights.

We have made progress, we have made great progress in every part of this country. We have made great progress in the South, we've made it in the West, the North and in the East, but we must now focus the direction of that progress towards the realization of a full program of civil rights for all.

This convention must set out more specifically the direction in which our party efforts are to go. We can be proud that we can be guided by the courageous trail blazing of two great Democratic Presidents. We can be proud of the fact that our great and beloved immortal leader, Franklin Roosevelt gave us guidance. And we can be proud of the fact, we can be proud of the fact that Harry Truman has had the courage to give to the people of America the new emancipation proclamation.

It seems to me, it seems to me that the Democratic Party needs to make definite pledges of the kind suggested in the minority report to maintain the trust and the confidence placed in it by the people of all races and all sections of this country. Sure we are here as Democrats, but my good friends, we're here as Americans. We are here as the believers in the principle and ideology of democracy. And I firmly believe that as men concerned with our country's future, we must specify in our platform the guarantees which we have mentioned in the minority report.

Yes this is far more than a party matter. Every citizen in this country has a stake in the emergence of the United States as a leader of the free world. That world is being challenged by the world of slavery. For us to play our part effectively we must be in a morally sound position. We can't use a double standard. There's no room for double standards in American politics for measuring our own and other people's policies. Our demands for democratic practices in other lands will be no more effective than the guarantee of those practices in our own country.

Friends, delegates, I do not believe that there can be any compromise on the guarantees of the civil rights which we have mentioned in the minority report. In spite of my desire for unanimous agreement on the entire platform, in spite of my desire to see everybody here in honest and unanimous agreement, there are some matters which I think must be stated clearly and without qualification.

There can be no hedging. The newspaper headlines are wrong, there will be no hedging and there will be no watering down if you please of the instruments and the principles of the civil rights program. To those who say that we are rushing this issue of civil rights, I say to them we are 172 years late. To those who say that this civil rights program is an infringement on state's rights, I say this, the time has arrived in America for the Democratic Party to get out of the shadows of state's rights to walk forthrightly into the bright sunshine of human rights. People—people—human beings, this is the issue of the 20th century. People of all kinds, all sorts of people—and these people are looking to America for leadership and they are looking to America for precept and example.

My good friends, my fellow Democrats, I ask you for a calm consideration of our historic opportunity. Let us do forget the evil passions and the blindness of the past. In these times of world, political and spiritual, above all spiritual crisis, we cannot and we must not turn from the path so plainly before us. That path has already led us through many valleys of the shadow of death. And now is the time to recall those who were left on that path of American freedom. For all of us here, for the millions who have sent us, for the whole two billion members of the human family, our land is now more than ever before, the last best hope on earth. And I know that we can, and I know that we shall begin here the fuller and richer realization of that hope. That promise of a land where all men are truly free and equal, and each man uses his freedom and equality wisely and well.

My good friends, I ask my party, I ask the Democratic party to march down the high road of progressive democracy. I ask this convention, I ask this convention to say in unmistakable terms that we proudly hail and we courageously support our President and leader, Harry Truman and his great fight for civil rights in America.

HARRY S. TRUMAN

Speech to the Democratic National Convention

Philadelphia, July 15, 1948

I AM SORRY that the microphones are in the way, but I must leave them the way they are because I have got to be able to see what I am doing—as I am always able to see what I am doing.

I can't tell you how very much I appreciate the honor which you have just conferred upon me. I shall continue to try to deserve it.

I accept the nomination.

And I want to thank this convention for its unanimous nomination of my good friend and colleague, Senator Barkley of Kentucky. He is a great man, and a great public servant. Senator Barkley and I will win this election and make these Republicans like it—don't you forget that!

We will do that because they are wrong and we are right, and I will prove it to you in just a few minutes.

This convention met to express the will and reaffirm the beliefs of the Democratic Party. There have been differences of opinion, and that is the democratic way. Those differences have been settled by a majority vote, as they should be.

Now it is time for us to get together and beat the common enemy. And that is up to you.

We have been working together for victory in a great cause. Victory has become a habit of our party. It has been elected four times in succession, and I am convinced it will be elected a fifth time next November.

The reason is that the people know that the Democratic Party is the people's party, and the Republican Party is the party of special interest, and it always has been and always will be.

The record of the Democratic Party is written in the accomplishments of the last 16 years. I don't need to repeat them.

They have been very ably placed before this convention by the keynote speaker, the candidate for Vice President, and by the permanent chairman.

Confidence and security have been brought to the people by the Democratic Party. Farm income has increased from less than $2½ billion in 1932 to more than $18 billion in 1947. Never in the world were the farmers of any republic or any kingdom or any other country as prosperous as the farmers of the United States; and if they don't do their duty by the Democratic Party, they are the most ungrateful people in the world!

Wages and salaries in this country have increased from 29 billion in 1933 to more than $128 billion in 1947. That's labor, and labor never had but one friend in politics, and that is the Democratic Party and Franklin D. Roosevelt.

And I say to labor what I have said to the farmers: they are the most ungrateful people in the world if they pass the Democratic Party by this year.

The total national income has increased from less than $40 billion in 1933 to $203 billion in 1947, the greatest in all the history of the world. These benefits have been spread to all the people, because it is the business of the Democratic Party to see that the people get a fair share of these things.

This last, worst 80th Congress proved just the opposite for the Republicans.

The record on foreign policy of the Democratic Party is that the United States has been turned away permanently from isolationism, and we have converted the greatest and best of the Republicans to our viewpoint on that subject.

The United States has to accept its full responsibility for leadership in international affairs. We have been the backers and the people who organized and started the United Nations, first started under that great Democratic President, Woodrow Wilson, as the League of Nations. The League was sabotaged by the Republicans in 1920. And we must see that the United Nations continues a strong and growing body, so we can have everlasting peace in the world.

We removed trade barriers in the world, which is the best asset we can have for peace. Those trade barriers must not be put back into operation again.

We have started the foreign aid program, which means the

recovery of Europe and China, and the Far East. We instituted the program for Greece and Turkey, and I will say to you that all these things were done in a cooperative and bipartisan manner. The Foreign Relations Committees of the Senate and House were taken into the full confidence of the President in every one of these moves, and don't let anybody tell you anything else.

As I have said time and time again, foreign policy should be the policy of the whole Nation and not the policy of one party or the other. Partisanship should stop at the water's edge; and I shall continue to preach that through this whole campaign.

I would like to say a word or two now on what I think the Republican philosophy is; and I will speak from actions and from history and from experience.

The situation in 1932 was due to the policies of the Republican Party control of the Government of the United States. The Republican Party, as I said a while ago, favors the privileged few and not the common everyday man. Ever since its inception, that party has been under the control of special privilege; and they have completely proved it in the 80th Congress. They proved it by the things they did *to* the people, and not *for* them. They proved it by the things they failed to do.

Now, let's look at some of them—just a few.

Time and time again I recommended extension of price control before it expired June 30, 1946. I asked for that extension in September 1945, in November 1945, in a Message on the State of the Union in 1946; and that price control legislation did not come to my desk until June 30, 1946, on the day on which it was supposed to expire. And it was such a rotten bill that I couldn't sign it. And 30 days after that, they sent me one just as bad. I had to sign it, because they quit and went home.

They said, when OPA died, that prices would adjust themselves for the benefit of the country. They have been adjusting themselves all right! They have gone all the way off the chart in adjusting themselves, at the expense of the consumer and for the benefit of the people that hold the goods.

I called a special session of the Congress in November 1947 —November 17, 1947—and I set out a 10-point program for the welfare and benefit of this country, among other things standby controls. I got nothing. Congress has still done nothing.

Way back 4½ years ago, while I was in the Senate, we passed a housing bill in the Senate known as the Wagner-Ellender-Taft bill. It was a bill to clear the slums in the big cities and to help to erect low-rent housing. That bill, as I said, passed the Senate 4 years ago. It died in the House. That bill was reintroduced in the 80th Congress as the Taft-Ellender-Wagner bill. The name was slightly changed, but it is practically the same bill. And it passed the Senate, but it was allowed to die in the House of Representatives; and they sat on that bill, and finally forced it out of the Banking and Currency Committee, and the Rules Committee took charge, and it still is in the Rules Committee.

But desperate pleas from Philadelphia in that convention that met here 3 weeks ago couldn't get that housing bill passed. They passed a bill they called a housing bill, which isn't worth the paper it's written on.

In the field of labor we needed moderate legislation to promote labor-management harmony, but Congress passed instead that so-called Taft-Hartley Act, which has disrupted labor-management relations and will cause strife and bitterness for years to come if it is not repealed, as the Democratic platform says it ought to be repealed.

On the Labor Department, the Republican platform of 1944 said, if they were in power, that they would build up a strong Labor Department. They have simply torn it up. Only one bureau is left that is functioning, and they cut the appropriation of that so it can hardly function.

I recommended an increase in the minimum wage. What did I get? Nothing. Absolutely nothing.

I suggested that the schools in this country are crowded, teachers underpaid, and that there is a shortage of teachers. One of our greatest national needs is more and better schools. I urged the Congress to provide $300 million to aid the States in the present educational crisis. Congress did nothing about it. Time and again I have recommended improvements in the social security law, including extending protection to those not now covered, and increasing the amount of benefits, to reduce the eligibility age of women from 65 to 60 years. Congress studied the matter for 2 years, but couldn't find the time to extend or increase the benefits. But they did find time to take social security benefits away from 750,000 people, and they passed that over my veto.

I have repeatedly asked the Congress to pass a health program. The Nation suffers from lack of medical care. That situation can be remedied any time the Congress wants to act upon it.

Everybody knows that I recommended to the Congress the civil rights program. I did that because I believed it to be my duty under the Constitution. Some of the members of my own party disagree with me violently on this matter. But they stand up and do it openly! People can tell where they stand. But the Republicans all professed to be for these measures. But Congress failed to act. They had enough men to do it, they could have had cloture, they didn't have to have a filibuster. They had enough people in that Congress that would vote for cloture.

Now everybody likes to have low taxes, but we must reduce the national debt in times of prosperity. And when tax relief can be given, it ought to go to those who need it most, and not those who need it least, as this Republican rich man's tax bill did when they passed it over my veto on the third try.

The first one of these was so rotten that they couldn't even stomach it themselves. They finally did send one that was somewhat improved, but it still helps the rich and sticks a knife into the back of the poor.

Now the Republicans came here a few weeks ago, and they wrote a platform. I hope you have all read that platform. They adopted the platform, and that platform had a lot of promises and statements of what the Republican Party is for, and what they would do if they were in power. They promised to do in that platform a lot of things I have been asking them to do that they have refused to do when they had the power.

The Republican platform cries about cruelly high prices. I have been trying to get them to do something about high prices ever since they met the first time.

Now listen! This is equally as bad, and as cynical. The Republican platform comes out for slum clearance and low-rental housing. I have been trying to get them to pass that housing bill ever since they met the first time, and it is still resting in the Rules Committee, that bill.

The Republican platform favors educational opportunity and promotion of education. I have been trying to get Congress to do something about that ever since they came there, and that bill is at rest in the House of Representatives.

The Republican platform is for extending and increasing social security benefits. Think of that! Increasing social security benefits! Yet when they had the opportunity, they took 750,000 off the social security rolls!

I wonder if they think they can fool the people of the United States with such poppycock as that!

There is a long list of these promises in that Republican platform. If it weren't so late, I would tell you all about them. I have discussed a number of these failures of the Republican 80th Congress. Every one of them is important. Two of them are of major concern to nearly every American family. They failed to do anything about high prices, they failed to do anything about housing.

My duty as President requires that I use every means within my power to get the laws the people need on matters of such importance and urgency.

I am therefore calling this Congress back into session July 26th.

On the 26th day of July, which out in Missouri we call "Turnip Day," I am going to call Congress back and ask them to pass laws to halt rising prices, to meet the housing crisis—which they are saying they are for in their platform.

At the same time I shall ask them to act upon other vitally needed measures such as aid to education, which they say they are for; a national health program; civil rights legislation, which they say they are for; an increase in the minimum wage, which I doubt very much they are for; extension of the social security coverage and increased benefits, which they say they are for; funds for projects needed in our program to provide public power and cheap electricity. By indirection, this 80th Congress has tried to sabotage the power policies the United States has pursued for 14 years. That power lobby is as bad as the real estate lobby, which is sitting on the housing bill.

I shall ask for adequate and decent laws for displaced persons in place of this anti-Semitic, anti-Catholic law which this 80th Congress passed.

Now, my friends, if there is any reality behind that Republican platform, we ought to get some action from a short session of the 80th Congress. They can do this job in 15 days, if they want to do it. They will still have time to go out and run for office.

They are going to try to dodge their responsibility. They are going to drag all the red herrings they can across this campaign, but I am here to say that Senator Barkley and I are not going to let them get away with it.

Now, what that worst 80th Congress does in this special session will be the test. The American people will not decide by listening to mere words, or by reading a mere platform. They will decide on the record, the record as it has been written. And in the record is the stark truth, that the battle lines of 1948 are the same as they were in 1932, when the Nation lay prostrate and helpless as a result of Republican misrule and inaction.

In 1932 we were attacking the citadel of special privilege nd greed. We were fighting to drive the money changers from the temple. Today, in 1948, we are now the defenders of the stronghold of democracy and of equal opportunity, the haven of the ordinary people of this land and not of the favored classes or the powerful few. The battle cry is just the same now as it was in 1932, and I paraphrase the words of Franklin D. Roosevelt as he issued the challenge, in accepting nomination in Chicago: "This is more than a political call to arms. Give me your help, not to win votes alone, but to win in this new crusade to keep America secure and safe for its own people."

Now my friends, with the help of God and the wholehearted push which you can put behind this campaign, we can save this country from a continuation of the 80th Congress, and from misrule from now on.

I must have your help. You must get in and push, and win this election. The country can't afford another Republican Congress.

MARGARET CHASE SMITH

Declaration of Conscience

Washington, D.C., June 1, 1950

M R. PRESIDENT, I would like to speak briefly and simply about a serious national condition. It is a national feeling of fear and frustration that could result in national suicide and the end of everything that we Americans hold dear. It is a condition that comes from the lack of effective leadership either in the legislative branch or the executive branch of our Government. That leadership is so lacking that serious and responsible proposals are being made that national advisory commissions be appointed to provide such critically needed leadership.

I speak as briefly as possible because too much harm has already been done with irresponsible words of bitterness and selfish political opportunism. I speak as simply as possible because the issue is too great to be obscured by eloquence. I speak simply and briefly in the hope that my words will be taken to heart.

Mr. President, I speak as a Republican. I speak as a woman. I speak as a United States Senator. I speak as an American.

The United States Senate has long enjoyed world-wide respect as the greatest deliberative body in the world. But recently that deliberative character has too often been debased to the level of a forum of hate and character assassination sheltered by the shield of congressional immunity.

It is ironical that we Senators can in debate in the Senate, directly or indirectly, by any form of words, impute to any American who is not a Senator any conduct or motive unworthy or unbecoming an American—and without that non-Senator American having any legal redress against us—yet if we say the same thing in the Senate about our colleagues we can be stopped on the grounds of being out of order.

It is strange that we can verbally attack anyone else without restraint and with full protection, and yet we hold ourselves above the same type of criticism here on the Senate floor. Surely the United States Senate is big enough to take self-criticism and self-appraisal. Surely we should be able to take the same kind of character attacks that we "dish out" to outsiders.

I think that it is high time for the United States Senate and its Members to do some real soul searching and to weigh our consciences as to the manner in which we are performing our duty to the people of America and the manner in which we are using or abusing our individual powers and privileges.

I think it is high time that we remembered that we have sworn to uphold and defend the Constitution. I think it is high time that we remembered that the Constitution, as amended, speaks not only of the freedom of speech but also of trial by jury instead of trial by accusation.

Whether it be a criminal prosecution in court or a character prosecution in the Senate, there is little practical distinction when the life of a person has been ruined.

Those of us who shout the loudest about Americanism in making character assassinations are all too frequently those who, by our own words and acts, ignore some of the basic principles of Americanism—

The right to criticize.

The right to hold unpopular beliefs.

The right to protest.

The right of independent thought.

The exercise of these rights should not cost one single American citizen his reputation or his right to a livelihood nor should he be in danger of losing his reputation or livelihood merely because he happens to know some one who holds unpopular beliefs. Who of us does not? Otherwise none of us could call our souls our own. Otherwise thought control would have set in.

The American people are sick and tired of being afraid to speak their minds lest they be politically smeared as Communists or Fascists by their opponents. Freedom of speech is not what it used to be in America. It has been so abused by some that it is not exercised by others.

The American people are sick and tired of seeing innocent people smeared and guilty people whitewashed. But there have been enough proved cases, such as the Amerasia case, the Hiss case, the Coplon case, the Gold case, to cause Nation-wide distrust and strong suspicion that there may be something to the unproved, sensational accusations.

As a Republican, I say to my colleagues on this side of the aisle that the Republican Party faces a challenge today that is not unlike the challenge which it faced back in Lincoln's day. The Republican Party so successfully met that challenge that it emerged from the Civil War as the champion of a united nation—in addition to being a party which unrelentingly fought loose spending and loose programs.

Today our country is being psychologically divided by the confusion and the suspicions that are bred in the United States Senate to spread like cancerous tentacles of "know nothing, suspect everything" attitudes. Today we have a Democratic administration which has developed a mania for loose spending and loose programs. History is repeating itself—and the Republican Party again has the opportunity to emerge as the champion of unity and prudence.

The record of the present Democratic administration has provided us with sufficient campaign issues without the necessity of resorting to political smears. America is rapidly losing its position as leader of the world simply because the Democratic administration has pitifully failed to provide effective leadership.

The Democratic administration has completely confused the American people by its daily contradictory grave warnings and optimistic assurances, which show the people that our Democratic administration has no idea of where it is going.

The Democratic administration has greatly lost the confidence of the American people by its complacency to the threat of communism here at home and the leak of vital secrets to Russia through key officials of the Democratic administration. There are enough proved cases to make this point without diluting our criticism with unproved charges.

Surely these are sufficient reasons to make it clear to the American people that it is time for a change and that a Republican victory is necessary to the security of the country. Surely it is clear that this Nation will continue to suffer so long as it is governed by the present ineffective Democratic administration.

Yet to displace it with a Republican regime embracing a

philosophy that lacks political integrity or intellectual honesty would prove equally disastrous to the Nation. The Nation sorely needs a Republican victory. But I do not want to see the Republican Party ride to political victory on the Four Horsemen of Calumny—fear, ignorance, bigotry, and smear.

I doubt if the Republican Party could do so, simply because I do not believe the American people will uphold any political party that puts political exploitation above national interest. Surely we Republicans are not so desperate for victory.

I do not want to see the Republican Party win that way. While it might be a fleeting victory for the Republican Party, it would be a more lasting defeat for the American people. Surely it would ultimately be suicide for the Republican Party and the two-party system that has protected our American liberties from the dictatorship of a one-party system.

As members of the minority party, we do not have the primary authority to formulate the policy of our Government. But we do have the responsibility of rendering constructive criticism, of clarifying issues, of allaying fears by acting as responsible citizens.

As a woman, I wonder how the mothers, wives, sisters, and daughters feel about the way in which members of their families have been politically mangled in Senate debate—and I use the word "debate" advisedly.

As a United States Senator, I am not proud of the way in which the Senate has been made a publicity platform for irresponsible sensationalism. I am not proud of the reckless abandon in which unproved charges have been hurled from this side of the aisle. I am not proud of the obviously staged, undignified countercharges which have been attempted in retaliation from the other side of the aisle.

I do not like the way the Senate has been made a rendezvous for vilification, for selfish political gain at the sacrifice of individual reputations and national unity. I am not proud of the way we smear outsiders from the floor of the Senate and hide behind the cloak of congressional immunity and still place ourselves beyond criticism on the floor of the Senate.

As an American, I am shocked at the way Republicans and Democrats alike are playing directly into the Communist design of "confuse, divide, and conquer." As an American, I do not want a Democratic administration white wash or cover up any more than I want a Republican smear or witch hunt.

As an American, I condemn a Republican Fascist just as much as I condemn a Democrat Communist. I condemn a Democrat Fascist just as much as I condemn a Republican Communist. They are equally dangerous to you and me and to our country. As an American, I want to see our Nation recapture the strength and unity it once had when we fought the enemy instead of ourselves.

It is with these thoughts that I have drafted what I call a Declaration of Conscience. I am gratified that the Senator from New Hampshire [Mr. TOBEY], the Senator from Vermont [Mr. AIKEN], the Senator from Oregon [Mr. MORSE], the Senator from New York [Mr. IVES], the Senator from Minnesota [Mr. THYE], and the Senator from New Jersey [Mr. HENDRICKSON] have concurred in that declaration and have authorized me to announce their concurrence.

The declaration reads as follows:

STATEMENT OF SEVEN REPUBLICAN SENATORS

1. We are Republicans. But we are Americans first. It is as Americans that we express our concern with the growing confusion that threatens the security and stability of our country. Democrats and Republicans alike have contributed to that confusion.

2. The Democratic administration has intially created the confusion by its lack of effective leadership, by its contradictory grave warnings and optimistic assurances, by its complacency to the threat of communism here at home, by its oversensitiveness to rightful criticism, by its petty bitterness against its critics.

3. Certain elements of the Republican Party have materially added to this confusion in the hopes of riding the Republican Party to victory through the selfish political exploitation of fear, bigotry, ignorance, and intolerance. There are enough mistakes of the Democrats for Republicans to criticize constructively without resorting to political smears.

4. To this extent, Democrats and Republicans alike have unwittingly, but undeniably, played directly into the Communist design of "confuse, divide, and conquer."

5. It is high time that we stopped thinking politically as Republicans and Democrats about elections and started thinking patriotically as Americans about national security based on individual freedom. It is high time that we all stopped being tools and victims of totalitarian

techniques—techniques that, if continued here unchecked, will surely end what we have come to cherish as the American way of life.

MARGARET CHASE SMITH,
Maine.

CHARLES W. TOBEY,
New Hampshire.

GEORGE D. AIKEN,
Vermont.

WAYNE L. MORSE,
Oregon.

IRVING M. IVES,
New York.

EDWARD J. THYE,
Minnesota.

ROBERT C. HENDRICKSON,
New Jersey.

WILLIAM FAULKNER

Nobel Prize Address

Stockholm, December 10, 1950

I FEEL that this award was not made to me as a man, but to my work—a life's work in the agony and sweat of the human spirit, not for glory and least of all for profit, but to create out of the materials of the human spirit something which did not exist before. So this award is only mine in trust. It will not be difficult to find a dedication for the money part of it commensurate with the purpose and significance of its origin. But I would like to do the same with the acclaim too, by using this moment as a pinnacle from which I might be listened to by the young men and women already dedicated to the same anguish and travail, among whom is already that one who will some day stand here where I am standing.

Our tragedy today is a general and universal physical fear so long sustained by now that we can even bear it. There are no longer problems of the spirit. There is only the question: When will I be blown up? Because of this, the young man or woman writing today has forgotten the problems of the human heart in conflict with itself which alone can make good writing because only that is worth writing about, worth the agony and the sweat.

He must learn them again. He must teach himself that the basest of all things is to be afraid; and, teaching himself that, forget it forever, leaving no room in his workshop for anything but the old verities and truths of the heart, the old universal truths lacking which any story is ephemeral and doomed—love and honor and pity and pride and compassion and sacrifice. Until he does so, he labors under a curse. He writes not of love but of lust, of defeats in which nobody loses anything of value, of victories without hope and, worst of all, without pity or compassion. His griefs grieve on no universal bones, leaving no scars. He writes not of the heart but of the glands.

Until he relearns these things, he will write as though he stood among and watched the end of man. I decline to accept the end of man. It is easy enough to say that man is immortal simply because he will endure: that when the last ding-dong of doom has clanged and faded from the last worthless rock hanging tideless in the last red and dying evening, that even then there will still be one more sound: that of his puny inexhaustible voice, still talking. I refuse to accept this. I believe that man will not merely endure: he will prevail. He is immortal, not because he alone among creatures has an inexhaustible voice, but because he has a soul, a spirit capable of compassion and sacrifice and endurance. The poet's, the writer's, duty is to write about these things. It is his privilege to help man endure by lifting his heart, by reminding him of the courage and honor and hope and pride and compassion and pity and sacrifice which have been the glory of his past. The poet's voice need not merely be the record of man, it can be one of the props, the pillars to help him endure and prevail.

DOUGLAS MacARTHUR

Address to Congress

Washington, D.C., April 19, 1951

M R. PRESIDENT, MR. SPEAKER, AND DISTINGUISHED
MEMBERS OF THE CONGRESS: I stand on this rostrum
with a sense of deep humility and great pride   humility in the
wake of those great American architects of our history who
have stood here before me, pride in the reflection that this forum of legislative debate represents human liberty in the
purest form yet devised. Here are centered the hopes and aspirations and faith of the entire human race.

I do not stand here as advocate for any partisan cause, for
the issues are fundamental and reach quite beyond the realm of
partisan consideration. They must be resolved on the highest
plane of national interest if our course is to prove sound and
our future protected. I trust, therefore, that you will do me the
justice of receiving that which I have to say as solely expressing
the considered viewpoint of a fellow American. I address you
with neither rancor nor bitterness in the fading twilight of life
with but one purpose in mind—to serve my country.

The issues are global and so interlocked that to consider the
problems of one sector, oblivious to those of another, is but to
court disaster for the whole.

While Asia is commonly referred to as the gateway to Europe, it is no less true that Europe is the gateway to Asia, and
the broad influence of the one cannot fail to have its impact
upon the other.

There are those who claim our strength is inadequate to
protect on both fronts—that we cannot divide our effort. I can
think of no greater expression of defeatism. If a potential enemy can divide his strength on two fronts, it is for us to counter
his effort.

The Communist threat is a global one. Its successful advance
in one sector threatens the destruction of every other sector.

You cannot appease or otherwise surrender to Communism in Asia without simultaneously undermining our efforts to halt its advance in Europe.

Beyond pointing out these simple truisms, I shall confine my discussion to the general areas of Asia. Before one may objectively assess the situation now existing there, he must comprehend something of Asia's past and the revolutionary changes which have marked her course up to the present. Long exploited by the so-called colonial powers, with little opportunity to achieve any degree of social justice, individual dignity, or a higher standard of life such as guided our own noble administration of the Philippines, the peoples of Asia found their opportunity in the war just past to throw off the shackles of colonialism and now see the dawn of new opportunity, a heretofore unfelt dignity and the self-respect of political freedom.

Mustering half of the earth's population and 60 per cent of its natural resources, these peoples are rapidly consolidating a new force, both moral and material, with which to raise the living standard and erect adaptations of the design of modern progress to their own distinct cultural environments. Whether one adheres to the concept of colonization or not, this is the direction of Asian progress and it may not be stopped. It is a corollary to the shift of the world economic frontiers, as the whole epicenter of world affairs rotates back toward the area whence it started. In this situation it becomes vital that our own country orient its policies in consonance with this basic evolutionary condition rather than pursue a course blind to the reality that the colonial era is now past and the Asian peoples covet the right to shape their own free destiny. What they seek now is friendly guidance, understanding, and support, not imperious direction; the dignity of equality, not the shame of subjugation. Their prewar standard of life, pitifully low, is infinitely lower now in the devastation left in war's wake. World ideologies play little part in Asian thinking and are little understood. What the peoples strive for is the opportunity for a little more food in their stomachs, a little better clothing on their backs, a little firmer roof over their heads, and the realization of the normal nationalist urge for political freedom. These political-social conditions have but an indirect bearing upon our own national security, but form a backdrop to contemporary planning which must be thoughtfully considered if we are to avoid the pitfalls of unrealism.

Of more direct and immediate bearing upon our national security are the changes wrought in the strategic potential of the Pacific Ocean in the course of the past war. Prior thereto, the western strategic frontier of the United States lay on the littoral line of the Americas with an exposed island salient extending out through Hawaii, Midway, and Guam to the Philippines. That salient proved not an outpost of strength but an avenue of weakness along which the enemy could and did attack. The Pacific was a potential area of advance for any predatory force intent upon striking at the bordering land areas.

All this was changed by our Pacific victory. Our strategic frontier then shifted to embrace the entire Pacific Ocean, which became a vast moat to protect us as long as we hold it. Indeed, it acts as a protective shield for all of the Americas and all free lands of the Pacific Ocean area. We control it to the shores of Asia by a chain of islands extending in an arc from the Aleutians to the Mariannas held by us and our free allies. From this island chain we can dominate with sea and air power every Asiatic port from Vladivostok to Singapore and prevent any hostile movement into the Pacific. Any predatory attack from Asia must be an amphibious effort. No amphibious force can be successful without control of the sea lanes and the air over those lanes in its avenue of advance. With naval and air supremacy and modest ground elements to defend bases, any major attack from continental Asia toward us or our friends of the Pacific would be doomed to failure. Under such conditions the Pacific no longer represents menacing avenues of approach for a prospective invader—it assumes instead the friendly aspect of a peaceful lake. Our line of defense is a natural one and can be maintained with a minimum of military effort and expense. It envisions no attack against anyone nor does it provide the bastions essential for offensive operations, but properly maintained would be an invincible defense against aggression.

The holding of this littoral defense line in the Western Pacific is entirely dependent upon holding all segments thereof, for any major breach of that line by an unfriendly power would render vulnerable to determined attack every other major segment. This is a military estimate as to which I have yet to find a military leader who will take exception. For that reason I have strongly recommended in the past as a matter of military urgency that under no circumstances must Formosa fall under Communist control. Such an eventuality would at once threaten the freedom of the Philippines and the loss of Japan, and might well force our western frontier back to the coasts of California, Oregon, and Washington.

To understand the changes which now appear upon the Chinese mainland, one must understand the changes in Chinese character and culture over the past 50 years. China up to 50 years ago was completely nonhomogeneous, being compartmented into groups divided against each other. The warmaking tendency was almost nonexistent, as they still followed the tenets of the Confucian ideal of pacifist culture. At the turn of the century, under the regime of Chan So Lin, efforts toward greater homogeneity produced the start of a nationalist urge. This was further and more successfully developed under the leadership of Chiang Kai-shek, but has been brought to its greatest fruition under the present regime, to the point that it has now taken on the character of a united nationalism of increasingly dominant aggressive tendencies. Through these past 50 years, the Chinese people have thus become militarized in their concepts and in their ideals. They now constitute excellent soldiers with competent staffs and commanders. This has produced a new and dominant power in Asia which for its own purposes is allied with Soviet Russia, but which in its own concepts and methods has become aggressively imperialistic with a lust for expansion and increased power normal to this type of imperialism. There is little of the ideological concept either one way or another in the Chinese make-up. The standard of living is so low and the capital accumulation has been so thoroughly dissipated by war that the masses are desperate and avid to follow any leadership which seems to promise the alleviation of local stringencies. I have from the beginning believed that the Chinese Communists' support of the North Koreans was the dominant one. Their interests are at present parallel to those of the Soviet, but I believe that the aggressiveness recently displayed not only in Korea, but also in Indochina and Tibet, and pointing potentially toward the south, reflects predominantly the same lust for the expansion of power which has animated every would-be conqueror since the beginning of time.

The Japanese people since the war have undergone the greatest reformation recorded in modern history. With a commendable will, eagerness to learn, and marked capacity to understand, they have, from the ashes left in war's wake, erected in Japan an edifice dedicated to the primacy of individual liberty and personal dignity, and in the ensuing process there has been created a truly representative government committed to the advance of political morality, freedom of economic enterprise, and social justice. Politically, economically and socially Japan is now abreast of many free nations of the earth and will not again fail the universal trust. That it may be counted upon to wield a profoundly beneficial influence over the course of events in Asia is attested by the magnificent manner in which the Japanese people have met the recent challenge of war, unrest and confusion surrounding them from the outside, and checked Communism within their own frontiers without the slightest slackening in their forward progress. I sent all four of our occupation divisions to the Korean battlefront without the slightest qualms as to the effect of the resulting power vacuum upon Japan. The results fully justified my faith. I know of no nation more serene, orderly and industrious— nor in which higher hopes can be entertained for future constructive service in the advance of the human race.

Of our former ward, the Philippines, we can look forward in confidence that the existing unrest will be corrected and a strong and healthy nation will grow in the longer aftermath of war's terrible destructiveness. We must be patient and understanding and never fail them, as in our hour of need they did not fail us. A Christian nation, the Philippines stand as a mighty bulwark of Christianity in the Far East, and its capacity for high moral leadership in Asia is unlimited.

On Formosa, the Government of the Republic of China has had the opportunity to refute by action much of the malicious gossip which so undermined the strength of its leadership on the Chinese mainland. The Formosan people are receiving a just and enlightened administration with majority representation on the organs of government, and politically, economically and socially they appear to be advancing along sound and constructive lines.

With this brief insight into the surrounding areas I now turn to the Korean conflict. While I was not consulted prior to the President's decision to intervene in support of the Republic of Korea, that decision, from a military standpoint, proved a sound one, as we hurled back the invader and decimated his forces. Our victory was complete and our objectives within reach when Red China intervened with numerically superior ground forces. This created a new war and an entirely new situation—a situation not contemplated when our forces were committed against the North Korean invaders—a situation which called for new decisions in the diplomatic sphere to permit the realistic adjustment of military strategy. Such decisions have not been forthcoming.

While no man in his right mind would advocate sending our ground forces into continental China and such was never given a thought, the new situation did urgently demand a drastic revision of strategic planning if our political aim was to defeat this new enemy as we had defeated the old.

Apart from the military need as I saw it to neutralize the sanctuary protection given the enemy north of the Yalu, I felt that military necessity in the conduct of the war made mandatory:

1. The intensification of our economic blockade against China;

2. The imposition of a naval blockade against the China coast;

3. Removal of restrictions on air reconnaissance of China's coastal areas and of Manchuria;

4. Removal of restrictions on the forces of the Republic of China on Formosa with logistical support to contribute to their effective operations against the common enemy.

For entertaining these views, all professionally designed to support our forces committed to Korea and bring hostilities to an end with the least possible delay and at a saving of countless American and Allied lives, I have been severely criticized in lay circles, principally abroad, despite my understanding that from a military standpoint the above views have been fully shared in the past by practically every military leader concerned with the Korean campaign, including our own Joint Chiefs of Staff.

I called for reinforcements, but was informed that reinforcements were not available. I made clear that if not permitted to destroy the enemy build-up bases north of the Yalu; if not permitted to utilize the friendly Chinese force of some 600,000 men on Formosa; if not permitted to blockade the China coast to prevent the Chinese Reds from getting succor from without; and if there were to be no hope of major reinforcements, the position of the command from the military standpoint forbade victory. We could hold in Korea by constant maneuver and at an approximate area where our supply line advantages were in balance with the supply line disadvantages of the enemy, but we could hope at best for only an indecisive campaign, with its terrible and constant attrition upon our forces if the enemy utilized his full military potential. I have constantly called for the new political decisions essential to a solution. Efforts have been made to distort my position. It has been said that I was in effect a warmonger. Nothing could be further from the truth. I know war as few other men now living know it, and nothing to me is more revolting. I have long advocated its complete abolition as its very destructiveness on both friend and foe has rendered it useless as a means of settling international disputes. Indeed, on the 2d of September, 1945, just following the surrender of the Japanese nation on the battleship *Missouri*, I formally cautioned as follows:

Men since the beginning of time have sought peace. Various methods through the ages have been attempted to devise an international process to prevent or settle disputes between nations. From the very start, workable methods were found insofar as individual citizens were concerned, but the mechanics of an instrumentality of larger international scope have never been successful. Military alliances, balances of power, leagues of nations, all in turn failed, leaving the only path to be by way of the crucible of war. The utter destructiveness of war now blots out this alternative. We have had our last chance. If we will not devise some greater and more equitable system, Armageddon will be at our door. The problem basically is theological and involves a spiritual recrudescence and improvement of human character that will synchronize with our almost matchless advances in science, art, literature, and all material and cultural developments of the past 2,000 years. It must be of the spirit if we are to save the flesh.

But once war is forced upon us, there is no other alternative than to apply every available means to bring it to a swift end. War's very object is victory—not prolonged indecision. In war, indeed, there can be no substitute for victory.

There are some who for varying reasons would appease Red China. They are blind to history's clear lesson. For history teaches with unmistakable emphasis that appeasement but begets new and bloodier war. It points to no single instance where the end has justified that means—where appeasement has led to more than a sham peace. Like blackmail, it lays the basis for new and successively greater demands, until, as in blackmail, violence becomes the only other alternative. Why, my soldiers asked of me, surrender military advantages to an enemy in the field? I could not answer. Some may say to avoid spread of the conflict into an all-out war with China; others, to avoid Soviet intervention. Neither explanation seems valid. For China is already engaging with the maximum power it can commit and the Soviet will not necessarily mesh its actions with our moves. Like a cobra, any new enemy will more likely strike whenever it feels that the relativity in military or other potential is in its favor on a world-wide basis.

The tragedy of Korea is further heightened by the fact that as military action is confined to its territorial limits, it condemns that nation, which it is our purpose to save, to suffer the devastating impact of full naval and air bombardment, while the enemy's sanctuaries are fully protected from such attack and devastation. Of the nations of the world, Korea alone, up to now, is the sole one which has risked its all against Communism. The magnificence of the courage and fortitude of the Korean people defies description. They have chosen to risk death rather than slavery. Their last words to me were "don't scuttle the Pacific."

I have just left your fighting sons in Korea. They have met all tests there and I can report to you without reservations, they are splendid in every way. It was my constant effort to preserve them and end this savage conflict honorably and with the least loss of time and a minimum sacrifice of life. Its growing bloodshed has caused me the deepest anguish and anxiety. Those gallant men will remain often in my thoughts and in my prayers always.

I am closing my 52 years of military service. When I joined the Army, even before the turn of the century, it was the fulfillment of all my boyish hopes and dreams. The world has turned over many times since I took the oath on the Plain at West Point, and the hopes and dreams have long since vanished. But I still remember the refrain of one of the most popular barrack ballads of that day, which proclaimed, most proudly, that "Old soldiers never die. They just fade away."

And like the old soldier of that ballad, I now close my military career and just fade away—an old soldier who tried to do his duty as God gave him the light to see that duty.

Goodbye.

RICHARD M. NIXON

"Checkers" Speech

Hollywood, California, September 23, 1952

MY FELLOW AMERICANS:
 I come before you tonight as a candidate for the Vice Presidency and as a man whose honesty and integrity have been questioned.

The usual political thing to do when charges are made against you is to either ignore them or to deny them without giving details.

I believe we've had enough of that in the United States, particularly with the present Administration in Washington, D.C. To me the office of the Vice Presidency of the United States is a great office, and I feel that the people have got to have confidence in the integrity of the men who run for that office and who might obtain it.

I have a theory, too, that the best and only answer to a smear or to an honest misunderstanding of the facts is to tell the truth. And that's why I'm here tonight. I want to tell you my side of the case.

I am sure that you have read the charge and you've heard it that I, Senator Nixon, took $18,000 from a group of my supporters.

Now, was that wrong? And let me say that it was wrong— I'm saying, incidentally, that it was wrong and not just illegal. Because it isn't a question of whether it was legal or illegal, that isn't enough. The question is, was it morally wrong?

I say that it was morally wrong if any of that $18,000 went to Senator Nixon for my personal use. I say that it was morally wrong if it was secretly given and secretly handled. And I say that it was morally wrong if any of the contributors got special favors for the contributions that they made.

And now to answer those questions let me say this:

Not one cent of the $18,000 or any other money of that

type ever went to me for my personal use. Every penny of it was used to pay for political expenses that I did not think should be charged to the taxpayers of the United States.

It was not a secret fund. As a matter of fact, when I was on "Meet the Press," some of you may have seen it last Sunday— Peter Edson came up to me after the program and he said, "Dick, what about this fund we hear about?" And I said, Well, there's no secret about it. Go out and see Dana Smith, who was the administrator of the fund. And I gave him his address, and I said that you will find that the purpose of the fund simply was to defray political expenses that I did not feel should be charged to the Government.

And third, let me point out, and I want to make this particularly clear, that no contributor to this fund, no contributor to any of my campaign, has ever received any consideration that he would not have received as an ordinary constituent.

I just don't believe in that and I can say that never, while I have been in the Senate of the United States, as far as the people that contributed to this fund are concerned, have I made a telephone call for them to an agency, or have I gone down to an agency in their behalf. And the record will show that, the records which are in the hands of the Administration.

But then some of you will say and rightly, "Well, what did you use the fund for, Senator? Why did you have to have it?"

Let me tell you in just a word how a Senate office operates First of all, a Senator gets $15,000 a year in salary. He gets enough money to pay for one trip a year, a round trip that is, for himself and his family between his home and Washington, D.C.

And then he gets an allowance to handle the people that work in his office, to handle his mail. And the allowance for my State of California is enough to hire thirteen people.

And let me say, incidentally, that that allowance is not paid to the Senator—it's paid directly to the individuals that the Senator puts on his payroll, that all of these people and all of these allowances are for strictly official business. Business, for example, when a constituent writes in and wants you to go down to the Veterans Administration and get some information about his GI policy. Items of that type for example.

But there are other expenses which are not covered by the

Government. And I think I can best discuss those expenses by asking you some questions. Do you think that when I or any other Senator makes a political speech, has it printed, should charge the printing of that speech and the mailing of that speech to the taxpayers?

Do you think, for example, when I or any other Senator makes a trip to his home state to make a purely political speech that the cost of that trip should be charged to the taxpayers?

Do you think when a Senator makes political broadcasts or political television broadcasts, radio or television, that the expense of those broadcasts should be charged to the taxpayers?

Well, I know what your answer is. The same answer that audiences give me whenever I discuss this particular problem. The answer is, "no." The taxpayers shouldn't be required to finance items which are not official business but which are primarily political business.

But then the question arises, you say, "Well, how do you pay for these and how can you do it legally?"

And there are several ways that it can be done, incidentally, and that it is done legally in the United States Senate and in the Congress.

The first way is to be a rich man. I don't happen to be a rich man so I couldn't use that.

Another way that is used is to put your wife on the payroll. Let me say, incidentally, my opponent, my opposite number for the Vice Presidency on the Democratic ticket, does have his wife on the payroll. And has had her on his payroll for the ten years—the past ten years.

Now just let me say this. That's his business and I'm not critical of him for doing that. You will have to pass judgment on that particular point. But I have never done that for this reason. I have found that there are so many deserving stenographers and secretaries in Washington that needed the work that I just didn't feel it was right to put my wife on the payroll.

My wife's sitting over here. She's a wonderful stenographer. She used to teach stenography and she used to teach shorthand in high school. That was when I met her. And I can tell you folks that she's worked many hours at night and many hours on Saturdays and Sundays in my office and she's done a fine job. And I'm proud to say tonight that in the six years I've been in the House and the Senate of the United States, Pat Nixon has never been on the Government payroll.

There are other ways that these finances can be taken care of. Some who are lawyers, and I happen to be a lawyer, continue to practice law. But I haven't been able to do that. I'm so far away from California that I've been so busy with my Senatorial work that I have not engaged in any legal practice.

And also as far as law practice is concerned, it seemed to me that the relationship between an attorney and the client was so personal that you couldn't possibly represent a man as an attorney and then have an unbiased view when he presented his case to you in the event that he had one before the Government.

And so I felt that the best way to handle these necessary political expenses of getting my message to the American people and the speeches I made, the speeches that I had printed, for the most part, concerned this one message—of exposing this Administration, the communism in it, the corruption in it— the only way that I could do that was to accept the aid which people in my home state of California who contributed to my campaign and who continued to make these contributions after I was elected were glad to make.

And let me say I am proud of the fact that not one of them has ever asked me for a special favor. I'm proud of the fact that not one of them has ever asked me to vote on a bill other than as my own conscience would dictate. And I am proud of the fact that the taxpayers by subterfuge or otherwise have never paid one dime for expenses which I thought were political and shouldn't be charged to the taxpayers.

Let me say, incidentally, that some of you may say, "Well, that's all right, Senator; that's your explanation, but have you got any proof?"

And I'd like to tell you this evening that just about an hour ago we received an independent audit of this entire fund.

I suggested to Gov. Sherman Adams, who is the chief of staff of the Dwight Eisenhower campaign, that an independent audit and legal report be obtained. And I have that audit here in my hand.

It's an audit made by the Price, Waterhouse & Co. firm, and the legal opinion by Gibson, Dunn & Crutcher, lawyers in Los

Angeles, the biggest law firm and incidentally one of the best ones in Los Angeles.

I'm proud to be able to report to you tonight that this audit and this legal opinion is being forwarded to General Eisenhower. And I'd like to read to you the opinion that was prepared by Gibson, Dunn & Crutcher and based on all the pertinent laws and statutes, together with the audit report prepared by the certified public accountants.

"It is our conclusion that Senator Nixon did not obtain any financial gain from the collection and disbursement of the fund by Dana Smith; that Senator Nixon did not violate any Federal or state law by reason of the operation of the fund, and that neither the portion of the fund paid by Dana Smith directly to third persons nor the portion paid to Senator Nixon to reimburse him for designated office expenses constituted income to the Senator which was either reportable or taxable as income under applicable tax laws. (signed) Gibson, Dunn & Crutcher by Alma H. Conway."

Now that, my friends, is not Nixon speaking, but that's an independent audit which was requested because I want the American people to know all the facts and I'm not afraid of having independent people go in and check the facts, and that is exactly what they did.

But then I realize that there are still some who may say, and rightly so, and let me say that I recognize that some will continue to smear regardless of what the truth may be, but that there has been understandably some honest misunderstanding on this matter, and there's some that will say:

"Well, maybe you were able, Senator, to fake this thing. How can we believe what you say? After all, is there a possibility that maybe you got some sums in cash? Is there a possibility that you may have feathered your own nest?"

And so now what I am going to do—and incidentally this is unprecedented in the history of American politics—I am going at this time to give to this television and radio audience a complete financial history; everything I've earned; everything I've spent; everything I owe. And I want you to know the facts. I'll have to start early.

I was born in 1913. Our family was one of modest circumstances and most of my early life was spent in a store out in

East Whittier. It was a grocery store—one of those family enterprises. The only reason we were able to make it go was because my mother and dad had five boys and we all worked in the store.

I worked my way through college and to a great extent through law school. And then, in 1940, probably the best thing that ever happened to me happened. I married Pat—sitting over here. We had a rather difficult time after we were married, like so many of the young couples who may be listening to us. I practiced law; she continued to teach school. I went into the service.

Let me say that my service record was not a particularly unusual one. I went to the South Pacific. I guess I'm entitled to a couple of battle stars. I got a couple of letters of commendation but I was just there when the bombs were falling and then I returned. I returned to the United States and in 1946 I ran for the Congress.

When we came out of the war, Pat and I—Pat during the war had worked as a stenographer and in a bank and as an economist for a Government agency—and when we came out the total of our savings from both my law practice, her teaching and all the time that I was in the war—the total for that entire period was just a little less than $10,000. Every cent of that, incidentally, was in Government bonds.

Well that's where we start when I go into politics. Now what have I earned since I went into politics? Well here it is—I jotted it down, let me read the notes. First of all I've had my salary as a Congressman and as a Senator. Second, I have received a total in this past six years of $1,600 from estates which were in my law firm at the time that I severed my connection with it.

And, incidentally, as I said before, I have not engaged in any legal practice and have not accepted any fees from business that came into the firm after I went into politics. I have made an average of approximately $1,500 a year from non-political speaking engagements and lectures. And then, fortunately, we've inherited a little money. Pat sold her interest in her father's estate for $3,000 and I inherited $1,500 from my grandfather.

We live rather modestly. For four years we lived in an

apartment in Park Fairfax, in Alexandria, Va. The rent was $80 a month. And we saved for the time that we could buy a house.

Now, that was what we took in. What did we do with this money? What do we have today to show for it? This will surprise you, because it is so little, I suppose, as standards generally go, of people in public life. First of all, we've got a house in Washington which cost $41,000 and on which we owe $20,000.

We have a house in Whittier, Calif., which cost $13,000 and on which we owe $3,000. My folks are living there at the present time.

I have just $4,000 in life insurance, plus my G.I. policy which I've never been able to convert and which will run out in two years. I have no life insurance whatever on Pat. I have no life insurance on our two youngsters, Patricia and Julie. I own a 1950 Oldsmobile car. We have our furniture. We have no stocks and bonds of any type. We have no interest of any kind, direct or indirect, in any business.

Now, that's what we have. What do we owe? Well, in addition to the mortgage, the $20,000 mortgage on the house in Washington, the $10,000 one on the house in Whittier, I owe $4,500 to the Riggs Bank in Washington, D.C., with interest 4½ per cent.

I owe $3,500 to my parents and the interest on that loan which I pay regularly, because it's the part of the savings they made through the years they were working so hard, I pay regularly 4 per cent interest. And then I have a $500 loan which I have on my life insurance.

Well, that's about it. That's what we have and that's what we owe. It isn't very much but Pat and I have the satisfaction that every dime that we've got is honestly ours. I should say this—that Pat doesn't have a mink coat. But she does have a respectable Republican cloth coat. And I always tell her that she'd look good in anything.

One other thing I probably should tell you, because if I don't they'll probably be saying this about me too, we did get something—a gift—after the election. A man down in Texas heard Pat on the radio mention the fact that our two youngsters would like to have a dog. And, believe it or not, the day before we left on this campaign trip we got a message from

Union Station in Baltimore saying they had a package for us. We went down to get it. You know what it was.

It was a little cocker spaniel dog in a crate that he sent all the way from Texas. Black and white spotted. And our little girl—Trisha, the 6-year-old—named it Checkers. And you know the kids love the dog and I just want to say this right now, that regardless of what they say about it, we're gonna keep it.

It isn't easy to come before a nation-wide audience and air your life as I've done. But I want to say some things before I conclude that I think most of you will agree on. Mr. Mitchell, the chairman of the Democratic National Committee, made the statement that if a man couldn't afford to be in the United States Senate he shouldn't run for the Senate.

And I just want to make my position clear. I don't agree with Mr. Mitchell when he says that only a rich man should serve his Government in the United States Senate or in the Congress.

I don't believe that represents the thinking of the Democratic party, and I know that it doesn't represent the thinking of the Republican party.

I believe that it's fine that a man like Governor Stevenson who inherited a fortune from his father can run for President. But I also feel that it's essential in this country of ours that a man of modest means can also run for President. Because, you know, remember Abraham Lincoln, you remember what he said: "God must have loved the common people—he made so many of them."

And now I'm going to suggest some courses of conduct.

First of all, you have read in the papers about other funds now. Mr. Stevenson, apparently, had a couple. One of them in which a group of business people paid and helped to supplement the salaries of state employes. Here is where the money went directly into their pockets.

And I think that what Mr. Stevenson should do should be to come before the American people as I have, give the names of the people that have contributed to that fund; give the names of the people who put this money into their pockets at the same time that they were receiving money from their state government, and see what favors, if any, they gave out for that.

I don't condemn Mr. Stevenson for what he did. But until the facts are in there there is a doubt that will be raised.

And as far as Mr. Sparkman is concerned, I would suggest the same thing. He's had his wife on the payroll. I don't condemn him for that. But I think that he should come before the American people and indicate what outside sources of income he has had.

I would suggest that under the circumstances both Mr. Sparkman and Mr. Stevenson should come before the American people as I have and make a complete financial statement as to their financial history. And if they don't it will be an admission that they have something to hide. And I think that you will agree with me.

Because folks, remember, a man that's to be President of the United States, a man that's to be Vice President of the United States must have the confidence of all the people. And that's why I'm doing what I'm doing, and that's why I suggest that Mr. Stevenson and Mr. Sparkman since they are under attack should do what they are doing.

Now, let me say this: I know that this is not the last of the smears. In spite of my explanation tonight other smears will be made; others have been made in the past. And the purpose of the smears, I know, is this—to silence me, to make me let up.

Well, they just don't know who they're dealing with. I'm going to tell you this: I remember in the dark days of the Hiss case some of the same columnists, some of the same radio commentators who are attacking me now and misrepresenting my position were violently opposing me at the time I was after Alger Hiss.

But I continued the fight because I knew I was right. And I can say to this great television and radio audience that I have no apologies to the American people for my part in putting Alger Hiss where he is today.

And as far as this is concerned, I intend to continue the fight.

Why do I feel so deeply? Why do I feel that in spite of the smears, the misunderstandings, the necessities for a man to come up here and bare his soul as I have? Why is it necessary for me to continue this fight?

And I want to tell you why. Because, you see, I love my country. And I think my country is in danger. And I think that

the only man that can save America at this time is the man that's running for President on my ticket—Dwight Eisenhower.

You say, "Why do I think it's in danger?" and I say look at the record. Seven years of the Truman-Acheson Administration and what's happened? Six hundred million people lost to the Communists, and a war in Korea in which we have lost 117,000 American casualties.

And I say to all of you that a policy that results in a loss of 600,000,000 to the Communists and a war which costs us 117,000 American casualties isn't good enough for America.

And I say that those in the State Department that made the mistakes which caused that war and which resulted in those losses should be kicked out of the State Department just as fast as we can get 'em out of there.

And let me say that I know Mr. Stevenson won't do that. Because he defends the Truman policy and I know that Dwight Eisenhower will do that, and that he will give America the leadership that it needs.

Take the problem of corruption. You've read about the mess in Washington. Mr. Stevenson can't clean it up because he was picked by the man, Truman, under whose Administration the mess was made. You wouldn't trust a man who made the mess to clean it up—that's Truman. And by the same token you can't trust the man who was picked by the man that made the mess to clean it up—and that's Stevenson.

And so I say, Eisenhower, who owes nothing to Truman, nothing to the big city bosses, he is the man that can clean up the mess in Washington.

Take communism. I say that as far as that subject is concerned, the danger is great to America. In the Hiss case they got the secrets which enabled them to break the American secret State Department code. They got secrets in the atomic bomb case which enabled 'em to get the secret of the atomic bomb, five years before they would have gotten it by their own devices.

And I say that any man who called the Alger Hiss case a "red herring" isn't fit to be President of the United States. I say that a man who like Mr. Stevenson has pooh-poohed and ridiculed the Communist threat in the United States—he said that they

are phantoms among ourselves; he's accused us that have attempted to expose the Communists of looking for Communists in the Bureau of Fisheries and Wildlife—I say that a man who says that isn't qualified to be President of the United States.

And I say that the only man who can lead us in this fight to rid the Government of both those who are Communists and those who have corrupted this Government is Eisenhower, because Eisenhower, you can be sure, recognizes the problem and he knows how to deal with it.

Now let me say that, finally, this evening I want to read to you just briefly excerpts from a letter which I received, a letter which, after all this is over, no one can take away from me. It reads as follows:

"Dear Senator Nixon,

"Since I'm only 19 years of age I can't vote in this Presidential election but believe me if I could you and General Eisenhower would certainly get my vote. My husband is in the Fleet Marines in Korea. He's a corpsman on the front lines and we have a two-month-old son he's never seen. And I feel confident that with great Americans like you and General Eisenhower in the White House, lonely Americans like myself will be united with their loved ones now in Korea.

"I only pray to God that you won't be too late. Enclosed is a small check to help you in your campaign. Living on $85 a month is all I can afford at present. But let me know what else I can do."

Folks, it's a check for $10, and it's one that I will never cash.

And just let me say this. We hear a lot about prosperity these days but I say, why can't we have prosperity built on peace rather than prosperity built on war? Why can't we have prosperity and an honest government in Washington, D.C., at the same time. Believe me, we can. And Eisenhower is the man that can lead this crusade to bring us that kind of prosperity.

And, now, finally, I know that you wonder whether or not I am going to stay on the Republican ticket or resign.

Let me say this: I don't believe that I ought to quit because I'm not a quitter. And, incidentally, Pat's not a quitter. After all, her name was Patricia Ryan and she was born on St. Patrick's Day, and you know the Irish never quit.

But the decision, my friends, is not mine. I would do

nothing that would harm the possibilities of Dwight Eisenhower to become President of the United States. And for that reason I am submitting to the Republican National Committee tonight through this television broadcast the decision which it is theirs to make.

Let them decide whether my position on the ticket will help or hurt. And I am going to ask you to help them decide. Wire and write the Republican National Committee whether you think I should stay on or whether I should get off. And whatever their decision is, I will abide by it.

But just let me say this last word. Regardless of what happens I'm going to continue this fight. I'm going to campaign up and down America until we drive the crooks and the Communists and those that defend them out of Washington. And remember, folks, Eisenhower is a great man. Believe me. He's a great man. And a vote for Eisenhower is a vote for what's good for America.

MARTIN LUTHER KING, JR.

Speech to the Montgomery Improvement Association

Montgomery, Alabama, December 5, 1955

M Y FRIENDS, we are certainly very happy to see each of
you out this evening. We are here this evening for serious business. [*Audience:*] (*Yes*) We are here in a general sense
because first and foremost we are American citizens (*That's
right*) and we are determined to apply our citizenship to the
fullness of its meaning. (*Yeah, That's right*) We are here also
because of our love for democracy (*Yes*), because of our deep-
seated belief that democracy transformed from thin paper to
thick action (*Yes*) is the greatest form of government on earth.
(*That's right*)

But we are here in a specific sense because of the bus situation in Montgomery. (*Yes*) We are here because we are determined to get the situation corrected. This situation is not at all
new. The problem has existed over endless years. (*That's right*)
For many years now, Negroes in Montgomery and so many
other areas have been inflicted with the paralysis of crippling
fear (*Yes*) on buses in our community. (*That's right*) On so many
occasions, Negroes have been intimidated and humiliated and
impressed—oppressed—because of the sheer fact that they
were Negroes. (*That's right*) I don't have time this evening to
go into the history of these numerous cases. Many of them now
are lost in the thick fog of oblivion (*Yes*), but at least one stands
before us now with glaring dimensions. (*Yes*)

Just the other day, just last Thursday to be exact, one of the
finest citizens in Montgomery (*Amen*)—not one of the finest
Negro citizens (*That's right*), but one of the finest citizens in
Montgomery—was taken from a bus (*Yes*) and carried to jail
and arrested (*Yes*) because she refused to get up to give her seat
to a white person. (*Yes, That's right*) Now the press would have
us believe that she refused to leave a reserved section for

Negroes (*Yes*), but I want you to know this evening that there is no reserved section. (*All right*) The law has never been clarified at that point. (*Hell no*) Now I think I speak with, with legal authority—not that I have any legal authority, but I think I speak with legal authority behind me (*All right*)—that the law, the ordinance, the city ordinance has never been totally clarified. (*That's right*)

Mrs. Rosa Parks is a fine person. (*Well, Well said*) And, since it had to happen, I'm happy that it happened to a person like Mrs. Parks (*Yes*), for nobody can doubt the boundless outreach of her integrity. (*Sure enough*) Nobody can doubt the height of her character (*Yes*), nobody can doubt the depth of her Christian commitment and devotion to the teachings of Jesus. (*All right*) And I'm happy, since it had to happen, it happened to a person that nobody can call a disturbing factor in the community. (*All right*) Mrs. Parks is a fine Christian person, unassuming, and yet there is integrity and character there. And just because she refused to get up, she was arrested.

And you know, my friends, there comes a time when people get tired of being trampled over by the iron feet of oppression. [*Sustained applause*] There comes a time, my friends, when people get tired of being plunged across the abyss of humiliation, where they experience the bleakness of nagging despair. (*Keep talking*) There comes a time when people get tired of being pushed out of the glittering sunlight of life's July and left standing amid the piercing chill of an alpine November. (*That's right*) [*Applause*] There comes a time. (*Yes sir. Teach*) [*Applause continues*]

We are here, we are here this evening because we are tired now. (*Yes*) [*Applause*] And I want to say that we are not here advocating violence. (*No*) We have never done that. (*Repeat that, Repeat that*) [*Applause*] I want it to be known throughout Montgomery and throughout this nation (*Well*) that we are Christian people. (*Yes*) [*Applause*] We believe in the Christian religion. We believe in the teachings of Jesus. (*Well*) The only weapon that we have in our hands this evening is the weapon of protest. (*Yes*) [*Applause*] That's all.

And certainly, certainly, this is the glory of America, with all of its faults. (*Yeah*) This is the glory of our democracy. If we were incarcerated behind the iron curtains of a Communistic nation we couldn't do this. If we were dropped in the dungeon of a totalitarian regime we couldn't do this. (*All right*) But the great glory of American democracy is the right to protest for right. (*That's right*) [*Applause*] My friends, don't let anybody make us feel that we are to be compared in our actions with the Ku Klux Klan or with the White Citizens' Council. [*Applause*] There will be no crosses burned at any bus stops in Montgomery. (*Well, That's right*) There will be no white persons pulled out of their homes and taken out on some distant road and lynched for not cooperating. [*Applause*] There will be nobody amid, among us who will stand up and defy the Constitution of this nation. [*Applause*] We only assemble here because of our desire to see right exist. [*Applause*] My friends, I want it to be known that we're going to work with grim and bold determination to gain justice on the buses in this city. [*Applause*]

And we are not wrong, we are not wrong in what we are doing. (*Well*) If we are wrong, the Supreme Court of this nation is wrong. (*Yes sir*) [*Applause*] If we are wrong, the Constitution of the United States is wrong. (*Yes*) [*Applause*] If we are wrong, God Almighty is wrong. (*That's right*) [*Applause*] If we are wrong, Jesus of Nazareth was merely a utopian dreamer that never came down to earth. (*Yes*) [*Applause*] If we are wrong, justice is a lie. (*Yes*) Love has no meaning. [*Applause*] And we are determined here in Montgomery to work and fight until justice runs down like water (*Yes*) [*Applause*], and righteousness like a mighty stream. (*Keep talking*) [*Applause*]

I want to say that in all of our actions, we must stick together. (*That's right*) [*Applause*] Unity is the great need of the hour (*Well, That's right*), and if we are united we can get many of the things that we not only desire but which we justly deserve. (*Yeah*) And don't let anybody frighten you. (*Yeah*) We are not afraid of what we are doing (*Oh no*), because we are doing it within the law. (*All right*) There is never a time in our American democracy that we must ever think we are wrong when we protest. (*Yes sir*) We reserve that right. When labor all over this nation came to see that it would be trampled over by capitalistic power, it was nothing wrong with labor getting together and organizing and protesting for its rights. (*That's right*)

We, the disinherited of this land, we who have been oppressed so long, are tired of going through the long night of captivity. And now we are reaching out for the daybreak of freedom and justice and equality. [*Applause*] May I say to you, my friends, as I come to a close, and just giving some idea of why we are assembled here, that we must keep—and I want to stress this, in all of our doings, in all of our deliberations here this evening and all of the week and while—whatever we do, we must keep God in the forefront. (*Yeah*) Let us be Christian in all of our actions. (*That's right*) But I want to tell you this evening that it is not enough for us to talk about love, love is one of the pivotal points of the Christian faith. There is another side called justice. And justice is really love in calculation. (*All right*) Justice is love correcting that which revolts against love. (*Well*)

The Almighty God himself is not the only, not the God just standing out saying through Hosea, "I love you, Israel." He's also the God that stands up before the nations and said: "Be still and know that I'm God (*Yeah*), that if you don't obey me I will break the backbone of your power (*Yeah*) and slap you out of the orbits of your international and national relationships." (*That's right*) Standing beside love is always justice, and we are only using the tools of justice. Not only are we using the tools of persuasion, but we've come to see that we've got to use the tools of coercion. Not only is this thing a process of education, but it is also a process of legislation. [*Applause*]

And as we stand and sit here this evening and as we prepare ourselves for what lies ahead, let us go out with the grim and bold determination that we are going to stick together. [*Applause*] We are going to work together. [*Applause*] Right here in Montgomery, when the history books are written in the future (*Yes*), somebody will have to say, "There lived a race of people (*Well*), a *black* people (*Yes sir*), fleecy locks and black complexion (*Yes*), a people who had the moral courage to stand up for their rights. [*Applause*] And thereby they injected a new meaning into the veins of history and of civilization." And we're going to do that. God grant that we will do it before it is too late. (*Oh yeah*) As we proceed with our program, let us think of these things. (*Yes*) [*Applause*]

DWIGHT D. EISENHOWER

Second Inaugural Address

Washington, D.C., January 21, 1957

M R. CHAIRMAN, Mr. Vice President, Mr. Chief Justice, Mr. Speaker, members of my family and friends, my countrymen, and the friends of my country wherever they may be:

We meet again, as upon a like moment four years ago, and again you have witnessed my solemn oath of service to you.

I, too, am a witness, today testifying in your name to the principles and purposes to which we, as a people, are pledged.

Before all else, we seek, upon our common labor as a nation, the blessings of Almighty God. And the hopes in our hearts fashion the deepest prayers of our whole people.

May we pursue the right—without self-righteousness.

May we know unity—without conformity.

May we grow in strength—without pride in self.

May we, in our dealings with all peoples of the earth, ever speak truth and serve justice.

And so shall America—in the sight of all men of good will—prove true to the honorable purposes that bind and rule us as a people in all this time of trial through which we pass.

We live in a land of plenty, but rarely has this earth known such peril as today.

In our nation work and wealth abound. Our population grows. Commerce crowds our rivers and rails, our skies, harbors and highways. Our soil is fertile, our agriculture productive. The air rings with the song of our industry—rolling mills and blast furnaces, dynamos, dams and assembly lines—the chorus of America the bountiful.

Now this is our home—yet this is not the whole of our world. For our world is where our full destiny lies—with men, of all peoples and all nations, who are or would be free. And for them—and so for us—this is no time of ease or of rest.

In too much of the earth there is want, discord, danger. New forces and new nations stir and strive across the earth, with power to bring, by their fate, great good or great evil to the free world's future. From the deserts of North Africa to the islands of the South Pacific one third of all mankind has entered upon an historic struggle for a new freedom: freedom from grinding poverty. Across all continents, nearly a billion people seek, sometimes almost in desperation, for the skills and knowledge and assistance by which they may satisfy from their own resources, the material wants common to all mankind.

No nation, however old or great, escapes this tempest of change and turmoil. Some, impoverished by the recent World War, seek to restore their means of livelihood. In the heart of Europe, Germany still stands tragically divided. So is the whole continent divided. And so, too, all the world.

The divisive force is International Communism and the power that it controls.

The designs of that power, dark in purpose, are clear in practice. It strives to seal forever the fate of those it has enslaved. It strives to break the ties that unite the free. And it strives to capture—to exploit for its own greater power—all forces of change in the world, especially the needs of the hungry and the hopes of the oppressed.

Yet the world of International Communism has itself been shaken by a fierce and mighty force: the readiness of men who love freedom to pledge their lives to that love. Through the night of their bondage, the unconquerable will of heroes has struck with the swift, sharp thrust of lightning. Budapest is no longer merely the name of a city; henceforth it is a new and shining symbol of man's yearning to be free.

Thus across all the globe there harshly blow the winds of change. And, we—though fortunate be our lot—know that we can never turn our backs to them.

We look upon this shaken earth, and we declare our firm and fixed purpose—the building of a peace with justice in a world where moral law prevails.

The building of such a peace is a bold and solemn purpose. To proclaim it is easy. To serve it will be hard. And to attain it, we must be aware of its full meaning—and ready to pay its full price.

We know clearly what we seek, and why.

We seek peace, knowing that peace is the climate of freedom. And now, as in no other age, we seek it because we have been warned, by the power of modern weapons, that peace may be the only climate possible for human life itself.

Yet this peace we seek cannot be born of fear alone: it must be rooted in the lives of nations. There must be justice, sensed and shared by all peoples, for, without justice the world can know only a tense and unstable truce. There must be law, steadily invoked and respected by all nations, for without law, the world promises only such meager justice as the pity of the strong upon the weak. But the law of which we speak, comprehending the values of freedom, affirms the equality of all nations, great and small.

Splendid as can be the blessings of such a peace, high will be its cost: in toil patiently sustained, in help honorably given, in sacrifice calmly borne.

We are called to meet the price of this peace.

To counter the threat of those who seek to rule by force, we must pay the costs of our own needed military strength, and help to build the security of others.

We must use our skills and knowledge and, at times, our substance, to help others rise from misery, however far the scene of suffering may be from our shores. For wherever in the world a people knows desperate want, there must appear at least the spark of hope, the hope of progress—or there will surely rise at last the flames of conflict.

We recognize and accept our own deep involvement in the destiny of men everywhere. We are accordingly pledged to honor, and to strive to fortify, the authority of the United Nations. For in that body rests the best hope of our age for the assertion of that law by which all nations may live in dignity.

And beyond this general resolve, we are called to act a responsible role in the world's great concerns or conflicts—whether they touch upon the affairs of a vast region, the fate of an island in the Pacific, or the use of a canal in the Middle East. Only in respecting the hopes and cultures of others will we practice the equality of all nations. Only as we show willingness and wisdom in giving counsel—in receiving counsel—and in sharing burdens, will we wisely perform the work of peace.

For one truth must rule all we think and all we do. No people can live to itself alone. The unity of all who dwell in freedom is their only sure defense. The economic need of all nations—in mutual dependence—makes isolation an impossibility: not even America's prosperity could long survive if other nations did not also prosper. No nation can longer be a fortress, lone and strong and safe. And any people, seeking such shelter for themselves, can now build only their own prison.

Our pledge to these principles is constant, because we believe in their rightness.

We do not fear this world of change. America is no stranger to much of its spirit. Everywhere we see the seeds of the same growth that America itself has known. The American experiment has, for generations, fired the passion and the courage of millions elsewhere seeking freedom, equality, opportunity. And the American story of material progress has helped excite the longing of all needy peoples for some satisfaction of their human wants. These hopes that we have helped to inspire, we can help to fulfill.

In this confidence, we speak plainly to all peoples.

We cherish our friendship with all nations that are or would be free. We respect, no less, their independence. And when, in time of want or peril, they ask our help, they may honorably receive it; for we no more seek to buy their sovereignty than we would sell our own. Sovereignty is never bartered among free men.

We honor the aspirations of those nations which, now captive, long for freedom. We seek neither their military alliance nor any artificial imitation of our society. And they can know the warmth of the welcome that awaits them when, as must be, they join again the ranks of freedom.

We honor, no less in this divided world than in a less tormented time, the people of Russia. We do not dread, rather do we welcome, their progress in education and industry. We wish them success in their demands for more intellectual freedom, greater security before their own laws, fuller enjoyment of the rewards of their own toil. For as such things come to pass, the more certain will be the coming of that day when our peoples may freely meet in friendship.

So we voice our hope and our belief that we can help to heal this divided world. Thus may the nations cease to live in trembling before the menace of force. Thus may the weight of fear and the weight of arms be taken from the burdened shoulders of mankind.

This, nothing less, is the labor to which we are called and our strength dedicated.

And so the prayer of our people carries far beyond our own frontiers, to the wide world of our duty and our destiny.

May the light of freedom, coming to all darkened lands, flame brightly—until at last the darkness is no more.

May the turbulence of our age yield to a true time of peace, when men and nations shall share a life that honors the dignity of each, the brotherhood of all.

Thank you very much.

JOHN F. KENNEDY

Speech to the Greater Houston Ministerial Association

Houston, September 12, 1960

REVEREND MEZA, Reverend Reck, I'm grateful for your generous invitation to speak my views.

While the so-called religious issue is necessarily and properly the chief topic here tonight, I want to emphasize from the outset that we have far more critical issues to face in the 1960 election; the spread of Communist influence, until it now festers 90 miles off the coast of Florida—the humiliating treatment of our President and Vice President by those who no longer respect our power—the hungry children I saw in West Virginia, the old people who cannot pay their doctor bills, the families forced to give up their farms—an America with too many slums, with too few schools, and too late to the moon and outer space.

These are the real issues which should decide this campaign. And they are not religious issues—for war and hunger and ignorance and despair know no religious barriers.

But because I am a Catholic, and no Catholic has ever been elected President, the real issues in this campaign have been obscured—perhaps deliberately, in some quarters less responsible than this. So it is apparently necessary for me to state once again—not what kind of church I believe in, for that should be important only to me—but what kind of America I believe in.

I believe in an America where the separation of church and state is absolute—where no Catholic prelate would tell the President (should he be Catholic) how to act, and no Protestant minister would tell his parishioners for whom to vote—where no church or church school is granted any public funds or political preference—and where no man is denied public office merely because his religion differs from the President who might appoint him or the people who might elect him.

I believe in an America that is officially neither Catholic, Protestant nor Jewish—where no public official either requests or accepts instructions on public policy from the Pope, the National Council of Churches or any other ecclesiastical source—where no religious body seeks to impose its will directly or indirectly upon the general populace or the public acts of its officials—and where religious liberty is so indivisible that an act against one church is treated as an act against all.

For while this year it may be a Catholic against whom the finger of suspicion is pointed, in other years it has been, and may someday be again, a Jew—or a Quaker—or a Unitarian—or a Baptist. It was Virginia's harassment of Baptist preachers, for example, that helped lead to Jefferson's statute of religious freedom. Today I may be the victim—but tomorrow it may be you—until the whole fabric of our harmonious society is ripped at a time of great national peril.

Finally, I believe in an America where religious intolerance will someday end—where all men and all churches are treated as equal—where every man has the same right to attend or not attend the church of his choice—where there is no Catholic vote, no anti-Catholic vote, no bloc voting of any kind—and where Catholics, Protestants and Jews, at both the lay and pastoral level, will refrain from those attitudes of disdain and division which have so often marred their works in the past, and promote instead the American ideal of brotherhood.

That is the kind of America in which I believe. And it represents the kind of Presidency in which I believe—a great office that must neither be humbled by making it the instrument of any one religious group nor tarnished by arbitrarily withholding its occupancy from the members of any one religious group. I believe in a President whose religious views are his own private affair, neither imposed by him upon the Nation or imposed by the Nation upon him as a condition to holding that office.

I would not look with favor upon a President working to subvert the first amendment's guarantees of religious liberty. Nor would, our system of checks and balances permit him to do so—and neither do I look with favor upon those who would work to subvert Article VI of the Constitution by requiring a religious test—even by indirection—for it. If they disagree with that safeguard they should be out openly working to repeal it.

I want a Chief Executive whose public acts are responsible to all groups and obligated to none—who can attend any ceremony, service, or dinner his office may appropriately require of him—and whose fulfillment of his Presidential oath is not limited or conditioned by any religious oath, ritual, or obligation.

This is the kind of America I believe in—and this is the kind I fought for in the South Pacific, and the kind my brother died for in Europe. No one suggested then that we might have a "divided loyalty." that we did "not believe in liberty" or that we belonged to a disloyal group that threatened the "freedoms for which our forefathers died."

And in fact this is the kind of America for which our forefathers died—when they fled here to escape religious test oaths that denied office to members of less favored churches—when they fought for the Constitution, the Bill of Rights, and the Virginia Statute of Religious Freedom—and when they fought at the shrine I visited today, the Alamo. For side by side with Bowie and Crockett died McCafferty and Bailey and Carey—but no one knows whether they were Catholics or not. For there was no religious test at the Alamo.

I ask you tonight to follow in that tradition—to judge me on the basis of my record of 14 years in Congress—on my declared stands against an Ambassador to the Vatican, against unconstitutional aid to parochial schools, and against any boycott of the public schools (which I have attended myself)—instead of judging me on the basis of these pamphlets and publications we all have seen that carefully select quotations out of context from the statements of Catholic church leaders, usually in other countries, frequently in other centuries, and always omitting, of course, the statement of the American Bishops in 1948 which strongly endorsed church-state separation, and which more nearly reflects the views of almost every American Catholic.

I do not consider these other quotations binding upon my public acts—why should you? But let me say, with respect to other countries, that I am wholly opposed to the state being used by any religious group, Catholic or Protestant, to compel, prohibit, or persecute the free exercise of any other religion. And I hope that you and I condemn with equal fervor those nations which deny their Presidency to Protestants and those which deny it to Catholics. And rather than cite the misdeeds of those who differ, I would cite the record of the Catholic Church in such nations as Ireland and France—and the independence of such statesmen as Adenauer and De Gaulle.

But let me stress again that these are my views—for, contrary to common newspaper usage, I am not the Catholic candidate for President. I am the Democratic Party's candidate for President who happens also to be a Catholic. I do not speak for my Church on public matters—and the Church does not speak for me.

Whatever issue may come before me as President—on birth control, divorce, censorship, gambling or any other subject—I will make my decision in accordance with these views, in accordance with what my conscience tells me to be the national interest, and without regard to outside religious pressures or dictates. And no power or threat of punishment could cause me to decide otherwise.

But if the time should ever come—and I do not concede any conflict to be even remotely possible—when my office would require me to either violate my conscience or violate the national interest, then I would resign the office; and I hope any conscientious public servant would do the same.

But I do not intend to apologize for these views to my critics of either Catholic or Protestant faith—nor do I intend to disavow either my views or my Church in order to win this election.

If I should lose on the real issues, I shall return to my seat in the Senate, satisfied that I had tried my best and was fairly judged. But if this election is decided on the basis that 40 million Americans lost their chance of being President on the day they were baptized, then it is the whole Nation that will be the loser, in the eyes of Catholics and non-Catholics around the world, in the eyes of history, and in the eyes of our own people.

But if, on the other hand, I should win the election, then I shall devote every effort of mind and spirit to fulfilling the oath of the Presidency—practically identical, I might add, to the oath I have taken for 14 years in the Congress. For, without reservation, I can "solemnly swear that I will faithfully execute the office of President of the United States, and will to the best of my ability preserve, protect, and defend the Constitution * * * so help me God."

DWIGHT D. EISENHOWER

Farewell Address

Washington, D.C., January 17, 1961

MY FELLOW AMERICANS:
 Three days from now, after half a century in the service of our country, I shall lay down the responsibilities of office as, in traditional and solemn ceremony, the authority of the Presidency is vested in my successor.

This evening I come to you with a message of leave-taking and farewell, and to share a few final thoughts with you, my countrymen.

Like every other citizen, I wish the new President, and all who will labor with him, Godspeed. I pray that the coming years will be blessed with peace and prosperity for all.

Our people expect their President and the Congress to find essential agreement on issues of great moment, the wise resolution of which will better shape the future of the Nation.

My own relations with the Congress, which began on a remote and tenuous basis when, long ago, a member of the Senate appointed me to West Point, have since ranged to the intimate during the war and immediate post-war period, and, finally, to the mutually interdependent during these past eight years.

In this final relationship, the Congress and the Administration have, on most vital issues, cooperated well, to serve the national good rather than mere partisanship, and so have assured that the business of the Nation should go forward. So, my official relationship with the Congress ends in a feeling, on my part, of gratitude that we have been able to do so much together.

We now stand ten years past the midpoint of a century that has witnessed four major wars among great nations. Three of these involved our own country. Despite these holocausts America is today the strongest, the most influential and most productive nation in the world. Understandably proud of this pre-eminence, we yet realize that America's leadership and prestige depend, not merely upon our unmatched material progress, riches and military strength, but on how we use our power in the interests of world peace and human betterment.

Throughout America's adventure in free government, our basic purposes have been to keep the peace; to foster progress in human achievement, and to enhance liberty, dignity and integrity among people and among nations. To strive for less would be unworthy of a free and religious people. Any failure traceable to arrogance, or our lack of comprehension or readiness to sacrifice would inflict upon us grievous hurt both at home and abroad.

Progress toward these noble goals is persistently threatened by the conflict now engulfing the world. It commands our whole attention, absorbs our very beings. We face a hostile ideology—global in scope, atheistic in character, ruthless in purpose, and insidious in method. Unhappily the danger it poses promises to be of indefinite duration. To meet it successfully, there is called for, not so much the emotional and transitory sacrifices of crisis, but rather those which enable us to carry forward steadily, surely, and without complaint the burdens of a prolonged and complex struggle—with liberty the stake. Only thus shall we remain, despite every provocation, on our charted course toward permanent peace and human betterment.

Crises there will continue to be. In meeting them, whether foreign or domestic, great or small, there is a recurring temptation to feel that some spectacular and costly action could become the miraculous solution to all current difficulties. A huge increase in newer elements of our defense; development of unrealistic programs to cure every ill in agriculture; a dramatic expansion in basic and applied research—these and many other possibilities, each possibly promising in itself, may be suggested as the only way to the road we wish to travel.

But each proposal must be weighed in the light of a broader consideration: the need to maintain balance in and among national programs—balance between the private and the public economy, balance between cost and hoped for advantage—balance between the clearly necessary and the comfortably desirable; balance between our essential requirements as a nation and the duties imposed by the nation upon the individual; balance between actions of the moment and the national welfare of the future. Good judgment seeks balance and progress; lack of it eventually finds imbalance and frustration.

The record of many decades stands as proof that our people and their government have, in the main, understood these truths and have responded to them well, in the face of stress and threat. But threats, new in kind or degree, constantly arise. I mention two only.

A vital element in keeping the peace is our military establishment. Our arms must be mighty, ready for instant action, so that no potential aggressor may be tempted to risk his own destruction.

Our military organization today bears little relation to that known by any of my predecessors in peacetime, or indeed by the fighting men of World War II or Korea.

Until the latest of our world conflicts, the United States had no armaments industry. American makers of plowshares could, with time and as required, make swords as well. But now we can no longer risk emergency improvisation of national defense; we have been compelled to create a permanent armaments industry of vast proportions. Added to this, three and a half million men and women are directly engaged in the defense establishment. We annually spend on military security more than the net income of all United States corporations.

This conjunction of an immense military establishment and a large arms industry is new in the American experience. The total influence—economic, political, even spiritual—is felt in every city, every State house, every office of the Federal government. We recognize the imperative need for this development. Yet we must not fail to comprehend its grave implications. Our toil, resources and livelihood are all involved; so is the very structure of our society.

In the councils of government, we must guard against the acquisition of unwarranted influence, whether sought or unsought, by the military-industrial complex. The potential for the disastrous rise of misplaced power exists and will persist.

We must never let the weight of this combination endanger our liberties or democratic processes. We should take nothing for granted. Only an alert and knowledgeable citizenry can compel the proper meshing of the huge industrial and military machinery of defense with our peaceful methods and goals, so that security and liberty may prosper together.

Akin to, and largely responsible for the sweeping changes in our industrial-military posture, has been the technological revolution during recent decades.

In this revolution, research has become central; it also becomes more formalized, complex, and costly. A steadily increasing share is conducted for, by, or at the direction of, the Federal government.

Today, the solitary inventor, tinkering in his shop, has been overshadowed by task forces of scientists in laboratories and testing fields. In the same fashion, the free university, historically the fountainhead of free ideas and scientific discovery, has experienced a revolution in the conduct of research. Partly because of the huge costs involved, a government contract becomes virtually a substitute for intellectual curiosity. For every old blackboard there are now hundreds of new electronic computers.

The prospect of domination of the nation's scholars by Federal employment, project allocations, and the power of money is ever present—and is gravely to be regarded.

Yet, in holding scientific research and discovery in respect, as we should, we must also be alert to the equal and opposite danger that public policy could itself become the captive of a scientific-technological elite.

It is the task of statesmanship to mold, to balance, and to integrate these and other forces, new and old, within the principles of our democratic system—ever aiming toward the supreme goals of our free society.

Another factor in maintaining balance involves the element of time. As we peer into society's future, we—you and I, and our government—must avoid the impulse to live only for today, plundering, for our own ease and convenience, the precious resources of tomorrow. We cannot mortgage the material assets of our grandchildren without risking the loss also of their political and spiritual heritage. We want democracy to survive for all generations to come, not to become the insolvent phantom of tomorrow.

Down the long lane of the history yet to be written America knows that this world of ours, ever growing smaller, must avoid becoming a community of dreadful fear and hate, and be, instead, a proud confederation of mutual trust and respect.

Such a confederation must be one of equals. The weakest must come to the conference table with the same confidence as do we, protected as we are by our moral, economic, and military strength. That table, though scarred by many past frustrations, cannot be abandoned for the certain agony of the battlefield.

Disarmament, with mutual honor and confidence, is a continuing imperative. Together we must learn how to compose differences, not with arms, but with intellect and decent purpose. Because this need is so sharp and apparent I confess that I lay down my official responsibilities in this field with a definite sense of disappointment. As one who has witnessed the horror and the lingering sadness of war—as one who knows that another war could utterly destroy this civilization which has been so slowly and painfully built over thousands of years—I wish I could say tonight that a lasting peace is in sight.

Happily, I can say that war has been avoided. Steady progress toward our ultimate goal has been made. But, so much remains to be done. As a private citizen, I shall never cease to do what little I can to help the world advance along that road.

So—in this my last good night to you as your President—I thank you for the many opportunities you have given me for public service in war and peace. I trust that in that service you find some things worthy; as for the rest of it, I know you will find ways to improve performance in the future.

You and I—my fellow citizens—need to be strong in our faith that all nations, under God, will reach the goal of peace with justice. May we be ever unswerving in devotion to principle, confident but humble with power, diligent in pursuit of the Nation's great goals.

To all the peoples of the world, I once more give expression to America's prayerful and continuing aspiration:

We pray that peoples of all faiths, all races, all nations, may have their great human needs satisfied; that those now denied opportunity shall come to enjoy it to the full; that all who yearn for freedom may experience its spiritual blessings; that those who have freedom will understand, also, its heavy responsibilities; that all who are insensitive to the needs of others will learn charity; that the scourges of poverty, disease and ignorance will be made to disappear from the earth, and that, in the goodness of time, all peoples will come to live together in a peace guaranteed by the binding force of mutual respect and love.

JOHN F. KENNEDY

Inaugural Address

Washington, D.C., January 20, 1961

V ICE PRESIDENT JOHNSON, Mr. Speaker, Mr. Chief Justice, President Eisenhower, Vice President Nixon, President Truman, Reverend Clergy, fellow citizens:

We observe today not a victory of party but a celebration of freedom—symbolizing an end as well as a beginning—signifying renewal as well as change. For I have sworn before you and Almighty God the same solemn oath our forebears prescribed nearly a century and three quarters ago.

The world is very different now. For man holds in his mortal hands the power to abolish all forms of human poverty and all forms of human life. And yet the same revolutionary beliefs for which our forebears fought are still at issue around the globe—the belief that the rights of man come not from the generosity of the state but from the hand of God.

We dare not forget today that we are the heirs of that first revolution. Let the word go forth from this time and place, to friend and foe alike, that the torch has been passed to a new generation of Americans—born in this century, tempered by war, disciplined by a hard and bitter peace, proud of our ancient heritage—and unwilling to witness or permit the slow undoing of those human rights to which this nation has always been committed, and to which we are committed today at home and around the world.

Let every nation know, whether it wishes us well or ill, that we shall pay any price, bear any burden, meet any hardship, support any friend, oppose any foe to assure the survival and the success of liberty.

This much we pledge—and more.

To those old allies whose cultural and spiritual origins we share, we pledge the loyalty of faithful friends. United, there is little we cannot do in a host of cooperative ventures. Divided, there is little we can do—for we dare not meet a powerful challenge at odds and split asunder.

To those new states whom we welcome to the ranks of the free, we pledge our word that one form of colonial control shall not have passed away merely to be replaced by a far more iron tyranny. We shall not always expect to find them supporting our view. But we shall always hope to find them strongly supporting their own freedom—and to remember that, in the past, those who foolishly sought power by riding the back of the tiger ended up inside.

To those peoples in the huts and villages of half the globe struggling to break the bonds of mass misery, we pledge our best efforts to help them help themselves, for whatever period is required—not because the communists may be doing it, not because we seek their votes, but because it is right. If a free society cannot help the many who are poor, it cannot save the few who are rich.

To our sister republics south of our border, we offer a special pledge—to convert our good words into good deeds—in a new alliance for progress—to assist free men and free governments in casting off the chains of poverty. But this peaceful revolution of hope cannot become the prey of hostile powers. Let all our neighbors know that we shall join with them to oppose aggression or subversion anywhere in the Americas. And let every other power know that this Hemisphere intends to remain the master of its own house.

To that world assembly of sovereign states, the United Nations, our last best hope in an age where the instruments of war have far outpaced the instruments of peace, we renew our pledge of support—to prevent it from becoming merely a forum for invective—to strengthen its shield of the new and the weak—and to enlarge the area in which its writ may run.

Finally, to those nations who would make themselves our adversary, we offer not a pledge but a request: that both sides begin anew the quest for peace, before the dark powers of destruction unleashed by science engulf all humanity in planned or accidental self-destruction.

We dare not tempt them with weakness. For only when our arms are sufficient beyond doubt can we be certain beyond doubt that they will never be employed.

But neither can two great and powerful groups of nations take comfort from our present course—both sides overburdened by the cost of modern weapons, both rightly alarmed by the steady spread of the deadly atom, yet both racing to alter that uncertain balance of terror that stays the hand of mankind's final war.

So let us begin anew—remembering on both sides that civility is not a sign of weakness, and sincerity is always subject to proof. Let us never negotiate out of fear. But let us never fear to negotiate.

Let both sides explore what problems unite us instead of belaboring those problems which divide us.

Let both sides, for the first time, formulate serious and precise proposals for the inspection and control of arms—and bring the absolute power to destroy other nations under the absolute control of all nations.

Let both sides seek to invoke the wonders of science instead of its terrors. Together let us explore the stars, conquer the deserts, eradicate disease, tap the ocean depths and encourage the arts and commerce.

Let both sides unite to heed in all corners of the earth the command of Isaiah—to "undo the heavy burdens . . . (and) let the oppressed go free."

And if a beach-head of cooperation may push back the jungle of suspicion, let both sides join in creating a new endeavor, not a new balance of power, but a new world of law, where the strong are just and the weak secure and the peace preserved.

All this will not be finished in the first one hundred days. Nor will it be finished in the first one thousand days, nor in the life of this Administration, nor even perhaps in our lifetime on this planet. But let us begin.

In your hands, my fellow citizens, more than mine, will rest the final success or failure of our course. Since this country was founded, each generation of Americans has been summoned to give testimony to its national loyalty. The graves of young Americans who answered the call to service surround the globe.

Now the trumpet summons us again—not as a call to bear arms, though arms we need—not as a call to battle, though embattled we are—but a call to bear the burden of a long twilight struggle, year in and year out, "rejoicing in hope, patient in tribulation"—a struggle against the common enemies of man: tyranny, poverty, disease and war itself.

Can we forge against these enemies a grand and global alliance, North and South, East and West, that can assure a more fruitful life for all mankind? Will you join in that historic effort?

In the long history of the world, only a few generations have been granted the role of defending freedom in its hour of maximum danger. I do not shrink from this responsibility—I welcome it. I do not believe that any of us would exchange places with any other people or any other generation. The energy, the faith, the devotion which we bring to this endeavor will light our country and all who serve it—and the glow from that fire can truly light the world.

And so, my fellow Americans: ask not what your country can do for you—ask what you can do for your country.

My fellow citizens of the world: ask not what America will do for you, but what together we can do for the freedom of man.

Finally, whether you are citizens of America or citizens of the world, ask of us here the same high standards of strength and sacrifice which we ask of you. With a good conscience our only sure reward, with history the final judge of our deeds, let us go forth to lead the land we love, asking His blessing and His help, but knowing that here on earth God's work must truly be our own.

JOHN F. KENNEDY

Address at American University

Washington, D.C., June 10, 1963

PRESIDENT ANDERSON, members of the faculty, board of trustees, distinguished guests, my old colleague, Senator Bob Byrd, who has earned his degree through many years of attending night law school, while I am earning mine in the next 30 minutes, ladies and gentlemen:

It is with great pride that I participate in this ceremony of the American University, sponsored by the Methodist Church, founded by Bishop John Fletcher Hurst, and first opened by President Woodrow Wilson in 1914. This is a young and growing university, but it has already fulfilled Bishop Hurst's enlightened hope for the study of history and public affairs in a city devoted to the making of history and to the conduct of the public's business. By sponsoring this institution of higher learning for all who wish to learn, whatever their color or their creed, the Methodists of this area and the Nation deserve the Nation's thanks, and I commend all those who are today graduating.

Professor Woodrow Wilson once said that every man sent out from a university should be a man of his nation as well as a man of his time, and I am confident that the men and women who carry the honor of graduating from this institution will continue to give from their lives, from their talents, a high measure of public service and public support.

"There are few earthly things more beautiful than a university," wrote John Masefield, in his tribute to English universities —and his words are equally true today. He did not refer to spires and towers, to campus greens and ivied walls. He admired the splendid beauty of the university, he said, because it was "a place where those who hate ignorance may strive to know, where those who perceive truth may strive to make others see."

I have, therefore, chosen this time and this place to discuss a topic on which ignorance too often abounds and the truth is too rarely perceived—yet it is the most important topic on earth: world peace.

What kind of peace do I mean? What kind of peace do we seek? Not a Pax Americana enforced on the world by American weapons of war. Not the peace of the grave or the security of the slave. I am talking about genuine peace, the kind of peace that makes life on earth worth living, the kind that enables men and nations to grow and to hope and to build a better life for their children—not merely peace for Americans but peace for all men and women—not merely peace in our time but peace for all time.

I speak of peace because of the new face of war. Total war makes no sense in an age when great powers can maintain large and relatively invulnerable nuclear forces and refuse to surrender without resort to those forces. It makes no sense in an age when a single nuclear weapon contains almost ten times the explosive force delivered by all of the allied air forces in the Second World War. It makes no sense in an age when the deadly poisons produced by a nuclear exchange would be carried by wind and water and soil and seed to the far corners of the globe and to generations yet unborn.

Today the expenditure of billions of dollars every year on weapons acquired for the purpose of making sure we never need to use them is essential to keeping the peace. But surely the acquisition of such idle stockpiles—which can only destroy and never create—is not the only, much less the most efficient, means of assuring peace.

I speak of peace, therefore, as the necessary rational end of rational men. I realize that the pursuit of peace is not as dramatic as the pursuit of war—and frequently the words of the pursuer fall on deaf ears. But we have no more urgent task.

Some say that it is useless to speak of world peace or world law or world disarmament—and that it will be useless until the leaders of the Soviet Union adopt a more enlightened attitude. I hope they do. I believe we can help them do it. But I also believe that we must reexamine our own attitude—as individuals and as a Nation—for our attitude is as essential as theirs. And every graduate of this school, every thoughtful citizen who despairs of war and wishes to bring peace, should begin by looking inward—by examining his own attitude toward the possibilities of peace, toward the Soviet Union, toward the course of the cold war and toward freedom and peace here at home.

First: Let us examine our attitude toward peace itself. Too many of us think it is impossible. Too many think it unreal. But that is a dangerous, defeatist belief. It leads to the conclusion that war is inevitable—that mankind is doomed—that we are gripped by forces we cannot control.

We need not accept that view. Our problems are man-made—therefore, they can be solved by man. And man can be as big as he wants. No problem of human destiny is beyond human beings. Man's reason and spirit have often solved the seemingly unsolvable—and we believe they can do it again.

I am not referring to the absolute, infinite concept of universal peace and good will of which some fantasies and fanatics dream. I do not deny the value of hopes and dreams but we merely invite discouragement and incredulity by making that our only and immediate goal.

Let us focus instead on a more practical, more attainable peace—based not on a sudden revolution in human nature but on a gradual evolution in human institutions—on a series of concrete actions and effective agreements which are in the interest of all concerned. There is no single, simple key to this peace—no grand or magic formula to be adopted by one or two powers. Genuine peace must be the product of many nations, the sum of many acts. It must be dynamic, not static, changing to meet the challenge of each new generation. For peace is a process—a way of solving problems.

With such a peace, there will still be quarrels and conflicting interests, as there are within families and nations. World peace, like community peace, does not require that each man love his neighbor—it requires only that they live together in mutual tolerance, submitting their disputes to a just and peaceful settlement. And history teaches us that enmities between nations, as between individuals, do not last forever. However fixed our likes and dislikes may seem, the tide of time and events will often bring surprising changes in the relations between nations and neighbors.

So let us persevere. Peace need not be impracticable, and war need not be inevitable. By defining our goal more clearly, by making it seem more manageable and less remote, we can help all peoples to see it, to draw hope from it, and to move irresistibly toward it.

Second: Let us reexamine our attitude toward the Soviet Union. It is discouraging to think that their leaders may actually believe what their propagandists write. It is discouraging to read a recent authoritative Soviet text on *Military Strategy* and find, on page after page, wholly baseless and incredible claims—such as the allegation that "American imperialist circles are preparing to unleash different types of wars . . . that there is a very real threat of a preventive war being unleashed by American imperialists against the Soviet Union . . . and that the political aims of the American imperialists are to enslave economically and politically the European and other capitalist countries . . . and to achieve world domination . . . by means of aggressive wars."

Truly, as it was written long ago: "The wicked flee when no man pursueth." Yet it is sad to read these Soviet statements—to realize the extent of the gulf between us. But it is also a warning—a warning to the American people not to fall into the same trap as the Soviets, not to see only a distorted and desperate view of the other side, not to see conflict as inevitable, accommodation as impossible, and communication as nothing more than an exchange of threats.

No government or social system is so evil that its people must be considered as lacking in virtue. As Americans, we find communism profoundly repugnant as a negation of personal freedom and dignity. But we can still hail the Russian people for their many achievements—in science and space, in economic and industrial growth, in culture and in acts of courage.

Among the many traits the peoples of our two countries have in common, none is stronger than our mutual abhorrence of war. Almost unique, among the major world powers, we have never been at war with each other. And no nation in the history of battle ever suffered more than the Soviet Union suffered in the course of the Second World War. At least 20 million lost their lives. Countless millions of homes and farms were burned or sacked. A third of the nation's territory, including nearly two thirds of its industrial base, was turned into a wasteland—a loss equivalent to the devastation of this country east of Chicago.

Today, should total war ever break out again—no matter how—our two countries would become the primary targets. It is an ironic but accurate fact that the two strongest powers are the two in the most danger of devastation. All we have built, all we have worked for, would be destroyed in the first 24 hours. And even in the cold war, which brings burdens and dangers to so many countries, including this Nation's closest allies—our two countries bear the heaviest burdens. For we are both devoting massive sums of money to weapons that could be better devoted to combating ignorance, poverty, and disease. We are both caught up in a vicious and dangerous cycle in which suspicion on one side breeds suspicion on the other, and new weapons beget counterweapons.

In short, both the United States and its allies, and the Soviet Union and its allies, have a mutually deep interest in a just and genuine peace and in halting the arms race. Agreements to this end are in the interests of the Soviet Union as well as ours—and even the most hostile nations can be relied upon to accept and keep those treaty obligations, and only those treaty obligations, which are in their own interest.

So, let us not be blind to our differences—but let us also direct attention to our common interests and to the means by which those differences can be resolved. And if we cannot end now our differences, at least we can help make the world safe for diversity. For, in the final analysis, our most basic common link is that we all inhabit this small planet. We all breathe the same air. We all cherish our children's future. And we are all mortal.

Third: Let us reexamine our attitude toward the cold war, remembering that we are not engaged in a debate, seeking to pile up debating points. We are not here distributing blame or pointing the finger of judgment. We must deal with the world as it is, and not as it might have been had the history of the last 18 years been different.

We must, therefore, persevere in the search for peace in the hope that constructive changes within the Communist bloc might bring within reach solutions which now seem beyond us. We must conduct our affairs in such a way that it becomes in the Communists' interest to agree on a genuine peace. Above all, while defending our own vital interests, nuclear powers must avert those confrontations which bring an adversary to a choice of either a humiliating retreat or a nuclear war. To adopt that kind of course in the nuclear age would be evidence only of the bankruptcy of our policy—or of a collective death-wish for the world.

To secure these ends, America's weapons are nonprovocative, carefully controlled, designed to deter, and capable of selective use. Our military forces are committed to peace and disciplined in self-restraint. Our diplomats are instructed to avoid unnecessary irritants and purely rhetorical hostility.

For we can seek a relaxation of tensions without relaxing our guard. And, for our part, we do not need to use threats to prove that we are resolute. We do not need to jam foreign broadcasts out of fear our faith will be eroded. We are unwilling to impose our system on any unwilling people—but we are willing and able to engage in peaceful competition with any people on earth.

Meanwhile, we seek to strengthen the United Nations, to help solve its financial problems, to make it a more effective instrument for peace, to develop it into a genuine world security system—a system capable of resolving disputes on the basis of law, of insuring the security of the large and the small, and of creating conditions under which arms can finally be abolished.

At the same time we seek to keep peace inside the non-Communist world, where many nations, all of them our friends, are divided over issues which weaken Western unity, which invite Communist intervention or which threaten to erupt into war. Our efforts in West New Guinea, in the Congo, in the Middle East, and in the Indian subcontinent, have been persistent and patient despite criticism from both sides. We have also tried to set an example for others—by seeking to adjust small but significant differences with our own closest neighbors in Mexico and in Canada.

Speaking of other nations, I wish to make one point clear. We are bound to many nations by alliances. Those alliances exist because our concern and theirs substantially overlap. Our commitment to defend Western Europe and West Berlin, for example, stands undiminished because of the identity of our vital interests. The United States will make no deal with the Soviet Union at the expense of other nations and other peoples, not merely because they are our partners, but also because their interests and ours converge.

Our interests converge, however, not only in defending the frontiers of freedom, but in pursuing the paths of peace. It is our hope—and the purpose of allied policies—to convince the Soviet Union that she, too, should let each nation choose its own future, so long as that choice does not interfere with the choices of others. The Communist drive to impose their political and economic system on others is the primary cause of world tension today. For there can be no doubt that, if all nations could refrain from interfering in the self-determination of others, the peace would be much more assured.

This will require a new effort to achieve world law—a new context for world discussions. It will require increased understanding between the Soviets and ourselves. And increased understanding will require increased contact and communication. One step in this direction is the proposed arrangement for a direct line between Moscow and Washington, to avoid on each side the dangerous delays, misunderstandings, and misreadings of the other's actions which might occur at a time of crisis.

We have also been talking in Geneva about other first-step measures of arms control, designed to limit the intensity of the arms race and to reduce the risks of accidental war. Our primary long-range interest in Geneva, however, is general and complete disarmament—designed to take place by stages, permitting parallel political developments to build the new institutions of peace which would take the place of arms. The pursuit of disarmament has been an effort of this Government since the 1920's. It has been urgently sought by the past three administrations. And however dim the prospects may be today, we intend to continue this effort—to continue it in order that all countries, including our own, can better grasp what the problems and possibilities of disarmament are.

The one major area of these negotiations where the end is in sight, yet where a fresh start is badly needed, is in a treaty to outlaw nuclear tests. The conclusion of such a treaty, so near and yet so far, would check the spiraling arms race in one of its most dangerous areas. It would place the nuclear powers in a position to deal more effectively with one of the greatest hazards which man faces in 1963, the further spread of nuclear arms. It would increase our security—it would decrease the prospects of war. Surely this goal is sufficiently important to require our steady pursuit, yielding neither to the temptation to give up the whole effort nor the temptation to give up our insistence on vital and responsible safeguards.

I am taking this opportunity, therefore, to announce two important decisions in this regard.

First: Chairman Khrushchev, Prime Minister Macmillan, and I have agreed that high-level discussions will shortly begin in Moscow looking toward early agreement on a comprehensive test ban treaty. Our hopes must be tempered with the caution of history—but with our hopes go the hopes of all mankind.

Second: To make clear our good faith and solemn convictions on the matter, I now declare that the United States does not propose to conduct nuclear tests in the atmosphere so long as other states do not do so. We will not be the first to resume. Such a declaration is no substitute for a formal binding treaty, but I hope it will help us achieve one. Nor would such a treaty be a substitute for disarmament, but I hope it will help us achieve it.

Finally, my fellow Americans, let us examine our attitude toward peace and freedom here at home. The quality and spirit of our own society must justify and support our efforts abroad. We must show it in the dedication of our own lives—as many of you who are graduating today will have a unique opportunity to do, by serving without pay in the Peace Corps abroad or in the proposed National Service Corps here at home.

But wherever we are, we must all, in our daily lives, live up to the age-old faith that peace and freedom walk together. In too many of our cities today, the peace is not secure because freedom is incomplete.

It is the responsibility of the executive branch at all levels of government—local, State, and National—to provide and protect that freedom for all of our citizens by all means within their authority. It is the responsibility of the legislative branch at all levels, wherever that authority is not now adequate, to make it adequate. And it is the responsibility of all citizens in all sections of this country to respect the rights of all others and to respect the law of the land.

All this is not unrelated to world peace. "When a man's ways please the Lord," the Scriptures tell us, "he maketh even his enemies to be at peace with him." And is not peace, in the last analysis, basically a matter of human rights—the right to live out our lives without fear of devastation—the right to breathe air as nature provided it—the right of future generations to a healthy existence?

While we proceed to safeguard our national interests, let us also safeguard human interests. And the elimination of war and arms is clearly in the interest of both. No treaty, however much it may be to the advantage of all, however tightly it may be worded, can provide absolute security against the risks of deception and evasion. But it can—if it is sufficiently effective in its enforcement and if it is sufficiently in the interests of its signers—offer far more security and far fewer risks than an unabated, uncontrolled, unpredictable arms race.

The United States, as the world knows, will never start a war. We do not want a war. We do not now expect a war. This generation of Americans has already had enough—more than enough—of war and hate and oppression. We shall be prepared if others wish it. We shall be alert to try to stop it. But we shall also do our part to build a world of peace where the weak are safe and the strong are just. We are not helpless before that task or hopeless of its success. Confident and unafraid, we labor on—not toward a strategy of annihilation but toward a strategy of peace.

JOHN F. KENNEDY

Address to the Nation on Civil Rights

Washington, D.C., June 11, 1963

G OOD EVENING, MY FELLOW CITIZENS:
   This afternoon, following a series of threats and defiant statements, the presence of Alabama National Guardsmen was required on the University of Alabama to carry out the final and unequivocal order of the United States District Court of the Northern District of Alabama. That order called for the admission of two clearly qualified young Alabama residents who happened to have been born Negro.

That they were admitted peacefully on the campus is due in good measure to the conduct of the students of the University of Alabama, who met their responsibilities in a constructive way.

I hope that every American, regardless of where he lives, will stop and examine his conscience about this and other related incidents. This Nation was founded by men of many nations and backgrounds. It was founded on the principle that all men are created equal, and that the rights of every man are diminished when the rights of one man are threatened.

Today we are committed to a worldwide struggle to promote and protect the rights of all who wish to be free. And when Americans are sent to Viet-Nam or West Berlin, we do not ask for whites only. It ought to be possible, therefore, for American students of any color to attend any public institution they select without having to be backed up by troops.

It ought to be possible for American consumers of any color to receive equal service in places of public accommodation, such as hotels and restaurants and theaters and retail stores, without being forced to resort to demonstrations in the street, and it ought to be possible for American citizens of any color to register and to vote in a free election without interference or fear of reprisal.

It ought to be possible, in short, for every American to enjoy the privileges of being American without regard to his race or his color. In short, every American ought to have the right to be treated as he would wish to be treated, as one would wish his children to be treated. But this is not the case.

The Negro baby born in America today, regardless of the section of the Nation in which he is born, has about one-half as much chance of completing a high school as a white baby born in the same place on the same day, one-third as much chance of completing college, one-third as much chance of becoming a professional man, twice as much chance of becoming unemployed, about one-seventh as much chance of earning $10,000 a year, a life expectancy which is 7 years shorter, and the prospects of earning only half as much.

This is not a sectional issue. Difficulties over segregation and discrimination exist in every city, in every State of the Union, producing in many cities a rising tide of discontent that threatens the public safety. Nor is this a partisan issue. In a time of domestic crisis men of good will and generosity should be able to unite regardless of party or politics. This is not even a legal or legislative issue alone. It is better to settle these matters in the courts than on the streets, and new laws are needed at every level, but law alone cannot make men see right.

We are confronted primarily with a moral issue. It is as old as the scriptures and is as clear as the American Constitution.

The heart of the question is whether all Americans are to be afforded equal rights and equal opportunities, whether we are going to treat our fellow Americans as we want to be treated. If an American, because his skin is dark, cannot eat lunch in a restaurant open to the public, if he cannot send his children to the best public school available, if he cannot vote for the public officials who represent him, if, in short, he cannot enjoy the full and free life which all of us want, then who among us would be content to have the color of his skin changed and stand in his place? Who among us would then be content with the counsels of patience and delay?

One hundred years of delay have passed since President Lincoln freed the slaves, yet their heirs, their grandsons, are not fully free. They are not yet freed from the bonds of injustice. They are not yet freed from social and economic oppression.

And this Nation, for all its hopes and all its boasts, will not be fully free until all its citizens are free.

We preach freedom around the world, and we mean it, and we cherish our freedom here at home, but are we to say to the world, and much more importantly, to each other that this is a land of the free except for the Negroes; that we have no second-class citizens except Negroes; that we have no class or caste system, no ghettoes, no master race except with respect to Negroes?

Now the time has come for this Nation to fulfill its promise. The events in Birmingham and elsewhere have so increased the cries for equality that no city or State or legislative body can prudently choose to ignore them.

The fires of frustration and discord are burning in every city, North and South, where legal remedies are not at hand. Redress is sought in the streets, in demonstrations, parades, and protests which create tensions and threaten violence and threaten lives.

We face, therefore, a moral crisis as a country and as a people. It cannot be met by repressive police action. It cannot be left to increased demonstrations in the streets. It cannot be quieted by token moves or talk. It is a time to act in the Congress, in your State and local legislative body and, above all, in all of our daily lives.

It is not enough to pin the blame on others, to say this is a problem of one section of the country or another, or deplore the fact that we face. A great change is at hand, and our task, our obligation, is to make that revolution, that change, peaceful and constructive for all.

Those who do nothing are inviting shame as well as violence. Those who act boldly are recognizing right as well as reality.

Next week I shall ask the Congress of the United States to act, to make a commitment it has not fully made in this century to the proposition that race has no place in American life or law. The Federal judiciary has upheld that proposition in a series of forthright cases. The executive branch has adopted that proposition in the conduct of its affairs, including the employment of Federal personnel, the use of Federal facilities, and the sale of federally financed housing.

But there are other necessary measures which only the Congress can provide, and they must be provided at this session. The old code of equity law under which we live commands for every wrong a remedy, but in too many communities, in too many parts of the country, wrongs are inflicted on Negro citizens and there are no remedies at law. Unless the Congress acts, their only remedy is in the street.

I am, therefore, asking the Congress to enact legislation giving all Americans the right to be served in facilities which are open to the public—hotels, restaurants, theaters, retail stores, and similar establishments.

This seems to me to be an elementary right. Its denial is an arbitrary indignity that no American in 1963 should have to endure, but many do.

I have recently met with scores of business leaders urging them to take voluntary action to end this discrimination and I have been encouraged by their response, and in the last 2 weeks over 75 cities have seen progress made in desegregating these kinds of facilities. But many are unwilling to act alone, and for this reason, nationwide legislation is needed if we are to move this problem from the streets to the courts.

I am also asking Congress to authorize the Federal Government to participate more fully in lawsuits designed to end segregation in public education. We have succeeded in persuading many districts to desegregate voluntarily. Dozens have admitted Negroes without violence. Today a Negro is attending a State-supported institution in every one of our 50 States, but the pace is very slow.

Too many Negro children entering segregated grade schools at the time of the Supreme Court's decision 9 years ago will enter segregated high schools this fall, having suffered a loss which can never be restored. The lack of an adequate education denies the Negro a chance to get a decent job.

The orderly implementation of the Supreme Court decision, therefore, cannot be left solely to those who may not have the economic resources to carry the legal action or who may be subject to harassment.

Other features will be also requested, including greater protection for the right to vote. But legislation, I repeat, cannot solve this problem alone. It must be solved in the homes of every American in every community across our country.

In this respect, I want to pay tribute to those citizens North and South who have been working in their communities to make life better for all. They are acting not out of a sense of legal duty but out of a sense of human decency.

Like our soldiers and sailors in all parts of the world they are meeting freedom's challenge on the firing line, and I salute them for their honor and their courage.

My fellow Americans, this is a problem which faces us all— in every city of the North as well as the South. Today there are Negroes unemployed, two or three times as many compared to whites, inadequate in education, moving into the large cities, unable to find work, young people particularly out of work without hope, denied equal rights, denied the opportunity to eat at a restaurant or lunch counter or go to a movie theater, denied the right to a decent education, denied almost today the right to attend a State university even though qualified. It seems to me that these are matters which concern us all, not merely Presidents or Congressmen or Governors, but every citizen of the United States.

This is one country. It has become one country because all of us and all the people who came here had an equal chance to develop their talents.

We cannot say to 10 percent of the population that you can't have that right; that your children can't have the chance to develop whatever talents they have; that the only way that they are going to get their rights is to go into the streets and demonstrate. I think we owe them and we owe ourselves a better country than that.

Therefore, I am asking for your help in making it easier for us to move ahead and to provide the kind of equality of treatment which we would want ourselves; to give a chance for every child to be educated to the limit of his talents.

As I have said before, not every child has an equal talent or an equal ability or an equal motivation, but they should have the equal right to develop their talent and their ability and their motivation, to make something of themselves.

We have a right to expect that the Negro community will be

responsible, will uphold the law, but they have a right to expect that the law will be fair, that the Constitution will be color blind, as Justice Harlan said at the turn of the century.

This is what we are talking about and this is a matter which concerns this country and what it stands for, and in meeting it I ask the support of all our citizens.

Thank you very much.

JOHN F. KENNEDY

Speech in the Rudolph Wilde Platz

Berlin, June 26, 1963

I AM PROUD to come to this city as the guest of your distinguished Mayor, who has symbolized throughout the world the fighting spirit of West Berlin. And I am proud to visit the Federal Republic with your distinguished Chancellor who for so many years has committed Germany to democracy and freedom and progress, and to come here in the company of my fellow American, General Clay, who has been in this city during its great moments of crisis and will come again if ever needed.

Two thousand years ago the proudest boast was "*civis Romanus sum.*" Today, in the world of freedom, the proudest boast is "*Ich bin ein Berliner.*"

I appreciate my interpreter translating my German!

There are many people in the world who really don't understand, or say they don't, what is the great issue between the free world and the Communist world. Let them come to Berlin. There are some who say that communism is the wave of the future. Let them come to Berlin. And there are some who say in Europe and elsewhere we can work with the Communists. Let them come to Berlin. And there are even a few who say that it is true that communism is an evil system, but it permits us to make economic progress. *Lass' sie nach Berlin kommen.* Let them come to Berlin.

Freedom has many difficulties and democracy is not perfect, but we have never had to put a wall up to keep our people in, to prevent them from leaving us. I want to say, on behalf of my countrymen, who live many miles away on the other side of the Atlantic, who are far distant from you, that they take the greatest pride that they have been able to share with you, even from a distance, the story of the last 18 years. I know of no town, no city, that has been besieged for 18 years that still lives with the vitality and the force, and the hope and the determination of the city of West Berlin. While the wall is the most obvious and vivid demonstration of the failures of the Communist system, for all the world to see, we take no satisfaction in it, for it is, as your Mayor has said, an offense not only against history but an offense against humanity, separating families, dividing husbands and wives and brothers and sisters, and dividing a people who wish to be joined together.

What is true of this city is true of Germany—real, lasting peace in Europe can never be assured as long as one German out of four is denied the elementary right of free men, and that is to make a free choice. In 18 years of peace and good faith, this generation of Germans has earned the right to be free, including the right to unite their families and their nation in lasting peace, with good will to all people. You live in a defended island of freedom, but your life is part of the main. So let me ask you, as I close, to lift your eyes beyond the dangers of today, to the hopes of tomorrow, beyond the freedom merely of this city of Berlin, or your country of Germany, to the advance of freedom everywhere, beyond the wall to the day of peace with justice, beyond yourselves and ourselves to all mankind.

Freedom is indivisible, and when one man is enslaved, all are not free. When all are free, then we can look forward to that day when this city will be joined as one and this country and this great Continent of Europe in a peaceful and hopeful globe. When that day finally comes, as it will, the people of West Berlin can take sober satisfaction in the fact that they were in the front lines for almost two decades.

All free men, wherever they may live, are citizens of Berlin, and, therefore, as a free man, I take pride in the words "*Ich bin ein Berliner.*"

MARTIN LUTHER KING, JR.

Address to the March on Washington

August 28, 1963

I AM happy to join with you today in what will go down in history as the greatest demonstration for freedom in the history of our nation. [*Applause*]

Fivescore years ago, a great American, in whose symbolic shadow we stand today, signed the Emancipation Proclamation. This momentous decree came as a great beacon light of hope to millions of Negro slaves who had been seared in the flames of withering injustice. It came as a joyous daybreak to end the long night of their captivity.

But one hundred years later, the Negro still is not free. [*Audience:*] (*My Lord*) One hundred years later, the life of the Negro is still sadly crippled by the manacles of segregation and the chains of discrimination. One hundred years later, the Negro lives on a lonely island of poverty in the midst of a vast ocean of material prosperity. One hundred years later (*My Lord*) [*Applause*], the Negro is still languished in the corners of American society and finds himself an exile in his own land. And so we've come here today to dramatize a shameful condition.

In a sense we've come to our nation's capital to cash a check. When the architects of our republic wrote the magnificent words of the Constitution and the Declaration of Independence (*Yeah*), they were signing a promissory note to which every American was to fall heir. This note was a promise that all men, yes, black men as well as white men, would be guaranteed the "unalienable Rights of Life, Liberty, and the pursuit of Happiness." It is obvious today that America has defaulted on this promissory note insofar as her citizens of color are concerned. Instead of honoring this sacred obligation, America has given the Negro people a bad check, a check which has come back marked "insufficient funds." [*Sustained applause*]

But we refuse to believe that the bank of justice is bankrupt.

(*My Lord*) [*Laughter*] (*Sure enough*) We refuse to believe that there are insufficient funds in the great vaults of opportunity of this nation. And so we've come to cash this check (*Yes*), a check that will give us upon demand the riches of freedom (*Yes*) and the security of justice. [*Applause*]

We have also come to this hallowed spot to remind America of the fierce urgency of now. This is no time (*My Lord*) to engage in the luxury of cooling off or to take the tranquilizing drug of gradualism. [*Applause*] Now is the time to make real the promises of democracy. (*My Lord*) Now is the time to rise from the dark and desolate valley of segregation to the sunlit path of racial justice. Now is the time [*Applause*] to lift our nation from the quicksands of racial injustice to the solid rock of brotherhood. Now is the time [*Applause*] to make justice a reality for all of God's children.

It would be fatal for the nation to overlook the urgency of the moment. This sweltering summer of the Negro's legitimate discontent will not pass until there is an invigorating autumn of freedom and equality. Nineteen sixty-three is not an end, but a beginning. And those who hope that the Negro needed to blow off steam and will now be content will have a rude awakening if the nation returns to business as usual. [*Applause*] There will be neither rest nor tranquillity in America until the Negro is granted his citizenship rights. The whirlwinds of revolt will continue to shake the foundations of our nation until the bright day of justice emerges.

But there is something that I must say to my people, who stand on the warm threshold which leads into the palace of justice: In the process of gaining our rightful place, we must not be guilty of wrongful deeds. Let us not seek to satisfy our thirst for freedom by drinking from the cup of bitterness and hatred. (*My Lord*) [*Applause*] We must forever conduct our struggle on the high plane of dignity and discipline. We must not allow our creative protest to degenerate into physical violence. Again and again, we must rise to the majestic heights of meeting physical force with soul force. The marvelous new militancy which has engulfed the Negro community must not lead us to a distrust of all white people, for many of our white brothers, as evidenced by their presence here today, have come to realize that their destiny is tied up with our destiny.

[*Applause*] And they have come to realize that their freedom is inextricably bound to our freedom. We cannot walk alone.

And as we walk, we must make the pledge that we shall always march ahead. We cannot turn back. There are those who are asking the devotees of civil rights, "When will you be satisfied?" (*Never*)

We can never be satisfied as long as the Negro is the victim of the unspeakable horrors of police brutality. We can never be satisfied [*Applause*] as long as our bodies, heavy with the fatigue of travel, cannot gain lodging in the motels of the highways and the hotels of the cities. [*Applause*] We cannot be satisfied as long as the Negro's basic mobility is from a smaller ghetto to a larger one. We can never be satisfied as long as our children are stripped of their selfhood and robbed of their dignity by signs stating "for whites only." [*Applause*] We cannot be satisfied as long as a Negro in Mississippi cannot vote and a Negro in New York believes he has nothing for which to vote. (*Yes*) [*Applause*] No, no, we are not satisfied and we will not be satisfied until justice rolls down like waters and righteousness like a mighty stream. [*Applause*]

I am not unmindful that some of you have come here out of great trials and tribulations. (*My Lord*) Some of you have come fresh from narrow jail cells. Some of you have come from areas where your quest for freedom left you battered by the storms of persecution (*Yes*) and staggered by the winds of police brutality. You have been the veterans of creative suffering. Continue to work with the faith that unearned suffering is redemptive. Go back to Mississippi (*Yes*), go back to Alabama, go back to South Carolina, go back to Georgia, go back to Louisiana, go back to the slums and ghettos of our northern cities, knowing that somehow this situation can and will be changed. (*Yes*) Let us not wallow in the valley of despair.

I say to you today, my friends [*Applause*], so even though we face the difficulties of today and tomorrow, I still have a dream. (*Yes*) It is a dream deeply rooted in the American dream.

I have a dream that one day (*Yes*) this nation will rise up and live out the true meaning of its creed: "We hold these truths to be self-evident, that all men are created equal." (*Yes*) [*Applause*]

I have a dream that one day on the red hills of Georgia, the sons of former slaves and the sons of former slave owners will be able to sit down together at the table of brotherhood.

I have a dream that one day even the state of Mississippi, a state sweltering with the heat of injustice (*Well*), sweltering with the heat of oppression, will be transformed into an oasis of freedom and justice.

I have a dream (*Well*) [*Applause*] that my four little children will one day live in a nation where they will not be judged by the color of their skin but by the content of their character. (*My Lord*) I have a dream today. [*Applause*]

I have a dream that one day down in Alabama, with its vicious racists, with its governor having his lips dripping with the words of "interposition" and "nullification" (*Yes*), one day right there in Alabama little black boys and black girls will be able to join hands with little white boys and white girls as sisters and brothers. I have a dream today. [*Applause*]

I have a dream that one day every valley shall be exalted (*Yes*), and every hill and mountain shall be made low; the rough places will be made plain, and the crooked places will be made straight (*Yes*); and the glory of the Lord shall be revealed, and all flesh shall see it together. (*Yes*)

This is our hope. This is the faith that I go back to the South with. (*Yes*) With this faith we will be able to hew out of the mountain of despair a stone of hope. (*Yes*) With this faith we will be able to transform the jangling discords of our nation into a beautiful symphony of brotherhood. (*Talk about it*) With this faith (*My Lord*) we will be able to work together, to pray together, to struggle together, to go to jail together, to stand up for freedom together, knowing that we will be free one day. [*Applause*] This will be the day [*Applause continues*], this will be the day when all of God's children (*Yes*) will be able to sing with new meaning:

> My country, 'tis of thee (*Yes*), sweet land of liberty,
>   of thee I sing.
> Land where my fathers died, land of the pilgrim's
>   pride (*Yes*),
> From every mountainside, let freedom ring!

And if America is to be a great nation, this must become true.

And so let freedom ring (*Yes*) from the prodigious hilltops of New Hampshire.

Let freedom ring from the mighty mountains of New York.

Let freedom ring from the heightening Alleghenies of Pennsylvania. (*Yes, That's right*)

Let freedom ring from the snowcapped Rockies of Colorado. (*Well*)

Let freedom ring from the curvaceous slopes of California. (*Yes*)

But not only that: Let freedom ring from Stone Mountain of Georgia. (*Yes*)

Let freedom ring from Lookout Mountain of Tennessee. (Yes)

Let freedom ring from every hill and molehill of Mississippi. (*Yes*)

From every mountainside, let freedom ring. [*Applause*]

And when this happens [*Applause continues*], when we allow freedom ring, when we let it ring from every village and every hamlet, from every state and every city (*Yes*), we will be able to speed up that day when all of God's children, black men and white men, Jews and Gentiles, Protestants and Catholics, will be able to join hands and sing in the words of the old Negro spiritual:

> Free at last! (*Yes*) Free at last!
> Thank God Almighty, we are free at last! [*Applause*]

BETTY FRIEDAN

The Crisis in Women's Identity

San Francisco, 1964

I AM DELIGHTED to be here. Women all over this country are on the verge of completing the massive delayed revolution that needs to be won for women. It is a delayed revolution because all the rights that would make women free and equal citizens of this country, persons able to develop to their full potential in society, were won on paper long ago. The last of these rights, the right to vote, was won the year before I was born. But we are not really free and equal if the feminine mystique keeps us from freely using our rights; if the only world we really are free to move in is the so-called woman's world of home; if we are asked to make an unreal choice no man is ever asked to make; if we think, as girls, that we have to choose somehow between love, marriage and motherhood and the chance to devote ourselves seriously to some challenge, some interest that would enable us to grow to our full human potential.

Are we really free and equal if we are forced to make such a choice, or half-choice, because of lack of support from our society—because we have not received simple institutional help in combining marriage and motherhood with work in the professions, politics, or any of the other frontiers beyond the home? If girls today still have no image of themselves as individual human beings, if they think their only road to status, to identity, in society is to grab that man—according to all the images of marriage from the ads, the television commercials, the movies, the situation comedies, and all the experts who counsel them—and if therefore they think they must catch him at nineteen and begin to have babies and that split-level dream house so soon that they never have time to make other choices, to take other active moves in society, to risk themselves in trial-and-error efforts, are they, are we, really free and equal? Are we confined by that simple age-old destiny that depends only on our sexual biology and chance, or do we actually have the freedom of choice that is open to us as women today in America?

I say that the only thing that stands in women's way today is this false image, this feminine mystique, and the self-denigration of women that it perpetuates. This mystique makes us try to beat ourselves down in order to be feminine, makes us deny or feel freakish about our own abilities as people. It keeps us from moving freely on the road that is open to us. It keeps us from recognizing and solving the small, but real problems that remain.

Whether you know it or not, you have—in your own lives, in your own persons—moved beyond this false image. You yourselves deny the feminine mystique; you deny the very images of women that come at you from all sides. There are no heroines today in America, not as far as the public image is concerned. There are sex objects and there are drudges. We see this on television every day.

You here, however, are the new image of women: as person, as heroine. You live actively in society. You are not solely dependent on your husbands and your children for your identity. You do not live your life vicariously through them. You do not wait passively for that wise man to make the decisions that will shape your society, but move in and help shape society yourself, and begin to make it a more human world. You bridge that old, obsolete division that splits life into man's world of thought and action and woman's world of love. With little help from society, you have begun to make a new pattern in which marriage, motherhood, homemaking—the traditional roles of women—are merged with the possibility of women as individuals, as decision-makers, as creators of the future.

But because of the feminine mystique, you have not felt fully free and confident even as you have moved on this road. You have felt guilty; you have endured jeers, sneers, snickers, perhaps not from your own husband—who, I suspect, supports you more than the image would admit—but from the image-makers, and perhaps from your less adventurous neighbors, who are less willing to assume the role of heroine.

Your presence here today, however, is a testament to the fact that you are beginning to become conscious of the task that is before you. You are beginning to become conscious of the moment in history in which you stand, and this consciousness is what we need now.

Someone said to me in St. Louis that I wasn't actually telling women to do anything new, that I was only helping to make them conscious of the road on which they were already moving. I would accept this. I think we must become conscious of it in order to finish the job. Otherwise we keep repeating over and over again the same arguments with ourselves, the same conflicts, the same decisions, instead of moving ahead and facing the new problems that need to be solved, and asking, in voices loud enough to be heard, for what we need from society. We do not know how strong we could be if we affirmed ourselves as women and joined together, instead of each woman feeling freakish and isolated, as if no one else but herself had the brains and the courage to look beyond that young peak of marriage and childbirth that the feminine mystique enshrines.

You know that you have brains as well as breasts, and you use them. You know what you are capable of, but you could use it for yourselves and for other women with so much more freedom if you could only break through those self-denigrating blocks. It is not laws, nor great obstacles, nor the heels of men that are grinding women down in America today. Men as well as women are victims of the feminine mystique. We must simply break through this curtain in the minds of *women* in order to get on with the massive delayed revolution. And there *are* massive numbers of us, if we stop to realize how many of us have already moved beyond the feminine mystique and how many more are ready to move.

I am speaking not only of the women who work outside the home in industry, but of every woman who works in society, for they all have made a certain advance from the isolation of household drudgery Unfortunately, far too many women are taking jobs too soon in order to put their husbands through law, engineering, graduate or theological school, because these women do not take themselves and their own abilities seriously enough to put themselves through schools. Consequently, too many women of the one-out-of-three who work outside the home are concentrating on the housework jobs of industry—which are going to be replaced by the machine, anyway, just as much of the drudgery of our housework at home has been replaced by the machine. Even more of this household drudgery could be done by machines if the massive resources of American technology were devoted to it, instead of to selling women things they do not need and convincing them that running the washing machine is as creative, scientific and challenging as solving the genetic code.

All of these women in industry housework, however, are now in a position, with the proper training, to move ahead to the kinds of work that cannot be replaced by the machine. With them in the massive revolution are the great numbers of women who engage in volunteer community leadership, work that requires a great deal of human strength, thought and initiative. To a certain extent, their work is often more in tune with the rapid change in our society than that of the existing professions. Committed, innovative volunteer work is done almost completely by women in America, and thus is not recognized for what it is by our society. Therefore, by sneaking around the corner, it manages to innovate in ways that the conformity, the resistance to change, structured into the existing professions does not permit.

I think, however, if we break through that denigrating image of women enshrined in the feminine mystique and take ourselves seriously, society may begin to take us seriously. The disparagement of volunteer work in America will stop, and the false line between the professional and the volunteer will be redrawn. As it is, professionals have such a low opinion of the woman volunteer that they dream up work to keep her busy, use her far below her own ability merely to raise money or hold teas or lick envelopes—or they break the jobs up into little segments that someone with even a small IQ could do. And yet we hear that they cannot find the professionals that they need to solve the social problems in the community, and that there aren't enough trained group workers to do what needs to be done in the hospitals, the schools, and the health and welfare agencies.

If all the volunteers resigned tomorrow, much of this work, not all, would still have to be done, but it might be done with a more serious use of women's real abilities.

I would add also to the massiveness of this revolution the great numbers of women who are doing the housework of politics, who, trapped in the feminine mystique, acquiesce merely to lick envelopes, take nominal posts in ladies' aid auxiliaries, collect furniture for auctions, and second nominating speeches. Freed from their self-denigration, however, they could hold policy-making positions, run for the county committee, serve on the town committee, run for the state Senate or Congress, go to law school and become a judge, or even run for Vice President. I won't say President, for I think that may be premature, but it might help the revolution if a woman had enough courage to try. Above all, women in America need higher aspirations in politics. We know more than we think we know politically, and we are not using this knowledge.

Of all the passions open to man and woman, politics is the one that a woman can most easily embrace and move ahead in, creating a new pattern of politics, marriage and motherhood. Only self-denigration stops women in politics.

In addition, there are the great number of women who could be artists, who *are* artists but do not take themselves seriously as such. In *The New York Times* recently, there were some interesting figures that showed an enormous increase in the number of Americans who answered "Artist" on the census blank, who defined themselves professionally as painters, sculptors, art teachers, writers, poets, playwrights, television writers, all the rest. This great increase was almost completely made up of men. All that keeps a woman of talent from being an artist is her false image of herself, the fear of making the commitment to discipline herself—and of being tested. She doesn't even run across the problems that an American woman has, say, in wanting to become a physicist. Even if as a young girl she does not absorb the notion that physics is unfeminine, she may find it hard to want to have children and go to the physics laboratory at the same time. However, you can paint at home. It is only for lack of taking herself seriously that a woman who paints does not become an artist—or that a woman who wants to become a physicist doesn't work out some sort of accommodation for both children and a career.

I also add to the massive, delayed revolution many of the young women who fell hook, line and sinker for the feminine mystique, used it as a rationalization for evading their own choices, and married early. They thought that all they had to do was to get that man at nineteen and that would take care of the rest of their life, and then they woke up at twenty-five or thirty-five or forty-five with the four children, the house and the husband, and realized they had to face a future ahead in which they would not be able to live through others. Such a woman, whose children are already moving out the door, finally asks herself what she is going to do with her life, and begins, even if late, to face and make some choices of her own. These great numbers of women are now trying to go back to college to get the education they gave up too easily and too soon, and they are getting more or less—too often less—a helping hand from the educators. Some of the universities are breaking through formal barriers and helping these women to grow to their full potential by admitting them to part-time college or graduate work—since part-time study is usually the only answer today for a woman who is still responsible for small children. Some universities may even provide part-time nursery schools so that women may continue to study even during those years; in this way they will not emerge as displaced people when their last child goes off to school, and they will not have to contribute to the population explosion by having baby after baby for lack of anything else creative to do. Perhaps the colleges and universities will even begin to be a little less rigid and understand that a woman who has had the strength to innovate in the community—who has led in solving new problems in education, politics, mental health, and in all the other problems that women have worked on in their suburbs and cities in recent years—may have learned something that is the equivalent of an academic thesis.

Finally, there are the great numbers of young girls for whom, thank heaven, the choices are still ahead. If they only see through the false image, they can so easily make the little choices—not the false big ones such as marriage versus career, but the little ones—that, if made all along, will easily create a new image of woman. And even if their choices involve effort, work, a few conflicts and problems that have to be solved, these are easier problems than that desperate emptiness a woman faces at thirty-five or forty after she realizes that all her life cannot be lived in lifelong full-time motherhood. These young girls can decide in high school "I would like to be a physicist, I would like to be a teacher, I would like to be a nurse, I would like to be an astronaut." Not "What do you want to be, little girl?" "I would like to be a mommy." "What do you want to be, little boy?" "I would like to be a cowboy." Of course he is going to be a husband and father; of course she is going to be a wife and mother. But the choices she must make in school are to learn what else she can be and do herself, because if she does not make these choices when she is young, she will not even try to do the work, to make the effort that will take her to our new frontiers.

Of course, if the revolution is going to be so massive, there is going to be resistance to it. In the last year or so, the problem of women in America has been put on the table. The President's Commission on the Status of Women has made its report. My book and others like it have stimulated discussions among women who have too long suppressed their own aspirations as people, and we are beginning to see some resistance.

There was a story in the *New Yorker* a few months ago called "An Educated American Woman," by John Cheever. It was about an educated woman who fought a zoning battle in her neighborhood, who was taking a French course at Columbia and who was writing a book. She was punished. The baby-sitter left her child alone and he died. Her husband left her for a motherly woman. No more education, no more zoning battles, and, heaven forbid, no more books.

In one of the Doris Day movies, she too was fighting a zoning battle, and the implication was, as a result, no sex: her man left her bed. Obviously, no more zoning battles for her. In the latest one, *The Thrill of It All*, Doris Day is an obstetrician's wife who gets a chance to do television commercials. She enjoys it, but her husband doesn't like it very much. He, by his great scientific ingenuity, is helping one of his patients, a poor, embittered, sophisticated career woman, to finally have a baby at the age of forty. In the end, the baby is born in a taxicab on the East River Drive, with Doris helping to deliver it and the obstetrician galloping up on a horse. Doris Day says, "Now I know what life is all about, helping you to deliver this baby." But of course, how foolish can the audience be, she can't help him deliver a baby in the operating room tomorrow, so what will she do? Aha, she'll have another baby herself, that's the answer. But the real life Doris Days can't go on having babies forever.

Recently you may have seen an advertising campaign by one of the women's service magazines. There are three obviously neurotic women. One says, "I read this wonderful poem; it was such an escape." Dreamy, neurotic escape. A second one, a very hard, bitter, career woman with a hat pulled down, says, "I read this article about India in such and such a magazine. It kept me occupied coming home on the five thirty-five." Another woman who looks as if something is wrong with her says, "I read a wonderful novel by so-and-so." Then we see the fourth one, healthy and wholesome, Mrs. Average Housewife: "I read about a new paint for the children's room. I won't use it, Jim will." The magazine only a homemaker could love. No articles about India, no poems, no great literature here, only service to home and children.

Redbook magazine had a story about a woman who felt guilty because she just sat home and baked cookies and fooled around while her neighbor made petitions to improve the schools. This neighbor said, "Goodness, how are women ever going to assume their equality if you are just going to sit on your behind and make cookies?" Then a mousy little wren came to town who wouldn't even *sign* the petitions; she literally did nothing but bake cookies. And the guilty woman discovered that this mousy little wren, who didn't even bother to look attractive, had been a physicist. But she saw no greater thing in the world to do now than to bake cookies in her own home. This was evidently supposed to mean that it was all phony, the idea that women could make petitions and campaign for the school board or be physicists or dream of doing something else besides bake cookies in their own kitchens.

Margaret Mead, who has contributed much to our knowledge of the plasticity of the human male and female but who has also helped to create the feminine mystique, had an article in *Redbook* attacking the report of the President's Commission on the Status of Women because, she said, it assumed that political life and work would be important to women and did not emphasize enough that women must be full-time wives and mothers. This woman, who is a world-famous, far-traveled anthropologist, declares approvingly that more and more educated women are choosing to be full-time wives and mothers. Margaret Mead even asked that if women really finish the job that the President's Commission says needs to be done, "who will be there to bandage the child's knee and listen to the husband's troubles and give the human element in the world?" Somehow she never explains how the woman is going to listen to the husband's troubles during the eight hours of the day when the husband is at the office, and how she is going to bandage the child's knee when the child isn't there but is at school.

Thus the resistance to the revolution even shows up in the ranks of what I call "capital C" Career women, women who would not be caught dead themselves behind a dishpan, and who from their vantage point back from the expedition in New Guinea or behind the television microphone, say, "But what greater thing can a woman do but drudgery for those she loves, and how many really rewarding, satisfying things in the world are there to do anyway—look at taxi drivers?" Somehow this is always at Radcliffe or Harvard, where the choices open to women, or men, are far more than being taxi drivers. Or, they sneer, how many women have abilities to do anything beyond housework? Of course, these women know *they* have such abilities, but they are exceptional.

I don't think they are so exceptional. I think that 50 percent of the women are above average, just as 50 percent aren't. And I think that while all women have to get dressed, eat dinner, make meals and keep houses clean, these tasks can hardly use all the abilities of an above-average woman—or the whole life-span abilities of a below-average woman, either. For we are going to live, my generation, to be seventy-five, and our daughters may live to be one hundred. No matter how much they will love their children, how much they will want to be wives and mothers and truly enjoy motherhood, it will be such a small part of their lives. It would deprive them of their real choices to say that they should think of themselves only, or even primarily, in terms of their sexual difference from man (long live it) and never in terms of their unique human abilities, whatever they may be.

There is also resistance on the part of some men, but not of as many as you think. I am increasingly surprised at the numbers of men who really do have a full regard for their wives as human beings, who want them to have full lives of their own, who are weary of the burden and the guilt of having to make up to a woman for all the life she misses beyond the home, for the world she has no part in. Men are weary of coming home from that tough, complex rat race in society only to be met by a pent-up wife who feels short-changed in the narrow world of home—and finds him somehow inadequate because he can't give her all that magic fulfillment she has been told to expect from marriage. But perhaps he is not inadequate at all; perhaps she is merely asking for too much from marriage. Perhaps for a woman, as for a man, marriage and love, while two of the basic, great values of life, cannot be all of life. For it is a fact that most men do not spend most of the hours of their day, most of the years of their lives, preoccupied with love or sex, as much as those passions are overglorified in the public image today. These images are directed at women, and they are directed at women to sell them something.

Do we really have to keep on acquiescing to the sexual sell, and is it really essential to the American economy? I have a hunch that if women were released to develop their full potential, they might want things that would keep the American economy alive just as much as those eighty-eight ways to get that man or keep him, or those magical powders that will keep the sink pure white. Perhaps more of the American economy might go to research and education, perhaps there might be other changes, but I hardly think keeping the American housewife in a state of perpetual frustration and emptiness and nagging discontent is essential to the American economy.

I think there are some men who may resist this massive, delayed revolution because they have had too much smothering from mothers who need them for an identity, and thus feel insecure in their own ability to move as human beings in the world. They may think they need a woman as a doormat. They may need someone whom they can think of as inferior so that they can feel superior. But I doubt that it is really going to solve any man's problem for his wife to beat herself down, to project a phony inferiority. Isn't it pretty contemptuous of man to say that his ego is so weak that he needs her to pretend to be something that she isn't, in order to make him feel like a big boy? I happen to think men are stronger than that. It might be better for both men and women if they could accept each other for what they are. It might even free men from the binds of the masculine mystique. Someone else will have to write a book about that.

I think all of these resistances are not that great. Our own self-denigration of ourselves as women and perhaps our own fears are the main problems. For it is an unknown road we now must take, and if we move on it, we take risks. It takes courage. We face a more complex life when we begin to create this new image of woman and to put all of these pieces of ourselves together. We risk being tested, being measured. We risk exposing ourselves if we insert ourselves into the human story instead of living through our husbands and children. The longer we hide in our homes evading the challenges of the society that is moving and changing so fast outside our doors, the more we may be afraid to move, the more we may wish, insist, somehow, that we can and only need to be wives and mothers, this is all, this is the greatest thing in life. And it is indeed the bedrock of life, the beginning.

But it isn't all, it can't be all for women today. And if it has to be all for some women too old or too frightened to risk a more complex road, it is not too late for most women. Most women have more strength than they imagine. We do not know what strength we have.

I will tell you something that might make you feel good; it makes me feel good. There is a study not yet published that is being done at Washington University Medical School about the growth of the self in women, the ego, identity, whatever you want to call it. Do you know who has the most mature and the strongest self of all, the most autonomous ego? The committed woman volunteer. Her sense of identity is much stronger than that little housewife. Much stronger, interestingly enough, than the professional social worker in the same field. Why? Because she pioneered on an unknown road; because she had to structure a growth pattern for herself, not a pattern already there and structured by society; because in many cases she innovated; and because she imposed a discipline on herself that was not imposed by the demands of the pay-check. She is living this new image of woman, she is showing the way. And so are you, whether you realize it or not.

We must all say yes to ourselves as women, and no to that outworn, obsolete image, the feminine mystique. We must stop denigrating ourselves, stop acquiescing in the remaining prejudices the mystique enshrines. We must recognize and af-firm each other in the massiveness of our own numbers and our own strength and ask for all women what we all need to move freely ahead. One does not move freely and joyously ahead if one is always torn by conflicts and guilts, nor if one feels like a freak in a man's world, if one is always walking a tightrope between being a good wife and mother and fulfilling one's commitments to society—with no help from society. If we ask, I think we can get simple institutional solutions from society to these real problems. Well-run five- or eight-hour-a-day nursery schools or day-care centers are needed, and mater-nity leaves that are real and not just on paper—so that the staff doesn't become mysteriously reduced when you get pregnant. Real credit needs to be given for the work you have done as volunteers. More part-time patterns are needed in all profes-sions for mothers. Above all, women must assume real political equality and take their place as decision-makers in political life.

We must ask for these things ourselves, for no one will hand women anything, any more than society has handed Negroes anything. It was only when they said for themselves, in 1963, the young ones and the old ones, we will no longer eat, live, work, go to school, or even go to the toilet as anything less than free and full and equal human beings, that the rights they won on paper a hundred years ago began to be a reality, and our society began to take them seriously.

American women—the only majority, perhaps, that is still treated like a rather unequal minority—do not have the un-comfortable suffering of the Negro. But they will not be free and equal members of society until they take themselves seri-ously and finish the work of the delayed revolution. Each and every woman must in her own life stop denigrating herself and must help to win these things for other women.

I have three children. I love them. I would not have missed having them for the world. They are a great fulfillment of my life. But my children no more fulfill, no more define me as a woman; my love for and my life with my husband no more defines or fulfills me as a woman, than the work I do, the non-sexual passions, the questions and the search that made me write my book—and the wish to help write the human story that makes me urge you to affirm your own identity as full human beings and to help create this new image of women as *people*, both for your daughters and for our society.

MALCOLM X

The Ballot or the Bullet

Cleveland, April 3, 1964

M R. MODERATOR, Brother Lomax, brothers and sisters, friends and enemies: I just can't believe everyone in here is a friend and I don't want to leave anybody out. The question tonight, as I understand it, is "The Negro Revolt, and Where Do We Go From Here?" or "What Next?" In my little humble way of understanding it, it points toward either the ballot or the bullet.

Before we try and explain what is meant by the ballot or the bullet, I would like to clarify something concerning myself. I'm still a Muslim, my religion is still Islam. That's my personal belief. Just as Adam Clayton Powell is a Christian minister who heads the Abyssinian Baptist Church in New York, but at the same time takes part in the political struggles to try and bring about rights to the black people in this country; and Dr. Martin Luther King is a Christian minister down in Atlanta, Georgia, who heads another organization fighting for the civil rights of black people in this country; and Rev. Galamison, I guess you've heard of him, is another Christian minister in New York who has been deeply involved in the school boycotts to eliminate segregated education; well, I myself am a minister, not a Christian minister, but a Muslim minister; and I believe in action on all fronts by whatever means necessary.

Although I'm still a Muslim, I'm not here tonight to discuss my religion. I'm not here to try and change your religion. I'm not here to argue or discuss anything that we differ about, because it's time for us to submerge our differences and realize that it is best for us to first see that we have the same problem, a common problem—a problem that will make you catch hell whether you're a Baptist, or a Methodist, or a Muslim, or a nationalist. Whether you're educated or illiterate, whether you live on the boulevard or in the alley, you're going to catch hell just like I am. We're all in the same boat and we all are going to catch the same hell from the same man. He just happens to be a white man. All of us have suffered here, in this country, political oppression at the hands of the white man, economic exploitation at the hands of the white man, and social degradation at the hands of the white man.

Now in speaking like this, it doesn't mean that we're anti-white, but it does mean we're anti-exploitation, we're anti-degradation, we're anti-oppression. And if the white man doesn't want us to be anti-him, let him stop oppressing and exploiting and degrading us. Whether we are Christians or Muslims or nationalists or agnostics or atheists, we must first learn to forget our differences. If we have differences, let us differ in the closet; when we come out in front, let us not have anything to argue about until we get finished arguing with the man. If the late President Kennedy could get together with Khrushchev and exchange some wheat, we certainly have more in common with each other than Kennedy and Khrushchev had with each other.

If we don't do something real soon, I think you'll have to agree that we're going to be forced either to use the ballot or the bullet. It's one or the other in 1964. It isn't that time is running out—time has run out! 1964 threatens to be the most explosive year America has ever witnessed. The most explosive year. Why? It's also a political year. It's the year when all of the white politicians will be back in the so-called Negro community jiving you and me for some votes. The year when all of the white political crooks will be right back in your and my community with their false promises, building up our hopes for a letdown, with their trickery and their treachery, with their false promises which they don't intend to keep. As they nourish these dissatisfactions, it can only lead to one thing, an explosion; and now we have the type of black man on the scene in America today—I'm sorry, Brother Lomax—who just doesn't intend to turn the other cheek any longer.

Don't let anybody tell you anything about the odds are against you. If they draft you, they send you to Korea and make you face 800 million Chinese. If you can be brave over there, you can be brave right here. These odds aren't as great as those odds. And if you fight here, you will at least know what you're fighting for.

I'm not a politician, not even a student of politics; in fact, I'm not a student of much of anything. I'm not a Democrat, I'm not a Republican, and I don't even consider myself an American. If you and I were Americans, there'd be no problem. Those Hunkies that just got off the boat, they're already Americans; Polacks are already Americans; the Italian refugees are already Americans. Everything that came out of Europe, every blue-eyed thing, is already an American. And as long as you and I have been over here, we aren't Americans yet.

Well, I am one who doesn't believe in deluding myself. I'm not going to sit at your table and watch you eat, with nothing on my plate, and call myself a diner. Sitting at the table doesn't make you a diner, unless you eat some of what's on that plate. Being here in America doesn't make you an American. Being born here in America doesn't make you an American. Why, if birth made you American, you wouldn't need any legislation, you wouldn't need any amendments to the Constitution, you wouldn't be faced with civil-rights filibustering in Washington, D.C., right now. They don't have to pass civil-rights legislation to make a Polack an American.

No, I'm not an American. I'm one of the 22 million black people who are the victims of Americanism. One of the 22 million black people who are the victims of democracy, nothing but disguised hypocrisy. So, I'm not standing here speaking to you as an American, or a patriot, or a flag-saluter, or a flag-waver—no, not I. I'm speaking as a victim of this American system. And I see America through the eyes of the victim. I don't see any American dream; I see an American nightmare.

These 22 million victims are waking up. Their eyes are coming open. They're beginning to see what they used to only look at. They're becoming politically mature. They are realizing that there are new political trends from coast to coast. As they see these new political trends, it's possible for them to see that every time there's an election the races are so close that they have to have a recount. They had to recount in Massachusetts to see who was going to be governor, it was so close. It was the same way in Rhode Island, in Minnesota, and in many other parts of the country. And the same with Kennedy and Nixon when they ran for president. It was so close they had to count all over again. Well, what does this mean? It means that when white people are evenly divided, and black people have a bloc of votes of their own, it is left up to them to determine who's going to sit in the White House and who's going to be in the dog house.

It was the black man's vote that put the present administration in Washington, D.C. Your vote, your dumb vote, your ignorant vote, your wasted vote put in an administration in Washington, D.C., that has seen fit to pass every kind of legislation imaginable, saving you until last, then filibustering on top of that. And your and my leaders have the audacity to run around clapping their hands and talk about how much progress we're making. And what a good president we have. If he wasn't good in Texas, he sure can't be good in Washington, D.C. Because Texas is a lynch state. It is in the same breath as Mississippi, no different; only they lynch you in Texas with a Texas accent and lynch you in Mississippi with a Mississippi accent. And these Negro leaders have the audacity to go and have some coffee in the White House with a Texan, a Southern cracker—that's all he is—and then come out and tell you and me that he's going to be better for us because, since he's from the South, he knows how to deal with the Southerners. What kind of logic is that? Let Eastland be president, he's from the South too. He should be better able to deal with them than Johnson.

In this present administration they have in the House of Representatives 257 Democrats to only 177 Republicans. They control two-thirds of the House vote. Why can't they pass something that will help you and me? In the Senate, there are 67 senators who are of the Democratic Party. Only 33 of them are Republicans. Why, the Democrats have got the government sewed up, and you're the one who sewed it up for them. And what have they given you for it? Four years in office, and just now getting around to some civil-rights legislation. Just now, after everything else is gone, out of the way, they're going to sit down now and play with you all summer long—the same old giant con game that they call filibuster. All those are in cahoots together. Don't you ever think they're not in cahoots together, for the man that is heading the civil-rights filibuster is a man from Georgia named Richard Russell. When Johnson became president, the first man he asked for when he got back to Washington, D.C., was "Dicky"—that's how tight they are. That's his boy, that's his pal, that's his buddy. But they're playing that old con game. One of them makes believe he's for you, and he's got it fixed where the other one is so tight against you, he never has to keep his promise.

So it's time in 1964 to wake up. And when you see them coming up with that kind of conspiracy, let them know your eyes are open. And let them know you got something else that's wide open too. It's got to be the ballot or the bullet. The ballot or the bullet. If you're afraid to use an expression like that, you should get on out of the country, you should get back in the cotton patch, you should get back in the alley. They get all the Negro vote, and after they get it, the Negro gets nothing in return. All they did when they got to Washington was give a few big Negroes big jobs. Those big Negroes didn't need big jobs, they already had jobs. That's camouflage, that's trickery, that's treachery, window-dressing. I'm not trying to knock out the Democrats for the Republicans, we'll get to them in a minute. But it is true—you put the Democrats first and the Democrats put you last.

Look at it the way it is. What alibis do they use, since they control Congress and the Senate? What alibi do they use when you and I ask, "Well, when are you going to keep your promise?" They blame the Dixiecrats. What is a Dixiecrat? A Democrat. A Dixiecrat is nothing but a Democrat in disguise. The titular head of the Democrats is also the head of the Dixiecrats, because the Dixiecrats are a part of the Democratic Party. The Democrats have never kicked the Dixiecrats out of the party. The Dixiecrats bolted themselves once, but the Democrats didn't put them out. Imagine, these lowdown Southern segregationists put the Northern Democrats down. But the Northern Democrats have never put the Dixiecrats down. No, look at that thing the way it is. They have got a con game going on, a political con game, and you and I are in the middle. It's time for you and me to wake up and start looking at it like it is, and trying to understand it like it is; and then we can deal with it like it is.

The Dixiecrats in Washington, D.C., control the key committees that run the government. The only reason the Dixiecrats control these committees is because they have seniority. The only reason they have seniority is because they come from states where Negroes can't vote. This is not even a government that's based on democracy. It is not a government that is made up of representatives of the people. Half of the people in the South can't even vote. Eastland is not even supposed to be in Washington. Half of the senators and congressmen who occupy these key positions in Washington, D.C., are there illegally, are there unconstitutionally.

I was in Washington, D.C., a week ago Thursday, when they were debating whether or not they should let the bill come onto the floor. And in the back of the room where the Senate meets, there's a huge map of the United States, and on that map it shows the location of Negroes throughout the country. And it shows that the Southern section of the country, the states that are most heavily concentrated with Negroes, are the ones that have senators and congressmen standing up filibustering and doing all other kinds of trickery to keep the Negro from being able to vote. This is pitiful. But it's not pitiful for us any longer; it's actually pitiful for the white man, because soon now, as the Negro awakens a little more and sees the vise that he's in, sees the bag that he's in, sees the real game that he's in, then the Negro's going to develop a new tactic.

These senators and congressmen actually violate the constitutional amendments that guarantee the people of that particular state or county the right to vote. And the Constitution itself has within it the machinery to expel any representative from a state where the voting rights of the people are violated. You don't even need new legislation. Any person in Congress right now, who is there from a state or a district where the voting rights of the people are violated, that particular person should be expelled from Congress. And when you expel him, you've removed one of the obstacles in the path of any real meaningful legislation in this country. In fact, when you expel them, you don't need new legislation, because they will be replaced by black representatives from counties and districts where the black man is in the majority, not in the minority.

If the black man in these Southern states had his full voting rights, the key Dixiecrats in Washington, D.C., which means the key Democrats in Washington, D.C., would lose their seats. The Democratic Party itself would lose its power. It would cease to be powerful as a party. When you see the amount of power that would be lost by the Democratic Party if it were to lose the Dixiecrat wing, or branch, or element, you can see where it's against the interests of the Democrats to give voting rights to Negroes in states where the Democrats have been in complete power and authority, ever since the Civil War. You just can't belong to that party without analyzing it.

I say again, I'm not anti-Democrat, I'm not anti-Republican, I'm not anti-anything. I'm just questioning their sincerity, and some of the strategy that they've been using on our people by promising them promises that they don't intend to keep. When you keep the Democrats in power, you're keeping the Dixiecrats in power. I doubt that my good Brother Lomax will deny that. A vote for a Democrat is a vote for a Dixiecrat. That's why, in 1964, it's time now for you and me to become more politically mature and realize what the ballot is for; what we're supposed to get when we cast a ballot; and that if we don't cast a ballot, it's going to end up in a situation where we're going to have to cast a bullet. It's either a ballot or a bullet.

In the North, they do it a different way. They have a system that's known as gerrymandering, whatever that means. It means when Negroes become too heavily concentrated in a certain area, and begin to gain too much political power, the white man comes along and changes the district lines. You may say, "Why do you keep saying white man?" Because it's the white man who does it. I haven't ever seen any Negro changing any lines. They don't let him get near the line. It's the white man who does this. And usually, it's the white man who grins at you the most, and pats you on the back, and is supposed to be your friend. He may be friendly, but he's not your friend.

So, what I'm trying to impress upon you, in essence, is this: You and I in America are faced not with a segregationist conspiracy, we're faced with a government conspiracy. Everyone who's filibustering is a senator—that's the government. Everyone who's finagling in Washington, D.C., is a congressman—that's the government. You don't have anybody putting blocks in your path but people who are a part of the government. The same government that you go abroad to fight for and die for is the government that is in a conspiracy to deprive you of your voting rights, deprive you of your economic opportunities, deprive you of decent housing, deprive you of decent education. You don't need to go to the employer alone, it is the government itself, the government of America, that is responsible for the oppression and exploitation and degradation of black people in this country. And you should drop it in their lap. This government has failed the Negro. This so-called democracy has failed the Negro. And all these white liberals have definitely failed the Negro.

So, where do we go from here? First, we need some friends. We need some new allies. The entire civil-rights struggle needs a new interpretation, a broader interpretation. We need to look at this civil-rights thing from another angle—from the inside as well as from the outside. To those of us whose philosophy is black nationalism, the only way you can get involved in the civil-rights struggle is give it a new interpretation. That old interpretation excluded us. It kept us out. So, we're giving a new interpretation to the civil-rights struggle, an interpretation that will enable us to come into it, take part in it. And these handkerchief-heads who have been dillydallying and pussyfooting and compromising—we don't intend to let them pussyfoot and dillydally and compromise any longer.

How can you thank a man for giving you what's already yours? How then can you thank him for giving you only part of what's already yours? You haven't even made progress, if what's being given to you, you should have had already. That's not progress. And I love my Brother Lomax, the way he pointed out we're right back where we were in 1954. We're not even as far up as we were in 1954. We're behind where we were in 1954. There's more segregation now than there was in 1954. There's more racial animosity, more racial hatred, more racial violence today in 1964, than there was in 1954. Where is the progress?

And now you're facing a situation where the young Negro's coming up. They don't want to hear that "turn-the-other-cheek" stuff, no. In Jacksonville, those were teenagers, they were throwing Molotov cocktails. Negroes have never done that before. But it shows you there's a new deal coming in. There's new thinking coming in. There's new strategy coming in. It'll be Molotov cocktails this month, hand grenades next month, and something else next month. It'll be ballots, or it'll be bullets. It'll be liberty, or it will be death. The only difference about this kind of death—it'll be reciprocal. You know what is meant by "reciprocal"? That's one of Brother Lomax's words, I stole it from him. I don't usually deal with those big words because I don't usually deal with big people. I deal with small people. I find you can get a whole lot of small people and whip hell out of a whole lot of big people. They haven't got anything to lose, and they've got everything to gain. And they'll let you know in a minute: "It takes two to tango; when I go, you go."

The black nationalists, those whose philosophy is black nationalism, in bringing about this new interpretation of the entire meaning of civil rights, look upon it as meaning, as Brother Lomax has pointed out, equality of opportunity. Well, we're justified in seeking civil rights, if it means equality of opportunity, because all we're doing there is trying to collect for our investment. Our mothers and fathers invested sweat and blood. Three hundred and ten years we worked in this country without a dime in return—I mean without a *dime* in return. You let the white man walk around here talking about how rich this country is, but you never stop to think how it got rich so quick. It got rich because you made it rich.

You take the people who are in this audience right now. They're poor, we're all poor as individuals. Our weekly salary individually amounts to hardly anything. But if you take the salary of everyone in here collectively it'll fill up a whole lot of baskets. It's a lot of wealth. If you can collect the wages of just these people right here for a year, you'll be rich—richer than rich. When you look at it like that, think how rich Uncle Sam had to become, not with this handful, but millions of black people. Your and my mother and father, who didn't work an eight-hour shift, but worked from "can't see" in the morning until "can't see" at night, and worked for nothing, making the white man rich, making Uncle Sam rich.

This is our investment. This is our contribution—our blood. Not only did we give of our free labor, we gave of our blood.

Every time he had a call to arms, we were the first ones in uniform. We died on every battlefield the white man had. We have made a greater sacrifice than anybody who's standing up in America today. We have made a greater contribution and have collected less. Civil rights, for those of us whose philosophy is black nationalism, means: "Give it to us now. Don't wait for next year. Give it to us yesterday, and that's not fast enough."

I might stop right here to point out one thing. Whenever you're going after something that belongs to you, anyone who's depriving you of the right to have it is a criminal. Understand that. Whenever you are going after something that is yours, you are within your legal rights to lay claim to it. And anyone who puts forth any effort to deprive you of that which is yours, is breaking the law, is a criminal. And this was pointed out by the Supreme Court decision. It outlawed segregation. Which means segregation is against the law. Which means a segregationist is breaking the law. A segregationist is a criminal. You can't label him as anything other than that. And when you demonstrate against segregation, the law is on your side. The Supreme Court is on your side.

Now, who is it that opposes you in carrying out the law? The police department itself. With police dogs and clubs. Whenever you demonstrate against segregation, whether it is segregated education, segregated housing, or anything else, the law is on your side, and anyone who stands in the way is not the law any longer. They are breaking the law, they are not representatives of the law. Any time you demonstrate against segregation and a man has the audacity to put a police dog on you, kill that dog, kill him, I'm telling you, kill that dog. I say it, if they put me in jail tomorrow, kill—that—dog. Then you'll put a stop to it. Now, if these white people in here don't want to see that kind of action, get down and tell the mayor to tell the police department to pull the dogs in. That's all you have to do. If you don't do it, someone else will.

If you don't take this kind of stand, your little children will grow up and look at you and think "shame." If you don't take an uncompromising stand—I don't mean go out and get violent; but at the same time you should never be nonviolent unless you run into some nonviolence. I'm nonviolent with those who are nonviolent with me. But when you drop that violence on me, then you've made me go insane, and I'm not responsible for what I do. And that's the way every Negro should get. Any time you know you're within the law, within your legal rights, within your moral rights, in accord with justice, then die for what you believe in. But don't die alone. Let your dying be reciprocal. This is what is meant by equality. What's good for the goose is good for the gander.

When we begin to get in this area, we need new friends, we need new allies. We need to expand the civil-rights struggle to a higher level—to the level of human rights. Whenever you are in a civil-rights struggle, whether you know it or not, you are confining yourself to the jurisdiction of Uncle Sam. No one from the outside world can speak out in your behalf as long as your struggle is a civil-rights struggle. Civil rights comes within the domestic affairs of this country. All of our African brothers and our Asian brothers and our Latin-American brothers cannot open their mouths and interfere in the domestic affairs of the United States. And as long as it's civil rights, this comes under the jurisdiction of Uncle Sam.

But the United Nations has what's known as the charter of human rights, it has a committee that deals in human rights. You may wonder why all of the atrocities that have been committed in Africa and in Hungary and in Asia and in Latin America are brought before the UN, and the Negro problem is never brought before the UN. This is part of the conspiracy. This old, tricky, blue-eyed liberal who is supposed to be your and my friend, supposed to be in our corner, supposed to be subsidizing our struggle, and supposed to be acting in the capacity of an adviser, never tells you anything about human rights. They keep you wrapped up in civil rights. And you spend so much time barking up the civil-rights tree, you don't even know there's a human-rights tree on the same floor.

When you expand the civil-rights struggle to the level of human rights, you can then take the case of the black man in this country before the nations in the UN. You can take it before the General Assembly. You can take Uncle Sam before a world court. But the only level you can do it on is the level of human rights. Civil rights keeps you under his restrictions, under his jurisdiction. Civil rights keeps you in his pocket. Civil rights means you're asking Uncle Sam to treat you right. Human rights are something you were born with. Human rights are your God-given rights. Human rights are the rights that are recognized by all nations of this earth. And any time any one violates your human rights, you can take them to the world court. Uncle Sam's hands are dripping with blood, dripping with the blood of the black man in this country. He's the earth's number-one hypocrite. He has the audacity—yes, he has—imagine him posing as the leader of the free world. The free world!—and you over here singing "We Shall Overcome." Expand the civil-rights struggle to the level of human rights, take it into the United Nations, where our African brothers can throw their weight on our side, where our Asian brothers can throw their weight on our side, where our Latin-American brothers can throw their weight on our side, and where 800 million Chinamen are sitting there waiting to throw their weight on our side.

Let the world know how bloody his hands are. Let the world know the hypocrisy that's practiced over here. Let it be the ballot or the bullet. Let him know that it must be the ballot or the bullet.

When you take your case to Washington, D.C., you're taking it to the criminal who's responsible; it's like running from the wolf to the fox. They're all in cahoots together. They all work political chicanery and make you look like a chump before the eyes of the world. Here you are walking around in America, getting ready to be drafted and sent abroad, like a tin soldier, and when you get over there, people ask you what are you fighting for, and you have to stick your tongue in your cheek. No, take Uncle Sam to court, take him before the world.

By ballot I only mean freedom. Don't you know—I disagree with Lomax on this issue—that the ballot is more important than the dollar? Can I prove it? Yes. Look in the UN. There are poor nations in the UN; yet those poor nations can get together with their voting power and keep the rich nations from making a move. They have one nation—one vote, everyone has an equal vote. And when those brothers from Asia, and Africa and the darker parts of this earth get together, their voting power is sufficient to hold Sam in check. Or Russia in check. Or some other section of the earth in check. So, the ballot is most important.

Right now, in this country, if you and I, 22 million African-Americans—that's what we are—Africans who are in America. You're nothing but Africans. Nothing but Africans. In fact, you'd get farther calling yourself African instead of Negro. Africans don't catch hell. You're the only one catching hell. They don't have to pass civil-rights bills for Africans. An African can go anywhere he wants right now. All you've got to do is tie your head up. That's right, go anywhere you want. Just stop being a Negro. Change your name to Hoogagagooba. That'll show you how silly the white man is. You're dealing with a silly man. A friend of mine who's very dark put a turban on his head and went into a restaurant in Atlanta before they called themselves desegregated. He went into a white restaurant, he sat down, they served him, and he said, "What would happen if a Negro came in here?" And there he's sitting, black as night, but because he had his head wrapped up the waitress looked back at him and says, "Why, there wouldn't no nigger dare come in here."

So, you're dealing with a man whose bias and prejudice are making him lose his mind, his intelligence, every day. He's frightened. He looks around and sees what's taking place on this earth, and he sees that the pendulum of time is swinging in your direction. The dark people are waking up. They're losing their fear of the white man. No place where he's fighting right now is he winning. Everywhere he's fighting, he's fighting someone your and my complexion. And they're beating him. He can't win any more. He's won his last battle. He failed to win the Korean War. He couldn't win it. He had to sign a truce. That's a loss. Any time Uncle Sam, with all his machinery for warfare, is held to a draw by some rice-eaters, he's lost the battle. He had to sign a truce. America's not supposed to sign a truce. She's supposed to be bad. But she's not bad any more. She's bad as long as she can use her hydrogen bomb, but she can't use hers for fear Russia might use hers. Russia can't use hers, for fear that Sam might use his. So, both of them are weaponless. They can't use the weapon because each's weapon nullifies the other's. So the only place where action can take place is on the ground. And the white man can't win another war fighting on the ground. Those days are over. The black man knows it, the brown man knows it, the red man knows it, and the yellow man knows it. So they engage him in guerrilla warfare. That's not his style. You've got to have heart to be a guerrilla warrior, and he hasn't got any heart. I'm telling you now.

I just want to give you a little briefing on guerrilla warfare because, before you know it, before you know it—It takes heart to be a guerrilla warrior because you're on your own. In conventional warfare you have tanks and a whole lot of other people with you to back you up, planes over your head and all that kind of stuff. But a guerrilla is on his own. All you have is a rifle, some sneakers and a bowl of rice, and that's all you need—and a lot of heart. The Japanese on some of those islands in the Pacific, when the American soldiers landed, one Japanese sometimes could hold the whole army off. He'd just wait until the sun went down, and when the sun went down they were all equal. He would take his little blade and slip from bush to bush, and from American to American. The white soldiers couldn't cope with that. Whenever you see a white soldier that fought in the Pacific, he has the shakes, he has a nervous condition, because they scared him to death.

The same thing happened to the French up in French Indochina. People who just a few years previously were rice farmers got together and ran the heavily-mechanized French army out of Indochina. You don't need it—modern warfare today won't work. This is the day of the guerrilla. They did the same thing in Algeria. Algerians, who were nothing but Bedouins, took a rifle and sneaked off to the hills, and de Gaulle and all of his highfalutin' war machinery couldn't defeat those guerrillas. Nowhere on this earth does the white man win in a guerrilla warfare. It's not his speed. Just as guerrilla warfare is prevailing in Asia and in parts of Africa and in parts of Latin America, you've got to be mighty naive, or you've got to play the black man cheap, if you don't think someday he's going to wake up and find that it's got to be the ballot or the bullet.

I would like to say, in closing, a few things concerning the Muslim Mosque, Inc., which we established recently in New York City. It's true we're Muslims and our religion is Islam, but we don't mix our religion with our politics and our economics and our social and civil activities—not any more. We keep our religion in our mosque. After our religious services are over, then as Muslims we become involved in political action, economic action and social and civic action. We become involved with anybody, anywhere, any time and in any manner that's designed to eliminate the evils, the political, economic and social evils that are afflicting the people of our community.

The political philosophy of black nationalism means that the black man should control the politics and the politicians in his own community; no more. The black man in the black community has to be re-educated into the science of politics so he will know what politics is supposed to bring him in return. Don't be throwing out any ballots. A ballot is like a bullet. You don't throw your ballots until you see a target, and if that target is not within your reach, keep your ballot in your pocket. The political philosophy of black nationalism is being taught in the Christian church. It's being taught in the NAACP. It's being taught in CORE meetings. It's being taught in SNCC meetings. It's being taught in Muslim meetings. It's being taught where nothing but atheists and agnostics come together. It's being taught everywhere. Black people are fed up with the dillydallying, pussyfooting, compromising approach that we've been using toward getting our freedom. We want freedom *now*, but we're not going to get it saying "We Shall Overcome." We've got to fight until we overcome.

The economic philosophy of black nationalism is pure and simple. It only means that we should control the economy of our community. Why should white people be running all the stores in our community? Why should white people be running the banks of our community? Why should the economy of our community be in the hands of the white man? Why? If a black man can't move his store into a white community, you tell me why a white man should move his store into a black community. The philosophy of black nationalism involves a re-education program in the black community in regards to economics. Our people have to be made to see that any time you take your dollar out of your community and spend it in a community where you don't live, the community where you live will get poorer and poorer, and the community where you spend your money will get richer and richer. Then you wonder why where you live is always a ghetto or a slum area. And where you and I are concerned, not only do we lose it when we spend it out of the community, but the white man has got all our stores in the community tied up; so that though we spend it in the community, at sundown the man who runs the store takes it over across town somewhere. He's got us in a vise.

So the economic philosophy of black nationalism means in every church, in every civic organization, in every fraternal order. it's time now for our people to become conscious of the importance of controlling the economy of our community. If we own the stores, if we operate the businesses, if we try and establish some industry in our own community, then we're developing to the position where we are creating employment for our own kind. Once you gain control of the economy of your own community, then you don't have to picket and boycott and beg some cracker downtown for a job in his business.

The social philosophy of black nationalism only means that we have to get together and remove the evils, the vices, alcoholism, drug addiction, and other evils that are destroying the moral fiber of our community. We ourselves have to lift the level of our community, the standard of our community to a higher level, make our own society beautiful so that we will be satisfied in our own social circles and won't be running around here trying to knock our way into a social circle where we're not wanted.

So I say, in spreading a gospel such as black nationalism, it is not designed to make the black man re-evaluate the white man—you know him already—but to make the black man re-evaluate himself. Don't change the white man's mind—you can't change his mind, and that whole thing about appealing to the moral conscience of America—America's conscience is bankrupt. She lost all conscience a long time ago. Uncle Sam has no conscience. They don't know what morals are. They don't try and eliminate an evil because it's evil, or because it's illegal, or because it's immoral; they eliminate it only when it threatens their existence. So you're wasting your time appealing to the moral conscience of a bankrupt man like Uncle Sam. If he had a conscience, he'd straighten this thing out with no more pressure being put upon him. So it is not necessary to change the white man's mind. We have to change our own mind. You can't change his mind about us. We've got to change our own minds about each other. We have to see each other with new eyes. We have to see each other as brothers and sisters. We have to come together with warmth so we can develop unity and harmony that's necessary to get this problem solved ourselves. How can we do this? How can we avoid jealousy? How can we avoid the suspicion and the divisions that exist in the community? I'll tell you how.

I have watched how Billy Graham comes into a city, spreading what he calls the gospel of Christ, which is only white nationalism. That's what he is. Billy Graham is a white nationalist; I'm a black nationalist. But since it's the natural tendency for leaders to be jealous and look upon a powerful figure like Graham with suspicion and envy, how is it possible for him to come into a city and get all the cooperation of the church leaders? Don't think because they're church leaders that they don't have weaknesses that make them envious and jealous—no, everybody's got it. It's not an accident that when they want to choose a cardinal over there in Rome, they get in a closet so you can't hear them cussing and fighting and carrying on.

Billy Graham comes in preaching the gospel of Christ, he evangelizes the gospel, he stirs everybody up, but he never tries to start a church. If he came in trying to start a church, all the churches would be against him. So, he just comes in talking about Christ and tells everybody who gets Christ to go to any church where Christ is; and in this way the church cooperates with him. So we're going to take a page from his book.

Our gospel is black nationalism. We're not trying to threaten the existence of any organization, but we're spreading the gospel of black nationalism. Anywhere there's a church that is also preaching and practicing the gospel of black nationalism, join that church. If the NAACP is preaching and practicing the gospel of black nationalism, join the NAACP. If CORE is spreading and practicing the gospel of black nationalism, join CORE. Join any organization that has a gospel that's for the uplift of the black man. And when you get into it and see them pussyfooting or compromising, pull out of it because that's not black nationalism. We'll find another one.

And in this manner, the organizations will increase in number and in quantity and in quality, and by August, it is then our intention to have a black nationalist convention which will consist of delegates from all over the country who are interested in the political, economic and social philosophy of black nationalism. After these delegates convene, we will hold a seminar, we will hold discussions, we will listen to everyone. We want to hear new ideas and new solutions and new answers. And at that time, if we see fit then to form a black nationalist party, we'll form a black nationalist party. If it's necessary to form a black nationalist army, we'll form a black nationalist army. It'll be the ballot or the bullet. It'll be liberty or it'll be death.

It's time for you and me to stop sitting in this country, letting some cracker senators, Northern crackers and Southern crackers, sit there in Washington, D.C., and come to a conclusion in their mind that you and I are supposed to have civil rights. There's no white man going to tell me anything about *my* rights. Brothers and sisters, always remember, if it doesn't take senators and congressmen and presidential proclamations to give freedom to the white man, it is not necessary for legislation or proclamation or Supreme Court decisions to give freedom to the black man. You let that white man know, if this is a country of freedom, let it be a country of freedom; and if it's not a country of freedom, change it.

We will work with anybody, anywhere, at any time, who is genuinely interested in tackling the problem head-on, nonviolently as long as the enemy is nonviolent, but violent when the enemy gets violent. We'll work with you on the voter-registration drive, we'll work with you on rent strikes, we'll work with you on school boycotts—I don't believe in any kind of integration; I'm not even worried about it because I know you're not going to get it anyway; you're not going to get it because you're afraid to die; you've got to be ready to die if you try and force yourself on the white man, because he'll get just as violent as those crackers in Mississippi, right here in Cleveland. But we will still work with you on the school boycotts because we're against a segregated school system. A segregated school system produces children who, when they graduate, graduate with crippled minds. But this does not mean that a school is segregated because it's all black. A segregated school means a school that is controlled by people who have no real interest in it whatsoever.

Let me explain what I mean. A segregated district or community is a community in which people live, but outsiders control the politics and the economy of that community. They never refer to the white section as a segregated community. It's the all-Negro section that's a segregated community. Why? The white man controls his own school, his own bank, his own economy, his own politics, his own everything, his own community—but he also controls yours. When you're under someone else's control, you're segregated. They'll always give you the lowest or the worst that there is to offer, but it doesn't mean you're segregated just because you have your own. You've got to *control* your own. Just like the white man has control of his, you need to control yours.

You know the best way to get rid of segregation? The white man is more afraid of separation than he is of integration. Segregation means that he puts you away from him, but not far enough for you to be out of his jurisdiction; separation means you're gone. And the white man will integrate faster than he'll let you separate. So we will work with you against the segregated school system because it's criminal, because it is absolutely destructive, in every way imaginable, to the minds of the children who have to be exposed to that type of crippling education.

Last but not least, I must say this concerning the great controversy over rifles and shotguns. The only thing that I've ever said is that in areas where the government has proven itself either unwilling or unable to defend the lives and the property of Negroes, it's time for Negroes to defend themselves. Article number two of the constitutional amendments provides you and me the right to own a rifle or a shotgun. It is constitutionally legal to own a shotgun or a rifle. This doesn't mean you're going to get a rifle and form battalions and go out looking for white folks, although you'd be within your rights—I mean, you'd be justified; but that would be illegal and we don't do anything illegal. If the white man doesn't want the black man buying rifles and shotguns, then let the government do its job. That's all. And don't let the white man come to you and ask you what you think about what Malcolm says—why, you old

Uncle Tom. He would never ask you if he thought you were going to say, "Amen!" No, he is making a Tom out of you.

So, this doesn't mean forming rifle clubs and going out looking for people, but it is time, in 1964, if you are a man, to let that man know. If he's not going to do his job in running the government and providing you and me with the protection that our taxes are supposed to be for, since he spends all those billions for his defense budget, he certainly can't begrudge you and me spending $12 or $15 for a single-shot, or double-action. I hope you understand. Don't go out shooting people, but any time, brothers and sisters, and especially the men in this audience—some of you wearing Congressional Medals of Honor, with shoulders this wide, chests this big, muscles that big—any time you and I sit around and read where they bomb a church and murder in cold blood, not some grownups, but four little girls while they were praying to the same god the white man taught them to pray to, and you and I see the government go down and can't find who did it.

Why, this man—he can find Eichmann hiding down in Argentina somewhere. Let two or three American soldiers, who are minding somebody else's business way over in South Vietnam, get killed, and he'll send battleships, sticking his nose in their business. He wanted to send troops down to Cuba and make them have what he calls free elections—this old cracker who doesn't have free elections in his own country. No, if you never see me another time in your life, if I die in the morning, I'll die saying one thing: the ballot or the bullet, the ballot or the bullet.

If a Negro in 1964 has to sit around and wait for some cracker senator to filibuster when it comes to the rights of black people, why, you and I should hang our heads in shame. You talk about a march on Washington in 1963, you haven't seen anything. There's some more going down in '64. And this time they're not going like they went last year. They're not going singing "We Shall Overcome." They're not going with white friends. They're not going with placards already painted for them. They're not going with round-trip tickets. They're going with one-way tickets.

And if they don't want that non-nonviolent army going down there, tell them to bring the filibuster to a halt. The black nationalists aren't going to wait. Lyndon B. Johnson is the head of the Democratic Party. If he's for civil rights, let him go into the Senate next week and declare himself. Let him go in there right now and declare himself. Let him go in there and denounce the Southern branch of his party. Let him go in there right now and take a moral stand—right now, not later. Tell him, don't wait until election time. If he waits too long, brothers and sisters, he will be responsible for letting a condition develop in this country which will create a climate that will bring seeds up out of the ground with vegetation on the end of them looking like something these people never dreamed of. In 1964, it's the ballot or the bullet. Thank you.

BARRY GOLDWATER

Speech to the
Republican National Convention

San Francisco, July 16, 1964

M Y GOOD FRIEND and great Republican, Dick Nixon and your charming wife, Pat; my running mate—that wonderful Republican who has served us so well for so long—Bill Miller and his wife, Stephanie; to Thruston Morton, who's done such a commendable job in chairmaning this convention; to Mr. Herbert Hoover, who I hope is watching, and to that great American and his wife, General and Mrs. Eisenhower. To my own wife, my family, and to all of my fellow Republicans here assembled, and Americans across this great nation:

From this moment, united and determined, we will go forward together dedicated to the ultimate and undeniable greatness of the whole man.

Together we will win.

I accept your nomination with a deep sense of humility. I accept, too, the responsibility that goes with it, and I seek your continued help and your continued guidance. My fellow Republicans, our cause is too great for any man to feel worthy of it. Our task would be too great for any man did he not have with him the heart and the hands of this great Republican party.

And I promise you tonight that every fibre of my being is consecrated to our cause, that nothing shall be lacking from the struggle that can be brought to it by enthusiasm, by devotion and plain hard work.

In this world no person, no party can guarantee anything, but what we can do and what we shall do is to deserve victory and victory will be ours. The Good Lord raised this mighty Republican—Republic to be a home for the brave and to flourish as the land of the free—not to stagnate in the swampland of collectivism, not to cringe before the bully of Communism.

Now my fellow Americans, the tide has been running against

freedom. Our people have followed false prophets. We must, and we shall, return to proven ways—not because they are old, but because they true.

We must, and we shall, set the tide running again in the cause of freedom. And this party, with its every action, every word, every breath and every heart beat, has but a single resolve, and that is freedom.

Freedom made orderly for this nation by our constitutional government. Freedom under a government limited by laws of nature and of nature's God. Freedom balanced so that order lacking liberty will not become the slavery of the prison cell; balanced so that liberty lacking order will not become the license of the mob and of the jungle.

Now, we Americans understand freedom, we have earned it; we have lived for it, and we have died for it. This nation and its people are freedom's models in a searching world. We can be freedom's missionaries in a doubting world.

But, ladies and gentlemen, first we must renew freedom's mission in our own hearts and in our own homes.

During four futile years the Administration which we shall replace has distorted and lost that faith. It has talked and talked and talked and talked the words of freedom but it has failed and failed and failed in the works of freedom.

Now failure cements the wall of shame in Berlin; failures blot the sands of shame at the Bay of Pigs; failures marked the slow death of freedom in Laos; failures infest the jungles of Vietnam, and failures haunt the houses of our once great alliances and undermine the greatest bulwark ever erected by free nations, the NATO community.

Failures proclaim lost leadership, obscure purpose, weakening wills and the risk of inciting our sworn enemies to new aggressions and to new excesses.

And because of this Administration we are tonight a world divided. We are a nation becalmed. We have lost the brisk pace of diversity and the genuis of individual creativity. We are plodding along at a pace set by centralized planning, red tape, rules without responsibility and regimentation without recourse.

Rather than useful jobs in our country, people have been

offered bureaucratic make-work; rather than moral leadership, they have been given bread and circuses; they have been given spectacles, and, yes, they've even been given scandals.

Tonight there is violence in our streets, corruption in our highest offices, aimlessness among our youth, anxiety among our elderly, and there's a virtual despair among the many who look beyond material success toward the inner meaning of their lives. And where examples of morality should be set, the opposite is seen. Small men seeking great wealth or power have too often and too long turned even the highest levels of public service into mere personal opportunity.

Now, certainly simple honesty is not too much to demand of men in government. We find it in most. Republicans demand it from everyone.

They demand it from everyone no matter how exalted or protected his position might be.

The growing menace in our country tonight, to personal safety, to life, to limb and property, in homes, in churches, on the playgrounds and places of business, particularly in our great cities, is the mounting concern or should be of every thoughtful citizen in the United States. Security from domestic violence, no less than from foreign aggression, is the most elementary and fundamental purpose of any government, and a government that cannot fulfill this purpose is one that cannot long command the loyalty of its citizens.

History shows us, demonstrates that nothing, nothing prepares the way for tyranny more than the failure of public officials to keep the streets safe from bullies and marauders.

Now we Republicans see all this as more—much more—than the result of mere political differences, or mere political mistakes. We see this as the result of a fundamentally and absolutely wrong view of man, his nature and his destiny.

Those who seek to live your lives for you, to take your liberty in return for relieving you of yours; those who elevate the state and downgrade the citizen, must see ultimately a world in which earthly power can be substituted for Divine Will. And this nation was founded upon the rejection of that notion and upon the acceptance of God as the author of freedom.

Now those who seek absolute power, even though they seek

it to do what they regard as good, are simply demanding the right to enforce their own version of heaven on earth, and let me remind you they are the very ones who always create the most hellish tyranny.

Absolute power does corrupt, and those who seek it must be suspect and must be opposed. Their mistaken course stems from false notions, ladies and gentlemen, of equality. Equality, rightly understood as our founding fathers understood it, leads to liberty and to the emancipation of creative differences; wrongly understood, as it has been so tragically in our time, it leads first to conformity and then to despotism.

Fellow Republicans, it is the cause of Republicanism to resist concentrations of power, private or public, which enforce such conformity and inflict such despotism.

It is the cause of Republicanism to insure that power remains in the hands of the people—and, so help us God, that is exactly what a Republican President will do with the help of a Republican Congress.

It is further the cause of Republicanism to restore a clear understanding of the tyranny of man over man in the world at large. It is our cause to dispel the foggy thinking which avoids hard decisions in the delusion that a world of conflict will somehow resolve itself into a world of harmony, if we just don't rock the boat or irritate the forces of aggression—and this is hogwash.

It is, further, the cause of Republicanism to remind ourselves, and the world, that only the strong can remain free; that only the strong can keep the peace.

Now I needn't remind you, or my fellow Americans regardless of party, that Republicans have shouldered this hard responsibility and marched in this cause before. It was Republican leadership under Dwight Eisenhower that kept the peace, and passed along to this Administration the mightiest arsenal for defense the world has ever known.

And I needn't remind you that it was the strength and the believable will of the Eisenhower years that kept the peace by using our strength, by using it in the Formosa Strait, and in Lebanon, and by showing it courageously at all times.

It was during those Republican years that the thrust of Communist imperialism was blunted. It was during those years of

Republican leadership that this world moved closer not to war but closer to peace than at any other time in the last three decades.

And I needn't remind you, but I will, that it's been during Democratic years that our strength to deter war has been stilled and even gone into a planned decline. It has been during Democratic years that we have weakly stumbled into conflicts, timidly refusing to draw our own lines against aggression, deceitfully refusing to tell even our own people of our full participation and tragically letting our finest men die on battlefields unmarked by purpose, unmarked by pride or the prospect of victory.

Yesterday it was Korea; tonight it is Vietnam. Make no bones of this. Don't try to sweep this under the rug. We are at war in Vietnam. And yet the President, who is the Commander in Chief of our forces, refuses to say, refuses to say mind you, whether or not the objective over there is victory, and his Secretary of Defense continues to mislead and misinform the American people, and enough of it has gone by.

And I needn't remind you, but I will, it has been during Democratic years that a billion persons were cast into Communist captivity and their fate cynically sealed.

Today—today in our beloved country we have an Administration which seems eager to deal with Communism in every coin known—from gold to wheat; from consulates to confidence, and even human freedom itself.

Now the Republican cause demands that we brand communism as the principal disturber of peace in the world today. Indeed, we should brand it as the only significant disturber of the peace. And we must make clear that until its goals of conquest are absolutely renounced, and its relations with all nations tempered, Communism and the governments it now controls are enemies of every man on earth who is or wants to be free.

Now, we here in America can keep the peace only if we remain vigilant, and only if we remain strong. Only if we keep our eyes open and keep our guard up can we prevent war.

And I want to make this abundantly clear—I don't intend to let peace or freedom be torn from our grasp because of lack of strength, or lack of will—and that I promise you Americans.

I believe, that we must look beyond the defense of freedom today to its extension tomorrow. I believe that the Communism which boasts it will bury us will instead give way to the forces of freedom. And I can see in the distant and yet recognizable future the outlines of a world worthy of our dedication, our every risk, our every effort, our every sacrifice along the way. Yes, a world that will redeem the suffering of those who will be liberated from tyranny.

I can see, and I suggest that all thoughtful men must contemplate, the flowering of an Atlantic civilization, the whole world of Europe reunified and free, trading openly across its borders, communicating openly across the world.

This is a goal far, far more meaningful than a moon shot.

It's a truly inspiring goal for all free men to set for themselves during the latter half of the twentieth century. I can see and all free men must thrill to the events of this Atlantic civilization joined by a straight ocean highway to the United States. What a destiny! What a destiny can be ours to stand as a great central pillar linking Europe, the Americas and the venerable and vital peoples and cultures of the Pacific.

I can see a day when all the Americas—North and South— will be linked in a mighty system—a system in which the errors and misunderstandings of the past will be submerged one by one in a rising tide of prosperity and interdependence.

We know that the misunderstandings of centuries are not to be wiped away in a day or wiped away in an hour. But we pledge, we pledge, that human sympathy—what our neighbors to the South call an attitude of sympatico—no less than enlightened self-interest will be our guide.

And I can see this Atlantic civilization galvanizing and guiding emergent nations everywhere. Now I know this freedom is not the fruit of every soil. I know that our own freedom was achieved through centuries by unremitting efforts by brave and wise men. And I know that the road to freedom is a long and a challenging road, and I know also that some men may walk away from it, that some men resist challenge, accepting the false security of governmental paternalism.

And I pledge that the America I envision in the years ahead will extend its hand in help, in teaching and in cultivation so that all new nations will be at least encouraged to go our way;

so that they will not wander down the dark alleys of tyranny or to the dead-end streets of collectivism.

My fellow Republicans, we do no man a service by hiding freedom's light under a bushel of mistaken humility.

I seek an America proud of its past, proud of its ways, proud of its dreams and determined actively to proclaim them. But our examples to the world must, like charity, begin at home.

In our vision of a good and decent future, free and peaceful, there must be room, room for the liberation of the energy and the talent of the individual, otherwise our vision is blind at the outset.

We must assure a society here which while never abandoning the needy, or forsaking the helpless, nurtures incentives and opportunity for the creative and the productive.

We must know the whole good is the product of many single contributions. And I cherish the day when our children once again will restore as heroes the sort of men and women who, unafraid and undaunted, pursue the truth, strive to cure disease, subdue and make fruitful our natural environment, and produce the inventive engines of production, science and technology.

This nation, whose creative people have enhanced this entire span of history, should again thrive upon the greatness of all those things which we—we as individual citizens—can and should do.

During Republican years, this again will be a nation of men and women, of families proud of their role, jealous of their responsibilities, unlimited in their aspirations—a nation where all who can will be self-reliant.

We Republicans see in our constitutional form of government the great framework which assures the orderly but dynamic fulfillment of the whole man, and we see the whole man as the great reason for instituting orderly government in the first place.

We see in private property and in economy based upon and fostering private property the one way to make government a durable ally of the whole man rather than his determined enemy.

We see in the sanctity of private property the only durable foundation for constitutional government in a free society.

And beyond that we see and cherish diversity of ways, diversity of thoughts, of motives, and accomplishments. We don't seek to live anyone's life for him. We only seek to secure his rights, guarantee him opportunity, guarantee him opportunity to strive with government performing only those needed and constitutionally sanctioned tasks which cannot otherwise be performed.

We, Republicans, seek a government that attends to its inherent responsibilities of maintaining a stable monetary and fiscal climate, encouraging a free and a competitive economy and enforcing law and order.

Thus do we seek inventiveness, diversity and creative difference within a stable order, for we Republicans define government's role where needed at many, many levels, preferably through the one closest to the people involved: our towns and our cities, then our counties, then our states then our regional contacts and only then the national government.

That, let me remind you, is the land of liberty built by decentralized power. On it also we must have balance between the branches of government at every level.

Balance, diversity, creative difference—these are the elements of Republican equation. Republicans agree, Republican agree heartily, to disagree on many, many of their applications. But we have never disagreed on the basic fundamental issues of why you and I are Republicans.

This is a party—this Republican party is a party for free men. Not for blind followers and not for conformists.

Back in 1858 Abraham Lincoln said this of the Republican party, and I quote him because he probably could have said it during the last week or so: It was composed of strained, discordant, and even hostile elements. End of the quote, in 1858.

Yet all of these elements agreed on one paramount objective: to arrest the progress of slavery, and place it in the course of ultimate extinction.

Today, as then, but more urgently and more broadly than then, the task of preserving and enlarging freedom at home and of safeguarding it from the forces of tyranny abroad is great enough to challenge all our resources and to require all our strength.

Anyone who joins us in all sincerity we welcome. Those,

those who do not care for our cause, we don't expect to enter our ranks in any case. And let our Republicanism so focused and so dedicated not be made fuzzy and futile by unthinking and stupid labels.

I would remind you that extremism in the defense of liberty is no vice!

And let me remind you also that moderation in the pursuit of justice is no virtue!

By the—the beauty of the very system we Republicans are pledged to restore and revitalize, the beauty of this Federal system of ours is in its reconciliation of diversity with unity. We must not see malice in honest differences of opinion, and no matter how great, so long as they are not inconsistent with the pledges we have given to each other in and through our Constitution.

Our Republican cause is not to level out the world or make its people conform in computer-regimented sameness. Our Republican cause is to free our people and light the way for liberty throughout the world. Ours is a very human cause for very humane goals. This party, its good people, and its unquestionable devotion to freedom will not fulfill the purposes of this campaign which we launch here now until our cause has won the day, inspired the world, and shown the way to a tomorrow worthy of all our yesteryears.

I repeat, I accept your nomination with humbleness, with pride and you and I are going to fight for the goodness of our land. Thank you.

RONALD REAGAN

Speech on Behalf of Barry Goldwater

Los Angeles, October 27, 1964

T HANK YOU very much. Thank you, and good evening. The sponsor has been identified, but unlike most television programs, the performer hasn't been provided with a script. As a matter of fact, I have been permitted to choose my own words and discuss my own ideas regarding the choice that we face in the next few weeks.

I have spent most of my life as a Democrat. I recently have seen fit to follow another course. I believe that the issues confronting us cross party lines. Now, one side in this campaign has been telling us that the issues of this election are the maintenance of peace and prosperity. The line has been used "We've never had it so good!"

But I have an uncomfortable feeling that this prosperity isn't something upon which we can base our hopes for the future. No nation in history has ever survived a tax burden that reached a third of its national income. Today thirty-seven cents out of every dollar earned in this country is the tax collector's share, and yet our government continues to spend 17 million dollars a day more than the government takes in. We haven't balanced our budget twenty-eight out of the last thirty-four years. We have raised our debt limit three times in the last twelve months, and now our national debt is one and a half times bigger than all the combined debts of all the nations of the world. We have 15 billion dollars in gold in our treasury—we don't own an ounce. Foreign dollar claims are 27.3 billion dollars, and we have just had announced that the dollar of 1939 will now purchase forty-five cents in its total value.

As for the peace that we would preserve, I wonder who among us would like to approach the wife or mother whose husband or son has died in Vietnam and ask them if they think this is a peace that should be maintained indefinitely. Do they mean peace, or do they mean we just want to be left in peace? There can be no real peace while one American is dying someplace in the world for the rest of us. We are at war with the most dangerous enemy that has ever faced mankind in his long climb from the swamp to the stars, and it has been said if we lose that war, and in so doing lose this way of freedom of ours, history will record with the greatest astonishment that those who had the most to lose did the least to prevent its happening. Well, I think it's time we ask ourselves if we still know the freedoms that were intended for us by the Founding Fathers.

Not too long ago two friends of mine were talking to a Cuban refugee, a businessman who had escaped from Castro, and in the midst of his story one of my friends turned to the other and said, "We don't know how lucky we are." And the Cuban stopped and said, "How lucky you are! I had someplace to escape to." In that sentence he told us the entire story. If we lose freedom here, there is no place to escape to. This is the last stand on earth.

And this idea that government is beholden to the people, that it has no other source of power except the sovereign people, is still the newest and most unique idea in all the long history of man's relation to man. This is the issue of this election. Whether we believe in our capacity for self-government or whether we abandon the American Revolution and confess that a little intellectual elite in a far-distant capital can plan our lives for us better than we can plan them ourselves.

You and I are told increasingly that we have to choose between a left or right, but I would like to suggest that there is no such thing as a left or right. There is only an up or down—up to man's age-old dream—the ultimate in individual freedom consistent with law and order—or down to the ant heap of totalitarianism, and regardless of their sincerity, their humanitarian motives, those who would trade our freedom for security have embarked on this downward course.

In this vote-harvesting time they use terms like the "Great Society," or as we were told a few days ago by the President, we must accept a "greater government activity in the affairs of the people." But they have been a little more explicit in the past and among themselves—and all of the things that I now will quote have appeared in print. These are not Republican accusations. For example, they have voices that say "the cold war will end through our acceptance of a not undemocratic socialism." Another voice says that the profit motive has become outmoded, it must be replaced by the incentives of the welfare state; or our traditional system of individual freedom is incapable of solving the complex problems of the twentieth century.

Senator Fulbright has said at Stanford University that the Constitution is outmoded. He referred to the president as our moral teacher and our leader, and he said he is hobbled in his task by the restrictions in power imposed on him by this antiquated document. He must be freed so that he can do for us what he knows is best.

And Senator Clark of Pennsylvania, another articulate spokesman, defines liberalism as "meeting the material needs of the masses through the full power of centralized government." Well, I for one resent it when a representative of the people refers to you and me—the free men and women of this country—as "the masses." This is a term we haven't applied to ourselves in America. But beyond that, "the full power of centralized government"—this was the very thing the Founding Fathers sought to minimize. They knew that governments don't control *things*. A government can't control the economy without controlling people. And they knew when a government sets out to do that, it must use force and coercion to achieve its purpose. They also knew, those Founding Fathers, that outside of its legitimate functions, government does nothing as well or as economically as the private sector of the economy.

Now, we have no better example of this than the government's involvement in the farm economy over the last thirty years. Since 1955 the cost of this program has nearly doubled. One-fourth of farming in America is responsible for 85 percent of the farm surplus. Three-fourths of farming is out on the free market and has known a 21 percent increase in the per capita consumption of all its produce. You see, that one-fourth of farming is regulated and controlled by the federal government. In the last three years we have spent forty-three dollars in the feed grain program for every dollar bushel of corn we don't grow.

Senator Humphrey last week charged that Barry Goldwater as president would seek to eliminate farmers. He should do his homework a little better, because he will find out that we have had a decline of 5 million in the farm population under these government programs. He will also find that the Democratic administration has sought to get from Congress an extension of the farm program to include that three-fourths that is now free. He will find that they have also asked for the right to imprison farmers who wouldn't keep books as prescribed by the federal government. The secretary of agriculture asked for the right to seize farms through condemnation and resell them to other individuals. And contained in that same program was a provision that would have allowed the federal government to remove 2 million farmers from the soil.

At the same time there has been an increase in the Department of Agriculture employees. There is now one for every thirty farms in the United States, and still they can't tell us how sixty-six shiploads of grain headed for Austria disappeared without a trace, and Billie Sol Estes never left shore!

Every responsible farmer and farm organization has repeatedly asked the government to free the farm economy, but who are farmers to know what is best for them? The wheat farmers voted against a wheat program. The government passed it anyway. Now the price of bread goes up; the price of wheat to the farmers goes down.

Meanwhile, back in the city, under urban renewal the assault on freedom carries on. Private property rights are so diluted that public interest is almost anything that a few government planners decide it should be. In a program that takes from the needy and gives to the greedy, we see such spectacles as in Cleveland, Ohio, a million-and-a-half-dollar building completed only three years ago must be destroyed to make way for what government officials call a "more compatible use of the land." The President tells us he is now going to start building public housing units in the thousands where heretofore we have only built them in the hundreds. But FHA and the Veterans Administration tell us that they have 120,000 housing units they've taken back through mortgage foreclosures.

For three decades we have sought to solve the problems of unemployment through government planning, and the more the plans fail, the more the planners plan. The latest is the Area Redevelopment Agency. They have just declared Rice County, Kansas, a depressed area. Rice County, Kansas, has two hundred oil wells, and the 14,000 people there have over thirty million dollars on deposit in personal savings in their banks. When the government tells you you are depressed, lie down and be depressed!

We have so many people who can't see a fat man standing beside a thin one without coming to the conclusion that the fat man got that way by taking advantage of the thin one! So they are going to solve all the problems of human misery through government and government planning. Well, now if government planning and welfare had the answer, and they've had almost thirty years of it, shouldn't we expect government to read the score to us once in a while? Shouldn't they be telling us about the decline each year in the number of people needing help? . . . the reduction in the need for public housing?

But the reverse is true. Each year the need grows greater, the program grows greater. We were told four years ago that seventeen million people went to bed hungry each night. Well, that was probably true. They were all on a diet! But now we are told that 9.3 million families in this country are poverty-stricken on the basis of earning less than $3,000 a year. Welfare spending is ten times greater than in the dark depths of the Depression. We are spending 45 billion dollars on welfare. Now do a little arithmetic, and you will find that if we divided the 45 billion dollars up equally among those 9 million poor families, we would be able to give each family $4,600 a year, and this added to their present income should eliminate poverty! Direct aid to the poor, however, is running only about $600 per family. It seems that someplace there must be some overhead.

So now we declare "war on poverty," or "you, too, can be a Bobby Baker!" How do they honestly expect us to believe that if we add 1 billion dollars to the 45 billion we are spending . . . one more program to the thirty-odd we have—and remember, this new program doesn't replace any, it just duplicates existing programs . . . do they believe that poverty is suddenly going to disappear by magic? Well, in all fairness I should explain that there is one part of the new program that isn't duplicated. This is the youth feature. We are now going to solve the dropout problem, juvenile delinquency, by reinstituting something like the old CCC camps, and we are going to put our young people in camps, but again we do some arithmetic, and we find that we are going to spend each year just on room and board for each young person that we help $4,700 a year! We can send them to Harvard for $2,700! Don't get me wrong. I'm not suggesting that Harvard is the answer to juvenile delinquency!

But seriously, what are we doing to those we seek to help? Not too long ago, a judge called me here in Los Angeles. He told me of a young woman who had come before him for a divorce. She had six children, was pregnant with her seventh. Under his questioning, she revealed her husband was a laborer earning $250 a month. She wanted a divorce so that she could get an $80 raise. She is eligible for $330 a month in the Aid to Dependent Children Program. She got the idea from two women in her neighborhood who had already done that very thing.

Yet anytime you and I question the schemes of the do-gooders, we are denounced as being against their humanitarian goals. They say we are always "against" things, never "for" anything. Well, the trouble with our liberal friends is not that they are ignorant, but that they know so much that isn't so! We are for a provision that destitution should not follow unemployment by reason of old age, and to that end we have accepted social security as a step toward meeting the problem.

But we are against those entrusted with this program, when they practice deception regarding its fiscal shortcomings, when they charge that any criticism of the program means that we want to end payments to those people who depend on them for a livelihood. They have called it insurance to us in a hundred million pieces of literature. But then they appeared before the Supreme Court and they testified that it was a welfare program. They only use the term "insurance" to sell it to the people. And they said social security dues are a tax for the general use of the government, and the government has used that tax. There is no fund, because Robert Byers, the actuarial head, appeared before a congressional committee and admitted that social security as of this moment is $298 billion in the hole! But he said there should be no cause for worry because as long as they have the power to tax, they could always take away from the people whatever they needed to bail them out of trouble! And they are doing just that.

A young man, twenty-one years of age, working at an average salary . . . his social security contribution would, in the open market, buy him an insurance policy that would guarantee $220 a month at age sixty-five. The government promises $127! He could live it up until he is thirty-one and then take out a policy that would pay more than social security. Now, are we so lacking in business sense that we can't put this program on a sound basis so that people who do require those payments will find that they can get them when they are due . . . that the cupboard isn't bare? Barry Goldwater thinks we can.

At the same time, can't we introduce voluntary features that would permit a citizen to do better on his own, to be excused upon presentation of evidence that he had made provisions for the nonearning years? Should we not allow a widow with children to work, and not lose the benefits supposedly paid for by her deceased husband? Shouldn't you and I be allowed to declare who our beneficiaries will be under these programs, which we cannot do? I think we are for telling our senior citizens that no one in this country should be denied medical care because of a lack of funds. But I think we are against forcing all citizens, regardless of need, into a compulsory government program, especially when we have such examples, as announced last week, when France admitted that their medicare program was now bankrupt. They've come to the end of the road.

In addition, was Barry Goldwater so irresponsible when he suggested that our government give up its program of deliberate planned inflation so that when you do get your social security pension, a dollar will buy a dollar's worth, and not forty-five cents worth?

I think we are for the international organization, where the nations of the world can seek peace. But I think we are against subordinating American interests to an organization that has become so structurally unsound that today you can muster a two-thirds vote on the floor of the General Assembly among nations that represent less than 10 percent of the world's population. I think we are against the hypocrisy of assailing our allies because here and there they cling to a colony, while we engage in a conspiracy of silence and never open our mouths about the millions of people enslaved in Soviet colonies in the satellite nations.

I think we are for aiding our allies by sharing of our material blessings with those nations which share in our fundamental beliefs, but we are against doling out money government to government, creating bureaucracy, if not socialism, all over the world. We set out to help 19 countries. We are helping 107. We spent $146 billion. With that money, we bought a 2-million-dollar yacht for Haile Selassie. We bought dress suits for Greek undertakers, extra wives for Kenya government officials. We bought a thousand TV sets for a place where they have no electricity. In the last six years, fifty-two nations have bought $7 billion of our gold, and all fifty-two are receiving foreign aid from us. No government ever voluntarily reduces itself in size. Government programs, once launched, never disappear. Actually, a government bureau is the nearest thing to eternal life we'll ever see on this earth!

Federal employees number 2.5 million, and federal, state, and local, one out of six of the nation's work force is employed by government. These proliferating bureaus with their thousands of regulations have cost us many of our constitutional safeguards. How many of us realize that today federal agents can invade a man's property without a warrant? They can impose a fine without a formal hearing, let alone a trial by jury, and they can seize and sell his property in auction to enforce the payment of that fine. In Chicot County, Arkansas, James Wier overplanted his rice allotment. The government obtained a $17,000 judgment, and a U.S. marshal sold his 950-acre farm at auction. The government said it was necessary as a warning to others to make the system work! Last February 19th, at the University of Minnesota, Norman Thomas, six times candidate for president on the Socialist Party ticket, said, "If Barry Goldwater became president, he would stop the advance of socialism in the United States." I think that's exactly what he will do!

As a former Democrat, I can tell you Norman Thomas isn't the only man who has drawn this parallel to socialism with the present administration. Back in 1936, Mr. Democrat himself, Al Smith, the great American, came before the American people and charged that the leadership of his party was taking the party of Jefferson, Jackson, and Cleveland down the road under the banners of Marx, Lenin, and Stalin. And he walked away from his party, and he never returned to the day he died, because to this day, the leadership of that party has been taking that party, that honorable party, down the road in the image of the labor socialist party of England. Now it doesn't require expropriation or confiscation of private property or business to impose socialism upon a people. What does it mean whether you hold the deed or the title to your business or property if the government holds the power of life and death over that business or property? Such machinery already exists. The government can find some charge to bring against any concern it chooses to prosecute. Every businessman has his own tale of harassment. Somewhere a perversion has taken place. Our natural, inalienable rights are now considered to be a dispensation from government, and freedom has never been so fragile, so close to slipping from our grasp as it is at this moment. Our Democratic opponents seem unwilling to debate these issues. They want to make you and I think that this is a contest between two men . . . that we are to choose just between two personalities. Well, what of this man they would destroy . . . and in destroying, they would destroy that which he represents, the ideas that you and I hold dear.

Is he the brash and shallow and trigger-happy man they say he is? Well, I have been privileged to know him "when." I knew him long before he ever dreamed of trying for high office, and I can tell you personally I have never known a man in my life I believe so incapable of doing a dishonest or dishonorable thing.

This is a man who in his own business, before he entered politics, instituted a profit-sharing plan, before unions had ever thought of it. He put in health and medical insurance for all his employees. He took 50 percent of the profits before taxes and set up a retirement plan, and a pension plan for all his employees. He sent monthly checks for life to an employee who was ill and couldn't work. He provided nursing care for the children of mothers who work in the stores. When Mexico was ravaged by the floods from the Rio Grande, he climbed in his airplane and flew medicine and supplies down there.

An ex-GI told me how he met him. It was the week before Christmas during the Korean War, and he was at the Los Angeles airport trying to get a ride home to Arizona, and he said that there were a lot of servicemen there and no seats available on the planes. Then a voice came over the loudspeaker and said, "Any men in uniform wanting a ride to Arizona, go to runway such-and-such," and they went down there, and there was a fellow named Barry Goldwater sitting in his plane. Every day in the weeks before Christmas, all day long, he would load up the plane, fly to Arizona, fly them to their homes, then fly back over to get another load.

During the hectic split-second timing of a campaign, this is a man who took time out to sit beside an old friend who was dying of cancer. His campaign managers were understandably impatient, but he said, "There aren't many left who care what happens to her. I'd like her to know that I care." This is a man who said to his nineteen-year-old son, "There is no foundation like the rock of honesty and fairness, and when you begin to build your life upon that rock, with the cement of the faith in God that you have, then you have a real start!" This is not a man who could carelessly send other people's sons to war. And that is the issue of this campaign that makes all of the other problems I have discussed academic, unless we realize that we are in a war that must be won.

Those who would trade our freedom for the soup kitchen of the welfare state have told us that they have a utopian solution of peace without victory. They call their policy "accommodation." And they say if we only avoid any direct confrontation with the enemy, he will forget his evil ways and learn to love us. All who oppose them are indicted as warmongers. They say we offer simple answers to complex problems. Well, perhaps there is a simple answer . . . not an easy one . . . but a simple one, if you and I have the courage to tell our elected officials that we want our *national* policy based upon what we know in our hearts is morally right.

We cannot buy our security, our freedom from the threat of the bomb by committing an immorality so great as saying to a billion human beings now in slavery behind the Iron Curtain,

"Give up your dreams of freedom because to save our own skin, we are willing to make a deal with your slave-masters." Alexander Hamilton said, "A nation which can prefer disgrace to danger is prepared for a master, and deserves one!" Let's set the record straight. There is no argument over the choice between peace and war, but there is only one guaranteed way you can have peace . . . and you can have it in the next second . . . surrender!

Admittedly there is a risk in any course we follow other than this, but every lesson in history tells us that the greater risk lies in appeasement, and this is the specter our well-meaning liberal friends refuse to face . . . that their policy of accommodation is appeasement, and it gives no choice between peace and war, only between fight or surrender. If we continue to accommodate, continue to back and retreat, eventually we have to face the final demand—the ultimatum. And what then? When Nikita Khrushchev has told his people he knows what our answer will be? He has told them that we are retreating under the pressure of the cold war, and someday when the time comes to deliver the ultimatum, our surrender will be voluntary because by that time we will have been weakened from within spiritually, morally, and economically. He believes this because from our side he has heard voices pleading for "peace at any price" or "better Red than dead," or as one commentator put it, he would rather "live on his knees than die on his feet." And therein lies the road to war, because those voices don't speak for the rest of us. You and I know and do not believe that life is so dear and peace so sweet as to be purchased at the price of chains and slavery. If nothing in life is worth dying for, when did this begin—just in the face of this enemy?—or should Moses have told the children of Israel to live in slavery under the pharaohs? Should Christ have refused the cross? Should the patriots at Concord Bridge have thrown down their guns and refused to fire the shot heard round the world? The martyrs of history were not fools, and our honored dead who gave their lives to stop the advance of the Nazis didn't die in vain! Where, then, is the road to peace? Well, it's a simple answer after all.

You and I have the courage to say to our enemies, "There is a price we will not pay." There is a point beyond which they must not advance! This is the meaning in the phrase of Barry Goldwater's "peace through strength!" Winston Churchill said that "the destiny of man is not measured by material computation. When great forces are on the move in the world, we learn we are spirits—not animals." And he said, "There is something going on in time and space, and beyond time and space, which, whether we like it or not, spells duty." You and I have a rendezvous with destiny. We will preserve for our children this, the last best hope of man on earth, or we will sentence them to take the last step into a thousand years of darkness.

We will keep in mind and remember that Barry Goldwater has faith in us. He has faith that you and I have the ability and the dignity and the right to make our own decisions and determine our own destiny.

Thank you.

MARIO SAVIO

Speech in Sproul Plaza

Berkeley, California, December 2, 1964

Y OU KNOW, I just want to say one brief thing about something the previous speaker said. I didn't want to spend too
much time on that because I don't think it's important enough,
but one thing is worth considering. He's the, he's the nominal
head of an organization supposedly representative of the under-
graduates, whereas in fact under the Kerr directives it derives
its authority, its delegated power, from the administration. It's
totally unrepresentative of the graduate students and TAs. But
he made the following statement, I quote: "I would ask all
those who are not definitely committed to the FSM cause to
stay away from demonstration." Alright, now, listen to this:
"For all upper division students who are interested in allevi-
ating the TA shortage problem, I would encourage you to
offer your services to department chairmen and advisers." That
has two things: a strikebreaker and a fink! (*Applause.*)

I'd like to say, I'd like to say one other thing about a union
problem. Upstairs, you may have noticed already on the second
floor of Sproul Hall, Locals 40 and 127 of the Painters' Union
are painting the inside of the second floor of Sproul Hall.
Now, apparently that action had been planned sometime in
the past. I've tried to contact those unions. Unfortunately, and
it tears my heart out, they're as bureaucratized as the administration—it's difficult to get through to anyone in authority
there. Very sad. We're still, we're still making an attempt. Those
people up there have no desire to interfere with what we're
doing. I would ask that they be considered, and that they not
be heckled in any way, and, I think that, you know, while
there's unfortunately no sense of, no sense of solidarity at this
point between unions and students, there at least need be no,
you know, excessively hard feelings between the two groups.

Now. There are at least two ways in which sit-ins, and civil

disobedience, and whatever, at least two major ways in which
it can occur. One, when a law exists, is promulgated, which is
totally unacceptable to people and they violate it again and
again and again until it's rescinded, repealed. Alright. But
there's another way, there's another way.

Sometimes the form of the law is such as to render impossible its effective violation as a method to have it repealed. Sometimes the grievances of people are more, extend more, to more
than just the law, extend to a whole mode of arbitrary power, a
whole mode of arbitrary exercise of arbitrary power. And that's
what we have here. We have an autocracy which, which runs
this university. It's managed! We were told the following: If
President Kerr actually tried to get something more liberal out
of the Regents in his telephone conversation, why didn't he
make some public statement to that effect? And the answer we
received, from a well-meaning liberal, was the following. He
said: "Would you ever imagine the manager of a firm making a
statement publicly in opposition to his board of directors?"
That's the answer! Now I ask you to consider: If this is a firm,
and if the Board of Regents are the board of directors, and if
President Kerr in fact is the manager, then I'll tell you something, the faculty are a bunch of employees, and we're the raw
materials! But we're a bunch of raw materials that don't mean
to be, have any process upon us, don't mean to be made into
any product, don't mean, don't mean to end up being bought
by some clients of the University, be they the government, be
they industry, be they organized labor, be they anyone! We're
human beings! (*Applause.*)

And that, that brings me to the second mode of civil disobedience. There is a time when the operation of the machine
becomes so odious, makes you so sick at heart, that you can't
take part; you can't even passively take part. And you've got to
put your bodies upon the gears and upon the wheels, upon the
levers, upon all the apparatus, and you've got to make it stop.
And you've got to indicate to the people who run it, to the
people who own it, that unless you're free, the machine will be
prevented from working at all! (*Applause.*)

That doesn't mean—and it will be interpreted to mean, unfortunately, by the bigots who run the *Examiner*, for example
—that doesn't mean that you have to break anything. One

thousand people, sitting down someplace, not letting anybody by, not letting anything happen, can stop any machine,
including this machine, and it will stop!

We're going to do the following, and the greater the number of people, the safer they'll be, and the more effective it will
be. We're going, once again, to march up to the second floor
of Sproul Hall. And we're going to conduct our lives for a
while in the second floor of Sproul Hall. We'll show movies,
for example. We tried to get *Un Chant d'amour. (Laughter.)*
Unfortunately, that's tied up in the courts because of a lot of
squeamish moral mothers for a moral America and other
people on the outside, the same people who get all their ideas
out of the *San Francisco Examiner.* Sad, sad. But Mr. Landau,
Mr. Landau has gotten us some other films.

Likewise, we'll do something, we'll do something that hasn't
occurred at this university in a good long time. We're going to
have *real classes* up there—there are going to be Freedom
Schools conducted up there, we're going to have classes on the
First and Fourteenth Amendments! *(Applause.)* We're going
to spend our time learning about the things this university is
afraid that we know. We're going to learn about freedom up
there, and we're going to learn by doing!

Now, we've had some good long rallies. We've had some
good long rallies, and I think I'm sicker of rallies than anyone
else here. It's not going to be long. I'd like to introduce one
last person, one last person before we enter Sproul Hall. And
the person is Joan Baez.

MARTIN LUTHER KING, JR.

Nobel Prize Address

Oslo, December 10, 1964

YOUR MAJESTY, Your Royal Highness, Mr. President, ex-cellencies, ladies and gentlemen: I accept the Nobel Prize for Peace at a moment when twenty-two million Negroes of the United States are engaged in a creative battle to end the long night of racial injustice. I accept this award on behalf of a civil rights movement which is moving with determination and a majestic scorn for risk and danger to establish a reign of freedom and a rule of justice.

I am mindful that only yesterday in Birmingham, Alabama, our children, crying out for brotherhood, were answered with fire hoses, snarling dogs, and even death. I am mindful that only yesterday in Philadelphia, Mississippi, young people seeking to secure the right to vote were brutalized and murdered. I am mindful that debilitating and grinding poverty afflicts my people and chains them to the lowest rung of the economic ladder.

Therefore, I must ask why this prize is awarded to a move-ment which is beleaguered and committed to unrelenting struggle, and to a movement which has not yet won the very peace and brotherhood which is the essence of the Nobel Prize. After contemplation, I conclude that this award, which I receive on behalf of that movement, is a profound recognition that nonviolence is the answer to the crucial political and moral questions of our time: the need for man to overcome op-pression and violence without resorting to violence and oppression.

Civilization and violence are antithetical concepts. Negroes of the United States, following the people of India, have dem-onstrated that nonviolence is not sterile passivity, but a power-ful moral force which makes for social transformation. Sooner or later, all the peoples of the world will have to discover a way to live together in peace, and thereby transform this pending cosmic elegy into a creative psalm of brotherhood. If this is to be achieved, man must evolve for all human conflict a method which rejects revenge, aggression, and retaliation. The foundation of such a method is love.

The torturous road which has led from Montgomery, Alabama, to Oslo bears witness to this truth, and this is a road over which millions of Negroes are traveling to find a new sense of dignity. This same road has opened for all Americans a new era of progress and hope. It has led to a new civil rights bill, and it will, I am convinced, be widened and lengthened into a superhighway of justice as Negro and white men in increasing numbers create alliances to overcome their common problems.

I accept this award today with an abiding faith in America and an audacious faith in the future of mankind. I refuse to accept despair as the final response to the ambiguities of history.

I refuse to accept the idea that the "is–ness" of man's present nature makes him morally incapable of reaching up for the eternal "ought–ness" that forever confronts him.

I refuse to accept the idea that man is mere flotsam and jetsam in the river of life, unable to influence the unfolding events which surround him.

I refuse to accept the view that mankind is so tragically bound to the starless midnight of racism and war that the bright daybreak of peace and brotherhood can never become a reality.

I refuse to accept the cynical notion that nation after nation must spiral down a militaristic stairway into the hell of nuclear annihilation.

I believe that unarmed truth and unconditional love will have the final word in reality. This is why right, temporarily defeated, is stronger than evil triumphant.

I believe that even amid today's mortar bursts and whining bullets, there is still hope for a brighter tomorrow.

I believe that wounded justice, lying prostrate on the blood-flowing streets of our nations, can be lifted from this dust of shame to reign supreme among the children of men.

I have the audacity to believe that peoples everywhere can have three meals a day for their bodies, education and culture for their minds, and dignity, equality, and freedom for their spirits.

I believe that what self-centered men have torn down, men other-centered can build up.

I still believe that one day mankind will bow before the altars of God and be crowned triumphant over war and bloodshed, and nonviolent redemptive goodwill proclaimed the rule of the land. And the lion and the lamb shall lie down together, and every man shall sit under his own vine and fig tree, and none shall be afraid.

I still believe that we shall overcome.

This faith can give us courage to face the uncertainties of the future. It will give our tired feet new strength as we continue our forward stride toward the city of freedom. When our days become dreary with low-hovering clouds and our nights become darker than a thousand midnights, we will know that we are living in the creative turmoil of a genuine civilization struggling to be born.

Today I come to Oslo as a trustee, inspired and with renewed dedication to humanity. I accept this prize on behalf of all men who love peace and brotherhood. I say I come as a trustee, for in the depths of my heart I am aware that this prize is much more than an honor to me personally. Every time I take a flight I am always mindful of the many people who make a successful journey possible, the known pilots and the unknown ground crew. You honor the dedicated pilots of our struggle, who have sat at the controls as the freedom movement soared into orbit. You honor, once again, Chief Lutuli of South Africa, whose struggles with and for his people are still met with the most brutal expression of man's inhumanity to man. You honor the ground crew, without whose labor and sacrifice the jet flights to freedom could never have left the earth. Most of these people will never make the headlines, and their names will never appear in *Who's Who*. Yet, when years have rolled past and when the blazing light of truth is focused on this marvelous age in which we live, men and women will know and children will be taught that we have a finer land, a better people, a more noble civilization because these humble children of God were willing to suffer for righteousness' sake.

I think Alfred Nobel would know what I mean when I say I accept this award in the spirit of a curator of some precious heirloom which he holds in trust for its true owners: all those to whom truth is beauty, and beauty, truth, and in whose eyes the beauty of genuine brotherhood and peace is more precious than diamonds or silver or gold. Thank you. [*Applause*]

LYNDON B. JOHNSON

Address to Congress on Voting Rights

Washington, D.C., March 15, 1965

MR. SPEAKER, MR. PRESIDENT, MEMBERS OF THE CONGRESS:

I speak tonight for the dignity of man and the destiny of democracy.

I urge every member of both parties, Americans of all religions and of all colors, from every section of this country, to join me in that cause.

At times history and fate meet at a single time in a single place to shape a turning point in man's unending search for freedom. So it was at Lexington and Concord. So it was a century ago at Appomattox. So it was last week in Selma, Alabama.

There, long-suffering men and women peacefully protested the denial of their rights as Americans. Many were brutally assaulted. One good man, a man of God, was killed.

There is no cause for pride in what has happened in Selma. There is no cause for self-satisfaction in the long denial of equal rights of millions of Americans. But there is cause for hope and for faith in our democracy in what is happening here tonight.

For the cries of pain and the hymns and protests of oppressed people have summoned into convocation all the majesty of this great Government—the Government of the greatest Nation on earth.

Our mission is at once the oldest and the most basic of this country: to right wrong, to do justice, to serve man.

In our time we have come to live with moments of great crisis. Our lives have been marked with debate about great issues; issues of war and peace, issues of prosperity and depression. But rarely in any time does an issue lay bare the secret heart of America itself. Rarely are we met with a challenge, not to our growth or abundance, our welfare or our security, but rather to the values and the purposes and the meaning of our beloved Nation.

The issue of equal rights for American Negroes is such an issue. And should we defeat every enemy, should we double our wealth and conquer the stars, and still be unequal to this issue, then we will have failed as a people and as a nation.

For with a country as with a person, "What is a man profited, if he shall gain the whole world, and lose his own soul?"

There is no Negro problem. There is no Southern problem. There is no Northern problem. There is only an American problem. And we are met here tonight as Americans—not as Democrats or Republicans—we are met here as Americans to solve that problem.

This was the first nation in the history of the world to be founded with a purpose. The great phrases of that purpose still sound in every American heart, North and South: "All men are created equal"—"government by consent of the governed"—"give me liberty or give me death." Well, those are not just clever words, or those are not just empty theories. In their name Americans have fought and died for two centuries, and tonight around the world they stand there as guardians of our liberty, risking their lives.

Those words are a promise to every citizen that he shall share in the dignity of man. This dignity cannot be found in a man's possessions; it cannot be found in his power, or in his position. It really rests on his right to be treated as a man equal in opportunity to all others. It says that he shall share in freedom, he shall choose his leaders, educate his children, and provide for his family according to his ability and his merits as a human being.

To apply any other test—to deny a man his hopes because of his color or race, his religion or the place of his birth—is not only to do injustice, it is to deny America and to dishonor the dead who gave their lives for American freedom.

Our fathers believed that if this noble view of the rights of man was to flourish, it must be rooted in democracy. The most basic right of all was the right to choose your own leaders. The history of this country, in large measure, is the history of the expansion of that right to all of our people.

Many of the issues of civil rights are very complex and most difficult. But about this there can and should be no argument. Every American citizen must have an equal right to vote. There is no reason which can excuse the denial of that right. There is no duty which weighs more heavily on us than the duty we have to ensure that right.

Yet the harsh fact is that in many places in this country men and women are kept from voting simply because they are Negroes.

Every device of which human ingenuity is capable has been used to deny this right. The Negro citizen may go to register only to be told that the day is wrong, or the hour is late, or the official in charge is absent. And if he persists; and if he manages to present himself to the registrar, he may be disqualified because he did not spell out his middle name or because he abbreviated a word on the application.

And if he manages to fill out an application he is given a test. The registrar is the sole judge of whether he passes this test. He may be asked to recite the entire Constitution, or explain the most complex provisions of State law. And even a college degree cannot be used to prove that he can read and write.

For the fact is that the only way to pass these barriers is to show a white skin.

Experience has clearly shown that the existing process of law cannot overcome systematic and ingenious discrimination. No law that we now have on the books—and I have helped to put three of them there—can ensure the right to vote when local officials are determined to deny it.

In such a case our duty must be clear to all of us. The Constitution says that no person shall be kept from voting because of his race or his color. We have all sworn an oath before God to support and to defend that Constitution. We must now act in obedience to that oath.

Wednesday I will send to Congress a law designed to eliminate illegal barriers to the right to vote.

The broad principles of that bill will be in the hands of the Democratic and Republican leaders tomorrow. After they have reviewed it, it will come here formally as a bill. I am grateful for this opportunity to come here tonight at the invitation of the leadership to reason with my friends, to give them my views, and to visit with my former colleagues.

I have had prepared a more comprehensive analysis of the legislation which I had intended to transmit to the clerk tomorrow but which I will submit to the clerks tonight. But I want to really discuss with you now briefly the main proposals of this legislation.

This bill will strike down restrictions to voting in all elections —Federal, State, and local—which have been used to deny Negroes the right to vote.

This bill will establish a simple, uniform standard which cannot be used, however ingenious the effort, to flout our Constitution.

It will provide for citizens to be registered by officials of the United States Government if the State officials refuse to register them.

It will eliminate tedious, unnecessary law-suits which delay the right to vote.

Finally, this legislation will ensure that properly registered individuals are not prohibited from voting.

I will welcome the suggestions from all of the Members of Congress—I have no doubt that I will get some—on ways and means to strengthen this law and to make it effective. But experience has plainly shown that this is the only path to carry out the command of the Constitution.

To those who seek to avoid action by their National Government in their own communities; who want to and who seek to maintain purely local control over elections, the answer is simple:

Open your polling places to all your people.

Allow men and women to register and vote whatever the color of their skin.

Extend the rights of citizenship to every citizen of this land.

There is no constitutional issue here. The command of the Constitution is plain.

There is no moral issue. It is wrong—deadly wrong—to deny any of your fellow Americans the right to vote in this country.

There is no issue of States rights or national rights. There is only the struggle for human rights.

I have not the slightest doubt what will be your answer.

The last time a President sent a civil rights bill to the Congress it contained a provision to protect voting rights in Federal elections. That civil rights bill was passed after 8 long months of debate. And when that bill came to my desk from the Congress for my signature, the heart of the voting provision had been eliminated.

This time, on this issue, there must be no delay, no hesitation and no compromise with our purpose.

We cannot, we must not, refuse to protect the right of every American to vote in every election that he may desire to participate in. And we ought not and we cannot and we must not wait another 8 months before we get a bill. We have already waited a hundred years and more, and the time for waiting is gone.

So I ask you to join me in working long hours—nights and weekends, if necessary—to pass this bill. And I don't make that request lightly. For from the window where I sit with the problems of our country I recognize that outside this chamber is the outraged conscience of a nation, the grave concern of many nations, and the harsh judgment of history on our acts.

But even if we pass this bill, the battle will not be over. What happened in Selma is part of a far larger movement which reaches into every section and State of America. It is the effort of American Negroes to secure for themselves the full blessings of American life.

Their cause must be our cause too. Because it is not just Negroes, but really it is all of us, who must overcome the crippling legacy of bigotry and injustice.

And we shall overcome.

As a man whose roots go deeply into Southern soil I know how agonizing racial feelings are. I know how difficult it is to reshape the attitudes and the structure of our society.

But a century has passed, more than a hundred years, since the Negro was freed. And he is not fully free tonight.

It was more than a hundred years ago that Abraham Lincoln, a great President of another party, signed the Emancipation Proclamation, but emancipation is a proclamation and not a fact.

A century has passed, more than a hundred years, since equality was promised. And yet the Negro is not equal.

A century has passed since the day of promise. And the promise is unkept.

The time of justice has now come. I tell you that I believe sincerely that no force can hold it back. It is right in the eyes of man and God that it should come. And when it does, I think that day will brighten the lives of every American.

For Negroes are not the only victims. How many white children have gone uneducated, how many white families have lived in stark poverty, how many white lives have been scarred by fear, because we have wasted our energy and our substance to maintain the barriers of hatred and terror?

So I say to all of you here, and to all in the Nation tonight, that those who appeal to you to hold on to the past do so at the cost of denying you your future.

This great, rich, restless country can offer opportunity and education and hope to all: black and white, North and South, sharecropper and city dweller. These are the enemies: poverty, ignorance, disease. They are the enemies and not our fellow man, not our neighbor. And these enemies too, poverty, disease and ignorance, we shall overcome.

Now let none of us in any sections look with prideful righteousness on the troubles in another section, or on the problems of our neighbors. There is really no part of America where the promise of equality has been fully kept. In Buffalo as well as in Birmingham, in Philadelphia as well as in Selma, Americans are struggling for the fruits of freedom.

This is one Nation. What happens in Selma or in Cincinnati is a matter of legitimate concern to every American. But let each of us look within our own hearts and our own communities, and let each of us put our shoulder to the wheel to root out injustice wherever it exists.

As we meet here in this peaceful, historic chamber tonight, men from the South, some of whom were at Iwo Jima, men from the North who have carried Old Glory to far corners of the world and brought it back without a stain on it, men from the East and from the West, are all fighting together without regard to religion, or color, or region, in Viet-Nam. Men from every region fought for us across the world 20 years ago.

And in these common dangers and these common sacrifices the South made its contribution of honor and gallantry no less than any other region of the great Republic—and in some instances, a great many of them, more.

And I have not the slightest doubt that good men from everywhere in this country, from the Great Lakes to the Gulf of Mexico, from the Golden Gate to the harbors along the Atlantic, will rally together now in this cause to vindicate the freedom of all Americans. For all of us owe this duty; and I believe that all of us will respond to it.

Your President makes that request of every American.

The real hero of this struggle is the American Negro. His actions and protests, his courage to risk safety and even to risk his life, have awakened the conscience of this Nation. His demonstrations have been designed to call attention to injustice, designed to provoke change, designed to stir reform.

He has called upon us to make good the promise of America. And who among us can say that we would have made the same progress were it not for his persistent bravery, and his faith in American democracy.

For at the real heart of battle for equality is a deep-seated belief in the democratic process. Equality depends not on the force of arms or tear gas but upon the force of moral right; not on recourse to violence but on respect for law and order.

There have been many pressures upon your President and there will be others as the days come and go. But I pledge you tonight that we intend to fight this battle where it should be fought: in the courts, and in the Congress, and in the hearts of men.

We must preserve the right of free speech and the right of free assembly. But the right of free speech does not carry with it, as has been said, the right to holler fire in a crowded theater. We must preserve the right to free assembly, but free assembly does not carry with it the right to block public thoroughfares to traffic.

We do have a right to protest, and a right to march under conditions that do not infringe the constitutional rights of our neighbors. And I intend to protect all those rights as long as I am permitted to serve in this office.

We will guard against violence, knowing it strikes from our hands the very weapons which we seek—progress, obedience to law, and belief in American values.

In Selma as elsewhere we seek and pray for peace. We seek order. We seek unity. But we will not accept the peace of stifled rights, or the order imposed by fear, or the unity that stifles protest. For peace cannot be purchased at the cost of liberty.

In Selma tonight, as in every—and we had a good day there—as in every city, we are working for just and peaceful settlement. We must all remember that after this speech I am making tonight, after the police and the FBI and the Marshals have all gone, and after you have promptly passed this bill, the people of Selma and the other cities of the Nation must still live and work together. And when the attention of the Nation has gone elsewhere they must try to heal the wounds and to build a new community.

This cannot be easily done on a battleground of violence, as the history of the South itself shows. It is in recognition of this that men of both races have shown such an outstandingly impressive responsibility in recent days—last Tuesday, again today.

The bill that I am presenting to you will be known as a civil rights bill. But, in a larger sense, most of the program I am recommending is a civil rights program. Its object is to open the city of hope to all people of all races.

Because all Americans just must have the right to vote. And we are going to give them that right.

All Americans must have the privileges of citizenship regardless of race. And they are going to have those privileges of citizenship regardless of race.

But I would like to caution you and remind you that to exercise these privileges takes much more than just legal right. It requires a trained mind and a healthy body. It requires a decent home, and the chance to find a job, and the opportunity to escape from the clutches of poverty.

Of course, people cannot contribute to the Nation if they are never taught to read or write, if their bodies are stunted from hunger, if their sickness goes untended, if their life is spent in hopeless poverty just drawing a welfare check.

So we want to open the gates to opportunity. But we are also going to give all our people, black and white, the help that they need to walk through those gates.

My first job after college was as a teacher in Cotulla, Tex., in a small Mexican-American school. Few of them could speak English, and I couldn't speak much Spanish. My students were poor and they often came to class without breakfast, hungry.

They knew even in their youth the pain of prejudice. They never seemed to know why people disliked them. But they knew it was so, because I saw it in their eyes. I often walked home late in the afternoon, after the classes were finished, wishing there was more that I could do. But all I knew was to teach them the little that I knew, hoping that it might help them against the hardships that lay ahead.

Somehow you never forget what poverty and hatred can do when you see its scars on the hopeful face of a young child.

I never thought then, in 1928, that I would be standing here in 1965. It never even occurred to me in my fondest dreams that I might have the chance to help the sons and daughters of those students and to help people like them all over this country.

But now I do have that chance—and I'll let you in on a secret—I mean to use it. And I hope that you will use it with me.

This is the richest and most powerful country which ever occupied the globe. The might of past empires is little compared to ours. But I do not want to be the President who built empires, or sought grandeur, or extended dominion.

I want to be the President who educated young children to the wonders of their world. I want to be the President who helped to feed the hungry and to prepare them to be taxpayers instead of taxeaters.

I want to be the President who helped the poor to find their own way and who protected the right of every citizen to vote in every election.

I want to be the President who helped to end hatred among his fellow men and who promoted love among the people of all races and all regions and all parties.

I want to be the President who helped to end war among the brothers of this earth.

And so at the request of your beloved Speaker and the Senator from Montana, the majority leader; the Senator from Illinois, the minority leader; Mr. McCulloch, and other Members of both parties, I came here tonight—not as President Roosevelt came down one time in person to veto a bonus bill, not as President Truman came down one time to urge the passage of a railroad bill—but I came down here to ask you to share this task with me and to share it with the people that we both work for. I want this to be the Congress, Republicans and Democrats alike, which did all these things for all these people.

Beyond this great chamber, out yonder in 50 States, are the people that we serve. Who can tell what deep and unspoken hopes are in their hearts tonight as they sit there and listen. We all can guess, from our own lives, how difficult they often find their own pursuit of happiness, how many problems each little family has. They look most of all to themselves for their futures. But I think that they also look to each of us.

Above the pyramid on the great seal of the United States it says—in Latin—"God has favored our undertaking."

God will not favor everything that we do. It is rather our duty to divine His will. But I cannot help believing that He truly understands and that He really favors the undertaking that we begin here tonight.

LYNDON B. JOHNSON

Address at Howard University

Washington, D.C., June 4, 1965

D R. NABRIT, MY FELLOW AMERICANS:
I am delighted at the chance to speak at this important and this historic institution. Howard has long been an outstanding center for the education of Negro Americans. Its students are of every race and color and they come from many countries of the world. It is truly a working example of democratic excellence.

Our earth is the home of revolution. In every corner of every continent men charged with hope contend with ancient ways in the pursuit of justice. They reach for the newest of weapons to realize the oldest of dreams, that each may walk in freedom and pride, stretching his talents, enjoying the fruits of the earth.

Our enemies may occasionally seize the day of change, but it is the banner of our revolution they take. And our own future is linked to this process of swift and turbulent change in many lands in the world. But nothing in any country touches us more profoundly, and nothing is more freighted with meaning for our own destiny than the revolution of the Negro American.

In far too many ways American Negroes have been another nation: deprived of freedom, crippled by hatred, the doors of opportunity closed to hope.

In our time change has come to this Nation, too. The American Negro, acting with impressive restraint, has peacefully protested and marched, entered the courtrooms and the seats of government, demanding a justice that has long been denied. The voice of the Negro was the call to action. But it is a tribute to America that, once aroused, the courts and the Congress, the President and most of the people, have been the allies of progress.

Thus we have seen the high court of the country declare that discrimination based on race was repugnant to the Constitution, and therefore void. We have seen in 1957, and 1960, and again in 1964, the first civil rights legislation in this Nation in almost an entire century.

As majority leader of the United States Senate, I helped to guide two of these bills through the Senate. And, as your President, I was proud to sign the third. And now very soon we will have the fourth—a new law guaranteeing every American the right to vote.

No act of my entire administration will give me greater satisfaction than the day when my signature makes this bill, too, the law of this land.

The voting rights bill will be the latest, and among the most important, in a long series of victories. But this victory—as Winston Churchill said of another triumph for freedom—"is not the end. It is not even the beginning of the end. But it is, perhaps, the end of the beginning."

That beginning is freedom; and the barriers to that freedom are tumbling down. Freedom is the right to share, share fully and equally, in American society—to vote, to hold a job, to enter a public place, to go to school. It is the right to be treated in every part of our national life as a person equal in dignity and promise to all others.

But freedom is not enough. You do not wipe away the scars of centuries by saying: Now you are free to go where you want, and do as you desire, and choose the leaders you please.

You do not take a person who, for years, has been hobbled by chains and liberate him, bring him up to the starting line of a race and then say, "you are free to compete with all the others," and still justly believe that you have been completely fair.

Thus it is not enough just to open the gates of opportunity. All our citizens must have the ability to walk through those gates.

This is the next and the more profound stage of the battle for civil rights. We seek not just freedom but opportunity. We seek not just legal equity but human ability, not just equality as a right and a theory but equality as a fact and equality as a result.

For the task is to give 20 million Negroes the same chance as every other American to learn and grow, to work and share in society, to develop their abilities—physical, mental and spiritual, and to pursue their individual happiness.

To this end equal opportunity is essential, but not enough, not enough. Men and women of all races are born with the same range of abilities. But ability is not just the product of birth. Ability is stretched or stunted by the family that you live with, and the neighborhood you live in—by the school you go to and the poverty or the richness of your surroundings. It is the product of a hundred unseen forces playing upon the little infant, the child, and finally the man.

This graduating class at Howard University is witness to the indomitable determination of the Negro American to win his way in American life.

The number of Negroes in schools of higher learning has almost doubled in 15 years. The number of nonwhite professional workers has more than doubled in 10 years. The median income of Negro college women tonight exceeds that of white college women. And there are also the enormous accomplishments of distinguished individual Negroes—many of them graduates of this institution, and one of them the first lady ambassador in the history of the United States.

These are proud and impressive achievements. But they tell only the story of a growing middle class minority, steadily narrowing the gap between them and their white counterparts.

But for the great majority of Negro Americans—the poor, the unemployed, the uprooted, and the dispossessed—there is a much grimmer story. They still, as we meet here tonight, are another nation. Despite the court orders and the laws, despite the legislative victories and the speeches, for them the walls are rising and the gulf is widening.

Here are some of the facts of this American failure.

Thirty-five years ago the rate of unemployment for Negroes and whites was about the same. Tonight the Negro rate is twice as high.

In 1948 the 8 percent unemployment rate for Negro teenage boys was actually less than that of whites. By last year that rate had grown to 23 percent, as against 13 percent for whites unemployed.

Between 1949 and 1959, the income of Negro men relative

to white men declined in every section of this country. From 1952 to 1963 the median income of Negro families compared to white actually dropped from 57 percent to 53 percent.

In the years 1955 through 1957, 22 percent of experienced Negro workers were out of work at some time during the year. In 1961 through 1963 that proportion had soared to 29 percent.

Since 1947 the number of white families living in poverty has decreased 27 percent while the number of poorer nonwhite families decreased only 3 percent.

The infant mortality of nonwhites in 1940 was 70 percent greater than whites. Twenty-two years later it was 90 percent greater.

Moreover, the isolation of Negro from white communities is increasing, rather than decreasing as Negroes crowd into the central cities and become a city within a city.

Of course Negro Americans as well as white Americans have shared in our rising national abundance. But the harsh fact of the matter is that in the battle for true equality too many—far too many—are losing ground every day.

We are not completely sure why this is. We know the causes are complex and subtle. But we do know the two broad basic reasons. And we do know that we have to act.

First, Negroes are trapped—as many whites are trapped—in inherited, gateless poverty. They lack training and skills. They are shut in, in slums, without decent medical care. Private and public poverty combine to cripple their capacities.

We are trying to attack these evils through our poverty program, through our education program, through our medical care and our other health programs, and a dozen more of the Great Society programs that are aimed at the root causes of this poverty.

We will increase, and we will accelerate, and we will broaden this attack in years to come until this most enduring of foes finally yields to our unyielding will.

But there is a second cause—much more difficult to explain, more deeply grounded, more desperate in its force. It is the devastating heritage of long years of slavery; and a century of oppression, hatred, and injustice.

For Negro poverty is not white poverty. Many of its causes and many of its cures are the same. But there are differences—

deep, corrosive, obstinate differences—radiating painful roots into the community, and into the family, and the nature of the individual.

These differences are not racial differences. They are solely and simply the consequence of ancient brutality, past injustice, and present prejudice. They are anguishing to observe. For the Negro they are a constant reminder of oppression. For the white they are a constant reminder of guilt. But they must be faced and they must be dealt with and they must be overcome, if we are ever to reach the time when the only difference between Negroes and whites is the color of their skin.

Nor can we find a complete answer in the experience of other American minorities. They made a valiant and a largely successful effort to emerge from poverty and prejudice.

The Negro, like these others, will have to rely mostly upon his own efforts. But he just can not do it alone. For they did not have the heritage of centuries to overcome, and they did not have a cultural tradition which had been twisted and battered by endless years of hatred and hopelessness, nor were they excluded—these others—because of race or color—a feeling whose dark intensity is matched by no other prejudice in our society.

Nor can these differences be understood as isolated infirmities. They are a seamless web. They cause each other. They result from each other. They reinforce each other.

Much of the Negro community is buried under a blanket of history and circumstance. It is not a lasting solution to lift just one corner of that blanket. We must stand on all sides and we must raise the entire cover if we are to liberate our fellow citizens.

One of the differences is the increased concentration of Negroes in our cities. More than 73 percent of all Negroes live in urban areas compared with less than 70 percent of the whites. Most of these Negroes live in slums. Most of these Negroes live together—a separated people.

Men are shaped by their world. When it is a world of decay, ringed by an invisible wall, when escape is arduous and uncertain, and the saving pressures of a more hopeful society are unknown, it can cripple the youth and it can desolate the men.

There is also the burden that a dark skin can add to the

search for a productive place in our society. Unemployment strikes most swiftly and broadly at the Negro, and this burden erodes hope. Blighted hope breeds despair. Despair brings indifferences to the learning which offers a way out. And despair, coupled with indifferences, is often the source of destructive rebellion against the fabric of society.

There is also the lacerating hurt of early collision with white hatred or prejudice, distaste or condescension. Other groups have felt similar intolerance. But success and achievement could wipe it away. They do not change the color of a man's skin. I have seen this uncomprehending pain in the eyes of the little, young Mexican-American schoolchildren that I taught many years ago. But it can be overcome. But, for many, the wounds are always open.

Perhaps most important—its influence radiating to every part of life—is the breakdown of the Negro family structure. For this, most of all, white America must accept responsibility. It flows from centuries of oppression and persecution of the Negro man. It flows from the long years of degradation and discrimination, which have attacked his dignity and assaulted his ability to produce for his family.

This, too, is not pleasant to look upon. But it must be faced by those whose serious intent is to improve the life of all Americans.

Only a minority—less than half—of all Negro children reach the age of 18 having lived all their lives with both of their parents. At this moment, tonight, little less than two-thirds are at home with both of their parents. Probably a majority of all Negro children receive federally-aided public assistance sometime during their childhood.

The family is the cornerstone of our society. More than any other force it shapes the attitude, the hopes, the ambitions, and the values of the child. And when the family collapses it is the children that are usually damaged. When it happens on a massive scale the community itself is crippled.

So, unless we work to strengthen the family, to create conditions under which most parents will stay together—all the rest: schools, and playgrounds, and public assistance, and private concern, will never be enough to cut completely the circle of despair and deprivation.

There is no single easy answer to all of these problems.

Jobs are part of the answer. They bring the income which permits a man to provide for his family.

Decent homes in decent surroundings and a chance to learn—an equal chance to learn—are part of the answer.

Welfare and social programs better designed to hold families together are part of the answer.

Care for the sick is part of the answer.

An understanding heart by all Americans is another big part of the answer.

And to all of these fronts—and a dozen more—I will dedicate the expanding efforts of the Johnson administration.

But there are other answers that are still to be found. Nor do we fully understand even all of the problems. Therefore, I want to announce tonight that this fall I intend to call a White House conference of scholars, and experts, and outstanding Negro leaders—men of both races—and officials of Government at every level.

This White House conference's theme and title will be "To Fulfill These Rights."

Its object will be to help the American Negro fulfill the rights which, after the long time of injustice, he is finally about to secure.

To move beyond opportunity to achievement.

To shatter forever not only the barriers of law and public practice, but the walls which bound the condition of many by the color of his skin.

To dissolve, as best we can, the antique enmities of the heart which diminish the holder, divide the great democracy, and do wrong—great wrong—to the children of God.

And I pledge you tonight that this will be a chief goal of my administration, and of my program next year, and in the years to come. And I hope, and I pray, and I believe, it will be a part of the program of all America.

For what is justice?

It is to fulfill the fair expectations of man.

Thus, American justice is a very special thing. For, from the first, this has been a land of towering expectations. It was to be a nation where each man could be ruled by the common consent of all—enshrined in law, given life by institutions, guided by men themselves subject to its rule. And all—all of every station and origin—would be touched equally in obligation and in liberty.

Beyond the law lay the land. It was a rich land, glowing with more abundant promise than man had ever seen. Here, unlike any place yet known, all were to share the harvest.

And beyond this was the dignity of man. Each could become whatever his qualities of mind and spirit would permit—to strive, to seek, and, if he could, to find his happiness.

This is American justice. We have pursued it faithfully to the edge of our imperfections, and we have failed to find it for the American Negro.

So, it is the glorious opportunity of this generation to end the one huge wrong of the American Nation and, in so doing, to find America for ourselves, with the same immense thrill of discovery which gripped those who first began to realize that here, at last, was a home for freedom.

All it will take is for all of us to understand what this country is and what this country must become.

The Scripture promises: "I shall light a candle of understanding in thine heart, which shall not be put out."

Together, and with millions more, we can light that candle of understanding in the heart of all America.

And, once lit, it will never again go out.

ROBERT F. KENNEDY

Address at the University of Cape Town

South Africa, June 6, 1966

I COME HERE this evening because of my deep interest and affection for a land settled by the Dutch in the mid-seventeenth century, then taken over by the British, and at last independent; a land in which the native inhabitants were at first subdued, but relations with whom remain a problem to this day; a land which defined itself on a hostile frontier; a land which has tamed rich natural resources through the energetic application of modern technology; a land which was once the importer of slaves, and now must struggle to wipe out the last traces of that former bondage. I refer, of course, to the United States of America. [Laughter and applause.]

But I am glad to come here to South Africa and glad to come here to Cape Town. I am already greatly enjoying my visit here. I am making an effort to meet and exchange views with people of all walks of life, and all segments of South African opinion, including those who represent the views of the government. Today I am glad to meet with the National Union of South African Students. For a decade, NUSAS has stood and worked for the principles of the Universal Declaration of Human Rights—principles which embody the collective hopes of men of good will all around the globe.

Your work, at home and in international student affairs, has brought great credit to yourselves and to your country. I know the National Student Association in the United States feels a particularly close relationship to this organization. And I wish to thank especially Mr. Ian Robertson, who first extended the invitation on behalf of NUSAS; I wish to thank him for his kindness to me in inviting me. I am very sorry that he cannot be with us here this evening. [Applause.] I was happy to have had the opportunity to meet and speak with him earlier this evening, and I presented him with a copy of *Profiles in*

Courage, which is the book which was written by President John Kennedy and was signed to him by President Kennedy's widow, Mrs. John Kennedy. [Applause.]

This is a Day of Affirmation, a celebration of liberty. We stand here in the name of freedom.

At the heart of that western freedom and democracy is the belief that the individual man, the child of God, is the touchstone of value, and all society, all groups and states, exist for that person's benefit. Therefore the enlargement of liberty for individual human beings must be the supreme goal and the abiding practice of any western society.

The first element of this individual liberty is the freedom of speech: the right to express and communicate ideas, to set oneself apart from the dumb beasts of field and forest; the right to recall governments to their duties and to their obligations; above all, the right to affirm one's membership and allegiance to the body politic—to society—to the men with whom we share our land, our heritage, and our children's future.

Hand in hand with freedom of speech goes the power to be heard, to share in the decisions of government which shape men's lives. Everything that makes man's life worthwhile—family, work, education, a place to rear one's children and a place to rest one's head—all this depends on decisions of government; all can be swept away by a government which does not heed the demands of its people—and I mean all of its people. Therefore, the essential humanity of men can be protected and preserved only where government must answer—not just to the wealthy, not just to those of a particular religion, not just to those of a particular race, but to all the people. [Applause.]

And even government by the consent of the governed, as in our own Constitution, must be limited in its power to act against its people; so that there may be no interference with the right to worship, but also no interference with the security of the home; no arbitrary imposition of pains or penalties on an ordinary citizen by officials high or low; no restriction on the freedom of men to seek education or to seek work or opportunity of any kind, so that each man may become all that he is capable of becoming. [Applause.]

These are the sacred rights of western society. These were

the essential differences between us and Nazi Germany, as they were between Athens and Persia.

They are the essence of our differences with communism today. I am unalterably opposed to communism because it exalts the state over the individual and over the family, and because its system contains the lack of freedom of speech, of protest, of religion, and of the press, which is the characteristic of a totalitarian regime. The way of opposition to communism, however, is not to imitate its dictatorship, but to enlarge individual human freedom. [Applause.] There are those in every land who would label as Communist every threat to their privilege. But may I say to you, as I have seen on my travels in all sections of the world, reform is not communism. [Applause.] And the denial of freedom, in whatever name, only strengthens the very communism it claims to oppose. [Applause.]

Many nations have set forth their own definitions and declarations of these principles. And there have often been wide and tragic gaps between promise and performance, ideal and reality. Yet the great ideals have constantly recalled us to our own duties. And—with painful slowness—we in the United States have extended and enlarged the meaning and the practice of freedom to all of our people.

For two centuries, my own country has struggled to overcome the self-imposed handicap of prejudice and discrimination based on nationality, on social class or race—discrimination profoundly repugnant to the theory and to the command of our Constitution. Even as my father grew up in Boston, Massachusetts, signs told him that No Irish Need Apply. Two generations later President Kennedy became the first Irish Catholic and the first Catholic to head the nation; but how many men of ability had, before 1961, been denied the opportunity to contribute to the nation's progress because they were Catholic, or because they were of Irish extraction? How many sons of Italian or Jewish or Polish parents slumbered in the slums— untaught, unlearned, their potential lost forever to our nation and to the human race? Even today, what price will we pay before we have assured full opportunity to millions of Negro Americans?

In the last five years we have done more to assure equality to our Negro citizens, and to help the deprived, both white and black, than in the hundred years before that time. But much, much more remains to be done. For there are millions of Negroes untrained for the simplest of jobs, and thousands every day denied their full and equal rights under the law; and the violence of the disinherited, the insulted, the injured, looms over the streets of Harlem, and of Watts, and of the South Side of Chicago.

But a Negro American trains now as an astronaut, one of mankind's first explorers into outer space; another is the chief barrister of the United States government, and dozens sit on the benches of our court; and another, Dr. Martin Luther King, is the second man of African descent to win the Nobel Peace Prize for his nonviolent efforts for social justice between all of the races. [Applause.]

We have passed laws prohibiting discrimination in education, in employment, in housing; but these laws alone cannot overcome the heritage of centuries—of broken families and stunted children, and poverty and degradation and pain.

So the road toward equality of freedom is not easy, and great cost and danger march alongside all of us. We are committed to peaceful and nonviolent change, and that is important for all to understand—though change is unsettling. Still, even in the turbulence of protest and struggle is greater hope for the future, as men learn to claim and achieve for themselves the rights formerly petitioned from others.

And most important of all, all of the panoply of government power has been committed to the goal of equality before the law, as we are now committing ourselves to the achievement of equal opportunity in fact.

We must recognize the full human equality of all of our people—before God, before the law, and in the councils of government. We must do this, not because it is economically advantageous, although it is; not because the laws of God command it, although they do; not because people in other lands wish it so. We must do it for the single and fundamental reason that it is the right thing to do. [Applause.]

We recognize that there are problems and obstacles before the fulfillment of these ideals in the United States, as we recognize that other nations, in Latin America and in Asia and in

Africa, have their own political, economic, and social problems, their unique barriers to the elimination of injustices.

In some, there is concern that change will submerge the rights of a minority, particularly where that minority is of a different race from that of the majority. We in the United States believe in the protection of minorities; we recognize the contributions that they can make and the leadership that they can provide; and we do not believe that any people—whether majority or minority, or individual human beings—are "expendable" in the cause of theory or of policy. We recognize also that justice between men and nations is imperfect, and that humanity sometimes progresses very slowly indeed.

All do not develop in the same manner and at the same pace. Nations, like men, often march to the beat of different drummers, and the precise solutions of the United States can neither be dictated nor transplanted to others. And that is not our intention. What is important, however, is that all nations must march toward increasing freedom; toward justice for all; toward a society strong and flexible enough to meet the demands of all of its people, whatever their race, and the demands of a world of immense and dizzying change that faces us all.

In a few hours, the plane that brought me to this country crossed over oceans and countries which have been a crucible of human history. In minutes we traced migrations of men over thousands of years; seconds, the briefest glimpse, and we passed battlefields on which millions of men once struggled and died. We could see no national boundaries, no vast gulfs or high walls dividing people from people; only nature and the works of man—homes and factories and farms—everywhere reflecting man's common effort to enrich his life. Everywhere new technology and communications bring men and nations closer together, the concerns of one inevitably become the concerns of all. And our new closeness is stripping away the false masks, the illusion of differences which is the root of injustice and of hate and of war. Only earth-bound man still clings to the dark and poisoning superstition that his world is bounded by the nearest hill, his universe ends at river shore, his common humanity is enclosed in the tight circle of those who share his town or his views and the color of his skin. [Applause.]

It is your job, the task of young people in this world, to strip the last remnants of that ancient, cruel belief from the civilization of man.

Each nation has different obstacles and different goals, shaped by the vagaries of history and of experience. Yet as I talk to young people around the world I am impressed not by the diversity but by the closeness of their goals, their desires and their concerns and their hope for the future. There is discrimination in New York, the racial inequality of apartheid in South Africa, and serfdom in the mountains of Peru. People starve to death in the streets of India, a former prime minister is summarily executed in the Congo, intellectuals go to jail in Russia, and thousands are slaughtered in Indonesia; wealth is lavished on armaments everywhere in the world. These are different evils; but they are the common works of man. They reflect the imperfections of human justice, the inadequacy of human compassion, the defectiveness of our sensibility toward the sufferings of our fellows; they mark the limit of our ability to use knowledge for the well-being of our fellow human beings throughout the world. [Applause.] And therefore they call upon common qualities of conscience and indignation, a shared determination to wipe away the unnecessary sufferings of our fellow human beings at home and around the world.

It is these qualities which make of our youth today the only true international community. More than this, I think that we could agree on what kind of a world we would all want to build. It would be a world of independent nations, moving toward international community, each of which protected and respected the basic human freedoms. It would be a world which demanded of each government that it accept its responsibility to ensure social justice. It would be a world of constantly accelerating economic progress—not material welfare as an end in itself, but as a means to liberate the capacity of every human being to pursue his talents and to pursue his hopes. It would, in short, be a world that we would all be proud to have built.

Just to the north of here are lands of challenge and of opportunity—rich in natural resources, land and minerals and people. Yet they are also lands confronted by the greatest odds—overwhelming ignorance, internal tensions and strife, and great obstacles of climate and geography. Many of these nations, as colonies, were oppressed and were exploited. Yet they have not estranged themselves from the broad traditions of the West; they are hoping and they are gambling their progress and their stability on the chance that we will meet our responsibilities to them to help them overcome their poverty.

In the world we would like to build, South Africa could play an outstanding role and a role of leadership in that effort. This country is without question a preeminent repository of the wealth and the knowledge and the skill of this continent. Here are the greater part of Africa's research scientists and steel production, most of its reservoirs of coal and of electric power. Many South Africans have made major contributions to African technical development and world science; the names of some are known wherever men seek to eliminate the ravages of tropical disease and of pestilence. In your faculties and councils, here in this very audience, are hundreds and thousands of men and women who could transform the lives of millions for all time to come.

But the help and the leadership of South Africa or of the United States cannot be accepted if we—within our own countries or in our relationships with others—deny individual integrity, human dignity, and the common humanity of man. [Applause.] If we would lead outside our own borders, if we would help those who need our assistance, if we would meet our responsibilities to mankind, we must first, all of us, demolish the borders which history has erected between men within our own nations—barriers of race and religion, social class and ignorance.

Our answer is the world's hope; it is to rely on youth. The cruelties and the obstacles of this swiftly changing planet will not yield to obsolete dogmas and outworn slogans. It cannot be moved by those who cling to a present which is already dying, who prefer the illusion of security to the excitement and danger which comes with even the most peaceful progress.

This world demands the qualities of youth; not a time of life but a state of mind, a temper of the will, a quality of the imagination, a predominance of courage over timidity, of the appetite for adventure over the life of ease—a man like the chancellor of this university. [Applause.] It is a revolutionary world that we all live in, and thus, as I have said in Latin America and in Asia, and in Europe and in my own country, the United States, it is the young people who must take the lead. Thus you, and your young compatriots everywhere, have had thrust upon you a greater burden of responsibility than any generation that has ever lived.

"There is," said an Italian philosopher, "nothing more difficult to take in hand, more perilous to conduct, or more uncertain in its success than to take the lead in the introduction of a new order of things." Yet this is the measure of the task of your generation, and the road is strewn with many dangers.

First, is the danger of futility: the belief there is nothing one man or one woman can do against the enormous array of the world's ills—against misery, against ignorance or injustice and violence. Yet many of the world's great movements, of thought and action, have flowed from the work of a single man. A young monk began the Protestant Reformation, a young general extended an empire from Macedonia to the borders of the earth, and a young woman reclaimed the territory of France. It was a young Italian explorer who discovered the New World, and thirty-two-year-old Thomas Jefferson who proclaimed that all men are created equal.

"Give me a place to stand," said Archimedes, "and I will move the world." These men moved the world, and so can we all. Few will have the greatness to bend history; but each of us can work to change a small portion of the events, and in the total of all these acts will be written the history of this generation. Thousands of Peace Corps volunteers are making a difference in the isolated villages and the city slums of dozens of countries. Thousands of unknown men and women in Europe resisted the occupation of the Nazis and many died, but all added to the ultimate strength and freedom of their countries. It is from numberless diverse acts of courage such as these that human history is shaped. Each time a man stands up for an ideal, or acts to improve the lot of others, or strikes out against injustice, he sends forth a tiny ripple of hope, and crossing each other from a million different centers of energy and daring those ripples build a current which can sweep down the mightiest walls of oppression and resistance.

"If Athens shall appear great to you," said Pericles, "consider then that her glories were purchased by valiant men, and by men who learned their duty." That is the source of all greatness in all societies, and it is the key to progress in our time.

The second danger is that of expediency; of those who say that hopes and beliefs must bend before immediate necessities. Of course, if we would act effectively we must deal with the world as it is. We must get things done. But if there was one thing that President Kennedy stood for that touched the most profound feelings of young people around the world, it was the belief that idealism, high aspirations, and deep convictions are not incompatible with the most practical and efficient of programs—that there is no basic inconsistency between ideals and realistic possibilities, no separation between the deepest desires of heart and of mind and the rational application of human effort to human problems. It is not realistic or hardheaded to solve problems and take action unguided by ultimate moral aims and values, although we all know some who claim that it is so. In my judgment, it is thoughtless folly. For it ignores the realities of human faith and of passion and of belief—forces ultimately more powerful than all of the calculations of our economists or of our generals. Of course to adhere to standards, to idealism, to vision in the face of immediate dangers takes great courage and takes self-confidence. But we also know that only those who dare to fail greatly, can ever achieve greatly.

It is this new idealism which is also, I believe, the common heritage of a generation which has learned that while efficiency can lead to the camps at Auschwitz, or the streets of Budapest, only the ideals of humanity and love can climb the hills of the Acropolis. [Applause.]

A third danger is timidity. Few men are willing to brave the disapproval of their fellows, the censure of their colleagues, the wrath of their society. Moral courage is a rarer commodity than bravery in battle or great intelligence. It is the one essential, vital quality of those who seek to change a world which yields most painfully to change. Aristotle tells us: "At the Olympic games it is not the finest or the strongest men who are crowned, but those who enter the lists. . . . So too in the life of the honorable and the good it is they who act rightly who win the prize." I believe that in this generation those with the courage to enter the conflict will find themselves with companions in every corner of the world.

For the fortunate amongst us, the fourth danger, my friends, is comfort, the temptation to follow the easy and familiar paths of personal ambition and financial success so grandly spread before those who have the privilege of an education. But that is not the road history has marked out for us. There is a Chinese curse which says, "May he live in interesting times." Like it or not we live in interesting times. They are times of danger and uncertainty; but they are also the most creative of any time in the history of mankind. And everyone here will ultimately be judged—will ultimately judge himself—on the effort he has contributed to building a new world society and the extent to which his ideals and goals have shaped that effort.

So we part, I to my country and you to remain. We are—if a man of forty can claim the privilege—fellow members of the world's largest younger generation. Each of us have our own work to do. I know at times you must feel very alone with your problems and with your difficulties. But I want to say how impressed I am with what you stand for and the effort you are making; and I say this not just for myself but men and women all over the world. And I hope you will often take heart from the knowledge that you are joined with your fellow young people in every land, they struggling with their problems and you with yours, but all joined in a common purpose; that, like the young people of my own country and of every country that I have visited, you are all in many ways more closely united to the brothers of your time than to the older generation in any of these nations. You are determined to build a better future. President Kennedy was speaking to the young people of America, but beyond them to young people everywhere, when he said, "the energy, the faith, the devotion which we bring to this endeavor will light our country and all who serve it—and the glow from that fire can truly light the world."

And, he added, "With a good conscience our only sure reward, with history the final judge of our deeds, let us go forth to lead the land we love, asking His blessing and His help, but knowing that here on earth God's work must truly be our own." [Extended applause.]

MARTIN LUTHER KING, JR.

Speech on the Vietnam War

New York City, April 4, 1967

MR. CHAIRMAN, ladies and gentlemen, I need not pause to say how very delighted I am to be here tonight, and how very delighted I am to see you expressing your concern about the issues that will be discussed tonight by turning out in such large numbers. I also want to say that I consider it a great honor to share this program with Dr. Bennett, Dr. Commager, and Rabbi Heschel, some of the distinguished leaders and personalities of our nation. And of course it's always good to come back to Riverside Church. Over the last eight years, I have had the privilege of preaching here almost every year in that period, and it is always a rich and rewarding experience to come to this great church and this great pulpit.

I come to this magnificent house of worship tonight because my conscience leaves me no other choice. I join you in this meeting because I am in deepest agreement with the aims and work of the organization which has brought us together, Clergy and Laymen Concerned About Vietnam. The recent statements of your executive committee are the sentiments of my own heart, and I found myself in full accord when I read its opening lines: "A time comes when silence is betrayal." That time has come for us in relation to Vietnam.

The truth of these words is beyond doubt, but the mission to which they call us is a most difficult one. Even when pressed by the demands of inner truth, men do not easily assume the task of opposing their government's policy, especially in time of war. Nor does the human spirit move without great difficulty against all the apathy of conformist thought within one's own bosom and in the surrounding world. Moreover, when the issues at hand seem as perplexing as they often do in the case of this dreadful conflict, we are always on the verge of being mesmerized by uncertainty. But we must move on.

Some of us who have already begun to break the silence of the night have found that the calling to speak is often a vocation of agony, but we must speak. We must speak with all the humility that is appropriate to our limited vision, but we must speak. And we must rejoice as well, for surely this is the first time in our nation's history that a significant number of its religious leaders have chosen to move beyond the prophesying of smooth patriotism to the high grounds of a firm dissent based upon the mandates of conscience and the reading of history. Perhaps a new spirit is rising among us. If it is, let us trace its movements and pray that our own inner being may be sensitive to its guidance. For we are deeply in need of a new way beyond the darkness that seems so close around us.

Over the past two years, as I have moved to break the betrayal of my own silences and to speak from the burnings of my own heart, as I have called for radical departures from the destruction of Vietnam, many persons have questioned me about the wisdom of my path. At the heart of their concerns, this query has often loomed large and loud: "Why are you speaking about the war, Dr. King? Why are you joining the voices of dissent?" "Peace and civil rights don't mix," they say. "Aren't you hurting the cause of your people?" they ask. And when I hear them, though I often understand the source of their concern, I am nevertheless greatly saddened, for such questions mean that the inquirers have not really known me, my commitment, or my calling. Indeed, their questions suggest that they do not know the world in which they live. In the light of such tragic misunderstanding, I deem it of signal importance to try to state clearly, and I trust concisely, why I believe that the path from Dexter Avenue Baptist Church—the church in Montgomery, Alabama, where I began my pastorate —leads clearly to this sanctuary tonight.

I come to this platform tonight to make a passionate plea to my beloved nation. This speech is not addressed to Hanoi or to the National Liberation Front. It is not addressed to China or to Russia. Nor is it an attempt to overlook the ambiguity of the total situation and the need for a collective solution to the tragedy of Vietnam. Neither is it an attempt to make North Vietnam or the National Liberation Front paragons of virtue, nor to overlook the role they must play in the successful resolution of the problem. While they both may have justifiable reasons to be suspicious of the good faith of the United States, life and history give eloquent testimony to the fact that conflicts are never resolved without trustful give and take on both sides. Tonight, however, I wish not to speak with Hanoi and the National Liberation Front, but rather to my fellow Americans.

Since I am a preacher by calling, I suppose it is not surprising that I have seven major reasons for bringing Vietnam into the field of my moral vision. There is at the outset a very obvious and almost facile connection between the war in Vietnam and the struggle I and others have been waging in America. A few years ago there was a shining moment in that struggle. It seemed as if there was a real promise of hope for the poor, both black and white, through the poverty program. There were experiments, hopes, new beginnings. Then came the buildup in Vietnam, and I watched this program broken and eviscerated as if it were some idle political plaything of a society gone mad on war. And I knew that America would never invest the necessary funds or energies in rehabilitation of its poor so long as adventures like Vietnam continued to draw men and skills and money like some demonic, destructive suction tube. So I was increasingly compelled to see the war as an enemy of the poor and to attack it as such.

Perhaps a more tragic recognition of reality took place when it became clear to me that the war was doing far more than devastating the hopes of the poor at home. It was sending their sons and their brothers and their husbands to fight and to die in extraordinarily high proportions relative to the rest of the population. We were taking the black young men who had been crippled by our society and sending them eight thousand miles away to guarantee liberties in Southeast Asia which they had not found in southwest Georgia and East Harlem. So we have been repeatedly faced with the cruel irony of watching Negro and white boys on TV screens as they kill and die together for a nation that has been unable to seat them together in the same schools. So we watch them in brutal solidarity burning the huts of a poor village, but we realize that they would hardly live on the same block in Chicago. I could not be silent in the face of such cruel manipulation of the poor.

My third reason moves to an even deeper level of awareness,

for it grows out of my experience in the ghettos of the North over the last three years, especially the last three summers. As I have walked among the desperate, rejected, and angry young men, I have told them that Molotov cocktails and rifles would not solve their problems. I have tried to offer them my deepest compassion while maintaining my conviction that social change comes most meaningfully through nonviolent action. But they asked, and rightly so, "What about Vietnam?" They asked if our own nation wasn't using massive doses of violence to solve its problems, to bring about the changes it wanted. Their questions hit home, and I knew that I could never again raise my voice against the violence of the oppressed in the ghettos without having first spoken clearly to the greatest purveyor of violence in the world today: my own government. For the sake of those boys, for the sake of this government, for the sake of the hundreds of thousands trembling under our violence, I cannot be silent.

For those who ask the question, "Aren't you a civil rights leader?" and thereby mean to exclude me from the movement for peace, I have this further answer. In 1957, when a group of us formed the Southern Christian Leadership Conference, we chose as our motto: "To save the soul of America." We were convinced that we could not limit our vision to certain rights for black people, but instead affirmed the conviction that America would never be free or saved from itself until the descendants of its slaves were loosed completely from the shackles they still wear. In a way we were agreeing with Langston Hughes, that black bard of Harlem, who had written earlier:

> O, yes, I say it plain,
> America never was America to me,
> And yet I swear this oath—
> America will be!

Now it should be incandescently clear that no one who has any concern for the integrity and life of America today can ignore the present war. If America's soul becomes totally poisoned, part of the autopsy must read "Vietnam." It can never be saved so long as it destroys the deepest hopes of men the world over. So it is that those of us who are yet determined that "America will be" are led down the path of protest and dissent, working for the health of our land.

As if the weight of such a commitment to the life and health of America were not enough, another burden of responsibility was placed upon me in 1964. And I cannot forget that the Nobel Peace Prize was also a commission, a commission to work harder than I had ever worked before for the brotherhood of man. This is a calling that takes me beyond national allegiances.

But even if it were not present, I would yet have to live with the meaning of my commitment to the ministry of Jesus Christ. To me, the relationship of this ministry to the making of peace is so obvious that I sometimes marvel at those who ask me why I am speaking against the war. Could it be that they do not know that the Good News was meant for all men—for communist and capitalist, for their children and ours, for black and for white, for revolutionary and conservative? Have they forgotten that my ministry is in obedience to the one who loved his enemies so fully that he died for them? What then can I say to the Vietcong or to Castro or to Mao as a faithful minister of this one? Can I threaten them with death or must I not share with them my life?

Finally, as I try to explain for you and for myself the road that leads from Montgomery to this place, I would have offered all that was most valid if I simply said that I must be true to my conviction that I share with all men the calling to be a son of the living God. Beyond the calling of race or nation or creed is this vocation of sonship and brotherhood. Because I believe that the Father is deeply concerned, especially for His suffering and helpless and outcast children, I come tonight to speak for them. This I believe to be the privilege and the burden of all of us who deem ourselves bound by allegiances and loyalties which are broader and deeper than nationalism and which go beyond our nation's self-defined goals and positions. We are called to speak for the weak, for the voiceless, for the victims of our nation, for those it calls "enemy," for no document from human hands can make these humans any less our brothers.

And as I ponder the madness of Vietnam and search within myself for ways to understand and respond in compassion, my mind goes constantly to the people of that peninsula. I speak now not of the soldiers of each side, not of the ideologies of the Liberation Front, not of the junta in Saigon, but simply of the people who have been living under the curse of war for almost three continuous decades now. I think of them, too, because it is clear to me that there will be no meaningful solution there until some attempt is made to know them and hear their broken cries.

They must see Americans as strange liberators. The Vietnamese people proclaimed their own independence in 1954—in 1945 rather—after a combined French and Japanese occupation and before the communist revolution in China. They were led by Ho Chi Minh. Even though they quoted the American Declaration of Independence in their own document of freedom, we refused to recognize them. Instead, we decided to support France in its reconquest of her former colony. Our government felt then that the Vietnamese people were not ready for independence, and we again fell victim to the deadly Western arrogance that has poisoned the international atmosphere for so long. With that tragic decision we rejected a revolutionary government seeking self-determination and a government that had been established not by China—for whom the Vietnamese have no great love—but by clearly indigenous forces that included some communists. For the peasants this new government meant real land reform, one of the most important needs in their lives.

For nine years following 1945 we denied the people of Vietnam the right of independence. For nine years we vigorously supported the French in their abortive effort to recolonize Vietnam. Before the end of the war we were meeting 80 percent of the French war costs. Even before the French were defeated at Dien Bien Phu, they began to despair of their reckless action, but we did not. We encouraged them with our huge financial and military supplies to continue the war even after they had lost the will. Soon we would be paying almost the full costs of this tragic attempt at recolonization.

After the French were defeated, it looked as if independence and land reform would come again through the Geneva Agreement. But instead there came the United States, determined that Ho should not unify the temporarily divided nation, and the peasants watched again as we supported one of the most vicious modern dictators, our chosen man, Premier Diem. The peasants watched and cringed as Diem ruthlessly rooted out all opposition, supported their extortionist landlords, and refused even to discuss reunification with the North. The peasants watched as all of this was presided over by United States influence and then by increasing numbers of United States troops who came to help quell the insurgency that Diem's methods had aroused. When Diem was overthrown they may have been happy, but the long line of military dictators seemed to offer no real change, especially in terms of their need for land and peace.

The only change came from America as we increased our troop commitments in support of governments which were singularly corrupt, inept, and without popular support. All the while the people read our leaflets and received the regular promises of peace and democracy and land reform. Now they languish under our bombs and consider us, not their fellow Vietnamese, the real enemy. They move sadly and apathetically as we herd them off the land of their fathers into concentration camps where minimal social needs are rarely met. They know they must move on or be destroyed by our bombs.

So they go, primarily women and children and the aged. They watch as we poison their water, as we kill a million acres of their crops. They must weep as the bulldozers roar through their areas preparing to destroy the precious trees. They wander into the hospitals with at least twenty casualties from American firepower for one Vietcong-inflicted injury. So far we may have killed a million of them, mostly children. They wander into the towns and see thousands of the children, homeless, without clothes, running in packs on the streets like animals. They see the children degraded by our soldiers as they beg for food. They see the children selling their sisters to our soldiers, soliciting for their mothers.

What do the peasants think as we ally ourselves with the landlords and as we refuse to put any action into our many words concerning land reform? What do they think as we test out our latest weapons on them, just as the Germans tested out new medicine and new tortures in the concentration camps of Europe? Where are the roots of the independent Vietnam we claim to be building? Is it among these voiceless ones?

We have destroyed their two most cherished institutions: the family and the village. We have destroyed their land and their crops. We have cooperated in the crushing of the nation's only noncommunist revolutionary political force, the unified Buddhist Church. We have supported the enemies of the peasants of Saigon. We have corrupted their women and children and killed their men.

Now there is little left to build on, save bitterness. Soon the only solid physical foundations remaining will be found at our military bases and in the concrete of the concentration camps we call "fortified hamlets." The peasants may well wonder if we plan to build our new Vietnam on such grounds as these. Could we blame them for such thoughts? We must speak for them and raise the questions they cannot raise. These, too, are our brothers.

Perhaps a more difficult but no less necessary task is to speak for those who have been designated as our enemies. What of the National Liberation Front, that strangely anonymous group we call "VC" or "communists"? What must they think of the United States of America when they realize that we permitted the repression and cruelty of Diem, which helped to bring them into being as a resistance group in the South? What do they think of our condoning the violence which led to their own taking up of arms? How can they believe in our integrity when now we speak of "aggression from the North" as if there were nothing more essential to the war? How can they trust us when now we charge them with violence after the murderous reign of Diem and charge them with violence while we pour every new weapon of death into their land? Surely we must understand their feelings, even if we do not condone their actions. Surely we must see that the men we supported pressed them to their violence. Surely we must see that our own computerized plans of destruction simply dwarf their greatest acts.

How do they judge us when our officials know that their membership is less than 25 percent communist, and yet insist on giving them the blanket name? What must they be thinking when they know that we are aware of their control of major sections of Vietnam, and yet we appear ready to allow national elections in which this highly organized political parallel government will not have a part? They ask how we can speak of free elections when the Saigon press is censored and controlled by the military junta. And they are surely right to wonder what kind of new government we plan to help form without them, the only party in real touch with the peasants. They question our political goals and they deny the reality of a peace settlement from which they will be excluded. Their questions are frighteningly relevant. Is our nation planning to build on political myth again, and then shore it up upon the power of a new violence?

Here is the true meaning and value of compassion and nonviolence, when it helps us to see the enemy's point of view, to hear his questions, to know his assessment of ourselves. For from his view we may indeed see the basic weaknesses of our own condition, and if we are mature, we may learn and grow and profit from the wisdom of the brothers who are called the opposition.

So, too, with Hanoi. In the North, where our bombs now pummel the land, and our mines endanger the waterways, we are met by a deep but understandable mistrust. To speak for them is to explain this lack of confidence in Western words, and especially their distrust of American intentions now. In Hanoi are the men who led the nation to independence against the Japanese and the French, the men who sought membership in the French Commonwealth and were betrayed by the weakness of Paris and the willfulness of the colonial armies. It was they who led a second struggle against French domination at tremendous costs, and then were persuaded to give up the land they controlled between the thirteenth and seventeenth parallel as a temporary measure at Geneva. After 1954 they watched us conspire with Diem to prevent elections which could have surely brought Ho Chi Minh to power over a united Vietnam, and they realized they had been betrayed again. When we ask why they do not leap to negotiate, these things must be remembered.

Also, it must be clear that the leaders of Hanoi considered the presence of American troops in support of the Diem regime to have been the initial military breach of the Geneva Agreement concerning foreign troops. They remind us that they did not begin to send troops in large numbers and even supplies into the South until American forces had moved into the tens of thousands.

Hanoi remembers how our leaders refused to tell us the truth about the earlier North Vietnamese overtures for peace, how the president claimed that none existed when they had clearly been made. Ho Chi Minh has watched as America has spoken of peace and built up its forces, and now he has surely heard the increasing international rumors of American plans for an invasion of the North. He knows the bombing and shelling and mining we are doing are part of traditional pre-invasion strategy. Perhaps only his sense of humor and of irony can save him when he hears the most powerful nation of the world speaking of aggression as it drops thousands of bombs on a poor, weak nation more than eight hundred, or rather, eight thousand miles away from its shores.

At this point I should make it clear that while I have tried in these last few minutes to give a voice to the voiceless in Vietnam and to understand the arguments of those who are called "enemy," I am as deeply concerned about our own troops there as anything else. For it occurs to me that what we are submitting them to in Vietnam is not simply the brutalizing process that goes on in any war where armies face each other and seek to destroy. We are adding cynicism to the process of death, for they must know after a short period there that none of the things we claim to be fighting for are really involved. Before long they must know that their government has sent them into a struggle among Vietnamese, and the more sophisticated surely realize that we are on the side of the wealthy, and the secure, while we create a hell for the poor.

Somehow this madness must cease. We must stop now. I speak as a child of God and brother to the suffering poor of Vietnam. I speak for those whose land is being laid waste, whose homes are being destroyed, whose culture is being subverted. I speak for the poor of America who are paying the double price of smashed hopes at home, and dealt death and corruption in Vietnam. I speak as a citizen of the world, for the world as it stands aghast at the path we have taken. I speak as one who loves America, to the leaders of our own nation:

The great initiative in this war is ours; the initiative to stop it must be ours.

This is the message of the great Buddhist leaders of Vietnam. Recently one of them wrote these words, and I quote:

Each day the war goes on the hatred increases in the heart of the Vietnamese and in the hearts of those of humanitarian instinct. The Americans are forcing even their friends into becoming their enemies. It is curious that the Americans, who calculate so carefully on the possibilities of military victory, do not realize that in the process they are incurring deep psychological and political defeat. The image of America will never again be the image of revolution, freedom, and democracy, but the image of violence and militarism.

Unquote.

If we continue, there will be no doubt in my mind and in the mind of the world that we have no honorable intentions in Vietnam. If we do not stop our war against the people of Vietnam immediately, the world will be left with no other alternative than to see this as some horrible, clumsy, and deadly game we have decided to play. The world now demands a maturity of America that we may not be able to achieve. It demands that we admit that we have been wrong from the beginning of our adventure in Vietnam, that we have been detrimental to the life of the Vietnamese people. The situation is one in which we must be ready to turn sharply from our present ways. In order to atone for our sins and errors in Vietnam, we should take the initiative in bringing a halt to this tragic war.

I would like to suggest five concrete things that our government should do immediately to begin the long and difficult process of extricating ourselves from this nightmarish conflict:

Number one: End all bombing in North and South Vietnam.

Number two: Declare a unilateral cease-fire in the hope that such action will create the atmosphere for negotiation.

Three: Take immediate steps to prevent other battlegrounds in Southeast Asia by curtailing our military buildup in Thailand and our interference in Laos.

Four: Realistically accept the fact that the National Liberation Front has substantial support in South Vietnam and must thereby play a role in any meaningful negotiations and any future Vietnam government.

Five: Set a date that we will remove all foreign troops from Vietnam in accordance with the 1954 Geneva Agreement. [*Sustained applause*]

Part of our ongoing [*Applause continues*], part of our ongoing commitment might well express itself in an offer to grant asylum to any Vietnamese who fears for his life under a new regime which included the Liberation Front. Then we must make what reparations we can for the damage we have done. We must provide the medical aid that is badly needed, making it available in this country if necessary. Meanwhile [*Applause*], meanwhile, we in the churches and synagogues have a continuing task while we urge our government to disengage itself from a disgraceful commitment. We must continue to raise our voices and our lives if our nation persists in its perverse ways in Vietnam. We must be prepared to match actions with words by seeking out every creative method of protest possible.

As we counsel young men concerning military service, we must clarify for them our nation's role in Vietnam and challenge them with the alternative of conscientious objection. [*Sustained applause*] I am pleased to say that this is a path now chosen by more than seventy students at my own alma mater, Morehouse College, and I recommend it to all who find the American course in Vietnam a dishonorable and unjust one. [*Applause*] Moreover, I would encourage all ministers of draft age to give up their ministerial exemptions and seek status as conscientious objectors. [*Applause*] These are the times for real choices and not false ones. We are at the moment when our lives must be placed on the line if our nation is to survive its own folly. Every man of humane convictions must decide on the protest that best suits his convictions, but we must all protest.

Now there is something seductively tempting about stopping there and sending us all off on what in some circles has become a popular crusade against the war in Vietnam. I say we must enter that struggle, but I wish to go on now to say something even more disturbing.

The war in Vietnam is but a symptom of a far deeper malady within the American spirit, and if we ignore this sobering reality [*Applause*], and if we ignore this sobering reality, we will find ourselves organizing "clergy and laymen concerned" com-

mittees for the next generation. They will be concerned about
Guatemala and Peru. They will be concerned about Thailand
and Cambodia. They will be concerned about Mozambique
and South Africa. We will be marching for these and a dozen
other names and attending rallies without end unless there is a
significant and profound change in American life and policy.
[*Sustained applause*] So such thoughts take us beyond Vietnam, but not beyond our calling as sons of the living God.

In 1957 a sensitive American official overseas said that it
seemed to him that our nation was on the wrong side of a world
revolution. During the past ten years we have seen emerge a
pattern of suppression which has now justified the presence of
U.S. military advisors in Venezuela. This need to maintain
social stability for our investments accounts for the counter-
revolutionary action of American forces in Guatemala. It tells
why American helicopters are being used against guerrillas in
Cambodia and why American napalm and Green Beret forces
have already been active against rebels in Peru.

It is with such activity in mind that the words of the late
John F. Kennedy come back to haunt us. Five years ago he said,
"Those who make peaceful revolution impossible will make violent revolution inevitable." [*Applause*] Increasingly, by choice
or by accident, this is the role our nation has taken, the role of
those who make peaceful revolution impossible by refusing to
give up the privileges and the pleasures that come from the immense profits of overseas investments. I am convinced that if
we are to get on the right side of the world revolution, we as a
nation must undergo a radical revolution of values. We must
rapidly begin [*Applause*], we must rapidly begin the shift from
a thing-oriented society to a person-oriented society. When
machines and computers, profit motives and property rights,
are considered more important than people, the giant triplets
of racism, extreme materialism, and militarism are incapable of
being conquered.

A true revolution of values will soon cause us to question
the fairness and justice of many of our past and present policies. On the one hand we are called to play the Good Samaritan on life's roadside, but that will be only an initial act. One
day we must come to see that the whole Jericho Road must be
transformed so that men and women will not be constantly

beaten and robbed as they make their journey on life's highway. True compassion is more than flinging a coin to a beggar. It comes to see that an edifice which produces beggars needs restructuring. [*Applause*]

A true revolution of values will soon look uneasily on the glaring contrast of poverty and wealth. With righteous indignation, it will look across the seas and see individual capitalists of the West investing huge sums of money in Asia, Africa, and South America, only to take the profits out with no concern for the social betterment of the countries, and say, "This is not just." It will look at our alliance with the landed gentry of South America and say, "This is not just." The Western arrogance of feeling that it has everything to teach others and nothing to learn from them is not just.

A true revolution of values will lay hand on the world order and say of war, "This way of settling differences is not just." This business of burning human beings with napalm, of filling our nation's homes with orphans and widows, of injecting poisonous drugs of hate into the veins of peoples normally humane, of sending men home from dark and bloody battlefields physically handicapped and psychologically deranged, cannot be reconciled with wisdom, justice, and love. A nation that continues year after year to spend more money on military defense than on programs of social uplift is approaching spiritual death. [*Sustained applause*]

America, the richest and most powerful nation in the world, can well lead the way in this revolution of values. There is nothing except a tragic death wish to prevent us from reordering our priorities so that the pursuit of peace will take precedence over the pursuit of war. There is nothing to keep us from molding a recalcitrant status quo with bruised hands until we have fashioned it into a brotherhood.

This kind of positive revolution of values is our best defense against communism. [*Applause*] War is not the answer. Communism will never be defeated by the use of atomic bombs or nuclear weapons. Let us not join those who shout war and, through their misguided passions, urge the United States to relinquish its participation in the United Nations. These are days which demand wise restraint and calm reasonableness. We must not engage in a negative anticommunism, but rather in a positive thrust for democracy [*Applause*], realizing that our greatest defense against communism is to take offensive action in behalf of justice. We must with positive action seek to remove those conditions of poverty, insecurity, and injustice, which are the fertile soil in which the seed of communism grows and develops.

These are revolutionary times. All over the globe men are revolting against old systems of exploitation and oppression, and out of the wounds of a frail world, new systems of justice and equality are being born. The shirtless and barefoot people of the land are rising up as never before. The people who sat in darkness have seen a great light. We in the West must support these revolutions.

It is a sad fact that because of comfort, complacency, a morbid fear of communism, and our proneness to adjust to injustice, the Western nations that initiated so much of the revolutionary spirit of the modern world have now become the arch antirevolutionaries. This has driven many to feel that only Marxism has a revolutionary spirit. Therefore, communism is a judgment against our failure to make democracy real and follow through on the revolutions that we initiated. Our only hope today lies in our ability to recapture the revolutionary spirit and go out into a sometimes hostile world declaring eternal hostility to poverty, racism, and militarism. With this powerful commitment we shall boldly challenge the status quo and unjust mores, and thereby speed the day when every valley shall be exalted, and every mountain and hill shall be made low [*Audience:*] (*Yes*); the crooked shall be made straight, and the rough places plain.

A genuine revolution of values means in the final analysis that our loyalties must become ecumenical rather than sectional. Every nation must now develop an overriding loyalty to mankind as a whole in order to preserve the best in their individual societies.

This call for a worldwide fellowship that lifts neighborly concern beyond one's tribe, race, class, and nation is in reality a call for an all-embracing and unconditional love for all mankind. This oft misunderstood, this oft misinterpreted concept, so readily dismissed by the Nietzsches of the world as a weak and cowardly force, has now become an absolute necessity for the survival of man. When I speak of love I am not speaking of some sentimental and weak response. I'm not speaking of that force which is just emotional bosh. I am speaking of that force which all of the great religions have seen as the supreme unifying principle of life. Love is somehow the key that unlocks the door which leads to ultimate reality. This Hindu-Muslim-Christian-Jewish-Buddhist belief about ultimate reality is beautifully summed up in the first epistle of Saint John: "Let us love one another (*Yes*), for love is God. (*Yes*) And every one that loveth is born of God and knoweth God. He that loveth not knoweth not God, for God is love. . . . If we love one another, God dwelleth in us and his love is perfected in us." Let us hope that this spirit will become the order of the day.

We can no longer afford to worship the god of hate or bow before the altar of retaliation. The oceans of history are made turbulent by the ever-rising tides of hate. History is cluttered with the wreckage of nations and individuals that pursued this self-defeating path of hate. As Arnold Toynbee says: "Love is the ultimate force that makes for the saving choice of life and good against the damning choice of death and evil. Therefore the first hope in our inventory must be the hope that love is going to have the last word." Unquote.

We are now faced with the fact, my friends, that tomorrow is today. We are confronted with the fierce urgency of now. In this unfolding conundrum of life and history, there is such a thing as being too late. Procrastination is still the thief of time. Life often leaves us standing bare, naked, and dejected with a lost opportunity. The tide in the affairs of men does not remain at flood—it ebbs. We may cry out desperately for time to pause in her passage, but time is adamant to every plea and rushes on. Over the bleached bones and jumbled residues of numerous civilizations are written the pathetic words, "Too late." There is an invisible book of life that faithfully records our vigilance or our neglect. Omar Khayyam is right: "The moving finger writes, and having writ moves on."

We still have a choice today: nonviolent coexistence or violent coannihilation. We must move past indecision to action. We must find new ways to speak for peace in Vietnam and justice throughout the developing world, a world that borders on our doors. If we do not act, we shall surely be dragged down the long, dark, and shameful corridors of time reserved for those who possess power without compassion, might without morality, and strength without sight.

Now let us begin. Now let us rededicate ourselves to the long and bitter, but beautiful, struggle for a new world. This is the calling of the sons of God, and our brothers wait eagerly for our response. Shall we say the odds are too great? Shall we tell them the struggle is too hard? Will our message be that the forces of American life militate against their arrival as full men, and we send our deepest regrets? Or will there be another message—of longing, of hope, of solidarity with their yearnings, of commitment to their cause, whatever the cost? The choice is ours, and though we might prefer it otherwise, we must choose in this crucial moment of human history.

As that noble bard of yesterday James Russell Lowell eloquently stated:

Once to every man and nation comes a moment to decide,
In the strife of Truth and Falsehood, for the good or evil side;
Some great cause, God's new Messiah offering each the bloom
    or blight,
And the choice goes by forever 'twixt that darkness and that
    light.

Though the cause of evil prosper, yet 'tis truth alone is strong
Though her portions be the scaffold, and upon the throne be
    wrong
Yet that scaffold sways the future, and behind the dim unknown
Standeth God within the shadow, keeping watch above his
    own.

And if we will only make the right choice, we will be able to transform this pending cosmic elegy into a creative psalm of peace. If we will make the right choice, we will be able to transform the jangling discords of our world into a beautiful symphony of brotherhood. If we will but make the right choice, we will be able to speed up the day, all over America and all over the world, when justice will roll down like waters, and righteousness like a mighty stream. [*Sustained applause*]

MARTIN LUTHER KING, JR.

Sermon at National Cathedral

Washington, D.C., March 31, 1968

I NEED NOT pause to say how very delighted I am to be here this morning, to have the opportunity of standing in this very great and significant pulpit. And I do want to express my deep personal appreciation to Dean Sayre and all of the cathedral clergy for extending the invitation.

It is always a rich and rewarding experience to take a brief break from our day-to-day demands and the struggle for freedom and human dignity and discuss the issues involved in that struggle with concerned friends of goodwill all over our nation. And certainly it is always a deep and meaningful experience to be in a worship service. And so for many reasons, I'm happy to be here today.

I would like to use as a subject from which to preach this morning: "Remaining Awake Through a Great Revolution." The text for the morning is found in the Book of Revelation. There are two passages there that I would like to quote, in the sixteenth chapter of that book: "Behold, I make all things new; former things are passed away."

I am sure that most of you have read that arresting little story from the pen of Washington Irving entitled "Rip Van Winkle." The one thing that we usually remember about the story is that Rip Van Winkle slept twenty years. But there is another point in that little story that is almost completely overlooked. It was the sign in the end, from which Rip went up in the mountain for his long sleep.

When Rip Van Winkle went up into the mountains, the sign had a picture of King George the Third of England. When he came down twenty years later, the sign had a picture of George Washington, the first president of the United States. When Rip Van Winkle looked up at the picture of George Washington—

and looking at the picture, he was amazed—he was completely lost. He knew not who he was.

And this reveals to us that the most striking thing about the story of Rip Van Winkle is not merely that Rip slept twenty years, but that he slept through a revolution. While he was peacefully snoring up in the mountain a revolution was taking place that at points would change the course of history—and Rip knew nothing about it. He was asleep. Yes, he slept through a revolution. And one of the great liabilities of life is that all too many people find themselves living amid a great period of social change, and yet they fail to develop the new attitudes, the new mental responses, that the new situation demands. They end up sleeping through a revolution.

There can be no gainsaying of the fact that a great revolution is taking place in the world today. In a sense it is a triple revolution: that is, a technological revolution, with the impact of automation and cybernation; then there is a revolution in weaponry, with the emergence of atomic and nuclear weapons of warfare; then there is a human rights revolution, with the freedom explosion that is taking place all over the world. Yes, we do live in a period where changes are taking place. And there is still the voice crying through the vista of time, saying, "Behold, I make all things new; former things are passed away."

Now, whenever anything new comes into history it brings with it new challenges and new opportunities. And I would like to deal with the challenges that we face today as a result of this triple revolution that is taking place in the world today.

First, we are challenged to develop a world perspective. No individual can live alone, no nation can live alone, and anyone who feels that he can live alone is sleeping through a revolution. The world in which we live is geographically one. The challenge that we face today is to make it one in terms of brotherhood.

Now, it is true that the geographical oneness of this age has come into being to a large extent through modern man's scientific ingenuity. Modern man through his scientific genius has been able to dwarf distance and place time in chains. And our jet planes have compressed into minutes distances that once took weeks and even months. All of this tells us that our world is a neighborhood.

Through our scientific and technological genius, we have made of this world a neighborhood and yet we have not had the ethical commitment to make of it a brotherhood. But somehow, and in some way, we have got to do this. We must all learn to live together as brothers or we will all perish together as fools. We are tied together in the single garment of destiny, caught in an inescapable network of mutuality. And whatever affects one directly affects all indirectly. For some strange reason I can never be what I ought to be until you are what you ought to be. And you can never be what you ought to be until I am what I ought to be. This is the way God's universe is made; this is the way it is structured.

John Donne caught it years ago and placed it in graphic terms: "No man is an island entire of itself. Every man is a piece of the continent, a part of the main." And he goes on toward the end to say, "Any man's death diminishes me because I am involved in mankind; therefore never send to know for whom the bell tolls; it tolls for thee." We must see this, believe this, and live by it if we are to remain awake through a great revolution.

Secondly, we are challenged to eradicate the last vestiges of racial injustice from our nation. I must say this morning that racial injustice is still the black man's burden and the white man's shame.

It is an unhappy truth that racism is a way of life for the vast majority of white Americans, spoken and unspoken, acknowledged and denied, subtle and sometimes not so subtle—the disease of racism permeates and poisons a whole body politic. And I can see nothing more urgent than for America to work passionately and unrelentingly—to get rid of the disease of racism.

Something positive must be done. Everyone must share in the guilt as individuals and as institutions. The government must certainly share the guilt; individuals must share the guilt; even the church must share the guilt.

We must face the sad fact that at eleven o'clock on Sunday morning when we stand to sing "In Christ there is no East or West," we stand in the most segregated hour of America.

The hour has come for everybody, for all institutions of the public sector and the private sector, to work to get rid of racism. And now if we are to do it we must honestly admit certain things and get rid of certain myths that have constantly been disseminated all over our nation.

One is the myth of time. It is the notion that only time can solve the problem of racial injustice. And there are those who often sincerely say to the Negro and his allies in the white community, "Why don't you slow up? Stop pushing things so fast. Only time can solve the problem. And if you will just be nice and patient and continue to pray, in a hundred or two hundred years the problem will work itself out."

There is an answer to that myth. It is that time is neutral. It can be used either constructively or destructively. And I am sorry to say this morning that I am absolutely convinced that the forces of ill will in our nation, the extreme rightists of our nation—the people on the wrong side—have used time much more effectively than the forces of goodwill. And it may well be that we will have to repent in this generation. Not merely for the vitriolic words and the violent actions of the bad people, but for the appalling silence and indifference of the good people who sit around and say "Wait on time."

Somewhere we must come to see that human progress never rolls in on the wheels of inevitability. It comes through the tireless efforts and the persistent work of dedicated individuals who are willing to be coworkers with God. And without this hard work, time itself becomes an ally of the primitive forces of social stagnation. So we must help time and realize that the time is always ripe to do right.

Now, there is another myth that still gets around: It is a kind of overreliance on the bootstrap philosophy. There are those who still feel that if the Negro is to rise out of poverty, if the Negro is to rise out of the slum conditions, if he is to rise out of discrimination and segregation, he must do it all by himself. And so they say the Negro must lift himself by his own bootstraps.

They never stop to realize that no other ethnic group has been a slave on American soil. The people who say this never stop to realize that the nation made the black man's color a stigma. But beyond this they never stop to realize the debt that they owe a people who were kept in slavery two hundred and forty-four years.

In 1863 the Negro was told that he was free as a result of the Emancipation Proclamation being signed by Abraham Lincoln. But he was not given any land to make that freedom meaningful. It was something like keeping a person in prison for a number of years and suddenly discovering that that person is not guilty of the crime for which he was convicted. And you just go up to him and say, "Now you are free," but you don't give him any bus fare to get to town. You don't give him any money to get some clothes to put on his back or to get on his feet again in life.

Every court of jurisprudence would rise up against this, and yet this is the very thing that our nation did to the black man. It simply said, "You're free," and it left him there penniless, illiterate, not knowing what to do. And the irony of it all is that at the same time the nation failed to do anything for the black man, though . . . Congress was giving away millions of acres of land in the West and the Midwest. Which meant that it was willing to undergird its white peasants from Europe with an economic floor.

But not only did it give the land, it built land-grant colleges to teach them how to farm. Not only that, it provided county agents to further their expertise in farming; not only that, as the years unfolded it provided low interest rates so that they could mechanize their farms. And to this day thousands of these very persons are receiving millions of dollars in federal subsidies every year not to farm. And these are so often the very people who tell Negroes that they must lift themselves by their own bootstraps. It's all right to tell a man to lift himself by his own bootstraps, but it is a cruel jest to say to a bootless man that he ought to lift himself by his own bootstraps.

We must come to see that the roots of racism are very deep in our country, and there must be something positive and massive in order to get rid of all the effects of racism and the tragedies of racial injustice.

There is another thing closely related to racism that I would like to mention as another challenge. We are challenged to rid our nation and the world of poverty. Like a monstrous octopus, poverty spreads its nagging, prehensile tentacles into hamlets and villages all over our world. Two-thirds of the people of the world go to bed hungry tonight. They are ill-housed; they are ill-nourished; they are shabbily clad. I've seen it in Latin America; I've seen it in Africa; I've seen this poverty in Asia.

I remember some years ago Mrs. King and I journeyed to that great country known as India. And I never will forget the experience. It was a marvelous experience to meet and talk with the great leaders of India, to meet and talk with and to speak to thousands and thousands of people all over that vast country. These experiences will remain dear to me as long as the cords of memory shall lengthen.

But I say to you this morning, my friends, there were those depressing moments. How can one avoid being depressed when he sees with his own eyes evidence of millions of people going to bed hungry at night? How can one avoid being depressed when he sees with his own eyes God's children sleeping on the sidewalks at night? In Bombay more than a million people sleep on the sidewalks every night. In Calcutta more than six hundred thousand sleep on the sidewalks every night. They have no beds to sleep in; they have no houses to go in. How can one avoid being depressed when he discovers that out of India's population of more than five hundred million people, some four hundred and eighty million make an annual income of less than ninety dollars a year. And most of them have never seen a doctor or a dentist.

As I noticed these things, something within me cried out, "Can we in America stand idly by and not be concerned?" And an answer came: "Oh no!" Because the destiny of the United States is tied up with the destiny of India and every other nation. And I started thinking of the fact that we spend in America millions of dollars a day to store surplus food, and I said to myself, "I know where we can store that food free of charge— in the wrinkled stomachs of millions of God's children all over the world who go to bed hungry at night." And maybe we spend far too much of our national budget establishing military bases around the world rather than bases of genuine concern and understanding.

Not only do we see poverty abroad, I would remind you that in our own nation there are about forty million people who are poverty-stricken. I have seen them here and there. I have seen them in the ghettos of the North; I have seen them in the rural areas of the South; I have seen them in Appalachia. I have just been in the process of touring many areas of our country, and I must confess that in some situations I have literally found myself crying.

I was in Marks, Mississippi, the other day, which is in Quitman County, the poorest county in the United States. I tell you, I saw hundreds of little black boys and black girls walking the streets with no shoes to wear. I saw their mothers and fathers trying to carry on a little Head Start program, but they had no money. The federal government hadn't funded them, but they were trying to carry on. They raised a little money here and there; trying to get a little food to feed the children; trying to teach them a little something.

And I saw mothers and fathers who said to me not only were they unemployed, they didn't get any kind of income—no old-age pension, no welfare check, no anything. I said, "How do you live?" And they say, "Well, we go around, go around to the neighbors and ask them for a little something. When the berry season comes, we pick berries. When the rabbit season comes, we hunt and catch a few rabbits. And that's about it."

And I was in Newark and Harlem just this week. And I walked into the homes of welfare mothers. I saw them in conditions—no, not with wall-to-wall carpet, but wall-to-wall rats and roaches. I stood in an apartment and this welfare mother said to me, "The landlord will not repair this place. I've been here two years and he hasn't made a single repair." She pointed out the walls with all the ceiling falling through. She showed me the holes where the rats came in. She said, "Night after night we have to stay awake to keep the rats and roaches from getting to the children." I said, "How much do you pay for this apartment?" She said, "A hundred and twenty-five dollars." I looked, and I thought, and said to myself, "It isn't worth sixty dollars." Poor people are forced to pay more for less. Living in conditions day in and day out where the whole area is constantly drained without being replenished. It becomes a kind of domestic colony. And the tragedy is, so often these forty million people are invisible because America is so affluent, so rich. Because our expressways carry us from the ghetto, we don't see the poor.

Jesus told a parable one day, and he reminded us that a man went to hell because he didn't see the poor. His name was Dives. He was a rich man. And there was a man by the name of Lazarus who was a poor man, but not only was he poor, he was sick. Sores were all over his body, and he was so weak that he could hardly move. But he managed to get to the gate of Dives every day, wanting just to have the crumbs that would fall from his table. And Dives did nothing about it. And the parable ends saying, "Dives went to hell, and there was a fixed gulf now between Lazarus and Dives."

There is nothing in that parable that said Dives went to hell because he was rich. Jesus never made a universal indictment against all wealth. It is true that one day a rich young ruler came to him, and he advised him to sell all, but in that instance Jesus was prescribing individual surgery and not setting forth a universal diagnosis. And if you will look at that parable with all of its symbolism, you will remember that a conversation took place between heaven and hell, and on the other end of that long-distance call between heaven and hell was Abraham in heaven talking to Dives in hell.

Now, Abraham was a very rich man. If you go back to the Old Testament, you see that he was the richest man of his day, so it was not a rich man in hell talking with a poor man in heaven; it was a little millionaire in hell talking with a multi-millionaire in heaven. Dives didn't go to hell because he was rich; Dives didn't realize that his wealth was his opportunity. It was his opportunity to bridge the gulf that separated him from his brother Lazarus. Dives went to hell because he passed by Lazarus every day and he never really saw him. He went to hell because he allowed his brother to become invisible. Dives went to hell because he maximized the minimum and minimized the maximum. Indeed, Dives went to hell because he sought to be a conscientious objector in the war against poverty.

And this can happen to America, the richest nation in the world—and nothing's wrong with that—this is America's opportunity to help bridge the gulf between the haves and the have-nots. The question is whether America will do it. There is nothing new about poverty. What is new is that we now have the techniques and the resources to get rid of poverty. The real question is whether we have the will.

In a few weeks some of us are coming to Washington to see if the will is still alive or if it's alive in this nation. We are coming to Washington in a Poor People's Campaign. Yes, we are going to bring the tired, the poor, the huddled masses. We are going to bring those who have known long years of hurt and neglect. We are going to bring those who have come to feel that life is a long and desolate corridor with no exit signs. We are going to bring children and adults and old people, people who have never seen a doctor or a dentist in their lives.

We are not coming to engage in any histrionic gesture. We are not coming to tear up Washington. We are coming to demand that the government address itself to the problem of poverty. We read one day, "We hold these truths to be self-evident, that all men are created equal, that they are endowed by their Creator with certain inalienable Rights, that among these are Life, Liberty, and the pursuit of Happiness." But if a man doesn't have a job or an income, he has neither life nor liberty nor the possibility for the pursuit of happiness. He merely exists.

We are coming to ask America to be true to the huge promissory note that it signed years ago. And we are coming to engage in dramatic nonviolent action, to call attention to the gulf between promise and fulfillment; to make the invisible visible.

Why do we do it this way? We do it this way because it is our experience that the nation doesn't move around questions of genuine equality for the poor and for black people until it is confronted massively, dramatically in terms of direct action.

Great documents are here to tell us something should be done. We met here some years ago in the White House conference on civil rights. And we came out with the same recommendations that we will be demanding in our campaign here, but nothing has been done. The president's commission on technology, automation, and economic progress recommended these things some time ago. Nothing has been done. Even the urban coalition of mayors of most of the cities of our country and the leading businessmen have said these things should be done. Nothing has been done. The Kerner Commission came out with its report just a few days ago and then made specific recommendations. Nothing has been done.

And I submit that nothing will be done until people of

goodwill put their bodies and their souls in motion. And it will be the kind of soul force brought into being as a result of this confrontation that I believe will make the difference.

Yes, it will be a Poor People's Campaign. This is the question facing America. Ultimately a great nation is a compassionate nation. America has not met its obligations and its responsibilities to the poor.

One day we will have to stand before the God of history and we will talk in terms of things we've done. Yes, we will be able to say we built gargantuan bridges to span the seas, we built gigantic buildings to kiss the skies. Yes, we made our submarines to penetrate oceanic depths. We brought into being many other things with our scientific and technological power.

It seems that I can hear the God of history saying, "That was not enough! But I was hungry, and ye fed me not. I was naked, and ye clothed me not. I was devoid of a decent sanitary house to live in, and ye provided no shelter for me. And consequently, you cannot enter the kingdom of greatness. If ye do it unto the least of these, my brethren, ye do it unto me." That's the question facing America today.

I want to say one other challenge that we face is simply that we must find an alternative to war and bloodshed. Anyone who feels—and there are still a lot of people who feel that way—that war can solve the social problems facing mankind is sleeping through a great revolution. President Kennedy said on one occasion, "Mankind must put an end to war or war will put an end to mankind." The world must hear this. I pray God that America will hear this before it is too late, because today we're fighting a war.

I am convinced that it is one of the most unjust wars that has ever been fought in the history of the world. Our involvement in the war in Vietnam has torn up the Geneva Accord. It has strengthened the military-industrial complex; it has strengthened the forces of reaction in our nation. It has put us against the self-determination of a vast majority of the Vietnamese people, and put us in the position of protecting a corrupt regime that is stacked against the poor.

It has played havoc with our domestic destinies. This day we are spending five hundred thousand dollars to kill every Vietcong soldier. Every time we kill one we spend about five hundred thousand dollars, while we spend only fifty-three dollars a year for every person characterized as poverty-stricken in the so-called poverty program, which is not even a good skirmish against poverty.

Not only that, it has put us in a position of appearing to the world as an arrogant nation. And here we are ten thousand miles away from home, fighting for the so-called freedom of the Vietnamese people, when we have not even put our own house in order. And we force young black men and young white men to fight and kill in brutal solidarity. Yet when they come back home they can't hardly live on the same block together.

The judgment of God is upon us today. And we could go right down the line and see that something must be done— and something must be done quickly. We have alienated ourselves from other nations so we end up morally and politically isolated in the world. There is not a single major ally of the United States of America that would dare send a troop to Vietnam, and so the only friends that we have now are a few client-nations like Taiwan, Thailand, South Korea, and a few others.

This is where we are. "Mankind must put an end to war or war will put an end to mankind," and the best way to start is to put an end to war in Vietnam, because if it continues, we will inevitably come to the point of confronting China, which could lead the whole world to nuclear annihilation.

It is no longer a choice, my friends, between violence and nonviolence. It is either nonviolence or nonexistence. And the alternative to disarmament, the alternative to a greater suspension of nuclear tests, the alternative to strengthening the United Nations and thereby disarming the whole world, may well be a civilization plunged into the abyss of annihilation, and our earthly habitat would be transformed into an inferno that even the mind of Dante could not imagine.

This is why I felt the need of raising my voice against that war and working wherever I can to arouse the conscience of our nation on it. I remember so well when I first took a stand against the war in Vietnam. The critics took me on and they had their say in the most negative and sometimes most vicious way.

One day a newsman came to me and said, "Dr. King, don't you think you're going to have to stop now opposing the war and move more in line with the administration's policy? As I understand it, it has hurt the budget of your organization, and people who once respected you have lost respect for you. Don't you feel that you've really got to change your position?" I looked at him and I had to say, "Sir, I'm sorry you don't know me. I'm not a consensus leader. I do not determine what is right and wrong by looking at the budget of the Southern Christian Leadership Conference. I've not taken a sort of Gallup poll of the majority opinion." Ultimately a genuine leader is not a searcher for consensus but a molder of consensus.

On some positions, cowardice asks the question, Is it expedient? And then expedience comes along and asks the question, Is it politic? Vanity asks the question, Is it popular? Conscience asks the question, Is it right?

There comes a time when one must take the position that is neither safe nor politic nor popular, but he must do it because conscience tells him it is right. I believe today that there is a need for all people of goodwill to come with a massive act of conscience and say in the words of the old Negro spiritual, "We ain't gonna study war no more." This is the challenge facing modern man.

Let me close by saying that we have difficult days ahead in the struggle for justice and peace, but I will not yield to a politic of despair. I'm going to maintain hope as we come to Washington in this campaign. The cards are stacked against us. This time we will really confront a Goliath. God grant that we will be that David of truth set out against the Goliath of injustice, the Goliath of neglect, the Goliath of refusing to deal with the problems, and go on with the determination to make America the truly great America that it is called to be.

I say to you that our goal is freedom, and I believe we are going to get there because however much she strays away from it, the goal of America is freedom. Abused and scorned though we may be as a people, our destiny is tied up in the destiny of America.

Before the Pilgrim fathers landed at Plymouth, we were here. Before Jefferson etched across the pages of history the majestic words of the Declaration of Independence, we were here. Before the beautiful words of "The Star-Spangled Banner" were written, we were here.

For more than two centuries our forebears labored here without wages. They made cotton king, and they built the homes of their masters in the midst of the most humiliating and oppressive conditions. And yet out of a bottomless vitality they continued to grow and develop. If the inexpressible cruelties of slavery couldn't stop us, the opposition that we now face will surely fail.

We're going to win our freedom because both the sacred heritage of our nation and the eternal will of the almighty God are embodied in our echoing demands. And so, however dark it is, however deep the angry feelings are, and however violent explosions are, I can still sing "We Shall Overcome."

We shall overcome because the arc of the moral universe is long, but it bends toward justice.

We shall overcome because Carlyle is right: "No lie can live forever."

We shall overcome because William Cullen Bryant is right: "Truth, crushed to earth, will rise again."

We shall overcome because James Russell Lowell is right: As we were singing earlier today,

> Truth forever on the scaffold,
> Wrong forever on the throne.
> Yet that scaffold sways the future.
> And behind the dim unknown stands God,
> Within the shadow keeping watch above his own.

With this faith we will be able to hew out of the mountain of despair the stone of hope. With this faith we will be able to transform the jangling discords of our nation into a beautiful symphony of brotherhood.

Thank God for John, who centuries ago out on a lonely, obscure island called Patmos caught vision of a new Jerusalem descending out of heaven from God, who heard a voice saying, "Behold, I make all things new; former things are passed away."

God grant that we will be participants in this newness and this magnificent development. If we will but do it, we will bring about a new day of justice and brotherhood and peace. And that day the morning stars will sing together and the sons of God will shout for joy. God bless you.

MARTIN LUTHER KING, JR.

Speech at Mason Temple

Memphis, April 3, 1968

THANK YOU very kindly, my friends. As I listened to Ralph Abernathy and his eloquent and generous introduction and then thought about myself, I wondered who he was talking about. [*Laughter*] It's always good to have your closest friend and associate to say something good about you, and Ralph Abernathy is the best friend that I have in the world.

I'm delighted to see each of you here tonight in spite of a storm warning. You reveal that you are determined [*Audience:*] (*Right*) to go on anyhow. (*Yeah, All right*) Something is happening in Memphis, something is happening in our world. And you know, if I were standing at the beginning of time with the possibility of taking a kind of general and panoramic view of the whole of human history up to now, and the Almighty said to me, "Martin Luther King, which age would you like to live in?" I would take my mental flight by Egypt (*Yeah*), and I would watch God's children in their magnificent trek from the dark dungeons of Egypt through, or rather, across the Red Sea, through the wilderness, on toward the Promised Land. And in spite of its magnificence, I wouldn't stop there. (*All right*)

I would move on by Greece, and take my mind to Mount Olympus. And I would see Plato, Aristotle, Socrates, Euripides, and Aristophanes assembled around the Parthenon [*Applause*], and I would watch them around the Parthenon as they discussed the great and eternal issues of reality. But I wouldn't stop there. (*Oh yeah*)

I would go on even to the great heyday of the Roman Empire (*Yes*), and I would see developments around there, through various emperors and leaders. But I wouldn't stop there. (*Keep on*)

I would even come up to the day of the Renaissance and get

a quick picture of all that the Renaissance did for the cultural and aesthetic life of man. But I wouldn't stop there. (*Yeah*)

I would even go by the way that the man for whom I'm named had his habitat, and I would watch Martin Luther as he tacks his ninety-five theses on the door at the church of Wittenberg. But I wouldn't stop there. (*All right*)

I would come on up even to 1863 and watch a vacillating president by the name of Abraham Lincoln finally come to the conclusion that he had to sign the Emancipation Proclamation. But I wouldn't stop there. (*Yeah*) [*Applause*]

I would even come up to the early thirties and see a man grappling with the problems of the bankruptcy of his nation, and come with an eloquent cry that "we have nothing to fear but fear itself." But I wouldn't stop there. (*All right*)

Strangely enough, I would turn to the Almighty and say, "If you allow me to live just a few years in the second half of the twentieth century, I will be happy." [*Applause*]

Now that's a strange statement to make because the world is all messed up. The nation is sick, trouble is in the land, confusion all around. That's a strange statement. But I know, somehow, that only when it is dark enough can you see the stars. (*All right, Yes*) And I see God working in this period of the twentieth century in a way that men in some strange way are responding. Something is happening in our world. (*Yeah*) The masses of people are rising up. And wherever they are assembled today, whether they are in Johannesburg, South Africa; Nairobi, Kenya; Accra, Ghana; New York City; Atlanta, Georgia; Jackson, Mississippi; or Memphis, Tennessee, the cry is always the same: "We want to be free." [*Applause*]

And another reason that I'm happy to live in this period is that we have been forced to a point where we are going to have to grapple with the problems that men have been trying to grapple with through history, but the demands didn't force them to do it. Survival demands that we grapple with them. (*Yes*) Men for years now have been talking about war and peace. But now no longer can they just talk about it. It is no longer a choice between violence and nonviolence in this world; it's nonviolence or nonexistence. That is where we are today. [*Applause*]

And also, in-the human rights revolution, if something isn't done and done in a hurry to bring the colored peoples of the world out of their long years of poverty, their long years of hurt and neglect, the whole world is doomed. (*All right*) [*Applause*] Now I'm just happy that God has allowed me to live in this period, to see what is unfolding. And I'm happy that he's allowed me to be in Memphis. (*Oh yeah*)

I can remember [*Applause*], I can remember when Negroes were just going around, as Ralph has said so often, scratching where they didn't itch and laughing when they were not tickled. [*Laughter, applause*] But that day is all over. (*Yeah*) [*Applause*] We mean business now and we are determined to gain our rightful place in God's world. (*Yeah*) [*Applause*] And that's all this whole thing is about. We aren't engaged in any negative protest and in any negative arguments with anybody. We are saying that we are determined to be men. We are determined to be people. (*Yeah*) We are saying [*Applause*], we are saying that we are God's children. (*Yeah*) [*Applause*] And if we are God's children, we don't have to live like we are forced to live.

Now what does all of this mean in this great period of history? It means that we've got to stay together. (*Yeah*) We've got to stay together and maintain unity. You know, whenever Pharaoh wanted to prolong the period of slavery in Egypt, he had a favorite, favorite formula for doing it. What was that? He kept the slaves fighting among themselves. [*Applause*] But whenever the slaves get together, something happens in Pharaoh's court, and he cannot hold the slaves in slavery. When the slaves get together, that's the beginning of getting out of slavery. [*Applause*] Now let us maintain unity.

Secondly, let us keep the issues where they are. (*Right*) The issue is injustice. The issue is the refusal of Memphis to be fair and honest in its dealings with its public servants, who happen to be sanitation workers. [*Applause*] Now we've got to keep attention on that. (*That's right*) That's always the problem with a little violence. You know what happened the other day, and the press dealt only with the window breaking. (*That's right*) I read the articles. They very seldom get around to mentioning the fact that 1,300 sanitation workers are on strike, and that

Memphis is not being fair to them, and that Mayor Loeb is in dire need of a doctor. They didn't get around to that. (*Yeah*) [*Applause*]

Now we're going to march again, and we've got to march again (*Yeah*), in order to put the issue where it is supposed to be (*Yeah*) [*Applause*] and force everybody to see that there are thirteen hundred of God's children here suffering (*That's right*), sometimes going hungry, going through dark and dreary nights wondering how this thing is going to come out. That's the issue. (*That's right*) And we've got to say to the nation, we know how it's coming out. For when people get caught up with that which is right and they are willing to sacrifice for it, there is no stopping point short of victory. [*Applause*]

We aren't going to let any mace stop us. We are masters in our nonviolent movement in disarming police forces. They don't know what to do. I've seen them so often. I remember in Birmingham, Alabama, when we were in that majestic struggle there, we would move out of the Sixteenth Street Baptist Church day after day. By the hundreds we would move out, and Bull Connor would tell them to send the dogs forth, and they did come. But we just went before the dogs singing, "Ain't gonna let nobody turn me around." [*Applause*] Bull Connor next would say, "Turn the fire hoses on." (*Yeah*) And as I said to you the other night, Bull Connor didn't know history. He knew a kind of physics that somehow didn't relate to the trans-physics that we knew about. And that was the fact that there was a certain kind of fire that no water could put out. [*Applause*] And we went before the fire hoses. (*Yeah*) We had known water. (*All right*) If we were Baptist or some other denominations, we had been immersed. If we were Methodist and some others, we had been sprinkled. But we knew water. That couldn't stop us. [*Applause*]

And we just went on before the dogs and we would look at them, and we'd go on before the water hoses and we would look at it. And we'd just go on singing, "Over my head, I see freedom in the air." (*Yeah*) [*Applause*] And then we would be thrown into paddy wagons, and sometimes we were stacked in there like sardines in a can. (*All right*) And they would throw us in, and old Bull would say, "Take 'em off." And they did, and we would just go on in the paddy wagon singing, "We Shall

Overcome." (*Yeah*) And every now and then we'd get in jail, and we'd see the jailers looking through the windows being moved by our prayers (*Yes*) and being moved by our words and our songs. (*Yes*) And there was a power there which Bull Connor couldn't adjust to (*All right*), and so we ended up transforming Bull into a steer, and we won our struggle in Birmingham. [*Applause*]

Now we've got to go on in Memphis just like that. I call upon you to be with us when we go out Monday. (*Yes*) Now about injunctions. We have an injunction and we're going into court tomorrow morning (*Go ahead*) to fight this illegal, unconstitutional injunction. All we say to America is be true to what you said on paper. [*Applause*] If I lived in China or even Russia, or any totalitarian country, maybe I could understand some of these illegal injunctions. Maybe I could understand the denial of certain basic First Amendment privileges, because they haven't committed themselves to that over there. But somewhere I read of the freedom of assembly. Somewhere I read (*Yes*) of the freedom of speech. (*Yes*) Somewhere I read (*All right*) of the freedom of press. (*Yes*) Somewhere I read (*Yes*) that the greatness of America is the right to protest for right. [*Applause*] And so just as I say we aren't going to let any dogs or water hoses turn us around, we aren't going to let any injunction turn us around. [*Applause*] We are going on. We need all of you.

You know, what's beautiful to me is to see all of these ministers of the Gospel. (*Amen*) It's a marvelous picture. (*Yes*) Who is it that is supposed to articulate the longings and aspirations of the people more than the preacher? Somehow the preacher must have a kind of fire shut up in his bones (*Yes*), and whenever injustice is around he must tell it. (*Yes*) Somehow the preacher must be an Amos, who said, "When God speaks, who can but prophesy?" (*Yes*) Again with Amos, "Let justice roll down like waters and righteousness like a mighty stream." (*Yes*) Somehow the preacher must say with Jesus, "The spirit of the Lord is upon me (*Yes*), because He hath anointed me (*Yes*), and He's anointed me to deal with the problems of the poor." (*Go ahead*)

And I want to commend the preachers, under the leadership of these noble men: James Lawson, one who has been in this struggle for many years. He's been to jail for struggling; he's been kicked out of Vanderbilt University for this struggling; but he's still going on, fighting for the rights of his people. [*Applause*] Reverend Ralph Jackson, Billy Kiles; I could just go right on down the list, but time will not permit. But I want to thank all of them, and I want you to thank them because so often preachers aren't concerned about anything but themselves. [*Applause*] And I'm always happy to see a relevant ministry. It's all right to talk about long white robes over yonder, in all of its symbolism, but ultimately people want some suits and dresses and shoes to wear down here. [*Applause*] It's all right to talk about streets flowing with milk and honey, but God has commanded us to be concerned about the slums down here and His children who can't eat three square meals a day. [*Applause*] It's all right to talk about the new Jerusalem, but one day God's preacher must talk about the new New York, the new Atlanta, the new Philadelphia, the new Los Angeles, the new Memphis, Tennessee. [*Applause*] This is what we have to do.

Now the other thing we'll have to do is this: always anchor our external direct action with the power of economic withdrawal. Now we are poor people, individually we are poor when you compare us with white society in America. We are poor. Never stop and forget that collectively, that means all of us together, collectively we are richer than all the nations in the world, with the exception of nine. Did you ever think about that? After you leave the United States, Soviet Russia, Great Britain, West Germany, France, and I could name the others, the American Negro collectively is richer than most nations of the world. We have an annual income of more than thirty billion dollars a year, which is more than all of the exports of the United States and more than the national budget of Canada. Did you know that? That's power right there, if we know how to pool it. (*Yeah*) [*Applause*]

We don't have to argue with anybody. We don't have to curse and go around acting bad with our words. We don't need any bricks and bottles; we don't need any Molotov cocktails. (*Yes*) We just need to go around to these stores (*Yes sir*), and to these massive industries in our country (*Amen*), and say, "God sent us by here (*All right*) to say to you that you're not treating His children right. (*That's right*) And we've come by here to ask you to make the first item on your agenda fair treatment where God's children are concerned. Now if you are not prepared to do that, we do have an agenda that we must follow. And our agenda calls for withdrawing economic support from you." [*Applause*]

And so, as a result of this, we are asking you tonight (*Amen*) to go out and tell your neighbors not to buy Coca-Cola in Memphis. (*Yeah*) [*Applause*] Go by and tell them not to buy Sealtest milk. (*Yeah*) [*Applause*] Tell them not to buy—what is the other bread?—Wonder Bread. [*Applause*] And what is the other bread company, Jesse? Tell them not to buy Hart's bread. [*Applause*] As Jesse Jackson has said, up to now only the garbage men have been feeling pain. Now we must kind of redistribute the pain. [*Applause*] We are choosing these companies because they haven't been fair in their hiring policies, and we are choosing them because they can begin the process of saying they are going to support the needs and the rights of these men who are on strike. And then they can move on downtown and tell Mayor Loeb to do what is right. (*That's right, Speak*) [*Applause*]

Now not only that, we've got to strengthen black institutions. (*That's right, Yeah*) I call upon you to take your money out of the banks downtown and deposit your money in Tri-State Bank. (*Yeah*) [*Applause*] We want a "bank-in" movement in Memphis. (*Yes*) Go by the savings and loan association. I'm not asking you something that we don't do ourselves in SCLC. Judge Hooks and others will tell you that we have an account here in the savings and loan association from the Southern Christian Leadership Conference. We are telling you to follow what we're doing, put your money there. [*Applause*] You have six or seven black insurance companies here in the city of Memphis. Take out your insurance there. We want to have an "insurance-in." [*Applause*] Now these are some practical things that we can do. We begin the process of building a greater economic base, and at the same time, we are putting pressure where it really hurts. (*There you go*) And I ask you to follow through here. [*Applause*]

Now let me say as I move to my conclusion that we've got to give ourselves to this struggle until the end. (*Amen*) Nothing would be more tragic than to stop at this point in Memphis. We've got to see it through. [*Applause*] And when we have our march, you need to be there. If it means leaving work, if it means leaving school, be there. [*Applause*] Be concerned about your brother. You may not be on strike (*Yeah*), but either we go up together or we go down together. [*Applause*] Let us develop a kind of dangerous unselfishness.

One day a man came to Jesus and he wanted to raise some questions about some vital matters of life. At points he wanted to trick Jesus (*That's right*), and show him that he knew a little more than Jesus knew and throw him off base. [*Recording interrupted*] Now that question could have easily ended up in a philosophical and theological debate. But Jesus immediately pulled that question from midair and placed it on a dangerous curve between Jerusalem and Jericho. (*Yeah*) And he talked about a certain man who fell among thieves. (*Sure*) You remember that a Levite (*Sure*) and a priest passed by on the other side; they didn't stop to help him. Finally, a man of another race came by. (*Yes sir*) He got down from his beast, decided not to be compassionate by proxy. But he got down with him, administered first aid, and helped the man in need. Jesus ended up saying this was the good man, this was the great man because he had the capacity to project the "I" into the "thou," and to be concerned about his brother.

Now, you know, we use our imagination a great deal to try to determine why the priest and the Levite didn't stop. At times we say they were busy going to a church meeting, an ecclesiastical gathering, and they had to get on down to Jerusalem so they wouldn't be late for their meeting. (*Yeah*) At other times we would speculate that there was a religious law that one who was engaged in religious ceremonials was not to touch a human body twenty-four hours before the ceremony. (*All right*) And every now and then we begin to wonder whether maybe they were not going down to Jerusalem, or down to Jericho, rather, to organize a Jericho Road Improvement Association. [*Laughter*] That's a possibility. Maybe they felt that it was better to deal with the problem from the causal root, rather than to get bogged down with an individual effect. [*Laughter*]

But I'm going to tell you what my imagination tells me. It's possible that those men were afraid. You see, the Jericho Road is a dangerous road. (*That's right*) I remember when Mrs. King and I were first in Jerusalem. We rented a car and drove from Jerusalem down to Jericho. (*Yeah*) And as soon as we got on that road I said to my wife, "I can see why Jesus used this as the setting for his parable." It's a winding, meandering road. (*Yes*) It's really conducive for ambushing. You start out in Jerusalem, which is about twelve hundred miles, or rather, twelve hundred feet above sea level. And by the time you get down to Jericho fifteen or twenty minutes later, you're about twenty-two hundred feet below sea level. That's a dangerous road. (*Yes*) In the days of Jesus it came to be known as the "Bloody Pass." And you know, it's possible that the priest and the Levite looked over that man on the ground and wondered if the robbers were still around. (*Go ahead*) Or it's possible that they felt that the man on the ground was merely faking (*Yeah*), and he was acting like he had been robbed and hurt in order to seize them over there, lure them there for quick and easy seizure. (*Oh yeah*) And so the first question that the priest asked, the first question that the Levite asked was, "If I stop to help this man, what will happen to me?" (*All right*)

But then the Good Samaritan came by, and he reversed the question: "If I do not stop to help this man, what will happen to him?" That's the question before you tonight. (*Yes*) Not, "If I stop to help the sanitation workers, what will happen to my job?" Not, "If I stop to help the sanitation workers, what will happen to all of the hours that I usually spend in my office every day and every week as a pastor?" (*Yes*) The question is not, "If I stop to help this man in need, what will happen to me?" The question is, "If I do *not* stop to help the sanitation workers, what will happen to them?" That's the question. [*Applause*]

Let us rise up tonight with a greater readiness. Let us stand with a greater determination. And let us move on in these powerful days, these days of challenge, to make America what it ought to be. We have an opportunity to make America a better nation. (*Amen*)

And I want to thank God, once more, for allowing me to be here with you. (*Yes sir*) You know, several years ago I was in New York City autographing the first book that I had written. And while sitting there autographing books, a demented black woman came up. The only question I heard from her was, "Are you Martin Luther King?" And I was looking down writing and I said, "Yes."

The next minute I felt something beating on my chest. Before I knew it I had been stabbed by this demented woman. I was rushed to Harlem Hospital. It was a dark Saturday afternoon. And that blade had gone through, and the X rays revealed that the tip of the blade was on the edge of my aorta, the main artery. And once that's punctured you're drowned in your own blood; that's the end of you. (*Yes sir*) It came out in the *New York Times* the next morning that if I had merely sneezed, I would have died.

Well, about four days later, they allowed me, after the operation, after my chest had been opened and the blade had been taken out, to move around in the wheelchair in the hospital. They allowed me to read some of the mail that came in, and from all over the states and the world kind letters came in. I read a few, but one of them I will never forget. I had received one from the president and the vice president; I've forgotten what those telegrams said. I'd received a visit and a letter from the governor of New York, but I've forgotten what that letter said. (*Yes*)

But there was another letter (*All right*) that came from a little girl, a young girl who was a student at the White Plains High School. And I looked at that letter and I'll never forget it. It said simply, "Dear Dr. King: I am a ninth-grade student at the White Plains High School." She said, "While it should not matter, I would like to mention that I'm a white girl. I read in the paper of your misfortune and of your suffering. And I read that if you had sneezed, you would have died. And I'm simply writing you to say that I'm so happy that you didn't sneeze." (*Yes*) [*Applause*]

And I want to say tonight [*Applause*], I want to say tonight that I, too, am happy that I didn't sneeze. Because if I had sneezed (*All right*), I wouldn't have been around here in 1960 (*Well*), when students all over the South started sitting-in at lunch counters. And I knew that as they were sitting in, they were really standing up (*Yes sir*) for the best in the American dream and taking the whole nation back to those great wells of democracy, which were dug deep by the founding fathers in the Declaration of Independence and the Constitution.

If I had sneezed (*Yes*), I wouldn't have been around here in 1961, when we decided to take a ride for freedom and ended segregation in interstate travel. (*All right*)

If had sneezed (*Yes*), I wouldn't have been around here in 1962, when Negroes in Albany, Georgia, decided to straighten their backs up. And whenever men and women straighten their backs up, they are going somewhere, because a man can't ride your back unless it is bent.

If I had sneezed [*Applause*], if I had sneezed, I wouldn't have been here in 1963 (*All right*), when the black people of Birmingham, Alabama, aroused the conscience of this nation and brought into being the Civil Rights Bill.

If I had sneezed, I wouldn't have had a chance later that year, in August, to try to tell America about a dream that I had had. (*Yes*)

If I had sneezed [*Applause*], I wouldn't have been down in Selma, Alabama, to see the great movement there.

If I had sneezed, I wouldn't have been in Memphis to see a community rally around those brothers and sisters who are suffering. (*Yes*) I'm so happy that I didn't sneeze.

And they were telling me. [*Applause*] Now it doesn't matter now. (*Go ahead*) It really doesn't matter what happens now. I left Atlanta this morning, and as we got started on the plane—there were six of us—the pilot said over the public address system: "We are sorry for the delay, but we have Dr. Martin Luther King on the plane. And to be sure that all of the bags were checked, and to be sure that nothing would be wrong on the plane, we had to check out everything carefully. And we've had the plane protected and guarded all night."

And then I got into Memphis. And some began to say the threats, or talk about the threats that were out (*Yeah*), or what would happen to me from some of our sick white brothers.

Well, I don't know what will happen now; we've got some difficult days ahead. (*Amen*) But it really doesn't matter with me now, because I've been to the mountaintop. (*Yeah*) [*Applause*] And I don't mind. [*Applause continues*] Like anybody, I would like to live a long life—longevity has its place. But I'm not concerned about that now. I just want to do God's will. (*Yeah*) And He's allowed me to go up to the mountain. (*Go ahead*) And I've looked over (*Yes sir*), and I've seen the Promised Land. (*Go ahead*) I may not get there with you. (*Go ahead*) But I want you to know tonight (*Yes*), that we, as a people, will get to the Promised Land. [*Applause*] (*Go ahead, Go ahead*) And so I'm happy tonight; I'm not worried about anything; I'm not fearing any man. Mine eyes have seen the glory of the coming of the Lord. [*Applause*]

ROBERT F. KENNEDY

Remarks on the Assassination of Martin Luther King

Indianapolis, April 4, 1968

I HAVE bad news for you, for all of our fellow citizens, and people who love peace all over the world, and that is that Martin Luther King was shot and killed tonight. [*a huge gasp came from the people and then screams of "No! No!" Kennedy somberly went on.*] Martin Luther King dedicated his life to love and to justice for his fellow human beings, and he died because of that effort.

In this difficult day, in this difficult time for the United States, it is perhaps well to ask what kind of a nation we are and what direction we want to move in. For those of you who are black—considering the evidence there evidently is that there were white people who were responsible—you can be filled with bitterness, with hatred, and a desire for revenge. We can move in that direction as a country, in great polarization—black people amongst black, white people amongst white, filled with hatred toward one another.

Or we can make an effort, as Martin Luther King did, to understand and to comprehend, and to replace that violence, that stain of bloodshed that has spread across our land, with an effort to understand with compassion and love.

For those of you who are black and are tempted to be filled with hatred and distrust at the injustice of such an act, against all white people, I can only say that I feel in my own heart the same kind of feeling. I had a member of my family killed, but he was killed by a white man. But we have to make an effort in the United States, we have to make an effort to understand, to go beyond these rather difficult times.

My favorite poet was Aeschylus. He wrote: "In our sleep, pain which cannot forget falls drop by drop upon the heart until, in our own despair, against our will, comes wisdom through the awful grace of God."

What we need in the United States is not division; what we need in the United States is not hatred; what we need in the United States is not violence or lawlessness; but love and wisdom, and compassion toward one another, and a feeling of justice toward those who still suffer within our country, whether they be white or they be black.

So I shall ask you tonight to return home, to say a prayer for the family of Martin Luther King, that's true, but more importantly to say a prayer for our own country, which all of us love—a prayer for understanding and that compassion of which I spoke.

We can do well in this country. We will have difficult times; we've had difficult times in the past; we will have difficult times in the future. It is not the end of violence; it is not the end of lawlessness; it is not the end of disorder.

But the vast majority of white people and the vast majority of black people in this country want to live together, want to improve the quality of our life, and want justice for all human beings who abide in our land.

Let us dedicate ourselves to what the Greeks wrote so many years ago: to tame the savageness of man and make gentle the life of this world.

Let us dedicate ourselves to that, and say a prayer for our country and for our people.

BARBARA JORDAN

Statement to the House Judiciary Committee

Washington, D.C., July 25, 1974

T HANK YOU, Mr. Chairman.
   Mr. Chairman, I join my colleague, Mr. Rangel, in thanking you for giving the junior members of this committee the glorious opportunity of sharing the pain of this inquiry. Mr. Chairman, you are a strong man and it has not been easy but we have tried as best we can to give you as much assistance as possible.

Earlier today we heard the beginning of the Preamble to the Constitution of the United States, We, the people. It is a very eloquent beginning. But when that document was completed on the 17th of September in 1787 I was not included in that "We, the people." I felt somehow for many years that George Washington and Alexander Hamilton just left me out by mistake. But through the process of amendment, interpretation and court decision I have finally been included in "We, the people."

Today, I am an inquisitor, I believe hyperbole would not be fictional and would not overstate the solemnness that I feel right now. My faith in the Constitution is whole, it is complete, it is total. I am not going to sit here and be an idle spectator to the diminution, the subversion, the destruction of the Constitution.

"Who can so properly be the inquisitors for the nation as the representatives of the nation themselves?" (Federalist No. 65) The subject of its jurisdiction are those offenses which proceed from the misconduct of public men. That is what we are talking about. In other words, the jurisdiction comes from the abuse of violation of some public trust. It is wrong, I suggest, it is a misreading of the Constitution for any member here to assert that for a member to vote for an Article of Impeachment means that that member must be convinced that the President should be removed from office. The Constitution doesn't say that. The powers relating to impeachment are an essential check in the hands of this body, the legislature, against and upon the encroachment of the Executive. In establishing the division between the two branches of the legislature, the House and the Senate, assigning to the one the right to accuse and to the other the right to judge, the Framers of this Constitution were very astute. They did not make the accusers and the judges the same person.

We know the nature of impeachment. We have been talking about it awhile now. "It is chiefly designed for the President and his high ministers" to somehow be called into account. It is designed to "bridle" the Executive if he engages in excesses. "It is designed as a method of national inquest into the conduct of public men." (Hamilton, Federalist No. 65) The Framers confined in the Congress the power if need be, to remove the President in order to strike a delicate balance between a President swollen with power and grown tyrannical; and preservation of the independence of the Executive. The nature of impeachment is a narrowly channeled exception to the separation of powers maxim, the Federal Convention of 1787 said that. It limited impeachment to high crimes and misdemeanors and discounted and opposed the term, "maladministration." "It is to be used only for great misdemeanors," so it was said in the North Carolina ratification convention. And in the Virginia ratification convention: "We do not trust our liberty to a particular branch. We need one branch to check the others."

The North Carolina Ratification Convention: "No one need be afraid that officers who commit oppression will pass with immunity."

"Prosecutions of impeachments will seldom fail to agitate the passions of the whole community," said Hamilton in the Federalist Papers No. 65. "And to divide it into parties more or less friendly or inimical to the accused." I do not mean political parties in that sense.

The drawing of political lines goes to the motivation behind impeachment; but impeachment must proceed within the confines of the constitutional term, "high crimes and misdemeanors."

Of the impeachment process, it was Woodrow Wilson who said that "nothing short of the grossest offenses against the plain law of the land will suffice to give them speed and effectiveness. Indignation so great as to overgrow party interest may secure a conviction: but nothing else can."

Commonsense would be revolted if we engaged upon this process for petty reasons. Congress has a lot to do. Appropriations, tax reform, health insurance, campaign finance reform, housing, environmental protection, energy sufficiency, mass transportation. Pettiness cannot be allowed to stand in the face of such overwhelming problems. So today we are not being petty. We are trying to be big because the task we have before us is a big one.

This morning in a discussion of the evidence we were told that the evidence which purports to support the allegations of misuse of the CIA by the President is thin. We are told that that evidence is insufficient. What that recital of the evidence this morning did not include is what the President did know on June 23, 1972. The President did know that it was Republican money, that it was money from the Committee for the Re-Election of the President, which was found in the possession of one of the burglars arrested on June 17.

What the President did know on June 23 was the prior activities of E. Howard Hunt, which included his participation in the break-in of Daniel Ellsberg's psychiatrist, which included Howard Hunt's participation in the Dita Beard ITT affair, which included Howard Hunt's fabrication of cables designed to discredit the Kennedy administration.

We were further cautioned today that perhaps these proceedings ought to be delayed because certainly there would be new evidence forthcoming from the President of the United States. There has not even been an obfuscated indication that this committee would receive any additional materials from the President. The committee subpena is outstanding and if the President wants to supply that material, the committee sits here.

The fact is that on yesterday, the American people waited with great anxiety for 8 hours, not knowing whether their President would obey an order of the Supreme Court of the United States.

At this point I would like to juxtapose a few of the impeachment criteria with some of the President's actions.

Impeachment criteria: James Madison, from the Virginia Ratification Convention. "If the President be connected in any suspicious manner with any person and there be grounds to believe that he will shelter him, he may be impeached."

We have heard time and time again that the evidence reflects payment to the defendants of money. The President had knowledge that these funds were being paid and that these were funds collected for the 1972 Presidential campaign.

We know that the President met with Mr. Henry Petersen 27 times to discuss matters related to Watergate and immediately thereafter met with the very persons who were implicated in the information Mr. Petersen was receiving and transmitting to the President. The words are, "if the President be connected in any suspicious manner with any person and there be grounds to believe that he will shelter that person, he may be impeached."

Justice Story: "Impeachment is intended for occasional and extraordinary cases where a superior power acting for the whole people is put into operation to protect their rights and rescue their liberties from violations."

We know about the Huston plan. We know about the break-in of the psychiatrist's office. We know that there was absolute complete direction in August 1971 when the President instructed Ehrlichman to "do whatever is necessary." This instruction led to a surreptitious entry into Dr. Fielding's office.

"Protect their rights." "Rescue their liberties from violation."

The South Carolina Ratification Convention impeachment criteria: Those are impeachable "who behave amiss or betray their public trust."

Beginning shortly after the Watergate break-in and continuing to the present time the President has engaged in a series of public statements and actions designed to thwart the lawful investigation by Government prosecutors. Moreover, the President has made public announcements and assertions bearing on the Watergate case which the evidence will show he knew to be false.

These assertions, false assertions, impeachable, those who

misbehave. Those who "behave amiss or betray their public trust."

James Madison again at the Constitutional Convention: "A President is impeachable if he attempts to subvert the Constitution."

The Constitution charges the President with the task of taking care that the laws be faithfully executed, and yet the President has counseled his aides to commit perjury, willfully disregarded the secrecy of grand jury proceedings, concealed surreptitious entry, attempted to compromise a Federal judge while publicly displaying his cooperation with the processes of criminal justice.

"A President is impeachable if he attempts to subvert the Constitution."

If the impeachment provision in the Constitution of the United States will not reach the offenses charged here, then perhaps that 18th century Constitution should be abandoned to a 20th century paper shredder. Has the President committed offenses and planned and directed and acquiesced in a course of conduct which the Constitution will not tolerate? That is the question. We know that. We know the question. We should now forthwith proceed to answer the question. It is reason, and not passion, which must guide our deliberations, guide our debate, and guide our decision.

I yield back the balance of my time, Mr. Chairman.

RICHARD M. NIXON

Remarks on Leaving the White House

Washington, D.C., August 9, 1974

MEMBERS OF THE CABINET, members of the White House Staff, all of our friends here:

I think the record should show that this is one of those spontaneous things that we always arrange whenever the President comes in to speak, and it will be so reported in the press, and we don't mind, because they have to call it as they see it.

But on our part, believe me, it is spontaneous.

You are here to say goodby to us, and we don't have a good word for it in English—the best is *au revoir.* We will see you again.

I just met with the members of the White House staff, you know, those who serve here in the White House day in and day out, and I asked them to do what I ask all of you to do to the extent that you can and, of course, are requested to do so: to serve our next President as you have served me and previous Presidents—because many of you have been here for many years—with devotion and dedication, because this office, great as it is, can only be as great as the men and women who work for and with the President.

This house, for example—I was thinking of it as we walked down this hall, and I was comparing it to some of the great houses of the world that I have been in. This isn't the biggest house. Many, and most, in even smaller countries, are much bigger. This isn't the finest house. Many in Europe, particularly, and in China, Asia, have paintings of great, great value, things that we just don't have here and, probably, will never have until we are 1,000 years old or older.

But this is the best house. It is the best house, because it has something far more important than numbers of people who serve, far more important than numbers of rooms or how big it is, far more important than numbers of magnificent pieces of art.

This house has a great heart, and that heart comes from those who serve. I was rather sorry they didn't come down. We said goodby to them upstairs. But they are really great. And I recall after so many times I have made speeches, and some of them pretty tough, yet, I always come back, or after a hard day—and my days usually have run rather long—I would always get a lift from them, because I might be a little down but they always smiled.

And so it is with you. I look around here, and I see so many on this staff that, you know, I should have been by your offices and shaken hands, and I would love to have talked to you and found out how to run the world—everybody wants to tell the President what to do, and boy, he needs to be told many times —but I just haven't had the time. But I want you to know that each and every one of you, I know, is indispensable to this Government.

I am proud of this Cabinet. I am proud of all the members who have served in our Cabinet. I am proud of our sub-Cabinet. I am proud of our White House Staff. As I pointed out last night, sure, we have done some things wrong in this Administration, and the top man always takes the responsibility, and I have never ducked it. But I want to say one thing: We can be proud of it—5½ years. No man or no woman came into this Administration and left it with more of this world's goods than when he came in. No man or no woman ever profited at the public expense or the public till. That tells something about you.

Mistakes, yes. But for personal gain, never. You did what you believed in. Sometimes right, sometimes wrong. And I only wish that I were a wealthy man—at the present time, I have got to find a way to pay my taxes—[*laughter*]—and if I were, I would like to recompense you for the sacrifices that all of you have made to serve in government.

But you are getting something in government—and I want you to tell this to your children, and I hope the Nation's children will hear it, too—something in government service that is far more important than money. It is a cause bigger than yourself. It is the cause of making this the greatest nation in the world, the leader of the world, because without our leadership, the world will know nothing but war, possibly starvation or worse, in the years ahead. With our leadership it will know peace, it will know plenty.

We have been generous, and we will be more generous in the future as we are able to. But most important, we must be strong here, strong in our hearts, strong in our souls, strong in our belief, and strong in our willingness to sacrifice, as you have been willing to sacrifice, in a pecuniary way, to serve in government.

There is something else I would like for you to tell your young people. You know, people often come in and say, "What will I tell my kids?" They look at government and say, sort of a rugged life, and they see the mistakes that are made. They get the impression that everybody is here for the purpose of feathering his nest. That is why I made this earlier point—not in this Administration, not one single man or woman.

And I say to them, there are many fine careers. This country needs good farmers, good businessmen, good plumbers, good carpenters.

I remember my old man. I think that they would have called him sort of a little man, common man. He didn't consider himself that way. You know what he was? He was a streetcar motorman first, and then he was a farmer, and then he had a lemon ranch. It was the poorest lemon ranch in California, I can assure you. He sold it before they found oil on it. [*Laughter*] And then he was a grocer. But he was a great man, because he did his job, and every job counts up to the hilt, regardless of what happens.

Nobody will ever write a book, probably, about my mother. Well, I guess all of you would say this about your mother—my mother was a saint. And I think of her, two boys dying of tuberculosis, nursing four others in order that she could take care of my older brother for 3 years in Arizona, and seeing each of them die, and when they died, it was like one of her own.

Yes, she will have no books written about her. But she was a saint.

Now, however, we look to the future. I had a little quote in the speech last night from T.R. As you know, I kind of like to read books. I am not educated, but I do read books—[*laughter*]—and the T.R. quote was a pretty good one.

Here is another one I found as I was reading, my last night in the White House, and this quote is about a young man. He was a young lawyer in New York. He had married a beautiful girl, and they had a lovely daughter, and then suddenly she died, and this is what he wrote. This was in his diary.

He said, "She was beautiful in face and form and lovelier still in spirit. As a flower she grew and as a fair young flower she died. Her life had been always in the sunshine. There had never come to her a single great sorrow. None ever knew her who did not love and revere her for her bright and sunny temper and her saintly unselfishness. Fair, pure and joyous as a maiden, loving, tender and happy as a young wife. When she had just become a mother, when her life seemed to be just begun and when the years seemed so bright before her, then by a strange and terrible fate death came to her. And when my heart's dearest died, the light went from my life forever."

That was T.R. in his twenties. He thought the light had gone from his life forever—but he went on. And he not only became President but, as an ex-President, he served his country, always in the arena, tempestuous, strong, sometimes wrong, sometimes right, but he was a man.

And as I leave, let me say, that is an example I think all of us should remember. We think sometimes when things happen that don't go the right way; we think that when you don't pass the bar exam the first time—I happened to, but I was just lucky; I mean, my writing was so poor the bar examiner said, "We have just got to let the guy through." We think that when someone dear to us dies, we think that when we lose an election, we think that when we suffer a defeat that all is ended. We think, as T.R. said, that the light had left his life forever.

Not true. It is only a beginning, always. The young must know it; the old must know it. It must always sustain us, because the greatness comes not when things go always good for you, but the greatness comes and you are really tested, when you take some knocks, some disappointments, when sadness comes, because only if you have been in the deepest valley can you ever know how magnificent it is to be on the highest mountain.

And so I say to you on this occasion, as we leave, we leave proud of the people who have stood by us and worked for us and served this country.

We want you to be proud of what you have done. We want you to continue to serve in government, if that is your wish. Always give your best, never get discouraged, never be petty; always remember, others may hate you, but those who hate you don't win unless you hate them, and then you destroy yourself.

And so, we leave with high hopes, in good spirit, and with deep humility, and with very much gratefulness in our hearts. I can only say to each and every one of you, we come from many faiths, we pray perhaps to different gods—but really the same God in a sense—but I want to say for each and every one of you, not only will we always remember you, not only will we always be grateful to you but always you will be in our hearts and you will be in our prayers.

Thank you very much.

JIMMY CARTER

Address to the Nation on Energy Policy

Washington, D.C., July 15, 1979

G OOD EVENING.
This is a special night for me. Exactly 3 years ago, on July 15, 1976, I accepted the nomination of my party to run for President of the United States. I promised you a President who is not isolated from the people, who feels your pain, and who shares your dreams and who draws his strength and his wisdom from you.

During the past 3 years I've spoken to you on many occasions about national concerns, the energy crisis, reorganizing the Government, our Nation's economy, and issues of war and especially peace. But over those years the subjects of the speeches, the talks, and the press conferences have become increasingly narrow, focused more and more on what the isolated world of Washington thinks is important. Gradually, you've heard more and more about what the Government thinks or what the Government should be doing and less and less about our Nation's hopes, our dreams, and our vision of the future.

Ten days ago I had planned to speak to you again about a very important subject—energy. For the fifth time I would have described the urgency of the problem and laid out a series of legislative recommendations to the Congress. But as I was preparing to speak, I began to ask myself the same question that I now know has been troubling many of you. Why have we not been able to get together as a nation to resolve our serious energy problem?

It's clear that the true problems of our Nation are much deeper—deeper than gasoline lines or energy shortages, deeper even than inflation or recession. And I realize more than ever that as President I need your help. So, I decided to reach out and listen to the voices of America.

I invited to Camp David people from almost every segment

of our society—business and labor, teachers and preachers, Governors, mayors, and private citizens. And then I left Camp David to listen to other Americans, men and women like you. It has been an extraordinary 10 days, and I want to share with you what I've heard.

First of all, I got a lot of personal advice. Let me quote a few of the typical comments that I wrote down.

This from a southern Governor: "Mr. President, you are not leading this Nation—you're just managing the Government."

"You don't see the people enough any more."

"Some of your Cabinet members don't seem loyal. There is not enough discipline among your disciples."

"Don't talk to us about politics or the mechanics of government, but about an understanding of our common good."

"Mr. President, we're in trouble. Talk to us about blood and sweat and tears."

"If you lead, Mr. President, we will follow."

Many people talked about themselves and about the condition of our Nation. This from a young woman in Pennsylvania: "I feel so far from government. I feel like ordinary people are excluded from political power."

And this from a young Chicano: "Some of us have suffered from recession all our lives."

"Some people have wasted energy, but others haven't had anything to waste."

And this from a religious leader: "No material shortage can touch the important things like God's love for us or our love for one another."

And I like this one particularly from a black woman who happens to be the mayor of a small Mississippi town: "The bigshots are not the only ones who are important. Remember, you can't sell anything on Wall Street unless someone digs it up somewhere else first."

This kind of summarized a lot of other statements: "Mr. President, we are confronted with a moral and a spiritual crisis."

Several of our discussions were on energy, and I have a notebook full of comments and advice. I'll read just a few.

"We can't go on consuming 40 percent more energy than we produce. When we import oil we are also importing inflation plus unemployment."

"We've got to use what we have. The Middle East has only 5 percent of the world's energy, but the United States has 24 percent."

And this is one of the most vivid statements: "Our neck is stretched over the fence and OPEC has a knife."

"There will be other cartels and other shortages. American wisdom and courage right now can set a path to follow in the future."

This was a good one: "Be bold. Mr. President. We may make mistakes, but we are ready to experiment."

And this one from a labor leader got to the heart of it: "The real issue is freedom. We must deal with the energy problem on a war footing."

And the last that I'll read: "When we enter the moral equivalent of war, Mr. President, don't issue us BB guns."

These 10 days confirmed my belief in the decency and the strength and the wisdom of the American people, but it also bore out some of my longstanding concerns about our Nation's underlying problems.

I know, of course, being President, that government actions and legislation can be very important. That's why I've worked hard to put my campaign promises into law—and I have to admit, with just mixed success. But after listening to the American people I have been reminded again that all the legislation in the world can't fix what's wrong with America. So, I want to speak to you first tonight about a subject even more serious than energy or inflation. I want to talk to you right now about a fundamental threat to American democracy.

I do not mean our political and civil liberties. They will endure. And I do not refer to the outward strength of America, a nation that is at peace tonight everywhere in the world, with unmatched economic power and military might.

The threat is nearly invisible in ordinary ways. It is a crisis of confidence. It is a crisis that strikes at the very heart and soul and spirit of our national will. We can see this crisis in the growing doubt about the meaning of our own lives and in the loss of a unity of purpose for our Nation.

The erosion of our confidence in the future is threatening to destroy the social and the political fabric of America.

The confidence that we have always had as a people is not

simply some romantic dream or a proverb in a dusty book that we read just on the Fourth of July. It is the idea which founded our Nation and has guided our development as a people. Confidence in the future has supported everything else—public institutions and private enterprise, our own families, and the very Constitution of the United States. Confidence has defined our course and has served as a link between generations. We've always believed in something called progress. We've always had a faith that the days of our children would be better than our own.

Our people are losing that faith, not only in government itself but in the ability as citizens to serve as the ultimate rulers and shapers of our democracy. As a people we know our past and we are proud of it. Our progress has been part of the living history of America, even the world. We always believed that we were part of a great movement of humanity itself called democracy, involved in the search for freedom, and that belief has always strengthened us in our purpose. But just as we are losing our confidence in the future, we are also beginning to close the door on our past.

In a nation that was proud of hard work, strong families, close-knit communities, and our faith in God, too many of us now tend to worship self-indulgence and consumption. Human identity is no longer defined by what one does, but by what one owns. But we've discovered that owning things and consuming things does not satisfy our longing for meaning. We've learned that piling up material goods cannot fill the emptiness of lives which have no confidence or purpose.

The symptoms of this crisis of the American spirit are all around us. For the first time in the history of our country a majority of our people believe that the next 5 years will be worse than the past 5 years. Two-thirds of our people do not even vote. The productivity of American workers is actually dropping, and the willingness of Americans to save for the future has fallen below that of all other people in the Western world.

As you know, there is a growing disrespect for government and for churches and for schools, the news media, and other institutions. This is not a message of happiness or reassurance, but it is the truth and it is a warning.

These changes did not happen overnight. They've come upon us gradually over the last generation, years that were filled with shocks and tragedy.

We were sure that ours was a nation of the ballot, not the bullet, until the murders of John Kennedy and Robert Kennedy and Martin Luther King, Jr. We were taught that our armies were always invincible and our causes were always just, only to suffer the agony of Vietnam. We respected the Presidency as a place of honor until the shock of Watergate.

We remember when the phrase "sound as a dollar" was an expression of absolute dependability, until 10 years of inflation began to shrink our dollar and our savings. We believed that our Nation's resources were limitless until 1973, when we had to face a growing dependence on foreign oil.

These wounds are still very deep. They have never been healed.

Looking for a way out of this crisis, our people have turned to the Federal Government and found it isolated from the mainstream of our Nation's life. Washington, D.C., has become an island. The gap between our citizens and our Government has never been so wide. The people are looking for honest answers, not easy answers; clear leadership, not false claims and evasiveness and politics as usual.

What you see too often in Washington and elsewhere around the country is a system of government that seems incapable of action. You see a Congress twisted and pulled in every direction by hundreds of well-financed and powerful special interests. You see every extreme position defended to the last vote, almost to the last breath by one unyielding group or another. You often see a balanced and a fair approach that demands sacrifice, a little sacrifice from everyone, abandoned like an orphan without support and without friends.

Often you see paralysis and stagnation and drift. You don't like it, and neither do I. What can we do?

First of all, we must face the truth, and then we can change our course. We simply must have faith in each other, faith in our ability to govern ourselves, and faith in the future of this Nation. Restoring that faith and that confidence to America is now the most important task we face. It is a true challenge of this generation of Americans.

One of the visitors to Camp David last week put it this way: "We've got to stop crying and start sweating, stop talking and start walking, stop cursing and start praying. The strength we need will not come from the White House, but from every house in America."

We know the strength of America. We are strong. We can regain our unity. We can regain our confidence. We are the heirs of generations who survived threats much more powerful and awesome than those that challenge us now. Our fathers and mothers were strong men and women who shaped a new society during the Great Depression, who fought world wars, and who carved out a new charter of peace for the world.

We ourselves are the same Americans who just 10 years ago put a man on the Moon. We are the generation that dedicated our society to the pursuit of human rights and equality. And we are the generation that will win the war on the energy problem and in that process rebuild the unity and confidence of America.

We are at a turning point in our history. There are two paths to choose. One is a path I've warned about tonight, the path that leads to fragmentation and self-interest. Down that road lies a mistaken idea of freedom, the right to grasp for ourselves some advantage over others. That path would be one of constant conflict between narrow interests ending in chaos and immobility. It is a certain route to failure.

All the traditions of our past, all the lessons of our heritage, all the promises of our future point to another path, the path of common purpose and the restoration of American values. That path leads to true freedom for our Nation and ourselves. We can take the first steps down that path as we begin to solve our energy problem.

Energy will be the immediate test of our ability to unite this Nation, and it can also be the standard around which we rally. On the battlefield of energy we can win for our Nation a new confidence, and we can seize control again of our common destiny.

In little more than two decades we've gone from a position of energy independence to one in which almost half the oil we use comes from foreign countries, at prices that are going through the roof. Our excessive dependence on OPEC has already taken a tremendous toll on our economy and our people. This is the direct cause of the long lines which have made millions of you spend aggravating hours waiting for gasoline. It's a cause of the increased inflation and unemployment that we now face. This intolerable dependence on foreign oil threatens our economic independence and the very security of our Nation.

The energy crisis is real. It is worldwide. It is a clear and present danger to our Nation. These are facts and we simply must face them.

What I have to say to you now about energy is simple and vitally important.

Point one: I am tonight setting a clear goal for the energy policy of the United States. Beginning this moment, this Nation will never use more foreign oil than we did in 1977—never. From now on, every new addition to our demand for energy will be met from our own production and our own conservation. The generation-long growth in our dependence on foreign oil will be stopped dead in its tracks right now and then reversed as we move through the 1980's, for I am tonight setting the further goal of cutting our dependence on foreign oil by one-half by the end of the next decade—a saving of over 4½ million barrels of imported oil per day.

Point two: To ensure that we meet these targets, I will use my Presidential authority to set import quotas. I'm announcing tonight that for 1979 and 1980, I will forbid the entry into this country of one drop of foreign oil more than these goals allow. These quotas will ensure a reduction in imports even below the ambitious levels we set at the recent Tokyo summit.

Point three: To give us energy security, I am asking for the most massive peacetime commitment of funds and resources in our Nation's history to develop America's own alternative sources of fuel—from coal, from oil shale, from plant products for gasohol, from unconventional gas, from the Sun.

I propose the creation of an energy security corporation to lead this effort to replace 2½ million barrels of imported oil per day by 1990. The corporation will issue up to $5 billion in energy bonds, and I especially want them to be in small denominations so that average Americans can invest directly in America's energy security.

Just as a similar synthetic rubber corporation helped us win World War II, so will we mobilize American determination and ability to win the energy war. Moreover, I will soon submit legislation to Congress calling for the creation of this Nation's first solar bank, which will help us achieve the crucial goal of 20 percent of our energy coming from solar power by the year 2000.

These efforts will cost money, a lot of money, and that is why Congress must enact the windfall profits tax without delay. It will be money well spent. Unlike the billions of dollars that we ship to foreign countries to pay for foreign oil, these funds will be paid by Americans to Americans. These funds will go to fight, not to increase, inflation and unemployment.

Point four: I'm asking Congress to mandate, to require as a matter of law, that our Nation's utility companies cut their massive use of oil by 50 percent within the next decade and switch to other fuels, especially coal, our most abundant energy source.

Point five: To make absolutely certain that nothing stands in the way of achieving these goals, I will urge Congress to create an energy mobilization board which, like the War Production Board in World War II, will have the responsibility and authority to cut through the redtape, the delays, and the endless roadblocks to completing key energy projects.

We will protect our environment. But when this Nation critically needs a refinery or a pipeline, we will build it.

Point six: I'm proposing a bold conservation program to involve every State, county, and city and every average American in our energy battle. This effort will permit you to build conservation into your homes and your lives at a cost you can afford.

I ask Congress to give me authority for mandatory conservation and for standby gasoline rationing. To further conserve energy, I'm proposing tonight an extra $10 billion over the next decade to strengthen our public transportation systems. And I'm asking you for your good and for your Nation's security to take no unnecessary trips, to use carpools or public transportation whenever you can, to park your car one extra day per week, to obey the speed limit, and to set your thermostats to save fuel. Every act of energy conservation like this is more than just common sense—I tell you it is an act of patriotism.

Our Nation must be fair to the poorest among us, so we will increase aid to needy Americans to cope with rising energy prices. We often think of conservation only in terms of sacrifice. In fact, it is the most painless and immediate way of rebuilding our Nation's strength. Every gallon of oil each one of us saves is a new form of production. It gives us more freedom, more confidence, that much more control over our own lives.

So, the solution of our energy crisis can also help us to conquer the crisis of the spirit in our country. It can rekindle our sense of unity, our confidence in the future, and give our Nation and all of us individually a new sense of purpose.

You know we can do it. We have the natural resources. We have more oil in our shale alone than several Saudi Arabias. We have more coal than any nation on Earth. We have the world's highest level of technology. We have the most skilled work force, with innovative genius, and I firmly believe that we have the national will to win this war.

I do not promise you that this struggle for freedom will be easy. I do not promise a quick way out of our Nation's problems, when the truth is that the only way out is an all-out effort. What I do promise you is that I will lead our fight, and I will enforce fairness in our struggle, and I will ensure honesty. And above all, I will act.

We can manage the short-term shortages more effectively and we will, but there are no short-term solutions to our long-range problems. There is simply no way to avoid sacrifice.

Twelve hours from now I will speak again in Kansas City, to expand and to explain further our energy program. Just as the search for solutions to our energy shortages has now led us to a new awareness of our Nation's deeper problems, so our willingness to work for those solutions in energy can strengthen us to attack those deeper problems.

I will continue to travel this country, to hear the people of America. You can help me to develop a national agenda for the 1980's. I will listen and I will act. We will act together. These were the promises I made 3 years ago, and I intend to keep them.

Little by little we can and we must rebuild our confidence. We can spend until we empty our treasuries, and we may summon all the wonders of science. But we can succeed only if we tap our greatest resources—America's people, America's values, and America's confidence.

I have seen the strength of America in the inexhaustible resources of our people. In the days to come, let us renew that strength in the struggle for an energy-secure nation.

In closing, let me say this: I will do my best, but I will not do it alone. Let your voice be heard. Whenever you have a chance, say something good about our country. With God's help and for the sake of our Nation, it is time for us to join hands in America. Let us commit ourselves together to a rebirth of the American spirit. Working together with our common faith we cannot fail.

Thank you and good night.

EDWARD M. KENNEDY

Speech to the Democratic National Convention

New York City, August 12, 1980

I THANK YOU for your eloquent introduction. Well, things worked out a little different from the way I thought, but let me tell you, I still love New York.

My fellow Democrats and my fellow Americans.

I have come here tonight not to argue as a candidate but to affirm a cause.

I'm asking you to renew the commitment of the Democratic Party to economic justice. I am asking you to renew our commitment to a fair and lasting prosperity that can put America back to work.

This is the cause that brought me into the campaign and that sustained me for nine months, across a hundred thousand miles in 40 different states. We had our losses, but the pain of our defeat is far, far less than the pain of the people that I have met. We have learned that it is important to take issues seriously, but never to take ourselves too seriously.

The serious issue before us tonight is the cause for which the Democratic Party has stood in its finest hours, the cause that keeps our party young and makes it, in the second century of its age, the largest political party in this republic and the longest lasting political party on this planet.

Our cause has been, since the days of Thomas Jefferson, the cause of the common man and the common woman. Our commitment has been, since the days of Andrew Jackson, to all those he called "the humble members of society—the farmers, mechanics and laborers." On this foundation we have defined our values, refined our policies and refreshed our faith.

Now I take the unusual step of carrying the cause and the commitment of my campaign personally to our national convention. I speak out of a deep sense of urgency about the anguish and anxiety I have seen across America. I speak out of a deep belief in the ideals of the Democratic Party and in the potential of that party and of a President to make a difference. And I speak out of a deep trust in our capacity to proceed with boldness and a common vision that will feel and heal the suffering of our time and the divisions of our party.

The economic plank of this platform on its face concerns only material things, but it is also a moral issue that I raise tonight. It has taken many forms over many years. In this campaign, and in this country that we seek to lead, the challenge in 1980 is to give our voice and our vote for these fundamental democratic principles:

- Let us pledge that we will never misuse unemployment, high interest rates and human misery as false weapons against inflation.

- Let us pledge that employment will be the first priority of our economic policy.

- Let us pledge that there will be security for all those who are now at work. And let us pledge that there will be jobs for all who are out of work. And we will not compromise on the issues of jobs.

These are not simplistic pledges. Simply put, they are the heart of our tradition; and they have been the soul of our party across the generations. It is the glory and the greatness of our tradition to speak for those who have no voice, to remember those who are forgotten, to respond to the frustrations and fulfill the aspirations of all Americans seeking a better life in a better land.

We dare not forsake that tradition. We cannot let the great purposes of the Democratic Party become the bygone passages of history. We must not permit the Republicans to seize and run on the slogans of prosperity.

We heard the orators at their convention all trying to talk like Democrats. They proved that even Republican nominees can quote Franklin Roosevelt to their own purpose. The Grand Old Party thinks it has found a great new trick. But 40 years ago, an earlier generation of Republicans attempted the same trick. And Franklin Roosevelt himself replied: "Most Republican leaders have bitterly fought and blocked the forward surge of average men and women in their pursuit of happiness. Let us not be deluded that overnight those leaders have suddenly become the friends of average men and women. You know," he continued, "very few of us are that gullible."

And four years later, when the Republicans tried that trick again, Franklin Roosevelt asked: "Can the Old Guard pass itself off as the New Deal? I think not. We have all seen many marvelous stunts in the circus, but no performing elephant could turn a handspring without falling flat on its back."

The 1980 Republican convention was awash with crocodile tears for our economic distress, but it is by their long record and not their recent words that you shall know them.

The same Republicans who are talking about the crisis of unemployment have nominated a man who once said, and I quote, "Unemployment insurance is a prepaid vacation plan for freeloaders." And that nominee is no friend of labor.

The same Republicans who are talking about the problems of the inner cities have nominated a man who said, and I quote, "I have included in my morning and evening prayers every day the prayer that the Federal Government not bail out New York." And that nominee is no friend of this city and our great urban centers across this nation.

The same Republicans who are talking about security for the elderly have nominated a man who said just four years ago that participation in Social Security "should be made voluntary." And that nominee is no friend of the senior citizen of this nation.

The same Republicans who are talking about preserving the environment have nominated a man who last year made the preposterous statement, and I quote: "Eighty percent of air pollution comes from plants and trees." And that nominee is no friend of the environment.

And the same Republicans who are invoking Franklin Roosevelt have nominated a man who said in 1976, and these are his exact words: "Fascism was really the basis of the New Deal." And that nominee, whose name is Ronald Reagan, has no right to quote Franklin Delano Roosevelt.

The great adventure which our opponents offer is a voyage into the past. Progress is our heritage, not theirs. What is right for us as Democrats is also the right way for Democrats to win.

The commitment I seek is not to outworn views, but to old

values that will never wear out. Programs may sometimes become obsolete, but the ideal of fairness always endures. Circumstances may change, but the work of compassion must continue. It is surely correct that we cannot solve problems by throwing money at them, but it is also correct that we dare not throw out our national problems onto a scrap heap of inattention and indifference. The poor may be out of political fashion, but they are not without human needs. The middle class may be angry, but they have not lost the dream that all Americans can advance together.

The demand of our people in 1980 is not for smaller government or bigger government but for better government. Some say that government is always bad and that spending for basic social programs is the root of our economic evils. But we reply, the present inflation and recession costs our economy $200 billion a year. We reply, inflation and unemployment are the biggest spenders of all.

The task of leadership in 1980 is not to parade scapegoats or to seek refuge in reaction but to match our power to the possibilities of progress.

While others talked of free enterprise, it was the Democratic Party that acted—and we ended excessive regulation in the airline and trucking industry. We restored competition to the marketplace. And I take some satisfaction that this deregulation legislation that I sponsored and passed in the Congress of the United States.

As Democrats, we recognize that each generation of Americans has a rendevous with a different reality. The answers of one generation become the questions of the next generation, but there is a guiding star in the American firmament. It is as old as the revolutionary belief that all people are created equal, and as clear as the contemporary condition of Liberty City and the South Bronx. Again and again, Democratic leaders have followed that star, and they have given new meaning to the old values of liberty and justice for all.

We are the party of the New Freedom, the New Deal and the New Frontier. We have always been the party of hope. So this year, let us offer new hope—new hope to an America uncertain about the present but unsurpassed in its potential for the future.

To all those who are idle in the cities and industries of America, let us provide new hope for the dignity of useful work. Democrats have always believed that a basic civil right of all Americans is that their right to earn their own way. The party of the people must always be the party of full employment.

To all those who doubt the future of our economy, let us provide new hope for the reindustrialization of America. And let our vision reach beyond the next election or the next year to a new generation of prosperity. If we could rebuild Germany and Japan after World War II, then surely we can reindustrialize our own nation and revive our inner cities in the 1980's.

To all those who work hard for a living wage, let us provide new hope that their price of their employment shall not be an unsafe work place and a death at an earlier age.

To all those who inhabit our land, from California to the New York island, from the Redwood forest to the Gulf Stream waters, let us provide new hope that prosperity shall not be purchased by poisoning the air, the rivers and the natural resources that are the greatest gift of this continent. We must insist that our children and grandchildren shall inherit a land which they can truly call America the Beautiful.

To all those who see the worth of their work and their savings taken by inflation, let us offer new hope for a stable economy. We must meet the pressures of the present by invoking the full power of government to master increasing prices. In candor, we must say that the Federal budget can be balanced only by policies that bring us to a balanced prosperity of full employment and price restraint.

And to all those overburdened by an unfair tax structure, let us provide new hope for real tax reform. Instead of shutting down classrooms, let us shut off tax shelters. Instead of cutting out school lunches, let us cut off tax subsidies for expensive business lunches that are nothing more than food stamps for the rich.

The tax cut of our Republican opponent takes the name of tax reform in vain. It is a wonderfully Republican idea that would redistribute income in the wrong direction. It's good news for any of you with incomes over $200,000 a year. For the few of you, it offers a pot of gold worth $14,000. But the

Republican tax cut is bad news for the middle-income families. For the many of you, they plan a pittance of $200 a year. And that is not what the Democratic Party means when we say tax reform.

The vast majority of Americans cannot afford this panacea from a Republican nominee who has denounced the progressive income tax as the invention of Karl Marx. I am afraid he has confused Karl Marx with Theodore Roosevelt, that obscure Republican President who sought and fought for a tax system based on ability to pay. Theodore Roosevelt was not Karl Marx, and the Republican tax scheme is not tax reform.

Finally, we cannot have a fair prosperity and isolation from a fair society.

So I will continue to stand for a national health insurance. We must—we must not surrender—we must not surrender to the relentless medical inflation that can bankrupt almost anyone, and that may soon break the budgets of governments at every level.

Let us insist on real controls over what doctors and hospitals can charge. And let us resolve that the state of a family's health shall never depend on the size of a family's wealth.

The President, the Vice President, the members of Congress have a medical plan that meets their needs in full. And whenever senators and representatives catch a little cold, the Capitol physician will see them immediately, treat them promptly, fill a prescription on the spot. We do not get a bill even if we ask for it. And when do you think was the last time a member of Congress asked for a bill from the Federal Government?

And I say again as I have said before: If health insurance is good enough for the President, the Vice President, the Congress of the United States, then it's good enough for you and every family in America.

There were some—there were some who said we should be silent about our differences on issues during this convention. But the heritage of the Democratic Party has been a history of democracy. We fight hard because we care deeply about our principles and purposes. We did not flee this struggle. We welcome the contrast with the empty and expedient spectacle last month in Detroit where no nomination was contested, no question was debated and no one dared to raise any doubt or dissent.

Democrats can be proud that we chose a different course—and a different platform.

We can be proud that our party stands for investment in safe energy instead of a nuclear future that may threaten the future itself. We must not permit the neighborhoods of America to be permanently shadowed by the fear of another Three Mile Island.

We can be proud that our party stands for a fair housing law to unlock the doors of discrimination once and for all. The American house will be divided against itself so long as there is prejudice against any American buying or renting a home.

And we can be proud that our party stands plainly and publicly, and persistently for the ratification of the equal rights amendment. Women hold their rightful place at our convention; and women must have their rightful place in the Constitution of the United States. On this issue, we will not yield, we will not equivocate, we will not rationalize, explain or excuse. We will stand for E.R.A. and for the recognition at long last that our nation was made up of founding mothers as well as founding fathers.

A fair prosperity and a just society are within our vision and our grasp. And we do not have every answer. There are questions not yet asked, waiting for us in the recesses of the future.

But of this much we can be certain, because it is the lesson of all of our history:

Together a President and the people can make a difference. I have found that faith still alive wherever I have traveled across this land. So let us reject the counsel of retreat and the call to reaction. Let us go forward in the knowledge that history only helps those who help themselves. There will be setbacks and sacrifices in the years ahead. But I am convinced that we as a people are ready to give something back to our country in return for all it has given to us. Let this—let this be our commitment: Whatever sacrifices must be made will be shared—and shared fairly. And let this be our confidence at the end of our journey and always before us shines that ideal of liberty and justice for all.

In closing, let me say a few words to all those that I have met and all those who have supported me at this convention and across the country. There were hard hours on our journey. And often we sailed against the wind, but always we kept our rudder true. And there were so many of you who stayed the course and shared our hope. You gave your help; but even more, you gave your hearts. And because of you, this has been a happy campaign. You welcomed Joan, me and our family into your homes and neighborhoods, your churches, your campuses, your union halls. And when I think back on all the miles and all the months and all the memories, I think of you. And I recall the poet's words, and I say: "What golden friends I had." Among you, my golden friends across this land, I have listened and learned.

I have listened to Kenny Dubois, a glass-blower in Charleston, W. Va., who has 10 children to support but has lost his job after 35 years, just three years short of qualifying for his pension.

I have listened to the Trachta family, who farm in Iowa and who wonder whether they can pass the good life and the good earth on to their children.

I have listened to the grandmother in East Los Angeles—in East Oakland—who no longer has a phone to call her grandchildren, because she gave it up to pay the rent on her small apartment.

I have listened to young workers out of work, to students without the tuition for college and to families without the chance to own a home. I have seen the closed factories and the stalled assembly lines of Anderson, Ind., and Southgate, Calif. And I have seen too many—far too many—idle men and women desperate to work. I have seen too many—far too many—working families desperate to protect the value of their wages from the ravages of inflation.

Yet I have also sensed a yearning for new hope among the people in every state where I have been. And I have felt it in their handshakes; I saw it in their faces. And I shall never forget the mothers who carried children to our rallies. I shall always remember the elderly who have lived in an America of high purpose and who believe that it can all happen again.

Tonight, in their name, I have come here to speak for them.

And for their sake I ask you to stand with them. On their behalf I ask you to restate and reaffirm the timeless truth of our party.

I congratulate President Carter on his victory here. I am—I am confident that the Democratic Party will reunite on the basis of Democratic principles—and that together we will march toward a Democratic victory in 1980.

And someday, long after this convention, long after the signs come down, and the crowds stop cheering, and the bands stop playing, may it be said of our campaign that we kept the faith. May it be said of our party in 1980 that we found our faith again.

And may it be said of us, both in dark passages and in bright days, in the words of Tennyson that my brothers quoted and loved and that have special meaning for me now:

> I am a part of all that I have met . . .
> Tho' much is taken, much abides . . .
> That which we are, we are—
> One equal temper of heroic heart . . . strong in will
> To strive, to seek, to find and not to yield.

For me, a few hours ago, this campaign came to an end. For all those whose cares have been our concern, the work goes on, the cause endures, the hope still lives and the dream shall never die.

RONALD REAGAN

Address to Members of Parliament

London, June 8, 1982

M<small>Y</small> L<small>ORD</small> C<small>HANCELLOR</small>, M<small>R</small>. S<small>PEAKER</small>:
The journey of which this visit forms a part is a long one. Already it has taken me to two great cities of the West, Rome and Paris, and to the economic summit at Versailles. And there, once again, our sister democracies have proved that even in a time of severe economic strain, free peoples can work together freely and voluntarily to address problems as serious as inflation, unemployment, trade, and economic development in a spirit of cooperation and solidarity.

Other milestones lie ahead. Later this week, in Germany, we and our NATO allies will discuss measures for our joint defense and America's latest initiatives for a more peaceful, secure world through arms reductions.

Each stop of this trip is important, but among them all, this moment occupies a special place in my heart and in the hearts of my countrymen—a moment of kinship and homecoming in these hallowed halls.

Speaking for all Americans, I want to say how very much at home we feel in your house. Every American would, because this is, as we have been so eloquently told, one of democracy's shrines. Here the rights of free people and the processes of representation have been debated and refined.

It has been said that an institution is the lengthening shadow of a man. This institution is the lengthening shadow of all the men and women who have sat here and all those who have voted to send representatives here.

This is my second visit to Great Britain as President of the United States. My first opportunity to stand on British soil occurred almost a year and a half ago when your Prime Minister graciously hosted a diplomatic dinner at the British Embassy in Washington. Mrs. Thatcher said then that she hoped I was not distressed to find staring down at me from the grand staircase a portrait of His Royal Majesty King George III. She suggested it was best to let bygones be bygones, and in view of our two countries' remarkable friendship in succeeding years, she added that most Englishmen today would agree with Thomas Jefferson that "a little rebellion now and then is a very good thing." [*Laughter*]

Well, from here I will go to Bonn and then Berlin, where there stands a grim symbol of power untamed. The Berlin Wall, that dreadful gray gash across the city, is in its third decade. It is the fitting signature of the regime that built it.

And a few hundred kilometers behind the Berlin Wall, there is another symbol. In the center of Warsaw, there is a sign that notes the distances to two capitals. In one direction it points toward Moscow. In the other it points toward Brussels, headquarters of Western Europe's tangible unity. The marker says that the distances from Warsaw to Moscow and Warsaw to Brussels are equal. The sign makes this point: Poland is not East or West. Poland is at the center of European civilization. It has contributed mightily to that civilization. It is doing so today by being magnificently unreconciled to oppression.

Poland's struggle to be Poland and to secure the basic rights we often take for granted demonstrates why we dare not take those rights for granted. Gladstone, defending the Reform Bill of 1866, declared, "You cannot fight against the future. Time is on our side." It was easier to believe in the march of democracy in Gladstone's day—in that high noon of Victorian optimism.

We're approaching the end of a bloody century plagued by a terrible political invention—totalitarianism. Optimism comes less easily today, not because democracy is less vigorous, but because democracy's enemies have refined their instruments of repression. Yet optimism is in order, because day by day democracy is proving itself to be a not-at-all-fragile flower. From Stettin on the Baltic to Varna on the Black Sea, the regimes planted by totalitarianism have had more than 30 years to establish their legitimacy. But none—not one regime—has yet been able to risk free elections. Regimes planted by bayonets do not take root.

The strength of the Solidarity movement in Poland demonstrates the truth told in an underground joke in the Soviet Union. It is that the Soviet Union would remain a one-party nation even if an opposition party were permitted, because everyone would join the opposition party. [*Laughter*]

America's time as a player on the stage of world history has been brief. I think understanding this fact has always made you patient with your younger cousins—well, not always patient. I do recall that on one occasion, Sir Winston Churchill said in exasperation about one of our most distinguished diplomats: "He is the only case I know of a bull who carries his china shop with him." [*Laughter*]

But witty as Sir Winston was, he also had that special attribute of great statesmen—the gift of vision, the willingness to see the future based on the experience of the past. It is this sense of history, this understanding of the past that I want to talk with you about today, for it is in remembering what we share of the past that our two nations can make common cause for the future.

We have not inherited an easy world. If developments like the Industrial Revolution, which began here in England, and the gifts of science and technology have made life much easier for us, they have also made it more dangerous. There are threats now to our freedom, indeed to our very existence, that other generations could never even have imagined.

There is first the threat of global war. No President, no Congress, no Prime Minister, no Parliament can spend a day entirely free of this threat. And I don't have to tell you that in today's world the existence of nuclear weapons could mean, if not the extinction of mankind, then surely the end of civilization as we know it. That's why negotiations on intermediate-range nuclear forces now underway in Europe and the START talks—Strategic Arms Reduction Talks—which will begin later this month, are not just critical to American or Western policy; they are critical to mankind. Our commitment to early success in these negotiations is firm and unshakable, and our purpose is clear: reducing the risk of war by reducing the means of waging war on both sides.

At the same time there is a threat posed to human freedom by the enormous power of the modern state. History teaches the dangers of government that overreaches—political control taking precedence over free economic growth, secret police, mindless bureaucracy, all combining to stifle individual excellence and personal freedom.

Now, I'm aware that among us here and throughout Europe there is legitimate disagreement over the extent to which the public sector should play a role in a nation's economy and life. But on one point all of us are united—our abhorrence of dictatorship in all its forms, but most particularly totalitarianism and the terrible inhumanities it has caused in our time— the great purge, Auschwitz and Dachau, the Gulag, and Cambodia.

Historians looking back at our time will note the consistent restraint and peaceful intentions of the West. They will note that it was the democracies who refused to use the threat of their nuclear monopoly in the forties and early fifties for territorial or imperial gain. Had that nuclear monopoly been in the hands of the Communist world, the map of Europe—indeed, the world—would look very different today. And certainly they will note it was not the democracies that invaded Afghanistan or suppressed Polish Solidarity or used chemical and toxin warfare in Afghanistan and Southeast Asia.

If history teaches anything it teaches self-delusion in the face of unpleasant facts is folly. We see around us today the marks of our terrible dilemma—predictions of doomsday, antinuclear demonstrations, an arms race in which the West must, for its own protection, be an unwilling participant. At the same time we see totalitarian forces in the world who seek subversion and conflict around the globe to further their barbarous assault on the human spirit. What, then, is our course? Must civilization perish in a hail of fiery atoms? Must freedom wither in a quiet, deadening accommodation with totalitarian evil?

Sir Winston Churchill refused to accept the inevitability of war or even that it was imminent. He said, "I do not believe that Soviet Russia desires war. What they desire is the fruits of war and the indefinite expansion of their power and doctrines. But what we have to consider here today while time remains is the permanent prevention of war and the establishment of conditions of freedom and democracy as rapidly as possible in all countries."

Well, this is precisely our mission today: to preserve freedom as well as peace. It may not be easy to see; but I believe we live now at a turning point.

In an ironic sense Karl Marx was right. We are witnessing today a great revolutionary crisis, a crisis where the demands of the economic order are conflicting directly with those of the political order. But the crisis is happening not in the free, non-Marxist West, but in the home of Marxist-Leninism, the Soviet Union. It is the Soviet Union that runs against the tide of history by denying human freedom and human dignity to its citizens. It also is in deep economic difficulty. The rate of growth in the national product has been steadily declining since the fifties and is less than half of what it was then.

The dimensions of this failure are astounding: A country which employs one-fifth of its population in agriculture is unable to feed its own people. Were it not for the private sector, the tiny private sector tolerated in Soviet agriculture, the country might be on the brink of famine. These private plots occupy a bare 3 percent of the arable land but account for nearly one-quarter of Soviet farm output and nearly one-third of meat products and vegetables. Overcentralized, with little or no incentives, year after year the Soviet system pours its best resource into the making of instruments of destruction. The constant shrinkage of economic growth combined with the growth of military production is putting a heavy strain on the Soviet people. What we see here is a political structure that no longer corresponds to its economic base, a society where productive forces are hampered by political ones.

The decay of the Soviet experiment should come as no surprise to us. Wherever the comparisons have been made between free and closed societies—West Germany and East Germany, Austria and Czechoslovakia, Malaysia and Vietnam—it is the democratic countries that are prosperous and responsive to the needs of their people. And one of the simple but overwhelming facts of our time is this: Of all the millions of refugees we've seen in the modern world, their flight is always away from, not toward the Communist world. Today on the NATO line, our military forces face east to prevent a possible invasion. On the other side of the line, the Soviet forces also face east to prevent their people from leaving.

The hard evidence of totalitarian rule has caused in mankind an uprising of the intellect and will. Whether it is the growth of the new schools of economics in America or England or the appearance of the so-called new philosophers in France, there is one unifying thread running through the intellectual work of these groups—rejection of the arbitrary power of the state, the refusal to subordinate the rights of the individual to the superstate, the realization that collectivism stifles all the best human impulses.

Since the exodus from Egypt, historians have written of those who sacrificed and struggled for freedom—the stand at Thermopylae, the revolt of Spartacus, the storming of the Bastille, the Warsaw uprising in World War II. More recently we've seen evidence of this same human impulse in one of the developing nations in Central America. For months and months the world news media covered the fighting in El Salvador. Day after day we were treated to stories and film slanted toward the brave freedom-fighters battling oppressive government forces in behalf of the silent, suffering people of that tortured country.

And then one day those silent, suffering people were offered a chance to vote, to choose the kind of government they wanted. Suddenly the freedom-fighters in the hills were exposed for what they really are—Cuban-backed guerrillas who want power for themselves, and their backers, not democracy for the people. They threatened death to any who voted, and destroyed hundreds of buses and trucks to keep the people from getting to the polling places. But on election day, the people of El Salvador, an unprecedented 1.4 million of them, braved ambush and gunfire, and trudged for miles to vote for freedom.

They stood for hours in the hot sun waiting for their turn to vote. Members of our Congress who went there as observers told me of a women who was wounded by rifle fire on the way to the polls, who refused to leave the line to have her wound treated until after she had voted. A grandmother, who had been told by the guerrillas she would be killed when she returned from the polls, and she told the guerrillas, "You can kill me, you can kill my family, kill my neighbors, but you can't kill us all." The real freedom-fighters of El Salvador turned out to be the people of that country—the young, the old, the in-between.

Strange, but in my own country there's been little if any news coverage of that war since the election. Now, perhaps they'll say it's—well, because there are newer struggles now.

On distant islands in the South Atlantic young men are fighting for Britain. And, yes, voices have been raised protesting their sacrifice for lumps of rock and earth so far away. But those young men aren't fighting for mere real estate. They fight for a cause—for the belief that armed aggression must not be allowed to succeed, and the people must participate in the decisions of government—[*applause*]—the decisions of government under the rule of law. If there had been firmer support for that principle some 45 years ago, perhaps our generation wouldn't have suffered the bloodletting of World War II.

In the Middle East now the guns sound once more, this time in Lebanon, a country that for too long has had to endure the tragedy of civil war, terrorism, and foreign intervention and occupation. The fighting in Lebanon on the part of all parties must stop, and Israel should bring its forces home. But this is not enough. We must all work to stamp out the scourge of terrorism that in the Middle East makes war an ever-present threat.

But beyond the troublespots lies a deeper, more positive pattern. Around the world today, the democratic revolution is gathering new strength. In India a critical test has been passed with the peaceful change of governing political parties. In Africa, Nigeria is moving into remarkable and unmistakable ways to build and strengthen its democratic institutions. In the Caribbean and Central America, 16 of 24 countries have freely elected governments. And in the United Nations, 8 of the 10 developing nations which have joined that body in the past 5 years are democracies.

In the Communist world as well, man's instinctive desire for freedom and self-determination surfaces again and again. To be sure, there are grim reminders of how brutally the police state attempts to snuff out this quest for self-rule—1953 in East Germany, 1956 in Hungary, 1968 in Czechoslovakia, 1981 in Poland. But the struggle continues in Poland. And we know that there are even those who strive and suffer for freedom within the confines of the Soviet Union itself. How we conduct ourselves here in the Western democracies will determine whether this trend continues.

No, democracy is not a fragile flower. Still it needs cultivating. If the rest of this century is to witness the gradual growth of freedom and democratic ideals, we must take actions to assist the campaign for democracy.

Some argue that we should encourage democratic change in right-wing dictatorships, but not in Communist regimes. Well, to accept this preposterous notion—as some well-meaning people have—is to invite the argument that once countries achieve a nuclear capability, they should be allowed an undisturbed reign of terror over their own citizens. We reject this course.

As for the Soviet view, Chairman Brezhnev repeatedly has stressed that the competition of ideas and systems must continue and that this is entirely consistent with relaxation of tensions and peace.

Well, we ask only that these systems begin by living up to their own constitutions, abiding by their own laws, and complying with the international obligations they have undertaken. We ask only for a process, a direction, a basic code of decency, not for an instant transformation.

We cannot ignore the fact that even without our encouragement there has been and will continue to be repeated explosions against repression and dictatorships. The Soviet Union itself is not immune to this reality. Any system is inherently unstable that has no peaceful means to legitimize its leaders. In such cases, the very repressiveness of the state ultimately drives people to resist it, if necessary, by force.

While we must be cautious about forcing the pace of change, we must not hesitate to declare our ultimate objectives and to take concrete actions to move toward them. We must be staunch in our conviction that freedom is not the sole prerogative of a lucky few, but the inalienable and universal right of all human beings. So states the United Nations Universal Declaration of Human Rights, which, among other things, guarantees free elections.

The objective I propose is quite simple to state: to foster the infrastructure of democracy, the system of a free press, unions, political parties, universities, which allows a people to choose their own way to develop their own culture, to reconcile their own differences through peaceful means.

This is not cultural imperialism, it is providing the means for genuine self-determination and protection for diversity. Democracy already flourishes in countries with very different cultures and historical experiences. It would be cultural condescension, or worse, to say that any people prefer dictatorship to democracy. Who would voluntarily choose not to have the right to vote, decide to purchase government propaganda handouts instead of independent newspapers, prefer government to worker-controlled unions, opt for land to be owned by the state instead of those who till it, want government repression of religious liberty, a single political party instead of a free choice, a rigid cultural orthodoxy instead of democratic tolerance and diversity?

Since 1917 the Soviet Union has given covert political training and assistance to Marxist-Leninists in many countries. Of course, it also has promoted the use of violence and subversion by these same forces. Over the past several decades, West European and other Social Democrats, Christian Democrats, and leaders have offered open assistance to fraternal, political, and social institutions to bring about peaceful and democratic progress. Appropriately, for a vigorous new democracy, the Federal Republic of Germany's political foundations have become a major force in this effort.

We in America now intend to take additional steps, as many of our allies have already done, toward realizing this same goal. The chairmen and other leaders of the national Republican and Democratic Party organizations are initiating a study with the bipartisan American political foundation to determine how the United States can best contribute as a nation to the global campaign for democracy now gathering force. They will have the cooperation of congressional leaders of both parties, along with representatives of business, labor, and other major institutions in our society. I look forward to receiving their recommendations and to working with these institutions and the Congress in the common task of strengthening democracy throughout the world.

It is time that we committed ourselves as a nation—in both

the pubic and private sectors—to assisting democratic development.

We plan to consult with leaders of other nations as well. There is a proposal before the Council of Europe to invite parliamentarians from democratic countries to a meeting next year in Strasbourg. That prestigious gathering could consider ways to help democratic political movements.

This November in Washington there will take place an international meeting on free elections. And next spring there will be a conference of world authorities on constitutionalism and self-government hosted by the Chief Justice of the United States. Authorities from a number of developing and developed countries—judges, philosophers, and politicians with practical experience—have agreed to explore how to turn principle into practice and further the rule of law.

At the same time, we invite the Soviet Union to consider with us how the competition of ideas and values—which it is committed to support—can be conducted on a peaceful and reciprocal basis. For example, I am prepared to offer President Brezhnev an opportunity to speak to the American people on our television if he will allow me the same opportunity with the Soviet people. We also suggest that panels of our newsmen periodically appear on each other's television to discuss major events.

Now, I don't wish to sound overly optimistic, yet the Soviet Union is not immune from the reality of what is going on in the world. It has happened in the past—a small ruling elite either mistakenly attempts to ease domestic unrest through greater repression and foreign adventure, or it chooses a wiser course. It begins to allow its people a voice in their own destiny. Even if this latter process is not realized soon, I believe the renewed strength of the democratic movement, complemented by a global campaign for freedom, will strengthen the prospects for arms control and a world at peace.

I have discussed on other occasions, including my address on May 9th, the elements of Western policies toward the Soviet Union to safeguard our interests and protect the peace. What I am describing now is a plan and a hope for the long term—the march of freedom and democracy which will leave

Marxism-Leninism on the ash-heap of history as it has left other tyrannies which stifle the freedom and muzzle the self-expression of the people. And that's why we must continue our efforts to strengthen NATO even as we move forward with our Zero-Option initiative in the negotiations on intermediate-range forces and our proposal for a one-third reduction in strategic ballistic missile warheads.

Our military strength is a prerequisite to peace, but let it be clear we maintain this strength in the hope it will never be used, for the ultimate determinant in the struggle that's now going on in the world will not be bombs and rockets, but a test of wills and ideas, a trial of spiritual resolve, the values we hold, the beliefs we cherish, the ideals to which we are dedicated.

The British people know that, given strong leadership, time and a little bit of hope, the forces of good ultimately rally and triumph over evil. Here among you is the cradle of self-government, the Mother of Parliaments. Here is the enduring greatness of the British contribution to mankind, the great civilized ideas: individual liberty, representative government, and the rule of law under God.

I've often wondered about the shyness of some of us in the West about standing for these ideals that have done so much to ease the plight of man and the hardships of our imperfect world. This reluctance to use those vast resources at our command reminds me of the elderly lady whose home was bombed in the Blitz. As the rescuers moved about, they found a bottle of brandy she'd stored behind the staircase, which was all that was left standing. And since she was barely conscious, one of the workers pulled the cork to give her a taste of it. She came around immediately and said, "Here now—there now, put it back. That's for emergencies." [*Laughter*]

Well, the emergency is upon us. Let us be shy no longer. Let us go to our strength. Let us offer hope. Let us tell the world that a new age is not only possible but probable.

During the dark days of the Second World War, when this island was incandescent with courage, Winston Churchill exclaimed about Britain's adversaries, "What kind of a people do they think we are?" Well, Britain's adversaries found out what extraordinary people the British are. But all the democracies paid a terrible price for allowing the dictators to underestimate us. We dare not make that mistake again. So, let us ask ourselves, "What kind of people do we think we are?" And let us answer, "Free people, worthy of freedom and determined not only to remain so but to help others gain their freedom as well."

Sir Winston led his people to great victory in war and then lost an election just as the fruits of victory were about to be enjoyed. But he left office honorably, and, as it turned out, temporarily, knowing that the liberty of his people was more important than the fate of any single leader. History recalls his greatness in ways no dictator will ever know. And he left us a message of hope for the future, as timely now as when he first uttered it, as opposition leader in the Commons nearly 27 years ago, when he said, "When we look back on all the perils through which we have passed and at the mighty foes that we have laid low and all the dark and deadly designs that we have frustrated, why should we fear for our future? We have," he said, "come safely through the worst."

Well, the task I've set forth will long outlive our own generation. But together, we too have come through the worst. Let us now begin a major effort to secure the best—a crusade for freedom that will engage the faith and fortitude of the next generation. For the sake of peace and justice, let us move toward a world in which all people are at last free to determine their own destiny.

Thank you.

RONALD REAGAN

Address at Pointe-du-Hoc

Normandy, June 6, 1984

W E'RE HERE to mark that day in history when the Allied armies joined in battle to reclaim this continent to liberty. For 4 long years, much of Europe had been under a terrible shadow. Free nations had fallen, Jews cried out in the camps, millions cried out for liberation. Europe was enslaved, and the world prayed for its rescue. Here in Normandy the rescue began. Here the Allies stood and fought against tyranny in a giant undertaking unparalleled in human history.

We stand on a lonely, windswept point on the northern shore of France. The air is soft, but 40 years ago at this moment, the air was dense with smoke and the cries of men, and the air was filled with the crack of rifle fire and the roar of cannon. At dawn, on the morning of the 6th of June, 1944, 225 Rangers jumped off the British landing craft and ran to the bottom of these cliffs. Their mission was one of the most difficult and daring of the invasion: to climb these sheer and desolate cliffs and take out the enemy guns. The Allies had been told that some of the mightiest of these guns were here and they would be trained on the beaches to stop the Allied advance.

The Rangers looked up and saw the enemy soldiers at the edge of the cliffs shooting down at them with machineguns and throwing grenades. And the American Rangers began to climb. They shot rope ladders over the face of these cliffs and began to pull themselves up. When one Ranger fell, another would take his place. When one rope was cut, a Ranger would grab another and begin his climb again. They climbed, shot back, and held their footing. Soon, one by one, the Rangers pulled themselves over the top, and in seizing the firm land at the top of these cliffs, they began to seize back the continent of Europe. Two hundred and twenty-five came here. After 2 days of fighting, only 90 could still bear arms.

Behind me is a memorial that symbolizes the Ranger daggers that were thrust into the top of these cliffs. And before me are the men who put them there.

These are the boys of Pointe du Hoc. These are the men who took the cliffs. These are the champions who helped free a continent. These are the heroes who helped end a war.

Gentlemen, I look at you and I think of the words of Stephen Spender's poem. You are men who in your "lives fought for life . . . and left the vivid air signed with your honor."

I think I know what you may be thinking right now—thinking "we were just part of a bigger effort; everyone was brave that day." Well, everyone was. Do you remember the story of Bill Millin of the 51st Highlanders? Forty years ago today, British troops were pinned down near a bridge, waiting desperately for help. Suddenly, they heard the sound of bagpipes, and some thought they were dreaming. Well, they weren't. They looked up and saw Bill Millin with his bagpipes, leading the reinforcements and ignoring the smack of the bullets into the ground around him.

Lord Lovat was with him—Lord Lovat of Scotland, who calmly announced when he got to the bridge, "Sorry I'm a few minutes late," as if he'd been delayed by a traffic jam, when in truth he'd just come from the bloody fighting on Sword Beach, which he and his men had just taken.

There was the impossible valor of the Poles who threw themselves between the enemy and the rest of Europe as the invasion took hold, and the unsurpassed courage of the Canadians who had already seen the horrors of war on this coast. They knew what awaited them there, but they would not be deterred. And once they hit Juno Beach, they never looked back.

All of these men were part of a rollcall of honor with names that spoke of a pride as bright as the colors they bore: the Royal Winnipeg Rifles, Poland's 24th Lancers, the Royal Scots Fusiliers, the Screaming Eagles, the Yeomen of England's armored divisions, the forces of Free France, the Coast Guard's "Matchbox Fleet" and you, the American Rangers.

Forty summers have passed since the battle that you fought here. You were young the day you took these cliffs; some of you were hardly more than boys, with the deepest joys of life before you. Yet, you risked everything here. Why? Why did you do it? What impelled you to put aside the instinct for self-preservation and risk your lives to take these cliffs? What inspired all the men of the armies that met here? We look at you, and somehow we know the answer. It was faith and belief; it was loyalty and love.

The men of Normandy had faith that what they were doing was right, faith that they fought for all humanity, faith that a just God would grant them mercy on this beachhead or on the next. It was the deep knowledge—and pray God we have not lost it—that there is a profound, moral difference between the use of force for liberation and the use of force for conquest. You were here to liberate, not to conquer, and so you and those others did not doubt your cause. And you were right not to doubt.

You all knew that some things are worth dying for. One's country is worth dying for, and democracy is worth dying for, because it's the most deeply honorable form of government ever devised by man. All of you loved liberty. All of you were willing to fight tyranny, and you knew the people of your countries were behind you.

The Americans who fought here that morning knew word of the invasion was spreading through the darkness back home. They fought—or felt in their hearts, though they couldn't know in fact, that in Georgia they were filling the churches at 4 a.m., in Kansas they were kneeling on their porches and praying, and in Philadelphia they were ringing the Liberty Bell.

Something else helped the men of D-day: their rockhard belief that Providence would have a great hand in the events that would unfold here; that God was an ally in this great cause. And so, the night before the invasion, when Colonel Wolverton asked his parachute troops to kneel with him in prayer he told them: Do not bow your heads, but look up so you can see God and ask His blessing in what we're about to do. Also that night, General Matthew Ridgway on his cot, listening in the darkness for the promise God made to Joshua: "I will not fail thee nor forsake thee."

These are the things that impelled them; these are the things that shaped the unity of the Allies.

When the war was over, there were lives to be rebuilt and governments to be returned to the people. There were nations to be reborn. Above all, there was a new peace to be assured. These were huge and daunting tasks. But the Allies summoned strength from the faith, belief, loyalty, and love of those who fell here. They rebuilt a new Europe together.

There was first a great reconciliation among those who had been enemies, all of whom had suffered so greatly. The United States did its part, creating the Marshall plan to help rebuild our allies and our former enemies. The Marshall plan led to the Atlantic alliance—a great alliance that serves to this day as our shield for freedom, for prosperity, and for peace.

In spite of our great efforts and successes, not all that followed the end of the war was happy or planned. Some liberated countries were lost. The great sadness of this loss echoes down to our own time in the streets of Warsaw, Prague, and East Berlin. Soviet troops that came to the center of this continent did not leave when peace came. They're still there, uninvited, unwanted, unyielding, almost 40 years after the war. Because of this, allied forces still stand on this continent. Today, as 40 years ago, our armies are here for only one purpose—to protect and defend democracy. The only territories we hold are memorials like this one and graveyards where our heroes rest.

We in America have learned bitter lessons from two World Wars: It is better to be here ready to protect the peace, than to take blind shelter across the sea, rushing to respond only after freedom is lost. We've learned that isolationism never was and never will be an acceptable response to tyrannical governments with an expansionist intent.

But we try always to be prepared for peace; prepared to deter aggression; prepared to negotiate the reduction of arms; and, yes, prepared to reach out again in the spirit of reconciliation. In truth, there is no reconciliation we would welcome more than a reconciliation with the Soviet Union, so, together, we can lessen the risks of war, now and forever.

It's fitting to remember here the great losses also suffered by the Russian people during World War II: 20 million perished, a terrible price that testifies to all the world the necessity of ending war. I tell you from my heart that we in the United States do not want war. We want to wipe from the face of the Earth the terrible weapons that man now has in his hands. And I tell you, we are ready to seize that beachhead. We look for some sign from the Soviet Union that they are willing to move forward, that they share our desire and love for peace, and that they will give up the ways of conquest. There must be a changing there that will allow us to turn our hope into action.

We will pray forever that some day that changing will come. But for now, particularly today, it is good and fitting to renew our commitment to each other, to our freedom, and to the alliance that protects it.

We are bound today by what bound us 40 years ago, the same loyalties, traditions, and beliefs. We're bound by reality. The strength of America's allies is vital to the United States, and the American security guarantee is essential to the continued freedom of Europe's democracies. We were with you then; we are with you now. Your hopes are our hopes, and your destiny is our destiny.

Here, in this place where the West held together, let us make a vow to our dead. Let us show them by our actions that we understand what they died for. Let our actions say to them the words for which Matthew Ridgway listened: "I will not fail thee nor forsake thee."

Strengthened by their courage, heartened by their valor, and borne by their memory, let us continue to stand for the ideals for which they lived and died.

Thank you very much, and God bless you all.

JESSE JACKSON

Speech to the
Democratic National Convention

San Francisco, July 17, 1984

T HANK YOU VERY MUCH.
    Tonight we come together bound by our faith in a mighty God, with genuine respect and love for our country, and inheriting the legacy of a great party, the Democratic Party, which is the best hope for redirecting our nation on a more humane, just, and peaceful course.

This is not a perfect party. We are not a perfect people. Yet, we are called to a perfect mission. Our mission: to feed the hungry, to clothe the naked, to house the homeless, to teach the illiterate, to provide jobs for the jobless, and to choose the human race over the nuclear race.

We are gathered here this week to nominate a candidate and adopt a platform which will expand, unify, direct, and inspire our party and the nation to fulfill this mission. My constituency is the desperate, the damned, the disinherited, the disrespected, and the despised. They are restless and seek relief. They have voted in record numbers. They have invested the faith, hope, and trust that they have in us. The Democratic Party must send them a signal that we care. I pledge my best not to let them down.

There is the call of conscience, redemption, expansion, healing, and unity. Leadership must heed the call of conscience, redemption, expansion, healing, and unity, for they are the key to achieving our mission. Time is neutral and does not change things. With courage and initiative, leaders change things. No generation can choose the age or circumstance in which it is born, but through leadership it can choose to make the age in which it is born an age of enlightenment, an age of jobs, and peace, and justice. Only leadership—that intangible combination of gifts, the discipline, information, circumstance, courage, timing, will and divine inspiration—can lead us out of the crisis in which we find ourselves. Leadership can mitigate the misery of our nation. Leadership can part the waters and lead our nation in the direction of the Promised Land. Leadership can lift the boats stuck at the bottom.

I have had the rare opportunity to watch seven men, and then two, pour out their souls, offer their service, and heal, and heed the call of duty to direct the course of our nation. There is a proper season for everything. There is a time to sow and a time to reap. There's a time to compete and a time to cooperate. I ask for your vote on the first ballot as a vote for a new direction for this party and this nation—a vote of conviction, a vote of conscience. But I will be proud to support the nominee of this convention for the Presidency of the United States of America. (*Prolonged applause.*) Thank you.

I have—I have watched the leadership of our party develop and grow. My respect for both Mr. Mondale and Mr. Hart is great. I have watched them struggle with the crosswinds and crossfires of being public servants, and I believe they will both continue to try to serve us faithfully. I am elated by the knowledge that for the first time in our history a woman, Geraldine Ferraro, will be recommended to share our ticket.

Throughout this campaign, I've tried to offer leadership to the Democratic Party and the nation. If, in my high moments, I have done some good, offered some service, shed some light, healed some wounds, rekindled some hope, or stirred someone from apathy and indifference, or in any way along the way helped somebody, then this campaign has not been in vain.

For friends who loved and cared for me, and for a God who spared me, and for a family who understood, I am eternally grateful.

If, in my low moments, in word, deed or attitude, through some error of temper, taste, or tone, I have caused anyone discomfort, created pain, or revived someone's fears, that was not my truest self. If there were occasions when my grape turned into a raisin and my joy bell lost its resonance, please forgive me. Charge it to my head and not to my heart. My head, so limited in its finitude; my heart, which is boundless in its love for the human family. I am not a perfect servant. I am a public servant, doing my best against the odds. As I develop and serve, be patient. God is not finished with me yet.

This campaign has taught me much: that leaders must be tough enough to fight, tender enough to cry, human enough to make mistakes, humble enough to admit them, strong enough to absorb the pain, and resilient enough to bounce back and keep on moving.

For leaders, the pain is often intense. But you must smile through your tears and keep moving with the faith that there is a brighter side somewhere. I went to see Hubert Humphrey three days before he died. He had just called Richard Nixon from his dying bed, and many people wondered why. And I asked him. He said, "Jesse, from this vantage point, the sun setting in my life, all of the speeches, the political conventions, the crowds, and the great fights are behind me now. At a time like this you are forced to deal with your irreducible essence, forced to grapple with that which is really important to you. And what I've concluded about life," Hubert Humphrey said, "when all is said and done, we must forgive each other, and redeem each other, and move on."

Our party is emerging from one of its most hard-fought battles for the Democratic Party's presidential nomination in our history. But our healthy competition should make us better, not bitter. We must use—we must use the insight, wisdom, and experience of the late Hubert Humphrey as a balm for the wounds in our Party, this nation, and the world. We must forgive each other, redeem each other, regroup, and move on. Our flag is red, white, and blue, but our nation is a rainbow— red, yellow, brown, black, and white—and we're all precious in God's sight.

America—America is not like a blanket—one piece of unbroken cloth, the same color, the same texture, the same size. America is more like a quilt: many patches, many pieces, many colors, many sizes, all woven and held together by a common thread. The white, the Hispanic, the black, the Arab, the Jew, the woman, the Native American, the small farmer, the businessperson, the environmentalist, the peace activist, the young, the old, the lesbian, the gay, and the disabled make up the American quilt.

Even in our fractured state, all of us count and fit some-where. We have proven that we can survive without each other. But we have not proven that we can win and make progress without each other. We must come together.

From Fannie Lou Hamer in Atlantic City in 1964 to the Rainbow Coalition in San Francisco today, from the Atlantic to the Pacific, we have experienced pain but progress, as we ended America's apartheid laws. We got public accommodations. We secured voting rights. We obtained open housing, as young people got the right to vote. We lost Malcolm, Martin, Medgar, Bobby, John, and Viola. The team that got us here must be expanded, not abandoned.

Twenty years ago, tears welled up in our eyes as the bodies of Schwerner, Goodman, and Chaney were dredged from the depths of a river in Mississippi. Twenty years later, our communities, black and Jewish, are in anguish, anger, and pain. Feelings have been hurt on both sides. There is a crisis in communications. Confusion is in the air. We cannot afford to lose our way. We may agree to agree, or agree to disagree on issues; we must bring back civility to these tensions. We are co-partners in a long and rich religious history—the Judeo-Christian traditions. Many blacks and Jews have a shared passion for social justice at home and peace abroad. We must seek a revival of the spirit, inspired by a new vision and new possibilities. We must return to higher ground. We are bound by Moses and Jesus, but also connected with Islam and Muhammad. These three great religions, Judaism, Christianity, and Islam, were all born in the revered and holy city of Jerusalem.

We are bound by Dr. Martin Luther King Jr. and Rabbi Abraham Heschel, crying out from their graves for us to reach common ground. We are bound by shared blood and shared sacrifices. We are much too intelligent, much too bound by our Judeo-Christian heritage, much too victimized by racism, sexism, militarism, and anti-Semitism, much too threatened as historical scapegoats to go on divided one from another. We must turn from finger-pointing to clasped hands. We must share our burdens and our joys with each other once again. We must turn to each other and not on each other and choose higher ground.

Twenty years later—twenty years later we cannot be satisfied by just restoring the old coalition. Old wineskins must make room for new wine. We must heal and expand. The Rainbow Coalition is making room for Arab-Americans. They, too, know the pain and hurt of racial and religious rejection. They must not continue to be made pariahs. The Rainbow Coalition is making room for Hispanic Americans, who this very night are living under the threat of the Simpson-Mazzoli bill; and farm workers from Ohio who are fighting the Campbell Soup Company with a boycott to achieve legitimate workers' rights.

The Rainbow is making room for the Native American, the most exploited people of all, a people with the greatest moral claim amongst us. We support them as they seek the restoration of their ancient land and claim amongst us. We support them as they seek the restoration of land and water rights, as they seek to preserve their ancestral homeland and the beauty of a land that was once all theirs. They can never receive a fair share for all they have given us. They must finally have a fair chance to develop their great resources and to preserve their people and their culture. The Rainbow Coalition includes Asian Americans, now being killed in our streets—scapegoats for the failures of corporate, industrial, and economic policies. The Rainbow is making room for the young Americans. Twenty years ago, our young people were dying in a war for which they could not even vote. Twenty years later, young America has the power to stop a war in Central America and the responsibility to vote in great numbers. Young America must be politically active in 1984. The choice is war or peace. We must make room for young America. The Rainbow includes disabled veterans. The color scheme fits in the Rainbow. The disabled have their handicap revealed and their genius concealed; while the able-bodied have their genius revealed and their disability concealed. But ultimately, we must judge people by their values and their contribution. Don't leave anybody out. I would rather have Roosevelt in a wheelchair than Reagan on a horse.

The Rainbow is making room for small farmers. They have suffered tremendously under the Reagan regime. They will either receive 90 percent parity or 100 percent charity. We must address their concerns and make room for them. The Rainbow includes lesbians and gays. No American citizen ought be denied equal protection under the law. We must be unusually committed and caring as we expand our family to include new members. All of us must be tolerant and understanding as the fears and anxieties of the rejected and the party leadership express themselves in many different ways. Too often what we call hate—as if it were some deeply rooted philosophy or strategy —is simply ignorance, anxiety, paranoia, fear, and insecurity. To be strong leaders, we must be long-suffering as we seek to right the wrongs of our party and our nation. We must expand our party, heal our party, and unify our party. That is our mission in 1984.

We are often reminded that we live in a great nation, and we do. But it can be greater still. The Rainbow is mandating a new definition of greatness. We must not measure greatness from the mansion down, but the manger. Jesus said that we should not be judged by the bark we wear, but by the fruit that we bear. Jesus said that we must measure greatness by how we treat the least of these.

President Reagan says the nation is in recovery. Those 90,000 corporations that made a profit last year, but paid no federal taxes are recovering. The 37,000 military contractors who have benefited from Reagan's more than doubling the military budget in peacetime, surely they are recovering. The big corporations and rich individuals who received the bulk of a three-year multi-billion tax cut from Mr. Reagan are recovering. But no such recovery is under way for the least of these.

Rising tides don't lift all boats, particularly those stuck at the bottom. For the boats stuck at the bottom there's a misery index. This administration has made life more miserable for the poor. Its attitude has been contemptuous. Its policies and programs have been cruel and unfair to working people. They must be held accountable in November for increasing infant mortality among the poor. In Detroit, one of the great cities of the western world, babies are dying at the same rate as Honduras, the most underdeveloped nation in our hemisphere. This administration must be held accountable for policies that have contributed to the growing poverty in America. There are now 34 million people in poverty, 15 percent of our nation. Twenty-three million are white; 11 million black, Hispanic,

Asian, and others—mostly women and children. By the end of this year, there will be 41 million people in poverty. We cannot stand idly by. We must fight for a change now.

Under this regime we look at Social Security. The '81 budget cuts included nine permanent Social Security benefit cuts totaling 20 billion dollars over five years. Small businesses have suffered under Reagan tax cuts. Only 18 percent of total business tax cuts went to them, 82 percent to big business. Health care under Mr. Reagan has been sharply cut. Education under Mr. Reagan has been cut 25 percent. Under Mr. Reagan there are now 9.7 million female-head families. They represent 16 percent of all families. Half of all of them are poor. Seventy percent of all poor children live in a house headed by a woman, where there is no man. Under Mr. Reagan, the Administration has cleaned up only six of 546 priority toxic waste dumps. Farmers' real net income was only about half its level in 1979.

Many say that the race in November will be decided in the South. President Reagan is depending on the conservative South to return him to office. But the South, I tell you, is unnaturally conservative. The South is the poorest region in our nation and, therefore, the least to conserve. In his appeal to the South, Mr. Reagan is trying to substitute flags and prayer cloths for food, and clothing, and education, health care, and housing.

Mr. Reagan will ask us to pray, and I believe in prayer. I have come this way by the power of prayer. But then, we must watch false prophecy. He cuts energy assistance to the poor, cuts breakfast programs from children, cuts lunch programs from children, cuts job training from children, and then says to an empty table, "Let us pray." Apparently, he is not familiar with the structure of a prayer. You thank the Lord for the food that you are about to receive, not the food that just left. I think that we should pray, but don't pray for the food that left. Pray for the man that took the food to leave. We need a change! We need a change in November.

Under Mr. Reagan, the misery index has risen for the poor. The danger index has risen for everybody. Under this administration, we've lost the lives of our boys in Central America and Honduras, in Grenada, in Lebanon, in nuclear standoff in Europe. Under this administration, one-third of our children believe they will die in a nuclear war. The danger index is increasing in this world. All the talk about the defense against Russia: the Russian submarines are closer, and their missiles are more accurate. We live in a world tonight more miserable and a world more dangerous.

While Reaganomics and Reaganism is talked about often, so often we miss the real meaning. Reaganism is a spirit, and Reaganomics represents the real economic facts of life. In 1980, Mr. George Bush, a man with reasonable access to Mr. Reagan, did an analysis of Mr. Reagan's economic plan. Mr. George Bush concluded that Reagan's plan was "voodoo economics." He was right. Third-party candidate John Anderson said, "A combination of military spending, tax cuts, and a balanced budget by '84 would be accomplished with blue smoke and mirrors." They were both right.

Mr. Reagan talks about a dynamic recovery. There's some measure of recovery. Three and a half years later, unemployment has inched just below where it was when he took office in '81. There are still 8.1 million people officially unemployed; 11 million working only part-time. Inflation has come down, but let's analyze for a moment who has paid the price for this superficial economic recovery.

Mr. Reagan curbed inflation by cutting consumer demand. He cut consumer demand with conscious and callous fiscal and monetary policies. He used the federal budget to deliberately induce unemployment and curb social spending. He then weighed and supported tight monetary policies of the Federal Reserve Board to deliberately drive up interest rates, again to curb consumer demand created through borrowing. Unemployment reached 10.7 percent. We experienced skyrocketing interest rates. Our dollar inflated abroad. There were record bank failures, record farm foreclosures, record business bankruptcies; record budget deficits, record trade deficits. Mr. Reagan brought inflation down by destabilizing our economy and disrupting family life. He promised—he promised in 1980 a balanced budget. But instead we now have a record 200 billion dollar budget deficit. Under Mr. Reagan, the cumulative budget deficit for his four years is more than the sum total of deficits from George Washington to Jimmy Carter combined. I tell you, we need a change.

How is he paying for these short-term jobs? Reagan's economic recovery is being financed by deficit spending—200 billion dollars a year. Military spending, a major cause of this deficit, is projected over the next five years to be nearly two trillion dollars, and will cost about 40,000 dollars for every taxpaying family. When the government borrows 200 billion dollars annually to finance the deficit, this encourages the private sector to make its money off of interest rates as opposed to development and economic growth. Even money abroad— we don't have enough money domestically to finance the debt, so we are now borrowing money abroad, from foreign banks, governments and financial institutions: 40 billion dollars in 1983; 70 to 80 billion dollars in 1984—40 percent of our total; over 100 billion dollars—50 percent of our total—in 1985. By 1989, it is projected that 50 percent of all individual income taxes will be going just to pay for interest on that debt. The United States used to be the largest exporter of capital, but under Mr. Reagan we will quite likely become the largest debtor nation. About two weeks ago, on July the Fourth, we celebrated our Declaration of Independence, yet every day supply-side economics is making our nation more economically dependent and less economically free. Five to six percent of our Gross National Product is now being eaten up with President Reagan's budget deficits. To depend on foreign military powers to protect our national security would be foolish, making us dependent and less secure. Yet Reaganomics has us increasingly dependent on foreign economic sources. This consumer-led but deficit-financed recovery is unbalanced and artificial. We have a challenge as Democrats to point a way out.

Democracy guarantees opportunity, not success. Democracy guarantees the right to participate, not a license for either a majority or a minority to dominate. The victory for the Rainbow Coalition in the platform debates today was not whether we won or lost, but that we raised the right issues. We could afford to lose the vote; issues are non-negotiable. We could not afford to avoid raising the right questions. Our self-respect and our moral integrity were at stake. Our heads are perhaps bloody, but not bowed. Our back is straight. We can go home and face our people. Our vision is clear.

When we think, on this journey from slave-ship to

championship, that we have gone from the planks of the Boardwalk in Atlantic City in 1964 to fighting to help write the planks in the platform in San Francisco in '84, there is a deep and abiding sense of joy in our souls in spite of the tears in our eyes. Though there are missing planks, there is a solid foundation upon which to build. Our party can win, but we must provide hope which will inspire people to struggle and achieve; provide a plan that shows a way out of our dilemma and then lead the way.

In 1984, my heart is made to feel glad because I know there is a way out. Justice. The requirement for rebuilding America is justice. The linchpin of progressive politics in our nation will not come from the North; they, in fact, will come from the South. That is why I argue over and over again. We look from Virginia around to Texas, there's only one black Congressperson out of 115. Nineteen years later, we're locked out of the Congress, the Senate and the governor's mansion. What does this large black vote mean? Why do I fight to end second primaries and fight gerrymandering and annexation and at-large —why do we fight over that? Because I tell you, you cannot hold someone in the ditch unless you linger there with them. Unless you linger there.

If you want a change in this nation, you enforce that Voting Rights Act. We'll get 12 to 20 black, Hispanic, female, and progressive congresspersons from the South. We can save the cotton, but we've got to fight the boll weevils. We've got to make a judgment! We've got to make a judgment.

It is not enough to hope ERA will pass. How can we pass ERA? If blacks vote in great numbers, progressive whites win. It's the only way progressive whites win. If blacks vote in great numbers, Hispanics win. When blacks, Hispanics, and progressive whites vote, women win. When women win, children win. When women and children win, workers win. We must all come up together! We must come up together! (*Prolonged applause.*) Thank you.

For all—for all of our joy and excitement, we must not save the world and lose our souls. We should never short-circuit enforcing the Voting Rights Act at every level. When one of us rise, all of us will rise. Justice is the way out. Peace is the way out. We should not act as if nuclear weaponry is negotiable and debatable. In this world in which we live, we dropped the bomb on Japan and felt guilty, but in 1984 other folks also got bombs. This time, if we drop the bomb, six minutes later we, too, will be destroyed. It's not about dropping the bomb on somebody. It is about dropping the bomb on everybody. We must choose to develop minds over guided missiles, and think it out and not fight it out. It's time for a change!

Our foreign policy must be characterized by mutual respect, not by gunboat diplomacy, big-stick diplomacy, and threats. Our nation at its best feeds the hungry. Our nation at its worst, at its worst, will mine the harbors of Nicaragua, at its worst, will try to overthrow their government, at its worst, will cut aid to American education and increase the aid to El Salvador. At its worst, our nation will have partnerships with South Africa. That's a moral disgrace! It's a moral disgrace; it's a moral disgrace.

We look at Africa. We cannot just focus on apartheid in southern Africa. We must fight for trade with Africa, and not just aid to Africa. We cannot stand idly by and say we will not relate to Nicaragua unless they have elections there, and then embrace military regimes in Africa overthrowing democratic governments in Nigeria and Liberia and Ghana. We must fight for democracy all around the world and play the game by one set of rules.

Peace in this world. Our present formula for peace in the Middle East is inadequate. It will not work. There are 22 nations in the Middle East. Our nation must be able to talk and act and influence all of them. We must build upon Camp David, and measure human rights by one yardstick. In that region we have too many interests and too few friends.

There is a way out—jobs. Put America back to work. When I was a child growing up in Greenville, South Carolina, the Reverend Sample used to preach every so often a sermon relating to Jesus. And he said, "If I be lifted up, I'll draw all men unto me." I didn't quite understand what he meant as a child growing up, but I understand a little better now. If you raise up truth, it's magnetic. It has a way of drawing people. With all this confusion in this convention, the bright lights and parties and big fun, we must raise up the simple proposition: If we lift up a program to feed the hungry, they'll come running; if we lift up a program to study war no more, our youth will come running; if we lift up a program to put America back to work, and an alternative to welfare and despair, they will come working. If we cut that military budget without cutting our defense, and use that money to rebuild bridges and put steel workers back to work, and use that money and provide jobs for our cities, and use that money to build schools and pay teachers and educate our children, and build hospitals and train doctors and train nurses, the whole nation will come running to us.

As—as I leave you now, we vote in this convention and get ready to go back across this nation in a couple of days. In this campaign, I've tried to be faithful to my promise. I lived in el barrios, ghettos, in reservations and housing projects. I have a message for our youth. I challenge them to put hope in their brains, and not dope in their veins. I told them that like Jesus, I, too, was born in the slum. But just because you're born in the slum does not mean the slum is born in you, and you can rise above it if your mind is made up. I told them in every slum there are two sides. When I see a broken window—that's the slummy side. Train some youth to become a glazier—that's the sunny side. When I see a missing brick—that's the slummy side. Let that child in the union and become a brick mason and build—that's the sunny side. When I see a missing door—that's the slummy side. Train some youth to become a carpenter—that's the sunny side. And when I see the vulgar words and hieroglyphics of destitution on the walls—that's the slummy side. Train some youth to become a painter, an artist—that's the sunny side. We leave this place looking for the sunny side because there's a brighter side somewhere. I'm more convinced than ever that we can win. We'll vault up the rough side of the mountain. We can win. I just want young America to do me one favor, just one favor. Exercise the right to dream. You must face reality—that which is. But then dream of a reality that ought to be—that must be. Live beyond the pain of reality with the dream of a bright tomorrow. Use hope and imagination as weapons of survival and progress. Use love to motivate you and obligate you to serve the human family.

Young America, dream. Choose the human race over the nuclear race. Bury the weapons and don't burn the people.

Dream—dream of a new value system. Teachers who teach for life and not just for a living; teach because they can't help it. Dream of lawyers more concerned about justice than a judgeship. Dream of doctors more concerned about public health than personal wealth. Dream of preachers and priests who will prophesy and not just profiteer. Preach and dream!

Our time has come. Our time has come. Suffering breeds character. Character breeds faith. In the end, faith will not disappoint. Our time has come. Our faith, hope, and dreams will prevail. Our time has come. Weeping has endured for nights, but now joy cometh in the morning. Our time has come. No grave can hold our body down. Our time has come. No lie can live forever. Our time has come. We must leave racial battleground and come to economic common ground and moral higher ground. America, our time has come. We come from disgrace to amazing grace. Our time has come. Give me your tired, give me your poor, your huddled masses who yearn to breathe free and come November, there will be a change because our time has come.

Thank you and God bless you.

RONALD REAGAN

Address to the Nation on the Challenger Disaster

Washington, D.C., January 28, 1986

LADIES AND GENTLEMEN, I'd planned to speak to you to-night to report on the state of the Union, but the events of earlier today have led me to change those plans. Today is a day for mourning and remembering. Nancy and I are pained to the core by the tragedy of the shuttle *Challenger*. We know we share this pain with all of the people of our country. This is truly a national loss. Nineteen years ago, almost to the day, we lost three astronauts in a terrible accident on the ground. But we've never lost an astronaut in flight; we've never had a tragedy like this. And perhaps we've forgotten the courage it took for the crew of the shuttle. But they, the *Challenger* Seven, were aware of the dangers, but overcame them and did their jobs brilliantly. We mourn seven heroes: Michael Smith, Dick Scobee, Judith Resnik, Ronald McNair, Ellison Onizuka, Gregory Jarvis, and Christa McAuliffe. We mourn their loss as a nation together.

For the families of the seven, we cannot bear, as you do, the full impact of this tragedy. But we feel the loss, and we're thinking about you so very much. Your loved ones were daring and brave, and they had that special grace, that special spirit that says, "Give me a challenge, and I'll meet it with joy." They had a hunger to explore the universe and discover its truths. They wished to serve, and they did. They served all of us. We've grown used to wonders in this century. It's hard to dazzle us. But for 25 years the United States space program has been doing just that. We've grown used to the idea of space, and per-haps we forget that we've only just begun. We're still pioneers. They, the members of the *Challenger* crew, were pioneers.

And I want to say something to the schoolchildren of America who were watching the live coverage of the shuttle's take-off. I know it is hard to understand, but sometimes painful things like this happen. It's all part of the process of exploration and discovery. It's all part of taking a chance and expanding man's horizons. The future doesn't belong to the fainthearted; it belongs to the brave. The *Challenger* crew was pulling us into the future, and we'll continue to follow them.

I've always had great faith in and respect for our space program, and what happened today does nothing to diminish it. We don't hide our space program. We don't keep secrets and cover things up. We do it all up front and in public. That's the way freedom is, and we wouldn't change it for a minute. We'll continue our quest in space. There will be more shuttle flights and more shuttle crews and, yes, more volunteers, more civilians, more teachers in space. Nothing ends here; our hopes and our journeys continue. I want to add that I wish I could talk to every man and woman who works for NASA or who worked on this mission and tell them: "Your dedication and professionalism have moved and impressed us for decades. And we know of your anguish. We share it."

There's a coincidence today. On this day 390 years ago, the great explorer Sir Francis Drake died aboard ship off the coast of Panama. In his lifetime the great frontiers were the oceans, and an historian later said, "He lived by the sea, died on it, and was buried in it." Well, today we can say of the *Challenger* crew: Their dedication was, like Drake's, complete.

The crew of the space shuttle *Challenger* honored us by the manner in which they lived their lives. We will never forget them, nor the last time we saw them, this morning, as they prepared for their journey and waved goodbye and "slipped the surly bonds of earth" to "touch the face of God."

RONALD REAGAN

Speech at the Brandenburg Gate

Berlin, June 12, 1987

THANK YOU very much. Chancellor Kohl, Governing Mayor Diepgen, ladies and gentlemen: Twenty four years ago, President John F. Kennedy visited Berlin, speaking to the people of this city and the world at the city hall. Well, since then two other presidents have come, each in his turn, to Berlin. And today I, myself, make my second visit to your city.

We come to Berlin, we American Presidents, because it's our duty to speak, in this place, of freedom. But I must confess, we're drawn here by other things as well: by the feeling of history in this city, more than 500 years older than our own nation; by the beauty of the Grunewald and the Tiergarten; most of all, by your courage and determination. Perhaps the composer, Paul Lincke, understood something about American Presidents. You see, like so many Presidents before me, I come here today because wherever I go, whatever I do: "*Ich hab noch einen koffer in Berlin.*"

Our gathering today is being broadcast throughout Western Europe and North America. I understand that it is being seen and heard as well in the East. To those listening throughout Eastern Europe, I extend my warmest greetings and the good will of the American people. To those listening in East Berlin, a special word: Although I cannot be with you, I address my remarks to you just as surely as to those standing here before me. For I join you, as I join your fellow countrymen in the West, in this firm, this unalterable belief: *Es gibt nur ein Berlin.*

Behind me stands a wall that encircles the free sectors of this city, part of a vast system of barriers that divides the entire continent of Europe. From the Baltic, south, those barriers cut across Germany in a gash of barbed wire, concrete, dog runs, and guardtowers. Farther south, there may be no visible, no obvious wall. But there remain armed guards and checkpoints all the same—still a restriction on the right to travel, still an instrument to impose upon ordinary men and women the will of a totalitarian state. Yet it is here in Berlin where the wall emerges most clearly; here, cutting across your city, where the news photo and the television screen have imprinted this brutal division of a continent upon the mind of the world. Standing before the Brandenburg Gate, every man is a German, separated from his fellow men. Every man is a Berliner, forced to look upon a scar.

President von Weizsäcker has said: "The German question is open as long as the Brandenburg Gate is closed." Today I say: As long as this gate is closed, as long as this scar of a wall is permitted to stand, it is not the German question alone that remains open, but the question of freedom for all mankind. Yet I do not come here to lament. For I find in Berlin a message of hope, even in the shadow of this wall, a message of triumph.

In this season of spring in 1945, the people of Berlin emerged from their air-raid shelters to find devastation. Thousands of miles away, the people of the United States reached out to help. And in 1947 Secretary of State—as you've been told—George Marshall announced the creation of what would become known as the Marshall plan. Speaking precisely 40 years ago this month, he said: "Our policy is directed not against any country or doctrine, but against hunger, poverty, desperation, and chaos."

In the Reichstag a few moments ago, I saw a display commemorating this 40th anniversary of the Marshall plan. I was struck by the sign on a burnt-out, gutted structure that was being rebuilt. I understand that Berliners of my own generation can remember seeing signs like it dotted throughout the Western sectors of the city. The sign read simply: "The Marshall plan is helping here to strengthen the free world." A strong, free world in the West, that dream became real. Japan rose from ruin to become an economic giant. Italy, France, Belgium—virtually every nation in Western Europe saw political and economic rebirth; the European Community was founded.

In West Germany and here in Berlin, there took place an economic miracle, the *Wirtschaftswunder*. Adenauer, Erhard, Reuter, and other leaders understood the practical importance of liberty—that just as truth can flourish only when the journalist is given freedom of speech, so prosperity can come about only when the farmer and businessman enjoy economic freedom. The German leaders reduced tariffs, expanded free trade, lowered taxes. From 1950 to 1960 alone, the standard of living in West Germany and Berlin doubled.

Where four decades ago there was rubble, today in West Berlin there is the greatest industrial output of any city in Germany—busy office blocks, fine homes and apartments, proud avenues, and the spreading lawns of park land. Where a city's culture seemed to have been destroyed, today there are two great universities, orchestras and an opera, countless theaters, and museums. Where there was want, today there's abundance—food, clothing, automobiles—the wonderful goods of the Ku'damm. From devastation, from utter ruin, you Berliners have, in freedom, rebuilt a city that once again ranks as one of the greatest on Earth. The Soviets may have had other plans. But, my friends, there were a few things the Soviets didn't count on—*Berliner herz, Berliner humor, ja, und Berliner schnauze.* [*Laughter*]

In the 1950's, Khrushchev predicted: "We will bury you." But in the West today, we see a free world that has achieved a level of prosperity and well-being unprecedented in all human history. In the Communist world, we see failure, technological backwardness, declining standards of health, even want of the most basic kind—too little food. Even today, the Soviet Union still cannot feed itself. After these four decades, then, there stands before the entire world one great and inescapable conclusion: Freedom leads to prosperity. Freedom replaces the ancient hatreds among the nations with comity and peace. Freedom is the victor.

And now the Soviets themselves may, in a limited way, be coming to understand the importance of freedom. We hear much from Moscow about a new policy of reform and openness. Some political prisoners have been released. Certain foreign news broadcasts are no longer being jammed. Some economic enterprises have been permitted to operate with greater freedom from state control. Are these the beginnings of profound changes in the Soviet state? Or are they token gestures, intended to raise false hopes in the West, or to strengthen the Soviet system without changing it? We welcome change and openness; for we believe that freedom and security go together, that the advance of human liberty can only strengthen the cause of world peace.

There is one sign the Soviets can make that would be unmistakable, that would advance dramatically the cause of freedom and peace. General Secretary Gorbachev, if you seek peace, if you seek prosperity for the Soviet Union and Eastern Europe, if you seek liberalization: Come here to this gate! Mr. Gorbachev, open this gate! Mr. Gorbachev, tear down this wall!

I understand the fear of war and the pain of division that afflict this continent—and I pledge to you my country's efforts to help overcome these burdens. To be sure, we in the West must resist Soviet expansion. So we must maintain defenses of unassailable strength. Yet we seek peace; so we must strive to reduce arms on both sides. Beginning 10 years ago, the Soviets challenged the Western alliance with a grave new threat, hundreds of new and more deadly SS-20 nuclear missiles, capable of striking every capital in Europe. The Western alliance responded by committing itself to a counterdeployment unless the Soviets agreed to negotiate a better solution; namely, the elimination of such weapons on both sides. For many months, the Soviets refused to bargain in earnestness. As the alliance, in turn, prepared to go forward with its counterdeployment, there were difficult days—days of protests like those during my 1982 visit to this city—and the Soviets later walked away from the table.

But through it all, the alliance held firm. And I invite those who protested then—I invite those who protest today—to mark this fact: Because we remained strong, the Soviets came back to the table. And because we remained strong, today we have within reach the possibility, not merely of limiting the growth of arms, but of eliminating, for the first time, an entire class of nuclear weapons from the face of the Earth. As I speak, NATO ministers are meeting in Iceland to review the progress of our proposals for eliminating these weapons. At the talks in Geneva, we have also proposed deep cuts in strategic offensive weapons. And the Western allies have likewise made far-reaching proposals to reduce the danger of conventional war and to place a total ban on chemical weapons.

While we pursue these arms reductions, I pledge to you that we will maintain the capacity to deter Soviet aggression at any level at which it might occur. And in cooperation with many of our allies, the United States is pursuing the Strategic Defense Initiative—research to base deterrence not on the threat of offensive retaliation, but on defenses that truly defend; on systems, in short, that will not target populations, but shield them. By these means we seek to increase the safety of Europe and all the world. But we must remember a crucial fact: East and West do not mistrust each other because we are armed; we are armed because we mistrust each other. And our differences are not about weapons but about liberty. When President Kennedy spoke at the City Hall those 24 years ago, freedom was encircled, Berlin was under siege. And today, despite all the pressures upon this city, Berlin stands secure in its liberty. And freedom itself is transforming the globe.

In the Philippines, in South and Central America, democracy has been given a rebirth. Throughout the Pacific, free markets are working miracle after miracle of economic growth. In the industrialized nations, a technological revolution is taking place—a revolution marked by rapid, dramatic advances in computers and telecommunications.

In Europe, only one nation and those it controls refuse to join the community of freedom. Yet in this age of redoubled economic growth, of information and innovation, the Soviet Union faces a choice: It must make fundamental changes, or it will become obsolete. Today thus represents a moment of hope. We in the West stand ready to cooperate with the East to promote true openness, to break down barriers that separate people, to create a safer, freer world.

And surely there is no better place than Berlin, the meeting place of East and West, to make a start. Free people of Berlin: Today, as in the past, the United States stands for the strict observance and full implementation of all parts of the Four Power Agreement of 1971. Let us use this occasion, the 750th anniversary of this city, to usher in a new era, to seek a still fuller, richer life for the Berlin of the future. Together, let us maintain and develop the ties between the Federal Republic and the Western sectors of Berlin, which is permitted by the 1971 agreement.

And I invite Mr. Gorbachev: Let us work to bring the Eastern and Western parts of the city closer together, so that all the inhabitants of all Berlin can enjoy the benefits that come with life in one of the great cities of the world. To open Berlin still further to all Europe, East and West, let us expand the vital air access to this city, finding ways of making commercial air service to Berlin more convenient, more comfortable, and more economical. We look to the day when West Berlin can become one of the chief aviation hubs in all central Europe.

With our French and British partners, the United States is prepared to help bring international meetings to Berlin. It would be only fitting for Berlin to serve as the site of United Nations meetings, or world conferences on human rights and arms control or other issues that call for international cooperation. There is no better way to establish hope for the future than to enlighten young minds, and we would be honored to sponsor summer youth exchanges, cultural events, and other programs for young Berliners from the East. Our French and British friends, I'm certain, will do the same. And it's my hope that an authority can be found in East Berlin to sponsor visits from young people of the Western sectors.

One final proposal, one close to my heart: Sport represents a source of enjoyment and ennoblement, and you many have noted that the Republic of Korea—South Korea—has offered to permit certain events of the 1988 Olympics to take place in the North. International sports competitions of all kinds could take place in both parts of this city. And what better way to demonstrate to the world the openness of this city than to offer in some future year to hold the Olympic games here in Berlin, East and West?

In these four decades, as I have said, you Berliners have built a great city. You've done so in spite of threats—the Soviet attempts to impose the East-mark, the blockade. Today the city thrives in spite of the challenges implicit in the very presence of this wall. What keeps you here? Certainly there's a great deal to be said for your fortitude, for your defiant courage. But I believe there's something deeper, something that involves Berlin's whole look and feel and way of life—not mere sentiment. No one could live long in Berlin without being completely disabused of illusions. Something instead, that has seen the difficulties of life in Berlin but chose to accept them, that continues to build this good and proud city in contrast to a surrounding totalitarian presence that refuses to release human energies or aspirations. Something that speaks with a powerful voice of affirmation, that says yes to this city, yes to the future, yes to freedom. In a word, I would submit that what keeps you in Berlin is love—love both profound and abiding.

Perhaps this gets to the root of the matter, to the most fundamental distinction of all between East and West. The totalitarian world produces backwardness because it does such violence to the spirit, thwarting the human impulse to create, to enjoy, to worship. The totalitarian world finds even symbols of love and of worship an affront. Years ago, before the East Germans began rebuilding their churches, they erected a secular structure: the television tower at Alexander Platz. Virtually ever since, the authorities have been working to correct what they view as the tower's one major flaw, treating the glass sphere at the top with paints and chemicals of every kind. Yet even today when the Sun strikes that sphere—that sphere that towers over all Berlin—the light makes the sign of the cross. There in Berlin, like the city itself, symbols of love, symbols of worship, cannot be suppressed.

As I looked out a moment ago from the Reichstag, that embodiment of German unity, I noticed words crudely spray-painted upon the wall, perhaps by a young Berliner, "This wall will fall. Beliefs become reality." Yes, across Europe, this wall will fall. For it cannot withstand faith; it cannot withstand truth. The wall cannot withstand freedom.

And I would like, before I close, to say one word. I have read, and I have been questioned since I've been here about certain demonstrations against my coming. And I would like to say just one thing, and to those who demonstrate so. I wonder if they have ever asked themselves that if they should have the kind of government they apparently seek, no one would ever be able to do what they're doing again.

Thank you and God bless you all.

WILLIAM J. CLINTON

Speech at Mason Temple

Memphis, November 13, 1993

THANK YOU. Please sit down. Bishop Ford, Mrs. Mason, Bishop Owens, and Bishop Anderson; my bishops, Bishop Walker and Bishop Lindsey. Now, if you haven't had Bishop Lindsey's barbecue, you haven't had barbecue. And if you haven't heard Bishop Walker attack one of my opponents, you have never heard a political speech. [*Laughter*]

I am glad to be here. You have touched my heart. You've brought tears to my eyes and joy to my spirit. Last year I was with you over at the convention center. Two years ago your bishops came to Arkansas, and we laid a plaque at the point in Little Rock, Arkansas, at 8th and Gaines where Bishop Mason received the inspiration for the name of this great church. Bishop Brooks said from his pulpit that I would be elected President when most people thought I wouldn't survive. I thank him, and I thank your faith, and I thank your works, for without you I would not be here today as your President.

Many have spoken eloquently and well, and many have been introduced. I want to thank my good friend Governor McWherter and my friend Mayor Herenton for being with me today; my friend Congressman Harold Ford, we are glad to be in his congressional district. I would like to, if I might, introduce just three other people who are Members of the Congress. They have come here with me, and without them it's hard for me to do much for you. The President proposes and the Congress disposes. Sometimes they dispose of what I propose, but I'm happy to say that according to a recent report in Washington, notwithstanding what you may have heard, this Congress has given me a higher percentage of my proposals than any first-year President since President Eisenhower. And I thank them for that. Let me introduce my good friend, a visitor to Tennessee, Congressman Bill Jefferson from New Orleans,

Louisiana—please stand up; and an early supporter of my campaign, Congressman Bob Clement from Tennessee, known to many of you; and a young man who's going to be coming back to the people of Tennessee and asking them to give him a promotion next year, Congressman Jim Cooper from Tennessee, and a good friend. Please welcome him.

You know, in the last 10 months, I've been called a lot of things, but nobody's called me a bishop yet. [*Laughter*] When I was about 9 years old, my beloved and now departed grandmother, who was a very wise woman, looked at me and she said, "You know, I believe you could be a preacher if you were just a little better boy." [*Laughter*]

Proverbs says, "A happy heart doeth good like medicine, but a broken spirit dryeth the bone." This is a happy place, and I'm happy to be here. I thank you for your spirit.

By the grace of God and your help, last year I was elected President of this great country. I never dreamed that I would ever have a chance to come to this hallowed place where Martin Luther King gave his last sermon. I ask you to think today about the purpose for which I ran and the purpose for which so many of you worked to put me in this great office. I have worked hard to keep faith with our common efforts: to restore the economy, to reverse the politics of helping only those at the top of our totem pole and not the hard-working middle class or the poor; to bring our people together across racial and regional and political lines, to make a strength out of our diversity instead of letting it tear us apart; to reward work and family and community and try to move us forward into the 21st century. I have tried to keep faith.

Thirteen percent of all my Presidential appointments are African-Americans, and there are five African-Americans in the Cabinet of the United States, 2½ times as many as have ever served in the history of this great land. I have sought to advance the right to vote with the motor voter bill, supported so strongly by all the churches in our country. And next week it will be my great honor to sign the restoration of religious freedoms act, a bill supported widely by people across all religions and political philosophies to put back the real meaning of the Constitution, to give you and every other American the freedom to do what is most important in your life, to worship God as your spirit leads you.

I say to you, my fellow Americans, we have made a good beginning. Inflation is down. Interest rates are down. The deficit is down. Investment is up. Millions of Americans, including, I bet, some people in this room, have refinanced their homes or their business loans just in the last year. And in the last 10 months, this economy has produced more jobs in the private sector than in the previous 4 years.

We have passed a law called the family leave law, which says you can't be fired if you take a little time off when a baby is born or a parent is sick. We know that most Americans have to work, but you ought not to have to give up being a good parent just to take a job. If you can't succeed as a worker and a parent, this country can't make it.

We have radically reformed the college loan program, as I promised, to lower the cost of college loans and broaden the availability of it and make the repayment terms easier. And we have passed the national service law that will give in 3 years, 3 years from now, 100,000 young Americans the chance to serve their communities at home, to repair the frayed bonds of community, to build up the needs of people at the grassroots, and at the same time, earn some money to pay for a college education. It is a wonderful idea.

On April 15th when people pay their taxes, somewhere between 15 million and 18 million working families on modest incomes, families with children and incomes of under $23,000, will get a tax cut, not a tax increase, in the most important effort to ensure that we reward work and family in the last 20 years. Fifty million American parents and their children will be advantaged by putting the Tax Code back on the side of working American parents for a change.

Under the leadership of the First Lady we have produced a comprehensive plan to guarantee health care security to all Americans. How can we expect the American people to work and to live with all the changes in a global economy, where the average 18-year-old will change work seven times in a lifetime, unless we can simply say we have joined the ranks of all the other advanced countries in the world; you can have decent health care that's always there, that can never be taken away? It is time we did that, long past time. I ask you to help us achieve that.

But we have so much more to do. You and I know that most people are still working harder for the same or lower wages, that many people are afraid that their job will go away. We have to provide the education and training our people need, not just for our children but for our adults, too. If we cannot close this country up to the forces of change sweeping throughout the world, we have to at least guarantee people the security of being employable. They have to be able to get a new job if they're going to have to get a new job. We don't do that today, and we must, and we intend to proceed until that is done.

We have a guarantee that there will be some investment in those areas of our country, in the inner cities and in the destitute rural areas in the Mississippi Delta, of my home State and this State and Louisiana and Mississippi and other places like it throughout America. It's all very well to train people, but if they don't have a job, they can be trained for nothing. We must get investment into those places where the people are dying for work.

And finally, let me say, we must find people who will buy what we have to produce. We are the most productive people on Earth. That makes us proud. But what that means is that every year one person can produce more in the same amount of time. Now, if fewer and fewer people can produce more and more things, and yet you want to create more jobs and raise people's incomes, you have to have more customers for what it is you're making. And that is why I have worked so hard to sell more American products around the world; why I have asked that we be able to sell billions of dollars of computers we used not to sell to foreign countries and foreign interests, to put our people to work; why next week I am going all the way to Washington State to meet with the President of China and the Prime Minister of Japan and the heads of 13 other Asian countries, the fastest growing part of the world, to say, "We want to be your partners. We will buy your goods, but we want you to buy ours, too, if you please." That is why.

That is why I have worked so hard for this North American trade agreement that Congressman Ford endorsed today and

Congressman Jefferson endorsed and Congressman Cooper and Congressman Clement, because we know that Americans can compete and win only if people will buy what it is we have to sell. There are 90 million people in Mexico. Seventy cents of every dollar they spend on foreign goods, they spend on American goods.

People worry fairly about people shutting down plants in America and going not just to Mexico but to any place where the labor is cheap. It has happened. What I want to say to you, my fellow Americans, is nothing in this agreement makes that more likely. That has happened already. It may happen again. What we need to do is keep the jobs here by finding customers there. That's what this agreement does. It gives us a chance to create opportunity for people. I have friends in this audience, people who are ministers from my State, fathers and sons, people—I've looked out all over this vast crowd and I see people I've known for years. They know I spent my whole life working to create jobs. I would never knowingly do anything that would take a job away from the American people. This agreement will make more jobs. Now, we can also leave it if it doesn't work in 6 months. But if we don't take it, we'll lose it forever. We need to take it, because we have to do better.

But I guess what I really want to say to you today, my fellow Americans, is that we can do all of this and still fail unless we meet the great crisis of the spirit that is gripping America today.

When I leave you, Congressman Ford and I are going to a Baptist church near here to a town meeting he's having on health care and violence. I tell you, unless we do something about crime and violence and drugs that is ravaging the community, we will not be able to repair this country.

If Martin Luther King, who said, "Like Moses, I am on the mountaintop, and I can see the promised land, but I'm not going to be able to get there with you, but we will get there"—if he were to reappear by my side today and give us a report card on the last 25 years, what would he say? You did a good job, he would say, voting and electing people who formerly were not electable because of the color of their skin. You have more political power, and that is good. You did a good job, he would say, letting people who have the ability to do so live wherever they want to live, go wherever they want to go in this great country. You did a good job, he would say, elevating people of color into the ranks of the United States Armed Forces to the very top or into the very top of our Government. You did a very good job, he would say. He would say, you did a good job creating a black middle class of people who really are doing well, and the middle class is growing more among African-Americans than among non-African-Americans. You did a good job; you did a good job in opening opportunity.

But he would say, I did not live and die to see the American family destroyed. I did not live and die to see 13-year-old boys get automatic weapons and gun down 9-year-olds just for the kick of it. I did not live and die to see young people destroy their own lives with drugs and then build fortunes destroying the lives of others. That is not what I came here to do. I fought for freedom, he would say, but not for the freedom of people to kill each other with reckless abandon, not for the freedom of children to have children and the fathers of the children walk away from them and abandon them as if they don't amount to anything. I fought for people to have the right to work but not to have whole communities and people abandoned. This is not what I lived and died for.

My fellow Americans, he would say, I fought to stop white people from being so filled with hate that they would wreak violence on black people. I did not fight for the right of black people to murder other black people with reckless abandon.

The other day the Mayor of Baltimore, a dear friend of mine, told me a story of visiting the family of a young man who had been killed—18 years old—on Halloween. He always went out with little bitty kids so they could trick-or-treat safely. And across the street from where they were walking on Halloween, a 14-year-old boy gave a 13-year-old boy a gun and dared him to shoot the 18-year-old boy, and he shot him dead. And the Mayor had to visit the family.

In Washington, DC, where I live, your Nation's Capital, the symbol of freedom throughout the world, look how that freedom is being exercised. The other night a man came along the street and grabbed a 1-year-old child and put the child in his car. The child may have been the child of the man. And two people were after him, and they chased him in the car, and they just kept shooting with reckless abandon, knowing that baby was in the car. And they shot the man dead, and a bullet went through his body into the baby's body, and blew the little bootie off the child's foot.

The other day on the front page of our paper, the Nation's Capital, are we talking about world peace or world conflict? No, big article on the front page of the Washington Post about an 11-year-old child planning her funeral: "These are the hymns I want sung. This is the dress I want to wear. I know I'm not going to live very long." That is not the freedom, the freedom to die before you're a teenager is not what Martin Luther King lived and died for.

More than 37,000 people die from gunshot wounds in this country every year. Gunfire is the leading cause of death in young men. And now that we've all gotten so cool that everybody can get a semiautomatic weapon, a person shot now is 3 times more likely to die than 15 years ago, because they're likely to have three bullets in them. A hundred and sixty thousand children stay home from school every day because they are scared they will be hurt in their schools.

The other day I was in California at a town meeting, and a handsome young man stood up and said, "Mr. President, my brother and I, we don't belong to gangs. We don't have guns. We don't do drugs. We want to go to school. We want to be professionals. We want to work hard. We want to do well. We want to have families. And we changed our school because the school we were in was so dangerous. So when we stowed up to the new school to register, my brother and I were standing in line and somebody ran into the school and started shooting a gun. My brother was shot down standing right in front of me at the safer school." The freedom to do that kind of thing is not what Martin Luther King lived and died for, not what people gathered in this hallowed church for the night before he was assassinated in April of 1968. If you had told anybody who was here in that church on that night that we would abuse our freedom in that way, they would have found it hard to believe. And I tell you, it is our moral duty to turn it around.

And now I think finally we have a chance. Finally, I think, we have a chance. We have a pastor here from New Haven, Connecticut. I was in his church with Reverend Jackson when I was running for President on a snowy day in Connecticut to mourn the death of children who had been killed in that city. And afterward we walked down the street for more than a mile in the snow. Then, the American people were not ready. People would say, "Oh, this is a terrible thing, but what can we do about it?"

Now when we read that foreign visitors come to our shores and are killed at random in our fine State of Florida, when we see our children planning their funerals, when the American people are finally coming to grips with the accumulated weight of crime and violence and the breakdown of family and community and the increase in drugs and the decrease in jobs, I think finally we may be ready to do something about it.

And there is something for each of us to do. There are changes we can make from the outside in; that's the job of the President and the Congress and the Governors and the mayors and the social service agencies. And then there's some changes we're going to have to make from the inside out, or the others won't matter. That's what that magnificent song was about, isn't it? Sometimes there are no answers from the outside in; sometimes all the answers have to come from the values and the stirrings and the voices that speak to us from within.

So we are beginning. We are trying to pass a bill to make our people safer, to put another 100,000 police officers on the street, to provide boot camps instead of prisons for young people who can still be rescued, to provide more safety in our schools, to restrict the availability of these awful assault weapons, to pass the Brady bill and at least require people to have their criminal background checked before they get a gun, and to say, if you're not old enough to vote and you're not old enough to go to war, you ought not to own a handgun, and you ought not to use one unless you're on a target range.

We want to pass a health care bill that will make drug treatment available for everyone. And we also have to do it, we have to have drug treatment and education available to everyone and especially those who are in prison who are coming out. We have a drug czar now in Lee Brown, who was the police chief of Atlanta, of Houston, of New York, who understands these things. And when the Congress comes back next year, we will be moving forward on that.

We need this crime bill now. We ought to give it to the

American people for Christmas. And we need to move forward on all these other fronts. But I say to you, my fellow Americans, we need some other things as well. I do not believe we can repair the basic fabric of society until people who are willing to work have work. Work organizes life. It gives structure and discipline to life. It gives meaning and self-esteem to people who are parents. It gives a role model to children.

The famous African-American sociologist William Julius Wilson has written a stunning book called "The Truly Disadvantaged" in which he chronicles in breathtaking terms how the inner cities of our country have crumbled as work has disappeared. And we must find a way, through public and private sources, to enhance the attractiveness of the American people who live there to get investment there. We cannot, I submit to you, repair the American community and restore the American family until we provide the structure, the values, the discipline, and the reward that work gives.

I read a wonderful speech the other day given at Howard University in a lecture series funded by Bill and Camille Cosby, in which the speaker said, "I grew up in Anacostia years ago. Even then it was all black, and it was a very poor neighborhood. But you know, when I was a child in Anacostia, a 100 percent African-American neighborhood, a very poor neighborhood, we had a crime rate that was lower than the average of the crime rate of our city. Why? Because we had coherent families. We had coherent communities. The people who filled the church on Sunday lived in the same place they went to church. The guy that owned the drugstore lived down the street. The person that owned the grocery store lived in our community. We were whole." And I say to you, we have to make our people whole again.

This church has stood for that. Why do you think you have 5 million members in this country? Because people know you are filled with the spirit of God to do the right thing in this life by them. So I say to you, we have to make a partnership, all the Government agencies, all the business folks; but where there are no families, where there is no order, where there is no hope, where we are reducing the size of our armed services because we have won the cold war, who will be there to give structure, discipline, and love to these children? You must do that. And we must help you. Scripture says, you are the the Earth and the light of the world, that if your light shines before men they will give glory to the Father in heaven. That is what we must do.

That is what we must do. How would we explain it to Martin Luther King if he showed up today and said, yes, we won the cold war. Yes, the biggest threat that all of us grew up under, communism and nuclear war, communism gone, nuclear war receding. Yes, we developed all these miraculous technologies. Yes, we all have got a VCR in our home; it's interesting. Yes, we get 50 channels on the cable. Yes, without regard to race, if you work hard and play by the rules, you can get into a service academy or a good college, you'll do just great. How would we explain to him all these kids getting killed and killing each other? How would we justify the things that we permit that no other country in the world would permit? How could we explain that we gave people the freedom to succeed, and we created conditions in which millions abuse that freedom to destroy the things that make life worth living and life itself? We cannot.

And so I say to you today, my fellow Americans, you gave me this job, and we're making progress on the things you hired me to do. But unless we deal with the ravages of crime and drugs and violence and unless we recognize that it's due to the breakdown of the family, the community, and the disappearance of jobs, and unless we say some of this cannot be done by Government, because we have to reach deep inside to the values, the spirit, the soul, and the truth of human nature, none of the other things we seek to do will ever take us where we need to go.

So in this pulpit, on this day, let me ask all of you in your heart to say: We will honor the life and the work of Martin Luther King. We will honor the meaning of our church. We will, somehow, by God's grace, we will turn this around. We will give these children a future. We will take away their guns and give them books. We will take away their despair and give them hope. We will rebuild the families and the neighborhoods and the communities. We won't make all the work that has gone on here benefit just a few. We will do it together by the grace of God.

Thank you.

WILLIAM J. CLINTON

Speech at Central High School

Little Rock, Arkansas, September 25, 1997

GOVERNOR and Mrs. Huckabee; Mayor and Mrs. Dailey; my good friend Daisy Bates; and the families of Wiley Branton and Justice Thurgood Marshall. To the cochairs of this event, Mr. Howard, and all the faculty and staff here at Central High; to Fatima and her fellow students; to all my fellow Americans: Hillary and I are glad to be home, especially on this day. And we thank you for your welcome.

I would also be remiss if I did not say one other word, just as a citizen. You know, we just sent our daughter off to college, and for 8½ years she got a very good education in the Little Rock school district. And I want to thank you all for that.

On this beautiful, sunshiny day, so many wonderful words have already been spoken with so much conviction, I am reluctant to add to them. But I must ask you to remember once more and to ask yourselves, what does what happened here 40 years ago mean today? What does it tell us, most importantly, about our children's tomorrows?

Forty years ago, a single image first seared the heart and stirred the conscience of our Nation, so powerful most of us who saw it then recall it still: a 15-year-old girl wearing a crisp black and white dress, carrying only a notebook, surrounded by large crowds of boys and girls, men and women, soldiers and police officers, her head held high, her eyes fixed straight ahead. And she is utterly alone.

On September 4th, 1957, Elizabeth Eckford walked to this door for her first day of school, utterly alone. She was turned away by people who were afraid of change, instructed by ignorance, hating what they simply could not understand. And America saw her, haunted and taunted for the simple color of her skin, and in the image we caught a very disturbing glimpse of ourselves. We saw not "one Nation under God, indivisible, with liberty and justice for all," but two Americas, divided and unequal.

What happened here changed the course of our country here forever. Like Independence Hall, where we first embraced the idea that God created us all equal; like Gettysburg, where Americans fought and died over whether we would remain one Nation, moving closer to the true meaning of equality; like them, Little Rock is historic ground, for surely it was here at Central High that we took another giant step closer to the idea of America.

Elizabeth Eckford along with her eight schoolmates were turned away on September 4th, but the Little Rock Nine did not turn back. Forty years ago today, they climbed these steps, passed through this door, and moved our Nation. And for that, we must all thank them.

Today we honor those who made it possible, their parents first—as Eleanor Roosevelt said of them, "To give your child for a cause is even harder than to give yourself"; to honor my friend Daisy Bates and Wylie Branton and Thurgood Marshall, the NAACP, and all who guided these children; to honor President Eisenhower, Attorney General Brownell, and the men of the 101st Airborne who enforced the Constitution; to honor every student, every teacher, every minister, every Little Rock resident, black or white, who offered a word of kindness, a glance of respect, or a hand of friendship; to honor those who gave us the opportunity to be part of this day of celebration and rededication.

But most of all, we come to honor the Little Rock Nine. Most of us who have just watched these events unfold can never understand fully the sacrifice they made. Imagine, all of you, what it would be like to come to school one day and be shoved against lockers, tripped down stairways, taunted day after day by your classmates, to go all through school with no hope of going to a school play or being on a basketball team or learning in simple peace.

[*At this point, there was a disturbance in the audience.*]

Speaking of simple peace, I'd like a little of it today.

I want all these children here to look at these people. They persevered, they endured, and they prevailed. But it was at

great cost to themselves. As Melba said years later in her wonderful memoir, "Warriors Don't Cry," "My friends and I paid
for the integration of Little Rock Central High with our innocence."

Folks, in 1957 I was 11 years old, living 50 miles away in Hot
Springs, when the eyes of the world were fixed here. Like
almost all southerners then, I never attended school with a
person of another race until I went to college. But as a young
boy in my grandfather's small grocery store, I learned lessons
that nobody bothered to teach me in my segregated school.
My grandfather had a sixth grade education from a tiny rural
school. He never made a bit of money. But in that store, in the
way he treated his customers and encouraged me to play with
their children, I learned America's most profound lessons: We
really are all equal. We really do have the right to live in dignity. We really do have the right to be treated with respect. We
do have the right to be heard.

I never knew how he and my grandmother came to those
convictions, but I'll never forget how they lived them. Ironi-
cally, my grandfather died in 1957. He never lived to see America come around to his way of thinking. But I know he's
smiling down today, not on his grandson but on the Little Rock
Nine, who gave up their innocence so all good people could
have a chance to live their dreams.

But let me tell you something else that was true about that
time. Before Little Rock, for me and other white children, the
struggles of black people, whether we were sympathetic or
hostile to them, were mostly background music in our normal,
self-absorbed lives. We were all, like you, more concerned
about our friends and our lives, day-in and day-out. But then
we saw what was happening in our own backyard, and we all
had to deal with it. Where did we stand? What did we believe?
How did we want to live? It was Little Rock that made racial
equality a driving obsession in my life.

Years later, time and chance made Ernie Green my friend.
Good fortune brought me to the Governor's office, where I
did all I could to heal the wounds, solve the problems, open
the doors so we could become the people we say we want to be.

Ten years ago, the Little Rock Nine came back to the Governor's Mansion when I was there. I wanted them to see that

the power of the office that once had blocked their way now welcomed them. But like so many Americans, I can never fully repay my debt to these nine people. For with their innocence, they purchased more freedom for me, too, and for all white people—people like Hazel Brown Massery, the angry taunter of Elizabeth Eckford, who stood with her in front of this school this week as a reconciled friend. And with the gift of their innocence, they taught us that all too often what ought to be can never be for free.

Forty years later, what do you young people in this audience believe we have learned? Well, 40 years later, we know that we all benefit—all of us—when we learn together, work together, and come together. That is, after all, what it means to be an American.

Forty years later, we know, not withstanding some cynics, that all our children can learn, and this school proves it. Forty years later, we know when the constitutional rights of our citizens are threatened, the National Government must guarantee them. Talk is fine, but when they are threatened, you need strong laws faithfully enforced and upheld by independent courts.

Forty years later, we know there are still more doors to be opened, doors to be opened wider, doors we have to keep from being shut again now. Forty years later, we know freedom and equality cannot be realized without responsibility for self, family, and the duties of citizenship, or without a commitment to building a community of shared destiny and a genuine sense of belonging.

Forty years later, we know the question of race is more complex and more important than ever, embracing no longer just blacks and whites, or blacks and whites and Hispanics and Native Americans, but now people from all parts of the Earth coming here to redeem the promise of America.

Forty years later, frankly, we know we're bound to come back where we started. After all the weary years and silent tears, after all the stony roads and bitter rides, the question of race is, in the end, still an affair of the heart.

But if these are our lessons, what do we have to do? First, we must all reconcile. Then we must all face the facts of today. And finally we must act.

Reconciliation is important not only for those who practice bigotry but for those whose resentment of it lingers, for both are prisons from which our spirits must escape. If Nelson Mandela, who paid for the freedom of his people with 27 of the best years of his life, could invite his jailers to his inauguration and ask even the victims of violence to forgive their oppressors, then each of us can seek and give forgiveness.

And what are the facts? It is a fact, my fellow Americans, that there are still too many places where opportunity for education and work are not equal, where disintegration of family and neighborhood make it more difficult. But it is also a fact that schools and neighborhoods and lives can be turned around if, but only if, we are prepared to do what it takes. It is a fact that there are still too many places where our children die or give up before they bloom, where they are trapped in a web of crime and violence and drugs. But we know this too can be changed, but only if we are prepared to do what it takes.

Today, children of every race walk through the same door, but then they often walk down different halls. Not only in this school but across America, they sit in different classrooms. They eat at different tables. They even sit in different parts of the bleachers at the football game. Far too many communities are all white, all black, all Latino, all Asian. Indeed, too many Americans of all races have actually begun to give up on the idea of integration and the search for common ground. For the first time since the 1950's, our schools in America are re-segregating. The rollback of affirmative action is slamming shut the doors of higher education on a new generation, while those who oppose it have not yet put forward any other alternative.

In so many ways, we still hold ourselves back. We retreat into the comfortable enclaves of ethnic isolation. We just don't deal with people who are different from us. Segregation is no longer the law, but too often separation is still the rule. And we cannot forget one stubborn fact that has not yet been said as clearly as it should: There is still discrimination in America.

There are still people who can't get over it, who can't let it go, who can't go through the day unless they have somebody else to look down on. And it manifests itself in our streets and in our neighborhoods and in the workplace and in the schools. And it is wrong. And we have to keep working on it, not just with our voices but with our laws. And we have to engage each other in it.

Of course, we should celebrate our diversity. The marvelous blend of cultures and beliefs and races has always enriched America, and it is our meal ticket to the 21st century. But we also have to remember, with the painful lessons of the civil wars and the ethnic cleansing around the world, that any nation that indulges itself in destructive separatism will not be able to meet and master the challenges of the 21st century.

We have to decide—all you young people have to decide—will we stand as a shining example or a stunning rebuke to the world of tomorrow? For the alternative to integration is not isolation or a new separate but equal, it is disintegration.

Only the American idea is strong enough to hold us together. We believe, whether our ancestors came here in slave ships or on the *Mayflower,* whether they came through the portals of Ellis Island or on a plane to San Francisco, whether they have been here for thousands of years, we believe that every individual possesses the spark of possibility, born with an equal right to strive and work and rise as far as they can go, and born with an equal responsibility to act in a way that obeys the law, reflects our values, and passes them on to their children. We are white and black, Asian and Hispanic, Christian and Jew and Muslim, Italian- and Vietnamese- and Polish-Americans and goodness knows how many more today. But above all, we are still Americans. Martin Luther King said, "We are woven into a seamless garment of destiny. We must be one America."

The Little Rock Nine taught us that. We cannot have one America for free, not 40 years ago, not today. We have to act. All of us have to act. Each of us has to do something. Especially our young people must seek out people who are different from themselves and speak freely and frankly to discover they share the same dreams.

All of us should embrace the vision of a colorblind society, but recognize the fact that we are not there yet and we cannot slam shut the doors of educational and economic opportunity. All of us should embrace ethnic pride and we should revere religious conviction, but we must reject separation and isolation. All of us should value and practice personal responsibility for ourselves and our families. And all Americans, especially our young people, should give something back to their community through citizen service. All Americans of all races must insist on both equal opportunity and excellence in education. That is even more important today than it was for these nine people, and look how far they took themselves with their education.

The true battleground in education today is whether we honestly believe that every child can learn and we have the courage to set high academic standards we expect all our children to meet. We must not replace the tyranny of segregation with the tragedy of low expectations. I will not rob a single American child of his or her future. It is wrong.

My fellow Americans, we must be concerned not so much with the sins of our parents as with the success of our children, how they will live, and live together, in years to come. If those nine children could walk up those steps 40 years ago all alone, if their parents could send them into the storm armed only with schoolbooks and the righteousness of their cause, then surely together we can build one America, an America that makes sure no future generation of our children will have to pay for our mistakes with the loss of their innocence.

At this schoolhouse door today, let us rejoice in the long way we have come these 40 years. Let us resolve to stand on the shoulders of the Little Rock Nine and press on with confidence in the hard and noble work ahead. Let us lift every voice and sing, till Earth and Heaven ring, one America today, one America tomorrow, one America forever.

God bless the Little Rock Nine, and God bless the United States of America. Thank you.

BIOGRAPHICAL NOTES

NOTE ON THE TEXTS

NOTES

INDEX

Biographical Notes

John Peter Altgeld (December 30, 1847–March 12, 1902) Born in Niederselters in western Germany. Family immigrated to the United States in 1848 and settled on a farm near Newville, Ohio. Served with the Union Army in Virginia in 1864. Left Ohio in 1869 and settled in Savannah, Missouri, where he taught school and was admitted to the bar in 1871. Elected prosecuting attorney of Andrew County in 1874. Resigned in 1875 and moved to Chicago. Published *Our Penal Machinery and Its Victims* in 1884. Won election as a Democrat to the superior court of Cook County and served 1886–91. Elected governor of Illinois in 1892 and served 1893–97. Defeated for reelection after pardoning the three surviving anarchists convicted in the Haymarket bombing and protesting the use of federal troops in Illinois during the Pullman strike. Died in Joliet, Illinois.

Susan B. Anthony (February 15, 1820–March 13, 1906) Born in Adams, Massachusetts, the daughter of a textile manufacturer. Family moved to Battenville, New York, in 1826 and to Rochester in 1845. Educated at home and at boarding school near Philadelphia. Taught at the Canajoharie Academy, 1846–49. Began friendship with Elizabeth Cady Stanton in 1851. Helped found the Woman's State Temperance Society in 1852 and became active in the woman's rights movement. Served as an agent for the American Anti-Slavery Society, 1856–61. Organized petition drive with Stanton in support of the Thirteenth Amendment, 1863–64. Helped found the American Equal Rights Association in 1866. Published weekly newspaper *Revolution*, 1868–70. Served as an executive officer of the National Woman Suffrage Association, 1869–90. Arrested in Rochester for voting in the 1872 election and was fined $100. Edited *History of Woman Suffrage* (3 vols., 1881–86) with Stanton and Matilda Joslyn Gage. Served as vice-president of the National American Woman Suffrage Association, 1890–92, and succeeded Stanton as its president, 1892–1900. Died in Rochester.

William Jennings Bryan (March 19, 1860–July 26, 1925) Born in Salem, Illinois, the son of a lawyer and farmer. Graduated from Illinois College, 1881, and from Union College of Law, 1883. Practiced law in Jacksonville, Illinois, before moving to Lincoln, Nebraska, in 1887. Served in Congress as a Democrat, 1891–95. Became editor of the Omaha *World-Herald* and a successful lecturer. Won Democratic presidential nomination in 1896 and 1900 but was twice defeated by William McKinley. Founded *The Commoner*, successful weekly newspaper, in 1901. Won Democratic nomination in 1908 but was defeated by William Howard Taft. Became Secretary of State in the Wilson administration in 1913 and served until June 9, 1915, when he resigned, fearing that Wilson's response to the sinking of the *Lusitania* would lead to war with Germany. Published *The Commoner* as a monthly until 1923. Served as special prosecutor at the Scopes evolution trial in Dayton, Tennessee, in 1925; died in Dayton five days after the trial ended.

Benjamin F. Butler (November 5, 1818–January 11, 1893) Born in Deerfield, New Hampshire, the son of a merchant. Graduated from Waterville (now Colby) College in 1838. Admitted to the bar in 1840 and began practicing law in Lowell, Massachusetts. Served as a Democrat in the Massachusetts house of representatives, 1853, and in the Massachusetts senate, 1859. Commissioned as a major general in the Union Army in 1861. Military governor of New Orleans, May–December 1862. Relieved of command by Grant in 1865. Served in Congress as a Republican, 1867–75 and 1877–79, and was one of the House managers at the impeachment trial of Andrew Johnson in 1868. Elected governor of Massachusetts as a Democrat and served one-year term in 1883. Presidential candidate of the Greenback and Anti-Monopolist parties in 1884. Died in Washington, D.C.

Jimmy Carter (October 1, 1924–) Born James Earl Carter Jr. in Plains, Georgia, the son of a farmer and a nurse. Graduated from the U.S. Naval Academy in 1946 and served in the navy until 1953. Returned to Plains to run the family farm and warehouse. Served as a Democrat in the Georgia state senate, 1963–67. Governor of Georgia, 1971–75. Won Democratic presidential nomination in 1976 and defeated President Gerald Ford. President of the United States, 1977–81. Defeated for reelection by Ronald Reagan. Awarded Nobel Peace Prize in 2002.

Carrie Chapman Catt (June 9, 1859–March 9, 1947) Born Carrie Lane in Ripon, Wisconsin, the daughter of a farmer. Graduated from Iowa State Agricultural College in 1880. Taught school in Mason City, Iowa, 1881–83, and served as its superintendent of schools, 1883–85. Married Leo Chapman, a newspaper editor, in 1885, but was widowed in 1886. Became a professional lecturer. Worked as an organizer for the Iowa Woman Suffrage Association, 1889–92, and the National American Woman Suffrage Association, 1890–1900. Married George

Catt, an engineer, in 1890, and settled in Brooklyn in 1892. Succeeded Susan B. Anthony as president of NAWSA, 1900–4. Helped found the International Woman Suffrage Association in 1902 and served as its president until 1923. Husband died in 1905. Traveled around the world, 1911–12, on behalf of the IWSA. Succeeded Anna Howard Shaw as president of NAWSA in 1915 and served until the ratification of the Nineteenth Amendment in 1920. Helped found the League of Woman Voters in 1919. Founded the National Committee on the Cause and Cure of War in 1925. Died in New Rochelle, New York.

John Jay Chapman (March 2, 1862–November 4, 1933) Born in New York City, the son of a stockbroker. Graduated from Harvard in 1884 and was admitted to the New York bar in 1888. Became active in reform politics in New York City. Published *Emerson and Other Essays* (1898), *Causes and Consequences* (1898), *Practical Agitation* (1900), and a magazine, *The Political Nursery*, 1897–1901. Wrote plays. Later books included *William Lloyd Garrison* (1913), *Memories and Milestones* (1915), *Greek Genius and Other Essays* (1915), *Letters and Religion* (1924), and *New Horizons in American Life* (1932). Died in Poughkeepsie, New York.

Chief Joseph (c. 1840–September 21, 1904) Born in the Wallowa Valley in northeastern Oregon, the son of a Nez Percé leader, and named Hin-mah-too-yah-lat-kekt (Thunder Rolling Down the Mountain). Chosen as a leader of the Wallowa Nez Percé after the death of his father in 1871 and became known to whites as Joseph, after his father's baptismal name. Resisted attempts to move his people to a reservation in Idaho and joined other Nez Percé in their flight to Canada in 1877. Surrendered to the U.S. Army in northern Montana on October 5, 1877, and was sent to Indian Territory (Oklahoma). Traveled to Washington, D.C., in 1879 and met with President Rutherford B. Hayes in an unsuccessful attempt to win the return of his people to Oregon. Permitted in 1885 to settle on the Colville Reservation in northern Washington, where he died.

Grover Cleveland (March 18, 1837–June 24, 1908) Born Stephen Grover Cleveland in Caldwell, New Jersey, the son of a Presbyterian minister. Studied law in Buffalo, New York, and was admitted to the bar in 1859. Served as assistant district attorney, 1862–65, sheriff of Erie County, 1871–73, mayor of Buffalo, 1882, and governor of New York, 1883–84. Won Democratic presidential nomination in 1884 and defeated James G. Blaine. President of the United States, 1885–89. Defeated for reelection by Benjamin Harrison in 1888, but defeated

Harrison in 1892 and served second term as president, 1893–97. Retired to Princeton, New Jersey, where he died.

William J. Clinton (August 19, 1946–) Born William Jefferson Blythe III in Hope, Arkansas, the son of a nurse; his father died before his birth, and he later took the name of his stepfather. Graduated from Georgetown University in 1968 and from Yale Law School in 1973. Attorney general of Arkansas, 1977–79. Governor of Arkansas, 1979–81 and 1983–92. Won Democratic presidential nomination in 1992 and defeated President George H. W. Bush; won re-election in 1996 by defeating Robert Dole. President of the United States, 1993–2001.

Eugene V. Debs (November 5, 1855–October 20, 1926) Born in Terre Haute, Indiana, the son of a grocer. Began working in a railroad shop in 1870 and became a locomotive fireman. Helped found local lodge of the Brotherhood of Locomotive Firemen in 1875. Secretary-treasurer of the national Brotherhood, 1880–93. City clerk of Terre Haute, 1879–83. Served as a Democrat in the Indiana house of representatives in 1885. Founded American Railway Union in 1893. Led strike against Pullman Company that resulted in an injunction that crippled the union. Served six-month sentence for contempt in 1895. Founded Social Democratic Party of America in 1897 and was its presidential candidate in 1900. Presidential candidate of the Socialist Party in 1904, 1908, and 1912, when he received 6 percent of the vote. Convicted under the Espionage Act in 1918 for making an anti-war speech and sentenced to ten years imprisonment. Received more than 900,000 votes in the 1920 presidential election while in prison. Released in 1921 after President Harding commuted his sentence. Died in Elmhurst, Illinois.

Frederick Douglass (February 1818–February 20, 1895) Born Frederick Bailey in Talbot County, Maryland, the son of a slave mother and an unknown white man. Escaped to Philadelphia in 1838 and settled in New Bedford, Massachusetts, where he took the name Douglass. Became a lecturer for the American Anti-Slavery Society, led by William Lloyd Garrison, in 1841. Published *Narrative of the Life of Frederick Douglass, An American Slave* in 1845. Made successful lecture tour in Great Britain and Ireland, 1845–47, during which a group of English supporters purchased his manumission. Began publishing an antislavery newspaper, *North Star*, in Rochester, New York, in 1847. Attended the woman's rights convention held at Seneca Falls, New York, in 1848. Broke with Garrison and became an ally of Gerrit Smith, who advocated an antislavery interpretation of the Constitution and participation in electoral politics. Published *My Bondage and My Freedom* in 1855. Advocated emancipation and the enlistment of black soldiers at the outbreak of the Civil War and eventually became a supporter of Abraham Lincoln. Continued his advocacy of racial equality and woman's rights after the Civil War. Served as U.S. marshal, 1877–81, and recorder of deeds, 1877–86, for the District of Columbia. Published *Life and Times of Frederick Douglass* in 1881. Served as minister to Haiti, 1889–91. Died in Washington, D.C.

Dwight D. Eisenhower (October 14, 1890–March 28, 1969) Born in Denison, Texas, the son of a railroad worker. Family moved to Abilene, Kansas, in 1892. Graduated from the U.S. Military Academy in 1915 and served stateside during World War I. Held rank of lieutenant colonel in 1939. Served in war plans division of the army general staff, 1941–42. Commanded the Allied invasions of North Africa in 1942 and of Sicily and Italy in 1943. Appointed Supreme Commander, Allied Expeditionary Force, and commanded the invasion of northwest Europe, 1944–45. Promoted to General of the Army (five-star rank) in December 1944. Chief of Staff of the U.S. Army, 1945–48. President of Columbia University, 1948–50. Served as Supreme Allied Commander, Europe, 1950–52. Retired from the army to run for president as a Republican. Defeated Adlai Stevenson in the 1952 and 1956 elections and served as President of the United States, 1953–61. Died in Washington, D.C.

Robert Brown Elliott (August 11, 1842?–August 9, 1884) Born and educated in Liverpool, England. Learned printing trade and served in the Royal Navy. Immigrated to Boston and then moved to Charleston, South Carolina, where in 1867 he became associate editor of the *South Carolina Leader*. Delegate to the South Carolina constitutional convention in 1868. Served as a Republican in the state house of representatives, 1868–70. Admitted to the bar in 1868. Elected to Congress in 1870 and served, 1871–74. Speaker of the South Carolina house of representatives, 1874–76. Elected state attorney general in 1876, but was forced out of office in 1877. Worked as a Treasury Department inspector in Charleston, 1879–81, and New Orleans, 1881–82. Died in New Orleans.

William Faulkner (September 25, 1897–July 6, 1962) Born in New Albany, Mississippi, the son of a railroad manager who later owned a livery stable. Moved to Oxford, Mississippi, with his family in 1902. Joined Royal Air Force in 1918 and attended ground school in Canada. Enrolled at the University of Mississippi, 1920–21. Published

Soldiers' Pay in 1926, the first of 19 novels, including *The Sound and the Fury* (1929), *As I Lay Dying* (1930), *Light in August* (1932), *Absalom, Absalom!* (1936), *The Hamlet* (1940), and *Go Down, Moses* (1942). Worked intermittently as a screenwriter in Hollywood. Awarded Nobel Prize for Literature in 1950. Published last novel, *The Reivers*, in 1962. Died in Byhalia, Mississippi.

Betty Friedan (February 4, 1921–February 4, 2006) Born Bettye Naomi Goldstein in Peoria, Illinois, the daughter of a jewelry store owner. Graduated from Smith College in 1942 and studied psychology at the University of California, Berkeley. Worked for *U.E. News*, weekly newspaper of the United Electrical Workers, 1946–52. Married Carl Friedan in 1947 (divorced in 1969). Published *The Feminine Mystique* in 1963. Helped found the National Organization for Women in 1966, the National Association for the Repeal of Abortion Laws in 1969, and the National Women's Political Caucus in 1971. President of NOW, 1966–70. Published *It Changed My Life: Writings on the Women's Movement* (1976), *The Second Stage* (1981), *The Fountain of Age* (1993), and *Life So Far* (2000). Died in Washington, D.C.

Barry Goldwater (January 1, 1909–May 29, 1998) Born in Phoenix, Arizona Territory, the son of a successful department store owner. Attended University of Arizona before entering the family business in 1929. Served as a transport pilot in the U.S. Army Air Forces, 1941–45. Member of the Phoenix city council, 1949–52. Elected to the Senate as a Republican and served 1953–65. Won Republican presidential nomination in 1964, but was defeated by President Lyndon B. Johnson. Elected to the Senate in 1968 and served 1969–87. Died in Paradise Valley, Arizona.

Oliver Wendell Holmes, Jr. (March 8, 1841–March 6, 1935) Born in Boston, the son of the physician, poet, and essayist Oliver Wendell Holmes. Graduated from Harvard in 1861. Served as an officer with the 20th Massachusetts Volunteer Regiment, July 1861–July 1864, and was wounded at Ball's Bluff, Antietam, and the Second Battle of Fredericksburg. Graduated from Harvard Law School in 1866. Practiced law in Boston, wrote legal articles, and edited new edition of James Kent's *Commentaries on American Law*. Published *The Common Law* in 1881. Served as an associate justice of the Massachusetts supreme judicial court, 1883–99, as its chief justice, 1899–1902, and as an associate justice of the U.S. Supreme Court, 1902–32. Died in Washington, D.C.

Herbert Hoover (August 10, 1874–October 20, 1964) Born in West Branch, Iowa, the son of a blacksmith. Graduated from Stanford in 1895. Worked as a mining engineer in California, Nevada, Colorado, Australia, and in China, where he was trapped in Tientsin during the Boxer Rebellion. Served as chairman of the Commission for Relief in Belgium, 1914–20, U.S. Food Administrator, 1917–20, and director of the American Relief Administration, 1918–20; oversaw the distribution of food throughout Europe and the Near East. Secretary of Commerce in the administrations of Warren Harding and Calvin Coolidge, 1921–28. Won Republican presidential nomination in 1928 and defeated Governor Al Smith. President of the United States, 1929–33. Defeated for reelection by Franklin D. Roosevelt. Served as government coordinator for overseas food relief, 1946–47, and as chairman of commissions on government reorganization, 1947–49 and 1953–55. Died in New York City.

Hubert H. Humphrey (May 27, 1911–January 13, 1978) Born in Wallace, South Dakota, the son of a pharmacist. Worked in the family drug store before graduating from the University of Minnesota in 1939. Taught political science and served in wartime administrative positions. Helped merge the Minnesota Democratic and Farmer-Labor parties in 1944. Mayor of Minneapolis, 1945–48. Elected to the Senate as the D.F.L. candidate in 1948 and served 1949–64. Candidate for the Democratic presidential nomination in 1960. Senate majority whip, 1961–64. Elected Vice-President of the United States on ticket with Lyndon B. Johnson in 1964 and served from 1965 to 1969. Won Democratic presidential nomination in 1968 but lost election to Richard Nixon. Elected to the Senate in 1970 and served from 1971 until his death. Candidate for the Democratic nomination in 1972. Died in Waverly, Minnesota.

Robert G. Ingersoll (August 11, 1833–July 21, 1899) Born in Dresden, New York, the son of a Congregational minister. Family moved to Ohio, Wisconsin, and Illinois. Admitted to the bar in 1854 and established successful law practice in Peoria. Raised the 11th Illinois Volunteer Cavalry Regiment in 1861 and commanded it at Shiloh and Corinth. Captured in December 1862 and did not see further service after being paroled. Appointed attorney general of Illinois in 1867 and served until 1869. Campaigned for Republican candidates and became a popular orator and lecturer, known as the "Great Agnostic" for his advocacy of freethinking. Died in Dobbs Ferry, New York.

Jesse Jackson (October 8, 1941–) Born Jesse Burns in Greenville, South Carolina, the son of a single teenaged mother; later took the name of his stepfather. Attended University of Illinois. Arrested in civil rights protest in Greensboro, North Carolina, in 1963. Graduated from North Carolina Agricultural and Technical College in 1964. Became an organizer for the Southern Christian Leadership Conference in 1966 and directed Operation Breadbasket for the SCLC, 1967–71. Ordained as a Baptist minister in 1968. Founded Operation PUSH (People United to Serve Humanity) in 1971 and the National Rainbow Coalition in 1985. Candidate for the Democratic presidential nomination in 1984 and 1988.

Lyndon B. Johnson (August 27, 1908–January 22, 1973) Born in Stonewall, Texas, the son of a farmer. Graduated from Southwest Texas State Teachers College in 1930. Served as secretary to Congressman Richard Kleberg, 1931–35, and as state director of the National Youth Administration, 1935–37. Elected to Congress as a Democrat in 1937 and served until 1949. Served as an officer in the U.S. Navy, 1941–42. Elected to the Senate in 1948 and served 1949–61. Majority whip, 1951–53; minority leader, 1953–55; and majority leader, 1955–61. Candidate for the 1960 Democratic presidential nomination. Elected Vice-President of the United States on ticket with John F. Kennedy. Served from 1961 to November 22, 1963, when he became president following the assassination of President Kennedy. President of the United States, 1963–69. Defeated Senator Barry Goldwater in 1964 election; decided in 1968 not to seek another term. Died on his ranch near Johnson City, Texas.

Barbara Jordan (February 21, 1936–January 17, 1996) Born in Houston, Texas, the daughter of warehouse worker and a maid. Graduated from Texas Southern University in 1956 and from Boston University Law School in 1959. Practiced law in Houston. Elected as a Democrat to the Texas state senate and served 1966–72. Won election to the House of Representatives in 1972, becoming the first African-American member of Congress from Texas. Served from 1973 to 1979, when she retired from politics because of illness. Professor at the Lyndon B. Johnson School of Public Affairs at the University of Texas at Austin from 1979 until her death. Died in Austin.

Edward M. Kennedy (February 22, 1932–) Born in Brookline, Massachusetts, the son of a wealthy businessman; brother of John F. Kennedy and Robert F. Kennedy. Served in the U.S. Army, 1951–53. Graduated from Harvard in 1956 and from the University of Virginia Law School in 1959. Worked on the Senate and presidential campaigns of John F. Kennedy. Elected as a Democrat to the Senate in 1962 and has served from 1963 until the present. Majority whip, 1969–71. Candidate for the Democratic presidential nomination in 1980.

John F. Kennedy (May 29, 1917–November 22, 1963) Born in Brookline, Massachusetts, the son of a wealthy businessman; brother of Robert F. Kennedy and Edward M Kennedy. Graduated from Harvard in 1940. Served in the U.S. Navy, 1941–45, and commanded a torpedo boat in the South Pacific. Elected as a Democrat to Congress in 1946 and served 1947–53; elected to the Senate in 1952 and served 1953–60. Won the Democratic presidential nomination in 1960 and defeated Vice-President Richard M. Nixon. President of the United States from 1961 until his death. Assassinated by Lee Harvey Oswald in Dallas, Texas.

Robert F. Kennedy (November 20, 1925–June 6, 1968) Born in Brookline, Massachusetts, the son of a wealthy businessman; brother of John F. Kennedy and Edward M. Kennedy. Served in the U.S. Navy, 1944–46. Graduated from Harvard in 1948 and from the University of Virginia Law School in 1951. Attorney in the criminal division of the Department of Justice, 1951–52. Managed 1952 Senate campaign of John F. Kennedy. Served as a counsel for the Senate permanent subcommittee on investigations, 1953 and 1954–55. Chief counsel for Senate select committee investigating labor racketeering, 1957–60. Managed 1960 presidential campaign of John F. Kennedy. Attorney General of the United States, 1961–64. Elected to the Senate from New York in 1964 and served from 1965 until his death. Assassinated by Sirhan Sirhan in Los Angeles while campaigning for the Democratic presidential nomination.

Martin Luther King, Jr. (January 15, 1929–April 4, 1968) Born in Atlanta, Georgia, the son of a Baptist minister. Graduated from Morehouse College in 1948 and from Crozer Theological Seminary in 1951. Became pastor of the Dexter Avenue Baptist Church in 1954. Awarded Ph.D. in theology from Boston University in 1955. Led boycott of city buses as president of the Montgomery Improvement Association, 1955–56. Helped found the Southern Christian Leadership Conference in 1957 and became its chairman. Moved to Atlanta in 1960 and became co-pastor of Ebenezer Baptist Church with his father. Helped lead nonviolent civil rights protests in Atlanta, Albany, Georgia, and Birmingham, Alabama; wrote "Letter from Birmingham Jail" after his arrest in 1963. Awarded the Nobel Peace Prize in 1964. Helped lead march from Selma to Montgomery in 1965. Publicly opposed the war in Vietnam and campaigned against housing discrimination in northern cities. Assassinated by James Earl Ray during visit to Memphis in support of striking sanitation workers.

Robert M. La Follette, Sr. (June 14, 1855–June 18, 1925) Born in Primrose, Wisconsin, the son of a farmer. Graduated from the University of Wisconsin at Madison in 1879 and was admitted to the bar in 1880. Served as district attorney of Dane County, 1880–84. Elected to Congress as a Republican and served from 1885 to 1891. Governor of Wisconsin, 1901–6. Served in the Senate from 1906 until his death, and was succeeded by his son, Robert La Follette, Jr. Nominated for president by the Progressive Party in 1924; won 16 percent of the popular vote and the 13 electoral votes of Wisconsin. Died in Washington, D.C.

Abraham Lincoln (February 12, 1809–April 15, 1865) Born near Hodgenville, Kentucky, the son of a farmer and carpenter. Family moved to Indiana in 1816 and to Illinois in 1830. Settled in New Salem, Illinois, and worked as a storekeeper, surveyor, and postmaster. Served as a Whig in the state legislature, 1834–41. Began law practice in 1836 and moved to Springfield in 1837. Elected to Congress as a Whig and served 1847–49. Became a public opponent of the extension of slavery after the passage of the Kansas-Nebraska Act in 1854. Helped found the Republican Party of Illinois in 1856. Campaigned in 1858 for Senate seat held by Stephen Douglas and debated him seven times on the slavery issue; although the Illinois legislature reelected Douglas, the campaign brought Lincoln national prominence. Received Republican presidential nomination in 1860 and won election in a four-way contest; his victory led to the secession of the Southern states. Issued preliminary and final emancipation proclamations on September 22, 1862, and January 1, 1863. After long series of command changes, appointed Ulysses S. Grant commander of all Union forces in March 1864. Won reelection in 1864 by defeating Democrat George B. McClellan. Died in Washington, D.C., after being shot by John Wilkes Booth.

Henry Cabot Lodge (May 12, 1850–November 9, 1924) Born in Boston, the son of a successful merchant. Graduated from Harvard in 1871 and Harvard Law School in 1874; awarded a Ph.D. in history and government by Harvard in 1876. Wrote numerous historical works, including biographies of Alexander Hamilton (1882), Daniel Webster (1883), and George Washington (1888). Elected to the Massachusetts house of representatives as a Republican and served 1880–81. Served in Congress, 1887–93, and in the Senate from 1893 until his death. Died in Cambridge, Massachusetts.

Huey Long (August 30, 1893–September 10, 1935) Born near Winnfield, Louisiana, the son of a farmer. Studied law at the University of Oklahoma and Tulane, and was admitted to the bar in 1915. Served on the state railroad commission, 1918–21, and on the public service commission, 1921–28. Democratic governor of Louisiana, 1928–32. Served in the Senate from 1932 until his assassination in Baton Rouge by Dr. Carl Weiss.

Douglas MacArthur (January 26, 1880–April 5, 1964) Born near Little Rock, Arkansas, the son of an army officer who had commanded a Union regiment during the Civil War. Graduated from the U.S. Military Academy in 1903. Served in France during World War I. Superintendent of the Military Academy, 1919–22. Chief of Staff of the U.S. Army, 1930–35. Appointed commander of the Philippine military in 1936 and resigned from the U.S. Army in 1937. Recalled to active duty in 1941 and made commander of the U.S. Army in the Far East. Directed defense of the Philippines from the Japanese attack on December 7, 1941, until March 1942, when he was evacuated to Australia. Appointed Supreme Commander of Allied forces in the Southwest Pacific, and directed offensives in New Guinea, 1942–44, and the Philippines, 1944–45. Promoted to General of the Army (five-star rank) in December 1944. Accepted Japanese surrender in Tokyo Bay on September 2, 1945. Served as commander of the Allied occupation of Japan, 1945–51, and of United Nations forces in Korea, 1950–51. Relieved of his command by President Harry S. Truman on April 11, 1951, for publicly criticizing administration policy in the Korean War. Died in Washington, D.C.

Malcolm X (May 19, 1925–February 21, 1965) Born Malcolm Little in Omaha, Nebraska, the son of a Baptist minister. Attended school in Lansing, Michigan, through the seventh grade. Lived in Boston, New York City, and Michigan, 1941–46. Worked at a series of jobs while engaging in petty crime and street hustling. Arrested in Boston in 1946 for grand larceny, breaking and entering, and carrying a firearm. Served sentence in Charlestown, Concord, and Norfolk prisons; read extensively in prison libraries and was introduced to the teachings of Elijah Mohammad, the leader of the Nation of Islam. Paroled in 1952. Met Elijah Mohammad, took name Malcolm X, and became a minister of Temple No. 7 in New York City in 1954. Traveled throughout the United States and became the leading spokesman for the Nation of Islam. Collaborated with Alex Haley on posthumously published autobiography. Broke with Elijah Mohammad in March 1964. Made pilgrimage to Mecca and took name El-Hajj Malik El-Shabazz.

Founded Organization of Afro-American Unity in June 1964. Assassinated in New York City by members of the Nation of Islam.

George C. Marshall (December 31, 1880–October 16, 1959) Born in Uniontown, Pennsylvania, the son of a successful coal and coke merchant. Graduated from the Virginia Military Institute in 1901 and was commissioned in the army as a second lieutenant in 1902. Served as a staff officer in France, 1917–18, and as assistant commandant of the Infantry School at Fort Benning, Georgia, 1927–32. Chief of Staff of the U.S. Army, September 1939–November 1945. Served as a special envoy to China, 1945–46. Secretary of State, 1947–49, and Secretary of Defense, 1950–51, in the Truman administration. Awarded the Nobel Peace Prize in 1953. Died in Washington, D.C.

Richard M. Nixon (January 9, 1913–April 22, 1994) Born in Yorba Linda, California, the son of a lemon grower who later owned a gas station and grocery store. Graduated from Whittier College in 1934 and Duke Law School in 1937. Practiced law in Whittier. Served as an officer in the U.S. Navy, 1942–46. Elected as a Republican to Congress in 1946 and served 1947–50; elected to the Senate in 1950 and served 1950–53. Nominated for vice-president on ticket with Dwight D. Eisenhower in 1952. Vice-President of the United States, 1953–61. Won Republican presidential nomination in 1960, but was defeated by Senator John F. Kennedy. Unsuccessful candidate for governor of California in 1962. Won Republican presidential nomination in 1968 and defeated Vice-President Hubert H. Humphrey, and was reelected in 1972, defeating Senator George McGovern. President of the United States from 1969 until August 9, 1974, when he resigned to avoid impeachment for his role in the Watergate scandal. Died in New York City.

J. Robert Oppenheimer (April 22, 1904–February 18, 1967) Born in New York City, the son of a successful textile importer and a painter. Graduated from Harvard in 1925, studied at Cambridge University, and received a doctorate in physics from the University of Göttingen in 1927. Professor of physics at the University of California, Berkeley, and the California Institute of Technology, 1929–47. Became involved in research on nuclear weapons in 1941. Founding director of the Los Alamos Laboratory, 1943–45; oversaw the design and manufacture of the first atomic bombs. Director of the Institute for Advanced Study at Princeton, 1947–66. Chairman of the General Advisory Committee of the Atomic Energy Commission, 1947–52. Denied further security clearance by the Atomic Energy Commission in 1954, ending his role as a government advisor on nuclear weapons policy. Died in Princeton, New Jersey.

George S. Patton (November 11, 1885–December 21, 1945) Born in San Gabriel, California, the son of an attorney. Graduated from the U.S. Military Academy in 1909. Served with the Pershing expedition in Mexico in 1916. Commanded 1st Tank Brigade in 1918 and saw action in the St. Mihiel salient and the Meuse-Argonne, where he was wounded. Graduated from the Army War College in 1932. Commanded the Western Task Force in Morocco, November 1942, the II Corps in Tunisia, March–April 1943, the Seventh Army in Sicily, July–August 1943, and the Third Army in France, Belgium, Luxembourg, Germany, and Czechoslovakia, August 1944–May 1945. Died in Heidelberg, Germany, from injuries suffered in an automobile accident.

Ronald Reagan (February 6, 1911–June 5, 2004) Born in Tampico, Illinois, the son of a shoe salesman. Graduated from Eureka College in 1932. Worked as a radio announcer, 1932–37. Acted in movies and television, 1937–1965; his films included *Knute Rockne, All American* (1940), *Kings Row* (1942), *Bedtime for Bonzo* (1951), and *The Killers* (1964). President of the Screen Actors Guild, 1947–52 and 1959–60. Made speeches for General Electric, 1954–62. Elected as a Republican to two terms as governor of California and served, 1967–1975. Candidate for Republican presidential nomination in 1968 and 1976. Won nomination in 1980 and defeated President Jimmy Carter. Wounded in assassination attempt in 1981. Won reelection in 1984 by defeating Walter Mondale. President of the United States, 1981–89. Died in Los Angeles.

Franklin D. Roosevelt (January 30, 1882–April 12, 1945) Born in Hyde Park, New York, the son of a wealthy investor. Graduated from Harvard in 1904. Studied law at Columbia, passed the bar exam in 1907, and worked for a law firm in New York City. Elected as a Democrat to the New York state senate in 1910 and served 1911–13. Assistant Secretary of the Navy in the Wilson administration, 1913–20. Unsuccessful Democratic vice-presidential candidate in 1920. Contracted poliomyelitis in 1921 and lost the use of his legs. Elected governor of New York in 1928 and served 1929–32. Won Democratic presidential nomination in 1932 and defeated President Herbert Hoover; subsequently won reelection by defeating Alfred Landon, Wendell Wilkie, and Thomas Dewey. President of the United States from 1933 until his death in Warm Springs, Georgia.

Theodore Roosevelt (October 27, 1858–January 6, 1919) Born in New York City, the son of a wealthy investor and philanthropist. Graduated from Harvard in 1880. Elected as a Republican to the New York state assembly in 1881 and served 1882–84. Published *The Naval War of 1812* in 1882, the first of many works of history, biography, and natural history. Raised cattle on ranch in the Dakota Badlands, 1884–86. Served on U.S. Civil Service Commission, 1889–95, and on the New York City Police Commission, 1895–97. Assistant Secretary of the Navy in the McKinley administration, 1897–98. Commanded First U.S. Volunteer Cavalry (Rough Riders) in Cuba, 1898. Elected governor of New York in 1898 and served 1899–1900. Elected vice-president of the United States on the McKinley ticket in 1900, and became president on September 14, 1901, following the assassination of President McKinley. Defeated Alton B. Parker in 1904 election. President of the United States, 1901–9. Challenged President William Howard Taft for the Republican nomination in 1912, then ran as the Progressive candidate and was defeated by Woodrow Wilson. Wounded in assassination attempt during 1912 campaign. Died in Oyster Bay, New York.

Mario Savio (December 8, 1942–November 6, 1996) Born in Queens, New York, the son of a machine punch operator. Attended Manhattan College and Queens College before entering the University of California, Berkeley, in 1963. Arrested at civil rights protest in San Francisco in March 1964. Participated as volunteer in "Freedom Summer" civil rights project in Mississippi. Returned to Berkeley and in the fall of 1964 became a prominent leader in the Free Speech Movement opposed to the severe restrictions on political activity on campus. Left the university in the spring of 1965. Sentenced to 120 days in jail in 1967 for participating in a 1964 campus sit-in. Taught at an alternative school in southern California. Graduated from San Francisco State University in 1984 with B.A. in physics and received an M.S. from San Francisco State in 1989. Taught at Sonoma State University from 1990 until his death. Resumed political activism in opposition to ballot initiatives denying services to undocumented immigrants and curtailing affirmative action. Died in Sebastopol, California.

Carl Schurz (March 2, 1829–May 14, 1906) Born in Liblar, near Cologne, Germany, the son of a schoolmaster. Participated in the 1848 Revolution while a student at the University of Bonn, then fled to Switzerland in 1849. Returned to Germany in 1850 to help a former professor escape from prison. Immigrated to the United States in 1852 and settled in Philadelphia. Moved to Watertown, Wisconsin, in 1855. Began campaigning for Republican candidates among both German- and English-speaking voters. U.S. minister to Spain, 1861–62. Served as a general in the Union Army, 1862–65, commanding a division at Second Bull Run, Chancellorsville, Gettysburg, and Chattanooga. Edited newspapers in Detroit and St. Louis after the war. Elected to the Senate from Missouri as a Republican and served from 1869 to 1875. Helped lead the Liberal Republican movement opposed to Grant's reelection in 1872. Secretary of the Interior in the cabinet of Rutherford B. Hayes, 1877–81. Editor of the New York *Evening Post*, 1881–83. President of the National Civil Service Reform League, 1892–1901. Died in New York City.

Margaret Chase Smith (December 14, 1897–May 29, 1995) Born Margaret Chase in Skowhegan, Maine, the daughter of a barber. Graduated from high school in Skowhegan in 1916. Taught school, then worked as a telephone operator, newspaper executive, and as an office manager at a woolen mill. Married Clyde Smith in 1930, and was his secretary while he served in Congress, 1937–40. Elected to Congress as a Republican following her husband's death, and served 1940–49. Won election to the Senate in 1948 and served 1949–73. Died in Skowhegan.

Elizabeth Cady Stanton (November 12, 1815–October 26, 1902) Born Elizabeth Cady in Johnstown, New York, the daughter of a wealthy lawyer and landowner. Graduated from the Troy Female Seminary in 1833. Married Henry Stanton, an agent for the American Anti-Slavery Society, in 1840. Helped organize the woman's rights convention held in Seneca Falls, New York, in July 1848 and drafted its "Declaration of Rights and Sentiments." Began friendship with Susan B. Anthony in 1851. President of the Woman's State Temperance Society, 1852–53. Advocated woman's rights in appearances before the New York legislature in 1854 and 1860. Organized petition drive with Anthony in support of the Thirteenth Amendment, 1863–64. First vice-president of the American Equal Rights Association, 1866–68; opposed the Fourteenth and Fifteenth amendments because they did not enfranchise women. Edited weekly newspaper *Revolution*, 1868–70. President of the National Woman Suffrage Association, 1869–70 and 1877–90, and of its successor, the National American Woman Suffrage Association, 1890–92. Toured as a lyceum lecturer, 1870–79. Edited *History of Woman Suffrage* (3 vols., 1881–86) with Anthony and Matilda Joslyn Gage. Formed "Revising Committee" to annotate and publish *The Woman's Bible* (2 vols., 1895–98). Died in New York City.

Thaddeus Stevens (April 4, 1792–August 11, 1868) Born in Danville, Vermont, the son of a shoemaker. Graduated from Dartmouth College in 1814. Admitted to the bar in 1816 and began practicing law in Gettysburg, Pennsylvania. Became partner in an ironworks in 1826. Elected to the Pennsylvania house of representatives as an Anti-Masonic candidate and served 1833–35, 1837, and 1841. Served in Congress as an antislavery Whig, 1849–53, and as a Republican from 1859 until his death. Chairman of the House managers who presented the case against Andrew Johnson at his impeachment trial in 1868.

Mary Church Terrell (September 23, 1863–July 24, 1954) Born Mary Church in Memphis, Tennessee, the daughter of a businessman and a hairdresser who were both former slaves. Graduated from Oberlin College in 1884. Taught at Wilberforce University and at M Street High School in Washington, D.C. Married Robert Terrell, a lawyer, in 1891. Served on the District of Columbia Board of Education, 1895–1901 and 1906–11. Helped found the National Association of Colored Women and served as its first president, 1896–1901. Became a popular lecturer and wrote articles and short stories denouncing lynching, peonage, and segregation. Helped found the NAACP in 1909 and campaigned for woman suffrage. Widowed in 1925. Published autobiography *A Colored Woman in a White World* in 1940. Led campaign of court actions, boycotts, and picketing that desegregated restaurants in Washington, D.C., 1950–53. Died in Annapolis, Maryland.

Harry S. Truman (May 8, 1884–December 26, 1972) Born in Lamar, Missouri, the son of a farmer. Graduated from high school in Independence in 1901. Worked as a railroad timekeeper and bank clerk, then returned to the family farm in Grandview in 1906. Commanded field artillery battery in France in 1918 and saw action in the Vosges, the Saint-Mihiel salient, and the Meuse-Argonne. Opened men's clothing store in Kansas City in 1919 that failed in 1922. Elected as a Democrat to the Jackson County Court (county commission) in 1922; served 1922–24, and then as presiding judge, 1926–34. Served in the Senate, 1935–45, and as Vice-President of the United States from January 20 to April 12, 1945, when he became president following the death of Franklin D. Roosevelt. Defeated Thomas Dewey in 1948 election. President of the United States, 1945–53. Died in Kansas City, Missouri.

Sojourner Truth (c. 1797–November 26, 1883) Born Isabella in Hurley, Ulster County, New York, the child of Dutch-speaking slaves. Worked as a field hand and milkmaid on a farm in New Paltz, New

York. Emancipated on July 4, 1827, by the law that ended slavery in New York State. Moved in 1829 to New York City, where she worked as a domestic. Member of the "Kingdom of Matthias," a utopian religious commune, from 1832 to 1834. Renamed herself Sojourner Truth in 1843 and became an itinerant preacher. Settled in 1844 in Northampton, Massachusetts. *Narrative of Sojourner Truth,* written by Olive Gilbert, a white abolitionist to whom Truth had told her story, published in 1850. Became a traveling speaker for antislavery and woman's rights. Moved to Battle Creek, Michigan, in 1857. Helped with relief efforts for freed slaves during the Civil War, campaigned for President Lincoln's reelection, and participated in the desegregation of the streetcars in Washington, D.C. Campaigned for western land grants for African-Americans and supported temperance while continuing to speak for woman's rights. Published an expanded edition of her *Narrative* in 1875 with the aid of her friend Frances Titus. Died in Battle Creek.

Booker T. Washington (1856?–November 14, 1915) Born in Franklin County, Virginia, the son of an unknown white father and a slave cook, and named Booker Taliaferro; later adopted the name Washington. Worked as a child in a salt furnace and in a coal mine. Graduated from Hampton Normal and Agricultural Institute in 1875. Taught school in Malden, West Virginia, attended the Wayland Seminary for eight months, and then taught at Hampton, 1879–81. Founded the Tuskegee Normal and Industrial Institute in 1881 and served as its principal until his death. Delivered widely reported speech on race relations at the Atlanta Exposition in 1895. Founded the National Negro Business League and served as its president until his death. Published autobiography *Up From Slavery* in 1901. Advised Theodore Roosevelt and William Howard Taft on appointments of African-Americans to federal office. Died in Tuskegee, Alabama.

Ida B. Wells (July 6, 1862–March 25, 1931) Born in Holly Springs, Mississippi, the daughter of a carpenter and a cook, both of whom were slaves. Educated at Rusk University, a freedmen's school founded in Holly Springs in 1866. Taught school in Memphis, 1884–91. Began publishing articles in 1887, and in 1891 became a part-owner of the *Memphis Free Speech.* Published articles denouncing lynching; left Memphis after a mob destroyed the *Free Speech* offices in 1892. Made lecture tours in the United States and Britain and published pamphlets *Southern Horrors* (1892) and *A Red Record* (1895) as part of campaign against lynching. Married Ferdinand Barnett, a Chicago lawyer and newspaper editor, in 1895. Helped found the NAACP in 1909. Founded the Negro Fellowship League in 1910 and the Alpha Suffrage Club in 1913. Continued to investigate and write about incidents of racial violence. Died in Chicago.

Woodrow Wilson (December 28, 1856–February 3, 1924) Born Thomas Woodrow Wilson in Staunton, Virginia, the son of a Presbyterian minister. Graduated from the College of New Jersey (Princeton) in 1879. Admitted to the bar in Atlanta in 1882. Entered graduate school at John Hopkins in 1883. Published *Congressional Government* (1885), the first of several works on American history and politics. Awarded Ph.D. in 1886. Taught at Bryn Mawr, 1885–88, and Wesleyan, 1888–90. Professor of jurisprudence and political economy at Princeton, 1890–1902, and president of Princeton, 1902–10. Elected as a Democrat to the governorship of New Jersey in 1910 and served 1911–13. Won Democratic presidential nomination in 1912 and defeated Theodore Roosevelt and William Howard Taft; defeated Charles Evans Hughes in 1916 to win reelection. President of the United States, 1913–21. Suffered stroke on October 2, 1919, that left him an invalid for the remainder of his term. Awarded Nobel Peace Prize in 1919. Died in Washington, D.C.

Note on the Texts

This volume collects the texts of 83 speeches on political subjects given by 52 American public figures between 1865 and 1997 and presents them in the chronological order of their delivery. Although some of these speeches were first published posthumously, most of them were printed during the lifetime of the speaker, and some were revised by the speaker after initial delivery. With two exceptions, the texts presented in this volume are taken from the best printed sources available. Where there is more than one printed source, the text printed in this volume comes from the source that contains the fewest editorial alterations in spelling, capitalization, paragraphing, and punctuation. Because no complete printed sources were available of the speeches given by Mario Savio at the University of California, Berkeley, on December 2, 1964, and by Jesse Jackson to the Democratic National Convention in San Francisco on July 17, 1984, the Savio and Jackson speeches have been transcribed from audio recordings, and the texts of those transcriptions are presented in this volume.

This volume prints texts as they appear in the sources listed below, but with a few alterations in editorial procedure. In cases where earlier editors supplied in brackets words that were omitted from a source text by an obvious printer's error, or used a bracketed emendation to correct an obvious slip of the tongue made during the delivery of a speech, this volume removes the brackets and accepts the editorial emendation. Where an obvious slip of the tongue has been marked by "[sic]," the present volume omits the "[sic]" and corrects the error. Bracketed or parenthetical identifications of persons that appeared in the original printed texts have been retained in this volume, but bracketed insertions used by editors to expand abbreviations, clarify meaning, or translate foreign phrases have been deleted. In cases where brackets were used in a source text to indicate words added by the speaker to a quotation, this volume omits the brackets. The topical headings added to the texts of some speeches by earlier editors have been omitted in this volume.

In presenting their text of the sermon given by Martin Luther King, Jr., at National Cathedral on March 31, 1968, the editors of *A Knock at Midnight: Inspiration from the Great Sermons of Reverend Martin Luther King, Jr.*, omitted King's opening comments and printed them in a separate section titled "Material Omitted from Sermons"; this volume prints the comments at the beginning of the sermon (p. 668.4–8). Two errors made in the transcription of speeches are corrected in this volume, even though they were not corrected in the source texts: at 477.38, "believers and" becomes "believers in," and at 736.23, "soldiers—the" becomes "soldiers at the." An obvious slip of the tongue has also been corrected in the transcription of the speech by Mario Savio printed in the volume: at 618.18–19, "on First" becomes "on the First."

The following is a list of the speeches included in this volume, in the order of their appearance, giving the source of each text.

Abraham Lincoln: Speech on Reconstruction, Washington, D.C., April 11, 1865. *Abraham Lincoln: Speeches and Writings, 1859–1865*, ed. Don E. Fehrenbacher (New York: Library of America, 1989), 697–701. Copyright 1953 by The Abraham Lincoln Association. Reprinted with permission.

Thaddeus Stevens: Speech in Congress on Reconstruction, Washington, D.C., December 18, 1865. *Congressional Globe*, 39th Congress, First Session, 72–75.

Sojourner Truth: Speech at Meeting Commemorating Emancipation, Boston, January 1, 1871. *Narrative of Sojourner Truth, A Bondswoman of Olden Time* (Battle Creek, Michigan: Published for the Author, 1878), 213–16.

Susan B. Anthony: Is It a Crime for a Citizen of the United States to Vote? Monroe County, N.Y., March–April 1873, Ontario County, N.Y., May–June 1873. *An Account of the Proceedings on the Trial of Susan B. Anthony on the Charge of Illegal Voting at the Presidential Election of Nov. 1872* (Rochester, N.Y.: Daily Democrat and Chronicle Book Print, 1874), 151–178.

Robert Brown Elliott: Speech in Congress on the Civil Rights Bill, Washington, D.C., January 6, 1874. *Congressional Record*, 43rd Congress, First Session, 407–10.

Benjamin F. Butler: Speech in Congress on the Civil Rights Bill, Washington, D.C., January 7, 1874. *Congressional Record*, 43rd Congress, First Session, 457–58.

Frederick Douglass: Oration in Memory of Abraham Lincoln, Washington, D.C., April 14, 1876. *The Frederick Douglass Papers*, Series One, Volume 4, ed. John W. Blassingame and John R. McKivigan (New Haven: Yale University Press, 1991), 428–40. Copyright © 1991 by Yale University. Reprinted by permission of Yale University Press.

Robert G. Ingersoll: Speech Nominating James G. Blaine, Cincinnati, June 15, 1876. Robert G. Ingersoll, *The Ghosts, and Other Lectures* (Washington, D.C.: C. P. Farrell, 1878), 221–25.

Chief Joseph: Reply to General Howard, Bear Paw Mountains, Montana Territory, October 5, 1877. "The Surrender of Joseph," *Harper's Weekly*, November 17, 1877, 906.

Oliver Wendell Holmes, Jr.: Memorial Day Address, Keene, N.H., May 30, 1884. Oliver Wendell Holmes, Jr., *Dead, Yet Living: An Address Delivered* at Keene, N.H., *Memorial Day, May 30, 1884* (Boston: Ginn, Heath, and Company, 1884), 3–12.

Grover Cleveland: Address at the Dedication of the Statue of Liberty, New York City, October 28, 1886. *The Writings and Speeches of Grover Cleveland*, selected and edited by George F. Parker (New York: Cassell Publishing Company, 1892), 222.

Elizabeth Cady Stanton: The Solitude of Self, Washington, D.C., January 18, 1892. *Solitude of Self: Address Delivered by Mrs. Stanton Before the Committee of the Judiciary of the United States Congress, Monday, January 18, 1892* [Washington, D.C.: Government Printing Office, 1915], 1–8.

Ida B. Wells: Lynch Law in All Its Phases, Boston, February 13, 1893. *Our Day: A Record and Review of Current Reform*, May 1893, 333–47.

John Peter Altgeld: Labor Day Address, Chicago, September 8, 1893. *The Mind and Spirit of John Peter Altgeld: Selected Writings and Addresses*, ed. Henry M. Christman (Urbana: University of Illinois Press, 1960), 105–112. © 1960 by the Board of Trustees of the University of Illinois.

Booker T. Washington: Address at the Atlanta Exposition, September 18, 1895. *The Booker T. Washington Papers*, volume 3, ed. Louis R. Harlan (Urbana: University of Illinois Press, 1974), 583–87. © 1974 by the Board of Trustees of the University of Illinois.

William Jennings Bryan: Speech to the Democratic National Convention, Chicago, July 9, 1896. William J. Bryan, *The First Battle: A Story of the Campaign of 1896* (Chicago: W.B. Conkey Company, 1896), 199–206.

Theodore Roosevelt: The Strenuous Life, Chicago, April 10, 1899. *Theodore Roosevelt: Letters and Speeches*, ed. Louis Auchincloss (New York: Library of America, 2004), 755–66.

Carl Schurz: The Policy of Imperialism, Chicago, October 17, 1899. *Speeches, Correspondence and Political Papers of Carl Schurz*, Volume VI, ed. Frederic Bancroft (New York: G. P. Putnam's Sons, 1913), 77–120.

Theodore Roosevelt: The Man with the Muck-Rake, Washington, D.C., April 14, 1906. *The Works of Theodore Roosevelt*, National Edition, volume XVI, ed. Hermann Hagedorn (New York: Charles Scribner's Sons, 1926), 415–24.

Mary Church Terrell: What It Means to be Colored in the Capital of the United States, Washington, D.C., October 10, 1906. *The Independent*, January 24, 1907, 181–86.

Theodore Roosevelt: The New Nationalism, Osawatomie, Kansas, August 31, 1910. *Theodore Roosevelt: Letters and Speeches*, ed. Louis Auchincloss (New York: Library of America, 2004), 799–814.

John Jay Chapman, Speech at Prayer Meeting, Coatesville, Pennsylvania, August 18, 1912. John Jay Chapman, *Memories and Milestones* (New York: Moffat, Yard and Company, 1915), 225–32.

Woodrow Wilson: First Inaugural Address, Washington, D.C., March 4, 1913. *The Papers of Woodrow Wilson*, volume 27, ed. Arthur S. Link (Princeton, N.J.: Princeton University Press, 1978), 148–52. Copyright © 1978 by

Princeton University Press. Reprinted by permission of Princeton University Press.

Woodrow Wilson: Address to Congress on War with Germany, Washington, D.C., April 2, 1917. *The Papers of Woodrow Wilson*, volume 41, ed. Arthur S. Link (Princeton, N.J.: Princeton University Press, 1983), 519–27. Copyright © 1983 by Princeton University Press. Reprinted by permission of Princeton University Press.

Robert La Follette, Sr.: Speech in the Senate on Free Speech in Wartime, Washington, D.C., October 6, 1917. Robert C. Byrd, *The Senate, 1789–1989: Classic Speeches, 1830–1993,* ed. Wendy Wolff (Washington, D.C.: U.S. Government Printing Office, 1994), 521–40.

Carrie Chapman Catt: Address to Woman Suffrage Convention, Washington, D.C., December 1917. Carrie Chapman Catt, *An Address to the Congress of the United States* (New York: National Woman Suffrage Publishing Company, Inc., 1917), 1–21.

Eugene V. Debs: Speech to the Court, Cleveland, September 14, 1918. David Krasner, *Debs: His Authorized Life and Letters* (New York: Boni and Liveright, 1919), 48–54.

Woodrow Wilson: Address to the Senate on the League of Nations, Washington, D.C., July 10, 1919. *The Papers of Woodrow Wilson*, volume 61, ed. Arthur S. Link (Princeton, N.J.: Princeton University Press, 1989), 426–36. Copyright © 1989 by Princeton University Press. Reprinted by permission of Princeton University Press.

Henry Cabot Lodge: Speech in the Senate on the League of Nations, Washington, August 12, 1919. Henry Cabot Lodge, *The Senate and the League of Nations* (New York: Charles Scribner's Sons, 1925), 380–410. Copyright 1925 Charles Scribner's Sons.

Herbert Hoover: "Rugged Individualism" Speech, New York City, October 22, 1928. *The New Day: Campaign Speeches of Herbert Hoover, 1928* (Stanford: Stanford University Press, 1928), 149–76. Copyright 1928 by the Board of Trustees of Leland Stanford Junior University. Reprinted by permission of The Hoover Presidential Library Museum.

Franklin D. Roosevelt: Speech to the Democratic National Convention, Chicago, July 2, 1932. *The Public Papers and Addresses of Franklin Delano Roosevelt*, ed. Samuel I. Rosenman, vol. I (New York: Random House, 1938), 647–59. Copyright 1938 by Franklin Delano Roosevelt.

Franklin D. Roosevelt: Speech to the Commonwealth Club, San Francisco, September 23, 1932. *The Public Papers and Addresses of Franklin D. Roosevelt*, ed. Samuel I. Rosenman, volume I (New York: Random House, 1938), 742–56. Copyright 1938 by Franklin Delano Roosevelt.

Franklin D. Roosevelt: First Inaugural Address, Washington, D.C., March 4, 1933. *The Public Papers and Addresses of Franklin D. Roosevelt*, ed. Samuel I. Rosenman, volume II (New York: Random House, 1938), 11–16. Copyright 1938 by Franklin Delano Roosevelt.

Huey Long: Every Man a King, Washington, D.C., February 23, 1934. *Kingfish to America: Share Our Wealth; Selected Senatorial Papers of Huey*

P. Long, ed. Henry M. Christman (New York: Schocken Books, 1985), 35–46. Copyright © 1985 by Henry M. Christman.

Franklin D. Roosevelt: Speech to the Democratic National Convention, Philadelphia, June 27, 1936. *The Public Papers and Addresses of Franklin D. Roosevelt*, ed. Samuel I. Rosenman, volume V (New York: Random House, 1938), 230–36. Copyright 1938 by Franklin Delano Roosevelt.

Franklin D. Roosevelt: Second Inaugural Address, Washington, D.C., January 20, 1937. *The Public Papers and Addresses of Franklin D. Roosevelt*, ed. Samuel I. Rosenman, volume VI (New York: Random House, 1938), 1–6. Copyright 1938 by Franklin Delano Roosevelt.

Franklin D. Roosevelt: "Arsenal of Democracy" Fireside Chat, December 29, 1940. *The Public Papers and Addresses of Franklin D. Roosevelt*, ed. Samuel I. Rosenman, volume IX (New York: The Macmillan Company, 1941), 633–44. Copyright 1941 by Franklin Delano Rocsevelt.

Franklin D. Roosevelt: Eighth Annual Address to Congress, Washington, January 6, 1941. *The Public Papers and Addresses of Franklin D. Roosevelt*, ed. Samuel I. Rosenman, volume IX (New York: The Macmillan Company, 1941), 663–72. Copyright 1941 by Franklin Delano Roosevelt.

Franklin D. Roosevelt: Address to Congress on War with Japan, Washington, D.C., December 8, 1941. *The Public Papers and Addresses of Franklin D. Roosevelt*, ed. Samuel I. Rosenman, volume X (New York: Harper & Brothers, 1950), 514–15. Copyright, 1950, by Samuel I. Rosenman.

George S. Patton: Speech to Third Army Troops, England, Spring 1944. Transcription provided by Patton Museum of Cavalry and Armor, Fort Knox, Kentucky. Reprinted with permission.

Dwight D. Eisenhower: Address to the Allied Expeditionary Forces, England, June 6, 1944. *The Papers of Dwight David Eisenhower: The War Years, III*, ed. Alfred D. Chandler, Jr. (Baltimore: The John Hopkins Press, 1970), 1913. Copyright © 1970 by The John Hopkins Press. Reprinted by permission of The Johns Hopkins University Press.

Harry S. Truman: Statement on the Atomic Bomb, Washington, D.C., August 6, 1945. *Public Papers of the Presidents of the United States: Harry S. Truman, 1945* (Washington, D.C.: U.S. Government Printing Office, 1961), 197–200.

J. Robert Oppenheimer: Speech to Los Alamos Scientists, Los Alamos, N.M., November 2, 1945. *Robert Oppenheimer: Letters and Recollections*, ed. Alice Kimball Smith and Charles Weiner (Cambridge: Harvard University Press, 1980), 315–25. Copyright © 1980 by Alice Kimball Smith and Charles Weiner. Reprinted by permission.

George C. Marshall: Speech at Harvard University, Cambridge. Massachusetts, June 5, 1947. Forrest C. Pogue, *George C. Marshall: Statesman, 1945–1959* (New York: Viking, 1987), 525–28. Copyright © George C. Marshall Research Foundation, 1987. Used by permission of Viking Penguin, a division of Penguin Group (U.S.A.) Inc.

Hubert H. Humphrey: Speech to the Democratic National Convention, Philadelphia, July 14, 1948 *The Civil Rights Rhetoric of Hubert H.*

Humphrey 1948–1964, ed. Paula Wilson (Lanham, Md.: University Press of America, Inc.), 3–5. Copyright © 1996 by University Press of America, Inc. Reprinted by permission of the Minnesota Historical Society.

Harry S. Truman: Speech to the Democratic National Convention, Philadelphia, July 15, 1948. *Public Papers of the Presidents of the United States: Harry S. Truman, 1948* (Washington, D.C.: U.S. Government Printing Office, 1964), 406–10.

Margaret Chase Smith: Declaration of Conscience, Washington, D.C., June 1, 1950. *Congressional Record,* 81st Congress, Second Session, 7894–95.

William Faulkner: Nobel Prize Address, Stockholm, December 10, 1950. William Faulkner, *Essays, Speeches & Public Letters,* ed. James B. Meriwether (New York: Random House, 1965), 119–20. Copyright 1951 by Estelle Faulkner and Jill Faulkner Summers. Reprinted with permission.

Douglas MacArthur: Address to Congress, April 19, 1951. *A Soldier Speaks: Public Papers and Speeches of General of the Army Douglas MacArthur,* ed. Vorin E. Whan, Jr. (New York: Frederick A. Praeger, 1965), 243–52. © 1965 by Frederick A. Praeger, Inc. Reprinted with permission of the United States Military Academy at West Point.

Richard M. Nixon: "Checkers" Speech, Hollywood, California, September 23, 1952. *The New York Times,* September 24, 1952, 22.

Martin Luther King, Jr.: Speech to the Montgomery Improvement Association, Montgomery, Alabama, December 5, 1955. *A Call to Conscience: The Landmark Speeches of Dr. Martin Luther King, Jr.,* ed. Clayborne Carson and Kris Shepard (New York: Warner Books, 2002), 7–12. © 2000 The Heirs to the Estate of Martin Luther King, Jr. Reprinted by arrangement with the Estate of Martin Luther King, Jr., c/o Writers House, as agent for proprietor New York, NY.

Dwight D. Eisenhower: Second Inaugural Address, Washington, D.C., January 21, 1957. *Public Papers of the Presidents of the United States: Dwight D. Eisenhower, 1957* (Washington, D.C.: U.S. Government Printing Office, 1958), 60–65.

John F. Kennedy: Speech to the Greater Houston Ministerial Association, Houston, September 12, 1960. *Freedom of Communications: Final Report of the Committee on Commerce, United States Senate,* 87th Congress, First Session, Senate Report 994, Part I (Washington, D.C.: U.S. Government Printing Office, 1961), 208–10.

Dwight D. Eisenhower: Farewell Address, Washington, D.C., January 17, 1961. *Public Papers of the Presidents of the United States: Dwight D. Eisenhower, 1960–61* (Washington, D.C.: U.S. Government Printing Office, 1961), 1035–40.

John F. Kennedy: Inaugural Address, Washington, D.C., January 20, 1961. *Public Papers of the Presidents of the United States: John F. Kennedy, 1961* (Washington, D.C.: U.S. Government Printing Office, 1962), 1–3.

John F. Kennedy: Address at American University, Washington, D.C., June 10, 1963. *Public Papers of the Presidents of the United States: John F. Kennedy, 1963* (Washington, D.C.: U.S. Government Printing Office, 1964), 459–64.

John F. Kennedy: Address to the Nation on Civil Rights, June 11, 1963. *Public Papers of the Presidents of the United States: John F. Kennedy, 1963* (Washington, D.C.: U.S. Government Printing Office, 1964), 468–71.

John F. Kennedy: Speech in the Rudolph Wilde Platz, Berlin, June 26, 1963. *Public Papers of the Presidents of the United States: John F. Kennedy, 1963* (Washington, D.C.: U.S. Government Printing Office, 1964), 524–25.

Martin Luther King, Jr.: Address to the March on Washington, August 28, 1963. *A Call to Conscience: The Landmark Speeches of Dr. Martin Luther King, Jr.*, ed. Clayborne Carson and Kris Shepard (New York: Warner Books, 2002), 81–87. © 2000 The Heirs to the Estate of Martin Luther King, Jr. Reprinted by arrangement with the Estate of Martin Luther King, Jr., c/o Writers House as agent for proprietor, New York, NY.

Betty Friedan: The Crisis in Women's Identity. San Francisco, 1964. Betty Friedan, *It Changed My Life: Writings on the Women's Movement* (New York: Random House, 1976), 62–71. Copyright © 1964 by Betty Friedan. Reprinted by permission of the author, c/o Curtis Brown, Ltd.

Malcolm X: The Ballot or the Bullet, Cleveland, April 3, 1964. *Malcolm X Speaks: Selected Speeches and Statements*, ed. George Breitman (New York: Grove Press, Inc., 1966), 23–44. Copyright © 1965 by Betty Shabazz and Pathfinder Press. Reprinted by permission.

Barry Goldwater: Speech to the Republican National Convention, San Francisco, July 16, 1964. *The New York Times*, July 17, 1964, 10.

Ronald Reagan: Speech on Behalf of Barry Goldwater, Los Angeles, October 27, 1964. Ronald Reagan, *Speaking My Mind: Selected Speeches* (New York: Simon and Schuster, 1989). 25–36. Copyright © 1989 by Ronald W. Reagan. Reprinted courtesy the Ronald Reagan Presidential Foundation.

Mario Savio: Speech in Sproul Plaza, Berkeley, California, December 2, 1964. Transcription from audio recording. Copyright © 2006 by Lynne Hollander Savio. Reprinted with permission.

Martin Luther King, Jr.: Nobel Prize Address, Oslo, December 10. 1964. *A Call to Conscience: The Landmark Speeches of Dr. Martin Luther King, Jr.*, ed. Clayborne Carson and Kris Shepard (New York: Warner Books, 2002), 105–9. © 2000 The Heirs to the Estate of Martin Luther King, Jr. Reprinted by arrangement with the Estate of Martin Luther King, Jr., c/o Writers House as agent for proprietor, New York, NY.

Lyndon B. Johnson: Address to Congress on Voting Rights, Washington, D.C., March 15, 1965. *Public Papers of the Presidents of the United States: Lyndon B. Johnson, 1965*, Book I (Washington, D.C.: U.S. Government Printing Office, 1966), 281–87.

Lyndon B. Johnson: Address at Howard University. Washington, D.C., June 4, 1965. *Public Papers of the Presidents of the United States: Lyndon B. Johnson, 1965*, Book II (Washington, D.C.: U.S. Government Printing Office, 1966), 635–40.

Robert F. Kennedy: Address at the University of Cape Town, South Africa, June 6, 1966. Robert C. Byrd, *The Senate, 1789–1989: Classic Speeches,*

1830–1993, ed. Wendy Wolff (Washington, D.C.: U.S. Government Printing Office, 1994), 713–18.

Martin Luther King, Jr.: Speech on the Vietnam War, New York City, April 4, 1967. *A Call to Conscience: The Landmark Speeches of Dr. Martin Luther King, Jr.,* ed. Clayborne Carson and Kris Shepard (New York: Warner Books, 2002), 105–9. © 2000 The Heirs to the Estate of Martin Luther King, Jr. Reprinted by arrangement with the Estate of Martin Luther King, Jr., c/o Writers House as agent for proprietor, New York, NY.

Martin Luther King, Jr.: Sermon at National Cathedral, Washington, D.C., March 31, 1968. *A Knock at Midnight: Inspiration from the Great Sermons of Reverend Martin Luther King, Jr.,* ed. Clayborne Carson and Peter Holloran (New York: Warner Books, 1998), 205–24, 229. © 1997 The Heirs to the Estate of Martin Luther King, Jr. Reprinted by arrangement with the Estate of Martin Luther King, Jr., c/o Writers House as agent for proprietor, New York, NY.

Martin Luther King, Jr.: Speech at Mason Temple, Memphis, April 3, 1968. *A Call to Conscience: The Landmark Speeches of Dr. Martin Luther King, Jr.,* ed. Clayborne Carson and Kris Shepard (New York: Warner Books, 2002), 207–23. © 2000 The Heirs to the Estate of Martin Luther King, Jr. Reprinted by arrangement with the Estate of Martin Luther King, Jr., c/o Writers House as agent for proprietor, New York, NY.

Robert F. Kennedy: Remarks on the Assassination of Martin Luther King, Indianapolis, April 4, 1968. *RFK: Collected Speeches,* ed. Edwin O. Guthman and C. Richard Allen (New York: Viking, 1993), 356–57. Copyright © Edwin Guthman and C. Richard Allen, 1993. Reprinted by permission.

Barbara Jordan: Statement to the House Judiciary Committee, Washington, July 25, 1974. *Debate on Articles of Impeachment: Hearings of the Committee on the Judiciary, House of Representatives, Ninety-Third Congress, Second Session* (Washington, D.C.: U.S. Government Printing Office, 1974), 110–13.

Richard M. Nixon: Remarks on Leaving the White House, Washington, D.C., August 9, 1974. *Public Papers of the Presidents of the United States: Richard Nixon, 1974* (Washington, D.C.: U.S. Government Printing Office, 1975), 630–32.

Jimmy Carter: Address to the Nation on Energy Policy, Washington, D.C., July 15, 1979. *Public Papers of the Presidents of the United States: Jimmy Carter, 1979,* Book II (Washington, D.C.: U.S. Government Printing Office, 1980), 1235–41.

Edward M. Kennedy, Speech to the Democratic National Convention, New York, August 12, 1980. *The New York Times,* August 13, 1980, B2.

Ronald Reagan: Address to Members of Parliament, London, June 8, 1982. *Public Papers of the Presidents of the United States: Ronald Reagan, 1982,* Book I (Washington, D.C.: U.S. Government Printing Office, 1983), 742–48.

Ronald Reagan: Address at Pointe-du-Hoc, Normandy, June 6, 1984. *Public Papers of the Presidents of the United States: Ronald Reagan, 1984*, Book I (Washington, D.C.: U.S. Government Printing Office, 1986). 817–819.

Jesse Jackson: Speech to the Democratic National Convention, San Francisco, July 17, 1984. Transcription from audio recording. Copyright © 1984 by Jesse Jackson. Used by permission.

Ronald Reagan: Address to the Nation on the *Challenger* Disaster, Washington, D.C., January 28, 1986. *Public Papers of the Presidents of the United States: Ronald Reagan, 1986*, Book I (Washington, D.C.: U.S. Government Printing Office, 1988), 94–95.

Ronald Reagan: Speech at the Brandenburg Gate, Berlin, June 12, 1987. *Public Papers of the Presidents of the United States: Ronald Reagan, 1987*, Book I (Washington, D.C.: U.S. Government Printing Office, 1989), 634–37.

William J. Clinton: Speech at Mason Temple, Memphis, November 13, 1993. *Public Papers of the Presidents of the United States: William J. Clinton, 1993*, Book II (Washington, D.C.: U.S. Government Printing Office, 1994), 1981–86.

William J. Clinton: Speech at Central High School, Little Rock, September 25, 1997. *Public Papers of the Presidents of the United States: William J. Clinton, 1997*, Book II (Washington, D.C.: U.S. Government Printing Office, 1999), 1233–36.

This volume presents the texts of the printings chosen as sources here but does not attempt to reproduce features of their typographic design. The texts are printed without alteration except for the changes previously discussed and for the correction of typographical errors. Spelling, punctuation, and capitalization are often expressive features, and they are not altered, even when inconsistent or irregular. The following is a list of typographical errors corrected, cited by page and line number: 5.12, Government?; 20.11, me?; 27.32, York,; 28.4, Leigslature; 28.11, claause; 29.12, Republic.; 30.25, dilemna; 31.24, refues; 48.13, bounddary; 50.26, vol,; 56.30, comfort;; 72.24, thei rrights; 99.7, familar; 101.7, never; 101.39, brighest; 102.14, devine; 103.13, humilation; 105.14, alter; 105.15–16, concience; 105.15, responsiblity; 105.17, self-sovereignity; 105.28, sovereignity; 105.32, dependance; 106.15, artifical; 106.19, though; 106.33–34, emergies; 106.39, bakies; 108.30, feelings; 132.33, than; 293.1, is to; 296.15–16, constitutionl; 332.1, 1839; 476.22–23, county; 511.6, kids,; 514.22, beu nited; 550.7, cast; 595.26, enthusiasm by; 600.19, Americans; 600.39, help in; 602.15, though; 602.15, closets; 610.10, 127!; 631.35–36, Mcntana; . . . leader, . . . Illinois; . . . leader,; 670.1, tell; 695.21, solemness; 696.39, crime; 728.32, what.

Notes

In the notes below, the reference numbers denote page and line of this volume (the line count includes headings). No note is made for material included in the eleventh edition of *Merriam-Webster's Collegiate Dictionary*. Biblical quotations are keyed to the King James Version. Quotations from Shakespeare are keyed to *The Riverside Shakespeare*, ed. G. Blakemore Evans (Boston: Houghton Mifflin, 1974).

1.2 *Speech on Reconstruction*] Lincoln delivered this speech, his last public address, from a balcony at the White House. John Wilkes Booth was in the audience and was later reported by his co-conspirators to have said: "That means nigger citizenship. Now, by God, I'll put him through," and: "That is the last speech he'll ever make."

1.6 surrender . . . insurgent army] The Army of Northern Virginia surrendered at Appomattox Court House on April 9, 1865.

1.13 I myself, was near the front] Lincoln visited Grant's headquarters in City Point, Virginia, from March 24 to April 8, 1865, and toured Richmond after its evacuation.

2.11 One of them] Salmon P. Chase (1808–1873), who served as Secretary of the Treasury, 1861–64, and as Chief Justice of the Supreme Court, 1864–73.

2.34 Gen. Banks] Major General Nathaniel P. Banks (1816–1894) commanded the Department of the Gulf, December 1862–September 1864.

6.7 the message] The annual message sent to Congress by President Andrew Johnson on December 4, 1865.

8.7 Mr. Justice Grier, in the prize cases] Robert C. Grier (1794–1870) was an Associate Justice of the Supreme Court, 1846–1870. He wrote the majority opinion in the *Prize Cases* (1863), in which the Court upheld, 5–4, the legality of Lincoln's blockade proclamations in 1861.

8.9 Vattel] Emmerich de Vattel (1714–1767), a Swiss jurist and the author of *The Law of Nations* (1760; originally published in French in 1758).

8.26 Phillimore] Sir Robert Joseph Phillimore (1810–1885), author of *Commentaries on International Law* (4 vols., 1854–61).

9.15 *Halleck*] Henry W. Halleck (1815–1872), *International Law; or, Rules Regarding the Intercourse of States in Peace and War* (1861).

10.8 present able Chief Justice] See note 2.11.

11.1   *in pais*]   Outside of legal proceedings.

11.36–37   The Fortieth Congress]   Stevens gave this speech in the Thirty-ninth Congress (1865–67); the Fortieth Congress would meet from 1867 to 1869

12.1   Luther *vs.* Borden]   The case, decided in 1849, arose from the 1842 Dorr Rebellion in Rhode Island that led to the establishment of rival "People's" and "Freeholder's" state governments. The Court rejected the plaintiff's challenge to the legitimacy of the Freeholder's government, ruling that it was a political question to be decided by Congress and not the judiciary.

13.22   If the slaves are now free]   Ratification of the Thirteenth Amendment was declared complete on December 18, 1865, the day Stevens gave this speech.

15.5–6   prisoners at Andersonville]   Approximately 13,000 Union prisoners died from hunger, disease, and exposure in the Confederate prison camp at Andersonville, Georgia.

15.23   the Secretary of State]   William H. Seward (1801–1872), Secretary of State from 1861 to 1869.

15.29   revolted cities of Latium]   The cities revolted during the Latin War, 340–338 B.C.

16.9   Governor Perry]   Benjamin Franklin Perry (1805–1886) was appointed provisional governor of South Carolina by President Johnson in June 1865 and served until November, when James Orr, the first governor elected during Reconstruction, was inaugurated.

18.11–12   late Chief Justice]   Roger B. Taney (1777–1864) was Chief Justice of the Supreme Court, 1836–64, and the author of the majority opinion in the *Dred Scott* case, in which he wrote that blacks had "no rights which the white man was bound to respect."

19.2–3   *Speech . . . Emancipation*]   The text printed here originally appeared as part of an article in the *Boston Post* on January 2, 1871, and was included in the 1878, 1881, and 1884 printings of *Narrative of Sojourner Truth.* The *Boston Post* report of the "large gathering" in Tremont Temple described it as being held "under the auspices of the National Association for the Spread of Temperance and Night Schools among the Freed People of the South."

22.2–3   *Is It a Crime . . . Vote?*]   Anthony succeeded in registering to vote in Rochester on November 1, 1872, and cast a ballot in the election on November 5. After being indicted by a federal grand jury on January 24, 1873, for unlawfully voting in a congressional election, she gave this speech in all 29 postal districts in Monroe County, New York, where her trial was scheduled to be held. Anthony then made a second speaking tour through Ontario County after the prosecution succeeded in having the trial moved to Canandaigua. On June 17, 1873, she was tried before Supreme Court Justice

Ward Hunt (1810–1886), sitting as a circuit judge. Hunt rejected her legal arguments, directed the jury to convict, and fined Anthony $100, a fine she refused to pay. In 1875 the Supreme Court unanimously ruled in *Minor* v. *Happersett*, another suffrage case, that the Fourteenth Amendment did not give women the vote.

24.38   Luther Martin . . . report] Martin (c. 1748–1826) was attorney general of Maryland, 1778–1805 and 1818–22, and a delegate to the Constitutional Convention. His speech to the Maryland House of Delegates on November 29, 1787, was published in a pamphlet entitled *The Genuine Information*.

25.8–11   "Under every . . . administer them."] From a speech in the Constitutional Convention, August 7, 1787.

25.11–14   "Let it be . . . human nature."] From an address to the states from the Continental Congress, April 26, 1783.

25.24–25   B. Gratz Brown . . . Cowan] Benjamin Gratz Brown (1826–1885), was a Unionist senator from Missouri, 1863–67; Edgar Cowan (1815–1885) was a Republican senator from Pennsylvania, 1861–67.

25.28–26.2   Mr. President . . . liberties."] Cf. Brown's speech in the Senate on December 12, 1866.

26.3   Charles Sumner] Sumner (1811–1874) was a Free Soil, and then Republican, senator from Massachusetts, 1851–74.

26.8   one of his great speeches] Delivered in the Senate on March 7, 1866.

33.20–21   Associate Justice Miller] Samuel Miller (1816–1890) served as Associate Justice of the Supreme Court, 1862–90.

33.36   J. H. Mitchell] John H. Mitchell (1835–1905) was a Republican senator from Oregon, 1873–79, 1885–97, and 1901–5.

34.36   Webster, Worcester, and Bouvier] American lexicographers Noah Webster (1758–1843), Joseph Worcester (1784–1865), and John Bouvier (1787–1851).

35.3–4   Associate Justice Washington . . . said] Bushrod Washington (1762–1829), an associate justice of the Supreme Court, 1799–1829, decided *Corfield* v. *Coryell* (1823) while sitting as a circuit judge in eastern Pennsylvania.

35.13–20   Chief Judge Daniels . . . Associate Justice Taney] Peter Daniel (1784–1860) was an associate justice, 1841–60, who joined the majority in the *Dred Scott* case. The confusion of Justice Daniel with Chief Justice Roger B. Taney appeared in two newspaper reports of Anthony's speech as well as in the pamphlet version printed here, and probably reflects an error in her manuscript.

35.37   General Bates] Edward Bates (1793–1869) served as attorney general in the Lincoln administration, 1861–64.

36.40   Judge Bingham] John A. Bingham (1815–1900) was a Republican congressman from Ohio, 1855–63 and 1865–73, and served as a judge advocate in the Union Army.

37.1   Carpenter] Matthew H. Carpenter (1824–1881) was a Republican senator from Wisconsin, 1869–75 and 1879–81.

37.19   Judge Underwood, of Virginia] John C. Underwood (1809–1873) was a federal district judge in Virginia, 1864–73.

37.23–32   "If the people . . . legislation?"] Anthony quotes from an article Underwood published in *Woman's Journal*, November 25, 1871.

37.36   Judges Howard] Jacob Howard (1805–1871) was a Republican senator from Michigan, 1862–71

38.5–16   "Protection . . . of the state." From *Corfield* v. *Coryell* (see note 35.3–4).

39.19–20   second section . . . amendment] The second section allowed Congress to reduce the congressional representation of states that denied the vote to adult male citizens.

39.31–33   disenfranchise . . . Rhode Island] The Rhode Island state constitution of 1843 imposed substantial property and residency requirements on naturalized citizens seeking to vote.

39.39   A. T. Stewarts . . . Fentons] Alexander T. Stewart (1803–1876) was a wealthy New York City merchant and property owner; Roscoe Conkling (1829–1888) was a Republican senator from New York, 1867–81; Reuben Fenton (1819–1885) was the Republican governor of New York, 1865–68, and a senator, 1869–75.

43.28–36   James Otis . . . mercy of others."] James Otis (1725–1783), *The Rights of the British Colonies Asserted and Proved* (1764).

44.9–23   "Every man . . . our behalf."] The passage, attributed to Franklin in a speech by Charles Sumner, appeared in a pamphlet Franklin owned and endorsed with the heading "Some Good Whig Principles."

44.35–45.2   "The right of . . . property."] Thomas Paine, *Dissertation on First Principles of Government* (1795).

45.31   Senator Frelinghuysen] Frederick T. Frelinghuysen (1817–1885) was a Republican senator from New Jersey, 1866–69 and 1871–77.

46.11–12   Judge Stanley Mathews . . . Cincinnati convention] Matthews (1824–1889), a former Ohio state judge, spoke at the Liberal Republican convention that nominated Horace Greeley for president in 1872.

46.33   Benjamin F. Butler]   See Biographical Notes.

48.2   *Speech . . . Civil Rights Bill*]   Elliott spoke during a debate on a
bill guaranteeing equal access to public schools, public accommodations,
transportation facilities, and places of amusement, and forbidding racial discrimination in federal and state juries. In 1875 the bill became law without the
provision regarding schools. The provisions regarding public accommodations, transportation, and amusement were declared unconstitutional by the
Supreme Court in an 8–1 decision in 1883 on the grounds that racial discrimination by private individuals was not prohibited by the Thirteenth and Fourteenth Amendments.

48.22–23   grateful State . . . Fort Griswold]   Fort Griswold was captured by Benedict Arnold during his raid on New London, Connecticut, on
September 6, 1781.

49.13   Mr. BECK]   James B. Beck (1822–1890) was a Democratic congressman from Kentucky, 1867–75, and a senator, 1877–90.

50.4   Mr. STEPHENS]   Alexander H. Stephens (1812–1883) was a congressman from Georgia, 1843–59 and 1873–82, and served as vice-president of the
Confederate States of America, 1861–65.

50.19   *Lieber on Civil Liberty*]   Francis Lieber (1800–1872), *On Civil Liberty and Self-Government* (1853).

50.23–26   Natural liberty . . . *American Republic*]   The quotation from
Alexander Hamilton's pamphlet *The Farmer Refuted* (1775) appears in *History
of the Republic of the United States* (1857) by Hamilton's son, John Church
Hamilton (1792–1882).

51.4–9   Is it . . . maintained?]   From a speech by Hamilton in the Constitutional Convention on June 29, 1787, as recorded by Robert Yates.

51.10–15   "the sacred . . . mortal power."]   From *The Farmer Refuted*
(1775).

51.16   the Slaughter-house cases!]   The cases were decided 5–4 by the
Supreme Court on April 14, 1873.

53.21   Chancellor Kent]   James Kent (1763–1847) was chancellor of New
York, 1814–23, and the author of *Commentaries on American Law* (1826).

53.31–32   Associate Justice Miller]   See note 33.20–21.

59.25   Mr. DAWES]   Henry L. Dawes (1816–1903) was a Republican congressman from Massachusetts, 1857–75, and a senator, 1875–93.

62.19   harmless speculations in his study]   Stephens was the author of *A
Constitutional View of the Late War Between the States* (2 vols., 1868–70).

62.36–38   that gentleman shocked . . . corner-stone.]   In a speech delivered in Savannah, Georgia, on March 21, 1861.

63.21   Mr. HARRIS] John T. Harris (1823–1899) was a Democratic congressman from Virginia, 1859-61 and 1871–81.

66.29–31   "reaped down . . . Sabaoth,"] James 5:4.

66.35–40   "Entreat me . . . and me."] Ruth 1:16–17.

67.2   Speech . . . Civil Rights Bill] Butler was the floor manager for the bill.

70.30–31   the Commanding General] Ulysses S. Grant.

71.9   the caps] Percussion caps.

71.11   'Remember Fort Pillow!'] Confederate cavalrymen killed several dozen black soldiers after capturing Fort Pillow in Tennessee on April 12, 1864

72.16–17   "May my . . . ever fail] Cf. Psalm 137:5–6.

74.2   Oration . . . Abraham Lincoln] Douglass gave this speech at the dedication of the Freedmen's Memorial Monument to Abraham Lincoln in Lincoln Park, Washington, D.C.

76.23   Chief Justice] Morrison Waite (1816–1888) was Chief Justice of the Supreme Court, 1874–88.

76.26   President] Ulysses S. Grant.

78.12–14   Jefferson . . . rebellion to oppose.] Douglass paraphrases a letter Jefferson wrote to Jean Nicholas Démeunier on June 26, 1786.

78.22–24   strangely told us . . . we were born;] Lincoln met with a committee of African-Americans on August 14, 1862, and encouraged them to establish a colony in Central America.

78.27–28   he would save . . . with slavery] In a public letter to Horace Greeley, written on August 22, 1862.

78.28–29   revoked . . . General Frémont] On September 11, 1861, Lincoln revoked the proclamation issued on August 30 by John C. Frémont, the commanding general in Missouri, that emancipated the slaves of enemies of the Union.

78.30   refused to remove . . . the Potomac,] Lincoln appointed George B. McClellan as commander of the Army of the Potomac on July 27, 1861, and did not remove him until November 5, 1862.

79.18–19   he loved Caesar . . . Rome] Cf. Julius Caesar, III, ii, 21–22.

80.17   in a distant city] Boston.

82.6   wounded . . . of his friends.] Cf. Zechariah 13:6.

82.32–35   A spade, . . . you will.] Thomas Hood (1799–1845), "The Lay of the Laborer."

82.39   gluts]   Wedges.

83.40–84.1   an oath in heaven]   In his first inaugural address Lincoln said he had taken an "oath registered in Heaven" to preserve the Union.

85.2   *Speech Nominating James G. Blaine*]   Ingersoll gave this speech at the 1876 Republican National Convention, which eventually nominated Ohio governor Rutherford B. Hayes on the seventh ballot. Blaine (1830–1893) served as a congressman from Maine, 1863–76, as Speaker of the House, 1869–75, as a senator, 1876–81, and as Secretary of State, 1881 and 1889–92. An unsuccessful candidate at the 1876 and 1880 conventions, Blaine won the Republican nomination in 1884, but was defeated by Grover Cleveland.

85.4–5   Benjamin H. Bristow]   Bristow (1832–1896), a Kentucky Unionist, served as an officer in the Union Army, 1861–63, and was wounded at Shiloh. He later served as the U.S. district attorney for Kentucky, 1866–69, as Solicitor General of the United States, 1870–72, and as Secretary of the Treasury, 1874–76.

86.2   resumption]   The restoration of the currency on a specie basis, set for January 1, 1879, by the Specie Resumption Act of 1875.

86.19   certificate of moral . . . confederate congress.]   In the spring of 1876 Blaine was accused of having engaged in improper transactions in railroad bonds while serving as Speaker of the House. Blaine retrieved letters that allegedly incriminated him and, after refusing to turn them over to the subcommittee investigating the charges, read them aloud in the House chamber on June 5 during a speech proclaiming his innocence. The investigation by the House, which was controlled by the Democrats, was discontinued after the governor of Maine appointed Blaine to a vacant seat in the Senate on July 10, 1876.

87.19–20   Andersonville and Libby]   Andersonville prison camp in Georgia and Libby prison in Richmond, Virginia.

88.2   *Reply to General Howard*]   In May 1877 Chief Joseph (Hin-mah-too-yah-lat-kekt), the leader of the Wallowa band of the Nez Percé, and several other Nez Percé leaders reluctantly agreed to move their bands onto a reservation in Idaho. The following month a group of young warriors left their camp in southern Idaho and killed more than a dozen white settlers. After defeating an attack by U.S. cavalry at White Bird Canyon on June 17, several Nez Percé bands fled through Idaho, Montana, and Wyoming, traveling more than 1,200 miles and fighting several engagements with the army before being besieged at Bear Paw Mountain near the Canadian border on September 30. Chief Joseph sent this message through Captain John (Jokais), a Nez Percé interpreter, on the morning of October 5, 1877, and surrendered that afternoon. The message was translated by an army interpreter, written down by Lieutenant Charles E. S. Wood, and published in *Harper's Weekly* on November 17. The so-called "surrender speech" became widely known, in part because of the misperception by the army and the press that Joseph was the paramount leader and military commander of the Nez Percé, when in fact he was one of several leaders who made decisions in council.

88.4   General HOWARD] Brigadier General Oliver Otis Howard (1830–1909), commander of the Department of the Columbia.

88.6–7   LOOKING-GLASS . . . TA-HOOL-HOOL-SHUTE] Looking Glass, leader of the Alpowais Nez Percé, was killed at Bear Paw Mountain on October 1; Toohoolhoolzote, leader of the Pikunam Nez Percé, was killed on September 30.

89.2   *Memorial Day Address*] Holmes gave this speech to a Grand Army of the Republic post.

89.5   kept up Memorial Day] The holiday was first formally observed in 1868.

91.32   White Oak . . . Jerusalem Road.] The battle of White Oak Swamp, one of the Seven Days' Battles, was fought near Glendale, Virginia, on June 30, 1862; the battle of Antietam was fought in Maryland on September 17, 1862; Union troops fought along the Jerusalem Plank Road south of Petersburg, Virginia, June 22–23, 1864.

92.14   a lieutenant, and a captain] Lieutenant William Lowell Putnam (1840–61) and Captain Charles F. Cabot (c. 1837–1862).

92.19–21   I awoke . . . Ball's Bluff] Holmes was shot in the chest at Ball's Bluff, Virginia, on October 21, 1861.

92.26   another youthful lieutenant] James Jackson Lowell (1837–1862).

93.16–17   grandson . . . historic name] Colonel Paul Joseph Revere (1832–1863), commander of the 20th Massachusetts Volunteer Infantry Regiment, was mortally wounded at Gettysburg on July 2, 1863.

93.18   Fair Oaks] Battle fought outside Richmond, Virginia, May 31–June 1, 1862.

93.22   His brother, a surgeon] Edward H. R. Revere (1827–1862).

93.26–29   His senior associate . . . Western city.] Nathan Hayward (c. 1830–1866) died in St. Louis.

93.30   quiet figure] Major Henry Patten (1836–1864), mortally wounded at Deep Bottom, Virginia, on August 17, 1864

93.37–38   He entered . . . he fell] Major Henry L. Abbott (1842–1864) was killed in the Wilderness on May 6, 1864.

94.27   one grave and commanding presence] William Francis Bartlett (1840–1876), a Harvard student who was commissioned as a captain in the 20th Massachusetts in 1861. He lost a leg in the Peninsula Campaign in 1862, but remained in the army and organized another regiment. Bartlett was wounded at Port Hudson and in the Wilderness before being wounded and captured in the Petersburg mine crater battle on July 30, 1864.

94.36 beloved friend in a book] Francis W. Palfrey (1831–1889), *Memoir of William Francis Bartlett* (1878).

95.12 "wearing . . . like stars."] Sir Francis Hastings Doyle (1810–1888), "The Loss of the Birkenhead."

95.30–37 But when . . . than mine.] Emily Brontë, "Remembrance" (1846).

99.2 *The Solitude of Self*] Stanton delivered this address before the Judiciary Committee of the House of Representatives.

99.7 sixteenth amendment] The proposed woman suffrage amendment, later adopted as the Nineteenth Amendment.

99.28–29 Spencer . . . Allen] Herbert Spencer (1820–1903), English writer on philosophy, sociology, and evolution; Frederic Harrison (1831–1923), English jurist and historian; Grant Allen (1848–1899), Canadian-born writer on natural science and evolution who became a popular novelist.

104.24 Prince Krapotkin] Prince Pyotr Alekseyevich Kropotkin (1842–1921), a Russian anarchist, was imprisoned in Russia, 1874–76, and in France, 1883–86.

105.40 "Bear . . . burdens,"] Galatians 6:2.

106.8–9 "My God! . . . forsaken me?"] Matthew 27:46.

110.2 *Lynch Law . . . Phases*] Wells gave this speech in Tremont Temple.

112.28 Thomas Moss] Moss was a childhood friend of Mary Church Terrell (see Biographical Notes) and attended her wedding.

118.39–40 driven out of Crittenden Co.] In 1888 armed white men occupied the courthouse in Marion, Arkansas, the seat of Crittenden County, and expelled the county court judge, the county clerk, and 13 other African-Americans to Memphis.

119.29 A.M.E.] African Methodist Episcopal.

120.13 the pamphlets] *Southern Horrors: Lynch Law In All Its Phases*, published by Wells in 1892.

121.28 the decision . . . Supreme Court] In *Cruikshank* v. *United States* (1876) the Court overturned the convictions under federal law of three men who had engaged in mob violence against African-Americans, ruling that their actions did not violate any federal constitutional rights and were not subject to federal jurisdiction.

122.5–6   Judge Tourjee] Albion Tourgée (1838–1905) was a carpetbagger from Ohio who served as a superior court judge in North Carolina, 1868–74, and later wrote several novels set during Reconstruction, including *A Fool's Errand* (1879) and *Bricks Without Straw* (1880). In 1896 he unsuccessfully challenged the Louisiana railroad segregation law as the attorney for the plaintiff in *Plessy* v. *Ferguson*.

124.23–26   Garrison . . . Northampton County] Garrison was jailed in Baltimore in 1830 for 49 days after being convicted of criminal libel for publishing an article linking a Massachusetts merchant with the domestic slave trade. Nat Turner led a slave rebellion in Southampton County, Virginia, in 1831.

124.28   Elijah Lovejoy at Alton] Elijah P. Lovejoy (1802–1837), the editor of an antislavery newspaper, was killed by a mob in Alton, Illinois, on November 7, 1837.

124.30   fearless Charles Sumner] Sumner was badly beaten in the Senate chamber by South Carolina congressman Preston Brooks on May 22, 1856, two days after delivering his antislavery speech "The Crime Against Kansas."

125.3   White Liners] White supremacists who used violence to intimidate Republican voters in the 1875 Mississippi elections.

125.19–20   Repeal of the Civil Rights Law] See note 48.2.

126.11–16   General Butler. . . . "'The Beast] Benjamin F. Butler (see Biographical Notes) died on January 11, 1893. Butler became known in the Confederacy as "Beast Butler" after he ordered that "any female" who insulted Union soldiers in New Orleans "be treated as a woman of the town plying her avocation."

127.2–3   Hogg . . . Tillman] James S. Hogg (1851–1906) was governor of Texas, 1891–95; William J. Northen (1835–1913) was governor of Georgia, 1890–94; Benjamin R. Tillman (1847–1918) was governor of South Carolina, 1890–94, and a senator, 1895–1918.

127.8   Governor Buchanan] John P. Buchanan (1837–1930) was governor of Tennessee, 1891–93.

127.25–28   the party . . . overwhelming defeat] In the 1892 election the Republicans lost the presidency and control of the Senate and failed to regain control of the House of Representatives.

128.8–9   sounding brass and a tinkling cymbal] 1 Corinthians 13:1.

128.12–18   My country . . . Freedom does ring.] Cf. Samuel F. Smith (1808–1895), "America" (1832).

129.32   great . . . depression.] A panic on Wall Street on May 5, 1893, was followed by a stock market crash on June 27.

132.5   great drainage canal]   The Chicago Ship and Sanitary Canal, constructed between 1889 and 1900.

134.39–40   Shay's rebellion . . . whisky rebellion]   Shay's Rebellion in Massachusetts, 1786–87, was directed against high property taxes and farm foreclosures; the Whiskey Rebellion in western Pennsylvania in 1794 was directed against federal excise taxes on spirits.

137.2   *Address at the Atlanta Exposition*]   Washington delivered this address, which became known as the "Atlanta Compromise Speech," at the opening of the Cotton States and International Exposition.

139.23–24   "blessing him . . . takes."]   Cf. *The Merchant of Venice*, IV, i, 187.

139.27–30   "The laws . . . abreast."]   John Greenleaf Whittier, "Song of the Negro Boatmen" (1862).

142.2–3   *Speech . . . National Convention*]   Bryan made this speech during the platform debate over free silver. Proponents of the "free and unlimited coinage of silver" advocated backing the currency with silver as well as gold, with their relative value fixed at a ratio of 16 to 1. The convention endorsed free silver and on July 11 nominated Bryan for president on the fifth ballot.

142.14–16   commendation of . . . the administration]   The second Cleveland administration (1893–97) resisted agitation for free silver and sought to maintain bullion reserves at a level sufficient to keep the currency on a gold basis.

143.18–19   (Senator Hill)]   David B. Hill (1843–1910) was Democratic governor of New York, 1885–91, and a senator from New York, 1892–97

143.25   (ex-Governor Russell)]   William E. Russell (1857–1896) was Democratic governor of Massachusetts, 1891–94

145.7–10   income tax law . . . changed his mind,]   In 1894 Congress passed a flat two percent tax on all incomes above $4,000. The constitutionality of the law was challenged in *Pollock* v. *Farmers' Loan and Trust Co.* on the grounds that an income tax was a direct tax, constitutionally required to be apportioned among the states according to population. On April 4, 1895, the Supreme Court split 4–4 on the question of whether taxing private and corporate incomes constituted a direct tax. The subsequent reargument of the case was attended by the ailing Justice Howell Jackson (1832–1895), who had not participated in the earlier decision. Although Jackson voted to uphold the tax, Justice George Shiras changed sides, and on May 20, 1895, the Court ruled 5–4 that the income tax law was unconstitutional. The *Pollock* decision was overturned by the ratification of the Sixteenth Amendment in 1913.

145.19   Thomas Benton]   Thomas Hart Benton (1782–1858) was a Democratic senator from Missouri, 1821–51.

146.15   act of 1873]   The Coinage Act, which demonetized the silver dollar.

148.22   Mr. Carlisle]   John G. Carlisle (1834–1910) was a Democratic congressman from Kentucky, 1877–90, a senator, 1890–93, and Secretary of the Treasury in the Cleveland administration, 1893–97.

150.2   *The Strenuous Life*]   Roosevelt gave this speech at the Appomattox Day banquet of the Hamilton Club in Chicago.

153.25   "stern men . . . in their brains"]   James Russell Lowell, "Mason and Slidell," in *The Biglow Papers*, second series (1867).

155.34   Secretary Long and Admiral Dewey]   John Davis Long (1838–1915) was Secretary of the Navy, 1897–1902; George Dewey (1837–1917) commanded the squadron that defeated the Spanish in Manila Bay on May 1, 1898.

156.11   Santiago]   The American naval victory off Santiago, Cuba, on July 3, 1898.

161.2   *The Policy of Imperialism*]   Schurz gave this speech to the conference that expanded the New England Anti-Imperialist League, founded in 1898, into a national organization.

161.4–6   addressing the citizens . . . imperialism]   Schurz had delivered the convocation address at the University of Chicago on January 4, 1899. The address was published in pamphlet form as *American Imperialism*.

163.15   Aguinaldo]   Emilio Aguinaldo (1869–1964) led the Philippine independence movement until his capture by American troops on March 23, 1901.

164.35   Thomas M. Anderson]   Anderson (1836–1917) commanded the first American troops sent to the Philippines and arrived at Cavite on June 30, 1898.

166.1–2   Our Secretary of State]   William Rufus Day (1849–1923) served as Secretary of State, April–September 1898.

166.30–31   General Merritt]   Major General Wesley Merritt (1834–1910) commanded the American troops in the Philippines from July 25 to August 26, 1898.

166.35–36   in Paris.]   The treaty ending the Spanish-American War was signed in Paris on December 10, 1898.

167.30   Mr. Barrett]   John Barrett (1866–1938) was the American minister to Siam, 1894–98.

168.15–18   Lincoln . . . starved to death]   In the sixth Lincoln-Douglas debate, held in Quincy, Illinois, on October 13, 1858.

170.33–34   One evening . . . American lines]   The incident occurred on the outskirts of Manila on February 4, 1899.

171.4   General Otis]   Major General Elwell S. Otis (1838–1909) was military governor of the Philippines from August 1898 to May 1900.

172.1   McKinley said at Pittsburgh]   In a speech delivered on August 28, 1899.

172.34   ingenious Postmaster-General]   Charles Emory Smith (1842–1908) was the editor of the *Philadelphia Press*, 1880–90, U.S. minister to Russia, 1890–92, and Postmaster-General, 1898–1902.

175.14–15   "battle of Virden"]   Eight miners and four company guards were killed in a gun battle in Virden, Illinois, on October 12, 1898, that began when members of the United Mine Workers attempted to stop a train bringing strikebreakers into a coal mine.

175.39–40   soon afterwards . . . to attack,]   The American expedition arrived in Iloilo Bay on December 28, 1898, and received orders to occupy the town on February 8, 1899, after fighting had begun at Manila. U.S. troops captured Iloilo on February 11 in a battle during which the city was burned.

180.36–37   "eternal vigilance . . . liberty."]   Cf. John Philpot Curran (1750–1817) from his speech on the right of election of the Lord Mayor of Dublin, July 10, 1790: "The condition upon which God hath given liberty to man is eternal vigilance."

183.25–26   Shays's rebellion, our whisky war]   See note 134.39–40.

184.13   James Bryce or John Morley]   Bryce (1832–1922) was professor of civil law at Oxford, 1870–93, a Liberal member of Parliament, 1880–1907, British ambassador to the United States, 1907–13, and the author of *The American Commonwealth* (1888, revised 1910). Morley (1838–1923) was a Liberal member of Parliament, 1883–95 and 1896–1908, secretary of state for Ireland, 1892–95, and secretary of state for India, 1905–8.

185.4–6   San Domingo . . . Hawaii]   In 1870 President Grant submitted a treaty for the annexation of Santo Domingo to the Senate, which rejected it. The United States annexed Hawaii in 1898.

187.15–16   an article . . . *Century Magazine*]   "Thoughts on American Imperialism," published in September 1898.

188.12–13   enactment of the civil service law]   The Pendleton Act of 1883.

188.13–14   new foray . . . public service?]   The McKinley administration removed 4,000 employees from the civil service classification in June 1899.

194.21   "Our country, right or wrong!"]   Commodore Stephen Decatur (1779–1820), in a toast given at Norfolk, Virginia, in 1816, said: "Our country! In her intercourse with foreign nations may she always be in the right; but our country, right or wrong."

195.2   *The Man with the Muck-Rake*] Roosevelt gave this speech at the cornerstone laying for the House Office Building (now the Cannon House Office Building).

199.3–4   "Ecclesiastical Polity" . . . Hooker] *Of the Laws of Ecclesiastical Polity* (1594) by Richard Hooker (1554–1600), an Anglican theologian.

201.7–8   the railway-rate legislation] The Hepburn Act, signed by Roosevelt on June 29, 1906, gave the Interstate Commerce Commission power to regulate railroad rates.

204.2–3   *What It Means . . . United States*] Terrell gave this speech to the United Women's Club in Washington, D.C. It was published anonymously in *The Independent* on January 24, 1907.

204.20   a stranger in a strange land,] Exodus 2:22.

206.30   the Columbian Law School] An earlier name for the George Washington University Law School.

211.20   Representative Heflin,] James T. Heflin (1869–1951) was a Democratic congressman from Alabama, 1904–20, and a senator, 1920–30.

213.2   *The New Nationalism*] Roosevelt gave this speech at the dedication of the John Brown Memorial State Park.

214.29   as through a glass, darkly] See 1 Corinthians 13:12.

215.33–34   "I hold . . . ameliorating mankind."] From Lincoln's speech at Cincinnati, Ohio, February 12, 1861.

215.36–216.6   "Labor is prior to . . . any other rights] The quotations are from Lincoln's annual message to Congress, December 3, 1861.

216.6–13   "Nor should this lead . . . violence when built."] The quotations are from Lincoln's reply to the New York Workingmen's Democratic Republican Association, Washington, D.C., March 21, 1864.

219.39–220.1   The Hepburn Act . . . the last session] The Hepburn Act, giving the Interstate Commerce Commission power to regulate railroad rates, was signed by Roosevelt on June 29, 1906. The I.C.C. was strengthened by the Mann-Elkins Act, passed on June 18, 1910, which gave the commission the power to set original rates.

229.2   *Speech at Prayer Meeting*] Chapman gave this speech in a rented storeroom after advertising a prayer meeting to mark the anniversary of the lynching of Zachariah Walker. The meeting was attended by Mrs. Chapman and two other persons; his speech was published in *Harper's Weekly* on September 21, 1912.

229.5   most dreadful crime] On August 12, 1911, Zachariah Walker, an African-American steelworker, shot and killed a white steel company police officer in Coatesville during a scuffle. Walker was captured on the morning of

August 13 and taken to Coatesville Hospital for treatment of a self-inflicted gunshot wound. He was dragged from the hospital by a mob that night and burned alive.

229.8–9   attempt to prosecute . . . failed;] Fifteen men were indicted for the lynching. After juries acquitted seven of the accused men, the prosecution asked for a directed acquittal of the remaining defendants.

242.19   addressed . . . twenty-second of January] In his speech Wilson called for the war to end in "a peace without victory," freedom of the seas, and the establishment of "some definite concert of power" to prevent future wars.

242.20–21   addressed . . . third of February] Wilson announced that the United States was severing diplomatic relations with Germany.

243.31–32   the last few weeks in Russia?] A series of strikes and army mutinies that began in Petrograd (St. Petersburg) on February 23, 1917, led to the abdication of Tsar Nicholas II on March 2 and the formation of a Provisional Government.

244.29–30   intercepted note . . . Mexico City] Arthur Zimmerman, the German foreign minister, sent a telegram to the German minister in Mexico on January 19, 1917, proposing an alliance between Germany and Mexico with the aim of restoring Texas, New Mexico, and Arizona to Mexico. The British intercepted and deciphered the telegram, then presented it to the Wilson administration, which made it public on March 1, 1917.

245.19–20   governments . . . Germany] The United States declared war on Austria-Hungary on December 7, 1917, but did not go to war with Bulgaria and the Ottoman Empire.

247.2–3   *Speech . . . Wartime*] The text printed here was prepared by La Follette for publication in the *Congressional Record.*

248.5   Waller T. Burns] Burns (1858–1917) was a federal judge for the Southern District of Texas from 1902 until his death on November 17, 1917.

248.7–9   STONE . . . GORE] William J. Stone (1848–1918) was a Democratic congressman from Missouri, 1885–91, and a senator, 1903–18. Thomas W. Hardwick (1872–1944) was a Democratic congressman from Georgia, 1903–14, and a senator, 1914–19. James K. Vardaman (1861–1930) was the Democratic governor of Mississippi, 1904–8, and a senator, 1913–19. Asle J. Gronna (1858–1922) was a Republican congressman from North Dakota, 1905–11, and a senator, 1911–21. Thomas P. Gore (1870–1949) was a Democratic senator from Oklahoma, 1907–21 and 1931–37.

248.37   "with malice . . . all."] Cf. Lincoln's Second Inaugural Address, March 4, 1865.

256.9–10   criticized President Polk . . . the House] In a speech delivered on January 12, 1848.

256.23–24   Lincoln said:] In a letter to his law partner William H. Herndon, written on February 15, 1848.

256.36–37   John A. Andrew . . . Massachusetts] Andrew (1818–1867) was the Republican governor of Massachusetts, 1861–66.

257.19   Mr. McAdoo] William G. McAdoo (1863–1941) was Secretary of the Treasury, 1913–18. In 1914 he married Eleanor Wilson and became the president's son-in-law.

261.4   Senator Tom Corwin] Thomas Corwin (1794–1865) was a Whig congressman from Ohio, 1831–40, and a senator, 1845–50. He served as Secretary of the Treasury in the Fillmore administration, 1850–53, and as a Republican congressman, 1859–61.

262.22   Gladstone] William Gladstone (1809–1898) served as chancellor of the exchequer in the government of Lord Aberdeen, 1852–55.

262.28–29   the prime minister] Lord Salisbury (1830–1903) was prime minister of Conservative governments, 1885–85 and 1886–92, and a Unionist government, 1895–1902.

262.34   these two Republics] The Transvaal Republic and the Orange Free State.

264.12   Duke of Grafton] The Duke of Grafton (1735–1811) was prime minister, 1768–70.

270.18   *Ex parte Milligan*] In *Milligan* (1866) the Supreme Court unanimously overturned the conviction of an Indiana copperhead convicted of treason during the Civil War by a military commission established under executive authority. Five of the justices held that military trials of civilians could not be held as long as the civil courts remained open, while four justices held that Congress could authorize military trials for civilians.

271.34   Watson] David K. Watson (1849–1917), *The Constitution of the United States; Its History, Application, and Construction* (1910).

272.16   Mr. KING] William H. King (1863–1949) was a Democratic congressman from Utah, 1897–99 and 1900–1, and a senator, 1917–41.

272.28–29   Pomeroy . . . *United States*] First published in 1868 by John N. Pomeroy (1828–1885), who was then serving as dean of New York University Law School.

273.3   Elliot's *Debates*] Jonathan Elliot (1784–1845), *The Debates in the Several State Conventions on the Adoption of the Federal Constitution*, first published 1827–30.

273.11 Story, . . . Constitution] *Commentaries on the Constitution of the United States*, first published in 1833 by Joseph Story (1779–1845), an Associate Justice of the Supreme Court, 1811–45.

273.33 Ordronaux, . . . Legislation,] John Ordronaux (1830–1908), *Constitutional Legislation in the United States* (1891).

274.35 *Hinds' Precedents*] Asher C. Hinds (1863–1919), *Hinds' Precedents of the House of Representatives of the United States* (1907).

275.22 Panama Congress] A conference of Latin American republics held in Panama in 1826.

275.31 James Buchanan and John Forsyth,] Buchanan (1791–1868) was a congressman from Pennsylvania, 1821–31, minister to Russia, 1832–34, a senator, 1834–45, Secretary of State in the Polk administration, 1845–49, minister to Great Britain, 1853–56, and President of the United States, 1857–61. Forsyth (1780–1841) was a congressman from Georgia, 1813–18 and 1823–27, a senator, 1818–19 and 1829–34, and Secretary of State in the Jackson and Van Buren administrations, 1834–41.

276.2–4 monarchical government . . . European power.] In 1863 France established the Austrian archduke Maximilian as emperor of Mexico. Maximilian was overthrown and executed in 1867 after French troops were withdrawn from Mexico in response to an American ultimatum.

276.10 Secretary Seward] See note 15.23.

276.18–19 Mr. Henry Winter Davis] Davis (1817–1865) was a congressman from Maryland, 1855–61 and 1863–65.

278.15 Ashmun amendment] The amendment was introduced by George Ashmun on January 3, 1848, and approved, 85–81. Ashmun (1804–1870) was a Whig congressman from Massachusetts, 1845–51.

278.22–23 Mr. Venable] Abraham W. Venable (1799–1876) was a Democratic congressman from North Carolina, 1847–53.

282.27–29 terms set forth . . . January 22, 1917,] In the spring of 1917 the Provisional Government announced that it sought peace on the basis of national self-determination, while the more radical Petrograd Soviet called for a peace without annexations or indemnities. For Wilson's speech of January 22, 1917, see note 242.19.

286.2 *Address to Woman Suffrage Convention*] Catt delivered this address to the annual convention of the National American Woman Suffrage Association.

286.7 November 6, 1917] A woman suffrage amendment to the New York State constitution was approved by referendum on November 6, 1917.

288.26   Hon. Champ Clark] James Beauchamp (Champ) Clark (1850–1921) was a Democratic congressman from Missouri, 1893–95 and 1897–1921, and Speaker of the House, 1911–19.

288.39   Elihu Root,] Root (1845–1937) served as Secretary of War, 1899–1904, Secretary of State, 1905–9, and as a Republican senator from New York, 1909–15.

290.5–6   Great Britain . . . women,] The Representation of the People Act, passed in 1918, enfranchised all men over 21 and women over 30 who paid rates (local taxes) or were married to ratepayers. In 1928 the suffrage was extended to all women over 21.

290.28   France . . . women] Women were not enfranchised in France until 1944.

291.29   Mr. Asquith] Herbert Asquith (1852–1928) was prime minister of Great Britain, 1908–16.

293.12   the Sixty-fifth Congress] The Sixty-fifth Congress met from 1917 to 1919.

300.5   Livermore . . . Blake] Mary A. Livermore (1820–1905) was a suffragist, journalist, and advocate for temperance and women's education. Lillie Devereux Blake (1833–1913) was a suffragist, novelist, and journalist.

306.30–31   Vance Thompson] Thompson (1863–1925) wrote novels, plays, verse, essays, and literary criticism.

308.2   *Speech to the Court*] Debs was tried and convicted under the 1917 Espionage Act for inciting disloyalty in the armed forces and obstructing military recruiting by making an anti-war speech at Canton, Ohio, on June 16, 1918. He was sentenced to ten years in prison and began serving his sentence on April 13, 1919, when the Supreme Court unanimously upheld his conviction. Debs was released on December 25, 1921 after President Harding commuted his sentence.

308.22   names of two noble women] Kate Richards O'Hare and Rose Pastor Stokes, two Socialists imprisoned under the Espionage Act for making anti-war statements and whom Debs had praised in his speech at Canton.

309.8   preferred to go to prison] In 1895 Debs served a six-month sentence for contempt of court for defying an injunction during the 1894 Pullman railroad strike.

313.13–20   "He is true . . . the race."] James Russell Lowell, "On the Capture of Fugitive Slaves near Washington" (1845).

314.7   the earliest opportunity] Wilson attended the signing of the treaty on June 28 and returned to Washington, D.C., at midnight on July 8, 1919.

315.8   our associates] Brazil, Cuba, Guatemala, Haiti, Honduras, Nicaragua, and Panama declared war on Germany at various times following the U.S. declaration on April 6, 1917.

315.32   action at Château-Thierry] In early June 1918 American troops helped stop a major German offensive in heavy fighting around Château Thierry, a town on the Marne 40 miles east of Paris.

320.25–29   the Saar . . . distant date] The treaty placed the Saar basin under League of Nations administration until 1935, when its inhabitants voted in a plebiscite to rejoin Germany.

320.32–33   a State] Poland.

327.2   Speech . . . League of Nations] Lodge, the chairman of the Senate Foreign Relations Committee, reported a resolution ratifying the Versailles Treaty on November 6, 1919, that contained 14 reservations regarding the League of Nations covenant. President Wilson, who had suffered a major stroke on October 2, rejected the reservations, and the Lodge resolution was defeated in the Senate on November 19. A second resolution of ratification with modified reservations passed 49–35 on March 19, 1920, but failed to win the necessary two-thirds majority. In 1921 the Harding administration abandoned attempts to enter the League, and the United States signed and ratified separate peace treaties with Germany, Austria, and Hungary.

327.4   the Essays of Elia,] *The Essays of Elia* (1823) by Charles Lamb (1775–1834).

327.20–21   a project . . . Abbé de Saint-Pierre] Charles-Irénée Castel (1658–1743), *La projet de paix perpétuelle* (1713).

328.1   Kaunitz . . . Leopold] Prince von Kaunitz (1711–1794) was state chancellor of Austria, 1753–92; Leopold II (1747–1792) was grand duke of Tuscany, 1765–90, and Holy Roman Emperor, 1790–92.

328.10   Emperor Alexander] Alexander I (1777–1825) was Tsar of Russia, 1801–25.

328.24   treaty of Tilsit] A treaty between France and Russia signed in 1807.

328.28   Baroness von Krudener] Barbara Juliane von Krüdener (1764–1824), the widow of a Russian diplomat, underwent a religious conversion in 1804. She met Alexander I in Switzerland in 1813 and became his religious adviser and confidant.

329.29   Lord Castlereagh] Viscount Castlereagh (1769–1822) was the foreign secretary of Great Britain, 1812–22.

329.35   Troppau and Laibach] The Congress of Troppau was held in 1820 and the Congress of Laibach in 1821.

329.38   Congress of Verona] Held in 1822.

329.39   George Canning] Canning (1770–1827) was foreign secretary, 1807–9 and 1822–27, and prime minister, April–August 1827.

330.23   Metternich] Prince von Metternich (1773–1859) was foreign minister of Austria, 1809–48.

333.18   Clemenceau . . . Paderewski] Georges Clemenceau (1841–1929) was premier of France, 1917–20; Ignacy Paderewski (1860–1941) was prime minister of Poland, January–November 1919.

336.6   cession . . . Shantung] The Treaty of Versailles ceded to Japan the German concessions on the Shantung peninsula, including control of the port of Tsingtao (Qingdao), railways, mines, and the right to station troops.

336.24   King of the Hedjaz] Hussein (ca. 1854–1931), the sharif of Mecca from 1908 to 1916, became king of the Hejaz n 1916 at the beginning of the Arab revolt against the Ottoman Empire and ruled until his defeat in 1924 by Ibn Saud.

336.27   Emir Abdullah] Abdullah (1882–1951) was a son of Hussein. He was later emir of Transjordan, 1921–46, and king of Jordan, 1946–51.

336.28   Ibn Savond] Ibn Saud (c. 1880–1953), the sultan of Nejd, conquered the Hejaz in 1926 and united it with the Nejd in 1932 to form the kingdom of Saudi Arabia, which he ruled until his death.

337.8–11   Great Britain . . . Mosquito Coast] The British maintained a protectorate on the Mosquito Coast, 1687–1783 and 1816–60.

338.32–34   school laws . . international dispute?] The decision by the San Francisco board of education in 1906 to segregate Japanese schoolchildren caused a crisis in Japanese-American relations. It was resolved in 1907 when President Theodore Roosevelt reached a "gentlemen's agreement" with the Japanese government, under which the segregation policy was ended in return for severe restrictions on Japanese immigration to the continental United States.

340.30–31   England . . . seven] The original members of the league included Great Britain, Canada, Australia, South Africa, New Zealand, and India.

343.34   John Quincy Adams] Adams served as Secretary of State during the Monroe administration, 1817–25.

345.14   Mr. Olney] Richard Olney (1835–1917) was Secretary of State, 1895–97.

354.38   "*Post equitem sedet atra cura*,"] Horace, *Odes*, III, I, 40: "Behind the rider sits dark care."

359.16–18   Republican Congress . . . Democratic administration] The Republicans controlled both the House and the Senate during the last two years of the Wilson administration, 1919–21.

361.32   administration of Muscle Shoals] President Wilson authorized the U.S. Army Corps of Engineers in 1918 to build a dam and hydroelectric plant on the Tennessee River at Muscle Shoals, Alabama. In 1922 Republican Senator George W. Norris (1861–1944) introduced a bill calling for government operation of the power plant, while other proposals were advanced for leasing the facility to private companies. The Norris bill was passed by Congress in May 1928 but was vetoed by President Coolidge. In 1933 the Muscle Shoals project became part of the Tennessee Valley Authority.

362.30   Samuel Gompers] Gompers (1850–1924) was a founder of the American Federation of Labor and its president, 1886–95 and 1896–1924.

373.9–10   no control over the winds of Heaven] Roosevelt had flown from Albany, New York, to Chicago that day.

384.2   *Commonwealth Club*] An organization founded in 1903 to serve as a forum for discussing public issues.

385.29   Meredith Nicholson] Nicholson (1866–1947) was a novelist whose works included *The Main Chance* (1903), *A Hoosier Chronicle* (1912), and *The Cavalier of Tennessee* (1928). During the Roosevelt administration he served as minister to Paraguay, 1933–35, Venezuela, 1935–38, and Nicaragua, 1938–41.

387.10–17   "We have no . . . their families."] From a letter Jefferson wrote to Thomas Cooper on September 10, 1814.

390.25–26   Supreme Court . . . "rule of reason"] The rule, used for interpreting the 1890 Sherman Anti-Trust Act, was adopted in two cases decided in 1911, *United States* v. *Standard Oil Company of New Jersey* and *United States* v. *American Tobacco Co.*

391.3–14   "No man can . . . be absorbed."] Woodrow Wilson, *The New Freedom: A Call for the Emancipation of the Generous Energies of a People* (1913).

399.15–16   when there is . . . perish.] Cf. Proverbs 29:18.

399.27   not to be . . . minister] Matthew 20:28; Mark 10:45.

403.2   *Every Man a King*] Long delivered this speech in a radio broadcast.

407.2–3   Supreme Court . . . Minnesota case] In *Home Building and Loan Association* v. *Blaisdell*, decided 5–4 on January 8, 1934, the Court upheld the 1933 Minnesota mortgage moratorium law, ruling that it did not impair the obligation of contracts.

408.9–10   the rich . . . upon them;] See James 5:1.

423.29–30   "each age . . . to birth."] Arthur O'Shaughnessy (1844–1881), "Ode" (1874).

425.39–40   "to give light . . . peace."] Cf. Luke 1:79.

426.2   *"Arsenal . . . Chat*] Roosevelt delivered this speech in a radio broadcast from the White House.

427.28   the Greeks,] The Italian army invaded Greece on October 28, 1940, but was driven back into Albania by late December. On April 6, 1941, the Germans attacked Greece, and captured Athens on April 27.

438.12   Maximilian interlude in Mexico] See note 276.2–4.

439.20–22   "Those, who . . . nor safety."] Benjamin Franklin, in the reply to the governor of the Pennsylvania Assembly, November 11, 1755.

439.25–26   sounding brass . . . cymbal] Cf. 1 Corinthians 13:1.

447.14   Japanese Ambassador . . . colleague] Ambassador Kichisaburo Nomura (1887–1964) and special envoy Saburo Kurusu (1888–1954).

447.15–16   recent American message] On November 26, 1941, Secretary of State Cordell Hull presented a note to Nomura and Kurusu outlining the basis for an agreement between Japan and the United States. The document called for Japan to withdraw its troops from China and Indochina and to recognize the Chinese Nationalist government in return for the lifting of the embargo on U.S. exports to Japan.

447.28–29   American ships have . . . Honolulu.] These reports were incorrect.

449.2   *Speech to Third Army Troops*] Patton gave several versions of this speech while preparing for the campaign in France. The text printed here is a transcription in the collection of the Patton Museum of Cavalry and Armor, Fort Knox, Kentucky.

451.16   Gabes] A coastal city in central Tunisia.

453.2   *Address to the Allied Expeditionary Forces*] A recording of this speech was played on ships of the Allied invasion fleet and was broadcast in England and the United States on June 6, 1944.

454.2   *Statement on the Atomic Bomb*] This statement was released by the White House while President Truman was returning from Europe on the cruiser U.S.S. *Augusta*. Truman read a portion of the statement for a newsreel camera crew onboard the ship.

454.6   20,000 tons of T.N.T.] The yield of the Hiroshima bomb has subsequently been estimated as 15 kilotons.

454.8   British "Grand Slam"]   A 22,000 pound bomb used by the Royal
Air Force to destroy German railway viaducts and bridges in March and April
1945.

454.25–26   the V-1's and V-2's late]   The Germans began using V-1 cruise
missiles against England on June 13, 1944, and V-2 ballistic missiles on September 8, 1944.

456.7   ultimatum . . . Potsdam]   The ultimatum, issued by the United
States, Britain, and Nationalist China, called for the unconditional surrender
of the Japanese armed forces and warned that the "alternative for Japan is
prompt and utter destruction."

456.17–19   sites at Oak Ridge . . . New Mexico]   The Oak Ridge installation produced enriched uranium, the Hanford works in Washington State
produced plutonium, and the Los Alamos laboratory in New Mexico designed and manufactured the bombs.

458.2   *Speech to Los Alamos Scientists*]   Oppenheimer gave this speech in a
movie theater at the laboratory to 500 members of the Association of Los
Alamos Scientists. The ALAS was founded on August 30, 1945, to promote
the international control of atomic energy.

458.12   talk to you as a Director]   Oppenheimer resigned as director of
Los Alamos on October 16, 1945.

458.18   the Secretary of War]   Henry Stimson (1867–1950) served as Secretary of War from June 1940 until his resignation in September 1945, when
he was succeeded by Robert Patterson (1891–1952).

462.30   these first bombs . . . Nagasaki]   The type of bomb tested near
Alamogordo, New Mexico, on July 16 and dropped on Nagasaki on August
9, 1945, was an implosion design that used plutonium. It was more technically
sophisticated and made more efficient use of fissionable material than the gun
assembly design using uranium that was dropped on Hiroshima.

467.20   Bohr]   Niels Bohr (1885–1962) was awarded the 1922 Nobel Prize
in physics for his work on atomic structure. He escaped from Denmark in
September 1943 and came to the United States, where he advised President
Roosevelt to work with the Soviet Union on international control of atomic
energy.

468.11   Mr. Stimson]   See note 458.18.

468.40   message to Congress]   In a special message to Congress sent on
October 3, 1945, Truman called for the creation of an Atomic Energy Commission and expressed the hope that international discussion would lead to
the peaceful development of atomic energy and the renunciation of the
atomic bomb.

470.10–11   President's Navy Day speech] In a speech delivered in New
York City on October 27, 1945, Truman said that the "atomic bomb does not
alter the basic foreign policy of the United States" and declared that American possession of the bomb posed "no threat to any nation" and was "a
sacred trust."

472.2   *Speech at Harvard University*] Marshall gave this speech after receiving an honorary degree. His proposal for economic assistance to Europe
led to the establishment of the European Recovery Program in December
1947.

476.6   minority report] The minority report called for a federal anti-
lynching law, establishment of a Fair Employment Practices Commission, the
abolition of poll taxes, and desegregation of the armed forces. Its adoption
by the convention led to a walkout by Southern "Dixiecrats," who held a
States' Rights convention on July 17 and nominated South Carolina governor
Strom Thurmond (1902–2003) for president.

476.7   Congressman Biemiller] Andrew Biemiller (1906–1982) was a
Democratic congressman from Wisconsin, 1945–47 and 1949–51.

477.1   Alben Barkley] Barkley (1877–1956) was a Democratic congressman from Kentucky, 1913–27, a senator, 1927–49 and 1955–56, and Vice-
President of the United States, 1949–53.

480.2–3   *Speech . . . Convention*] Truman began this speech at 2 A.M.

481.2–3   the permanent chairman] Sam Rayburn (1882–1961), a Democratic congressman from Texas, 1913–61, and Speaker of the House, 1940–47
and 1949–61.

481.23   80th Congress] The Republicans controlled both the Senate and
the House during the 80th Congress, 1947–49.

482.2   program for Greece and Turkey] In the spring of 1947 Congress
granted Truman's request for military and economic aid for Greece and
Turkey in order to contain Soviet expansionism.

482.32   OPA] Office of Price Administration, a federal agency established in 1941 and abolished in 1947.

483.19   Taft-Hartley Act] The act, passed over Truman's veto on June
23, 1947, restricted union activity and strengthened the position of employers
in labor disputes.

484.8   civil rights program] In a message sent to Congress on February
2, 1948, Truman called for establishing a permanent Civil Rights Commission
and a civil rights division in the Department of Justice, a federal anti-lynching
law, legislation to protect voting rights, the prohibition of discrimination in

interstate transportation, and the establishment of a Fair Employment Practices Commission.

485.39   anti-Semitic, anti-Catholic law] The Displaced Persons Act of 1948 provided for the admission into the United States of 200,000 refugees who had entered Germany, Austria, or Italy on or before December 22, 1945. Truman reluctantly signed the act on June 25, 1948, while criticizing its eligibility requirements for excluding more than 90 percent of Jewish displaced persons, as well as many Catholic refugees.

487.2   *Declaration of Conscience*] Smith made this speech in the Senate while a select subcommittee continued its investigation of charges by Senator Joseph McCarthy of widespread Communist infiltration in the State Department. McCarthy first made his accusations in a speech in Wheeling, West Virginia, on February 9, 1950, and repeated them in the Senate on February 20. The subcommittee, headed by Senator Millard Tydings of Maryland, issued a report on July 20, 1950, highly critical of McCarthy.

488.40–489.1   Amerasia case . . . Gold case] Six persons, including two State Department employees, a naval officer, and the co-editors of *Amerasia*, a magazine sympathetic to the Chinese Communists, were arrested in June 1945 in connection with the unauthorized disclosure of government documents. Four of the accused were never indicted or prosecuted, and the remaining two entered pleas and paid fines. Alger Hiss (1904–1996), an employee of the State Department from 1936 to 1946, was accused of espionage for the Soviet Union in 1948 and convicted of perjury in January 1950. (Hiss was not charged with espionage because the statute of limitations had expired.) Judith Coplon, an employee of the Justice Department, was arrested in March 1949 while meeting with a Soviet intelligence officer. She was convicted of stealing classified documents in 1949 and of conspiracy to commit espionage in March 1950; both convictions were later overturned on appeal. Harry Gold (1910–1972) was arrested on May 22, 1950, and immediately confessed to having served as a courier for Klaus Fuchs, a German-born British physicist who spied for the Soviets while working at Los Alamos.

491.12–16   Mr. TOBEY . . . Mr. HENDRICKSON] Charles W. Tobey (1880–1953) was a Republican congressman from New Hampshire, 1933–39, and a senator, 1939–53. George D. Aiken (1892–1984) was a Republican senator from Vermont, 1941–75. Wayne L. Morse (1900–1974) was a Republican senator from Oregon, 1945–53, who then served in the Senate as an independent, 1953–55, and as a Democrat, 1955–69. Irving M. Ives (1896–1962) was a Republican senator from New York, 1947–59. Edward J. Thye (1896–1969) was a Republican senator from Minnesota, 1947–59. Robert C. Hendrickson (1898–1964) was a Republican senator from New Jersey, 1949–55.

495.2   *Address to Congress*] On April 11, 1951, Truman relieved MacArthur of his command for repeated insubordination.

498.15   Chan So Lin] Chang Tso-lin (Zhang Zuolin) was a Manchurian warlord who ruled over part of northern China from 1924 until 1928, when he was driven from Peking by the Nationalists and then assassinated by Japanese army officers.

498.18   Chiang Kai-shek] Chiang (1887–1975) became the leader of Nationalist China in 1928. The Communist victory in 1949 forced him to flee to Taiwan (Formosa), where he continued to lead the Nationalists until his death.

498.39   Korea . . . Tibet] The Chinese launched a major offensive against United Nations forces in North Korea on November 25, 1950, and captured Seoul on January 5, 1951. Their offensive was halted in late January, and by mid-April U.N. forces had retaken Seoul and were on a line close to the 38th parallel. In September–October 1950 the Viet Minh used Chinese-supplied weapons and Chinese bases to launch a successful offensive against the French along the northeastern Vietnamese-Chinese border. The Chinese army invaded Tibet in October 1950.

499.27–28   Philippines . . . existing unrest] The Communist-led Hukbalahap guerilla movement engaged in an insurrection against the Philippine government, 1946–55, that was eventually defeated with American assistance.

500.23   north of the Yalu] The Yalu River runs along most of the border between China and North Korea.

504.2   "Checkers" Speech] Nixon broadcast this speech from the El Capitan theater in Hollywood.

504.21   read the charge] The existence of the fund was revealed in a story in the New York Post on September 18, 1952.

505.5   "Meet the Press," . . . last Sunday] Nixon appeared on "Meet the Press," an NBC television news program, on September 14, 1952.

505.6   Peter Edson] Edson was a Washington columnist for the Newspaper Enterprise Association, 1941–64.

505.8   Dana Smith] Smith, an attorney in Los Angeles, served as the treasurer of the fund.

506.25–26   opposite number for the Vice Presidency] John J. Sparkman (1899–1985), the Democratic vice-presidential candidate in 1952, was a congressman from Alabama, 1937–46, and a senator, 1946–79.

507.35   Gov. Sherman Adams] Adams (1899–1986) was the Republican governor of New Hampshire, 1949–52, and later served as White House chief of staff, 1953–58.

509.12–13   service record . . . South Pacific] Nixon served in 1944 as a
navy supply officer on the Bougainville beachhead while it was being bombed
and shelled by the Japanese.

509.20   a Government agency] The Office of Price Administration.

510.15   Patricia and Julie] Patricia Nixon Cox (b. 1946) and Julie Nixon
Eisenhower (b. 1948).

511.10   Mr. Mitchell] Stephen A. Mitchell (1903–1974), a Chicago attorney, was chairman of the Democratic National Committee, 1952–55.

511.20–21   Governor Stevenson . . . father] Lewis Stevenson (1868–
1929) left an estate valued at $174,333, most of it in farmland.

512.23–24   the Hiss case] While serving on the House Committee on Un-
American Activities in 1948 Nixon had aggressively pursued the allegations
made against Hiss by Whittaker Chambers (1901–1961), a former Communist.

513.4   Truman-Acheson] Dean Acheson (1893–1971) served as Assistant
Secretary of State, 1941–45, Undersecretary of State, 1945–47, and Secretary
of State, 1949–53.

513.32–33   the atomic bomb case] In January 1950 Klaus Fuchs, a physicist who had worked at Los Alamos from 1944 to 1946, confessed to British
authorities that he had spied for the Soviet Union. The arrest and confession
of his courier Harry Gold (see note 488.40–489.1) led to the arrests in 1950
of David Greenglass, a former machinist at Los Alamos, and of Greenglass's
sister and brother-in-law, Ethel and Julius Rosenberg.

513.36–37   any man . . . "red herring"] At a press conference held on
August 5, 1948, Truman called the ongoing investigation into Soviet espionage by the House Committee on Un-American Activities a "red herring"
intended to distract the public from inflation.

516.2–3   *Speech to the Montgomery Improvement Association*] King gave
this speech at Holt Street Baptist Church during the first mass meeting of the
Montgomery Improvement Association, an organization founded by King
and several other African-American ministers and community leaders earlier
that day to conduct a boycott of Montgomery city buses. The boycott continued until December 21, 1956, when the buses began operating on a desegregated basis following a federal court decision declaring segregation on
Alabama intrastate buses to be unconstitutional.

516.28   just last Thursday] December 1, 1955.

517.8   Mrs. Rosa Parks] Parks (1913–2005), a seamstress, had served as the
secretary of the Montgomery branch of the NAACP since 1943.

518.6   White Citizens' Council] An organization founded in Mississippi
in 1954 to oppose desegregation by political, legal, and economic means.

518.26–27   justice runs . . . stream.] Cf. Amos 5:24.

520.3   *January 21, 1957*] Eisenhower took the presidential oath of office at the White House on Sunday, January 20, 1957, and then repeated it at the inaugural ceremony held on January 21.

521.28   Budapest] An uprising in Budapest on October 23, 1956, led to the collapse of the Communist regime. Soviet troops invaded Hungary on November 4 and suppressed the uprising in fighting that continued in Budapest until November 10. About 2,700 Hungarians were killed during the uprising, and more than 200 were subsequently executed.

525.11–12   humiliating treatment . . . Vice President] A planned visit by President Eisenhower to Japan was canceled in June 1960 because of violent street demonstrations against the recently signed U.S.-Japan security treaty. Vice-President Nixon was spat upon by a mob at the Caracas airport during a visit to Venezuela on May 13, 1958, and his limousine was attacked and nearly overturned.

525.16–17   too late . . . outer space.] The Soviet Union sent the first satellite into earth orbit in 1957, and in 1959 sent the first unmanned spacecraft to the moon.

526.13–14   Jefferson's statute of religious freedom] The statute, drafted in 1777 and adopted in 1786, abolished tax assessments in support of religious denominations in Virginia.

527.7–8   my brother died for] Joseph Kennedy Jr. (1915–1944), a naval officer, was killed on August 12, 1944, when his bomber exploded over England.

528.40   ***] The asterisks were used in the source text to indicate an ellipsis.

529.2   *Farewell Address*] Eisenhower delivered this address on television from the White House.

537.22–23   "undo . . . go free."] Isaiah 58:6.

537.40–538.1   "rejoicing . . . tribulation"] Romans 12:12.

539.5–6   Senator Bob Byrd] Robert C. Byrd (b. 1917) served as a Democratic congressman from West Virginia, 1953–59, and as a senator from 1959 until the present.

539.11   Bishop John Fletcher Hurst] Hurst (1834–1903) raised an endowment and secured a congressional charter while serving as chancellor of American University, 1891–1902.

539.27–28   "There are . . . Masefield] From an address given at the University of Sheffield in 1946 by John Masefield (1878–1967), the poet laureate of Great Britain, 1930–67.

542.9   Soviet text on *Military Strategy*] Edited by Marshal Vasily
Sokolovsky (1897–1968), *Military Strategy* was published in 1962 and translated in 1963.

542.19–20   "The wicked . . . pursueth."] Proverbs 28:1.

544.31   West New Guinea] The United States sponsored negotiations
between Indonesia and the Netherlands in 1962 that resulted in the transfer
of West New Guinea to Indonesian administration in 1963.

545.21   direct line . . . Washington] On June 20, 1963, the United
States and the Soviet Union agreed to establish a direct teletype link between
Moscow and Washington. The "hot line" became operational on August 30,
1963, and was first used for a diplomatic message on June 5, 1967, during the
Arab-Israeli war.

546.12   Khrushchev . . . Macmillan] Nikita Khrushchev (1894–1971)
was first secretary of the Communist Party of the Soviet Union, 1953–64, and
chairman of the Council of Ministers (premier), 1958–64. Harold Macmillan
(1894–1986) was prime minister of Great Britain, 1957–63

546.14–15   early agreement . . . test ban treaty.] The United States,
Britain, and the Soviet Union signed a limited test ban treaty on August 5,
1963, that prohibited nuclear tests in the atmosphere, underwater, or in outer
space, while permitting continued testing underground. (A comprehensive
test ban treaty was signed by the United States, Russia, China, Britain, and
France in September 1996, but was rejected by the U.S. Senate in 1999.)

547.4–6   "When a man's . . . with him."] Proverbs 16:7.

548.2   *Address . . . Civil Rights*] This speech was broadcast from the
White House.

548.5–7   threats and defiant statements . . . University of Alabama] On
the morning of June 11 Alabama Governor George Wallace (1919–1998), accompanied by scores of state troopers, defied Deputy Attorney General
Nicholas Katzenbach by refusing to step aside from the doorway of Foster
Auditorium and permit two African-American students to enter and register.
Wallace yielded in the afternoon after Alabama National Guardsmen acting
under federal authority arrived on campus to enforce the court order admitting the students.

551.8–11   Congress to enact . . . establishments.] The administration
submitted the bill to Congress on June 19, 1963; the final version was passed
by the House on July 2, 1964, and signed by President Johnson the same day.
Because the Supreme Court had ruled in 1883 that racial discrimination in
public accommodations by private individuals did not violate the Fourteenth
Amendment (see note 48.2), the Civil Rights Act of 1964 regulated public
accommodations under the commerce power. The constitutionality of the

public accommodations section of the act was upheld by the Supreme Court in two unanimous decisions on December 14, 1964.

551.22–24   asking Congress . . . public education] This provision was included in the bill passed in 1964.

553. 3   Justice Harlan . . . the century] In his dissent in *Plessy* v. *Ferguson* (1896), John Marshall Harlan (1833–1911) wrote: "Our Constitution is color-blind, and neither knows nor tolerates classes among citizens." (Harlan, an Associate Justice of the Supreme Court, 1877–1911, was also the sole dissenter in the 1883 case that overturned the Civil Rights Act of 1875.)

554.4–5   your distinguished Mayor] Willy Brandt (1913–1992), a Social Democrat, was mayor of West Berlin, 1957–1966, foreign minister of West Germany, 1966–69, and chancellor of West Germany, 1969–74.

554.7   your distinguished Chancellor] Konrad Adenauer (1876–1967), a Christian Democrat, was chancellor of West Germany, 1949–63.

554.10   General Clay] Lucius Clay (1897–1978) was military governor of the U.S. Occupation Zone in West Germany, 1947–49, and oversaw the Berlin Airlift during the Soviet blockade of the city, 1948–49.

554.12–13   "*civis Romanus sum.*"] I am a Roman citizen.

554.27   put a wall up] The East German government began building the Berlin Wall on August 13, 1961.

556.2   *Address to the March on Washington*] King gave this speech on the steps of the Lincoln Memorial to a crowd of 200,000 people attending the March for Jobs and Freedom.

558.19–20   justice rolls . . . stream.] Cf. Amos 5:24.

559.12   its governor] George Wallace (1919–1998) was the Democratic governor of Alabama, 1963–67, 1971–79, and 1983–87.

559.17–21   every valley . . . it together.] Cf. Isaiah 40:4–5.

559.33–37   My country . . . let freedom ring!] Samuel F. Smith (1808–1895), "America" (1832).

561.2   *The Crisis in Women's Identity*] Friedan gave this speech at the University of California, San Francisco.

567.15–17   President's Commission . . . report] The commission was established by President Kennedy on December 14, 1961, and submitted its report on October 11, 1963.

567.17   My book] *The Feminine Mystique* (1963).

567.20–21   *New Yorker* . . . John Cheever] The story was published in *The New Yorker* of November 2, 1963.

567.31   *The Thrill of It All*]   The film, directed by Norman Jewison, was released on July 17, 1963.

574.2   *The Ballot or the Bullet*]   Malcolm X gave this speech at a symposium sponsored by the Congress of Racial Equality (CORE), a civil rights organization founded in 1942.

574.4   Brother Lomax]   Louis Lomax (1922–1970), a freelance journalist whose books included *The Negro Revolt* (1962) and *When the Word Is Given: A Report on Elijah Muhammad, Malcolm X, and the Black Muslim World* (1963).

574.14   Adam Clayton Powell]   Powell (1908–1972) was a Democratic congressman from New York, 1945–67 and 1969–71.

574.20   Rev. Galamison]   Milton A. Galamison (1923–1988) was pastor of the Siloam Presbyterian Church in the Bedford-Stuyvesant section of Brooklyn, 1948–68. Galamison organized successful one-day school boycotts in February and March 1964 to protest de facto segregation in the New York City public school system.

577.12–13   filibustering on top of that]   Southern senators began a filibuster against the civil rights bill on March 30 that lasted until June 10, 1964, when the Senate voted 71–29 to end the debate.

577.25   Eastland]   James O. Eastland (1904–1986) was a Democratic senator from Mississippi, 1943–78, and chairman of the Senate Judiciary Committee, 1956–78.

578.2   Richard Russell]   Russell (1897–1971) was a Democratic senator from Georgia, 1933–71.

578.32   Dixiecrats bolted themselves once]   See note 476.6.

579.12   I was in Washington . . . Thursday]   During his visit to the Capitol on March 26 Malcolm X had his only encounter with Martin Luther King, Jr., when the two men met and shook hands in a Senate corridor.

579.15–16   huge map . . . location of Negroes]   The map had been introduced as an exhibit by Senator Richard Russell when he proposed equalizing racial proportions throughout all 50 states by relocating African-American families from the South.

581.39   Jacksonville]   Rioting began in Jacksonville, Florida, on March 23, 1964, when the police dispersed an antisegregation march by hundreds of African-American youths, and continued the following day. During the violence an African-American housekeeper, Johnnie Mae Chappell, was fatally shot in a racially motivated attack.

587.39   Muslim Mosque, Inc. . . . recently]   Malcolm X incorporated the organization on March 16, 1964.

588.19   SNCC] Student Nonviolent Coordinating Committee, a civil rights organization founded in 1960.

593.15–16   bomb a church . . . four little girls] Klansmen bombed the Sixteenth Street Baptist Church in Birmingham, Alabama, on September 15, 1963, killing Denise McNair, age 11, Cynthia Wesley, 14, Carole Robertson, 14, and Addie Mae Collins, 14.

593.18   the government . . . find who did it.] In September 1963 the FBI launched an extensive investigation into the Birmingham church bombing. A memorandum submitted to FBI director J. Edgar Hoover in 1965 identified four Klansmen—Robert Chambliss, Herman Cash, Thomas Blanton, Jr., and Bobby Frank Cherry—as suspects in the case. Hoover did not inform prosecutors of the Bureau's findings, and the FBI closed its investigation in 1968. Alabama attorney general Bill Baxley reopened the investigation in 1971, and Chambliss was convicted of murder on November 18, 1977; he died in prison in 1985. Cash died in 1994 without ever having been charged. In 2000 Blanton and Cherry were charged with murder. Blanton was convicted on May 1, 2001, and Cherry was found guilty on May 22, 2002; both men were sentenced to life imprisonment, and Cherry died in prison in 2004.

593.19–20   Eichmann . . . Argentina] Acolf Eichmann (1906–1962) was captured in Argentina by Israeli agents on May 11, 1960, and taken to Israel, where he was tried in 1961 and hanged on May 31, 1962. An officer in the SS, Eichmann headed the Jewish Department of the Reich Main Security Office, 1939–45, and played a major role in organizing the deportation of European Jews to extermination camps.

595.7–8   Bill Miller . . . Thruston Morton] William Miller (1914–1983), the Republican vice-presidential nominee in 1964, was a congressman from New York, 1951–65. Thruston Morton (1907–1982) was a Republican congressman from Kentucky, 1947–53, and a senator, 1957–68.

596.25   the Bay of Pigs] A brigade of 1,500 Cuban exiles trained and armed by the Central Intelligence Agency landed at the Bay of Pigs in southern Cuba on April 17, 1961, but were forced to surrender on April 19. President Kennedy was subsequently criticized for failing to provide the invasion with adequate air support.

596.26   death of freedom in Laos] The United States and North Vietnam signed an agreement in Geneva on July 23, 1962, pledging to respect the neutrality of Laos and to refrain from using its territory for military purposes. Despite the agreement the North Vietnamese failed to withdraw their troops from Laos.

598.37   the Formosa Strait] In September 1954 the Chinese Communists began shelling Quemoy and Matsu, islands in the Formosa (Taiwan) Strait occupied by the Chinese Nationalists, and in January 1955 attacked other Nationalist-held islands along the coast. After Congress passed a resolution authorizing the President to defend Quemoy and Matsu, the Eisenhower administration warned in March that an attack on the islands could result in the use of tactical nuclear weapons by the United States. The Communists halted their shelling of the islands on May 1, 1955, but resumed it on August 23, 1958. Eisenhower responded by sending naval forces to the region and declaring in a televised address on September 11 that the United States would resist aggression in the Formosa Strait. The Communists halted their bombardment on October 6, 1958, ending the crisis.

598.38   Lebanon] Following the overthrow of the pro-Western monarchy in Iraq on July 14, 1958, Eisenhower ordered U.S. Marines to land in Lebanon on July 15 as a demonstration of support for President Camille Chamoun, who had previously accused Egypt and Syria of trying to overthrow him. American forces were withdrawn from Lebanon on October 25, 1958.

599.17–18   his Secretary of Defense] Robert S. McNamara (b. 1916) was Secretary of Defense in the Kennedy and Johnson administrations, 1961–68.

600.3   boasts it will bury us] At a diplomatic reception held in Moscow on November 18, 1956, Nikita Khrushchev (see note 546.12) told a group of Western diplomats: "Whether you like it or not, history is on our side. We will bury you."

602.30–31   It was composed . . . hostile elements] In his "House Divided" speech delivered in Springfield, Illinois, on June 16, 1858, Lincoln had described the Republican Party of 1856: "Of *strange, discordant*, and even, *hostile* elements, we gathered from the four winds . . ."

605.35–36   "Great Society,"] President Johnson first used this term to describe his domestic agenda in a speech given in Ann Arbor, Michigan, on May 22, 1964.

606.8   Senator Fulbright] J. William Fulbright (1905–1995) was a Democratic congressman from Arkansas, 1943–45, and a senator, 1945–74.

606.14   Senator Clark] Joseph Clark (1901–1990) was a Democratic senator from Pennsylvania, 1957–69.

607.1   Senator Humphrey] See Biographical Notes.

607.10   secretary of agriculture] Orville Freeman (1918–2003) was Secretary of Agriculture in the Kennedy and Johnson administrations, 1961–69.

607.19   Billie Sol Estes] Estes (b. 1924), a Texas businessman and financial supporter of Lyndon Johnson, was convicted in 1963 on fraud charges that involved the manipulation of federal grain storage contracts.

608.35   Bobby Baker] Baker (b. 1928) served as a close aide to Lyndon Johnson when Johnson was Senate majority leader. He resigned as secretary to the Senate majority on October 7, 1963, after being accused of corrupt dealings involving defense contractors, and was convicted of fraud and tax evasion charges in 1967.

611.35   Norman Thomas] Thomas (1884–1968) was the Socialist presidential candidate, 1928–48.

612.2   Al Smith] Smith (1873–1944) was the Democratic candidate for president in 1928 and the governor of New York, 1919–20 and 1923–28.

614.3–4   Alexander Hamilton said, . . . one!"] The quotation has been attributed to Hamilton, but the source is unknown.

615.2–7   Winston Churchill . . . spells duty."] In a radio broadcast to the United States on June 16, 1941.

616.2   *Speech in Sproul Plaza*] In September 1964 a coalition of student groups began protesting the regulations restricting political advocacy on the campus of the University of California, Berkeley. On October 1 campus police arrested Jack Weinberg, a former graduate student who was soliciting funds in Sproul Plaza for the civil rights group CORE. Hundreds of students then prevented the police car carrying Weinberg from leaving the plaza, beginning a confrontation that lasted for 32 hours. Mario Savio, a student civil rights activist, addressed the crowd several times from the roof of the police car and helped negotiate an agreement that ended the blockade. After weeks of negotiations involving the Free Speech Movement (a student alliance formed after the police car incident), the university administration, and the faculty, a new speech policy was announced by the Board of Regents on November 20 that prohibited "illegal advocacy," and the administration began disciplinary action against Savio and three other FSM members. In response the FSM organized a sit-in at Sproul Hall on December 2 that ended the following morning when police sent by Governor Pat Brown arrested 800 people. In January 1965 the university administration yielded to pressure from the faculty and adopted a more permissive speech policy.

616.5   the previous speaker] Charles Powell, president of the ASUC (Associated Students of the University of California), the student government at Berkeley.

616.9   Kerr] Clark Kerr (1911–2003) was chancellor of the University of California, Berkeley, 1952–58, and president of the University of California, 1958–67.

616.18   a strikebreaker] Graduate students and teaching assistants were planning to strike on December 4 in support of the FSM.

618.9   *Un Chant d'amour*] A silent film (1950) directed by the French writer Jean Genet that depicted homosexual relationships inside a prison. In 1964 the film was exhibited in the San Francisco Bay Area by Saul Landau, a political activist associated with the San Francisco Mime Troupe, until he was warned by the Berkeley police to stop screening it.

618.27   Joan Baez] Baez (b. 1941), a folk singer and political activist, sang "We Shall Overcome" as the sit-in began.

619.15–16   Philadelphia, Mississippi . . . murdered.] Three civil rights workers, James Cheney, 21, an African-American from Mississippi, and Michael Schwerner, 24, and Andrew Goodman, 20, white volunteers from New York City, were murdered by Klansmen near Philadelphia, Mississippi, on June 21, 1964. Their bodies were buried under an earthen dam and not discovered until August 4.

621.8–10   And the lion . . . shall be afraid.] Cf. Isaiah 11:6, Micah 4:4.

621.28   Chief Lutuli] Albert Lutuli (c. 1898–1967), a Zulu chief and lay Methodist preacher, was president of the African National Congress, 1952–67. He was awarded the Nobel Peace Prize in 1961 for his opposition to apartheid.

623.14   last week in Selma, Alabama.] Several hundred civil rights demonstrators were beaten and tear-gassed by state police and sheriff's deputies as they crossed the Edmund Pettus bridge in Selma on Sunday, March 7, 1965.

623.17   a man of God, was killed] The Rev. James Reeb (1927–1965), a white Unitarian minister from Boston, was beaten in Selma on March 9 and died in a Birmingham hospital on March 11.

624.7–8   "What is a . . . own soul?"] Matthew 16:26; Mark 8:36.

625.33–34   a law . . . right to vote.] The administration submitted the voting rights bill to Congress on March 17. It was signed into law by President Johnson on August 6, 1965.

631.34–36   beloved Speaker . . . Mr. McCulloch] John McCormack (1891–1980) was a Democratic congressman from Massachusetts, 1928–71, and Speaker of the House, 1961–70. Mike Mansfield (1903–2001) was a Democratic congressman from Montana, 1943–53, a senator, 1953–77, and Senate majority leader, 1961–77. Everett Dirksen (1896–1969) was a Republican congressman from Illinois, 1933–49, a senator, 1951–69, and Senate minority leader, 1959–69. William McCulloch (1901–1980) was a Republican congressman from Ohio, 1947–73, and the ranking Republican member of the House Judiciary Committee.

634.14–16   Winston Churchill said . . . the beginning."] In a speech delivered on November 10, 1942, referring to the Allied victory at the battle of El Alamein, October 23–November 4.

635.20–21   first lady ambassador] Johnson had appointed Patricia R. Harris, a professor at Howard Law School, as ambassador to Luxembourg earlier in the day. Harris (1924–1985) graduated from Howard in 1945. She served in Luxembourg until 1967, and was Secretary of Housing and Urban

Development, 1977–79, and Secretary of Health and Human Services, 1979–81, in the Carter administration.

640.20–21   "I shall light . . . put out."] 2 Esdras 14:25.

641.2   *Address at the University of Cape Town*] Kennedy delivered this speech during a visit to South Africa, June 4–9, 1966, in which he spoke at four universities, toured Soweto, and met with Chief Albert Lutuli (see note 621.28).

641.29–32   Mr. Ian Robertson . . . cannot be with us] In May 1966 Robertson, the president of NUSAS, was placed under a five-year "banning" order that restricted his movements, prevented him from being quoted in the press, and prohibited him from meeting with more than one person at a time. (Albert Lutuli was also under a banning order when Kennedy met with him.)

644.8   a Negro . . . astronaut] Major Robert Henry Lawrence, Jr., (1935–1967) was killed in an airplane crash while training for spaceflight. In 1983 Colonel Guion Bluford (b. 1942) became the first African-American astronaut to reach space when he flew in the space shuttle.

644.9–10   chief barrister . . . government] Thurgood Marshall (1908–1993) served as Solicitor General of the United States, 1965–67, before being appointed to the Supreme Court.

644.12   second man of African descent] See note 621.28.

646.11–12   former prime minister . . . Congo] Patrice Lumumba (1925–1961), a leader of the Congolese independence movement, was the first prime minister of the Congo, June 23–September 5, 1960. He was arrested on December 1 by troops loyal to Colonel Joseph Mobutu and shot on January 17, 1961, by Katanga secessionists led by Moise Tshombe.

646.13   thousands are slaughtered in Indonesia;] At least 200,000 alleged Communists were killed by the Indonesian army and its supporters following a failed coup attempt on October 1, 1965.

648.7–10   "There is . . . order of things."] Niccolò Machiavelli, *The Prince* (1513).

650.31–33   President Kennedy . . . he said] In his Inaugural Address; see p. 538.10–13 and p. 538.21–25 in this volume.

651.9–10   Dr. Bennett . . . Rabbi Heschel] John C. Bennett (1902–1995) was the president of Union Theological Seminary, 1964–70. Henry Steele Commager (1902–1998) taught American history at New York University, Columbia, and Amherst. Abraham Joshua Heschel (1907–1972) was a prominent professor at Jewish Theological Seminary, 1945–72, who had joined King on the Selma to Montgomery March in 1965.

652.35   National Liberation Front]   An alliance of opponents of the South
Vietnamese regime, formed in 1960 and controlled by the leadership of the
Vietnamese Communist Party in Hanoi.

654.29–32   O, yes, . . . will be!]   Langston Hughes, "Let America Be
America Again" (1936).

656.32   Dien Bien Phu]   The Viet Minh began shelling the French base
at Dien Bien Phu on March 13, 1954, and captured it on May 7.

656.38–39   Geneva Agreement]   The conference on Indochina held in
Geneva, May 8–July 21, 1954, concluded with the signing of a cease-fire agreement between representatives of the Viet Minh and the French military that
provided for an exchange of prisoners and the "regrouping" of the opposing
armies north and south of a "provisional military demarcation line" near the
17th parallel. The "Final Declaration" of the conference called for holding in-
ternationally supervised elections throughout Vietnam in July 1956; it was not
signed by any of the attending delegations, and the United States and the
South Vietnamese government refused to "associate" themselves with it.

657.2   Premier Diem]   Ngo Dinh Diem (1901–1963) was premier of the
State of Vietnam, 1954–55, and president of the Republic of Vietnam, 1955–63.
He was overthrown in a military coup on November 1, 1963, and assassinated
the following day.

661.5–12   Each day . . . militarism.]   From *Vietnam: Lotus in a Sea of
Fire* (1967) by Thich Nhat Hanh (b. 1926), a Buddhist monk who went into
exile in 1966 after calling for the U.S. and South Vietnam to declare a unilateral ceasefire. King met Thich Nhat Hanh in 1966 and nominated him for the
Nobel Peace Prize in 1967.

663.20–22   John F. Kennedy . . . revolution inevitable."]   In a speech
given to a meeting of Latin American diplomats at the White House on
March 13, 1962.

665.11–12   The people . . . great light.]   Matthew 4:6.

665.26–29   every valley . . . plain.]   Isaiah 40:4.

666.8–12   "Let us love . . . in us."]   1 John 4:7–8, 12.

667.17–28   Once to every . . . his own.]   James Russell Lowell (1819–
1891), "Once To Every Man and Nation" (1849).

667.35–36   justice will . . . stream.]   Cf. Amos 5:24.

668.20–21   "Behold, I . . . away."]   Revelation 21:5; Revelation 21:4.

668.23–24   "Rip Van Winkle."]   The story was first published in *The
Sketch Book of Geoffrey Crayon, Gent.* (1819–20).

670.15–20   John Donne . . . for thee."]   *Devotions upon Emergent Occasions* (1624), XVII.

670.39–40   "In Christ . . . West,"] Hymn (1908) with words by William Dunkerley (1852–1941).

673.5–6   some years ago . . . India] King visited India in 1959.

675.1   a parable] See Luke 16:19–26.

676.3   Poor People's Campaign] King announced plans on December 4, 1967, for a campaign that would bring poor people to Washington, D.C., in the spring of 1968 to lobby and demonstrate for government help in securing jobs and income.

676.37   The Kerner Commission] The National Advisory Commission on Civil Disorders, led by Illinois Governor Otto Kerner, was appointed by President Johnson on July 27, 1967, following major riots in Newark, New Jersey, and Detroit. On March 1, 1968, the Commission issued its report, warning that "the nation is moving toward two societies, one black, one white—separate and unequal."

677.15–19   But I was . . . unto me."   Cf. Matthew 25:34–46.

677.25–27   President Kennedy . . . mankind."]   In a speech to the U.N. General Assembly, September 25, 1961.

680.17–18   Bryant . . . will rise again."]   "The Battlefield" (1839).

680.21–25   Truth forever . . . above his own.   See note 667.17–28.

681.2   *Mason Temple*]   The temple, completed in 1945, is part of the headquarters of the Church of God in Christ, and is named after Charles Harrison Mason (1866–1961), the founder of the Church.

681.4–5   Ralph Abernathy]   Abernathy (1926–1990), a Baptist minister, helped organize the Montgomery bus boycott in 1955 and the Southern Christian Leadership Conference in 1957. He was secretary-treasurer of SCLC, 1957–68, and succeeded King as its president, 1968–77.

681.10–11   a storm warning]   Tornado warnings had been broadcast in Memphis during the afternoon of April 3.

683.32–34   refusal of Memphis . . . sanitation workers]   Sanitation workers in Memphis went on strike on February 12, 1968. After the assassination of King, President Johnson sent the undersecretary of labor to Memphis to mediate a settlement, and the strike ended on April 16.

683.36   happened the other day]   On March 28 a march led by King in support of the strikers turned violent when groups of African-American youths began breaking store windows and looting. The police used clubs and tear gas to disperse the crowd, made 280 arrests, and fatally shot a 16-year-old suspected looter.

684.1   Mayor Loeb]   Henry Loeb was the mayor of Memphis, 1960–63 and 1968–71.

684.20   Bull Connor] Eugene "Bull" Connor (1897–1973) was public safety commissioner of Birmingham, Alabama, 1937–53 and 1957–63.

685.32–34   "When God . . . mighty stream."] Cf. Amos 3:8, 5:24.

685.35–37   "The spirit . . . the poor."] Cf. Luke 4:18.

685.40   James Lawson] Lawson (b. 1928) organized sit-ins in Nashville, Tennessee, in 1960 while a divinity student at Vanderbilt University, helped found the Student Nonviolent Coordinating Committee, and was jailed in Mississippi in 1961 for leading a Freedom Ride. An adviser to King on nonviolent strategy, Lawson became pastor of Centenary Methodist Church in Memphis in 1962, and in 1968 mobilized support from civil rights groups for the sanitation strike.

686.4   Reverend Ralph Jackson, Billy Kiles] H. Ralph Jackson and Samuel "Billy" Kyles were Memphis ministers.

687.28   Judge Hooks] Benjamin Hooks (b. 1925), a Baptist minister and an attorney, was a judge of the Shelby County criminal court, 1966–68. He later served as executive director of the NAACP, 1977–92.

688.15–16   he talked . . . among thieves.] See Luke 10:25–37.

689.1–2   Mrs. King . . . Jerusalem] In 1959, while returning from their trip to India.

689.39   the first book I had written] *Stride Toward Freedom: The Montgomery Story* (1958).

690.6–7   dark Saturday afternoon] King was stabbed on September 20, 1958.

690.21   governor of New York] Averell Harriman (1891–1986) was the Democratic governor of New York, 1955–59.

693.2–3   *Remarks . . . King*] Kennedy declared his candidacy for the Democratic presidential nomination on March 16, 1968, and began his primary campaign in Indiana on April 4 by speaking at several college campuses. After learning of King's death he went to a previously scheduled rally in an African-American neighborhood of Indianapolis, where he gave this speech while standing on a flatbed truck.

693.32–694.2 Aeschylus . . . grace of God."] Cf. *Agamemnon*, 179–83, as translated by Edith Hamilton in *The Greek Way* (1930): "And even in our sleep pain that cannot forget, falls drop by drop upon the heart, and in our own despite, against our will, comes wisdom to us by the awful grace of God."

695.2   *Statement . . . Committee*] The Committee began debating articles of impeachment against President Nixon on July 24, 1974, and voted to bring three articles before the House, July 26–30.

695.4   Mr. Chairman] Peter Rodino (1909–2005) was a Democratic congressman from New Jersey, 1949–89, and chairman of the House Judiciary Committee, 1973–89.

695.5   Mr. Rangel] Charles Rangel (b. 1930), a Democrat, has served in Congress from 1971 to the present.

697.16–19   misuse of the CIA . . . June 23, 1972] On June 23, 1972, Nixon ordered his chief of staff, H. R. Haldeman, to have the CIA tell the FBI that tracing money found on the Watergate burglars would compromise sensitive CIA operations.

697.24   E. Howard Hunt] Hunt (b. 1918) served in the CIA clandestine service, 1948–70, before becoming a White House consultant in 1971. He planned the Watergate break-in with G. Gordon Liddy, a former FBI agent who worked for the White House and the Committee to Re-elect the President.

697.25   break-in . . . Ellsberg's psychiatrist] On September 3, 1971, Hunt and Liddy directed a break-in at the Los Angeles offices of Dr. Lewis Fielding. They were seeking information with which to discredit Daniel Ellsberg, a former government official who had given the "Pentagon Papers," a secret Defense Department study of the Vietnam War, to the press.

697.26   Dita Beard ITT affair] On February 29, 1972, syndicated columnist Jack Anderson quoted a memorandum written by Dita Beard, a lobbyist for the conglomerate ITT, as evidence that ITT had donated $400,000 to the Republican Party in return for a favorable settlement of an antitrust suit. Using a CIA alias, Hunt flew in March to Denver and persuaded Beard to issue a statement denying that she had written the memorandum.

697.27–28   Hunt's fabrication . . . administration.] In September 1971 Hunt forged two cables implicating the Kennedy administration in the 1963 assassination of South Vietnamese President Ngo Dinh Diem.

697.39   President would obey . . . Court] On July 24, 1974, the Supreme Court unanimously ordered Nixon to turn over 64 tapes subpoenaed by the Watergate special prosecutor. The White House did not announce that Nixon would comply with the decision until about eight hours after it was handed down.

698.8   the defendants] Liddy, Hunt, and the five men arrested during the Watergate break-in on June 17 were indicted on September 15, 1972.

698.11   Mr. Henry Petersen] Petersen, the Assistant Attorney General in charge of the Criminal Division of the Justice Department, supervised the Watergate investigation until a special prosecutor was appointed in late May 1973.

698.19   Justice Story] See note 273.11.

698.23   the Huston plan] Tom Charles Huston, a lawyer on the White House staff, submitted a memorandum in July 1970 that called for using electronic surveillance, burglaries, and illegal mail opening to collect intelligence on "domestic security threats." The plan was approved by Nixon but was withdrawn after being rejected by FBI Director J. Edgar Hoover.

698.26   Ehrlichman] John Ehrlichman (1925–1999) served as a senior aide to Nixon, 1969–73.

700.2   *Remarks on Leaving the White House*] Nixon announced his resignation on August 8, 1974, effective at noon on August 9. He gave these remarks on the morning of August 9 and then left for California.

701.33   pay my taxes] The IRS announced in April 1974 that Nixon owed $476,431 in back taxes and interest after ruling that he had taken an improper deduction on the gift of his vice-presidential papers to the National Archives.

702.33–34   two boys dying of tuberculosis] Arthur Nixon (1918–1925) died of tubercular meningitis after a short illness. Harold Nixon (1909–1933) contracted tuberculosis in 1927.

702.39–40   little quote . . . T.R.] In his speech Nixon said: "Sometimes I have succeeded and sometimes I have failed, but always I have taken heart from what Theodore Roosevelt once said about the man in the arena, 'whose face is marred by dust and sweat and blood, who strives valiantly, who errs and comes short again and again because there is not effort without error and shortcoming, but who does actually strive to do the deed, who knows the great enthusiasms, the great devotions, who spends himself in a worthy cause, who at the best knows in the end the triumphs of high achievements and who at the worst, if he fails, at least fails while daring greatly.'" The quotation is from "Citizenship in a Republic," a speech Roosevelt gave in Paris at the Sorbonne on April 23, 1910.

703.5–7   He had married . . . she died,] Alice Lee Roosevelt died on February 14, 1884, two days after the birth of her daughter Alice.

705.2   *Address . . . Energy Policy*] Carter gave this speech from the White House during a period of severe gasoline shortages caused by the 1979 revolution in Iran.

706.8   a southern Governor] Bill Clinton, then serving his first term as governor of Arkansas.

709.13–14   until 1973 . . . foreign oil] The Organization of Arab Petroleum Exporting Countries announced an embargo on oil exports to the United States on October 17, 1973, in retaliation for American support of Israel. The embargo lasted until March 17, 1974.

711.29   recent Tokyo summit.] The economic summit, held June 28–29, was attended by the leaders of Britain, France, Italy, West Germany, Japan, Canada, and the U.S.

715.2–3   *Speech . . . Convention*]   Kennedy spoke to the convention the day before it voted to renominate President Carter.

715.5   your eloquent introduction]   Kennedy was introduced by Barbara Mikulski (b. 1936), a Democratic congresswoman from Maryland, 1977–87, and a senator from 1987 to the present.

717.19–20   bail out New York]   New York City avoided bankruptcy in 1976 with the help of federal loan guarantees.

718.32–33   Liberty City and the South Bronx]   Eighteen people were killed in rioting that broke out in the Liberty City section of Miami on May 17, 1980, following the acquittal of four white police officers charged in the beating death of an African-American motorcyclist. In the 1970s widespread arson devastated large portions of the South Bronx and made the area a national symbol of urban decay.

719.16–18   from California . . . Gulf Stream waters,]   Woody Guthrie, "This Land Is Your Land" (1940).

721.8–9   Three Mile Island.]   A pressure valve malfunction at the Three Mile Island nuclear power plant near Harrisburg, Pennsylvania, on March 28, 1979, resulted in a partial meltdown of a reactor core. There were no fatalities in the accident, which released only a very small amount of radiation.

721.20   E.R.A.]   The Equal Rights Amendment, forbidding the denial or abridgment of rights on account of sex, was proposed to the states by Congress on March 22, 1972, with a seven-year deadline for its ratification. After 35 states had ratified the amendment, Congress voted on October 6, 1978, to extend the deadline to June 30, 1982, but there were no further ratifications and the amendment did not go into effect.

722.8   Joan]   Joan Bennett Kennedy (b. 1936) was married to Edward M. Kennedy from 1958 to 1982.

723.16–20   I am a . . . not to yield."]   Alfred Lord Tennyson, "Ulysses" (1842).

724.7   economic summit at Versailles]   The meeting, held June 4–6, was attended by the leaders of Britain, France, Italy, West Germany, Japan, Canada, and the U.S.

725.5–6   Jefferson . . . very good thing."]   In a letter commenting on Shays's Rebellion, Jefferson wrote to James Madison on January 30, 1787: "I hold it that a little rebellion now and then is a good thing, & as necessary in the political world as storms in the physical."

725.24–25   Reform Bill of 1866]   The bill, a measure to extend the franchise by reducing property qualifications for voting, was defeated in 1866, but in 1867 a Conservative government led by Disraeli succeeded in passing a more comprehensive bill that doubled the size of the electorate.

725.35 From Stettin . . . the Black Sea] Cf. the speech given by Winston Churchill in Fulton, Missouri, on March 5, 1946: "From Stettin in the Baltic to Trieste in the Adriatic, an iron curtain has descended across the Continent."

725.40 Solidarity movement in Poland] A series of strikes that began in the Gdansk shipyards on August 14 forced the Communist government to sign an agreement on August 31, 1980, allowing the organization of independent unions. Solidarity was founded on September 17, 1980, and by early 1981 had become a movement that united millions of workers, farmers, students, and intellectuals in opposition to Communist rule. It was outlawed on December 13, 1981, when General Wojciech Jaruzelski, the prime minister of Poland, declared martial law.

726.9 one of our . . . diplomats] John Foster Dulles (1888–1959), Secretary of State in the Eisenhower administration, 1953–59.

727.10 the great purge] A purge of Soviet society that was carried out on the orders of Stalin, 1937–38, during which at least 680,000 people were executed and 1.5 million were sent to prison or forced labor camps.

727.11 Cambodia] At least one million people were executed, starved, or worked to death in Cambodia under the rule of the Khmer Rouge, 1975–78.

727.20–21 chemical and toxin . . . Southeast Asia] In 1980 the Carter administration accused the Soviet Union of using chemical weapons in Afghanistan and of supplying them to the Vietnamese for use in Laos and Cambodia. Secretary of State Alexander Haig announced on September 13, 1981, that samples collected in Southeast Asia had been found to contain mycotoxins (toxic compounds produced by fungal molds) and accused the Soviets of using them as weapons. The allegations were disputed by scientists from outside the government, who argued that the samples were of natural origin and that refugee accounts of chemical attacks were unreliable.

727.33–39 "I do not . . . countries."] From the "Iron Curtain" speech; see note 725.35.

729.3 new philosophers in France] A group of anti-Communist French intellectuals who came to prominence in the 1970s.

729.22–27 election day . . . El Salvador] The election for the Constituent Assembly was held on March 28, 1982. It was boycotted by the center-left parties, who feared that their candidates would be murdered if they participated. The voting produced a right-wing majority that threatened to elect Roberto D'Aubuisson, a former National Guard officer linked to right-wing death squads, as provisional president. After the Reagan administration warned that U.S. aid would be cut off if D'Aubuisson became president, the Assembly instead chose Alvaro Magaña, a banker supported by the armed forces.

730.4 distant islands in the South Atlantic] After Argentina seized the Falkland Islands on April 2, 1982, Britain sent a task force to the South Atlantic. By June 8 British troops had landed on East Falkland Island and were preparing an offensive that forced the Argentineans to surrender on June 14.

730.16 Lebanon] Israel invaded southern Lebanon on June 6, 1982, in a campaign directed against the Palestine Liberation Organization and Syrian occupation forces.

730.25–26 India . . . political parties.] The Congress Party, which had governed India since 1947, was defeated in the 1977 election, but was returned to power in 1980.

731.14 Chairman Brezhnev] Leonid Brezhnev (1906–1982) was general secretary of the Communist Party of the Soviet Union, 1964–82, and chairman of the Presidium of the Supreme Soviet (the Soviet head of state), 1977–82.

733.11 Chief Justice] Warren Burger (1907–1995) served as Chief Justice, 1969–86.

733.35–36 address of May 9th] Reagan delivered the commencement address at his alma mater, Eureka College in Illinois, on May 9, 1982.

734.5–6 Zero-Option . . . forces] On November 18, 1981, Reagan proposed that the Soviet Union dismantle its intermediate-range ballistic missiles in return for the cancellation of NATO plans for deploying U.S. cruise and ballistic missiles in Western Europe.

734.36–38 Winston Churchill . . . think we are?"] In an address to Congress on December 26, 1941.

735.6 lost an election] Churchill was defeated in the general election held on July 5, 1945.

737.8–10 "lives fought . . . your honor."] Stephen Spender (1909–1995), "I think continually of those who were truly great" (1933).

737.14–21 Bill Millin . . . Lord Lovat] Millin served as the personal piper of Brigadier Simon Fraser, The Lord Lovat (1911–1995), the commander of the 1st Special Service (Commando) Brigade.

737.26–27 valor of the Poles . . . rest of Europe] The 1st Polish Armored Division went into action in Normandy on August 8, 1944. In fierce fighting around Mont-Ormel, August 18–21, the Poles blocked the escape of German forces from the Falaise Pocket.

737.28–29 the Canadians . . . on this coast] More than 2,800 Canadian soldiers were killed or captured in the raid on Dieppe on August 19, 1942.

737.36 the Screaming Eagles] The U.S. 101st Airborne Division.

738.33–34   Colonel Wolverton] Lieutenant Colonel Robert Wolverton, commander of the 3rd Battalion, 506th Parachute Infantry Regiment, 101st Airborne Division. Wolverton was killed on D-Day.

738.37   Matthew Ridgway] Ridgway (1895–1993) commanded the 82nd Airborne Division, 1942–44. He successfully parachuted into Normandy on D-Day.

738.38–39   "I will . . . forsake thee."] Joshua 1:5.

742.6   seven men] Former Vice-President Walter Mondale, Senator Gary Hart (Colorado), Senator John Glenn (Ohio), Senator Alan Cranston (California), Senator Ernest Hollings (South Carolina), former Senator George McGovern (South Dakota), and former Governor Reubin Askew (Florida).

742.21–22   Geraldine Ferraro] Ferraro (b. 1935), the Democratic vice-presidential nominee in 1984, served in Congress, 1979–85.

742.32–34   low moments . . . someone's fears] *The Washington Post* reported on February 13, 1984, that Jackson had referred in conversation to Jews as "Hymies" and New York City as "Hymietown." Although Jackson apologized for his remarks on February 26, he created further controversy by his refusal to denounce anti-Semitic remarks made by Louis Farrakhan, the leader of the Nation of Islam.

744.5   Fannie Lou Hamer in Atlantic City] Hamer (1917–1977), a SNCC field secretary, helped found the Mississippi Freedom Democratic Party in 1964 and was vice-chairman of the delegation that challenged the seating of the all-white regular delegation at the 1964 Democratic National Convention. When the credentials committee offered the Freedom Democrats two at-large seats, the FDP rejected the offer.

744.10–11   Malcolm, . . . Viola.] Malcolm X; Martin Luther King; Medgar Evers (1925–1963), the field secretary of the Mississippi NAACP, 1954–63, who was shot outside his house in Jackson by a white supremacist; Robert F. Kennedy; John F. Kennedy; and Viola Liuzzo (1925–1965), a white civil rights volunteer from Detroit who was killed by Klansmen in Lowndes County, Alabama.

744.14   Schwerner, Goodman, and Chaney] See note 619.15–16.

744.29–30   Rabbi Abraham Heschel] See note 651.9–10.

745.7   the Simpson-Mazzoli bill] The bill, first introduced in 1982 and passed in 1986, established penalties for employers who hired illegal immigrants.

748.12   John Anderson] Anderson (b. 1922) was a Republican congressman from Illinois, 1961–81. In 1980 he received seven percent of the popular vote as an independent candidate for president.

750.16   Nineteen years later,] After the passage of the 1965 Voting Rights Act.

750.18–19   second primaries . . . at-large] Run-off primary elections, the annexation of minority neighborhoods and suburbs by larger jurisdictions, and the holding of at-large elections have all been criticized as measures intended to weaken the power of African-American voters.

750.26   boll weevils] Term used for Southern Democrats in Congress who supported Reagan administration policies.

750.28   ERA will pass] Unsuccessful attempts were made after 1982 to have Congress resubmit the ERA to the states (see note 721.18).

751.11   mine the harbors of Nicaragua] Using teams of Latin American mercenaries assisted by U.S. special operations forces, the CIA began mining Nicaraguan harbors in January 1984. The operation was revealed by *The Wall Street Journal* on April 6.

751.22   Nigeria and Liberia and Ghana.] Elected governments were overthrown in Nigeria in 1983, in Liberia in 1984, and in Ghana in 1981.

751.28   Camp David] The Egyptian-Israeli peace agreements negotiated at Camp David, Maryland, in September 1978.

754.11–12   Nineteen years ago, . . . ground.] On January 27, 1967, astronauts Virgil (Gus) Grissom, Edward White, and Roger Chaffee died in a flash fire inside their Apollo spacecraft while conducting a launch pad test at Cape Kennedy.

754.17–19   Michael Smith . . . Christa McAuliffe.] Smith, the shuttle pilot, Jarvis, a payload specialist, and McAuliffe, a high school teacher from Concord, New Hampshire, who had been chosen from among 11,000 applicants to undergo astronaut training, were all making their first space flights. Scobee, the mission commander, and Resnik, McNair, and Onizuka, all mission specialists, had each flown on a previous shuttle mission. Resnik was the second American woman to fly in space, and McNair was the second African-American.

755.30–31   "slipped the surly . . . God "] From the poem "High Flight," by John G. Magee, Jr. (1922–1941). Magee, an American volunteer serving as a fighter pilot in the Royal Canadian Air Force, was killed in a midair collision over England a few months after he sent a copy of the poem to his parents.

756.4–5   Chancellor Kohl, Governing Mayor Diepgen] Helmut Kohl (b. 1930), a Christian Democrat, was Chancellor of West Germany, 1982–90, and of Germany, 1990–98. Eberhard Diepgen (b. 1942), a Christian Democrat, was mayor of West Berlin, 1984–89, and of Berlin, 1991–2001.

756.8   two other presidents have come] Nixon in 1969 and Carter in 1978.

756.9   my second visit] Reagan visited Berlin on June 11, 1982.

756.16   Paul Lincke] Lincke (1866–1946) was a composer of operettas whose works included *Frau Luna* (1899) and *Lysistrata* (1902).

756.18–19   "*Ich . . . Berlin.*"] I still have a suitcase in Berlin.

756.28   *Es . . . Berlin.*] There is only one Berlin.

757.10   President von Weizsäcker] Richard von Weizsäcker (b. 1920) was President of West Germany, 1984–90, and of Germany, 1990–94.

757.39–40   Adenauer, Erhard, Reuter] For Adenauer, see note 554.7. Ludwig Erhard (1897–1977), a Christian Democrat, was economics minister, 1949–63, and Chancellor of West Germany, 1963–66. Ernst Reuter (1889–1953), a Social Democrat, was mayor of West Berlin, 1948–53.

758.19–20   *Berliner . . . schnauze.*] Berliner heart, Berliner humor, yes, and Berliner schnauze (snout).

759.7   Gorbachev] Mikhail Gorbachev (b. 1931) was general secretary of the Communist Party of the Soviet Union, 1985–91, president of the Presidium of the Supreme Soviet, 1989–90, and president of the Soviet Union, 1990–91.

759.33–34   eliminating . . . class of nuclear weapons] On December 8, 1987, Reagan and Gorbachev signed the Intermediate-Range Nuclear Forces (INF) Treaty in Washington, D.C. The treaty eliminated all American and Soviet land-based cruise and ballistic missiles with a range of between 500 and 5,500 kilometers.

760.4–5   Strategic Defense Initiative] Name for the ballistic missile defense program announced by Reagan on March 23, 1983, popularly known as "Star Wars."

763.2   *Mason Temple*] See note 680.2.

763.5–6   my bishops, . . . Lindsey] L.T. Walker and Donnie Lindsey, bishops of the Arkansas jurisdiction of the Church of God in Christ.

763.21–22   Governor McWherter . . . Mayor Herenton] Ned Ray McWherter (b. 1930) was the Democratic governor of Tennessee, 1987–95. Willie Herenton has served as mayor of Memphis from 1991 to the present; he is the first African-American to be elected to the office.

763.23   Congressman Harold Ford] Ford (b. 1945) served in Congress, 1975–97. (He was succeeded as the representative from the 9th Congressional District by his son, Harold Ford, Jr.)

763.34 Congressman Bill Jefferson] William Jefferson (b. 1947) has served in Congress from 1991 to the present.

764.2 Bob Clement] Robert Clement (b. 1943) served in Congress, 1988–2003.

764.5 Jim Cooper] James Cooper (b. 1954) served in Congress, 1983–95, and from 2003 until the present. In 1994 Cooper ran for the Senate but was defeated by Fred Dalton Thompson.

764.13–14 "A happy . . . the bone."] Proverbs 17.22.

764.31–32 five African-Americans . . . Cabinet] Mike Espy, Secretary of Agriculture, 1993–94, Ron Brown, Secretary of Commerce, 1993–96, Hazel O'Leary, Secretary of Energy, 1993–97, Jesse Brown, Secretary of Veterans Affairs, 1993–97, and Lee Brown, Director of the Office of National Drug Control Policy, 1993–96.

764.34 motor voter bill] The National Voter Registration Act, signed by Clinton on May 20, 1993, required states to provide voter registration facilities in government offices used to issue drivers licenses.

764.36–37 restoration of religious freedoms act] The act, signed by Clinton on November 16, 1993, overturned a 1990 Supreme Court decision that made it easier for states to pass generally applicable laws restricting religious practices. In 1997 the Supreme Court struck down part of the law as an unconstitutional exercise of congressional power against the states.

768.26 Mayor of Baltimore] Kurt Schmoke (b. 1949), the first African-American mayor of Baltimore, served 1987–99.

771.9–10 "The Truly Disadvantaged"] William Julius Wilson (b. 1935), *The Truly Disadvantaged: The Inner City, the Underclass, and Public Policy* (1987).

772.1–3 you are the . . . in heaven.] See Matthew 5:13–16.

773.5–6 Daisy Bates . . . Thurgood Marshall] Bates (c. 1914–1999), a leader of the Arkansas NAACP and publisher of the *Arkansas State Voice*, advised the Little Rock Nine during the integration crisis. She published a memoir, *The Long Shadow of Little Rock*, in 1962. Wiley Branton (1923–1988), an African-American attorney from Pine Bluff, Arkansas, first argued *Aaron* v. *Cooper*, the Little Rock desegregation case, in 1956. He later served as director of the Voter Education Project, 1962–65. Marshall (1908–1993) was director of the NAACP Legal Defense Fund, 1939–61, a federal appellate judge, 1962–65, Solicitor General of the United States, 1965–67, and an Associate Justice of the Supreme Court, 1967–91.

773.12–13 our daughter off to college] Chelsea Clinton (b. 1980) entered Stanford University in 1997.

774.11   her eight schoolmates] Minnie Jean Brown, Ernest Green, Thelma Mothershed, Melba Patillo, Gloria Ray, Terrence Roberts, Jefferson Thomas, and Carlotta Walls.

774.21   Brownell] Herbert Brownell, Jr., (1904–1996) was Attorney General in the Eisenhower administration from January 1953 to November 1957.

774.22   the 101st Airborne] After a large mob attacked the nine students on September 23, 1957, President Eisenhower sent more than 1,000 paratroopers to Little Rock to enforce the federal court order desegregating Central High School. The troops remained until November 27.

775.1–2   Melba . . . Cry,"] Melba Patillo Beals, *Warriors Don't Cry: A Searing Memoir of the Battle to Integrate Little Rock's Central High* (1994).

775.11   My grandfather] James Eldridge Cassidy (1898–1957), President Clinton's maternal grandfather.

779.27–28   one America today . . . forever.] Cf. George Wallace in his inaugural address as governor of Alabama, January 14, 1963: "segregation now, segregation tomorrow, segregation forever."

Index

Abdullah ibn al-Husayn, 336
Abbott. Henry, 93–94
Abernathy, Ralph, 681, 683
Abolitionism, 35, 81–82, 124, 128, 465
Acheson, Dean, 515
Adams, Charles Francis, 257
Adams, John, 43
Adams, John Quincy, 343
Adams, Sherman, 707
Adenauer, Konrad, 528, 554, 757
Affirmative action, 777
Afghanistan, 727
African-Americans, 2–4, 13–14, 16–21,
  26, 28–29, 32, 34–38, 40–42, 46,
  48–84, 110–28, 137–41, 175, 190,
  204–12, 229–32, 287, 299, 476–79,
  516–19, 548–53, 556–60, 572, 574–94,
  619–20, 623–40 643–44, 653–54,
  668–94, 743–45. 749–50, 764, 767–
  68, 771, 773–79
African Methodist Episcopal Church,
  119, 127
Agriculture Department, U.S.. 223,
  607
Aguinaldo, Emilio, 163–67, 171, 173,
  175, 182, 184, 195
Aid to Dependent Children program,
  609, 638
Aiken, George D., 491–92
Alabama, 15, 117, 548, 558–59
Alamo, 527
Alaska, 497
Albany, Ga., 691
Albany, N. Y., 301, 384
Alexander I, 328, 330
Algeria, 587
Allen, Grant, 99
Alliance for Progress, 536
Altgeld, John Peter, 129–36
Alton, Ill., 124
Amerasia case, 439
American Indians, 33, 88, 156, 159,
  287, 743, 745, 776, 778
American University, 539
Anderson, Hurst Robins, 539
Anderson, John, 748
Anderson, Thomas, M., 164–65

Andersonville Prison, 15, 87
Andrew, John A., 256
Anniston, Ala., 117
Anthony, Susan B., 22–47, 299–300
Antietam, battle of, 91–93
Apaches, 159
Appomattox, surrender at, 124, 623
Arab Americans, 743, 745
Arabs, 336–37, 587, 751
Area Redevelopment Agency, 608
Argentina, 542
Arizona, 159, 613
Arkansas, 111, 117, 611, 763, 766, 773
Arlington National Cemetery, 76
Army, U.S., 1, 3, 69–72, 75–76, 78–79,
  87, 89–97, 135, 153, 155–58, 166–71, 175–
  77, 179–80, 191, 213–17, 220–21, 227–
  28, 241, 254, 258, 267, 269–72, 277–
  78, 281–85, 304, 311–12, 315–17, 337,
  348–49, 351–52, 432–35, 441–42, 447–
  53, 455, 500–3, 513, 531, 548, 575, 583,
  585, 587, 593, 628, 653, 657–60, 662–
  63, 678, 736–40, 745, 768, 771, 774
Arnold, Benedict, 48
Articles of Confederation, 24
Ashmun Amendment, 278–79
Asian Americans, 745–46, 777
Asquith, Herbert, 291
Atlanta, Ga., 574, 586, 682, 686
Atlanta Exposition, 137–41
Atomic weapons, 454–57, 460–70, 493,
  501, 513, 522, 533, 536–37, 540, 543–47,
  586, 620, 664. 669, 678, 682, 724,
  726–27, 731, 734, 740–41, 747–48,
  750–51, 759–60, 772
Auschwitz concentration camp, 649,
  727
Australia, 293, 340
Austria, 431, 473, 607, 728
Austria-Hungary, 245, 289, 315, 318–19,
  321, 328–32, 343

Baez, Joan, 618
Bailey, Peter, 527
Baker, Bobby, 608
Ball's Bluff, battle of, 92
Baltimore, Md., 124

859

Bank of the United States (Second), 145

Banks, Nathaniel P., 2

Baptists, 526, 574, 684

Barbary pirates, 174

Barkley, Alben, 476–77, 480–81, 486

Barrett, John, 167

Bartlett, William F., 94–95

Barton, Clara, 300

Bates, Daisy, 773–74

Bates, Edward, 35–36

Bay of Pigs invasion, 596

Beals, Melba Patillo, 775

Beck, James B., 49, 51–52, 54, 56–57, 59–62

Bedouins, 336–37

Belgium, 185, 239, 351, 429, 431, 443, 757

Bennett, John C., 651

Benton, Thomas Hart, 145

Berkeley, Calif., 616

Berlin, Germany, 452, 544, 548, 554–55, 725, 739, 756–62

Berlin Wall, 554–55, 596, 725, 756–57, 759, 761–62

Biemiller, Andrew J., 476

Bill of Rights, 527

Bingham, John A., 36–37

Birmingham, Ala., 550, 593, 619, 684–85, 691

Black nationalism, 574–75, 581–83, 588–94, 687

Blackstone, William, 43

Blaine, James G., 85–87

Blake, Lillie Devereux, 300

Boer War, 262–64

Bohemia, 290, 318

Bohr, Niels, 467

Bolsheviks, 353

Borden, Robert Laird, 290

Boston, Mass., 19, 85, 110, 208–9, 257, 643

Bowie, James, 527

Brady, James, 770

Brandt, Willy, 554–55

Branton, Wiley, 773–74

Brazil, 342

Brezhnev, Leonid, 731, 733

Bright, John, 262

Bristow, Benjamin H., 85

Britain, 49, 92, 149, 159, 175, 184, 188, 253, 262–64, 328–34, 337, 340–42, 347, 466, 724–26, 729–30, 734–37, 761; American Revolution, 43, 90, 169–70, 192, 264–65; woman suffrage in, 290–91, 293, 299, 303, 307; World War I, 238, 241, 284–85, 351; World War II, 427–29, 432–33, 435–36, 438–39, 446, 449, 451, 453–55

Brown, B. Gratz, 25–26

Brown, John, 124, 213, 215

Brown, Lee, 770

Brown v. Board of Education, 551, 583, 633–34

Brownell, Herbert, 774

Bryan, William Jennings, 142–49, 408

Bryce, James, 184

Buchanan, James, 83, 275

Buchanan, John P., 127

Budapest, Hungary, 521, 649

Buddhism, 658, 661

Bunker Hill, battle of, 85, 264

Burger, Warren E., 733

Burke, Edmund, 192, 264

Burns, Waller T., 247–48

Bush, George H. W., 748

Butler, Benjamin F., 46–47, 67–73, 126

Byers, Robert, 609–10

Byrd, Robert C., 539

Cabot, Charles F., 92

California, 38, 46, 116, 294, 338, 384–85, 498, 505, 507–10, 702, 769

Cambodia, 663, 727

Camp David Accords, 751

Canada, 290, 293, 299, 307, 340, 342, 391, 544, 686, 737

Canning, George, 329–31, 334

Cape Town, South Africa, 641

Carey, William, 527

Carlisle, John G., 148

Carpenter, Matthew H., 37

Carter, Jimmy, 705–14, 723, 748

Carter, David K., 37

Castlereagh, viscount (Robert Stewart), 329

Castro, Fidel, 605, 655

Catholic University, 206

Catholicism, 287, 477, 485, 525–28, 560, 643

Catt, Carrie Chapman, 286–307

Central Intelligence Agency, 697

Cervera, Pascual, 173
Challenger disaster, 754–55
Chaney, James E., 744
Chang Tso-lin, 498
Chapman, John Jay, 229–32
Chase, Salmon P., 2, 10
Château-Thierry, battle of, 315
Chiang Kai-shek, 498
Chicago, Ill., 129, 132, 142, 150, 161,
  373, 486, 644, 653
Chief Joseph, 88
Child labor laws, 224, 304, 309–10
China, 152, 158, 186, 336, 340, 427,
  481, 498–502, 513, 575, 585, 598–99,
  652, 678, 685, 766
Chinese Americans, 38, 287–88
Churchill, Winston, 455, 615, 634,
  726–27, 734–35
Cincinnati, Ohio, 85
Civil rights, 484–85, 652–54, 744–45,
  749–50; address by Booker T.
  Washington, 137–41; address by
  John F. Kennedy, 548–53; address
  by Robert F. Kennedy, 641–50;
  and lynching, 110–28, 229–32;
  Montgomery bus boycott, 516–19;
  Nobel Prize address of Martin
  Luther King, 619–22; and
  segregation, 204–12; sermons by
  Martin Luther King, 668–92;
  speech by Benjamin F. Butler,
  67–73; speech by Hubert H.
  Humphrey, 476–79; speech by
  Malcolm X, 574–94; speech by
  Mary Church Terrell, 204–12;
  speech by Robert Brown Elliott,
  48–66; speech by William J.
  Clinton, 773–79; speeches by
  Lyndon B. Johnson, 623–40;
  speeches by Martin Luther King,
  Jr., 516–19, 556–60
Civil Rights Act (1866), 125
Civil Rights Act (1875), 125
Civil Rights Act (1957), 634
Civil Rights Act (1960), 634
Civil Rights Act (1964), 577, 579, 620,
  626–27, 634, 691
Civil rights bill (1874), 48–73
Civil service, 188, 363, 611, 683
Civil War, 1, 7–9, 14, 34, 45, 49, 54–
  55, 63–72, 75, 78–83, 86–87, 89–97,
  124–26, 135, 152, 183, 190, 209, 213–18,
  220, 226–27, 231, 292, 333, 344–45,
  412, 437, 465, 489, 580, 623, 774
Civil Works Administration, 412
Clark, James Beauchamp, 288
Clark, Joseph S., 606
Clarksville, Ga., 117
Clay, Henry, 252–56, 261–62, 266, 274–
  75
Clay, Lucius, 554
Clemenceau, Georges, 333, 342
Clement, Robert N., 764, 767
Clergy and Laymen Concerned About
  Vietnam, 651
Cleveland, Grover, 98, 345, 366, 612
Cleveland, Ohio, 308, 574, 591, 607
Clinton, Hillary Rodham, 765, 773
Clinton, William J.: speech at Central
  High School, 773–79; speech at
  Mason Temple, 763–72
Coatesville, Pa., 229–31
Coinage Act, 146
Cold War, 541, 543, 606, 614, 771–72
Colombia, 334
Commager, Henry Steele, 651
Committee for the Re-Election of the
  President, 697
Commonwealth Club, 384–85
Communism, 216, 353, 488–91, 495–96,
  498–502, 507, 513–15, 517, 521, 525, 530,
  536, 542–45, 554–55, 595, 598–600, 613,
  643, 656, 658, 664–65, 725–34, 758,
  772
Conant, James B., 472
Concentration camps, 431, 446, 649,
  657–58, 727, 736
Concord, battle of, 163, 614, 623
Confederate States of America, 1, 7–11,
  62–63, 80, 89, 135
Congo, 544, 646
Congress, Confederate, 11, 86
Congress, U.S., 76, 86–87, 124, 137,
  218, 225, 309, 312, 359, 361, 375, 400,
  402, 413–15, 433, 438, 442, 445, 456–
  57, 468, 481–86, 505–11, 529, 607, 672,
  709, 718, 720, 729, 732, 750, 763, 770;
  address by Douglas MacArthur, 495–
  503; and business, 201, 219–20; and
  civil rights, 50, 52, 55–59, 61–62, 64–
  65, 125, 484, 550–51, 577–80, 593, 625–
  27, 629, 631–34; declaration of

conscience by Margaret Chase Smith, 487–92; eighth annual address by Franklin D. Roosevelt, 437–46; energy policy, 705, 712; impeachment of Richard M. Nixon, 695–99; League of Nations address by Woodrow Wilson, 314–26; and military, 155–57, 267–72; and Reconstruction, 2, 4, 6–7, 10–18, 54–55; and Spanish-American War, 162, 168–69, 171, 173, 179–80, 277; and suffrage, 25–28, 38, 46–47, 294, 296, 301, 304–6; voting rights address by Lyndon B. Johnson, 623–32; war address by Franklin D. Roosevelt, 447–48; war address by Woodrow Wilson, 238–46; war powers of, 178–79, 181, 238, 240–41, 246, 252–56, 260–62, 266–85, 337, 348–49, 402, 448; woman suffrage address by Carrie Chapman Catt, 286–307

Congress of Aix-la-Chapelle, 329
Congress of Laibach, 329, 331
Congress of Racial Equality, 588, 590
Congress of Troppau, 329
Congress of Verona, 329, 331
Congressional debates: on 1874 civil rights bill, 48–73; on free speech in wartime, 247–85; on League of Nations, 327–55; on Reconstruction, 6–18
Connecticut, 48, 769–70
Connor, Eugene (Bull), 684–85
Conscription, 281, 284
Conservation, 222–23, 225, 234–35, 364, 368, 379, 400, 711–13, 719, 747
Constitution, U.S., 218, 250, 259, 265, 282–83, 401–2, 418, 422, 437, 488, 518, 526–28, 556, 601, 603, 606, 691, 708, 721, 764; amendments to, 4–5, 13–15, 18, 26, 29, 34, 37–40, 43, 45–47, 50, 53–56, 64, 99, 125, 576, 579, 592, 618, 685; and civil rights, 48–50, 58–59, 65, 67–68, 73, 484, 549, 553, 576, 625–26, 629, 633–34, 642–43, 774, 776; and gold standard, 146; and impeachment, 695–96, 699; and income tax, 145; and Reconstruction, 6–8, 10, 12–15, 18; and slavery, 13, 65, 77, 124; and

suffrage, 22, 24–30, 34–35, 39, 45–47, 99, 296, 304; war powers in, 178–79, 183, 193, 252–56, 260–62, 266–80, 337, 348
Constitutional Convention, 253–54, 256, 268, 274, 422, 695–96
Continental Congress, 24, 169–70
Coolidge, Calvin, 366, 375
Cooper, Jim, 764, 767
Coplon, Judith, 489
Copperheads, 14, 16, 18
Corporations, 200–2, 218–19, 224, 365–66, 376, 390, 392–93, 407, 746–47
Corwin, Thomas, 261, 274
Cotton, 14, 218, 310, 405, 680
Cotulla, Texas, 630–31, 638
Council of Europe, 733
Cowan, Edgar, 25
Coy, Ed, 121–22
Crimean War, 262
Crockett, Davy, 527
Cuba, 153–54, 156, 158–59, 161–63, 165–67, 172–73, 188–90, 277, 325, 346, 525, 593, 596, 605, 729
Czechoslovakia, 318, 431, 728, 730, 739

D-Day, 453, 736–40
Dachau concentration camp, 727
Dailey, Jim, 773
Daniel, Peter V., 35
Danzig, 320
Davis, Henry Winter, 276
Dawes, Henry L., 59
Day, Doris, 567–68
Day, William R., 166
De Gaulle, Charles, 528, 587
Debs, Eugene V., 308–13
Declaration of Independence, 16, 22–23, 25, 63, 214, 286–89, 299, 387, 394, 403–4, 556, 656, 676, 679, 691, 749, 774
Democratic Party, 13–14, 16, 18, 28, 36, 45–46, 72, 85, 142–49, 155, 233, 298, 301, 304–6, 345, 356, 359–60, 371, 373–75, 378–83, 387, 415, 441, 476–81, 486, 489–91, 506, 511, 528, 576–80, 594, 599, 604, 607, 611–12, 623–25, 631–32, 715–23, 732, 741–43, 749
Denmark, 299, 431
Depression of 1893, 129–33
Detroit, Mich., 720, 746

Dewey, George, 153, 162–64, 172, 193
Díaz, Porfirio, 183
Diem, Ngo Dinh, 657–59
Diepgen, Eberhard, 756
Dirksen, Everett M., 631
District of Columbia, slavery in, 79
Dixiecrats, 578–80
Dominican Republic, 185
Douglas, Stephen A., 168
Douglass, Frederick, 74–84, 128, 206
Dred Scott case, 34–36, 52
Dreyfus, Alfred, 192

East Germany, 555, 725, 728, 730, 739, 761–62
Eastland, James O., 577, 579
Eckford, Elizabeth, 773–74, 776
Edson, Peter, 505
Education, 4, 14, 58, 60–61, 86, 100, 102–4, 106–7, 111, 125, 140, 206, 210–12, 224, 328, 368–69, 411, 483, 485, 525, 527, 535, 548–49, 551–52, 565, 591–92, 616–18, 630–31, 635, 747, 752, 765–66, 773–79
Egypt, 159
Ehrlichman, John, 698
Eighteenth Amendment, 297, 304, 359–60, 378
Eisenhower, Dwight D., 507–8, 513–15, 525, 535, 595, 598, 763, 774; address about D-Day, 453; Farewell Address, 529–34; Second Inaugural Address, 520–24
El Salvador, 729–30, 751
Electric power, 359–60, 365, 368, 485
Elliot, Jonathan, 273
Elliott, Robert Brown, 48–66, 72
Ellsberg, Daniel, 597–98
Emancipation Proclamation, 2, 80, 555, 627, 672, 632
Energy policy, 705–14, 721
Equal rights amendment, 721, 750
Erhard, Ludwig, 757
Espionage Act, 308
Estes, Billie Sol, 607
Ethiopia, 611
European Community, 757
European Recovery Program, 472–75, 481–82, 739, 757
Evers, Medgar, 744

Fair Oaks, battle of, 93
Falklands War, 730
Family and Medical Leave Act, 765
Farm relief, 357, 359–60, 370, 379–81, 400, 411, 481, 606–7, 672
Faulkner, William, 493–94
Federal Bureau of Corporations, 219
Federal Housing Administration, 607
Federal Reserve Board, 748
Feminine mystique, 561–73
Ferraro, Geraldine A., 742
Fifteenth Amendment, 26, 29, 37, 39–40, 43, 45–47, 50, 54–57, 64, 125
Fleming, J. L., 118–19
Ford, Harold E., 763, 766
Forsyth, John, 275
Fort Griswold, 48
Fort Sumter, 64
Four Freedoms, 445
Four Powers Agreement, 760
Fourteen Points, 317, 324
Fourteenth Amendment, 26, 29, 34, 37–39, 45–47, 50, 53–59, 64
Fox, Charles James, 264
France, 50, 93, 98, 169–70, 192, 270, 276, 290, 306, 324, 328–33, 341–42, 344–45, 347, 352, 438, 528, 587, 610, 656, 659, 729, 736–40, 757, 761; World War I, 241, 285, 315–17, 351; World War II, 431
Franklin, Benjamin, 44, 292
Franz Ferdinand, 289
Fredericksburg, battle of, 92, 94
Free blacks, 13, 32
Free silver movement, 142–49
Free Speech Movement, 616–18
Frelinghuysen, Frederick J., 45
Frémont, John C., 78
French Revolution, 327, 333, 438
Friedan, Betty, 561–73
Fugitive slaves, 40, 77
Fulbright, J. William, 606

Galamison, Milton, 574
Garfield, James A., 187
Garrison, William Lloyd, 124, 128, 208
Geneva Conference (1954), 656, 659–60, 662, 677
Geneva disarmament talks, 545, 759
George III, 43, 192, 293, 725

George Washington University, 206, 211

Georgia, 40, 63, 117, 127, 137–41, 558, 653

German Americans, 246

Germany, 289–90, 306, 521, 719, 757; East Germany, 555, 725, 728, 730, 739, 761–62; Treaty of Versailles, 314, 317–21, 323–24, 333, 350; West Germany, 521, 528, 544, 548, 554–55, 724–25, 728, 732, 756–62; World War I, 238–46, 280–81, 284–85, 315–17, 350, 355; World War II, 426–27, 429–33, 436, 438, 440, 449–55, 463, 473, 643, 736

Gettysburg, battle of, 93, 292, 774

Ghana, 682, 751

Gladstone, William E., 262, 725

Gold, Harry, 489

Gold standard, 130, 142–49

Goldwater, Barry M., 595–603, 607, 611–15

Gompers, Samuel, 362–63

Good Neighbor Policy, 401, 424

Goodman, Andrew, 744

Gorbachev, Mikhail, 759, 761

Gore, Thomas P., 248

Grafton, duke of (Augustus Henry Fitzroy), 264

Graham, Billy, 590

Grant, Ulysses S., 1, 39, 45–46, 70, 76, 150, 152, 154, 217

Great Depression, 374–83, 391–93, 396, 398–402, 405–13, 418, 422, 424, 426, 486, 608–9, 682, 710

Great Society, 605, 636

Greater Houston Ministerial Association, 525–28

Greece, 427, 436, 482, 611

Greene, Nathanael, 48

Greenville, S. C., 751

Grenada, 747

Grier, Robert C., 8, 10

Gronna, Asle J., 248

Guam, 447, 497

Guatemala, 663

Gun control, 768–70

Haiti, 79

Hamer, Fannie Lou, 744

Hamilton, Alexander, 48–51, 350, 386–87, 614, 695–96

Hancock, John, 43

Hardwick, Thomas W., 248

Harlan, John Marshall, 553

Harpers Ferry, Va. [W. Va.], 124

Harris, John T., 63, 67

Harris, Patricia, 635

Harrison, Frederic, 99

Hart, Gary, 742

Hartford Convention, 135

Harvard Regiment, 91–95

Harvard University, 472, 609

Havana, Cuba, 189

Hawaii, 153, 183, 185, 430, 447, 497

Head Start program, 674

Health care, 357, 368, 444, 484–85, 610, 636, 720, 747, 752, 765–66, 770

Heflin, James T., 211

Hejaz, 336–37, 340

Hendrickson, Robert C., 491–92

Henry, Patrick, 43

Hepburn Act, 201, 209

Herenton, Willie W., 763

Heschel, Abraham, 651, 744

Hill, David B., 143, 146

Hinds, Asher C., 274–75

Hirohito, 447

Hiroshima, atomic bombing of, 454, 469

Hispanics, 630–31, 638, 743, 745–46, 750, 776–77

Hiss, Alger, 488–89, 512–13

Hitler, Adolf, 427

Ho Chi Minh, 656, 659–60

Hogg, James S., 127

Hollendale, Miss., 123

Hollywood, Calif., 504

Holmes, Oliver Wendell, Jr., 89–97

Honduras, 746–47

Hong Kong, 163–64, 447

Hoover, Herbert, 356–72, 377, 408–9, 595

Housing, 483–85, 550, 607–8, 721, 744, 747

Houston, Texas, 525

Howard, Jacob M., 37

Howard, Oliver O., 88

Howard University, 209, 633, 635, 771

Howe, I. G., 256

Howe, J. H., 37

Howe, Julia Ward, 300
Huckabee, Mike. 773
Hughes, Langston, 654
Hull, Cordell, 447
Human rights, 584–85, 626, 641, 669,
    683, 710, 725, 731, 751, 761
Humphrey, Hubert H., 476–79, 607,
    743
Hungary, 318, 332, 521, 584, 649, 730
Hunt, E. Howard, 697
Hurst, John Fletcher, 539
Husayn ibn Ali, 336–37

Ibn Saud, 336
Iceland, 299
Illinois, 42, 87, 124, 129, 132, 150, 175
Iloilo, Philippines, 175–76
Immigration, 287–88, 337–40, 351–52,
    357, 388, 391
Impeachment, 695–99
Imperialism, 153–94, 283, 319, 325,
    349, 496, 498, 542, 598, 611, 656,
    732
Income tax, 144–45, 200, 221, 279,
    293–94, 304, 720, 749
India, 159, 188, 544, 619, 646, 673,
    730
Indiana, 295
Indianapolis, Ind., 693
Indianola, Miss., 122
Indonesia, 544, 646
Ingersoll, Robert G., 85–87
Inquisition, 121, 331
Interstate commerce, 201, 219, 227
Interstate Commerce Commission,
    219
Ireland, 430, 528
Irish Americans, 38, 643
Israel, 730, 751
Italian Americans, 120, 576, 643
Italy, 120–21, 290, 331, 333, 347, 351,
    426–27, 430–32, 436, 757
Ives, Irving M., 491–92
Iwo Jima, battle of, 628

Jackson, Andrew, 49, 144–45, 366,
    612, 715
Jackson, H. Ralph, 686
Jackson, Jesse, 687, 741–53, 769
Jackson, Miss., 682
Jackson, Tenn., 123

Jacksonville, Fla., 581
Jamestown, Va., 426
Japan, 167, 333, 336–37, 339–40, 347,
    498–99, 719, 757, 766; World War II,
    426–27, 430–32, 436, 440, 447–48,
    451, 454–56, 462, 469, 497, 499, 501,
    587, 656, 659, 751
Jarvis, Gregory, 754
Jefferson, Thomas, 78, 143, 288, 343,
    350, 387, 390, 397, 408, 416, 477, 526,
    612, 648, 679, 715, 725
Jefferson, William J., 763, 767
Jerusalem Road, battle of, 91
Jews, 208, 287, 333, 477, 485, 526, 560,
    643, 736, 743–44
Johnson, Andrew, 6, 15–17, 54
Johnson, Lyndon B., 535, 577–78, 594,
    596, 599, 605–7, 660, 676; address at
    Howard University, 633–40; address
    on voting rights, 623–32
Jordan, Barbara, 695–99

Kansas, 116, 213–14, 217, 225, 608
Kaunitz, Wenzel Anton von, 327–28
Keene, N. H., 89
Kennedy, Edward M., 715–23
Kennedy, John F., 529, 575, 577, 596,
    641–43, 649–50, 663, 677, 693, 697,
    709, 723, 744, 756, 760; address at
    American University, 539–47; address
    on civil rights, 548–53; Inaugural
    Address, 535–38; speech in Berlin,
    554–55; speech to Greater Houston
    Ministerial Association, 525–28
Kennedy, Joseph, Jr., 527
Kennedy, Robert F., 709, 723, 744; on
    assassination of Martin Luther King,
    693–94; speech at University of Cape
    Town, 641–50
Kent, James, 53
Kentucky, 49, 59–61, 63
Kenya, 611, 682
Kerner Commission, 676
Kerr, Clark, 616–17
Khrushchev, Nikita, 546, 575, 614, 758
King, Martin Luther, Jr., 574, 644,
    709, 744, 764, 767–69, 772, 778;
    address to March on Washington,
    556–60; Nobel Prize address, 619–22;
    Robert F. Kennedy on assassination
    of, 693–94; sermon at Mason

Temple, 681–92; sermon at
National Cathedral, 668–80;
speech to Montgomery
Improvement Association, 516–19;
speech on Vietnam War, 651–67
King, William H., 272
Knights of White Liners, 125
Kohl, Helmut, 756
Korea: North Korea, 498, 500–1, 761;
South Korea, 500–2, 575, 678, 761
Korean War, 498–502, 513–14, 529,
531, 586, 599, 613
Kossuth, Lajos, 332
Kropotkin, Pyotr Alekseyevich, 104
Krüdener, Barbara Juliane von, 328
Ku Klux Klan, 125, 518
Kyes, Samuel, 686

La Follette, Robert M., Sr., 247–85
Labor, 85–86, 108, 129–36, 138, 143–
44, 149, 151, 200, 202, 205–8, 211–
12, 215–16, 224, 235–36, 304, 308–
10, 319, 357–58, 363, 367–69, 381,
411, 417, 433–34, 441, 473, 481, 483,
485, 518, 563–64, 616, 716–17, 722
Labor Department, U.S., 483
Laos, 596, 661
Lausanne, Stéphane, 342
Lawson, James, 685–86
League of Nations, 321–23, 327, 332–
49, 352–55, 481
Lebanon, 598, 730, 747
Lee, Robert E., 124
Lend-Lease, 442–43
Lenin, V. I., 612, 728, 732, 734
Leopold II, 328
Lewis, Will, 123
Lexington, battle of, 163, 264, 623
Libby Prison, 87
Liberia, 751
Lieber, Francis, 50
Lincoln, Abraham, 45, 150, 152, 154,
168, 183, 213, 215–16, 256, 261–62,
266, 274, 278–79, 286, 366, 408,
465, 489, 511, 549, 556, 602, 627,
672, 682; Frederick Douglass'
oration on, 74–84; speech on
Reconstruction, 1–5
Little Rock, Ark., 117, 763, 773–79
Liuzzo, Viola, 744
Livermore, Mary A., 300

Lloyd George, David, 262–64, 290
Lodge, Henry Cabot, 327–55
Loeb, Henry, 684, 687
Lomax, Louis E., 574–75, 580–82, 585
London, England, 724, 734
Long, Huey, 403–14
Long, John D., 155
Looking-Glass, 88
Los Alamos Laboratory, 456, 458
Los Angeles, Calif., 604, 609, 644, 686
Louisiana, 1–5, 52–53, 69–70, 117, 121,
123, 411, 438, 558, 766
Lovat, Lord (Simon Fraser), 737
Lovejoy, Elijah, 124
Lowell, James J., 92
Luther v. *Borden*, 12
Lutuli, Albert, 621
Lynching, 110–28, 175, 229–32, 518, 577

MacArthur, Douglas, 495–503
Macmillan, Harold, 546
Madison, James, 25, 274, 698–99
Malaysia, 447, 728
Malcolm X (Malcolm Little), 574–94,
744
Manchuria, 500
Mandela, Nelson, 777
Manifest Destiny, 190, 388
Manila, Philippines, 154, 156, 162–69,
171–72, 180, 189, 193
Mansfield, Michael J., 631
Mao Zedong, 655
March on Washington (1963), 556–60,
593, 691
Mariana Islands, 497
Marines, U.S., 451, 514
Marks, Miss., 674
Marshall, George C., 472–75, 757
Marshall, Thurgood, 773–74
Martin, Luther, 24–25
Marx, Karl, 612, 665, 720, 728, 732, 734
Maryland, 24
Mason, Charles H., 763
Mason Temple, 681, 763
Massachusetts, 42, 59–61, 85, 92, 143,
149, 576
Matthews, Stanley, 46
Maximilian, 345, 438
McAdoo, William G., 257
McAuliffe, Christa, 754
McCafferty, Edward, 527

McCormack, John W., 631
McCulloch, William M., 631
McDowell, Calvin, 112–15
McKinley, William, 147, 162, 167–69,
    171–76, 178–81, 187, 193, 277, 356
McNair, Ronald, 754
McNamara, Robert, 599
McWherter, Ned Ray, 763
Mead, Margaret, 568–69
Meade, George G., 78
Medicare, 610
Memphis, Tenn., 11–20, 127, 142,
    681–88, 691, 763
Merritt, Wesley, 166
Methodists, 190, 539, 574, 684
Metternich, Klemens von, 330–32
Mexican Americans, 630–31, 638
Mexican-American War, 173, 182, 252–
    62, 278–79
Mexico, 163, 173, 183, 244, 276, 344–
    45, 438, 544, 612–13, 767
Midway Island, 448, 497
Military-industrial complex, 531–32,
    677, 746
Miller, M. P., 175
Miller, Samuel F., 33, 53
Miller, William E., 595
Milligan, Ex parte, 270
Millin, Bill, 737
Minnesota, 407, 576
Mississippi, 111, 122, 558–59, 577, 591,
    674, 747, 766
Missouri, 485
Missouri, U.S.S., 501
Mitchell, John H., 33
Mitchell, Samuel, 511
Mondale, Walter F., 742
Monroe, James, 342–44, 350
Monroe Doctrine, 331, 341–45, 427
Montana, 88
Montgomery, Ala., 516–19, 620, 652,
    655
Montgomery Improvement
    Association, 516–19
Morehouse College, 662
Morley, John, 184
Morse, Wayne L., 491–92
Morton, Thruston, 595
Moscow, Russia, 546
Moss, Thomas, 112–16
Mozambique, 663

Muckrakers, 195–203
Munich Conference, 438
Muscle Shoals, Ala., 361
Muslims, 574–75, 587–88, 744

Nabrit, James M., 633
Nagasaki, atomic bombing of, 462
Naples, Italy, 331
Napoleon, Louis, 345
Napoleon Bonaparte, 147, 328, 438
Nashville, Tenn., 126
National Aeronautics and Space
    Administration, 755
National Association for the
    Advancement of Colored People,
    588, 590, 774
National banks, 145, 219
National Cathedral, 668
National and Community Service
    Trust Act, 765
National Council of Churches, 526
National Recovery Administration,
    412–13
National Service Corps, 546
National Student Association, 641
National Woman Suffrage Association,
    47, 299
Navy, U.S., 1, 153–58, 162–65, 171–73,
    186, 221, 241, 254, 267, 269–72, 277,
    337, 348–49, 352, 427, 433–35, 441–
    42, 447–48, 453, 497
Nazis, 427, 429–31, 453, 463, 473, 614,
    643, 648, 657
Netherlands, 431, 443
Neutrality, 238–40, 242, 266, 277–78,
    281, 299, 328, 343, 433
New Deal, 383, 400, 402, 717–18
New Freedom, 718
New Frontier, 718
New Hampshire, 296
New Jersey, 296
New Mexico, 295, 456
New Nationalism, 213–23
New Orleans, battle of, 49
New Orleans, La., 2, 52–53, 69–70, 117,
    120–21, 414
New York, 19, 22, 26–27, 31–32, 41, 47,
    143, 149, 183, 291–92, 294–97, 301,
    307, 378–79, 382–83, 394, 558, 690
New York City, 98, 170, 207–8, 301,
    356, 369–70, 574, 587, 644, 646, 651,

653–54, 674, 682, 686, 689–90, 715, 717–18
New Zealand, 340
Newark, N. J., 674
Newspapers, 111–12, 114, 116–20, 124, 126, 130, 187, 196–98, 225, 247–51, 265, 312, 363–64
Nez Percé, 88
Nicaragua, 337, 745, 747, 751
Nicholas I, 332
Nicholson, Meredith, 385
Nigeria, 730, 751
Nightingale, Taylor, 118–19
Nineteenth Amendment, 293–301, 304–7
Nixon, Julie, 510
Nixon, Patricia, 510–11
Nixon, Patricia Ryan, 506–7, 509–11, 514, 595
Nixon, Richard M., 520, 525, 535, 577, 595, 743; Barbara Jordan on impeachment of, 695–99; "Checkers" speech, 504–15; remarks on leaving White House, 700–4
Nobel, Alfred, 622
Nobel Prize, 493–94, 619–22, 644, 655
North, Frederick, 192
North American Free Trade Agreement, 766–67
North Atlantic Treaty Organization, 596, 724, 728, 734, 739–40, 759
North Carolina, 696
North Korea, 498, 500–1, 761
North Vietnam, 652–53, 656–62
Northen, William J., 127
Norway, 431, 440, 443
Nuclear test ban treaty, 545–47

Oak Ridge Laboratory, 456
Office of Price Administration, 482
Ohio, 46, 312, 745
Oil, 389, 705–7, 709–13
Oklahoma, 116
Olney, Richard, 345
Olympics, 761
Onizuka, Ellison, 754
Oppenheimer, J. Robert, 458–71
Organization of Petroleum Exporting Countries, 707, 710–11

Ord, Edward O. C., 70
Ordronaux, John, 273–74
Oregon, 33, 38, 498
Osawatomie, Kans., 213
Oslo, Norway, 619
Otis, Elwell S., 171
Otis, James, 43
Ottoman Empire, 315, 319, 321

Paderewski, Ignacy, 333
Paine, Thomas, 44–45
Panama, 334, 346
Panama Canal, 154, 197
Panama Congress, 275
Paris, France, 166, 314–16, 324–25
Paris, Texas, 121–22, 127
Parks, Rosa, 516–17
Parliament, 262–64, 290–91, 331, 724, 734–35
Patriotism, 189, 192, 194, 223, 248, 261, 274, 279, 291, 353–55
Patten, Henry, 93
Patton, George S., 449–52
Peace Corps, 546, 648
Pearl Harbor, attack on, 447–48, 454
Pendleton Act, 188
Pennsylvania, 183, 296
Perry, Benjamin Franklin, 16
Peru, 342, 646, 663
Petersburg, siege of, 1, 93–94
Petersen, Henry, 698
Philadelphia, Miss., 619
Philadelphia, Pa., 415–16, 476, 480, 483–84, 686
Philippines, 153–54, 156–93, 210, 325, 349, 447, 496–99, 760
Phillips, Wendell, 45, 128, 208
Phillips, William Alison, 331
Pilgrims, 679
Pitt, William (the Elder), 192, 264–65
Plymouth, Mass., 426, 679
Pointe-du-Hoc, France, 736
Poland, 318, 320, 333, 431, 725–27, 729–30, 737, 739
Polish Americans, 576, 643
Political parties, 296–98, 304–7
Polk, James K., 252, 255–56, 260–61, 278–79
Pomeroy, John N., 272
Poor People's Campaign, 676–77, 679
Port Hudson, siege of, 94

Portugal, 430
Potsdam Declaration, 456
Powell, Adam Clayton, 574
Prague, Czech Republic, 290, 739
Pratt, E. Spencer, 163–64, 166
Presidency, U.S., 2, 6–7, 10–12, 17, 77,
    83, 102, 178–82, 193, 233, 238, 240,
    242, 253–56, 260–62, 268–83, 314–
    15, 378, 398, 402, 425–26, 433, 436,
    438–40, 447–48, 484–85, 511–12,
    514, 525–29, 546, 565, 606, 695–704,
    709, 711, 721, 756, 763–64
President's Commission on the
    Status of Women, 567–69
Press, freedom of, 17–20, 124, 179–
    81, 193, 250, 265, 363–64
Prize Cases, 8–10
Prohibition, 297, 304, 359–60, 378
Protestantism, 99, 287, 477, 525–28,
    560, 574–75, 590
Prussia, 329–32, 343
Public debt, 13–14, 85, 357, 484, 604,
    749
Public lands, 33, 222, 387–91, 672
Public works, 378–79, 400, 411
Public Works Administration, 412
Puerto Rico, 153, 158
Puritans, 93–94
Putnam, William L., 92

Quakers, 23, 526

Race, 16–18, 25, 28–29, 38–40, 51, 53,
    55, 57, 59–73, 75, 77, 80–81, 110–11,
    117–18, 123–25, 128, 137–41, 175, 188,
    231, 287–88, 430, 477, 548–53, 619–
    50, 653, 670–80, 683–84, 691, 693–
    94, 743–45, 749–50, 753, 764, 767–
    68, 773–79
Railroads, 56, 67, 112, 125, 201, 219,
    362, 377, 389
Rainbow Coalition, 743-46, 749
Rangel, Charles B., 695
Rayville, La., 123
Reagan, Ronald W., 717, 719–20,
    745–49; address on *Challenger*
    disaster, 754–55; address on
    D-Day, 736–40 address to
    Parliament, 724–35; speech in
    Berlin, 756–62; speech supporting
    Barry Goldwater, 604–15

Reconstruction, 1–18, 28–29, 45, 54–55,
    66
Reconstruction Finance Corporation,
    389–90
Republican Party, 13–14, 17–18, 28, 35–
    37, 39, 45–46, 72, 85–87, 119, 127,
    147–48, 155, 298, 301, 304–6, 345,
    356–59, 365–66, 370, 372, 373–75, 381–
    83, 387, 390, 415, 441, 480–92, 510–11,
    515, 576–78, 580, 595–603, 605, 623–25,
    627, 631–32, 697, 716–17, 719–20, 732
Resnik, Judith, 754
Reuter, Ernst, 757
Revere, Edward H. R., 93
Revere, Paul, 93
Revere, Paul J., 93
Revolutionary War, 16, 29, 43–44, 48,
    78, 86, 90, 93, 149, 163, 169–70, 183,
    192, 213–14, 264–65, 286, 352, 375,
    386–87, 416–17, 422, 535, 605, 614,
    623, 668–69, 725
Rhode Island, 39, 576
Richmond, Virginia, 1, 69
Ridgway, Matthew, 738, 740
Robertson, Ian, 641
Robinson, Joseph T., 415
Rochester, N.Y., 301
Rockefeller, John D., 310–11
Romania, 319
Roosevelt, Eleanor, 774
Roosevelt, Franklin D., 408–9, 455,
    477, 481, 486, 631, 682, 716–17, 745;
    address on war with Japan, 447–48;
    "Arsenal of Democracy" fireside
    chat, 426–36; eighth annual address
    to Congress, 437–46; First Inaugural
    Address, 398–402; Second Inaugural
    Address, 421–25; speech to
    Commonwealth Club, 384–97;
    speech to Democratic National
    Convention (1932), 373–83; speech to
    Democratic National Convention
    (1936), 415–20
Roosevelt, Theodore, 345, 366, 390,
    397, 408, 702–3, 720; "Man with the
    Muck-Rake" speech, 195–203; "New
    Nationalism" speech, 213–28;
    "Strenuous Life" speech, 150–60
Root, Elihu, 288–89
Russell, Richard B., 578
Russell, William E., 143

Russia, 30, 104, 243–44, 281–82, 290, 299, 318, 328–33, 343, 366
Russian Revolution, 243, 281, 290

Saar, 320
St. Louis, Mo., 563
Saint-Pierre, abbé de (Charles-Irénée Castel), 327
Salisbury, marquis of (Robert Gascoyne-Cecil), 262–64
San Francisco, Calif., 384, 595, 741
Santiago, Cuba, 154, 156, 173
Saudi Arabia, 336–37, 713
Savio, Mario, 616–18
Sayre, Francis B., 668
Schouler, James, 278
Schwerner, Michael, 744
Scobee, Richard, 754
Scott, Winfield, 256
Scott v. Sanford, 35–36, 52
Secession, 3, 6, 8, 10–11, 14
Segregation, 54, 56–58, 64, 67–68, 112, 125, 204–12, 516–18, 548–49, 551–52, 556–58, 572, 574, 578, 580–81, 583, 586, 591–92, 634, 670–71, 691, 744, 773–79
Selassie, Haile, 611
Selma, Ala., 623, 627–30, 691
Seneca Falls, N.Y., 47
Serbia, 319
Seven Days' Battles, 92
Seward, William H., 15, 276
Shantung, China, 336
Share-the-Wealth movement, 403–14
Shays's Rebellion, 134, 183
Shenandoah Valley campaigns, 92
Sheridan, Philip, 217
Sherman, Roger, 273
Sherman, William T., 217
Silver v. Ladd, 33
Singapore, 163–64, 166, 497
Slaughterhouse Cases, 51–59, 64–65
Slave rebellions, 124
Slave trade, 79–80, 231
Slavery, 16–17, 40–42, 52, 55, 62–68, 74–75, 84, 89, 126, 135, 138, 161, 190, 209, 218, 257, 287, 582, 636, 641, 671, 679–80, 749, 778; abolition of, 2, 4–5, 13–15, 19–21, 26, 29, 34–35, 37–38, 45, 50, 53–57, 64, 66, 76, 78–82, 124–25, 152, 231, 465, 549, 556,

602, 627, 672, 682; and Constitution, 13, 65, 77, 124; in District of Columbia, 79; Dred Scott case, 35–36, 52; fugitive slaves, 40, 77
Smith, Al, 612
Smith, Charles E., 172
Smith, Dana, 505, 508
Smith, Henry, 122, 127
Smith, Margaret Chase, 487–92
Smith, Michael, 754
Social Security, 410, 444, 483–85, 609–10, 717, 747
Socialism, 225, 308–11, 358–60, 606, 611–12
Solidarity movement, 725–27
South Africa, 621, 641–50, 663, 682, 751, 777
South America, independence of, 275, 331, 343
South Carolina, 11, 15, 40, 48, 59, 127, 558, 698
South Korea, 500–2, 575, 678, 761
South Vietnam, 548, 593, 596, 656–61
Southern Christian Leadership Conference, 654, 679, 687
Soviet Union, 433, 489, 497–98, 502, 523, 540–43, 545–46, 586, 611, 614, 646, 652, 685, 725–28, 730–34, 739–40, 748, 758–61
Space program, 525, 600, 644, 710, 754–55
Spain, 121, 188, 275, 331
Spanish-American War, 153–76, 179, 183, 193, 277, 325, 349–50, 412, 437
Sparkman, John J., 506, 512
Speech, freedom of, 110, 124, 127, 247–85, 363–64, 387, 445, 487–91, 616, 629, 642–43, 685
Spencer, Herbert, 99
Stalin, Joseph, 612
Stanton, Elizabeth Cady, 99–109, 299–300
State Department, U.S., 121, 163, 513
States' rights, 45, 50–52, 56–57, 62–63, 72, 301, 303–4, 307, 478, 559, 626
Statue of Liberty, 98
Stephens, Alexander, 50–52, 54, 56–57, 62–63
Stevens, Thaddeus, 6–18, 25
Stevenson, Adlai E., 511–13
Stewart, Will, 112–13, 115

Stimson, Henry L., 456, 458, 468
Stock market crash, 376, 418
Stockholm, Sweden, 493
Stone, Lucy, 300
Stone, William J., 248
Story, Joseph, 273, 698
Stowe, Harriet Beecher, 300
Strategic Arms Reduction Talks, 726, 734
Strategic Defense Initiative, 760
Student Nonviolent Coordinating Committee, 588
Submarines, 238–44, 245, 348
Suez crisis, 522
Suffrage, 3–4, 12–14, 17, 22–47, 50, 54–57, 59–62, 64, 72, 99–100, 105, 125, 127, 218, 286–307, 548–49, 551, 558, 574–80, 585, 588, 593–94, 623–32, 634, 744–45, 750, 764, 767
Sumner, Charles, 26, 28–29, 124, 128, 208, 256–57, 261–62, 274
Supreme Court, U.S., 76, 121, 145, 271, 390, 407, 518, 591, 609; *Brown v. Board of Education*, 551, 583, 633–34; *Ex parte Milligan*, 270; and Nixon impeachment, 697; Prize Cases, 8–10; and Reconstruction, 6–12; *Scott v. Sanford*, 35–36, 52; *Silver v. Ladd*, 23; Slaughterhouse Cases, 51–59, 64–65
Sweden, 433
Switzerland, 185

Ta-hool-hool-shute, 88
Taft-Ellender-Wagner Bill, 483
Taft-Hartley Act, 483
Taiwan, 498–501, 598, 678
Taney, Roger B., 18, 35–36
Tariffs, 127, 146, 220, 235, 337–40, 357, 379, 381, 389, 391–92, 481
Tarnowski, Adam, 245
Tax cuts, 719–20, 746–48, 765
Tea Act, 43
Tennessee, 111–12, 116, 123, 127, 456, 763–64, 766
Terrell, Mary Church, 204–12
Terrorism, 730
Texarkana, Texas, 121–22
Texas, 121–22, 127, 247–48, 577
Thailand, 340, 661, 663, 678
Thatcher, Margaret, 724–25

Thirteenth Amendment, 4–5, 15, 26, 34, 37, 50, 53–57, 64
Thomas, George H., 217
Thomas, Norman, 611
Thompson, Vance, 306
Three Mile Island nuclear accident, 721
Thye, Edward J., 491–92
Tibet, 498
Tillman, Benjamin R., 127
Tobey, Charles W., 491–92
Tokyo economic summit conference, 712
Torres Bugallon, José, 171
Tourgée, Albion W., 122
Treaty of Chaumont, 328–29
Treaty of Paris (1815), 328–30, 332
Treaty of Paris (1898), 157, 166–69, 171, 174, 179
Treaty of Tilsit, 328
Treaty of Utrecht, 327
Treaty of Versailles, 314–15, 317–26, 336–37, 345, 347, 350, 353–55, 438
Treaty of Vienna, 328–29
Treitschke, Heinrich von, 306
Truman, Harry S, 458, 468–70, 477, 479, 489, 491, 500, 504, 507, 513, 535, 631 speech to Democratic National Convention, 480–86; statement on atomic bomb, 454–57
Truth, Sojourner, 19–21
Turkey, 319, 482
Turner, Nat, 124

Unitarians, 526
United Nations, 463, 467, 481, 522, 536, 542, 584–85, 610–11, 664, 678, 730–31, 762
Universal Declaration of Human Rights, 641, 731
University of Alabama, 548, 552
University of California, 616–18
University of Cape Town, 641

Van Valkenburg, Ellen, 31
Vardaman, James K., 248
Vatican, 526–27
Vattel, Emmerich, 8–9
Venable, Abraham W., 278–79
Venezuela, 663
Versailles economic summit conference, 724

Veterans Administration, 607
Vice-Presidency, U.S., 504, 506, 512, 565
Viet Cong, 655, 657–58
Vietnam, 498, 587, 656, 659, 728; North Vietnam, 652–53, 656–62; South Vietnam, 548, 593, 596, 656–61
Vietnam War, 548, 593, 596, 599, 604–5, 613, 628, 651–67, 677–78, 709, 745
Vilas, William F., 144
Virden, Ill., 175
Virginia, 2, 70–72, 124, 205, 526–27, 696, 698
Voltaire (François-Marie Arouet), 327
Voting Rights Act, 623–32, 634, 750

Wagner-Ellender-Taft Bill, 483
Wahabis, 336–37
Waite, Morrison R., 76
Wake Island, 448
Wall, Sarah E., 31
Walla Walla, Wash., 30
Wallace, George C., 559
Walsh, Thomas J., 373
War Department, U.S., 468
War of 1812, 49, 135, 438
War on Poverty, 608–9, 678
War Production Board, 712
Warsaw, Poland, 725, 729, 739
Washington, 30, 456, 498, 766
Washington, Booker T., 137–41
Washington, Bushrod, 35, 38
Washington, D.C., 1, 6, 20-21, 25, 48, 67, 74–75, 79, 99, 195, 204–12, 227, 233, 238, 247, 286, 300, 314, 327, 398, 403, 421, 426, 437, 447, 454, 487, 495, 505, 513–15, 520, 529, 535, 539, 548, 556–60, 579, 623, 633, 668, 676, 679, 695, 705, 709, 754, 768–69
Washington, George, 50, 163, 169–70, 181, 195, 213, 293, 343, 350, 354, 416, 695, 748
Washington University, 571
Watergate scandal, 697–98, 709
Watson, David K., 271–72
Webster, Daniel, 257–62, 266, 274–75, 408

Weedon, J. S., 31
Weizsäcker, Richard von, 757
Welfare, 606, 608–9, 613, 630, 638–39, 674, 752
Wells, Ida B., 110–28
West Germany, 521, 528, 544, 548, 554–55, 724–25, 728, 732, 756–62
West Indies, 437–38
West Virginia, 525
Whig Party, 260
Whiskey Rebellion, 134–35, 183
White Citizens Council, 518
White Oak Swamp, battle of, 91
Whittier, Calif., 509–10
Whittier, John Greenleaf, 128
Wier, James, 611
Wilderness Campaign, 93–94
Willard, Frances, 300
Wilson, William Julius, 771
Wilson, Woodrow, 247, 266, 270, 279–83, 286, 341, 366, 373–74, 390–92, 397, 481, 539, 697; address on League of Nations, 314–26; address on war with Germany, 238–46; First Inaugural Address, 233–37
Wolverton, Robert, 738
Women's rights, 223–24, 721, 750; speech by Betty Friedan, 561–73; speech by Carrie Chapman Catt, 286–307; speech by Elizabeth Cady Stanton, 99–109; speech by Susan B. Anthony, 22–47
World War I, 238–51, 253, 262, 265–67, 270, 273, 279–85, 286, 289–91, 299, 303–4, 307, 312, 315–18, 322–26, 343, 348–52, 355–59, 362, 365, 367, 375, 391, 412, 437–38, 463, 529, 710, 739
World War II, 426–57, 460, 462–63, 472–73, 496–97, 499, 501, 509, 521, 527, 529, 531, 540, 542–43, 587, 614, 628, 656–57, 659, 710, 712, 719, 729–30, 734–40, 757
Wyoming, 37, 293

Yorktown, battle of, 169
Yugoslavia, 319, 339

Zimmermann Note, 244

Library of Congress Cataloging-in-Publication Data:

American speeches.

     p. cm. — (The Library of America ; 166–167)
Contents: pt. 1. Political oratory from the Revolution to the
Civil War—pt. 2. Political oratory from Abraham Lincoln to Bill
Clinton.

    ISBN 1–931082–97–9 (v. 1 : alk. paper)—ISBN 1–931082–98–7
(v. 2 : alk. paper)

    1. United States—Politics and government—Sources.
2. United States—History—Sources. 3. Speeches, addresses, etc.,
American. 4. Political oratory—United States. I. Series: Library
of America (Series) ; 166–167.

E183.A498 2006
973—dc22   2006040928

THE LIBRARY OF AMERICA SERIES

The Library of America fosters appreciation and pride in America's literary heritage by publishing, and keeping permanently in print, authoritative editions of America's best and most significant writing. An independent nonprofit organization, it was founded in 1979 with seed money from the National Endowment for the Humanities and the Ford Foundation.

1. Herman Melville, *Typee, Omoo, Mardi* (1982)
2. Nathaniel Hawthorne, *Tales and Sketches* (1982)
3. Walt Whitman, *Poetry and Prose* (1982)
4. Harriet Beecher Stowe, *Three Novels* (1982)
5. Mark Twain, *Mississippi Writings* (1982)
6. Jack London, *Novels and Stories* (1982)
7. Jack London, *Novels and Social Writings* (1982)
8. William Dean Howells, *Novels 1875–1886* (1982)
9. Herman Melville, *Redburn, White-Jacket, Moby-Dick* (1983)
10. Nathaniel Hawthorne, *Collected Novels* (1983)
11. Francis Parkman, *France and England in North America*, vol. I (1983)
12. Francis Parkman, *France and England in North America*, vol. II (1983)
13. Henry James, *Novels 1871–1880* (1983)
14. Henry Adams, *Novels, Mont Saint Michel, The Education* (1983)
15. Ralph Waldo Emerson, *Essays and Lectures* (1983)
16. Washington Irving, *History, Tales and Sketches* (1983)
17. Thomas Jefferson, *Writings* (1984)
18. Stephen Crane, *Prose and Poetry* (1984)
19. Edgar Allan Poe, *Poetry and Tales* (1984)
20. Edgar Allan Poe, *Essays and Reviews* (1984)
21. Mark Twain, *The Innocents Abroad, Roughing It* (1984)
22. Henry James, *Literary Criticism: Essays, American & English Writers* (1984)
23. Henry James, *Literary Criticism: European Writers & The Prefaces* (1984)
24. Herman Melville, *Pierre, Israel Potter, The Confidence-Man, Tales & Billy Budd* (1985)
25. William Faulkner, *Novels 1930–1935* (1985)
26. James Fenimore Cooper, *The Leatherstocking Tales*, vol. I (1985)
27. James Fenimore Cooper, *The Leatherstocking Tales*, vol. II (1985)
28. Henry David Thoreau, *A Week, Walden, The Maine Woods, Cape Cod* (1985)
29. Henry James, *Novels 1881–1886* (1985)
30. Edith Wharton, *Novels* (1986)
31. Henry Adams, *History of the U.S. during the Administrations of Jefferson* (1986)
32. Henry Adams, *History of the U.S. during the Administrations of Madison* (1986)
33. Frank Norris, *Novels and Essays* (1986)
34. W.E.B. Du Bois, *Writings* (1986)
35. Willa Cather, *Early Novels and Stories* (1987)
36. Theodore Dreiser, *Sister Carrie, Jennie Gerhardt, Twelve Men* (1987)
37A. Benjamin Franklin, *Silence Dogood, The Busy-Body, & Early Writings* (1987)
37B. Benjamin Franklin, *Autobiography, Poor Richard, & Later Writings* (1987)
38. William James, *Writings 1902–1910* (1987)
39. Flannery O'Connor, *Collected Works* (1988)
40. Eugene O'Neill, *Complete Plays 1913–1920* (1988)
41. Eugene O'Neill, *Complete Plays 1920–1931* (1988)
42. Eugene O'Neill, *Complete Plays 1932–1943* (1988)
43. Henry James, *Novels 1886–1890* (1989)
44. William Dean Howells, *Novels 1886–1888* (1989)
45. Abraham Lincoln, *Speeches and Writings 1832–1858* (1989)
46. Abraham Lincoln, *Speeches and Writings 1859–1865* (1989)
47. Edith Wharton, *Novellas and Other Writings* (1990)
48. William Faulkner, *Novels 1936–1940* (1990)
49. Willa Cather, *Later Novels* (1990)

50. Ulysses S. Grant, *Memoirs and Selected Letters* (1990)
51. William Tecumseh Sherman, *Memoirs* (1990)
52. Washington Irving, *Bracebridge Hall, Tales of a Traveller, The Alhambra* (1991)
53. Francis Parkman, *The Oregon Trail, The Conspiracy of Pontiac* (1991)
54. James Fenimore Cooper, *Sea Tales: The Pilot, The Red Rover* (1991)
55. Richard Wright, *Early Works* (1991)
56. Richard Wright, *Later Works* (1991)
57. Willa Cather, *Stories, Poems, and Other Writings* (1992)
58. William James, *Writings 1878–1899* (1992)
59. Sinclair Lewis, *Main Street & Babbitt* (1992)
60. Mark Twain, *Collected Tales, Sketches, Speeches, & Essays 1852–1890* (1992)
61. Mark Twain, *Collected Tales, Sketches, Speeches, & Essays 1891–1910* (1992)
62. *The Debate on the Constitution: Part One* (1993)
63. *The Debate on the Constitution: Part Two* (1993)
64. Henry James, *Collected Travel Writings: Great Britain & America* (1993)
65. Henry James, *Collected Travel Writings: The Continent* (1993)
66. *American Poetry: The Nineteenth Century*, Vol. 1 (1993)
67. *American Poetry: The Nineteenth Century*, Vol. 2 (1993)
68. Frederick Douglass, *Autobiographies* (1994)
69. Sarah Orne Jewett, *Novels and Stories* (1994)
70. Ralph Waldo Emerson, *Collected Poems and Translations* (1994)
71. Mark Twain, *Historical Romances* (1994)
72. John Steinbeck, *Novels and Stories 1932–1937* (1994)
73. William Faulkner, *Novels 1942–1954* (1994)
74. Zora Neale Hurston, *Novels and Stories* (1995)
75. Zora Neale Hurston, *Folklore, Memoirs, and Other Writings* (1995)
76. Thomas Paine, *Collected Writings* (1995)
77. *Reporting World War II: American Journalism 1938–1944* (1995)
78. *Reporting World War II: American Journalism 1944–1946* (1995)
79. Raymond Chandler, *Stories and Early Novels* (1995)
80. Raymond Chandler, *Later Novels and Other Writings* (1995)
81. Robert Frost. *Collected Poems, Prose, & Plays* (1995)
82. Henry James *Complete Stories 1892–1898* (1996)
83. Henry James *Complete Stories 1898–1910* (1996)
84. William Bartram, *Travels and Other Writings* (1996)
85. John Dos Passos, *U.S.A.* (1996)
86. John Steinbeck, *The Grapes of Wrath and Other Writings 1936–1941* (1996)
87. Vladimir Nabokov, *Novels and Memoirs 1941–1951* (1996)
88. Vladimir Nabokov, *Novels 1955–1962* (1996)
89. Vladimir Nabokov, *Novels 1969–1974* (1996)
90. James Thurber, *Writings and Drawings* (1996)
91. George Washington, *Writings* (1997)
92. John Muir. *Nature Writings* (1997)
93. Nathanael West, *Novels and Other Writings* (1997)
94. *Crime Novels: American Noir of the 1930s and 40s* (1997)
95. *Crime Novels: American Noir of the 1950s* (1997)
96. Wallace Stevens, *Collected Poetry and Prose* (1997)
97. James Baldwin, *Early Novels and Stories* (1998)
98. James Baldwin, *Collected Essays* (1998)
99. Gertrude Stein, *Writings 1903–1932* (1998)
100. Gertrude Stein, *Writings 1932–1946* (1998)
101. Eudora Welty, *Complete Novels* (1998)
102. Eudora Welty, *Stories, Essays, & Memoir* (1998)
103. Charles Brockden Brown, *Three Gothic Novels* (1998)
104. *Reporting Vietnam: American Journalism 1959–1969* (1998)
105. *Reporting Vietnam: American Journalism 1969–1975* (1998)
106. Henry James, *Complete Stories 1874–1884* (1999)

107. Henry James, *Complete Stories 1884–1891* (1999)
108. *American Sermons: The Pilgrims to Martin Luther King Jr.* (1999)
109. James Madison, *Writings* (1999)
110. Dashiell Hammett, *Complete Novels* (1999)
111. Henry James, *Complete Stories 1864–1874* (1999)
112. William Faulkner, *Novels 1957–1962* (1999)
113. John James Audubon, *Writings & Drawings* (1999)
114. *Slave Narratives* (2000)
115. *American Poetry: The Twentieth Century,* Vol. 1 (2000)
116. *American Poetry: The Twentieth Century,* Vol. 2 (2000)
117. F. Scott Fitzgerald, *Novels and Stories 1920–1922* (2000)
118. Henry Wadsworth Longfellow, *Poems and Other Writings* (2000)
119. Tennessee Williams, *Plays 1937–1955* (2000)
120. Tennessee Williams, *Plays 1957–1980* (2000)
121. Edith Wharton, *Collected Stories 1891–1910* (2001)
122. Edith Wharton, *Collected Stories 1911–1937* (2001)
123. *The American Revolution: Writings from the War of Independence* (2001)
124. Henry David Thoreau, *Collected Essays and Poems* (2001)
125. Dashiell Hammett, *Crime Stories and Other Writings* (2001)
126. Dawn Powell, *Novels 1930–1942* (2001)
127. Dawn Powell, *Novels 1944–1962* (2001)
128. Carson McCullers, *Complete Novels* (2001)
129. Alexander Hamilton, *Writings* (2001)
130. Mark Twain, *The Gilded Age and Later Novels* (2002)
131. Charles W. Chesnutt, *Stories, Novels, and Essays* (2002)
132. John Steinbeck, *Novels 1942–1952* (2002)
133. Sinclair Lewis, *Arrowsmith, Elmer Gantry, Dodsworth* (2002)
134. Paul Bowles, *The Sheltering Sky, Let It Come Down, The Spider's House* (2002)
135. Paul Bowles, *Collected Stories & Later Writings* (2002)
136. Kate Chopin, *Complete Novels & Stories* (2002)
137. *Reporting Civil Rights: American Journalism 1941–1963* (2003)
138. *Reporting Civil Rights: American Journalism 1963–1973* (2003)
139. Henry James, *Novels 1896–1899* (2003)
140. Theodore Dreiser, *An American Tragedy* (2003)
141. Saul Bellow, *Novels 1944–1953* (2003)
142. John Dos Passos, *Novels 1920–1925* (2003)
143. John Dos Passos, *Travel Books and Other Writings* (2003)
144. Ezra Pound, *Poems and Translations* (2003)
145. James Weldon Johnson, *Writings* (2004)
146. Washington Irving, *Three Western Narratives* (2004)
147. Alexis de Tocqueville, *Democracy in America* (2004)
148. James T. Farrell, *Studs Lonigan: A Trilogy* (2004)
149. Isaac Bashevis Singer, *Collected Stories I* (2004)
150. Isaac Bashevis Singer, *Collected Stories II* (2004)
151. Isaac Bashevis Singer, *Collected Stories III* (2004)
152. Kaufman & Co., *Broadway Comedies* (2004)
153. Theodore Roosevelt, *The Rough Riders, An Autobiography* (2004)
154. Theodore Roosevelt, *Letters and Speeches* (2004)
155. H. P. Lovecraft, *Tales* (2005)
156. Louisa May Alcott, *Little Women, Little Men, Jo's Boys* (2005)
157. Philip Roth, *Novels & Stories 1959–1962* (2005)
158. Philip Roth, *Novels 1967–1972* (2005)
159. James Agee, *Let Us Now Praise Famous Men, A Death in the Family* (2005)
160. James Agee, *Film Writing & Selected Journalism* (2005)
161. Richard Henry Dana, Jr., *Two Years Before the Mast & Other Voyages* (2005)
162. Henry James, *Novels 1901–1902* (2006)
163. Arthur Miller, *Collected Plays 1944–1961* (2006)

164. William Faulkner, *Novels 1926–1929* (2006)
165. Philip Roth, *Novels 1973–1977* (2006)
166. *American Speeches: Part One* (2006)
167. *American Speeches: Part Two* (2006)
168. Hart Crane, *Complete Poems & Selected Letters* (2006)

This book is set in 10 point Linotron Galliard,
a face designed for photocomposition by Matthew Carter
and based on the sixteenth-century face Granjon. The paper
is acid-free lightweight opaque and meets the requirements
for permanence of the American National Standards Institute.
The binding material is Brillianta, a woven rayon cloth made
by Van Heek-Scholco Textielfabrieken, Holland. Compo-
sition by Dedicated Business Services. Printing by
Malloy Incorporated. Binding by Dekker Book-
binding. Designed by Bruce Campbell.

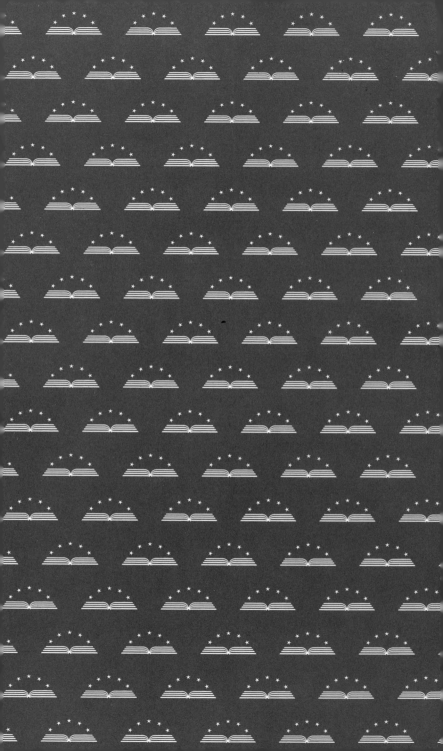